Remote Sensing for Ecology and Conservation

Techniques in Ecology and Conservation Series

Series Editor: William J. Sutherland

Remote Sensing for Ecology and Conservation

A Handbook of Techniques

Ned Horning,
Julie A. Robinson,
Eleanor J. Sterling,
Woody Turner,
and
Sacha Spector

OXFORD
UNIVERSITY PRESS

OXFORD
UNIVERSITY PRESS

Great Clarendon Street, Oxford OX2 6DP

Oxford University Press is a department of the University of Oxford.
It furthers the University's objective of excellence in research, scholarship,
and education by publishing worldwide in

Oxford New York

Auckland Cape Town Dar es Salaam Hong Kong Karachi
Kuala Lumpur Madrid Melbourne Mexico City Nairobi
New Delhi Shanghai Taipei Toronto

With offices in

Argentina Austria Brazil Chile Czech Republic France Greece
Guatemala Hungary Italy Japan Poland Portugal Singapore
South Korea Switzerland Thailand Turkey Ukraine Vietnam

Oxford is a registered trade mark of Oxford University Press
in the UK and in certain other countries

Published in the United States
by Oxford University Press Inc., New York

British Library Cataloguing in Publication Data

Data available

Library of Congress Cataloging in Publication Data

Data available

Typeset by SPI Publisher Services, Pondicherry, India
Printed in China
on acid-free paper by
Golden Cup Printing Co., Ltd.

ISBN 978–0–19–921994–0 (Hbk.)
       978–0–19–921995–7 (Pbk.)

1 3 5 7 9 10 8 6 4 2

Contents

Preface

Remote sensing has revolutionized our understanding of the Earth as an integrated system, giving us a growing capability to forecast changes in weather and climate and allowing observations of changes in land cover and land use. In general, biologists and ecologists have lagged behind their physical science counterparts in harnessing remote sensing to enhance their research and its applications. There are many perfectly good reasons for this. For one, the near global scales at which satellites have observed many phenomena on Earth's surface are simply too coarse for the local- or plot-scales at which most biologists and ecologists traditionally have worked. If you cannot detect a field site in the imagery, much less the organisms you are studying within it, how useful could the imagery be? While airborne sensors can overcome many of these issues of spatial scale, the costs of mounting an airborne campaign have often been daunting.

The need for relatively expensive and complex-to-operate computer hardware and software provided another disincentive to biologists and ecologists considering the potential utility of remote sensing. The rapidly growing remote sensing literature often discussed new techniques in a specialized terminology with little guidance for those outside the discipline. A number of books and articles over the years have addressed some biological applications of remote sensing. While engineers, physicists, and chemists still seem to dominate the development of new remote sensing techniques and much of the associated literature, biologists and ecologists across multiple specializations are discovering the benefits of using remote sensing as a tool, both to extend the spatial scales of their research beyond limited field observations and to apply their science to real world problems. Sensors with higher spatial and spectral resolutions are also bringing smaller sites into focus and in some cases allowing the identification of types of communities and species, and even the location of individual organisms. In addition, ecosystem-based approaches to science and management have emphasized the importance of investigating and understanding the broader context in which local communities and individuals function. It turns out that remote sensing is often quite good at providing elements of this broader context.

Improvements in related technologies have further promoted an awakening to the benefits of remote sensing and given it a broader role in the biological sciences. The advent of accurate and relatively inexpensive global positioning system (GPS) technology has provided an effective means for those in the field to place their data points into an accurate, global, and common geospatial reference frame. Essentially, all field data can now be easily georeferenced. The rise of geographic information system (GIS) software allows you to overlay and compare georeferenced digital data from disparate sources, lessening the challenge of using multi-scale inputs. Concomitant increases in computer capacity and the increasing simplification and availability of remote sensing software tools let you handle ever-larger amounts of satellite imagery faster and in a more user-friendly manner. Older remote sensing hands can recall the days when computational power was such that they were limited to working with only one quarter of a Landsat Multispectral Scanner scene (with 79 m pixels) at any given time on their computers. Today, computer systems easily handle full Landsat Enhanced Thematic Mapper Plus scenes (30 m pixels). The convergence of technologies and holistic approaches to ecology and much of biology are turning remote sensing into a much more commonly used tool.

We brought our backgrounds in ecology and conservation biology, along with experiences in the use of remote sensing, to the task of writing a book on remote sensing for ecologists, conservation biologists, and resource managers. We tried to write the book we had wished for back when we first learned remote sensing techniques, wrestled with issues of whether to use remote sensing for a project, and tried to decide what type of remote sensing was best and then employ it wisely. Our objective is to make the tool of remote sensing more accessible to professional communities that are in the relatively early stages of recognizing its strengths and exploring its applications. We realize that remote sensing is not the answer to all challenges faced by ecologists, conservation biologists, and resource managers. As such, we have sought to point out situations in which remote sensing might not be a good idea—where time and money would be better spent elsewhere.

There are a number of introductory remote sensing books, but we wanted this book to be different, focused on meeting the needs of biological scientists. Experience with elements of this book in other projects grew into a commitment to complete a more ambitious guide. We have organized the book's chapters along the lines of either large-scale biological units (e.g., vegetated lands, wetlands, marine and coastal systems, and the urban interface) or by topics of wide importance in the fields of ecology, conservation, and resource management (e.g., disturbance, fragmentation, reserve design, modeling, and global conservation). Other chapters introduce the well-established domains of climate remote sensing and terrain mapping. The initial chapters and the appendices offer a foundation in the areas of remote sensing most relevant to ecology and conservation biology, along with assessments of the tools available and a better understanding of when and when not to use remote sensing. Throughout the text, there is an emphasis on applications of remote sensing with examples and case studies showing the way.

We hope you will find this book a useful introduction to remote sensing or to particular areas of remote sensing that are new to you. It should also serve as a refresher for those more familiar with remotely sensed data and provide insights into new and helpful approaches to ecological problems.

May this book contribute to the growing recognition of remote sensing as an important spatially based tool for conservation and management and its text and online materials serve to promote a deeper investigation of remote sensing by ecologists and conservation biologists. In time, a basic understanding of remote sensing could become part of the toolkit of every ecologist, conservation biologist, and resource manager.

The challenges species, ecological communities, and ecosystems face are often regional to global in scale. If more ecologists, conservation biologists, and resource managers become proficient users of remote sensing to answer their questions, can a revolution in understanding within the biological sciences be far behind?

Acronyms List

Certain acronyms are used so frequently in remote sensing, especially agency names, satellite names, and sensor names, that they become a part of the lingo of the discipline. Rather than spell these out on every use in the book (they are sometimes used in every chapter), we list the most common acronyms here.

Common Satellites and Sensors

AERONET, Aerosol Robotic Network, ground-based federation of networks of calibrated sun photometers and radiometers

ADEOS, Advanced Earth Observing Satellite "Midori," I and II, JAXA

AIRS, Atmospheric Infrared Sounder sensor on the Aqua Earth Observing System satellite, NASA

AMSR-E, Advanced Microwave Scanning Radiometer-EOS, Japanese sensor on NASA Aqua Earth Observing System satellite, JAXA

AMSU, Advanced Microwave Sounding Unit, sensor on NOAA POES satellites; also flies aboard NASA Aqua and ESA/EUMETSAT MetOp satellites

ASCAT, Advanced Scatterometer sensor on the MetOp satellite, ESA/EUMET-SAT

ASTER, Advanced Spaceborne Thermal Emission and Reflection Radiometer, a Japanese sensor aboard the NASA Terra Earth Observing System satellite, METI

AVHRR, Advanced Very-high Resolution Radiometer sensor on the POES series of satellites, NOAA

AVIRIS, Airborne Visible/Infrared Imaging Spectrometer, airborne hyperspectral instrument, NASA

CALIPSO, Cloud-Aerosol Lidar and Infrared Pathfinder Satellite Observation, French-US clouds and aerosols satellite

CASI, Compact Airborne Spectrographic Imager, airborne instrument, ITRES Research Ltd.

CERES, Clouds and the Earth's Radiant Energy System sensor on the TRMM, Terra, and Aqua satellites, NASA

CZCS Coastal Zone Color Scanner sensor on the Nimbus 7 satellite

DMSP, Defense Meteorological Satellite Program, US Department of Defense: SSM/I, Special Sensor Microwave Imager

Envisat satellite, ESA:
  AATSR, Advanced Along-Track Scanning Radiometer
  ASAR, Advanced Synthetic Aperture Radar instrument
  MERIS, Medium Resolution Imaging Spectrometer sensor

EO-1, Earth Observing-1 satellite, NASA:
  ALI, Advanced Land Imager
  Hyperion, Hyperspectral Imager

LEISA, Linear Etalon Imaging Spectral Array Atmospheric Corrector (also LAC)

ERS, European Remote Sensing Satellite series

GeoEye, satellite, sensor, and commercial developer and operator (not an acronym, but spelled this way as a trade name and by convention)

GOES, Geostationary Operational Environmental Satellite series, NOAA

GPS, global positioning system, a method of locating position based on triangulation of position based on time to receive microwave signals from a set of dedicated satellites, US Department of Defense

GTOPO30, Global 30 Arc Second Elevation Data, a global digital elevation model developed from a variety of topographic data sets worldwide, USGS

HIRS, High Resolution Infrared Radiation Sounder, sensor on NOAA POES satellites

HRG, High Resolution Geometric sensor

HRV, Visible High-Resolution sensor

HRVIR, Visible and Infrared High-Resolution sensor

IKONOS, satellite and sensor (not an acronym, but spelled in all capitals as a trade name and by convention), developed and operated by GeoEye

INSAT, Indian series of geostationary satellites for meteorology and communications

Landsat satellite series, NASA/USGS:
    ETM + , Enhanced Thematic Mapper Plus sensor
    MSS, Multispectral Scanner sensor
    TM, Thematic Mapper sensor

Lidar, laser light detection and ranging, type of instrument, an acronym spelled in small letters by convention

MISR, Multi-angle Imaging SpectroRadiometer, sensor on Terra Earth Observing System satellite, NASA

MIVIS, Multispectral IR and Visible Imaging Spectrometer, airborne multispectral imager, Daedalus Enterprise Inc.

MODIS, Moderate Resolution Imaging Spectroradiometer, sensor on Terra and Aqua Earth Observing System satellites, NASA

MPLNET, Micro-pulse Lidar Network, ground-based lidar network for atmospheric observations

MSU, Microwave Sounding Unit, sensor on past POES satellites, NOAA

MTSAT, Japan's meteorological satellite series operated by the Japan Meteorological Agency

NPOESS, National Polar-orbiting Operational Environmental Satellite System

OMI, Ozone Monitoring Instrument, Dutch-Finnish instrument on the NASA Aura Earth Observing System satellite

POES, Polar-orbiting Operational Environmental Satellite, NOAA

POLDER, Polarization and Directionality of the Earth's Reflectances, CNES aerosol sensor that flew on two Japanese ADEOS satellites

PRISM, Panchromatic Remote-sensing Instrument for Stereo Mapping sensor on the Daichi Advanced Land Observing Satellite, JAXA

QuickBird, sensor on WorldView-1 satellite (not an acronym, but spelled this way as a trade name and by convention), developed and operated by DigitalGlobe

QuikSCAT, Quick Scatterometer, NASA satellite carrying the SeaWinds scatterometer; usually the data is referred to as QuikSCAT data

Radar, radio detection and ranging, type of instrument, an acronym spelled in small letters by convention

Radarsat, Radar Satellite series, CSA with NASA cooperation

ROSIS, Reflective Optics System Imaging Spectrometer, airborne hyperspectral instrument, DLR

SAR, synthetic aperture radar

SeaWiFS, Sea-viewing Wide Field-of-view Sensor on OrbView-2 satellite (also known as the SeaStar satellite), NASA provides access to non-real-time data for educational and research purposes

SIR-C, Shuttle Imaging Radar-C band, radar elevation instrument flown onboard the Space Shuttle, NASA

SORCE, Solar Radiation and Climate Experiment satellite, NASA

SPOT, Satellite Pour l'Observation de la Terre, satellite series operated by Spot Image for CNES

HRG, High Resolution Geometric sensor

HRV, Visible High-Resolution sensor

HRVIR, Visible and Infrared High-Resolution sensor

SRTM, Shuttle Radar Topography Mission, radar elevation instrument flown onboard the Space Shuttle, NASA

TOMS, Total Ozone Mapping Spectrometer, a NASA ozone sensor has flown onboard Nimbus 7 (NASA/NOAA), Meteor 3 (NASA/Russian Space Agency), ADEOS (JAXA), and Earth Probe (NASA) satellites

TOPEX/Poseidon satellite and set of two radar altimeters flown jointly by CNES/NASA, followed by Jason-1 and Jason-2 which had different instrumentation

TRMM, Tropical Rainfall Measuring Mission, a NASA/JAXA satellite

LIS, Lightning Imaging Sensor

TMI, TRMM Microwave Imager

VIRS, Visible and Infrared Scanner

X-SAR, Shuttle Imaging Radar X-band Synthetic Aperture Radar, German and Italian radar elevation instrument flown onboard the NASA Space Shuttle

Government Agencies

CNES, Centre National d'Études Spatiales, national space agency of France

CONAE, Comisión Nacional de Actividades Espaciales, space agency of Argentina

CSA, Canadian Space Agency, space agency of Canada

DLR, Deutsches Zentrum für Luft- und Raumfahrt, national space agency of Germany

ESA, European Space Agency

EUMETSAT, European Organisation for the Exploitation of Meteorological Satellites

JAXA, Japan Aerospace Exploration Agency, known earlier as NASDA. National Space Development Agency of Japan

METI, Ministry of Economy, Trade and Industry (Japan)

NASA, National Aeronautics and Space Administration (United States)

    GISS, Goddard Institute for Space Studies

    GSFC, Goddard Space Flight Center

    JPL, Jet Propulsion Laboratory (operated by California Institute of Technology for NASA)

    JSC, Johnson Space Center

NOAA, National Oceanic and Atmospheric Agency (United States)

    CLASS, Comprehensive Large Array-data Stewardship System

USGS, United States Geological Survey

    EROS, Earth Resources Observation and Science data center, USGS

Acknowledgments

We greatly appreciate the efforts of numerous friends and colleagues who contributed to the preparation of this book, and deeply apologize if we have inadvertently neglected to thank any of you. These individuals served as sounding boards for ideas and content, reviewed chapters, or provided guidance, references, images, or unpublished data: Geeta Acharya, Bob Adler, John Barras, Gary Borda, Bob Brakenridge, Mark Cochrane, Karl Didier, Peter Ersts, Sarah Federman, Gene Feldman, Jennifer Gebelein, Gary Geller, Scott Goetz, James Goodman, Matt Hansen, Eric Hochberg, Michelle Hofton, Chris Justice, Norman Kuring, Ramesh Kakar, Kevin Koy, Nadine Laporte, Matthew Levine, Hal Maring, Jeff Morisette, John Morrison, Debra Moskovits, Jesús Muñoz, Rama Nemani, Ross Nelson, Richard Pearson, Natalia Piland, Diego Fernández Prieto, Lori Randall, Mike Ramsey, Taylor Ricketts, Robert Rose, Eric Sanderson, Jeffrey Silverman, David Skole, Jared Stabach, Will Stefanov, Kaity Tsui, Erin Vintinner, and Wayne Walker.

A special thank you goes to Erica Fleishman for a thorough review of the manuscript and to Kevin Frey for editing.

We want to thank our families and support networks for their encouragement and understanding while we overcame the challenges of creating a book like this as each of us worked in nonacademic positions. Special thanks goes to Neil and Maggie Davidson; Kevin Frey; Nadia, Naina, and Nanja Horning; Sandra Markgraf; Sue Ann Robinson; Jennifer, Maddy, and Harry Turner; and Daphne Uviller, Talia and Gabriel Spector.

We also wish to extend our thanks to the series editor, William Sutherland, as well as to Oxford University Press staff, including Ian Sherman, Helen Eaton, Stephanie Gehrig, and Peter Prescott.

Abbreviations

AATSR	Advanced Along Track Scanning Radiometer
ADEOS	Advanced Earth Observation Satellite
AERONET	Aerosol Robotic Network
AIRS	Aqua Atmospheric Infrared Sounder
AISA	Airborne Image Spectrometer
ALI	Advanced Land Imager
ALOS	Advanced Land Observing Satellite
AMS	Autonomous Modular Sensor
AMSR-E	Advanced Microwave Scanning Radiometer for EOS
AMSU	Advanced Microwave Sounding Unit
AOD	Aerosol Optical Depth
ASAR	Advanced Synthetic Aperture Radar
ASCAT	Advanced Scatterometer
ASST	Averaged Sea Surface Temperature Product
ASTER	Advanced Spaceborne Thermal Emission and Reflection Radiometer
ATSR	Along Track Scanning Radiometer
AVHRR	Advanced Very-High Resolution Radiometer
AVIRIS	Airborne Visible/Infrared Imaging Spectrometer
AVO	Alaska Volcano Observatory
BAER	Burned Area Emergency Response
BRDF	Bi-directional Reflectance Distribution Function
CALIPSO	Cloud-Aerosol Lidar and Infrared Pathfinder Satellite Observation
CART	Classification and Regression Tree
CASI	Compact Airborne Spectrographic Imager
CBI	Composite Burn Index
CDOM	colored dissolved organic matter
CERES	Clouds and the Earth's Radiant Energy System
CHARTS	Compact Hydrographic Airborne Rapid Total Survey
CLASS	Comprehensive Large Array-data Stewardship System
CNES	Centre National d'Études Spatiales
CONAE	Comisión Nacional de Actividades Espaciales
CZCS	Coastal Zone Color Scanner
DAIS	Digital Airborne Imaging Spectrometer
DEM	Digital Elevation Model
DHW	Degree Heating Weeks
DMS	Dimethyl Sulfide
DMSP	Defense Meteorological Satellite Program
EAARL	Experimental Advanced Airborne Research Lidar

EM	Electromagnetic
EMS	Electromagnetic Spectrum
ENSO	El Niño/Southern Oscillation
EO-1	Earth Observing–1 satellite
EROS	Earth Resources Observation and Science
ERS	European Remote Sensing
ESA	European Space Agency
ET	Evapotranspiration
ETM +	Enhanced Thematic Mapper Plus Sensor
EUMETSAT	European Organisation for the Exploitation of Meteorological Satellites
EVI	Enhanced Vegetation Index
FAO	Food and Agriculture Organization
FPAR	Fraction of Photosynthetically Active Radiation
GARP	Genetic Algorithm for Rule-set Prediction
GCMs	General Circulation Models
GHCN	Global Historical Climatology Network
GIS	Geographic Information System
GISS	Goddard Institute for Space Studies
GLAS	Geoscience Laser Altimeter System
GLCF	Global Land Cover Facility
GLOVIS	Global Visualization Viewer
GOES	Geostationary Operational Environmental Satellite series
GPCP	Global Precipitation Climatology Project
GPS	Global Positioning System
GTOPO30	Global 30 Arc Second Elevation Data
GSFC	Goddard Space Flight Center
HAB	Harmful Algal Blooms
HIRS	High Resolution Infrared Radiation Sounder
HydroSHEDS	**Hydro**logical data and maps based on **SH**uttle **E**levation **D**erivatives at multiple **S**cales
ICESAT	Ice, Cloud, and land Elevation Satellite
IFSAR	Interferometric Synthetic Aperture Radar
IMS	Ice Mapping System
IMU	Inertial Measurement Unit
INSAT	Indian Series of Geostationary Satellites for Meteorology and Communications
IPCC	Intergovernmental Panel on Climate Change
ISCCP	International Satellite Cloud Climatology Project
ITCZ	Inter-Tropical Convergence Zone
JAXA	Japan Aerospace Exploration Agency
JPL	Jet Propulsion Laboratory
LAI	Leaf Area Index
LCCS	Land Cover Classification System

LEISA   Linear Etalon Imaging Spectral Array Atmospheric Corrector (also LAC)
LIS   Lightning Imaging Sensor
MERIS   Medium Resolution Imaging Spectrometer
METI   Ministry of Economy, Trade and Industry (Japan)
MHS   Microwave Humidity Sounder
MISR   Multi-angle Imaging SpectroRadiometer
MIVIS   Multispectral IR and Visible Imaging Spectrometer
MM5   Fifth generation Mesoscale Model
MNF   Maximum Noise Fraction
MODIS   Moderate Resolution Imaging Spectroradiometer
MPLNET   Micro-pulse Lidar Network
MSU   Microwave Sounding Unit
MSS   Multispectral Scanner Sensor
MTSAT   Meteorological Satellite
NASA   National Aeronautics and Space Administration
NBR   Normalized Burn Ratio
NDVI   Normalized Difference Vegetation Index
NGS   National Geodetic Survey
NOAA   National Oceanic and Atmospheric Administration
NPOESS   National Polar-orbiting Operational Environmental Satellite System
OC4   Ocean Chlorophyll 4 Algorithm
OMI   Ozone Monitoring Instrument
PAR   Photosynthetically Active Radiation
PCA   Principle Components Analysis
PNWR   Patuxent National Wildlife Refuge
PODAAC   Physical Oceanography Distributed Active Archive Center
POLDER   Polarization and Directionality of the Earth's Reflectances
PSU-NCAR   Pennsylvania State University—National Center for Atmospheric Research
QuikSCAT   Quick Scatterometer
RGB   Red, Green, Blue
RMS   Root-Mean-Square
ROC   Receiver Operator Curve
ROSIS   Reflective Optics System Imaging Spectrometer
SAGE   Stratospheric Aerosol and Gas Experiment
SAR   Synthetic Aperture Radar
SAVI   Soil Adjusted Vegetation Index
SeaWIFS   Sea-Viewing Wide Field-of-View Sensor on Orbview-2 Satellite
SEVIRI   Spinning Enhanced Visible and Infrared Imager
SHOALS   Scanning Hydrographic Operational Airborne Lidar Survey
SIR   Shuttle Imaging Radar
SLC   Scan Line Corrector
SMMR   Scanning Multichannel Microwave Radiometer

SORCE	Solar Radiation and Climate Experiment
SPOT	Satellite Pour l'Observation de la Terre
SRTM	Shuttle Radar Topography Mission
SSMI	Special Sensor Microwave Imager
SST	Sea Surface Temperature
SVI	Simple Vegetation Index
SWIR	Shortwave Infrared
TIN	Triangulated Irregular Networks
TIR	Thermal infrared imaging
TM	Thematic Mapper
TMI	TRMM Microwave Imager
TRMM	Tropical Rainfall Measuring Mission
UASS	Unmanned Aircraft Systems
UAV	Unmanned Aerial Vehicles
USGS	United States Geological Survey
VCF	Vegetation Continuous Fields
VGPM	Vertically Generalized Production Model
VIRS	Visible and Infrared Scanner
VNIR	Visible and Near-Infrared
X-SAR	Shuttle Imaging Radar X-band Synthetic Aperture Radar

Part I

Getting started: remote sensing fundamentals

1

Introduction: Why ecologists and conservation biologists use remote sensing

This chapter addresses a question that we hope occurs to many ecologists and conservation biologists: How can remotely sensed data and methods support the conservation of biological diversity? We highlight the contributions remote sensing technologies make toward advancing our understanding of Earth and its varied biomes. You can use this information for applications ranging from researching habitat use by species to making decisions on how best to manage a protected area.

The chapter starts off with an overview of the motivation behind this book and a description of the intended audience. We present a broad array of applications of remote sensing technologies in the field of conservation biology and conclude with a brief summary of the remaining chapters of this book.

1.1 Our aims and objectives

Our overarching goal in publishing this book is to increase awareness about, and use of, remotely sensed data and methods in conservation biology and ecology. The objective of this book is to make remote sensing tools accessible so that ecologists and conservation biologists can assess the tools they need, have enough information to recognize effective uses and abuses of remote sensing, and know when to try to use the tools themselves versus when to solicit help from others. The broadest definition of remote sensing refers to measuring a particular quality (such as the intensity of light reflected) of a feature without being in physical contact with the feature itself. The magnitude of objects observed can range from the microscopic to the astronomic. In this book, however, we will limit our definition of remote sensing to measurements acquired from either airborne or orbiting platforms, with the features of interest located on or just above the surface of the Earth. Furthermore, we will focus primarily on remotely sensed data recorded in an image format since these are the data most commonly used in biodiversity conservation applications.

Conservation biology has grown from local and regional studies of single species into a discipline concerned with the complex interactions of species and their environment at global, regional, and local scales as well as across scales.

Increasingly, remote sensing provides a crucial tool for the effective collection of the information needed to set conservation priorities and to develop and implement conservation plans. This book will also help ecologists do their work more effectively by incorporating remotely sensed data.

The perceived complexities of remotely sensed data and analysis often discourage conservation biologists and ecologists from using this valuable resource. With practice, however, researchers and practitioners will be able to create their own data sets based on remotely sensed data instead of using data from archives that might not meet their specific and often changing needs.

The book departs from the usual organization of a remote sensing textbook focused on sensors and algorithms, and instead is structured by biomes and applications to reflect the organization used in the disciplines of ecology and conservation biology. The emphasis is on applications and illustrated examples that show how goals were met.

1.2 Why remote sensing tools are important

Remote sensing is a valuable tool for evaluating the status and trends of ecological systems (Peterson and Parker 1998; Turner *et al.* 2003; McPhearson and Wallace 2008). To help you better understand how remote sensing is used in ecology and conservation science we have focused on five broad capabilities: observation, analysis and measurement, mapping, monitoring over time and space, and decision support.

1.2.1 Observation

We use the term "observation" to include the detection and identification of features such as a specific type of habitat or events such as fires or storms. With a number of satellite remote sensing systems providing daily coverage of the Earth, we are able to detect the presence of events such as wildfires (Fig. 1.1) and substantial changes in land cover (Fig. 1.2) anywhere in the world. Using meteorological remote sensing satellites we can locate and track storms that occur around the globe.

A unique quality of remotely sensed data is that it allows us to understand habitats in a broader landscape or global context. The term "habitat" is problematic. In its original manifestation it is specific to a particular species, and relates to the physical space within the landscape in which an organism lives and the abiotic and biotic resources it needs within that space (Morrison and Hall 2002). Researchers often use the term "habitat" to denote a more generalized concept for which we do not have a term in ecology—essentially to describe a subset of an ecosystem or an area that provides necessary and sufficient resources for several different species. In this book we define a habitat to be an environment suitable for individual species or groups of species to live and reproduce. These habitats can then be linked with information about water resources, land

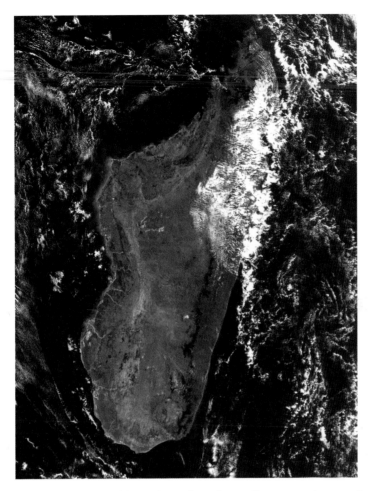

Fig. 1.1 Sensors that are able to detect heat from a fire are used to monitor the location of fires on a daily basis (Chapter 9). The red dots in this image of Madagascar show where a fire was detected by the MODIS sensor on the Terra satellite (June 4, 2003). With this capability it is possible to alert protected area or other land managers when a fire has been detected within or near a specific area of interest. Credit: MODIS Rapid Response Team, NASA.

cover, and fire and can provide a better understanding of connectivity across scales.

Remote sensing methods are commonly used to detect natural features. At one extreme is the use of satellite imagery to detect the occurrence of large mammals such as elephants (NASA 2005b), but it is more commonly used for identifying larger features or patterns such as habitats and land cover types. You can observe landscapes simply by viewing images acquired from aircraft or satellites or you can do sophisticated processing to facilitate the identification of specific features.

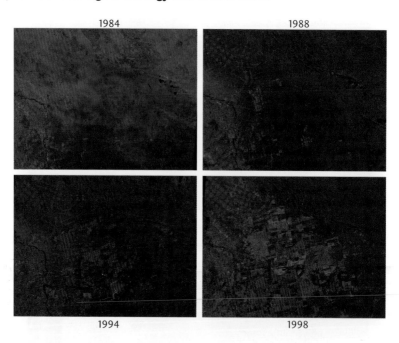

Fig. 1.2 Satellite data are often used to monitor changes in land cover over time (Chapter 4). These Landsat TM images show how deforestation progressed east of Santa Cruz, Bolivia, from 1984 to 1998. The various geometric patterns that appear in the images and expand over time are progressive clearing of forest for agriculture. Credit: Scientific Visualization Studio, NASA/GSFC.

Feature recognition algorithms developed for computer vision applications and available in specialized computer software automate the identification of specific features in an image. Although this software can help make the identification of objects easier, it is still difficult to improve upon the feature recognition abilities of the eye and brain.

At a finer scale, you can use remote sensing to provide information to more effectively enforce rules protecting natural resources (Souza *et al.* 2003). You can also use information from satellite and aerial platforms to locate areas where a landscape has changed in ways not supported by local laws. In the marine environment, remote sensing instruments can detect dumping of oil from ships (Fig. 1.3) or the occurrence of red tides.

1.2.2 Analysis and measurement

Remotely sensed platforms measure a number of biological and physical variables such as elevation, productivity, cloud type and coverage, land and water surface temperature, precipitation amount, wind velocity, and water quality. Sensors measure some of these variables directly (i.e., elevation and temperature). In

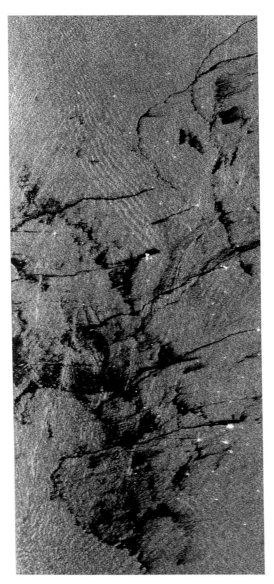

Fig. 1.3 This image from the NASA Spaceborne Imaging Radar C/X-Band Synthetic Aperture Radar instrument onboard the *Space Shuttle* shows oil slicks from an offshore drilling field about 150 km off the west coast of Mumbai, India (October 9, 1994). Radar instruments are ideal for detecting oil spills in water. When a radar signal hits the rough surface of an uncontaminated ocean surface much of the energy bounces back toward the sensor. When oil is on the ocean surface very little of the energy returns to the sensor. This is why oil on the ocean appears as black patches in the image. The bright spots are oil platforms and boats. Credit: NASA/JPL.

other cases, variables are derived using algorithms that continue to be developed and improved.

Remote sensing is an important input to a variety of models including those used for species, population, and ecosystem analysis. As our ability to measure biophysical variables improves, the explanatory and predictive accuracy of the models that use these data will also improve. These measurements are available at scales ranging from local- or plot-level studies all the way to global studies. Some measurements are available on demand or are generated at regular intervals using production systems, while others are custom products requiring substantial input from experienced analysts.

Working in a quickly changing world, conservation biologists often do not have the time or resources for widespread and detailed ecological surveys. Remote sensing provides the possibility for broad sampling from which you can infer information to solve a crisis more effectively.

1.2.3 Mapping

Conservation biology and ecology are both disciplines that have a spatial or geographic component, and remote sensing is a great tool for providing spatial information. Perhaps the best-known use of remotely sensed data is to document the conditions of a specific area at a specific time in the form of a map. This snapshot in time can be from a recent acquisition of data or from previous decades.

The creation of land use maps is a common application of remotely sensed data but there are several other types of maps that you can create to document conditions on land or in the water. Examples of maps of different features include soils, landforms, habitats, clouds, and coral distribution. In addition to mapping physical features, any of the biophysical variables mentioned in the previous section can be mapped to show how they vary over space.

Accuracy assessment is a key component of mapping, and we discuss this in greater detail in Section 2.2.

1.2.4 Monitoring over time and space

In addition to mapping features or variables at a single date in time, you can use remote sensing methods to monitor how they change over time. This temporal component is important for documenting how features have changed in the past, and predicting changes into the future. The frequency of monitoring depends on how frequently data are acquired and the phenomenon being monitored but it can range from continuous to several days to many years.

Another important characteristic of remote sensing is that there is a rich archive of data going back to the 1960s for satellite imagery and the early 1900s for aerial photography. This archive allows us to assess accurately how environments have changed from historic time periods; in many cases understanding past changes will explain why the current environment is the way it is and also helps us better understand drivers of change to more accurately predict how the environment will change in the future.

Some monitoring applications that are relevant to conservation of biological diversity include land cover and land use change, grassland conditions, oil-spill cleanup, wildfire fighting, monitoring of fire scars in tropical forests, postfire recovery, and changes in fragmentation patterns.

1.2.5 Decision support

Incorporating remotely sensed data into the decision-making process is a common way to benefit from its capabilities. You can use trend information derived from remotely sensed products to develop multiple management and policy scenarios, thereby providing guidance for more effective decisions, for instance in setting conservation priorities and finding optimum locations for protected areas (Menon and Bawa 1997), or in managing protected areas (Chapter 12). The applications section of this book presents specific examples of how remotely sensed data are used to support decision-making.

1.3 Organization of the book

We have written the chapters in this book to parallel treatments in the biological literature, rather than the remote sensing literature. The chapters have been divided into three parts and appendices:

1. Getting started: remote sensing fundamentals (Chapters 1–3)
2. Ecological systems and processes (Chapters 4–9)
3. Putting remote sensing into practice: conservation and ecology applications (Chapters 10–15)
4. Appendices

The chapters within each section provide an overview of how and why remote sensing is used in specific applications as well as case studies that illustrate uses of remotely sensed data. Although it is not necessary to read this book from cover to cover, we suggest that you read the chapters in the part "Getting Started" prior to reading the remainder of the book. This will help you establish the fundamental principles of remote sensing used throughout the book. Depending on the focus of your work, certain chapters may seem more relevant to you than others, but you may want to skim those other sections to read about application of specific techniques that could be relevant to your area of interest. The third part of the book, "Putting it into Practice: Conservation and Ecology Applications," builds on much of the information covered in the preceding chapters.

1.3.1 Getting started: remote sensing fundamentals

In the first three chapters we introduce how remote sensing is used in conservation and ecology, presenting fundamental concepts used throughout the book.

Before you decide to use remotely sensed data, it is important that you understand the benefits and limitations of remotely sensed data. A number of factors impose limitations, and these need to be assessed in order to make good decisions related to using remotely sensed data. A factor for you to consider is the level of detail that can be resolved from remotely sensed data and how this affects the type(s) of data suitable for a particular objective. Similarly, understanding how to evaluate the accuracy of products derived from remotely sensed data helps you become aware of the limitations of those products. Another limitation is the remote sensing expertise that you or those in your organization have. In some cases you will need to assess the capabilities within your institution to determine if it is necessary to look for additional expertise to achieve an objective or execute a project using remotely sensed data. These topics are covered in Chapter 2, "When to use remote sensing."

Before embarking on any project that works with remotely sensed data, it is a good idea to understand some of the fundamental concepts. This understanding will also help you better understand most of the chapters in this book. In Chapter 3, "Working with images," we begin with an overview of how to manipulate images in a computer and how they can be processed to make visual imagery that you can interpret on a computer monitor or in printed form. We also discuss what factors need to be considered when selecting imagery to help you decide what type of imagery is suitable for a particular task. This is helpful since the uses of remotely sensed data are extensive, and selecting imagery from the tremendous variety of remotely sensed data can be daunting. You will also have to make choices about the different types of software that can be used to visualize and process remotely sensed data. Using specialized software you can use image-processing techniques to reduce the negative effects of the atmosphere on the remote sensing signal and modify the geometry of an image so that it can be overlaid with a map. You can also use image interpretation and classification techniques that help you to identify and map features in an image. Even if you do not get involved with image processing it is helpful to know techniques for visualizing and processing remotely sensed data.

1.3.2 Ecological systems and processes

We organized this part so that chapters cover remote sensing of terrestrial, freshwater, and marine biomes as well as urban environments and the atmosphere. We also cover processes including climate and human-induced and natural disturbances. We start off with terrestrial biomes in Chapter 4, "Measuring and monitoring land cover, land use, and vegetation characteristics." One common use of remotely sensed data is to produce land use and land cover maps and maps that show how the landscape has changed over time. There are a number of steps involved in mapping vegetation cover that you should be familiar with. These range from defining the study area, to the categories that will be used for the mapping, to selecting appropriate imagery and analysis methods, and to measuring the accuracy when the map is finished. You can also use remotely sensed data acquired from different time periods to study how land cover has changed over time. These methods are similar to the ones used for mapping land use and land cover but the differences are important. In addition to mapping types of vegetation, you can also use remotely sensed data to measure other ecologically relevant measures of vegetation such as vegetation biomass.

Other features of the land that you can study using remotely sensed data are terrain, geology, and soils. We cover these topics in Chapter 5, "Terrain and soils." Some background information that you will need to understand includes how elevation is defined and how elevation data are acquired and processed. Using computer algorithms and elevation data it is possible to create a host of products that describe the physical features of the terrain such as slope, aspect, watercourses, ridges, and valleys. You can also use elevation data to improve the geometric and radiometric qualities of remotely sensed image data. Geologists commonly use remote sensing methods to study landforms and to classify different types of substrate materials based on their reflectance properties. Similar techniques can also be used to map soils. Unfortunately these methods are hindered in areas where the Earth surface is covered by vegetation. Mapping of global soil moisture is routinely measured using remote sensing instruments but the resolution tends to be very coarse, on the order of tens of kilometers. Finer-scale data can be acquired using aerial instruments.

Aquatic environments are also well served using remote sensing methods. This is especially important since their extent is so vast. In the marine realm you need to consider how the water surface, water column, and bottom affect a remote sensing signal. Knowing how to deal with these effects will allow you to use remote sensing techniques to measure water properties including chlorophyll, primary productivity, sea surface temperature, and salinity. Shallow benthic cover types such as coral reefs, seagrasses, and kelp can also be studied using remote sensing techniques. You can use these techniques for monitoring events such as algal blooms, for predicting coral bleaching, and for understanding the effects of ocean circulation on dispersal of larval fish. In order to measure and monitor all these features, you can use a mix of multispectral, hyperspectral, and lidar data. These topics are summed up in Chapter 6, "Marine and coastal environments."

Other aquatic environments are wetlands and inland waters. Chapter 7, "Wetlands—estuaries, inland wetlands, and freshwater lakes" covers these topics in detail. Use of remotely sensed data allows increased insight into the ecological functions of these complex interfaces between land and water such as wetlands, mangroves, saltwater and freshwater marshes, shorelines, streams, and lakes. Wetlands tend to be difficult to map because they are quite dynamic and often gradients between terrestrial and aquatic ecosystems. In wetland environments there are a number of remote sensing techniques similar to those used in terrestrial and marine environments. For example, you can measure wetland elevations and vegetation using terrestrial techniques and water quality and temperature using aquatic techniques. A range of sensors covers aquatic ecosystems including multispectral, hyperspectral, radar, lidar, and thermal instruments.

Monitoring climatic and atmospheric phenomena is also important in the fields of ecology and conservation. Remote sensing data have revolutionized climate science. Much of the money supporting remote sensing research is going into studying the five elements of Earth's climate system: clouds, aerosols, precipitation, winds, and temperature. In order to understand how remote sensing is applied to research on these phenomena it is helpful to have some background on clouds, aerosols, precipitation, winds, and temperature. With a fundamental understanding you can learn how remote sensing of these atmospheric parameters takes place. There are a number of climatic and atmospheric products based on remotely sensed data so you might not need to create these yourself but it is still helpful to know what products are available and how they were created. You can use output generated from global climate models to predict changes within ecosystems and this can be a powerful decision support tool. These topics are covered in Chapter 8, "Atmosphere and climate."

Identifying and monitoring the effects of natural and human disturbance on the environment is the focus of Chapter 9, "Disturbances: fires and floods." Remote sensing tools are well suited to observing events that are drivers of ecosystem disturbance such as fires, floods, volcanoes, and dams. These tools can also be used to predict the occurrence of these events, monitor the event as it progresses, and finally monitor changes long after the event has ended.

1.3.3 Putting it into practice: conservation applications

This final part ties together topics addressed in the earlier parts in the book by illustrating how you can apply them to conservation. Case studies highlight how scientists and managers have used remote sensing methods.

Understanding fragmentation and landscape metrics provides insight into how land cover is distributed, which can in turn be used to predict suitability for different flora and fauna. Remotely sensed data and products can be used to calculate a number of different measures including composition and connectivity as well as fractal dimension and route networks. These measures, which can be applied across scales from local to global, are the subject of Chapter 10, "Landscape fragmentation."

Another use of remotely sensed data is to study the interfaces between human-modified and natural environments, and to map urban extent and urban change. This is the focus of Chapter 11, "Human interfaces and urban change." Many of the techniques used for vegetation mapping, such as image rectification, image preprocessing, change detection approaches, texture analysis, and accuracy assessment, have been adapted to map and monitor human land uses and urban, suburban, and exurban environments.

Remotely sensed data can be used for planning, implementation, and monitoring of individual protected areas and in developing networks of protected areas in terrestrial as well as marine systems. At the global scale, remotely sensed data contributes to the analysis of protected area effectiveness. The issue of integrating social and economic data into protected area planning and monitoring is critical to the success of these initiatives. There are advantages and limitations to using remote sensing tools in this respect. As with other technologies, there can be stumbling blocks associated with the use of remotely sensed data due to the fundamental limitations of remote sensing and also a lack of knowledge of how to effectively use remote sensing methods. Chapter 12, "Protected area design and monitoring," addresses these fundamental conservation and management activities.

Remote sensing and fieldwork are complementary. Chapter 13, "Integrating field data", focuses on the use of remote sensing for inventory and monitoring and the integration of field-based measurement with remotely sensed data. You can use field-based instruments to relate conditions measured in the field with great detail and accuracy when compared with data collected from aerial and satellite platforms, which can image broad areas. You can collect field data that will help you more accurately interpret, classify, or predict biological and physical parameters (i.e., net primary productivity, soil moisture, percent tree cover) calculated from aerial or satellite remotely sensed data. You can also test the accuracy of products created from remotely sensed data. Although it is not considered a remote sensing technique, for the purposes of this book telemetry can be used with remotely sensed data to monitor how animals interact with their environment.

You can use many of the remotely sensed data and derived products discussed earlier to provide accurate information about species, ecosystems, and landscapes when more direct measurements are impractical. This is the focus of Chapter 14, "Linking remote sensing with modeling." Selecting appropriate data for a model requires that you define some fundamental components such as a problem statement, a model system's boundaries, a modeling approach, model variables, and what data are necessary to test and validate your model. A number of abiotic and biotic variables that are available from remote sensing-derived products can be used for modeling. Becoming familiar with the qualities of these products can help you more effectively conduct your modeling tasks.

The book concludes with Chapter 15, "Global conservation," which highlights how global remotely sensed data sets serve broad-scale conservation efforts. Remote sensing helps to bring a global approach to conservation. Starting with early images of the Earth from *Apollo* missions that helped awaken a global environmental consciousness, remotely sensed imagery has affected how we perceive our world in ways that have ramifications for both fundamental ecological research and conservation practice. By giving us the big picture, remote sensing has helped us develop measures for understanding the condition and trends of large, regional-scale patches of the Earth's surface, for example: vegetation indices, net primary productivity, land cover, and ocean color. Furthermore, combining these broad-scale data sets with fine-scale information on the species in a given area or the location of specific protected areas allows us to relate broad-scale changes back to particular species or areas of concern. The proliferation of both remote sensing products and ground-based inventories of species and ecosystems as well as collection of social, economic, and cultural information should enable a scientifically rigorous global ecology to drive successful strategies for global conservation.

1.3.4 Appendices

The appendices provide more detailed and practical information on topics that are not covered in depth in the main part of the book.

Appendix 1: The electromagnetic spectrum
Appendix 2: Image-processing software
Appendix 3: Open source software
Appendix 4: Satellites and sensors
Appendix 5: Visual interpretation
Appendix 6: Systems for observing climate and atmospheric phenomena

1.4 Remote sensing: a technology in development

When writing a book that is tightly linked to technology and instrumentation that is constantly changing, some of the details rapidly go out of date. This is certainly the case with remote sensing and its supporting technologies. To deal with this problem, we use high-level descriptions about the technology and applications that will remain relatively unchanged over the next several years. To address topics that do change rapidly, such as the software tools, sensors, and platforms, we have established a Web site that will be regularly updated to reflect the current status. This Web site is located at http://RemoteSensing4Conservation. amnh.org.

Enjoy reading this book. Remote sensing can be an accessible and powerful tool to study and manage the environment.

2

When to use remote sensing

Remote sensing technologies can benefit a large number of environmental conservation and management tasks. However, understanding the limitations is as important as understanding the benefits. While appropriate use of remotely sensed data can increase knowledge and expand understanding, inappropriate use can be expensive and create products that mislead, rather than inform. In this chapter we present the benefits as well as technical and practical limitations of remote sensing, emphasizing the importance of clearly understanding the accuracy of remote sensing data and analyses. The chapter concludes with practical advice on how an organization can assess its remote sensing capabilities and, if necessary, work with collaborators to add remote sensing expertise to projects.

2.1 Physical and practical limitations of remotely sensed imagery

There is no doubt that satellite and aerial remote sensing has greatly improved our ability to map land cover and to monitor a range of environmental phenomena. Still, there are fundamental limitations of remote sensing that are often understated or overlooked in the professional literature. We want to alert you to some of the limitations as well as highlight the trade-offs between limitations and benefits, some of which may not be intuitive. Throughout the book we present trends in remote sensing research and development to give a sense of how these issues evolve over time.

In other chapters, we discuss a number of limitations such as problems related to accurately aligning different imagery with a map base (Chapter 3); recording usable images in areas that are cloudy or hazy (Chapter 4); and recording data beneath a vegetative canopy (Chapter 4) or water surface (Chapters 6 and 7).

The issues discussed in this chapter focus on the applicability of remote sensing imagery and its derived products. Some of these issues are technical in nature such as the different qualities that affect how well a feature can be resolved in an image or factors related to image classification. Other limitations are more practical and may depend on the location of a particular project or available resources (financial, time, and human).

2.1.1 Resolution

Many discussions in remote sensing revolve around ways to detect more detail in an image. Different characteristics affect the details that can be resolved (seen) in imagery. These are traditionally referred to as the four types of image resolution: spatial, spectral, radiometric, and temporal.

Spatial resolution, which is often simply referred to as "resolution," is the size of a pixel in ground dimensions. A pixel is the smallest discrete scene element and image display unit. A common misconception about spatial resolution is that finer resolution is always better. Although a number of image providers offer imagery with a resolution of 1 m or less (Appendix 4), these are not always the best choice for a project. Fig. 2.1 illustrates a set of images throughout the book with spatial resolutions ranging from 1 m to 500 m. The 1 m IKONOS image certainly looks nice and we can see individual tree crowns, houses, and other details that are not visible in the other images. Why then would we even consider using other images?

A fine-resolution image requires more data (pixels) to cover a given area so the total area covered (the extent or footprint) by a fine-resolution image is usually smaller than for a coarse-resolution image (Fig. 2.2). This is an important consideration when conducting studies that cover a large area. "Mosaicing" or "tiling" multiple images to create a single seamless image to cover a study area can be a difficult task. As a general rule, it is best to use the fewest number of images that are practical to cover a study area. Related to this is the size of the data files—the finer the spatial resolution, the greater is the size of the data file. For example, there would be 100 times as many pixels in an image with 1 m resolution as there would be in an image with 10 m resolution resulting in a file 100 times larger.

Another limitation to using high-resolution imagery is that it can be costly, often tens of US dollars per square kilometer. As high-resolution imagery becomes more common and more providers appear in the marketplace, prices may come down, but they are likely to remain high enough in the foreseeable future to give users pause before purchasing.

A less obvious limitation is that high-resolution images are difficult to process using automated methods. Traditional classification methods that work on a pixel-by-pixel basis tend to perform poorly when the components of a feature of interest are resolved as individual features (Carleer *et al.* 2005). For example, in the IKONOS image in Fig. 2.1 we might be interested in delineating a forest class but when we run a traditional pixel-by-pixel classification on the image the classes produced are actually the components of the forest such as shadow, stems, leaves, and soil (Fig. 2.3). At a coarser spatial resolution a single pixel over a forest will contain a mixture of these components (i.e., shadow, stems, leaves, and soil) and it is this "mixed pixel" that is recognized as a forest. A technique called "spectral unmixing" (Chapters 6 and 7) can be used to estimate the relative abundance of specific components that are contained in an individual pixel (Liu and Wu 2005).

IKONOS, 1 m panchromatic merge,
1 m resolution

IKONOS multispectral, 4 m resolution

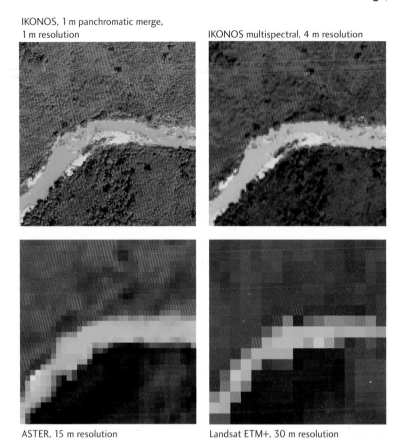

ASTER, 15 m resolution

Landsat ETM+, 30 m resolution

Fig. 2.1 The level of spatial detail varies as spatial resolution changes. These maps represent the view from satellite sensors with different spatial resolutions for a 500 × 500 m square on the ground of an area in central Vietnam. In the upper two images you can see individual tree crowns. The bottom two images integrate reflected energy from a much larger area and therefore less detail is visible. An image from MODIS has 500 m resolution (ground sampled distance), and would represent this area with a single pixel (not shown). Image details: IKONOS, 1 m panchromatic, 4 m multispectral resolution, subset from ID PO_91586, April 29, 2002; ASTER, 15 m, 8 November 2003; Landsat ETM+, 30 m, April 2, 2002. Credit: Ned Horning, American Museum of Natural History's Center for Biodiversity and Conservation, IKONOS images courtesy of GeoEye.

Automated analysis methods are being developed (Meinel and Neubert 2004; Carleer *et al.* 2005) that use feature recognition algorithms to group pixels into meaningful classes. These methods are able to group adjoining features such as the components seen in an image that make up a tree (shadows, leaves, and

MODIS footprint   Landsat ETM+ footprint

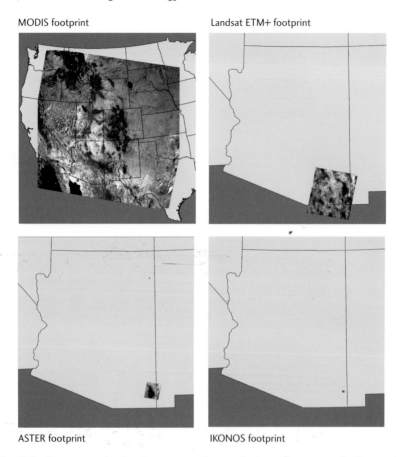

ASTER footprint   IKONOS footprint

Fig. 2.2 As a general rule, the coarser the resolution of a sensor the larger the footprint will be. The ground widths of the images represented are: MODIS—2330 km, Landsat ETM+—185 km, ASTER—60 km, and IKONOS—11 km. The footprint for the IKONOS image is only a speck at this scale. Credit: American Museum of Natural History's Center for Biodiversity and Conservation, IKONOS image courtesy of GeoEye.

branches) into an individual object such as a tree or a forest. However, the software programs supporting these methods are costly and complicated to use.

In most cases, the ideal imagery for a classification task will have a spatial resolution compatible with the desired scale of the final map representation of the data. Imagery with finer resolution than needed will make automated classification more difficult, while imagery with coarser resolution than needed will oversimplify and provide a map that does not meet the user's needs.

Spectral characteristics that affect the resolving power of an image include band width, band placement, and the number of bands. A band is a layer of an image and is described in more detail in Section 3.1.1. Information about the

IKONOS image   Classified image using pixel-by-pixel methods

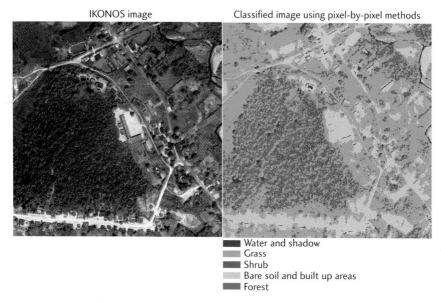

■ Water and shadow
▓ Grass
▨ Shrub
▨ Bare soil and built up areas
■ Forest

Fig. 2.3 Using conventional pixel-by-pixel classification algorithms to create maps using high-resolution remotely sensed data can cause problems since individual components of a feature much larger than the spatial resolution are classified instead of the feature itself. The IKONOS image on the left, with a spatial resolution of 1 m (covering a 400 × 400 m area, ID PO_91586, April 29, 2002), was classified using maximum likelihood methods to create a land cover map. Features with a smooth homogeneous surface such as a rooftops, roads, and bare soil are classified nicely. However, other features are misclassified as a set of multiple classes. For example, the forest in the leftmost portion of the image was classified as a mix of forest, shadow, shrub, and grass. Although these are the components of a forest, when we create a land cover map that kind of detail is usually not desired. New algorithms are being developed to address this problem. Credit: Ned Horning, American Museum of Natural History's Center for Biodiversity and Conservation, IKONOS image courtesy of GeoEye.

electromagnetic spectrum can be found in Appendix 1. Spectral bandwidth (often called "spectral resolution") is the range of wavelengths along the electromagnetic spectrum that are detected in a particular image band. Most multispectral sensors have relatively broad bands since they allow more light to reach the detector therefore providing a high signal-to-noise ratio, but for some applications narrow bands may be preferred. For example, narrow bands at carefully selected wavelengths can be used to detect small differences between similar vegetation.

Band placement defines the portion of the electromagnetic spectrum used for a particular image band. For example, one band might detect blue wavelengths and another band might detect thermal wavelengths. The particular properties of the features in which you are interested indicate which bands are important. For example, green vegetation largely absorbs red light and reflects most near-infrared light, so the red and near-infrared bands are useful for mapping vegetation.

The third spectral variable is the number of bands recorded by a sensor (sometimes also called "spectral resolution"). This is generally less important for visual interpretation since we are usually only interested in using one or three bands at a time, but it can become important when using automated classification approaches. The image classification process involves translating pixel values in a satellite image into meaningful categories. In other words, each pixel in an image is assigned a label such as forest or non-forest. Image products with many bands (usually over 100) are called "hyperspectral images." This is important because each of these bands can be thought of as a sample point recording radiance (light intensity) for a particular wavelength. If we plot these points we can create a spectral curve (Fig. 2.4). The more bands we have, the smoother the curve will be if we plot out the radiance values for all available bands at a particular pixel. The shape of these spectral curves is used to identify features in an image. Fig. 2.4 illustrates this concept by comparing two spectral curves; one from an Enhanced Landsat Thematic Mapper Plus (Landsat ETM+) image (7 bands with 6 in the visible and near-infrared wavelengths) and the other from a hyperspectral Hyperion image (242 bands). Hyperion is a test system to define whether future Earth remote sensing satellites should include hyperspectral sensors. In principle this highly detailed spectral information can be used to identify subtle differences in vegetation types. For example, tree diversity in moist tropical forests can be determined by spectranomics, the use of airborne hyperspectral sensors to measure the chemical properties of tree canopies (Asner and Martin 2008). Most of the work in hyperspectral remote sensing involves the use of airborne hyperspectral sensors with a high spatial resolution.

Sensitivity of the sensor (radiometric resolution) is defined by the dynamic range of the sensor as well as the number of units (digital numbers) that can represent the extremes of that range (quantization). The range between the minimum and maximum values permitted for a particular data type determines the detail that a sensor can measure between these extremes. Sensors have lower limits below which a signal is not registered and upper limits above which the sensor saturates and is unable to measure increases in radiance. For example, Landsat Thematic Mapper (Landsat TM) data values can range from 0 to 255 whereas IKONOS values range from 0 to 2048. This potential range of values is often referred to as the radiometric resolution of a sensor. Some sensors provide a low and high gain setting to provide the capability of recording high and low radiance values for a particular bandwidth using two bands instead of one.

Repeat frequency (temporal resolution) is the minimum time necessary for a particular remotely sensed feature to be recorded twice, and in the case of satellites is determined by the orbit track and the acquisition schedule. The frequency with which a sensor images an area can influence the ability to identify and define features that change over time, such as deciduous vegetation, or to

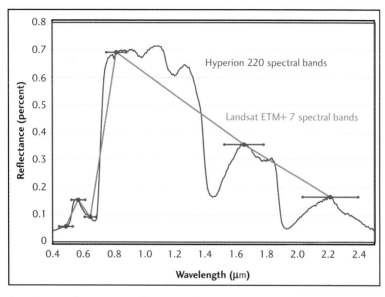

Fig. 2.4 Spectral sensitivity of sensors determines the level of detail that can be plotted in a spectral curve. This graph compares the spectral curves of Live Oak as they would be recorded by two different sensors. The Landsat ETM+ sensor measures radiance in six bands in the visible and near-infrared wavelengths (each shown by the red lines) and plotting reflectance data derived from these bands provides a fairly crude plot of line segments. In contrast, the Hyperion sensor has 242 bands and when plotting these data for the same vegetation the plot contains much more information about the spectral characteristics or signature. Reflectance data plotted on the graph are from the "veg_2grn.sli" spectral library that is packaged with ITT Visual Information Solutions ENVI version 4.5 software program. Credit: Ned Horning, American Museum of Natural History's Center for Biodiversity and Conservation.

record an event such as a flood. If sufficient images are acquired within the period of a year for a particular area, you can create temporal profiles (Fig. 2.5) using individual image bands or indices such as the vegetation indices discussed in Chapter 4. These temporal profiles or temporal signatures have been used to identify different types of vegetation (Defries and Townshend 1994). Having the possibility of a high repeat frequency also improves the chances of acquiring imagery without significant cloud cover, which is important for areas with persistent cloud cover.

The orbit of a satellite determines both its height above the Earth and how frequently it passes over the same spot on the ground (Wertz and Larson, 1999). Geostationary satellites have a very short repeat frequency, determined simply by the image acquisition frequency, since they follow the rotation of the Earth and maintain a constant position relative to features on the Earth. Because of orbital

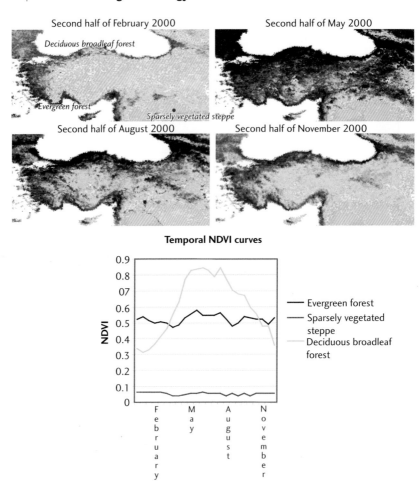

Fig. 2.5 Temporal profiles of vegetation indices such as the Normalized Difference Vegetation Index (NDVI) can be used to characterize different types of vegetation. The four images at the top of the figure represent NDVI values derived from Advanced Very High Resolution Radiometer (AVHRR) data for four different seasons in Turkey and surrounding areas. In these images, dark green indicates the highest NDVI values and tan the lowest. The graph plots the temporal profile for the area under the three red dots drawn on the upper left NDVI image. Each dot represents a different type of vegetation cover: deciduous broadleaf forest, evergreen forest, and sparsely vegetated steppe. The NDVI values used to create the plot are from 24 bimonthly composites for the year 2000. Credit: Ned Horning, American Museum of Natural History's Center for Biodiversity and Conservation.

dynamics, satellites in geosynchronous orbit are at 35,786 km from the Earth's surface directly over the equator and the sensors they carry typically produce imagery with a relatively low (kilometer-scale) spatial resolution (e.g., imagery from the US National Oceanic and Atmospheric Administration Geostationary Operational Environmental Satellite [GOES] program).

Most Earth remote sensing satellites are in a polar sun-synchronous orbit. This means that when they pass over a specific area on the ground, it is generally at the same time of day and that each passage over the equator is at different longitude. For example the Terra and Aqua pair of missions are designed so that the Aqua satellite crosses the equator at roughly 1:30 PM local time each day, while the Terra satellite observes the same area at 10:30–10:45 AM local time. Most sun-synchronous orbits used by Earth remote sensing missions are at an elevation on the order of hundreds of kilometers. Unique data can be found from manned spacecraft such as the NASA Space Shuttle and the International Space Station that are in low Earth orbit and can acquire images at very different times during the progression of their missions.

Some polar orbiting sensors with a very wide field-of-view can acquire multiple images of the same area in the same day (e.g., MODIS). Some sensors can also be pointed in different directions, which allow them to look to the side or forward and aft when acquiring imagery (e.g., SPOT). This capability effectively reduces the repeat time for which a feature can be recorded because the sensor is not limited to viewing directly beneath the satellite, that is, in a nadir orientation.

The repeat frequency for a particular sensor defines the maximum possible frequency for which a particular area can be imaged. This does not, however, mean that data are always acquired. Most satellite sensors are specifically tasked only to acquire specific images. For example, although Landsat data had been collected for years, it was not until the Landsat 7 long-term acquisition plan in 2001 that the satellite was tasked to cover coral reef areas in the Pacific (Arvidson *et al.* 2001). The amount of data a sensor can acquire throughout a day is limited by the onboard memory storage capacity, the network of receiving stations that can download imagery, and the energy available to the sensor.

Another quality related to repeat frequency is the timing of image acquisitions. Features that change over time, such as deciduous vegetation, and events, such as flooding, often have optimum or multiple instances at which they should be imaged. For example, the identification of deciduous vegetation is aided by acquiring imagery during leaf-on and during leaf-off periods. This timing is an important consideration when interpreting some features in an image.

2.1.2 Working at different scales: practical and conceptual limitations

Although remote sensing offers many data sets and techniques that allow you to work at, and even among, different scales, there are some practical limitations that must be understood when deciding to use remote sensing. These are usually related to the institutional or project resources available to work with remotely sensed data and the location of the study area.

As early as the conceptual development of a project, you should conduct some sort of formal or informal assessment of the benefits of remote sensing and, if remote sensing can contribute substantially to the project, the available resources and capabilities to work with such information. Section 2.3 presents some guidelines on assessing in-house capabilities.

Once you have decided to incorporate remote sensing into a project, the price and availability of imagery often limits what you can accomplish. Although image search capabilities are quite powerful and are improving all the time, it can still be time consuming to locate suitable imagery and at times the data you seek may not yet exist.

A growing archive of free satellite and aerial photography is available to the public but these data are not always suitable for a specific project. Most of the free satellite data has a medium or coarse (>15 m) spatial resolution and is limited to the contents of an archive. If you need high-resolution new images, you likely will have to purchase data. In some cases the cost can approach US$100/km^2 for on-demand, precision-corrected (processed so it precisely matches a map base) high-resolution imagery.

Locating usable imagery can also be problematic, especially if the project area is in a perennially cloudy region such as many areas in the tropics. It can be difficult to locate imagery if the timing of the acquisition is important such as for phenology studies, seasonal flooding, or to differentiate between deciduous and evergreen vegetation. In many archives such as the global Landsat GeoCover archive (Tucker *et al.* 2004) there might only be one image available within a 10-year time period. As of the end of 2008, digital imagery in the Landsat archive maintained by the US Geological Survey (USGS) is being distributed free of charge.

When searching for archived data it is possible that you will not be able to find what you are looking for. Even if the data formerly existed there is no guarantee that they are still available. Many of the archives of older historical data are difficult to search and become more expensive to access because of the need to locate old data and then convert it to a digital format. Requestors must often pay a fee for these types of services. A large number of data sets have been and continue to be lost due to the degradation of the photographic or digital media on which they are archived (Faundeen *et al.* 2004).

You may also find conceptual issues regarding scale that limit the application of remotely sensed data to the problem you are addressing, particularly when your work involves local human communities. For instance, Walker and Peters (2007) looked at forest change in two districts in Malawi using aerial photographs acquired in 1965 and 1995. While the photographs clearly showed forest loss through time, local communities did not perceive the same magnitude of loss. This disparity stemmed from the fact that community members focused on smaller pockets of available trees that could be overlooked when interpreting the aerial photos.

2.1.3 Using remote sensing to study social phenomena

Working on issues related to social phenomena requires collaboration with social scientists. The social science literature has several examples of projects using remotely sensed data (Turner 2003; Dennis *et al.* 2005; Ostrom and Nagendra 2006; Walker and Peters 2007). However, historically, remote sensing analysts have conducted social and economic analyses without appropriate consultation with social scientists (Turner 2003). Assessing the effects of the environment on humans, or vice versa, using traditional remote sensing methods will likely miss some important causal links between the social, political, and natural realms. For example, information about land tenure can only be inferred, not obtained conclusively, from remotely sensed data. To obtain information on property regimes (including land tenure) it is necessary to get the input of a social scientist or community member familiar with such institutional arrangements in your study area. When monitoring changes over time, temporal information captured by remotely sensed data does not necessarily correspond with the timing of social and political developments. For instance, you might lack remotely sensed data acquired at times that correspond with changes in natural resource policy or governance. As mentioned in Section 2.1.2, there is also a significant difference between how humans perceive space and the spatial information provided by remotely sensed data. In short, many features and events invisible to remote sensing analysts are critical for social scientific research. A thorough discussion of the integration of remote sensing and the social sciences is beyond the scope of this book, but we encourage you to think about collaborating with social scientists when dealing with the interactions between humans and their environment.

2.2 Accuracy

Remote sensing methods are often used to convert unprocessed (or minimally processed) aerial or satellite imagery to a product that can be used within a computer model or a geographic information system (GIS). Understanding and measuring the accuracy of these products is an important component of this process. The topic of image classification is addressed in detail in Chapters 3 and 4. In this section we will provide a basic understanding of the importance of accuracy assessment and how to interpret accuracy statistics. Details on how to design and implement an effective accuracy assessment will not be covered. For this sort of detail you can read some of the documents listed in the suggested reading section of the book's Web site.

2.2.1 Types of error

Accuracy can refer to either spatial accuracy or thematic accuracy (Vieira *et al.* 2004). *Spatial accuracy* refers to how well a derived product aligns with a reference map or other data from which accurate location information (i.e., latitude and longitude coordinates) can be obtained. This is directly related to the spatial qualities of the data from which the final product is derived (Wang and Ellis 2005). If you are using satellite imagery, the spatial accuracy of the final product will be dictated by the spatial accuracy of the satellite image that was used. Spatial error is sometimes presented as a root mean square error (RMSE) distance, such as ± 15 m from the "true" location, but it may also be presented as a proportion of the pixel dimension, such as plus/minus a half pixel.

Thematic accuracy specifies how well individual classes match what is actually on the ground. For example, if the thematic map indicates that there is forest at a particular location, is there actually forest on the ground? Error is inherent to the classification process and determining an acceptable level of error requires careful thought. Factors affecting thematic accuracy include: quality and type of the base data, experience of the analyst, processing methods, the analyst's familiarity with the area being classified, and the level of detail of the classification scheme.

When working with remote sensing image data, it is a good idea to limit the amount of processing steps to the minimum necessary to produce the end product. Each step in a processing chain alters the data in some way and with multiple steps these changes can become significant (see Box 2.1).

Box 2.1 Image degradation, an example

Certain image processing steps can degrade the quality of an image and it is a good idea to minimize these steps.

A small conservation organization wanted to create a land cover map for a protected area in a mountainous part of Madagascar. Since they were on a tight budget, they decided to look for some free imagery. They located an Enhanced Landsat Thematic Mapper Plus (ETM+) image, but it was in the wrong map projection to match their other geographic information system (GIS) data sets. The image was projected into a Universal Transverse Mercator (UTM) projection and all of their other data were projected using the Oblique Mercator projection. Fortunately they had some software that automatically re-projected the image from UTM coordinates to the Oblique Mercator projection.

After the satellite image was projected, the analyst decided to overlay some global positioning system (GPS) points that were collected using a very accurate GPS receiver to serve as control points for their project. What he found was that some areas seemed to match pretty well, but in other areas the control points were off by a few pixels. To fix this problem, the analyst followed a process called "image registration" that can warp the image to improve the match between the GPS control points and the image. After this process the match was not perfect but it was considered to be good enough to create the land cover map.

From this process it appears as if the image only went through two process-ing steps. Before the image was acquired by the nongovernmental organization (NGO), however, it had already undergone some processing to take it from its raw format, as it was recorded from the sensor, to the UTM projection. This involved two processing steps and in each the image values were modified. The work conducted by the NGO analyst, re-projecting the image and then the image registration, added two more processing steps with each modifying the image values some more (Jeong Chang 2003). Each of these processing steps involves a process called "resampling," whereby an image's pixel values are recalculated using a resampling algorithm such as nearest neighbor, bilinear, or cubic convolution. The distortions introduced by each step might be minimal but after resampling an image four times the changes can become significant enough to affect the land cover classification results.

Unfortunately, each of these steps was necessary in order to transform the image into the proper map projection. It would have been better to acquire an image that was in the right projection to reduce the processing steps but given the budget constraints this was not an option.

2.2.2 Defining acceptable accuracy

Spatial and thematic errors are inherent in the creation of products derived from remotely sensed data, so the goal is to produce a product with an acceptable level of error. Defining "acceptable" is often based more on available resources than on what is optimum for the project. Predicting the level of accuracy obtainable using a specific set of methods for a particular study is difficult, but experience and discussions with colleagues can help. Reading remote sensing journals can also help but journal articles tend to highlight the capabilities of a particular method without adequately discussing the limitations such as the time and cost required to produce the final product.

One guideline for creating a thematic map is to use the minimum number of classes that is practical because as the number of thematic classes increases, the accuracy of individual classes will decrease. A review of several dozen journal articles with forest classifications conducted by Ross Nelson (personal commu-nication, 2002) indicated the following typical land cover accuracy figures for land cover classifications using Landsat Thematic Mapper data:

- Forest/non-forest, water/no water, soil/vegetated: accuracies in the high 90 percent
- Conifer/hardwood: 80–90 percent
- Genus: 60–70 percent
- Species: 40–60 percent

These results indicate that the more thematic detail that we try to extract from the satellite image, the lower our accuracy will tend to be per class. For this reason, you will likely want to select the minimum number of classes that is practical.

2.2.3 Measuring and reporting accuracy

Conducting a proper accuracy assessment of a product created using remotely sensed data can be time consuming and costly, which is the primary reason why this important step is often not carried out in a mapping project. Time and again, accuracy assessment is included in the project design but later dropped or greatly modified in the interest of saving time or money. In these cases one can try to take an educated guess of what the accuracy is, based on the methods, experience, and data used, but in the end it is only a guess.

Methods for accuracy assessment come from the field of statistical sampling. To measure accuracy you compare the output from the remote sensing analysis (i.e., land cover map, elevation map, timber volume map) with the actual features observed in the field. For example, with a land cover map, you would compare a series of points on the map with the corresponding points in the field to build a statistical picture of how well they match. There are four steps involved in assessing accuracy: (1) develop a sample design, (2) collect validation data, (3) compile validation data, and (4) analyze these data.

A sample design is necessary to minimize bias. The following questions must be answered when developing a sample design:

- How many samples need to be selected?
- How will the samples be distributed?
- How will a sample area be defined?
- How will the field sampling be conducted?

The number and distribution of samples to use depend on the sampling framework that is selected. Most methods have formulas for calculating the appropriate number of sample points per class but more often than not the number of sample points per class is influenced by available time and money. A rule of thumb is to use 50 sample points per class (Congalton and Green 1999) but this is not always practical. We recommended that you work with someone familiar with sampling statistics or use guidelines from a book or journal article specializing in remote sensing accuracy assessment to ensure a sampling design robust enough to provide reliable statistics.

The sample area or sample unit can be individual pixels, clusters of homogeneous pixels, or polygons if the data are in a vector format. Due to the difficulty of accurately determining pixel boundaries on the ground, we do not recommend using individual pixels. When using groups of homogeneous pixels, the size depends a little on the resolution of the image. There are no set rules for this but higher resolution imagery would tend to use more pixels in a block than lower resolution imagery. A 3 × 3 pixel block seems to be common with Landsat imagery.

The last question is to determine how data (validation data) from the field will be collected. Two common approaches are to do field visits and to collect samples from aerial photographs or video. No matter what method is used, these data need to be accurately located on the image. The use of global positioning system (GPS) receivers has greatly facilitated this process. One popular method of recording field data is to use a digital camera with a GPS to record the location where the photograph was taken and a compass to record the direction the camera was pointed.

When collecting validation data, the same class labels that were used for the map data should be used to label the validation data. It is also important that data collected for validation are independent from those data that might have been collected to provide information used during the classification process. In other words, information that was used to improve the classification cannot be used to assess the accuracy of the classification. You can ensure these two data sets remain separate by setting aside a random subset of field data for future accuracy assessment.

One aspect of validation data that must be addressed is the time lag between collection of these data and the data used to create the map. If there is a significant difference in time between when the image used to create the map was acquired and when the validation data were collected, the image interpretation might be accurate but the feature could have changed.

It is difficult to develop a single method for accuracy assessment that works in all situations. There are many variables and these can change dramatically from one project to another. In many cases, adjustments to a theoretically ideal sampling design must be made to accommodate practical realities such as poor access to sample points in the field and lack of time or money to sample all of the sites. No matter what method you select, it is important to document these methods so the user of the final map knows how the accuracy was assessed.

Contingency tables (sometimes called "error matrices") are tools used to compile and present accuracy statistics (Table 2.1). A contingency table compares the agreement between the mapped data and the field data for the samples. Once the data are tabulated, you can use simple analysis methods to calculate accuracy statistics.

The result of an accuracy assessment typically provides you with an overall accuracy of the map and the accuracy for each class in the map. For example, in a land cover map the water class could be very accurate but some of the vegetation classes might be less accurate. This can have a significant effect on the utility of

Table 2.1 Contingency table for classified image in Fig. 2.6.

Ground reference		Satellite image map classes			
		Forest	Non-forest	Total	Correct (percent)
	Forest	900	0	900	100
	Non-forest	100	0	100	0
	Total	1000	0	1000	
	Correct (percent)	90	N/A		90

Note: This table represents the results from validating the classified image in Fig. 2.6. We randomly selected 1000 pixels in the classified image and verified them against the actual land cover in the field.

the map and, in some cases, may indicate that classes should be merged. Continuing the example, if two forest types, say deciduous and coniferous, are relatively inaccurate it might make sense to combine them into a single forest class with much higher accuracy.

2.2.4 Understanding accuracy statistics

Looking at accuracy statistics can be misleading if you do not understand what they represent. In this section, we will describe and compare some of the ways that accuracy is represented. We will start with a simple hypothetical example.

In Fig. 2.6, you can see that the map did not accurately represent the actual landscape since it classified the entire area as forest whereas 10 percent is actually non-forest. Clearly the overall map accuracy is 90 percent but one could say that the accuracy of the forest class is 100 percent since the entire area of the forest class was accurately classified as forest. As you can see, there are different ways to represent accuracy. Two types of accuracy, producer's accuracy and user's accuracy (also called "consumer's accuracy"), are illustrated in the contingency table (Story and Congalton 1986) (Table 2.1). It is best practice to report all three types of accuracy – overall, producer's, and user's; however, many times reports in the published literature only give the overall accuracy, which can be misleading. User's accuracy is especially important for management and decision-making.

Producer's accuracy is the probability that a reference sample (validation data) will be correctly classified in the map. In other words, if you know that a particular area is hardwood (you have been out on the ground to check), what is the probability that the digital map will correctly identify that pixel as hardwood?

Consumer's accuracy is the probability that a sample from the map matches what is actually on the ground. For example, if you select any hardwood pixel on

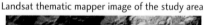

Fig. 2.6 Classifications generally simplify detail that is present in an image in order to produce a map. The Landsat ETM+ image shows a mountainous area that is mostly forested but roughly 10 percent of the image is non-forest (path 125, row 49, January 9, 2001). The green rectangle on the right is a map showing that the entire area is forested. Credit: Ned Horning, American Museum of Natural History's Center for Biodiversity and Conservation.

the classified map, what is the probability that you will be standing in a hardwood stand when you visit that pixel location in the field?

Common accuracy terms include:

- **Overall accuracy:** The overall probability that any pixel in the image is correctly classified; overall accuracy = (number pixels correctly classified)/(total number of pixels).
- **Producer's accuracy:** The probability that reference data of a given type is correctly classified; producer's accuracy (forest) = (number of pixels correctly classified as forest)/(number of ground reference pixels in forest).
- **Omission error:** Probability of excluding a pixel that should have been included in the class; omission error = 1 − producers accuracy.
- **Consumer's accuracy:** The probability that a point on the map matches what is on the ground; consumer's accuracy (forest) = (number of pixels correctly classified as forest)/(total number of pixels classified as forest).
- **Commission error:** Probability of including a pixel in a class when it should have been excluded; commission error = 1 − consumer's accuracy.

Other terms associated with accuracy assessments:

- **Average (class) accuracy:** The average of the individual class accuracies.
- **Average Accuracy:** The average of the producer's accuracies for each class; average accuracy = (sum of producer class accuracies)/number of classes).
- **Kappa:** An accuracy statistic that permits two or more contingency matrices to be compared. The statistic adjusts overall accuracy to account for chance agreement. Use kappa to statistically test for agreement between two contingency tables.

2.2.5 Trends in accuracy assessment

The use of a contingency table, as described earlier, is a common practice throughout the world to evaluate classification accuracy; however, it does not provide much detail about the errors themselves. To address these shortcomings, alternative methods are increasingly being developed and implemented. Two areas of accuracy assessment research that are being discussed in the remote sensing literature are:

- How to account for the spatial distribution and correlation of error, and
- How to measure error using methods such as probability and fuzzy set theory to account for the severity of the error instead of recording only if a class is correct or incorrect.

Traditionally, accuracy statistics provide per-class and overall map accuracy but there is no information on the spatial characteristics of these errors. For example, in some areas of the map, the accuracy might be quite high but in other areas the accuracy could be significantly less. This could happen for a variety of reasons, from having hazy conditions in one area of an image to different terrain conditions throughout an image causing varying solar illumination effects. Understanding how error is spatially distributed across an image can be useful when evaluating the utility of a particular map. One way to do this is simply to plot out the location of the reference samples used to validate the map indicating if that point was accurately classified or not using colors or symbols. The map can be inspected visually to see if errors are clustered in certain areas of the image. Research continues into mapping the accuracy of individual land cover types (Tran *et al.* 2005).

Another aspect of spatial distribution of error is spatial correlation of the error. For example, the likelihood that a pixel will be misclassified increases if its neighbor is misclassified (Congalton 1988). In addition, classification errors commonly occur on the boundaries between different categories such as different land cover types (Townshend *et al.* 2000) since land cover often changes along a gradient and the mixing of reflected energy from different land cover types is represented in a single pixel. This type of error highlights the problem associated with trying to define a discrete boundary between different land cover types that gradually change from one type to another. This is common in ecotones, which are transitions between two ecological communities. One approach to alleviate this mixed pixel problem is to map land cover as a continuous data set instead of classifying it into discrete classes. An example of this is the continuous fields data set described in Section 4.3.3.

Assessing the severity of error is another area of accuracy assessment research. Using a contingency table, you must decide whether or not a point or area is correctly classified. This binary approach does not take into consideration the severity of the error or the fact that more than one cover type can be present in the same area. For example, if an area is entirely covered by a pine forest, it clearly should be labeled as a pine forest, but if the forest is a mix of pine and oak, then it may be that either label is acceptable, at least to some degree; however, any pixel classified as water would be totally incorrect. Using fuzzy set theory (Zadeh 1965), it is possible to account for the degree to which the class is accurately labeled (its degree of class membership) in a particular area. One approach assigns a number from 1 through 5 to indicate the confidence in the class label for each possible cover type in each sample area as follows: 1 = absolutely incorrect, 2 = understandable but incorrect, 3 = reasonable or acceptable answer, 4 = good answer, and 5 = absolutely correct (Gopal and Woodcock 1994). Since one sample site can have varying degrees of class membership for different cover types, varying magnitudes of correctness or incorrectness can be calculated for each sample point and for each land cover class. Although this approach provides more information about accuracy, it also requires more effort to acquire the necessary field data to perform the validation since proportion of each land cover type must be noted, not just the primary cover.

2.3 Assessing in-house capabilities (institutional limitations)

Two factors that determine what can be accomplished using remote sensing technology are the ability of the individual or group of analysts who will be doing the work, and the hardware and software resources that are available. Deliberately assessing your available resources and capabilities reduces the chance that a project will be terminated due to misperceived complexities or that a project will be conducted without the resources necessary to produce useful products.

Deciding on the most effective way to move forward with a project involving remote sensing can be a challenging task. This is particularly true for a small organization without dedicated remote sensing specialists. This section provides insight into the evaluation process an organization can use to decide what kind of work should be hired out and when it makes sense to do work internally. A number of parameters must be evaluated to determine the most cost-effective way to move forward in the short and long term.

Unfortunately, there is no magic formula or standard response that works for all situations. We provide a series of questions to address when deciding how to proceed with a remote sensing project and explore the advantages and disadvantages of different options.

2.3.1 Doing work in-house or contracting out

If the resources are on hand and are available (image data, computer software and data storage, and remote sensing analysis experience relevant to the data and analysis type), it probably makes sense to use in-house resources for the project. This assumes that the person making this decision knows the capabilities and limitations of the in-house staff. If this is not the case, you may want to hire someone to evaluate staff capacity to see if the project requirements can be effectively met using in-house resources. If the resources are not available in-house, you should evaluate the options of:

- training existing staff
- hiring someone to do the work, or
- a combination of these

Many organizations cannot justify hiring a full-time remote sensing specialist because they do not have enough work to justify the expense of employing someone with suitable expertise and experience or purchasing the additional hardware and software required. One solution is to share an expert with other organizations either formally or informally. For example, some larger organizations have remote sensing experts on their staff and smaller organizations do not. These organizations can work out financial or in-kind agreements to foster collaboration and support. In academic settings, interdepartmental collaborations (with departments such as geography, geology, or agriculture) can provide access to remote sensing expertise outside the biology departments that often house ecologists and conservation biologists.

2.3.2 Training

To address the training options it is helpful to know what can be expected from different levels of training. All too often people are sent out for training to become proficient in using remote sensing methods but return to their jobs without sufficient experience to conduct adequately the tasks on their own. Many companies, including those that have developed software packages, offer basic remote sensing training combined with software training over 1–2 weeks that can get someone started carrying out the most common analyses. With remote sensing training, you can learn a lot in a relatively short period. However, a thorough knowledge of remote sensing entails a long-term educational invest-ment. Although many of the methods necessary to apply remote sensing tech-nology are not difficult to learn, there is no substitute for experience when designing and overseeing a remote sensing project.

Traditional introductory remote sensing courses tend to focus on learning the physics and algorithm (software) details of remote sensing with a focus on land cover classification. These courses tend to be scaled-down versions of college-level courses and students interested in only the basics or the more practical aspects of remote sensing often come away feeling a bit overwhelmed and not sure where to start. Another approach is to start by focusing on learning what can and cannot be done using remotely sensed data, how to acquire imagery for your area of interest, and how to interpret the imagery (the structure offered in this book).

Many of the short-term (less than 1 month) remote sensing courses are geared to train people to conduct some of the simpler and often time-consuming tasks common on most remote sensing projects, such as image classification or image rectification. People trained with these skills and guided by a remote sensing expert can be very effective at conducting remote sensing projects.

We have witnessed a number of instances in which people with some basic remote sensing training but not much experience or expert oversight conducted a project and after a significant effort produced a product that was effectively unusable. This reinforces the importance of considering options such as hiring a consultant or making an arrangement with an experienced organization to help design and oversee the project. In an arrangement of this type, someone with extensive training and experience can define the approach, be a resource for troubleshooting, and make sure the project is on track, while less experienced people conduct much of the time-consuming work and gain valuable experience. The key point here is that there is no substitute for experience and if sufficient experience is not available in-house, it would be wise to explore options for including experienced personnel in the project.

Another issue related to training courses has to do with the focus of the course. The type of available remote sensing courses varies widely from introductory to very specialized. For example, if you are interested in using remote sensing for land cover classification you would want a course that included that as an area of study. Some courses put a lot of emphasis on the use of a specific brand of software and other courses are more focused on the basic techniques with the assumption that if you understand the techniques you can learn to apply it using a variety of software. If you are training to become a remote sensing expert, you should expect to complete college-level training and acquire significant experience in the domain in which you plan to work. On the other hand if you are interested in using remote sensing as a tool to complement your knowledge in your particular area of expertise, an introductory course is more appropriate. Before you enroll in a short- or long-term course it is a good idea to correspond with the course organizers or instructors to make sure the course will meet your expectations.

2.3.3 Finding a good remote sensing consultant

Consulting organizations can range from one-person shops run out of the home to large corporations. Although there are lists of possible consultants available on the Internet as well as from various organizations, finding the right match for your project and budget constraints can require a lot of work. From our experience, learning from the experience of others is the best source of information for finding a reliable consultant. It is helpful to talk to colleagues who have used consultants for similar projects and get their feedback. If this is not practical, then request a list of previous clients from prospective consultants and talk to the clients to see if their needs were met. Try to get a feel for whether the relationship between the consultant and your organization will be compatible.

When drawing up a contract with a consultant you should define clearly the specifications for the products you want delivered, including archives of the data and methods that would allow future rework by a different analyst. It may be best to seek outside help (perhaps another consultant or an experienced colleague) to draft the specifications and, equally important, a plan to verify that the specification requirements have been met. All too often, a task is completed and months or years down the line it becomes evident that the products produced for a project are not sufficient to meet the goals for which the project was designed.

With a little work and some correspondence with colleagues, it is possible to make a good decision about moving forward with a remote sensing project.

2.4 Summary

From reading Chapter 1 and the rest of the book you can see that remote sensing technology has a lot to offer but it is important to use it wisely, understanding the capabilities and limitations of data and methods. Many of the choices require balancing trade-offs between parameters such as spatial resolution versus file size or cost, image footprint (size) versus ability to mosaic multiple images, and manual versus automated processing (Box 2.2). Although rules of thumb exist to help with some of these decisions, experience and trial and error are the best references for making informed choices. Moreover, it is important to keep in mind that products produced from remotely sensed imagery will always contain some errors. However, measuring and documenting these errors gives you a sense for their suitability for a given task.

Box 2.2 Working with trade-offs in change detection

When working with remotely sensed data you often have to make compromises. This is especially true when conducting a land cover change analysis in which case many environmental factors can confound the conceptually simple task of mapping changes in land cover using images acquired on two different dates. You simply do the best you can with the given resources.

A team of researchers at a university wanted to map land cover change between 1990 and 2000 for an area in central Vietnam. Fortunately they were able to locate two adjacent, nearly cloud-free, Landsat Thematic Mapper (TM) images that were acquired on the same day in February 1990 and covered their area of interest. Unfortunately, for the 2000 imagery they were not able to find adjacent Landsat ETM+ images with suitable cloud cover from the same day. The one image was acquired in January 2001, the end of the rainy season, and the other was acquired in April 2003, the end of the dry season. This posed two problems. The first is that there was more than 2 years difference between the more recently acquired images, meaning that the period of change would be different for the portions of the study site covered by the different images. The other problem is that the more recent imagery was acquired during two different times of the year and the vegetation and other cover types looked significantly different.

Clearly this situation is less than ideal but an approach was worked out to address the shortcomings. Having one of the four images acquired during a different time of the growing season did make the analysis more difficult since much of the detectable change was due to the difference in phenology and not due to actual change in the type of land cover. Although it was more time consuming than the classification methods they intended to use for the entire study area, they decided to use visual interpretation methods. Using this approach they were able to detect accurately changes in land cover. To address the problem of having an 11-year difference between the two dates for one part of the study area and a 13-year difference for the other, the analysts decided to keep the two parts of the study area separate for the analysis. In the end, they combined the land cover change maps from the two parts of the study area to make a singe map but the statistics were generated from their respective image pairs. For the intended use, they determined that for the visual product (the map) the time difference was not significant enough to note.

Working with images

There are two very different ways to envision a satellite image: as a photograph taken with a camera, or as a visual representation of spectral intensity data quantifying the light reflecting off of objects on a planet's surface. In working with satellite images, sometimes the objective is to highlight and accent the information in the image using tools to enhance the way the image looks—the same goal that a professional photographer might have when working in the darkroom with film or using Photoshop to manipulate digital photographs. Another objective could be to manipulate the image using automated processing methods within a remote sensing package that rely on a set of equations that quantify information about reflected light. With either approach the goal is to gain information about conditions observed on the ground.

At first glance, the image in Fig. 3.1 bears little resemblance to what most people would recognize as a terrestrial landscape. After all, its predominant colors are orange and bright turquoise. The use of colors in creating a visual image allows great breadth in the types of things one can identify on the ground, but also makes image interpretation an art. Even an inexperienced interpreter can make some sense of the image; more experienced interpreters with knowledge of the color scheme in use are able to determine finer details. For example, in Fig. 3.1 some of the more prominent features are a river (blue line on the left side of the image) a gradient of different vegetation (orange colors throughout the image that go from light to dark), and burn scars (turquoise patches).

Fig. 3.2 shows a portion of landscape represented in the satellite image in Fig. 3.1. The red dot in Fig. 3.1 indicates the location where the photograph was taken. This photograph shows what a human observer would see looking south (in this case toward the top of the satellite image) from the point represented by the red dot. The view in the photograph differs from the satellite image in two important ways. The first is the perspective from which the images were acquired. The photograph was taken with the camera oriented slightly off horizontal, while the satellite image was acquired with a sensor in space looking vertically down at the Earth. The other obvious difference is that the photograph shows much more landscape detail than the satellite image. The satellite image provides a somewhat abstract view of the landscape compared to the photograph.

Arguably, the most important skill in using remotely sensed imagery is the ability to associate what you see in the image with physical features on the

Fig. 3.1 The Landsat ETM+ image covers an area in Quang Nam Province in central Vietnam (path 125, row 49, 2 April 2002). The point under the yellow plus sign in the image represents the location where the photograph in Fig. 3.2 was taken. This image is oriented with south at the top of the page to match the photo. Credit: Ned Horning, American Museum of Natural History's Center for Biodiversity and Conservation.

Fig. 3.2 A photograph of a landscape in Quang Nam Province in central Vietnam (April 2002). The camera was pointed south when the picture was taken. Credit: American Museum of Natural History's Center for Biodiversity and Conservation.

landscape. In this chapter we will discuss the details necessary to work with remotely sensed imagery so that you can begin to interpret imagery and identify features in the landscape.

3.1 Choosing the right type of imagery

Remote sensors can be either active or passive. The primary difference between these two categories is the source of energy that is used to illuminate features on the ground. Active sensors provide their own energy whereas passive sensors rely on an external energy source, most commonly the sun. Two common active sensors are radar, an acronym for radio detection and ranging (Section 4.3.4.1), which measures the return of radio waves to a sensor, and lidar, an acronym for light detection and ranging, which measures the return of light from a laser. Data from these active sensors are increasingly common but imagery acquired using passive sensors is still used for the majority of projects. This is primarily because there is more passive remote sensing imagery, plus it is more accessible and straightforward to process and visualize.

One example of an operational passive satellite-based sensor that collects data during the night is the US Air Force Defense Meteorological Satellite Program (DMSP) Operational Linescan System (OLS) that has been used to produce a global nighttime lights product since 1994. The OLS is sensitive to faint lights such as those produced in and around urban areas. The nighttime light products are distributed by NOAA National Geophysical Data Center (NGDC) and can be used to estimate human population density and growth globally.

Cameras (without a flash) are the most common passive remote sensing devices. In the case of a digital camera, the recording media is an electronic image plate (sensor) and in the case of a film camera the media is film (the negative). In either case, the camera records the intensity of light reflected from a feature (such as a landscape) resulting in a picture that resembles the feature as viewed by the human eye.

3.1.1 Multispectral imaging

Remote sensing instruments (including cameras) are often capable of acquiring data in multiple bands or layers. Each band records a particular range of wavelengths (colors—refer to Section 2.1.1). In the case of a common color camera, three layers of data are recorded—one for each of the additive primary colors of light (red, blue, and green or RGB). These wavelengths of light correspond to the colors that can be perceived by the human eye, so when you acquire a color photograph it closely resembles the actual feature that was photographed.

Other, more sophisticated remote sensing instruments, such as those mounted in satellites, can acquire many different bands. These include bands that detect wavelengths of light, such as ultraviolet and infrared, outside the range that can be detected by the human eye. Hyperspectral imagers acquire data in dozens or even hundreds of different bands. These sensors provide multiple bands to improve our ability to identify features on the Earth's surface. Having the ability to view wavelengths of light outside of the range that can be seen by the human eye provides us with additional information that can be used to better characterize features of interest.

Fig. 3.3 shows the same Landsat image displaying different band combinations. The first image was created using bands similar to a digital camera—so the band closest in wavelength to red is displayed as red, the band closest in wavelength to green is displayed as green, and the band closest in wavelength to blue is displayed as blue (by convention this is noted as 3, 2, 1 display). Band combinations are typically listed in the order red, green, and blue, using a number assigned to each band that is unique to each remote sensing instrument. The other images were created using different band combinations using data from the visible and near-infrared portion of the spectrum. Any band can be displayed by any of the three primary colors, but only three bands can be displayed at a time. Note in Fig. 3.3 how different features are better highlighted with particular band combinations. There is no magic formula for determining the ideal band combination, and since changing the sequence of bands in an image is an easy task, often the best approach is to try a few different band combinations to see which one looks the best to you for the features in which you are interested. When interpreters become familiar with an instrument and its bands, they often find they prefer certain display combinations for particular purposes.

Fig. 3.4 shows the seven different bands that make up a Landsat ETM+ image. You can see how some bands are better than others for identifying particular features. For example, in the infrared bands (Landsat ETM+ bands 4, 5, and 7) you can clearly see the land–water interface, and the visible bands (Landsat ETM+ bands 1–3) show some variation within the river due to sediment. A true color (similar to a color photograph) representation with Landsat data would be RGB 3,2,1 (band 3 = red, band 2 = green, and band 1 = blue) but this often looks hazy because the shorter wavelength bands are more sensitive to small particulates and water vapor in the atmosphere. The images using other band combinations are referred to as "false color" images since the color schemes do not represent natural colors. Interpreters working with Landsat data often like to use 4,5,3 since this tends to do a good job separating a broad variety of features in the image.

3.1.2 Spatial resolution and scale

Another important quality of remotely sensed imagery is spatial resolution, the ground sampled distance or size of the area on the ground represented by a pixel. In most cases an image's resolution is labeled with a single number, such as 30 m, which represents the length of a side of a square pixel if it were projected onto the

Common Landsat band combinations

3,2,1 RGB
This color composite is as close to true color that we can get with a Landsat ETM+ image. It is also useful for studying aquatic habitats. The downside of this set of bands is that they tend to produce a hazy image.

4,3,2 RGB
This has similar qualities to the image with bands 3,2,1 however, since this includes the near-infrared channel (band 4) land–water boundaries are clearer and different types of vegetation are more apparent.

4,5,3 RGB
This is crisper than the two images above because the two shortest wavelength bands (bands 1 and 2) are not included. Different vegetation types can be more clearly defined and the land–water interface is very clear. Variations in moisture content are evident with this set of band. This is probably the most common band combination for Landsat imagery.

7,4,2 RGB
This has similar properties to the 4,5,3 band combination with the biggest difference being that vegetation is green. This is the band combination that was selected for the global Landsat mosaic created by NASA.

Fig. 3.3 Common band combinations for Landsat ETM+ data. The image covers the same area around Hue city in central Vietnam as shown in Fig. 3.4 (path 125, row 49, 21 April 2003). Credit: American Museum of Natural History's Center for Biodiversity and Conservation.

Landsat spectral band information (Bands 1–4)

Band 1　　(0.45–0.52 μm, blue-green)

Since this short wavelength of light penetrates better than the other bands it is often the band of choice for aquatic ecosystems. It is used to monitor sediment in water, mapping coral reefs, and water depth. Unfortunately, this is the noisest of the Landsat bands. For this reason it is rarely used for "pretty picture" type images.

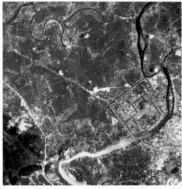

Band 2　　(0.52–0.60 μm, green)

This band has similar qualities to band 1 but not as extreme. The band matches the wavelength for the green we see when looking at vegetation.

Band 3　　(0.63–0.69 μm, red)

Since vegetation absorbs nearly all red light (it is sometimes called the chlorophyll absorption band) this band can be useful for distinguishing between vegetation and soil and in monitoring vegetation health.

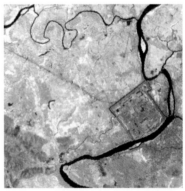

Band 4　　(0.76–0.90 μm, near infrared)

Since water absorbs nearly all light at this wavelength water bodies appear very dark. This contrasts with bright reflectance for soil and vegetation so it is a good band for defining the water–land interface.

Landsat spectral band information (Bands 5–7)

 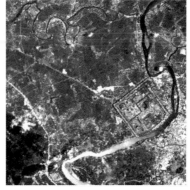

Band 5   (1.55–1.75 μm, mid-infrared)

Band 6   (10.40–12.50 μm, thermal infrared)

This band is very sensitive to moisture and is therefore used to monitor vegetation and soil moisture. It is also good at differentiating between clouds and snow.

This is a thermal band, which means it can be used to measure surface temperature. This is primarily used for geological applications but is also used to differentiate clouds from bright soils since clouds tend to be very cold. This is half the resolution of the other bands (60 m instead of 30 m)

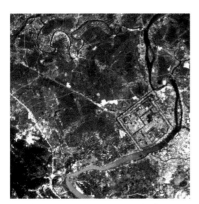

Band 7   (2.08–2.35 μm mid-infrared)

This band is used for monitoring vegetation moisture although generally band 5 is preferred for that application, as well as for soil and geology mapping.

Fig. 3.4 Landsat TM and ETM+ data include seven different bands, each representing a different portion of the electromagnetic spectrum. In order to work with Landsat band combinations (red, green, blue composites of three bands) first we must understand the qualities of each band. The image covers the same area around Hue city in central Vietnam as shown in Fig. 3.3 (path 125, row 49, 21 April 2003). Credit: American Museum of Natural History's Center for Biodiversity and Conservation.

Earth's surface. If the pixel were rectangular (not very common), then both the length and width would be provided.

So, how do you decide on an appropriate resolution for a particular project? A simple rule of thumb is that the resolution should be approximately one-tenth the size of the feature you want to examine. For example, if you want to be able to identify forest patches that are 1 ha (10,000 m²) in size, you would want a pixel resolution of approximately 32 m (=1024 m²). Unfortunately, in practice these rules of thumb are not always practical since other factors influence our ability to identify accurately features on the Earth's surface. If the contrast between features is low or the landscape is very heterogeneous, a finer resolution than the one calculated using the rule of thumb might be required to distinguish different features.

Another important point about resolution is that the information contained in a pixel does not represent a perfect square on the ground. A detector in a sensor recording energy for an individual pixel actually views a circle or ellipse on the ground. Furthermore, as can be seen in Fig. 3.5, approximately 50 percent of the information for a given pixel contains recorded energy from the surface area surrounding it. This tends to contribute to hazy borders between objects rather than the crisp border you might expect.

The contrast between features and the surrounding cover types greatly influences the size of a feature that you can detect with a given resolution. For example, there is a good chance that we would be able to detect a trail only a

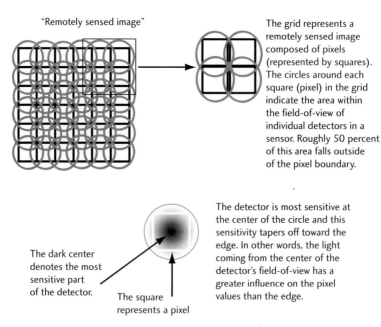

"Remotely sensed image"

The grid represents a remotely sensed image composed of pixels (represented by squares). The circles around each square (pixel) in the grid indicate the area within the field-of-view of individual detectors in a sensor. Roughly 50 percent of this area falls outside of the pixel boundary.

The dark center denotes the most sensitive part of the detector.

The square represents a pixel

The detector is most sensitive at the center of the circle and this sensitivity tapers off toward the edge. In other words, the light coming from the center of the detector's field-of-view has a greater influence on the pixel values than the edge.

Fig. 3.5 Area recorded by an individual detector in a satellite-based sensor. Credit: Ned Horning, American Museum of Natural History's Center for Biodiversity and Conservation.

few meters wide that cuts through a dense forest in imagery with 30 m pixels because of the stark contrast between the bright soil and the dark forest (Fig. 3.6). In other words, the light reflected from the trail is bright enough to raise the pixel value sufficiently for it to be discernable from the surrounding pixels. On the other hand, trying to map different forest types can be difficult because contrast between the different types might not be very high.

The heterogeneity of the landscape can also influence how well we detect a feature. If the landscape is very heterogeneous due to terrain or land cover variations, it is more difficult to detect any single feature than if the landscape were very homogeneous. Heterogeneity is sensitive to resolution. Some landscapes may appear relatively heterogeneous at a fine resolution but appear more homogeneous at a courser resolution (Fig. 3.7).

Experience is probably the best way to understand the limitations of a particular resolution. For every rule of thumb there will be numerous exceptions. Getting advice from others who are working on a similar project can be a great help.

Fig. 3.6 Landsat ETM+ image of an area around the town of Sakaraha, southern Madagascar (path 160, row 76, 23 August 2000). Linear features running from left to right are roads and paths. The lowest line is a paved road approximately 10 m wide. The road is very visible while passing through the forest but it is less visible when it passes through areas with little vegetation alongside the road. The two lines above the road are oil exploration paths ranging from roughly 3–10 m in width. Credit: Ned Horning, American Museum of Natural History's Center for Biodiversity and Conservation.

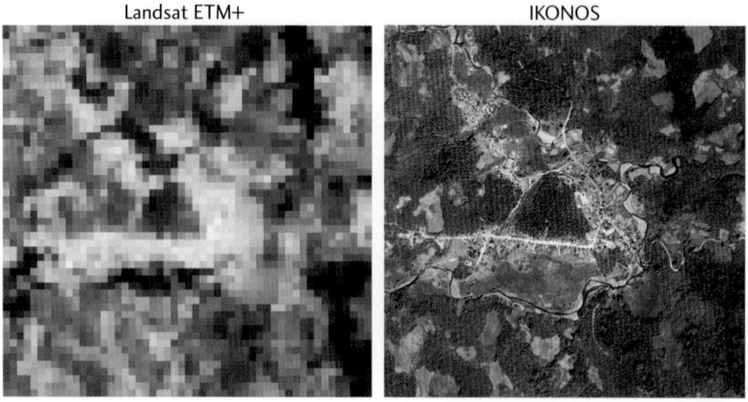

Landsat ETM+   IKONOS

Fig. 3.7 Comparison of spatial resolutions of an IKONOS image (1 m spatial resolution) and a Landsat ETM+ (30 m spatial resolution). At 1 m spatial resolution you
can identify individual buildings and rice fields. At 30 m spatial resolution these details
are integrated into single pixels giving us the impression of a more homogeneous
landscape. The images cover an area in Quang Nam Province, central Vietnam (Landsat
ETM+ image, path 125, row 49, 2 April 2002; IKONOS image, ID PO_91586, 29
April 2002). Credit: Ned Horning, American Museum of Natural History's Center for
Biodiversity and Conservation, IKONOS image courtesy of GeoEye.

3.1.3 Temporal options: seasonality and frequency of acquisitions

Seasonality and weather around the area of interest are important factors to
consider when requesting or interpreting imagery. In some regions you can only
acquire images during seasons without significant cloud cover. You also need to
bear in mind the state of the features you are interested in identifying. For
example, if you are interested in mapping the location of a deciduous forest, you
might want to acquire imagery when the leaves are on the trees. If you were
mapping deciduous and evergreen vegetation it might be helpful if you acquire
both leaf-on and leaf-off imagery. If you acquire multiple images of an area to
monitor a particular phenomenon such as land cover change it is probably best to
acquire the images using "anniversary" dates so all of the imagery is from roughly
the same time of the year to minimize changes that might be due to phenology.
As a general rule, the more frequently a satellite sensor can acquire an image over
your area of interest, the greater the chances that you will be able to find a
satisfactory cloud-free image.

3.1.4 Requesting imagery

As the remote sensing industry has matured, the ease of ordering imagery has
greatly improved. Most satellite vendors, private and government, provide user-
friendly Web sites to browse image archives for existing imagery and to place an
order for a new image acquisition. Unfortunately, understanding the details of

the various options can still be somewhat confusing, and it can require significant effort before the Web interfaces tell you how much your request might cost.

When you place an order for imagery, there are a wide range of questions that you will need to answer regarding the qualities of the product. These questions address the type of radiometric processing (adjusting the pixel values so that they represent physical values such as radiance or reflectance), geometric processing (adjusting the image so that it matches a particular orientation or a specific map projection), and file format for the image.

The simplest radiometric and geometric processing uses information recorded automatically on board the satellite or from ground-tracking stations. This type of processing is automated so it is relatively inexpensive. If more precise processing is necessary, then ancillary data must be used. For instance, you can use a digital elevation model to correct geometric distortions caused by terrain displacement or to normalize image pixel values by reducing the effect of shadow and brightly illuminated hillsides. This higher level of processing can significantly increase the price of the imagery. If appropriate software and properly trained image processing personnel are available, it is possible to do custom processing of the imagery in-house. When you evaluate the type of processing to request, you need to have an idea of the accuracy and precision required of the final product. For example, with geometric processing, is it acceptable if the location error of individual pixels is on the order of hundreds of meters, tens of meters, or less than 10 m?

Even though all the image vendors provide helpful information about the processing options, it is a good idea to have someone explain what specific options mean if they are not clear.

The price for satellite imagery ranges from free to more than US$100/km^2. The two factors that most directly affect the cost of imagery are spatial resolution (the finer the resolution, the more expensive is the imagery) and the level of processing requested. You may also be required to pay a sizable fee associated with requests that require the sensor to be programmed to acquire a new image. Sometimes these costs are presented on a sliding scale, with more requests requiring a rapid turnaround costing more.

The last issue regarding the purchase of satellite imagery has to do with licensing. In many cases you are purchasing a license to use the image and you do not own the image. The license agreements vary significantly but it is important that you understand the license since it details how you can share and publish imagery and products derived from the imagery.

3.1.5 Making the decision

So, how do you sift through all the differences in imagery and image distributors to select appropriate imagery? One possibility is to look at a list such as the one in Appendix 4. This list includes several commercial and government-operated satellite image products and their associated qualities. Despite all your research you might find that the imagery of choice is not practical due to its high cost or nonavailability. Locating the most appropriate imagery for a particular project is often a challenge, and throughout the remainder of this book we hope to provide you with enough information to make some reasonable choices when the "optimum" imagery is not accessible. As you begin using satellite imagery, it will become clear that the ideal situation is the exception and a good deal of thought must go into making the best of what is available.

It is always a good idea to talk with others who have done work similar to what you plan to do. Professional societies can be a source of information and there are a number of Internet news groups and list servers that discuss remote sensing (see the book's Web site) that can be good venues for getting answers to questions related to selecting appropriate imagery.

3.2 Software options

If image data are in a digital format, you will need to use computer software to visualize these images. There are several software options available for viewing remotely sensed imagery. In this section we give an overview of the different categories of software including common graphics software, GIS, and specialized remote sensing software.

3.2.1 Graphics software

Graphics software is the most common type of image-processing software, especially with the rise of digital photography. Unfortunately, not all of the software geared toward processing digital photography is appropriate for processing satellite imagery. The primary problem is that digital photo processing typically works with a color image made up of three "bands" (red, green, and blue), also known as "layers," whereas with satellite or other remotely sensed data the images can have several bands. Most basic graphics software packages work only with imagery that is either a single band (black and white) or a three-band (color) image.

More robust graphics software, such as Adobe Photoshop™, allows for manipulating image bands and can be quite useful for visualizing and enhancing satellite imagery (Horning and McPhearson 2005). The primary drawback is that graphics software cannot use geo-coding information in satellite images, which makes it difficult to overlay accurately vector data such as roads, towns, and contours, or to combine two or more images into one image known as a "mosaic." If you already have Photoshop or something similar (such as the GNU Image Manipulation Program [GIMP]) this may be a good place to begin looking at satellite imagery.

3.2.2 GIS software

Another type of software that can be used to view and in some cases analyze remotely sensed data is GIS software. Many GIS packages provide basic capabilities for displaying image data but many of the less expensive packages do not provide powerful graphic enhancement or processing capabilities. As the distinction between GIS and remote sensing becomes more blurred, the capabilities of GIS and specialized remote sensing software have converged.

The most common use of satellite imagery in GIS is as a backdrop for other data layers such as roads, rivers, political boundaries, and digital elevation data. This can be a very effective tool for illustrating the land cover for a particular area and can give the viewer a reasonably realistic view of the terrain.

3.2.3 Specialized remote sensing software

Image-processing software designed for use with satellite imagery has built-in capabilities that allow it to make use of geo-coding information, but it can be very expensive and difficult to use. This software, which remote sensing professionals use, provides sophisticated tools for visualizing imagery as well as a large suite of image-processing tools for the analyst. Automated land cover classification and geometric and radiometric correction are some types of processing that require this type of specialized software. Effectively using these tools requires a reasonable knowledge of remote sensing. There are several relatively simple open source and freeware proprietary software packages that provide a good entry for new users, but have limited capabilities. More comprehensive and complex proprietary and open source software requires additional experience to use properly. Workshops to train users in various remote sensing techniques are offered by the commercial software vendors as well as organizations supporting open source software. Information about different remote sensing software packages can be found in Appendix 2 and information about open source software can be found in Appendix 3.

3.2.4 Mathematical and visualization software

A specialty software, mathematical and visualization software is typically used to analyze the numbers that make up the imagery. It is not geared toward the casual user, and often requires a thorough knowledge of image processing and computer programming. In research environments, this type of software is used to create programs to analyze and visualize imagery in ways that cannot be done using the "canned" routines in the above-mentioned types of software.

3.2.5 Deciding which software to use

Deciding which type of software to acquire usually depends on your budget, experience, and the tasks that need to be performed. If you have experience with Photoshop and you are simply interested in working with visual images, Photoshop or a similar package would be a good place to start. A GIS package would be better suited for your needs if you are interested in integrating remote sensing images with other data, such as vector GIS layers, or if you want to have geospatial capabilities, such as locating a feature using geographic coordinates such as latitude and longitude, and you do not need to do much image analysis. If you need extensive image-processing capabilities and are willing to invest a little time in learning more sophisticated processing techniques, then it might be worth acquiring some of the more specialized remote sensing software.

3.3 Visualizing the data

The specific techniques you use to visualize satellite imagery depend on the type of software you use. Most GIS and remote sensing-focused software provides information on displaying and manipulating satellite imagery. In this section we will discuss some of the fundamental concepts necessary to manipulate remotely sensed imagery to make useful image products for display or interpretation.

3.3.1 Combining bands to make a color composite

When you create color composites of satellite image bands you can modify the way the image will look by assigning different satellite image bands to the red, green, and blue colors emitted by the computer monitor (Fig. 3.8). Different combinations of bands can be used to better visualize certain phenomena (Figs. 3.3 and 3.4). Under each image the band assignment (red, green, and blue) used to create the image is provided. These figures are some of the more common band combinations, but when you work with imagery you can experiment with other band combinations.

3.3.2 Image enhancements

When you first display a satellite image it will often look dark with little contrast. If the image looks nice when you first open it, there is a good possibility that either the image was previously enhanced or the software you are using might be automatically enhancing the image. If you need to enhance the image to improve the way it looks, you can use the image enhancement tools provided with your image-processing or GIS software to brighten the image and improve contrast to better identify objects of interest.

Before we start to discuss image enhancement, we need to understand our objectives and the limits within which we must work. Most computer monitors can display a range of pixel values from 0 through 255 where "0" represents no light (black) and "255" represents the light's full intensity (white). A challenge with most satellite imagery is that most of the pixel values are concentrated in a small portion of their potential data range (Fig. 3.9). You can redistribute (or scale) these image values to take advantage of the full range of available display values (0–255 on most computers; Fig. 3.9). The potential data range varies from sensor to sensor although two of the most common ranges are 0 through 255 and 0 through 1023. Regardless of the potential data range, it is possible to scale the original image values so they can be viewed on a computer display.

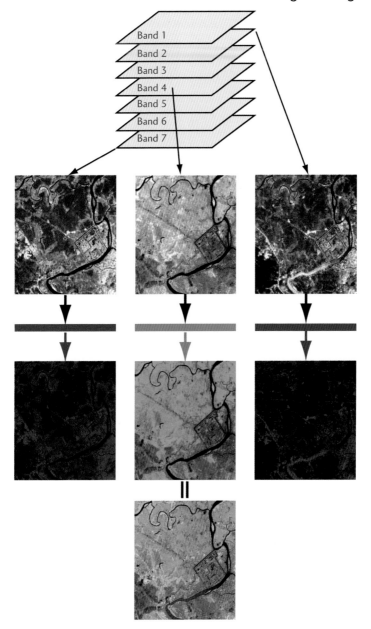

Fig. 3.8 A color rendition of a multispectral image created by selecting three bands from the image and then projecting each band through red, green, or blue light. Compositing these red, green, and blue single-color images produces the color image at the bottom of the figure. This is effectively the same process used to display digital color photographs with the exception that for multispectral images the analyst must select three bands necessary to create color images. (Landsat ETM+ image, path 125, row 49, 21 April 2003). Credit: Ned Horning, American Museum of Natural History's Center for Biodiversity and Conservation.

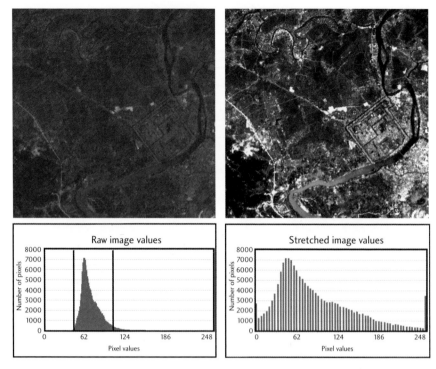

Fig. 3.9 The image on the left is an un-enhanced Landsat ETM+ band 3 (red, 630–690 nm) image and the histogram of pixel values is underneath. In the histogram we can see that the pixel values range from 42–220 but most of the values are between roughly 45 and 115, only a small portion of the available range of data values. The image on the right was brightened by assigning raw pixel values from 0–48 to 0 and values from 111–255 to 255. Values between 48 and 111 were then linearly assigned to values from 0 to 255 as is shown in the histogram on the right (Landsat ETM+ image, path 125, row 49, 21 April 2003). Credit: Ned Horning, American Museum of Natural History's Center for Biodiversity and Conservation.

Usually, the goal in image enhancement is to improve the ease of interpretation of an image so we can better identify the features of interest. We do this by modifying the histogram so that the full range (0–255) is utilized and the data are partitioned within the histogram to optimize visual interpretation.

There are a number of options for improving the way an image looks. The most familiar technique is to modify the image's brightness and contrast. Adjusting brightness and contrast is fairly intuitive but somewhat limited in its capabilities. Of these, the linear stretch is the most common. As illustrated in Fig. 3.9, a linear stretch clips off a portion of the histogram's tails and then effectively increases the dynamic range by stretching the remaining histogram over the full 0–255 data range. The pixel values in the lower portion of the histogram are automatically set to 0 and the values in the upper portion of the histogram that are clipped are set to 255. Most software programs allow the user to enter a variable to specify the extent of the histogram tail that will be clipped. This variable is either specified as a percentage of the histogram (i.e., 2 percent) that should be clipped or the clipping point is defined as the number of standard deviations (i.e., 2 SD) from the mean. You can use several methods, in addition to using brightness and contrast controls, to improve the appearance of an image. These include linear stretches, histogram equalization, and Gaussian stretches just to name a few (Fig. 3.10).

Another feature available in some image-processing software is one that lets you specify the area within the image from which the pixels will be selected to create the histogram. This is a very useful feature since it allows you to optimize the stretch for individual features such as a body of water or a forest. In Fig. 3.11, you can see the different effect of stretching an image using a histogram from the entire image or a histogram of only the water portion of the image. In the second image you can clearly see subtle differences in the water that are not visible in the first image. Of course, the second image looks washed out as a whole, but if our feature of interest is the water, then this enhancement provides information not available in the first image.

Depending on the software you are using to enhance the imagery, you may have several other options available to stretch the data to improve the way it looks. A good way to get a feel for the different enhancement options is to experiment with the different methods available to see which work best. Some software packages provide a graphic display of the histograms before and after enhancement. Studying these histograms provides a good foundation for understanding the fundamental changes that occur when an image is enhanced.

3.3.3 Image sharpening with a panchromatic band

Another type of image enhancement is called "image sharpening" or "image fusion", which combines a higher resolution (usually a single-band panchromatic) image with a lower resolution multispectral image to create a multispectral resolution image with more detail than the original multispectral image (Zhang 2004). An example of this is shown in Fig. 3.12. Various options for this panchromatic or pan sharpening are available in many of the remote sensing image-processing software packages. Although the output image has more spatial detail, this does not provide an image with the same qualities as if it were originally acquired at the higher resolution of the panchromatic image.

The higher resolution panchromatic image can come from any source but often it is from the same sensor that collected the multispectral data. For example, the Landsat ETM+ sensor collects multispectral imagery at a resolution of 30 m and has a panchromatic band (composed with data from all image bands or colors, hence panchromatic) at a resolution of 15 m (see Appendix 4 for other examples). The advantage of this system is that both images are acquired simultaneously and they cover identical areas on the ground.

Different contrast stretches and their associated histograms

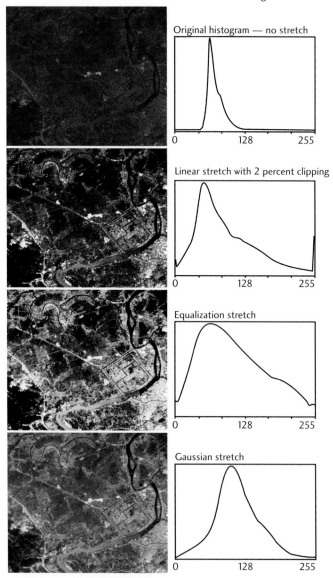

Fig. 3.10 These four images illustrate the result of adjusting the display of an image using different methods. The image on the top is the "raw" image and the three subsequent images have been enhanced using linear, histogram equalization, and Gaussian stretches. Next to each image is the image histogram. The histogram of the "raw" image shows that most of the data values are concentrated between approximately 45 and 115. In the linear stretch the data values from 49 to 111 are linearly stretched between the full data range of most computer displays, 0 to 255. Values less than 49 (the lowest 2 percent of all of the data values) are converted to 0 and those greater than 111 (the highest 2 percent of all of the data values) are converted to 255 (Landsat ETM+ image, path 125, row 49, 21 April 2003). Credit: Ned Horning, American Museum of Natural History's Center for Biodiversity and Conservation.

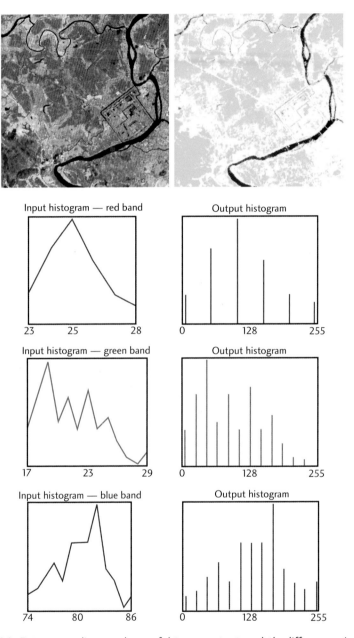

Fig. 3.11 Extreme scaling can be useful to accentuate subtle differences in pixel values for specific features, such as water. The right image was created by using the pixel values under the red box in the image (*left*) to generate the statistics used to scale the image. The input histograms show the relative number of pixels for the range of digital numbers (DNs) under the red square and the output histograms show how these values are stretched over the range from 0 to 255 to create the bottom image (Landsat ETM+ image, path 125, row 49, 21 April 2003). Credit: Ned Horning, American Museum of Natural History's Center for Biodiversity and Conservation.

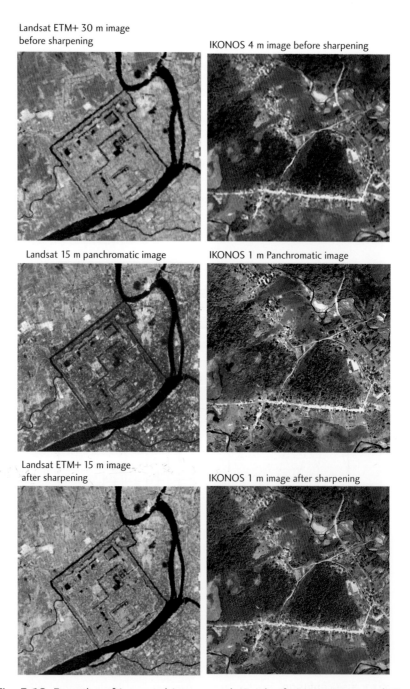

Landsat ETM+ 30 m image before sharpening

IKONOS 4 m image before sharpening

Landsat 15 m panchromatic image

IKONOS 1 m Panchromatic image

Landsat ETM+ 15 m image after sharpening

IKONOS 1 m image after sharpening

Fig. 3.12 Examples of improved image resolution by fusing coarser resolution multispectral data with finer resolution panchromatic data. The top row of images illustrates the fusing of Landsat ETM+ multispectral data with a spatial resolution of 30 m with Landsat ETM+ panchromatic data with a 15 m spatial resolution. The bottom row illustrates the same process using IKONOS 4 m multispectral and 1 m panchromatic data. Image data: Landsat ETM+ image, path 125, row 49, 21 April 2003; IKONOS image, ID PO_91586, 29 April 2002). Credit: Ned Horning, American Museum of Natural History's Center for Biodiversity and Conservation, IKONOS image courtesy of GeoEye.

3.3.4 Three-dimensional viewing

When you look at a satellite image of the Earth you can often tell if it is of a relatively flat or mountainous region. This is mostly due to the way the sun illuminates the scene, where the shadows are, and the way the human brain processes this type of information. Shadows can be very troublesome in image classification, but they can also provide critical information about the landscape and cues to help identify features on the ground. In some cases, however, our brains play tricks on us, and when we look at an image, the valleys look like mountains and the mountains look like valleys. Usually you can reverse this effect by turning the satellite image around so the shadows in the image fall toward the observer (Fig. 3.13).

A convenient way to improve or accentuate the visualization of terrain relief is to create a three-dimensional perspective image (Fig. 3.14). This type of view results from draping an image over a digital elevation model (DEM). Specialized software is required to create this effect, but fortunately there is free software available, and many remote sensing image-processing software packages include this capability (Appendix 2). The views are created by providing perspective information such as sun location (elevation and azimuth), viewer location

Fig. 3.13 Although shadows can help us identify features on the ground, they can also cause confusion. Areas with significant terrain displacement can create illusions in aerial and satellite images. This image of the Grand Canyon in Arizona, USA, is a digital color photograph taken by an astronaut on the International Space Station. Depending on the image's orientation, the canyon switches from appearing as a valley to appearing as a mountain. Turn the image upside down to see this effect. Credit: ISS001-E-6660, 19 February 2001, Image Science and Analysis Laboratory, NASA/JSC.

Photograph

Three-dimensional perspective using Landsat ETM+

Landsat ETM+ image used to create
the perspective image

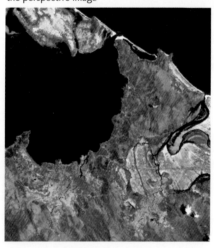

Fig. 3.14 By draping a satellite image over a digital elevation model (DEM) it is possible to create a three-dimensional perspective view. These images show a photograph taken from an elevated field location in central Vietnam, the three-dimensional view created using a Landsat ETM+ image draped over a DEM, and the Landsat image itself (Landsat ETM+ image, path 125, row 49, 21 April 2003; DEM from SRTM). Credit: Kevin Koy, American Museum of Natural History's Center for Biodiversity and Conservation.

(latitude or longitude and elevation), and terrain exaggeration to accentuate the terrain relief. Some software even allows you to fly above landscape as if you were in an airplane.

You can also drape satellite images over a land cover map or just about any other type of map. These three-dimensional tools are a lot of fun to work with, and they also provide information about a satellite image that you cannot easily see when viewing a standard two-dimensional image.

3.4 Additional processing

In some cases, when you order satellite imagery you can start using it immediately for your intended tasks. In other cases, you will need to process the imagery to correct further the geometric or radiometric properties of the image. This type of processing (often called "preprocessing") can range from simple to very complex. In this section, we present an overview of geometric and radiometric processing and provide information about the difficulty of the different types of processing.

3.4.1 Radiometric processing

The goal of most radiometric processing is to calibrate the image pixel values recorded by the sensor so that they either represent a physical property such as radiance or reflectance, or to normalize two or more images so similar features will have similar pixel values in all of the images. To understand how this is done we first have to understand what a satellite sensor sees as it records an image.

A common misconception is that a satellite sensor records reflectance from features on the ground. Instead, a satellite sensor simply measures radiance (energy) at the sensor for a particular range of wavelengths. Radiance is a measure of the energy recorded at the sensor. As we will see in the next section, the relation between radiance at the sensor and surface reflectance is not as strong as we would like.

Satellite sensors are typically calibrated before launch to accurately measure radiance but as the sensor ages it must be recalibrated to adjust for changes as the sensor degrades. Fortunately, most satellite sensors have the capability to calibrate themselves. When you order a radiometrically calibrated satellite image, you receive an image that has been calibrated using these on-board calibration data to provide sensor radiance. The image you receive, however, will not have the radiance values included in the image; rather, the image is in most cases scaled from 0 to 255 or 0 to 1023. The information you need for calculating the radiance value is often included in the image metadata. You can process these data for each band, often provided as gain and offset values or minimum and maximum radiance values, with most remote sensing image-processing software so you can calculate the actual radiance values. This step is necessary when comparing the digital numbers (pixel values) from two images or when you want to try to calculate reflectance values. If you are simply interested in a visual image, it is not necessary to calculate the at-sensor radiance values; the image will look the same whether you calculate physical radiance or not.

3.4.2 Reflectance: the holy grail of remote sensing

Surface reflectance is the ratio, expressed as a percent, of light that is reflected from the feature of interest on the Earth's surface to the light that is incident on that feature. Accurately calculating surface reflectance is arguably the holy grail of remote sensing, and is a difficult if not impossible task. If satellite instruments could easily measure surface reflectance, our job would be a lot easier and our land cover maps would be much more accurate.

Land cover mapping, and remote sensing interpretation in general, relies heavily on the assumption that features on the Earth have unique spectral signatures. A feature's spectral signature can be plotted as a spectral reflectance curve that indicates the reflectance values for that feature across the electromagnetic spectrum (Fig. 3.15). The job of an image analyst is to use specialized software to group image pixels into appropriate land cover categories based on

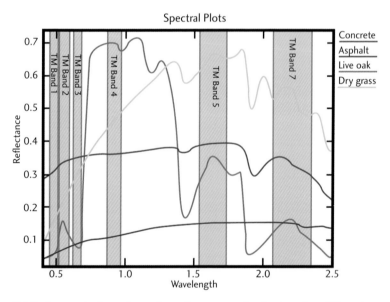

Fig. 3.15 Spectral plots show the reflectance of a feature for different wavelengths across the electromagnetic spectrum. This graph plots the reflectance curves for concrete, asphalt, live oak, and dry grass. The vertical bands on the graph illustrate the wavelengths that are recorded for the different Landsat TM bands. Band 6 is not included since its wavelength is beyond the limit of this graph. Credit: Ned Horning, American Museum of Natural History's Center for Biodiversity and Conservation.

the pixel values that we often assume to be directly related to the feature's reflectance. For example, all the pixels that have values similar to pixels that we know are water would be classified as water, and all the pixels that have values similar to pixels that we know are forest would be classified as forest, and so on until the entire image is classified into one land cover type or another. This sounds pretty straightforward, but in practice it can be very difficult because we cannot easily determine the actual reflectance of a surface feature on the ground from a satellite image.

One way to understand this problem is to contrast satellite remote sensing with reflectance measurements made in a laboratory. Important factors in determining reflectance include:

- Intensity of incoming radiation (that is the intensity of light energy as it hits the target)
- Intensity of the reflected radiation (that is the intensity of light energy just after it leaves the target)
- Orientation of the light source and detector relative to the target

In a laboratory setting with specialized equipment, it is straightforward to determine the reflectance properties of a material. The intensity of the light energy when it hits an object is easy to measure; the light path is quite short and the air quality is controlled so not much energy is lost between the light source and the target or the target and the detector; and the illumination and target orientation is known with high accuracy and precision.

The situation is very different for satellite remote sensing. We know the intensity of the light before it enters the Earth's atmosphere, but as it passes through the atmosphere it interacts with particulates (i.e., water vapor, dust, and smoke) that significantly alter the signal before and after interacting with the target (Fig. 3.16). A good deal of progress has been made in removing these atmospheric effects from an image but we are still unable to remove these effects with consistency and ease. Such effects become even more challenging if we are interested in knowing the reflectance of a benthic surface in a shallow aquatic environment. Then we need to remove atmospheric effects as well as water surface and column effects (Section 6.1).

As for illumination and detector orientation, we can calculate the position of the sun and the satellite when the image was acquired but it is much more difficult to know the orientation of the target (i.e., its slope and aspect). We can use digital elevation models to estimate these parameters but usually they only provide a rough estimate of the target orientation. For example, the same cover type may be found at two locations within an image—one in the shadow of a mountain and another oriented in such a way that the maximum amount of energy is reflected to the sensor (Fig. 3.17). It can be very difficult to process the two locations in such a way that they would have the same reflectance values.

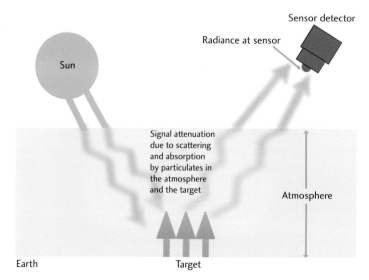

Fig. 3.16 The atmosphere modifies light from the sun before and after the light hits the Earth's surface. The sensor at the top of the atmosphere is not able to directly measure surface reflectances because of the atmospheric effects. To accurately calculate reflectance properties of the land cover on the surface of the earth we must remove these effects via atmospheric correction algorithms. Credit: Ned Horning, American Museum of Natural History's Center for Biodiversity and Conservation.

The bottom line is that similar land cover features can appear different within a single satellite image. There can also be a good deal of confusion between land cover classes that do not have drastically different reflectance signatures, such as different types of forests. This creates challenges for both automated and visual interpretation and classification methods.

3.4.3 Geometric processing

A geometrically corrected image can either be referenced either to a map (image-to-map registration) or to another image (image-to-image registration).

There are different levels of geometric correction that can be applied to satellite images to correct for inherent geometric errors. The simplest applies systematic corrections in which distortions caused by the sensor and movement of the satellite around the Earth are removed. This process often uses ephemeris data, a record of the location and velocity of the satellite at the time of image acquisition, to calculate the position in real-world coordinates, such as latitude or longitude or projected coordinates such as Universal Transverse Mercator (UTM). The resulting image has reasonable accuracy, often with positional displacement less than 50 m in areas with little terrain relief.

Fig. 3.17 Similar vegetation types can appear quite different under different illumination conditions. In this Landsat ETM+ image of a forested mountainous region in Vietnam similar forest types look very different because of their orientation to the sun. The black and dark green areas are dense forest located in the shadow of the mountains whereas the brighter green areas are oriented so that the sun is directly shining on the forest making it look much brighter. The forests on these two sides of the mountain are very similar but look very different in the Landsat image because of the difference in how they are illuminated. The shadows in this image are particularly severe because the sun is quite low in January during the morning overflight time (Landsat ETM+ image, path 125, row 49, 9 January 2001). Credit: Ned Horning, American Museum of Natural History's Center for Biodiversity and Conservation.

An intermediate process, often called "image registration," can be used to improve the positional accuracy of a satellite image. This involves using ground control points (GCPs) to increase the accuracy of the image's coordinate system. GCPs are locations with known real-world coordinates that can be located on the image and the ground. With this process the image is stretched or "warped" using a variety of algorithms to find the best fit of the satellite image to the GCPs. These algorithms are just a digital version of "rubber-sheeting," the old method of printing an aerial photo on a rubber sheet and stretching it to match a map reference. Unfortunately, in areas with significant terrain relief, this method usually produces only mediocre results unless you use dozens or hundreds of GCPs.

A more advanced geometric correction process is called "orthorectification." The process uses elevation information (usually from a digital elevation model) to correct distortions caused by terrain relief and is the preferred method in mountainous terrain. An orthorectified image is effectively an image map and has spatial qualities similar to a topographic map. In an image with level terrain, using simple image registration methods would produce similar results to an orthorectified image since elevation change is not a factor.

As a mapping product, an orthorectified image is superior to an image that has not been orthorectified because it has the best absolute positional accuracy. A problem can occur, however, when comparing an orthorectified image to a non-orthorectified image. In a comparison of two images, often used to determine changes in land cover over time, the relative positional accuracy between images (how well two coincident images are aligned to one another) is more important than the absolute positional accuracy, how well the image matches a map base. Trying to match an image geocorrected using simple image registration methods to an orthorectified one can be a very difficult and often impractical task because of the complex distortion corrections in an orthorectified image.

Matching two images that cover the same area can be done using a process called "image-to-image registration," as opposed to "image-to-map registration" discussed above. This is done by designating one image as the reference and registering the other image(s) to the reference image. The process involves selecting control points that can be located in both images and then applying the same algorithms that are used for image-to-map geo-referencing. When trying to achieve high relative accuracy between two or more satellite images it is often easiest to register two images that have undergone similar geometric processing. In other words, if you have one image that has been systematically corrected it is usually easiest to register that to another systematically corrected image rather than to combine it with an orthorectified image.

Depending on the accuracy, it may be impractical to try and align two or more orthorectified images in which different ortho-correction processes were used. If different methods were used, the distortions between the two images could be quite different, making the coregistration process very difficult. The best scenario is to have all of the images orthorectified using the same process so that they have high absolute and relative accuracy, although this is often not practical when working with limited time and financial resources.

The bottom line is that orthorectified images generally have higher absolute accuracy, but when relative accuracy is more important it may be better to use only systematically corrected images rather than mixing systematically corrected images with ortho-imagery. Often trial and error will dictate what works best in a specific situation.

3.5 Image interpretation and classification

Now that you have a satellite image and are able to view it on a computer monitor, you probably would like to be able to interpret it. The primary goal of image interpretation is to identify features in an image. These features can include objects or phenomena such as land cover, soil moisture, geologic formations, urban features, vehicles, or just about anything else that is identifiable in the image.

Features can be identified using visual or automated methods. With visual methods you can associate features you see in the image with objects you are familiar with on the ground. To do this you use visual cues in the image—such as tone (color), size, shape, texture and pattern, relative and absolute location, and shadows—to determine the identity of a particular feature. Visual interpretation can be performed with little formal training, but experience will increase the accuracy and precision with which you can identify features.

A variety of automated methods can be used to identify features in a satellite image. The most common approach is automated image classification. With this approach a computer algorithm groups pixels in the image into classes that the analyst defines. The result is typically a map such as a land cover map (Chapter 4).

Another approach is automated feature recognition wherein a computer algorithm locates specific features defined by the analyst. For example, an analyst could use a feature recognition approach to locate all of the houses in an image.

3.5.1 Visual interpretation

Methods to visually interpret satellite images are very similar to methods developed over 100 years ago to interpret aerial photographs. With the advent of fast computers and sophisticated algorithms for image classification the value of visual interpretation tends to be overlooked. Even with improved algorithms and speedy computers the human brain is still better at processing the vast amounts of information that are required to identify features in an image. Additional information about visual interpretation can be found in Appendix 5.

Some advantages of using image photoproducts with visual interpretation are:

- Less time required to create a usable product.
- Little, if any, expense incurred beyond the acquisition of the image.
- Aspects of image illumination that are otherwise challenging (such as shadows and brightly illuminated surfaces) can be used as an interpretation aid.
- Minimal remote sensing analysis expertise required to interpret the image.
- More brain power used.

Less time: A reliable land cover classification project can take months or years to complete. With photo interpretation methods, visualization can start immediately once the satellite data are in hand. All that is needed is a hardcopy of the image or a computer and some visualization software to view the image on a screen.

Less expense: Land cover classification projects can be very costly. Costs include the analyst's time for the classification and error analysis. This usually includes fieldwork for collecting location and testing data and can easily run into tens of thousands of dollars. Usually, the cost of the data is a small fraction of the total cost of a land cover classification project.

Image illumination: The uneven illumination of a satellite image is a source of problems for automated classification. A significant and sometimes futile effort can go into accounting for these effects. In visual interpretation, however, these problems can be used to aid in the interpretation of an image. The variations in illumination across an image are largely responsible for the appearance of relief on a satellite image, which is useful in identifying features on the image.

Less expertise: The level of expertise required to carry out a robust land cover classification is substantial and selecting appropriate methods is not always intuitive. Using photo interpretation methods to interpret an image requires training, but the level of training necessary to begin interpreting an image is less than the level required for conducting a land cover classification.

More brain power: The capability of the brain to interpret land cover features in a satellite image is still significantly more effective than that of a computer. A computer is very good at consistently applying a specific set of rules to classify an image but unfortunately in the practice these rules are not necessarily clear-cut or static.

Also, when a satellite image is classified, a thematic class replaces the visual cues that exist in the original image. In other words, the subtle changes throughout a forest that can be seen in an image photo are replaced by a single discrete class representing a particular feature such as forest (Fig. 3.18).

One of the best ways to improve your ability to make sense out of what you see in an image is to take it out into the field with you either as a hardcopy map, on a

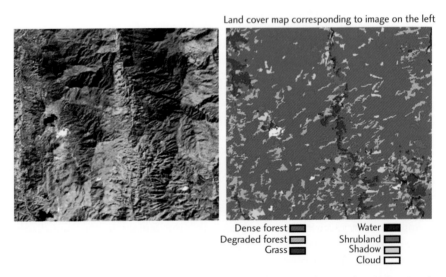

Land cover map corresponding to image on the left

Dense forest ▪ | Water ▪
Degraded forest ▫ | Shrubland ▪
Grass ▪ | Shadow ▫
| Cloud ▫

Fig. 3.18 When a satellite image is classified, a thematic class replaces the visual cues that exist in the original image. Through this process the subtle differences in color and texture that can be seen in an image photo are replaced by a single color representing a particular feature such as forest (Landsat ETM+ image, path 125, row 49, 9 January 2001). Credit: Ned Horning, American Museum of Natural History's Center for Biodiversity and Conservation.

laptop computer, or in a mobile device. If you can locate yourself on the image and orient the image properly (e.g., Figs. 3.1 and 3.2) you will be able to visit or at least view some of the areas in the image. By associating what you see on the ground with what is in the image you can begin to train your brain to correlate different shapes and colors in the image with actual features on the ground. Once you can identify a few different features in one area you can begin to look for similar features in another area. The importance of this type of experience cannot be overstated. In their early years of training, NASA astronauts participate in field exercises where they take aerial photographs, astronaut-acquired photographs, and satellite imagery into the field to practice these interpretation skills, in preparation for interpreting scenes they will see from orbit.

To help orient yourself on an image, you can overlay features such as roads, rivers, towns, and other landmarks. If you are using a GPS receiver, you can overlay grid lines with latitude and longitude or some other coordinate grid so you can pinpoint your location using GPS coordinates. A handy option if you have a GPS and a computer is to use a moving map or heads-up display. With this configuration your location is automatically plotted on the image and as you move across the terrain the display accurately tracks your location on the image (usually a cursor of one form or another). This can be done using GIS or remote sensing image-processing software.

Once you become consistent at accurately identifying image features, you can create thematic maps such as land cover by drawing polygons on the image to delimit clusters of pixels that represent a particular feature or land cover type. In effect you are classifying an image using visual methods. This is often called 'heads-up' or 'on-screen' digitizing since the interpreter is usually drawing boundaries on the computer screen. This can be somewhat time consuming, especially over a large area, but the results can be comparable to those obtained using automated methods.

3.5.2 Image classification

Classified images (or *maps* as they are often called) are frequently required for quantitative studies such as modeling and GIS data analysis. They are also easy to interpret since the different classes are discrete entities that are symbolized (usually using colors) so that individual classes can be easily identified.

In the remote sensing literature you will find comparisons of classification algorithms and approaches touting one method over another. Although these studies are valuable it is best to view them in the context within which the study was conducted. You may not get the same accuracy using similar methods for your application. Image classification remains an active area of research as scientists strive to improve classification accuracy and to provide guidance for selecting appropriate approaches for specific situations (Lu and Weng 2007). To facilitate the discussion of different methods, we group them into manual, automated, and hybrid approaches.

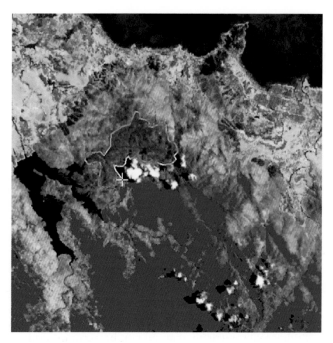

Fig. 3.19 On-screen digitizing involves an image analyst drawing polygons around land cover types of interest. In the image, the analyst has already digitized much of the forest area (colored dark green) and an area of forest is being digitized as can be seen by the polygon next to the cursor (white crosshair). We will show different classification techniques applied to this Landsat ETM+ image of northern Bach Ma National Park in central Vietnam in Figs. 3.20 through 3.23 (path 125, row 49, 21 April 2003). Credit: Ned Horning, American Museum of Natural History's Center for Biodiversity and Conservation.

3.5.2.1 Manual classification

Manual, or visual, classification of remotely sensed data is an effective method of classifying land cover especially when the analyst is familiar with the area being classified. This method uses skills originally developed for interpreting aerial photographs. It relies on the interpreter to employ visual cues such as tone, texture, shape, pattern, and relationship to other objects to identify the different land cover classes. The primary advantage of manual interpretation is its use of the brain to identify features in the image and relate them to features on the ground. The brain can still beat the computer in accurately identifying image features. Another advantage is that manual classification can be done without a computer using a hardcopy version of a satellite image.

The downside of manual interpretation is that it tends to be tedious and slow when compared with automated classification, and because it relies solely on a human interpreter it is more subjective. This constraint tends to limit the use of manual classification to smaller areas. Another drawback is that it is only able to incorporate three bands of data from a satellite image since the interpretation is usually done using a color image comprised of red, green, and blue bands. These drawbacks aside, manual classification of satellite imagery is still a reliable method for creating land cover maps.

The technique used in manual interpretation is fairly simple. The analyst views the image on either a computer screen or a hardcopy printout and then draws a polygon around areas that are identified as a particular land cover type (Fig. 3.19). If you do the land cover delineations on a computer screen you create the land cover map during the delineation process. If you use a hardcopy image for the interpretation the resulting map will have to be digitized to convert it into a machine-readable format.

3.5.2.2 Automated classification

The majority of classification methods fall in this category. With automated classification the analyst uses an algorithm and the computer's power to generate and apply specific rules to assign pixels to one class or another. Although creating these rules is often subjective in nature, the rules are applied systematically throughout the image, something that cannot be accomplished using visual methods. In general, humans are good at using size, shape, and location information to identify a feature in an image, but computers are far better at working with several layers of data (image bands and ancillary data).

Automated image classification algorithms can incorporate data from hundreds of satellite bands along with assorted ancillary data layers. Traditionally, automated algorithms tended to be limited to using only the pixel values in the image but there are now several approaches that allow a user to easily incorporate ancillary data layers such as elevation, slope, aspect, soil type, and a host of other biophysical layers to improve the classification accuracy.

In order for an automated classification algorithm to associate pixel values with the correct land cover category, some input from an analyst is necessary. When this information is provided before the algorithm is run the procedure is referred to as "supervised classification." With this approach the user identifies sample pixels (usually contiguous groups of pixels of a single cover type) in the image that can be used as representative examples for a particular land cover category and the sample pixels are used to train the algorithm to locate similar pixels in the image. A supervised classification results in a land cover map with all of the pixels labeled as a particular cover type (Fig. 3.20).

The other way to classify an image is to start by letting the computer group similar pixels together into unlabeled classes (clusters) and then have the analyst label the clusters with the appropriate land cover category. This approach is called "unsupervised classification" since the algorithm works without knowledge of existing land cover samples.

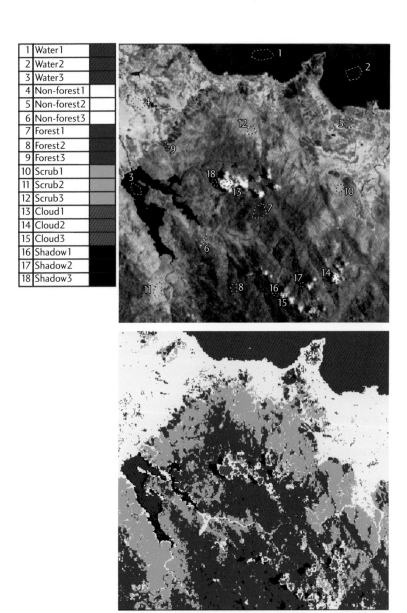

1	Water1	
2	Water2	
3	Water3	
4	Non-forest1	
5	Non-forest2	
6	Non-forest3	
7	Forest1	
8	Forest2	
9	Forest3	
10	Scrub1	
11	Scrub2	
12	Scrub3	
13	Cloud1	
14	Cloud2	
15	Cloud3	
16	Shadow1	
17	Shadow2	
18	Shadow3	

Fig. 3.20 The image in the upper right has 18 numbered polygons that represent samples of the cover types listed in the table next to the image (also called
training areas). Using the pixel values from these samples, the supervised classification algorithm analyzes each pixel in the satellite image to determine which
land cover class it most closely represents. The image on the bottom is the
resulting classified image. This first map has some areas that were not correctly
classified. We next refined the training areas by selecting additional areas and
modifying the existing areas to improve the classification accuracy. This iterative
process is often repeated several times (Landsat ETM+ image, path 125, row 49,
21 April 2003). Credit: Ned Horning, American Museum of Natural History's
Center for Biodiversity and Conservation.

Both supervised and unsupervised classification methods can produce reliable results; however, there are a greater variety of approaches in the supervised classification category. The primary difference between classification algorithms is the way in which they determine how an individual pixel is assigned to a land cover category.

We present a short overview of some of the more popular classification approaches to provide you with insight into the range of possibilities. Many of these algorithms come from the field of machine learning and they can be quite complex. Providing details of these algorithms is beyond the scope of this book. More detailed information is available in remote sensing textbooks, training courses, or on the Internet. The best way to get a feel for how these different algorithms work is to practice applying them using remote sensing software packages. Although it is not required, an understanding of how an algorithm works will help the analyst use the selected method more effectively. In addition, talking with someone with experience with the different classification approaches can be helpful in deciding which one to use.

ISODATA unsupervised classification: The ISODATA algorithm is the most common unsupervised classification tool. It uses cluster analysis techniques to create a user-defined number of clusters or classes in an image that must later be labeled to create a land cover map (Jensen 2005). Before you run an ISODATA program, you need to define several parameters that control how many clusters will be generated, the number of iterations that will be run, and other parameters that control how clusters are combined and split as the program runs.

When the program is finished, you will have an image with several classes that will not be labeled. For example, if you specified that the ISODATA program should create 25 classes, the output map will have 25 classes, each comprised of pixels with similar spectral characteristics. The next step is to label these classes with the correct land cover type. If you were trying to create a map with two classes, forest and non-forest, you would look at each of the 25 classes in the ISODATA output image and label them as either forest or non-forest (Fig. 3.21). In some cases, it will be difficult to decide how to label a particular class because it will contain more than one land cover type. When this happens you can choose to run the ISODATA program again to output more classes or you can have the ISODATA program run only on those classes that contain multiple land cover types, a technique known as "cluster-busting" (Jensen 2005).

Supervised statistical classification: With supervised statistical classification algorithms, the analyst must first locate and define samples of each class that are required for the final map (Richards and Jia 1986). For example if you were interested in creating a map with forest and non-forest classes you would select sample areas in the image that represent the different types of forest and non-forest. These sample areas are called "training areas." Remote sensing software that supports supervised classification provides tools to allow users to define and label training areas on an image. Once you select a sufficient number of training areas for each class you can run the supervised classification. The algorithm then

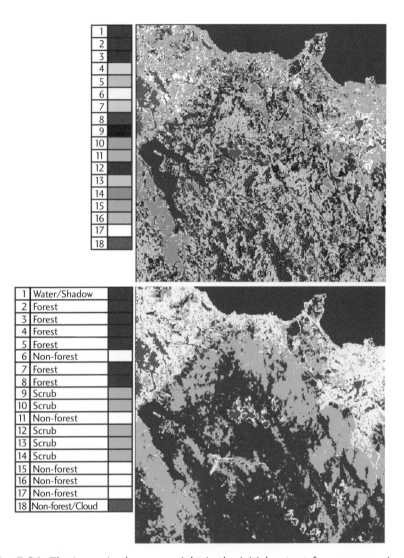

Fig. 3.21 The image in the upper right is the initial output from unsupervised classification using the ISODATA algorithm. This algorithm groups pixels with similar values to create the number of classes specified by the image analyst. In this case, we specified 18 classes, and each class identified by the algorithm is shown in a different color in the top map. Next, we labeled each of the classes as one of the land cover types. The table in the lower left shows how each of the classes were labeled to represent a smaller number of land cover classes. The lower right image is the resulting classified image map. Credit: Ned Horning, American Museum of Natural History's Center for Biodiversity and Conservation.

compares each pixel in the image with the different training areas to determine which training area is most "similar" to the pixel in the image. Similarity is defined statistically in analogous ways to the measurement of fit in a multiple regression with a variety of choices for measurement. Some of the more popular measurements are parallelepiped, minimum distance, maximum likelihood, and Mahalanobis distance (Jensen 2005; Richards and Jia 1986). Once you find the most similar training area, you can label the image pixel with the appropriate land cover class (Fig. 3.20).

The difference between the different types of supervised statistical classification algorithms is how they determine similarity between pixels. In general, the more complex algorithms take longer to process but they also tend to do a better job at assigning the right land cover label to image pixels.

Unsupervised and supervised classification methods represent the classic approaches to land cover mapping. Major packages all perform them, many free packages are available, and compared to some of the newer methods, they are relatively easy to learn and apply. They remain the workhorses of most land cover classifications.

Artificial neural net classification: Artificial neural network algorithms attempt to mimic the human learning process in associating the correct land cover class label to image pixels. Neural networks have their roots in the field of artificial intelligence and although the algorithm still pales in comparison with the human brain, its use in image classification has been quite successful. One advantage to using neural networks is that it is easy to incorporate ancillary data in the classification process. This in itself can greatly improve classification accuracy (Mas 2003).

Learning to conduct a neural network classification can be time consuming and is not as simple as the supervised statistical approach. There are a number of parameters that are not very intuitive and experience plays an important part in learning how to use these methods. Mas and Flores (2008) provide an overview of the use of artificial neural networks for remote sensing application along with strengths and limitations.

Binary decision tree classification: Decision trees are common machine-learning tools that are now widely used in the remote sensing arena. Decision trees are a set of binary rules that define how specific land cover classes should be assigned to individual pixels (Lieng *et al.* 2005). Fig. 3.22 illustrates a simple decision tree that was used to classify forest and non-forest classes using two Landsat TM bands. Each node represents a true or false decision, thereby creating a branch in the tree. The terminal node (the bottom tips of the tree) along each path defines an individual land cover class. This approach makes it easy to integrate ancillary data into the classification process (Lieng *et al.* 2005). A type of binary decision tree algorithm often used to classify remotely sensed data is the classification and regression tree (CART) algorithm.

Creating the rules for a decision tree requires decision tree generator software available in most popular statistics packages. This software takes sample data

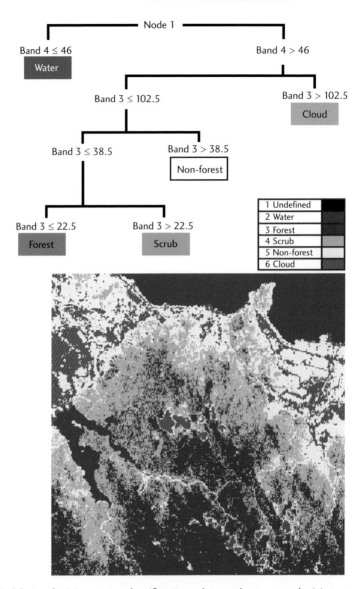

Fig. 3.22 In decision tree classification the analyst uses decision tree rule generation software to calculate a set of rules from a set of training sites that can be systematically applied to the satellite image to create land cover classes. In this simplistic example we used Landsat ETM+ bands 3 and 4 (red and near infrared) to develop a decision tree (top). The resulting classes can be displayed as a classified map with five land cover classes (bottom). The decision tree shows cutoffs applied to values of each pixel in each band, as determined by the rule generation software. In this example, if the pixel value for band 4 ≤ 46, it was designated as Water. If band 4 > 46 and band 3 > 102.5, then the pixel is labeled as Cloud. This process of successive testing continues until all of the pixels are classified. This example uses only two bands for illustration purposes. Normally you would use more bands and the resulting map would be much more accurate. Credit: Ned Horning, American Museum of Natural History's Center for Biodiversity and Conservation.

from training areas in the satellite imagery and ancillary data and works to define the most effective set of rules to determine the nodes in the decision tree. Experience is helpful when working with decision trees, as they require a good deal of editing (pruning) to produce suitable land cover maps.

A relatively new algorithm that uses a binary decision tree classification approach is called "random forest." The random forest algorithm creates several decision trees and then this collection of trees can be used to classify an image. Classification accuracy using random forests is higher than using a single tree approach such as CART (Gislason *et al.* 2006), and there is no need to edit the trees so it is much easier to use when compared to other binary decision tree approaches.

Image segmentation: Image segmentation is not a classification tool; rather it is a method used to group similar pixels into contiguous homogeneous areas or segments (Fig. 3.23). It can be thought of as a preprocessing step before classifying an image. The segmentation is done using sophisticated algorithms that compare a pixel's value with the values of the neighboring pixels. If neighboring pixels are relatively similar, then they are added to the contiguous group and if they are not, then another segment is started. These programs provide variables that allow an analyst to specify the relative size and sometimes even the shape of the segments (Blumberg & Zhu 2007).

Once an image has been segmented, it can be classified at the segment level instead of the pixel level. These segments are also called "objects" and the classification methods associated with this technique are often referred to as "object-based" or "object-oriented" classification. Analysts often employ these methods for mapping urban environments (Section 11.2). There are several advantages to this approach:

- It runs much faster since the number of segments is much less than the number of pixels in an image.
- The relative scale of the segmentation output can be specified so different segmentation runs can be used to capture features of different sizes.
- The classification algorithm can use the spectral characteristics (the pixel values) of an image as well as a host of other segment characteristics that describe the segment such as mean value, standard deviation, shape of the segments, and dimensions of the segment.
- The resulting image does not suffer from the "salt and pepper" effect common to pixel-by-pixel classifiers.

This approach holds a lot of promise for imagery with high spatial resolution as a way of removing unwanted information such as spaces between tree crowns when classifying forest types. Image segmentation is quite popular for classifying moderate resolution imagery as well. With moderate resolution imagery the accuracy obtained using this approach is often similar to other methods but the advantages mentioned above make it an appealing alternative. As with the

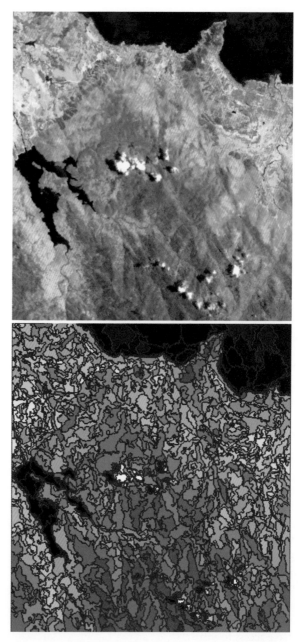

Fig. 3.23 Image segmentation groups together adjacent pixels that have similar pixel values. The image on the bottom is the result of a segmentation process applied to the image on the top. Segments are delimited with black lines (Landsat ETM+ image, path 125, row 49, 21 April 2003). Credit: Ned Horning, American Museum of Natural History's Center for Biodiversity and Conservation.

other newer methods, this classification approach requires experience to become proficient.

Fuzzy logic: Fuzzy logic methods can also be used in image classification. Fuzzy set theory as it relates to remote sensing image classification is based on the idea that boundaries between classes are not hard (crisp) but instead are soft, meaning that any pixel in a classified image can have partial membership in more than one class (Zhang and Foody 2001; Droj 2007). In other words, a pixel might partially belong to forest, soil, and shrub classes. With a hard classification, the pixel can only belong to a single class. As you can imagine, soft classifications more closely represent actual conditions on the ground than to do hard classifications.

In fuzzy cluster analysis, a method applied for image classification, one layer is created for each output class. Each pixel in an output layer will have a value between 0 and 1 assigned to it representing the degree of membership that pixel has in a particular class. For example, with a forest class each pixel would represent the "forestness" of that pixel using a value between 0 (definitely not forest) and 1 (definitely forest).

For practical purposes it is often necessary to create a product with a single, definitive hard classification output. Simply selecting the class that has the highest membership value can do this, or you can use more sophisticated methods that take into account contextual information about surrounding pixels. Both unsupervised and supervised classification methods have been developed that apply fuzzy logic classifiers but they are not common in remote sensing-focused image-processing packages. Fuzzy set theory is also used to assess the accuracy of a classified map as is discussed in Section 2.2.5.

3.5.2.3 Hybrid manual–automated classification

A hybrid approach combines the advantages of the automated and manual methods to produce a better land cover map. One hybrid approach is to use one of the automated classification methods to do an initial classification and then use manual methods to refine the classification and correct obvious errors. In this case, you use the manual methods to effectively edit the map output from the automated classification. With this approach you can get a reasonably good classification quickly with the automated approach and then use manual methods to refine the classes that did not get labeled correctly.

The editing process requires that the analyst be able to compare the classified map with either the original satellite image or some other imagery that can be used to identify land cover features. To compare a classified map with imagery it is helpful to have access to software that allows the analyst to flicker between two images (the land cover image and the original satellite image) or slide one image over the other on the computer display using a technique often called "swiping." By doing these comparisons, the analyst gets a sense of the quality of the classification. Errors can be corrected using tools common in many image-processing software packages.

Many remote sensing practitioners will not edit a classified map even if it is obvious that a certain area is misclassified. If the purpose of the land cover classification study is to produce the best map possible, then the analyst should use all means possible to meet that goal. In most cases, visually editing a classified map will improve the accuracy of the final product.

3.5.3 Accuracy assessment

An accuracy assessment should be part of any classification project so that accuracy of the individual classes can be determined. Since classified maps are not a perfect representation of reality, accuracy statistics provide objective information about the quality of the land cover classification. These assessments can be costly and unfortunately they are often dropped from a project because of time or cost limitations. More information about accuracy assessment is available in Section 2.2.

3.6 Summary

This chapter provides you with a basic understanding of remote sensing fundamentals. These fundamentals are covered in more detail in remote sensing textbooks and courses (see the book's Web site) but the information presented here is sufficient to grasp the methods and applications discussed throughout this book. Our aim is to provide a foundation necessary to appropriately use remotely sensed data without overwhelming you with technical details. The more you work with remotely sensed data the more comfortable you will become with these concepts and if necessary you can pursue more detailed and focused knowledge about remote sensing.

Part II

Ecological systems and processes

4

Measuring and monitoring land cover, land use, and vegetation characteristics

In terrestrial biomes, ecologists and conservation biologists commonly need to understand vegetation characteristics such as structure, primary productivity, and spatial distribution and extent. Fortunately, there are a number of airborne and satellite sensors capable of providing data from which you can derive this information.

We will begin this chapter with a discussion on mapping land cover and land use. This is followed by text on monitoring changes in land cover and concludes with a section on vegetation characteristics and how we can measure these using remotely sensed data. We provide a detailed example to illustrate the process of creating a land cover map from remotely sensed data to make management decisions for a protected area.

4.1 Land cover classification

This section provides an overview of land cover classification using remotely sensed data. We will describe different options for conducting land cover classification, including types of imagery, methods and algorithms, and classification schemes. Land cover mapping is not as difficult as it may appear, but you will need to make several decisions, choices, and compromises regarding image selection and analysis methods. Although it is beyond the scope of this chapter to provide details for all situations, after reading it you will be able to better assess your own needs and requirements. You will also learn the steps to carry out a land cover classification project while gaining an appreciation for the image classification process. That said, if you lack experience with land cover mapping, it always wise to seek appropriate training and, if possible, collaborate with someone who has land cover mapping experience (Section 2.3).

4.1.1 Land cover versus land use

Although the terms "land cover" and "land use" are sometimes used interchangeably they are different in important ways. Simply put, land cover is what covers the surface of the Earth and land use describes how people use the land (or water). Examples of land cover classes are: water, snow, grassland, deciduous forest, or bare soil. Land uses include: wildlife management area, agriculture, urban, or recreation. Some land cover maps include a mix of land cover and land use. For example, the map might have a "forest" (land cover) class and another class labeled "tree plantation" (land use). In a "pure" land cover map these would both be labeled "forest." Although there is nothing inherently wrong with mixing land cover and land use classes, it can sometimes lead to confusion. To avoid this confusion, it is important that each class on the map be clearly defined and distinct from other classes. One way to do this is to represent land cover using different colors while using different patterns or symbols overlaid on the map to represent land use.

Using image classification methods, ecologists and conservation biologists are able to identify and label land cover features to produce land cover maps from remotely sensed data. If you are able to place these land cover features into a use context you can create land use classes. For example, you can map forest as a land cover class but if you have information about how people use or manage the forest (usually obtained from field work) you can generate land use categories. Monitoring land cover and land use changes is an important tool to study whether and how policy affects the way people use natural resources (Thiha *et al.* 2007). These land use data are derived in different ways such as

- Map layers indicating how a particular area is managed such as wilderness, limited logging, or recreation provide direct information related to land use.
- Context of how one feature is situated in the landscape provides information about the likely use of that feature. For example, a forest area surrounded by an urban area is likely a park.
- Patterns of the land cover features often provide hints about how the land is used. For example, geometric shapes such as rectangles and circles can indicate agricultural fields.
- Sometimes the features themselves provide enough information to accurately label land use classes. For example, plantations tend to have a unique spectral response because all of the trees are the same age and the canopy is relatively even so plantations tend to look relatively smooth in texture on remotely sensed imagery.

The remainder of this section focuses on classifying land cover.

4.1.2 Options for output products

Land cover products can be grouped into two categories: classified maps and statistics. *Classified maps* are commonly used to represent land cover for a particular area. These maps group the landscape into discrete classes such as: forest, water, and grassland (see Fig. 3.18). One of the main advantages of this approach is that it provides mapped output in a format necessary for automated spatial analyses such as modeling and the calculation of landscape metrics. Statistics can be easily generated from these mapped products, so one effectively gets both output products when producing a classified map.

In spite of all of these advantages, classified maps have some disadvantages. For example, the classification process can be costly and time consuming. Classified maps also tend to be used for purposes for which they were not originally intended, often assuming that the map is more accurate than it is. A common example of this is using a land cover map created from satellite imagery that has much coarser resolution than necessary for the intended application (i.e., using a global 1 km resolution land cover map for a small protected area).

During the early years of satellite remote sensing, providing *statistics* summarizing the area covered by each land cover class offered the most common approach to land cover analysis simply because creating classified maps for large areas required too much computer power. To create change statistics you would develop a sampling strategy whereby small portions of the image are classified and, using statistics, generate estimates for the various cover types for the entire study area.

The primary disadvantage to the statistics-only approach is that there is no mapped output. In this age of spatial analysis, providing a visual representation is often a project requirement.

4.1.3 Comparing land cover maps with image photoproducts

Before we address the topic of land cover mapping we should first understand how a classified map differs from a remotely sensed image. A visual representation of a satellite image can be thought of as a photograph of the Earth's surface acquired from space. Methods to visually interpret satellite images are very similar to methods developed to interpret aerial photographs over 100 years ago. Using visual cues, such as tone, texture, shape, pattern, and relationships to other objects, an observer can identify many features in an image (see Section 3.5.1 and Appendix 5).

When using a land cover map it is important to keep in mind that it is an abstraction of actual land cover. When we classify a satellite image, thematic classes replace the visual cues that exist in the original image. For example, the subtle changes throughout a forest that can be seen in an image photo are replaced by a single color representing a particular feature such as forest (Fig. 3.18). Another feature of most land cover maps is that they portray different land cover classes as discrete entities with well-defined boundaries. In many cases, however, the actual change from one land cover type to another is gradual and this is easily visualized using the original image data. Defining a discrete boundary between land cover that transitions from one cover type to another in a continuous fashion often results in a somewhat arbitrary line drawn between those different classes.

Therefore, when would you choose to use the original image and when a classified map? First, in many quantitative studies the preferred data product would be a classified map in a digital format (as opposed to a hardcopy or paper format). One clear case for using classified data is in modeling (Chapter 14). When modeling, the algorithm needs to know the value of a particular parameter at a particular location, and that information is available in a classified image. For more qualitative studies, however, image representations of the data could be the product of choice. Examples of qualitative applications where image photo products might be preferred to land cover maps include:

- Planning protected area limits.
- Planning field work.
- Getting a broad-picture view of an area to understand land cover types and patterns.

4.1.4 Getting started

A good place to start is to define explicitly why you need to create a map and how will it be used. Reading this section will provide sufficient information regarding the factors that you will need to consider for a needs assessment. You should write down the results of a needs assessment for future reference. It will become obvious that there are several decisions that you need to make based upon how you will use the map. Accordingly, these decisions will determine many of your choices throughout the classification process. The next several sections detail the steps of a land cover mapping project.

4.1.5 Requirements for creating a land cover classification map

Creating a land cover map using remotely sensed imagery necessitates access to suitable imagery. There are several choices available and the process of selecting the appropriate imagery is described in Section 4.1.8.

You will also need some way to visualize and process the imagery. If the imagery is in a printed form, then viewing it is relatively straightforward and the classification process is essentially limited to visual interpretation methods. However, if the imagery is in digital form, you will need software to view and process the imagery. Software required for classifying imagery can range in price from free to tens of thousands of dollars (Appendix 2). There are several options available when using digital imagery and these are detailed in Section 3.5.2.

It is easy to focus on the skills needed to operate a particular piece of remote sensing software. However, the most important skill in our experience is the ability to accurately associate the features that can be seen in an image with what is on the ground. This ability comes from experience (Section 3.5.1 and Appendix 5).

Lastly, whether you are just learning image classification or you have been through some formal training such as workshops or university classes, it is always a good idea to get some feedback from experienced colleagues. Discussing your plan of action and periodically showing your progress to other remote-sensing practitioners is very helpful. They can sometimes suggest refinements and offer other options that will help improve the land cover map.

4.1.6 Define the study area

Once you identify how you will use the map you need to define the region to map. This can be a fairly easy task. When delineating the area to be mapped it might be important to include an area adjacent to the primary study area. This could be done to better understand the transition to the area outside of the study area. An easy way to do this is to create a buffer around the primary study area so you include adjacent areas (Fig. 4.1). You can create buffers using common geographic information system (GIS) software or image-processing software.

In some cases it can be difficult to reach consensus among project participants about the study area. For example, you might find that adding a small portion to a study area will involve the purchase of additional imagery and therefore increase the required resources to conduct the classification. After discussing

Fig. 4.1 We defined the scope of a land cover analysis of Bach Ma National Park in central Vietnam by including a 1.5 km buffer (transparent strip). The inside line of this buffer is the boundary for the park. By including the buffer in the land cover analysis of the protected area some of the land surrounding the park is included in the study (Landsat ETM+ image; path 125; row 49; April 21, 2003). Credit: Ned Horning, American Museum of Natural History's Center for Biodiversity and Conservation.

this situation with project participants you may decide that the additional cost to include the small portion of the study area cannot be justified and the study area will have to be modified.

4.1.7 Defining a classification scheme

A classification scheme effectively defines the legend that will be used for the final map. For example, will the map show forest and non-forest or will it have several or even dozens of different categories? Should the final map categories represent land cover or perhaps something else such as habitat or conservation importance? The way in which the map will be used, and some practical realities, will dictate the content of the classification scheme.

There are a large number of standardized classification schemes used for land use and land cover maps throughout the world. Some of the more common systems are listed in Table 4.1. An important point to remember is that no matter what classification scheme is selected, each class must be well defined and documented. For example, if you have a class called "Forest," you need to specify what constitutes a forest. Do the trees need to be a certain height? How dense do the trees or their canopies have to be? With this information it is possible for the user of the final map to clearly know what the different classes represent.

When choosing an appropriate classification scheme you should decide if compatibility with existing schemes is necessary or desirable. Some advantages of using an existing system are that the classes are already defined and the map you produce can be easily compared with other maps using the same system.

The Food and Agriculture Organization (FAO) of the United Nations developed the Land Cover Classification System (LCCS), which is gaining in popularity among land cover mapping projects around the world. The LCCS is supported by extensive documentation and a software tool that is freely available

Table 4.1 Examples of major land cover classification schemes designed for use with remotely sensed data.

Classification name	URL	Designed for sensor
Anderson	http://landcover.usgs.gov/pdf/anderson.pdf	Landsat and aerial photography
United States National Land Cover Data	http://eros.usgs.gov/products/landcover/nlcd.html	Landsat
FAO Land Cover Classification System	http://www.africover.org/LCCS.htm	N/A
Geocover-LC	http://www.mdafederal.com/geocover/geocoverlc	Landsat
Global Land Cover (IGBP DISCover/MOD12)	http://edcsns17.cr.usgs.gov/glcc/	AVHRR, MODIS

from FAO. An excerpt from the Summary of the LCCS User Manual (Gregorio and Jansen 2000) states:

> The Land Cover Classification System (LCCS) is a comprehensive, standardized *a priori* classification system, designed to meet specific user requirements, and created for mapping exercises, independent of the scale or means used to map. Any land cover identified anywhere in the world can be readily accommodated. The classification uses a set of independent diagnostic criteria that allow correlation with existing classifications and legends.

Defining mapping classes is often an iterative process. You must strike a balance between the classes you want, based on the map's purpose, and the classes that you can accurately and economically delimit. In general, greater detail translates to greater cost in time and money. A good rule of thumb is to select the minimum number of classes that are practical (Section 2.2.2).

When selecting classes, you can use a hierarchical or nonhierarchical approach. In a hierarchical approach, classes are nested such that major classes are broken into subclasses and these subclasses can further be broken into more detail. The advantage of such a system is that you can easily generalize the classes and it is easy to adapt to various scales (in general, the finer the map scale, the more detailed the hierarchy will be). A nonhierarchical approach, however, is designed for a specific purpose with a specific scale in mind. The advantage of a non-hierarchical system is that you can modify it to suit a specific application. In other words, you can more easily customize it for specific project goals since it can include a mix of detailed and generalized land cover classes.

When defining classes, you must decide how to classify mixed features such as transition and mosaic classes where multiple land cover types occur together. One approach is to explicitly define these classes as mixed or transition and the other is to ignore the fact that classes are mixed and define classes by the most common feature on the ground within a delineated unit. When deciding which approach to use in representing mixed features, you must take into account the nature of the features being mapped and how important mixed classes are relative to the intended use of the map. You should clearly document whichever method is used.

Another point that has to be considered with the classification scheme is the spatial detail that you will want in your map. A minimum mapping unit defines the smallest area that is delineated on a map. For instance if the minimum mapping unit is 1 ha, then any feature smaller than 1 ha would not be delineated as a unique feature. Instead it would be incorporated into another feature. Minimum mapping units can vary from class to class, so more important or rare classes would have a smaller minimum mapping unit to ensure that they are not lost as a result of inclusion in another class. In some cases no minimum mapping unit is used and all recognizable features are identified. No matter the approach, it is important that it meets the requirements of the needs assessment, is applied consistently, and is well documented. The level of detail that you can extract when creating a land cover map depends largely on the type of imagery that you use (Section 2.1.1).

4.1.8 Selecting imagery

Now that you have defined the classes you want to map, you will need to select imagery that will allow you to accurately define these classes. Selecting appropriate satellite imagery is, more often than not, limited by data availability and project budget. If the project budget is small, you may be restricted to using free or inexpensive imagery, which in turn affects the level of information that you can extract for the map. Ultimately, this may require that the project goals be adjusted to reflect the practical limitations.

The spatial detail of the information you need will dictate the required resolution of the imagery and this will significantly limit the list of possible image types that can be used. For example, if you were interested in identifying individual trees you would need fine-resolution satellite images or aerial photographs. If, at the other extreme, you wanted to create a global land cover map, you would look for imagery with a much coarser resolution. The selection of an appropriate image resolution is somewhat of an art and experience will improve your ability to know what can be reliably mapped using different image resolutions. One way to get a sense for the level of detail you can expect from a particular image type is to display the image on a computer monitor and zoom and roam around the image to see how well you can identify individual features. In general, if you can see your feature of interest on the screen, there is a good chance automated methods will properly classify it.

4.1.9 Image preprocessing

Preprocessing can be divided into two categories, radiometric and geometric (see Section 3.4 for more details on radiometric and geometric preprocessing). When conducting automated classification, improving the radiometric and geometric qualities of the data tends to improve classification accuracy since you are essentially reducing the noise in the image. With visual interpretation, however, this is not always the case. For example, in mountain environments there is often one side of a mountain that is brightly lit while the other side is in shadow. If not corrected, this effect will introduce problems for automated classification since the same land cover will look very different. However, with visual interpretation this illumination effect can actually help since it tends to accentuate three-dimensional features (Fig. 4.2). Moreover, a trained analyst is able to accurately classify and identify the vegetation even though the shadows and topography make the vegetation features appear like two distinct classes.

Geometric correction typically involves warping an image to match another image or some other reference data set (Section 3.4.3). Whenever an image is warped a resampling of the image pixels takes place, which degrades the original data to some degree (see Box 2.1). This has more of an influence when applying

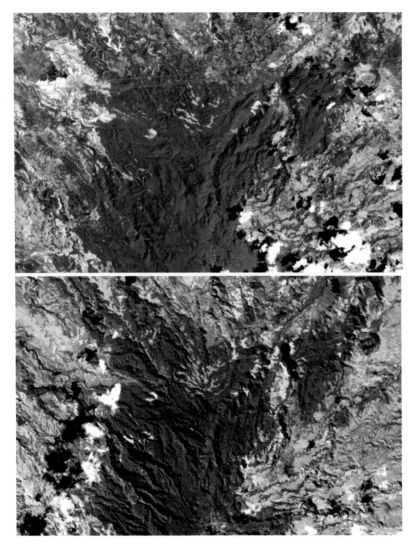

Fig. 4.2 Shadows can help improve the interpretability of an image. The top image of the northern part of Madagascar was acquired when the sun was high in the sky in the southern hemisphere (Landsat ETM+; path 159; row 69; December 4, 1999). The bottom image was acquired over the same area when the sun was significantly lower in the sky and therefore shadows are more pronounced (Landsat TM; path 159; row 69; June 25, 1984). You can see much more detail in the terrain in the lower image. Credit: Ned Horning, American Museum of Natural History's Center for Biodiversity and Conservation.

automated methods since the individual pixel values are modified. This effect may or may not be significant, depending on the application, but in general it is best to minimize the processing steps that involve resampling image pixels.

4.1.10 Ancillary data

In addition to satellite or aerial imagery, you can use other data to increase the accuracy of the classification. Some possible ancillary data types are digital elevation models (DEMs) and their derived data sets (slope and aspect), climate data such as precipitation and temperature, and vector overlays such as roads, rivers, and human population density. If there is a factor that affects the distribution of land cover that exists in a mapped form, you should try to incorporate it into the classification process. For example, DEMs often supplement satellite data when mapping land cover since specific vegetation classes are often limited to specific elevations or aspects.

Sometimes we might be aware of an attribute that we want to incorporate into the classification but there is no available data set that is appropriate for the study. For example, rainfall affects vegetation distribution but many rainfall data sets are too coarse to be useful in classifying vegetation. As time goes on, more of these environmental layers will be improved so that you can use them to map vegetation more accurately and at finer scales (Chapter 8).

Incorporating ancillary data into the classification process is not always easy. Some of the classification methods discussed in Section 3.5.2 allow the incorporation of assorted data sets but others are more restrictive. For the more restrictive methods, there are still some ways to utilize ancillary data. One is to use these data to stratify the study area into regions based on one or more environmental variables. We might use a DEM to create unique strata for elevation, slope, and aspect ranges. For example, we could create two elevation categories (below 500 m and 500 m or above) and four aspect categories (north, east, south, and west) and from these create the following eight strata: below 500 m north aspect, below 500 m east aspect, below 500 m south aspect, below 500 m west aspect, 500 m or above north aspect, 500 m or above east aspect, 500 m or above south aspect, and 500 m or above west aspect. The classification can then be carried out within each of the individual strata. Defining strata will generally have a positive effect on the accuracy of a classification product.

4.1.11 Classification methods

Image classification is covered in detail in Section 3.5.2. In the case of land cover classification, image pixels are assigned to categories (classes) that comprise different types of land cover defined by the classification scheme being implemented. There are dozens, if not hundreds, of classification methods you can use to group image pixels into meaningful categories. Unfortunately, there is not a single "best" approach to image classification. The choice you make depends on the algorithms available to you given the image-processing software you use, the data you have available, and your familiarity and experience with the different methods.

4.1.12 Field validation

Although land cover maps are often made without visiting the area in the image, there are good reasons why you should visit the area. The two primary reasons you would want to visit the area being mapped are to collect data to train the algorithm or the interpreter, and to collect data to evaluate the land cover map and estimate the accuracy of the individual classes, a process called validation. At a minimum, these data can be collected in one trip but often times two or more trips are preferred so that you can systematically collect validation information using a sampling design based on the classification results.

You must georeference your field data so that the point where you collected the data can be located on the imagery. Global positioning system (GPS) receivers are commonly used to record this location information. The type of information collected can range from detailed notes describing a site to a photograph of the site. Some of the detailed information that you can record includes type of vegetation, crown closure, slope, aspect, soil type, and other biological or physical characteristics that are important to identify the land cover type. If you take photographs it is a good idea to record the direction the camera was pointed and to make notes about the area to supplement the content in the photograph. For example, you could add information about species composition, tree height, and possibly land use.

When land cover maps are created without using field data from the region of interest it is difficult to interpret the accuracy of the final land cover map. An analyst with significant experience may be able to produce a land cover map of high quality but without validating information the true accuracy of the image classification quality is not known.

4.1.13 Accuracy assessment

In the needs assessment you should give some thought to the accuracy of the final map. The sampling statistics for this process are fairly straightforward but the practical issues such as limited access to the study area, insufficient funds to visit all of the sites, and a lack of time tend to impose limitations that must be accommodated in the sampling design. Dealing with this less than ideal situation may necessitate some creative solutions that require an understanding of statistics that are beyond the expertise of the image analyst. See Section 2.2 for more information about accuracy assessment.

4.1.14 Using the completed map

Classified maps are used for a host of quantitative analysis applications such as species or landscape modeling, fragmentation analysis, and setting conservation priority areas. They can also be used as visual aids in a presentation or as a layer in a GIS. No matter how a classified map is used, it is critical to have some information on the accuracy of the map. This information can come from a carefully planned accuracy assessment or some less rigorous qualitative methods but the source of the accuracy value should also be known. It is important to keep in mind that a classified map is only an approximate representation of the features on the ground. The accuracy of this representation can greatly affect the results of any quantitative analysis.

Another important characteristic of a classified map is spatial scale. This is especially important when using a land cover map to calculate landscape metrics. A coarse-scale land cover map will produce very different results than a finer-scale map when calculating most landscape metrics (Chapter 10).

4.2 Monitoring land cover change

Beyond studies of the fragmentation of target habitats, conservation biologists have an increasing need to evaluate the effects of change in the surrounding matrix of terrestrial or aquatic habitats. This section focuses specifically on issues relating to measuring and monitoring changes in land cover over time. We will present a number of different change detection approaches along with their strengths and weaknesses.

Remote sensing methods can be used to monitor changes within and between many different vegetation cover types such as grass, shrubs, and woodlands. This section uses forest monitoring to illustrate the fundamentals of remote sensing-based monitoring but similar approaches and issues are relevant for monitoring other land cover types.

Throughout this section, we refer to an early (older) and late (more recent) date image. Limiting change detection to two images is done to keep the examples simple, but in actual projects you can use more than two dates. After reading this section you will have sufficient information to understand how land cover change mapping works, and what approaches are available to answer your specific questions.

4.2.1 Reasons for mapping land cover change

Before starting a land cover change project it is important to define the objectives of the analysis. Reviewing these objectives will provide insight into what methods are necessary to achieve them. This seemingly obvious step is often skipped simply because someone decides that creating a land cover change map is a good idea. The person may not know why it is a good idea but it seems like the right thing to do.

Therefore, what are some reasons for conducting a land cover change analysis? Here is a list of common objectives:

- Identify areas of deforestation/reforestation.
- Identify or quantify seasonal patterns of change.

- Monitor growth of urban or rural populations.
- Predict future change based on past change.
- Provide input into climate or carbon budget models.
- Monitor changes in species habitat.
- Monitor changes in agriculture patterns.

4.2.2 Monitoring changes in forest cover

A very common type of change detection is monitoring changes in forest cover over time. This typically involves comparing two dates using one of the methods described below and noting where forests have been cleared or where they have grown back (Lu *et al.* 2004). The detection of a change from a dense forest to a cleared area is relatively straightforward and can be done with high accuracy (Section 2.2.2). We are often interested in other types of forest cover change such as selective logging, differentiation between young secondary and more mature forests, and changes in areas with low tree density such as woodlands. Monitoring these less dramatic types of forest cover change can be difficult largely because the changes are not abrupt, as they are with clear-cutting, but occur over a gradient. Determining where along that gradient change can be reliably detected is far from straightforward.

Although some progress is being made (Asner *et al.* 2005), monitoring forest degradation such as selective logging is still impractical at regional and global scales. High-resolution imagery that can detect gaps created in the canopy when a tree is removed can be used to detect some selective logging but in many dense forests these gaps in the canopy will close over a period of a few years.

Separating young secondary forests from more mature forests can also be difficult. Over time a newly planted forest will begin to be indistinguishable from a more mature forest when viewed on remotely sensed imagery. The length of time it takes for a young forest to resemble an older forest on remotely sensed imagery depends on a number of factors including the local environment, the type of forest, and type of remotely sensed data being used. One study demonstrated that you cannot distinguish between secondary and primary moist tropical forests 14 years after the primary forest was cut using Landsat Thematic Mapper data (Steininger 1996).

Monitoring changes in tree cover in an area with sparse trees can be troublesome. The lower the tree density the more the area will appear like the surrounding vegetation, often grassland or shrubs. In areas with low tree density the change in contrast after trees have been removed may not be great enough to detect.

4.2.3 Visual methods for monitoring land cover change

All too often we shun a simple visual approach to monitoring changes in land cover. With this approach two images from different dates are viewed simultaneously either by overlaying bands from the different dates (Fig. 4.3), displaying the images side by side, or rapidly switching between images acquired at different times using flicker or swipe options offered in many image-processing software products (Fig. 4.4). Creating a red, green, blue (RGB) color composite by

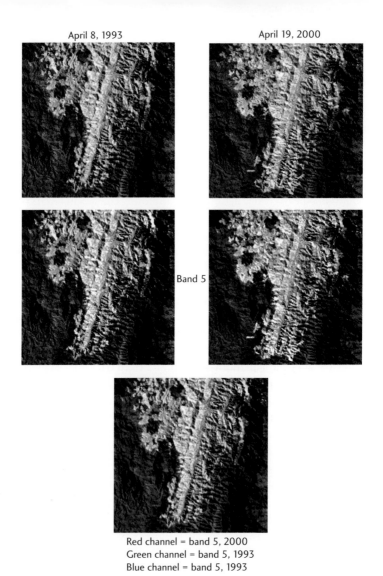

April 8, 1993   April 19, 2000

Band 5

Red channel = band 5, 2000
Green channel = band 5, 1993
Blue channel = band 5, 1993

Fig. 4.3 A way to quickly and easily visualize change is to create a color image using bands from images acquired on two different dates. The top row images are two-color composites of Landsat images from the same month in 1993 and 2000. The second row shows band 5 (mid-infrared) from these images. The multitemporal image at the bottom is a color composite image created using the two mid-infrared images from the two dates by assigning the band 5 image from 2000 to the red channel and the band 5 image from 1993 to the green and blue channels of the color composite. In the multitemporal image dark red patches indicate areas that have been converted from forest to non-forest. Placing this image next to the color composites in the top row provides a quick overview of changes in land cover over time. The same Landsat images will also be used in Figs. 4.4–4.6, 4.8, and 4.9 (path 158; row 72; TM on April 8, 1993; ETM+ on April 19, 2000). Credit: Ned Horning, American Museum of Natural History's Center for Biodiversity and Conservation.

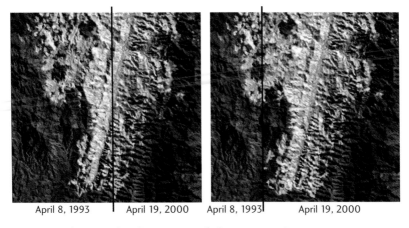

April 8, 1993   April 19, 2000   April 8, 1993   April 19, 2000

Fig. 4.4 Another visual technique is to flicker or swipe between images acquired on two different dates. We used a swipe function that is common in image-processing software to show changes between the two images in Fig. 4.3. With a swipe tool you superimpose one image over the other, and one date is displayed to the left of the swipe line (the black vertical line), while the other image is displayed to the right of the swipe line. By moving the line back and forth you can control the amount of each image displayed and the changes between the images become apparent. Credit: Ned Horning, American Museum of Natural History's Center for Biodiversity and Conservation.

mixing bands from images acquired on different dates is an excellent way to visualize change (Fig. 4.3). One way to do this with Landsat ETM+ imagery is to select band 5 (mid-infrared, 1.55–1.75 m) from the more recent date for the red output channel and band 5 from the older date for the green and blue output channels. When the image is displayed, areas that have undergone change will be displayed as different colors. For example, an area that was forest in the early date and cleared in the late date would appear red. Another band that is often used for this method is Landsat ETM+ band 3 (red, 0.63–0.69 m) although this tends to be noisier than band 5.

The primary advantage to visually comparing two images is that it can be done immediately after you acquire the data. Another advantage is that you can get a better sense of the actual landscape since you are effectively looking at a picture of the landscape rather than a map of discrete categories as in a classified map.

The downside to this approach is that it does not produce a quantitative product. That said, before this method is put to the side, it is important to ask yourself if a visual product can meet your needs.

4.2.4 Selecting a change detection method

There are dozens of ways to create land cover change maps and it is beyond the scope of this section to provide sufficient details to implement each one of these.

The purpose of this section is to provide an overview of the more common options (Mas 1999) and describe the advantages and limitations of each.

4.2.4.1 On-screen digitizing/editing

On-screen digitizing, or heads-up digitizing as it is sometimes called, is a manual method for creating land cover change maps relying on visual interpretation (Fig. 4.5). It involves an analyst drawing polygons that represent land cover change classes on a computer screen. This is the most subjective of the approaches but the human brain is still better at classifying the vast array of landscape features than a computer algorithm. The downside is that this approach is more susceptible to operator fatigue and bias than automated methods and tends to be slower in complex or large areas.

Visual interpretation of change is well suited for creating land cover change maps through the process of editing an existing land cover map. In this scenario, you create a land cover map for one time period (either the early date or the late date) using your method of choice. Validate this baseline map to assure that the quality is acceptable. Next, edit this land cover map using image editing

Fig. 4.5 Changes in land cover can also be mapped using manual hand digitization methods. To do this, it is helpful to display color composite images of each date as well as a color composite change image such as the one in Fig. 4.3. In this image an analyst has delineated a number of polygons that appear to be areas of deforestation. Credit: Ned Horning, American Museum of Natural History's Center for Biodiversity and Conservation.

procedures available with most image-processing software, by comparing the land cover map with both the image used to create the land cover map and the complementary image (if the land cover map represents the late date then the complementary image would be the early date satellite image). By comparing these three products, one can visually note areas that have changed from one cover type to another and edit the land cover map to represent this other time period. During the process of interpreting change, the analyst will occasionally find errors in the original land cover map and these errors can be corrected. This is an additional benefit of using a visual editing process. Updating or editing a land cover map to monitor changes in vegetation over time can often be done for a fraction of the cost required to produce the initial baseline map.

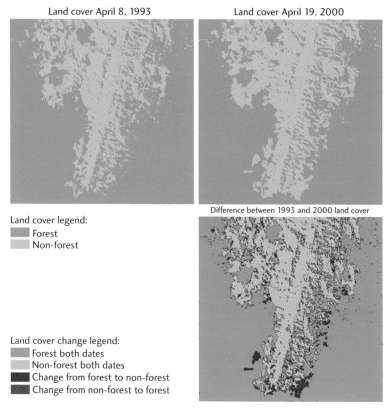

Fig. 4.6 A common and intuitive way to compare land cover from two different dates is to overlay the two land cover maps, a process termed post-classification change detection. The two independently classified land cover maps are illustrated in the top row and the result of overlaying them is shown in the bottom image. We performed classifications on the same Landsat images shown in Figs. 4.3–4.5. Credit: Ned Horning, American Museum of Natural History's Center for Biodiversity and Conservation.

4.2.4.2 Comparing two classified images (post-classification comparison)

This is likely the most common and intuitive change detection method. However, it rarely produces the most accurate results. In this method, you produce a land cover map for each of the two dates and then compare these two land cover maps using simple image math to determine the land cover change map (Fig. 4.6).

Logically, this approach makes a lot of sense and it has the advantage of directly providing land cover maps for the individual dates in addition to the change in land cover between the two dates. The problem is that the errors from each of the individual land cover maps are incorporated (they are cumulative) into the final change product, which makes the error of the final map significantly greater than that of the individual land cover maps.

One way to illustrate this multiplication of errors problem is to classify the same image twice and then overlay the resulting products as if they represented imagery acquired on different dates. When these images are overlaid, you will perceive changes in the land cover even though the exact same image was used to represent the early and late time period.

One instance where this method may be appropriate is when the images from the two dates have substantial variation not related to changes in vegetation cover. When this is the case some of the other change methods would tend to lump together the non-land cover changes with those related to changes in land cover. For example, if you are studying land cover change in an area with deciduous vegetation and one of the images was acquired with leaves on and the other with leaves off, the other change methods might have a difficult time differentiating between land cover change and changes due to phenology.

A variation of the post-classification method is to compare maps created at different times and using different methods to determine the changes in land cover over time. With this approach, when there is little or no control over the methods used to create the maps, the results can be questionable because you cannot assess the accuracy of the input maps.

Although comparing two classified images can produce acceptable results, alternative approaches often produce a higher-quality product for a given level of effort and resources.

4.2.4.3 Multi-date composite classification

With this approach the images from the two dates are combined into one multi-temporal image. This multi-temporal image is then classified using the automated classification method of choice such as those outlined in the land cover mapping section above. For example, it is common to combine Landsat TM bands 1–5 from the two dates to create a 10-band image containing all of the bands from the two dates (Fig. 4.7). This 10-band image is then used as input into the classification algorithm. This approach has the advantage of directly outputting the change classes, which effectively reduces the classification error when compared to the post-classification method described earlier. Although this method does not directly output land cover maps for the individual date, this information can be derived from the change classes.

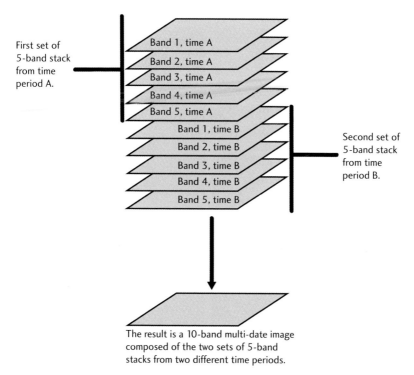

The result is a 10-band multi-date image composed of the two sets of 5-band stacks from two different time periods.

Fig. 4.7 Images from multiple dates can be combined to create a single, multi-date image. In this figure five bands from an image acquired on one date are combined with five bands from an image acquired on another date to create a 10-band multi-date image (although only three of these bands can ever be visualized in an image display, all the bands in the multi-date image can then be processed using automated methods similar to those used to create land cover maps, except the result would be a land cover change map (Landsat images are the same as shown in Fig. 4.3). Credit: Ned Horning, American Museum of Natural History's Center for Biodiversity and Conservation.

The limitations to this method are similar to those associated with automated land cover classification. Depending on the quality of the two images there may be sufficient variation across one or both images not related to changes in land cover. This would make it difficult to identify change consistently with reasonable accuracy.

4.2.4.4 Image math

When using an image math approach you can work with either individual bands or more commonly single-band image products such as vegetation indices or individual image bands from different dates. You then compare the single-band images from each of the two dates by subtracting or differencing them. Then you analyze the resulting image to determine the range of values that represent a change in land cover from one date to the next (Fig. 4.8). One approach is to

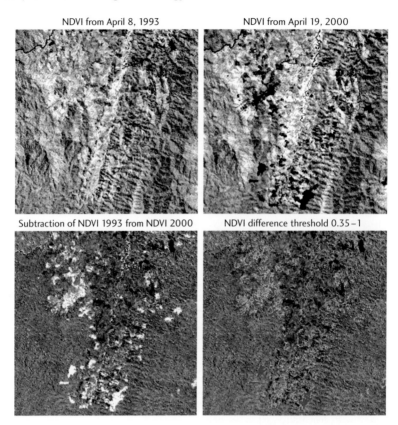

Fig. 4.8 Band math—subtracting the pixel values of one image from another—can give a quick overview of areas that have undergone change. These images show calculated Normalized Difference Vegetation Indices (NDVIs) for the two Landsat images shown in Fig. 4.3 (*top*). Then we calculated the difference between the two NDVI values for each pixel. The image resulting from the subtraction is in the lower left. When NDVI values are displayed, brighter pixels indicate the presence of vegetation. In the difference image, bright areas had high-NDVI values in the 1993 image and lower values in 2000. The image in the lower right highlights those pixels that had a significant drop in NDVI value between 1993 and 2000. These highlighted values can be used as a mask to restrict future processing to areas where a significant reduction in NDVI has been noted. As you can see, some of the highlighted areas did not change from forest to non-forest but from grass to cleared or burned land. This is because the change in NDVI value from grass to cleared or burned land is quite significant. NDVI highlights vegetation changes but does not discriminate between specific land cover types. Credit Ned Horning, American Museum of Natural History's Center for Biodiversity and Conservation.

create a Normalized Difference Vegetation Index (NDVI) (Section 4.3.1.1) image for each date and then subtract the NDVI images from each other to determine which pixels represent actual changes in land cover. Large differences in NDVI values between the two images would suggest that there has been a change in land cover between the two dates. When using this approach to map changes in land cover you must determine a threshold of change. The advantage to this approach is that it is easy and fast. The primary disadvantage is that while the output highlights areas that have experienced an increase or decrease in vegetation cover, it does not provide detailed information about what the land cover changed from or to. It is also sensitive to changes not related to land cover such as changes due to seasonality and changes in atmospheric conditions (clouds and haze).

This method is often used to create a mask (Fig. 4.8) highlighting areas that have undergone some sort of change. You can then use this mask with other methods to limit the analysis only to those areas that are suspected of undergoing actual land cover change.

4.2.4.5 Spectral change vectors

In spectral change vector analysis, changes in vegetation cover are noted by a change in brightness value (intensity) from one date to the next and the spectral direction of that change (change in color) as is illustrated in Fig. 4.9. For example, if an area was forested in the early image and was soil in the more recent image, there would be a change in intensity since soil tends to be bright in most spectral bands and forest tends to be darker and there would also be a notable directional component since the "color" of a forest is quite different from the "color" of bare soil.

Spectral change vector analysis provides two output images: intensity of the change vector and direction of the change vector. The intensity value is similar to what is calculated using image math although spectral change vector analysis typically uses multispectral imagery whereas image math is usually limited to single-band comparisons. This approach shares some of the drawbacks with image math but they are less severe and using the direction information in combination with the intensity information allows you to classify land cover change into different types.

4.2.4.6 Hybrid approach

You can also us a hybrid approach similar to that described in the land cover classification section above to leverage the advantages of both automated and manual methods.

4.2.5 Dealing with different data sources

Although it is best to use data from the same sensor, one of the practical realities of change detection is that you are often forced to use different types of imagery for the different time periods that are of interest. For example, if you want to calculate changes in land cover starting with a period before 1972 you will almost

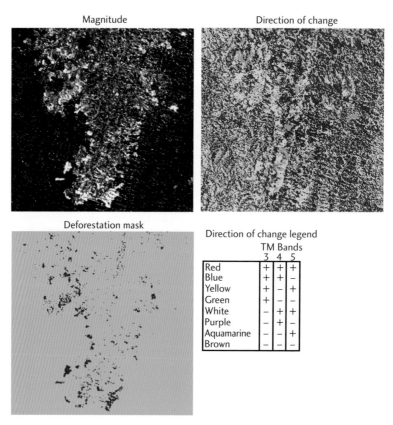

Magnitude · Direction of change

Deforestation mask

Direction of change legend

TM Bands

	3	4	5
Red	+	+	+
Blue	+	+	−
Yellow	+	−	+
Green	+	−	−
White	−	+	+
Purple	−	+	−
Aquamarine	−	−	+
Brown	−	−	−

Fig. 4.9 Spectral change vector analysis can be used to determine the magnitude of change between two dates and the spectral direction of that change. We calculated magnitude and the spectral direction of change using Landsat TM and ETM+ bands 3, 4, and 5 (red, near-infrared, and mid-infrared, for the two Landsat images shown in Fig. 4.3). The magnitude image shows you how much pixel values changed from one date to another, with brighter pixels representing greater change. The direction of change image indicates whether the pixel values for individual bands increased or decreased between the two dates. For example, the blue color shows that for bands 3 and 4 pixel values increased (+) from the earlier date to the more recent date and band 5 decreased (−) in value. In the deforestation mask the red color illustrates all pixels that have a magnitude greater than 35 and increases in pixel values for bands 3 and 5 and a decrease for band 4. This corresponds roughly with areas that have been deforested. In this example only three bands were used to more easily explain the process; however, more bands can be used. Credit: Ned Horning, American Museum of Natural History's Center for Biodiversity and Conservation.

certainly be limited to using aerial or satellite-based photography as data layers because digital imaging land remote sensing satellites did not exist before 1972. Another common example of using different types of data is comparing Landsat MSS, TM, and ETM+. Historic data from Landsat MSS has a lower spatial resolution and a more limited band set than TM and ETM+.

However, how do you deal with change detection when using different data types? One solution, and probably the most common when aerial photos are compared to satellite imagery, is to use the visual on-screen digitizing methods described above. This approach is easier if the two image types are both in digital format (the aerial photos can be scanned) and georeferenced so that they can be displayed in a coordinated manner on a computer screen.

If both data sets are multispectral in nature you can resample one of the data sets so that the pixel sizes for the two data sets are equal. When this is done the coarser resolution data set is usually resampled to equal the resolution of the other data set. This, of course, does not effectively increase the information content of the coarser resolution image but it does provide a data set that can be processed using the automated methods described above without compromising the detail of the higher-resolution image. Some GIS and remote sensing software packages allow you to combine imagery with different resolutions and in that case resampling would not be necessary.

4.2.6 Data normalization

There is a lot of debate in remote sensing circles about the practical value of normalizing images before conducting change detection classification (Song *et al.* 2001). Data normalization is primarily aimed at making the two images used as input for a land cover change analysis similar with respect to radiometric qualities so that the same land cover type on the two images has the same brightness value (digital number). In other words, it is an attempt to simulate the illumination and atmospheric conditions present when one of the images was acquired. The idea is that if the images are normalized, then it is much easier to note changes from one cover type to another since any change in brightness value between the two images will indicate a change in land cover. Even though this logic is quite sound, in practice it can be difficult to accomplish. There are two primary reasons for this. The first is that it is difficult to accurately create two normalized images. This is largely because the variations caused by illumination and atmospheric effects are rarely homogeneous across an image and simple and reliable methods to normalize imagery are still being perfected (Hashim *et al.* 2004). The second issue is that there is often a change in the state of the land cover between the two dates due to senescence, green-up, disease, or simply different growing conditions (growing degree days, water availability...) so the assumption that similar land cover types will look the same on both images is not always valid.

Although one can argue that any improvement gained from data normalization will improve classification accuracy, from our experience investing a significant effort into normalizing images using sophisticated algorithms does not always decrease the time spent on conducting the change detection or increase the accuracy of the output. Access to easy-to-use but complex data normalization algorithms is improving but in the past these capabilities have generally been restricted to expensive image-processing software programs. These algorithms may produce more accurate surface reflectance measurement but they often do not do as well normalizing the difference between the two images, which is important when doing change detection analysis (Song *et al.* 2001).

Two simple methods that you can use to normalize multi-date images are dark object subtraction and histogram matching. The dark object subtraction method works on the assumption that the darkest object in an image will have a very low (undetectable) surface reflectance in each of the image bands. To apply this approach you need to determine the lowest pixel value from the histogram of an image band and then subtract that value from all the pixels in that band. This process is repeated for all image bands. With histogram matching one of the images is used as a reference and the goal is to modify the histograms of the other images acquired on different dates so that they match as closely as possible. The closer histograms from the reference and other images are, the more similar the images will appear when visually inspected. The histogram matching process is available in most remote sensing software packages but it should only be used when the different images were acquired from the same sensor. Both of these normalization methods assume the atmosphere is uniform throughout the image.

4.2.7 Validating change detection results

Validating the results of a land cover change map can be difficult because one needs to determine what the land cover was for the time periods that are being compared. Typically when you assess the accuracy of a land cover map you can collect ground reference data on existing land cover but how do you go back in time to verify past land cover? The best answer to this is to use whatever information is available. In some cases you might be able to find aerial photos that can provide sufficient detail for the time period of interest. A possibility, although rarely practical, is to use interviews from people familiar with the landscape.

If you are putting in place a project to systematically monitor land cover change over time, it is advisable to set up permanent plots or use some other method for systematically sampling the same area so that the areas or plots can be checked every time a new layer is added to the land cover change series of maps. A simple way you can accomplish this is to periodically take photographs of an area from the same observation point (Section 13.1.3). This way you effectively keep a running tally of the change situation on the ground for specific areas.

4.2.8 Planning a land cover change project

Many of the issues that you address in a land cover mapping project (Section 4.1) must be addressed when mapping land cover change. For example, the change

Table 4.2 Biological and physical characteristics that affect the ease and resulting accuracy of mapping changes in forest cover over time.

Characteristic	Relatively easy	More difficult
Terrain	Flat terrain	High hills or mountains
Phenology	Predictable and homogeneous	Heterogeneous changes
Cloud cover	Rare morning clouds	Near continuous cloud coverage
Tree density	Closed canopy	Low percent crown closure
Fragmentation	Large contiguous coverage	Small patches of forest/non-forest

classes have to be thoughtfully selected so that they meet the objectives of the project and can be accurately delineated using the methods selected. The same goes for the selection of image dates that will be used for determining land cover change. The images have to provide sufficient spatial and spectral information to allow the detection of significant changes in the landscape. As for the selection of methods, it is important that the people doing the classification have sufficient experience in those methods so they can be performed reliably and consistently.

There are a number of additional issues that you must consider when creating a change detection map. The biological and physical characteristics of the area greatly impact the ease and accuracy for which land cover change can be monitored. Many of these characteristics are summarized in Table 4.2.

In a perfect world, all of the sensor and environmental conditions would be relatively equal in both the early and late date images but in practice many or even all of these are beyond your control and you just have to do the best you can with the available imagery.

Here is a list of some variables worth considering when selecting imagery for a land cover change project.

4.2.8.1 Sensor characteristics

Ideally one would like to use imagery from the same sensor to keep the sensor characteristics as consistent as possible. The more similar the characteristics of the sensors (Section 2.1.1), the more likely you are to have similar features on the ground appear similar in the two image dates.

Even using imagery from the same sensor is no guarantee that the sensor characteristics will equal since sensors degrade over time thereby changing the radiometric qualities of the sensor and in some cases causing a partial loss of data. The degradation of a sensor can often be compensated by applying published radiometric correction factors or simply by ordering radiometrically corrected imagery. As an example of the major changes that can occur, the Landsat ETM+ Scan Line Corrector (SLC) failed on May 31, 2003, and since that time, there are lost scan lines on the edges of each scene, with a 22 km swath in the middle that has full data (Markham *et al.* 2004).

4.2.8.2 Solar illumination

Images acquired under similar solar illumination configurations help ensure that ground features will appear similar on both early and late date imagery. If solar illumination angles are similar then shadowed areas as well as brightly illuminated areas will be similar in appearance for both dates. To accomplish this it is necessary for the imagery to be acquired during the same time of the year and the same time of the day. Some of these effects can be reduced using a DEM to normalize the effect of differencing illumination angles but this approach is not perfect (Riaño *et al.* 2003).

4.2.8.3 Atmospheric conditions

Ensuring similar atmospheric conditions between two dates of imagery is much harder to control than many of the other variables as it tends to change on an hourly or daily basis and is not always homogeneous across an image. Acquiring imagery at approximately the same time of the year can increase the chances of meeting this goal but it is certainly no guarantee. As with the solar illumination variable, atmospheric effects can be reduced using atmospheric correction algorithms but this too is an imperfect solution. See Section 4.2.6 on data normalization for more insight into this problem.

4.2.8.4 Soil moisture

Differences in soil moisture between two images acquired on different dates can affect change detection analysis in direct and indirect ways. It can directly affect interpretation of features when soil makes up a significant portion of the signal. This is especially noticeable when image bands that are sensitive to water, such as Landsat TM band 5, are used in the analysis.

Soil moisture can indirectly affect plant productivity (primary productivity is higher when plants have abundant water) thereby altering the reflectance characteristics of similar vegetation so it may appear as if the vegetation composition has changed (Mas 1999).

4.2.8.5 Acquisition date and frequency

The acquisition date of imagery is important for a number of reasons. In addition to those stated above, it is best to select a time of the year when you can most accurately differentiate the features in which you are most interested. This way it will be easier to detect changes in that cover type. For example, if you want to monitor changes in deciduous land cover, you would want to avoid using imagery acquired during green-up or senescence since the vegetation you are interested in is changing rapidly and it is nearly impossible to acquire an image from another time period with vegetation in the same state of green-up or senescence.

Another issue related to the acquisition date is the frequency of acquisition. If you are interested in monitoring changes over a relatively short period of time, you need to make sure that sufficient imagery is available for the focal time periods. The acquisition schedules for some sensors are predictable but even if you know when a satellite will acquire an image you are not able to predict if that image will be of sufficient quality (due to an array of environmental contaminants such as clouds or haze) to effectively perceive change in land cover. If the frequency for monitoring is on the order of several years then this is less of a concern.

Typically, you would try to acquire images from the same time of the year to reduce differences due to solar configuration and vegetation phenology.

4.2.8.6 Water levels

When working in areas with water, it is important to be aware of changes due to differences in water levels. If the change is permanent, it is certainly important to record it accordingly, but if it is periodic such as with tides and floods, then knowledge of these events and their timing should be considered when selecting imagery and during the interpretation phase. For example, the level of standing water in wetlands can vary greatly over time (Section 7.2). Viewing images acquired at times when water levels were not the same can present a very different picture of the wetland.

4.3 Vegetation characteristics

In terrestrial biomes, ecologists and conservation biologists need information about vegetation cover beyond what can be inferred from land cover maps. This section discusses ecologically relevant measures of vegetation that you can make using passive and active remote sensing sensors. Coverage of this topic includes how the measurements are made, how they compare with ground-based measurements, and how they can be used to understand the status or condition of the vegetation, the foundation of terrestrial ecosystems.

Some of the methods discussed in this chapter have been applied to global data sets to provide input to a number of models that require information about primary productivity. As remote sensing technology and algorithms improve, the ability to accurately monitor a variety of vegetation characteristics will increase.

There are a number of satellite image-based products that are being used to monitor vegetation over large areas around the world (Morton *et al.* 2005). For example, data collected from the MODIS sensor are used to create a number of products related to vegetation. These include (with the standard product reference)

- Vegetation indices (Section 4.3.1) (MOD13)
- Land cover (MOD12)
- Vegetation cover conversion (MOD44A)

- Vegetation continuous fields (VCF)/percent woody vegetation, herbaceous cover, and bare ground (MOD44B)
- Phenology (MOD12Q2)
- Leaf area index (LAI) (MOD15A2)
- Net primary productivity (MOD17A3)
- Fraction of absorbed photosynthetically active radiation (MOD15A2)

Measurements of these characteristics are based on the fact that reflectance, transmittance, and scattering of energy in a canopy are greatly affected by the structure and composition of the vegetation and how the vegetation components (leaves, branches, and trunk) interact with the spectrum of energy being used by a particular remote sensing instrument.

One quality that differentiates most of the vegetation characteristic data sets listed above from classified maps is that they are continuous representations of the attribute being mapped instead of discrete classes as is the case with land cover mapping.

4.3.1 Using vegetation indices

You can calculate vegetation indices with algorithms that rely on the fundamental principle that chlorophyll in green unstressed vegetation strongly absorbs red and blue wavelengths of light and strongly reflects infrared wavelengths (Glenn *et al.* 2008). This can be observed by looking at image bands recording red and infrared light (Fig. 4.10) or at a reflectance curve for vegetation (Fig. 3.15). Areas with a high density of green vegetation have a high vegetation index value and those with little or no green vegetation have a low value.

Vegetation indices have been used extensively for global studies to monitor changes in vegetation and have been effective in mapping droughts, desertification, phenology, and deforestation around the world. There are several reasons for this:

- There is a positive and strong relationship between vegetation indices and primary productivity (Tucker and Sellers 1986).
- The algorithms are, in general, simple and as a result they only require moderate computer power.
- Suitable imagery (at 1–4 km spatial resolution) has been acquired daily since 1978 for regions on Earth except the poles.

Most global products are available as multiday composites to reduce the effects of cloud cover and poor-quality data. Composites are created using a variety of periods such as 8 days, 10 days, 16 days, and monthly. Compositing routines use logic so that the "best" quality value for the composite period is selected. Historically, the "best" value simply equaled the highest index value during the compositing period. Now, more sophisticated logic incorporates several factors such as the number of "good" index values during the compositing period (Chen *et al.* 2003).

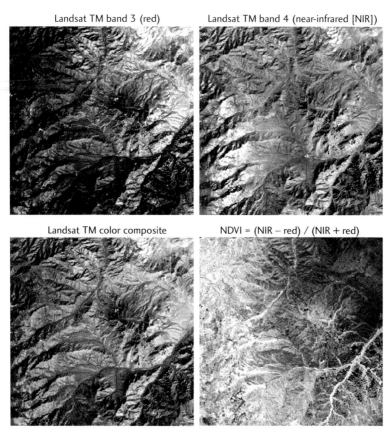

Landsat TM band 3 (red) Landsat TM band 4 (near-infrared [NIR])

Landsat TM color composite NDVI = (NIR − red) / (NIR + red)

Fig. 4.10 In an NDVI image, vegetation has a high value since chlorophyll in green vegetation heavily absorbs red wavelengths and reflects most of the near-infrared wavelengths of light. In this Landsat TM image of an area in southeastern Arizona you can see the heavily vegetated areas along streams and in the mountains toward the left portion of the image produce higher NDVI values then the sparsely vegetated areas toward the upper right corner of the image (Landsat ETM+ image; path 35; row 38; September 12, 2000). Credit: Ned Horning, American Museum of Natural History's Center for Biodiversity and Conservation.

In addition to primary productivity, vegetation indices have also been used to estimate parameters such as LAI. However, one of the limitations of using vegetation indices for these measures is that they are not very sensitive in high biomass and LAI environments since the indices saturate easily (Huete *et al.* 2002). To get around this problem you can use other algorithms. These improved algorithms are used to create a number of data products related to productivity that are based on the MODIS instruments (Appendix 4) on

NASA's Terra and Aqua satellites. MODIS provides near-daily global coverage at resolutions ranging from 250 m to 1 km.

We will discuss two common vegetation index algorithms: the NDVI and the Enhanced Vegetation Index (EVI). There are several other vegetation indices that have been described in the literature (Huete *et al.* 1997), such as the Simple Vegetation Index (SVI), Soil Adjusted Vegetation Index (SAVI), and the Modified SAVI (MSAVI), but the two indices presented below illustrate the basic principles of how vegetation indices work.

4.3.1.1 NDVI

The NDVI is the most common vegetation index and it has been in use since the 1970s (Rouse *et al.* 1973). It was applied to a global data set of coarse-resolution satellite imagery acquired by the National Oceanic and Atmospheric Administration (NOAA)-operated Advanced Very High Resolution Radiometer (AVHRR) sensors. The first AVHRR sensor was launched in 1978 and successive AVHRR instruments continue to provide nearly global coverage. Creating NDVI layers from this global data set proved to be an efficient way to get a good overall picture of primary productivity in terrestrial landscapes at a global scale (Tucker and Sellers 1986). The formula for the NDVI is:

$$NDVI = \frac{(NIR - Red)}{(NIR + Red)} \qquad (4.1)$$

where NIR = the near-infrared channel image value and Red is the red channel image value (Fig. 4.10). This generates a number between +1 and −1. Areas with a lot of unstressed green vegetation will have a value well above 0 and areas with no vegetation will be close to 0 and in some cases will have negative values. As a plant is stressed its productivity decreases so stressed vegetation will have NDVI values lower than unstressed vegetation (Kogan 2001).

4.3.1.2 EVI

The EVI was developed to improve upon the NDVI algorithm (Huete *et al.* 2002) and is gaining in popularity because it is offered as a MODIS data product.

The MODIS algorithm for EVI is:

$$EVI = G^* \left[\frac{(NIR - Red)}{(NIR + C_1 * Red - C_2 * Blue + L)} \right], \qquad (4.2)$$

where NIR = the near-infrared channel image value, Red is the red channel image value, Blue is the blue channel image value, and the four coefficients (they are constants when used with MODIS) are:

- Gain factor, $G = 2.5$
- Canopy background adjustment, $L = 1$

- Atmospheric aerosol resistance, $C_1 = 6$
- Atmospheric aerosol resistance, $C_2 = 7.5$

This is similar to the algorithm for NDVI but it adds corrections to reduce the effects of radiometric contaminants from the atmosphere and within a canopy. The canopy background adjustment coefficient L compensates for the different ways in which near infrared and red light behave (scattered and absorbed) inside and below a canopy. Soil moisture, surface litter, snow, and the type of soil all influence NDVI. The EVI is also more sensitive to variations in dense vegetation where NDVI tends to get saturated. The atmospheric aerosol resistance coefficients C_1 and C_2 reduce atmospheric effects in the red channel using data from the blue channel.

The EVI is more sensitive to canopy structure whereas NDVI is more sensitive to chlorophyll content so these two indices tend to complement each other. In fact, the MODIS Vegetation Indices product (MOD13) contains both NDVI and EVI products. It should also be noted that the imagery used to create the MODIS vegetation indices products are preprocessed to reduce the effects of viewing angle and solar illumination angles. If you need finer resolution than what is available from the MODIS products, you can always create your own vegetation indices using imagery with a finer spatial resolution and image-processing software (Appendix 2).

4.3.2 Principle components analysis (PCA)

Another technique that uses multispectral imagery to create a data set indicating the amount and status of green vegetation is PCA. Used throughout multivariate statistics, principal components analysis is a vector space transformation for multivariate data that transforms a number of correlated variables into a smaller number of uncorrelated variables called principal components. In remote sensing, it transforms a set of multiple bands into a new smaller set of principal components that describe the same image. Each successive component image will contain a lower percentage of the total variance. In other words, the first principle component image will contain most (often more than 85 percent) of the total variance from the original multispectral image and the second image will contain much less and the third even less variance.

A standardized PCA approach called the *Tasseled Cap transformation* has been developed for data sets acquired by different sensors. Using the Tasseled Cap transformation coefficients, it is possible to compare component images created using imagery from different times of the year or from different areas. The second principle component of a Tasseled Cap transform is called "greenness" and it is often compared with NDVI as an index of vegetation productivity. PCA can also be used to detect changes in land cover over time when applied to a time series vegetation index data set. When using a NDVI time series data set, the second principle component is considered the change component although the higher order components also are related to changes in land cover over time.

When interpreting the results of PCA you will need to identify the type of land cover change (i.e., seasonal, deforestation, and reforestation) that is most strongly associated with each of the component images.

We will also mention uses of PCA in other chapters in the book, and there is a detailed example using PCA with other classifications methods in Section 7.1. It can be used as a classification approach in its own right, and also for data reduction when there are a large number of bands.

4.3.3 Other MODIS vegetation data products

Two MODIS vegetation data products, in addition to the Vegetation Indices product (MOD13), that can help you understand vegetation cover and dynamics are the Global Land Cover Dynamics (MOD12Q2) and Vegetation Continuous Fields (MOD44B).

If you are interested in studying phenology, the MODIS Global Land Cover Dynamics data set (MOD12Q2) may be useful (Zhang *et al.* 2003c). The MOD12Q2 product includes a number of data sets with information about phenological cycles over a 12-month period including: onset of greenness increase, onset of greenness maximum, onset of greenness decrease, and onset of greenness minimum. These data are generated using a phenology detection algorithm that uses the MODIS EVI data set, described above, to track the green-up and senescence of vegetation around the globe. The algorithm uses data from other MODIS data sets to account for cloud cover, snow, and surface temperatures that are too low to support vegetation growth. One issue to keep in mind when using the MOD12Q2 product is that the EVI data used in the algorithm are available only every 16 days so the temporal scale is quite coarse. Consequently, the timing of greenness and senescence provided by the MOD12Q2 data set are only approximate.

The MODIS VCF data set (MOD44B) provides information about the density of vegetation (Hansen *et al.* 2003). Each pixel represents the percent cover within that pixel. For example, for percent tree cover each pixel would indicate the percent of that pixel that is covered by trees. A pixel value of 70 means that 70 percent of the pixel is covered by trees. This provides the ability to detect subtle differences in vegetation cover that would not be detectible in a typical land cover map. However, using the continuous fields approach requires that a separate layer be generated for each land cover type of interest. The MOD44B data set provides the following layers: tree cover, herbaceous cover, and bare cover at a spatial resolution of 500 m.

4.3.4 Using active sensors for vegetation mapping

Passive optical sensors that use the sun as the energy source are effective at providing information about the surface of a canopy but provide little information about what is under the canopy. To get subcanopy data we need to look at the different active sensors such as radar and lidar systems that emit their own energy source. These active sensors consist of a detector and signal generator whereas passive systems require only a detector. Radar is an acronym for radio detection and ranging. Radar systems operate in the microwave portion of the electromagnetic spectrum (Appendix 1) and because of this the signal is largely unaffected by clouds and rain so it can be considered an all-weather system. Lidar is an acronym for light detection and ranging and these systems operate in the visible and near-infrared portions of the electromagnetic spectrum.

Active sensors emit a signal and then measure its return properties. Since the signal is sent in regular pulses, the time it takes for the signal to return can be measured. It is this ability to measure different properties of the returned signal that allows active remote sensing systems to measure vegetation structure.

4.3.4.1 Radar systems

Radar is a rapidly evolving technology for measuring vegetation properties such as biomass, LAI, forest structure, and forest inventory information such as tree height and timber volume. Radar systems interact with materials differently from optical systems. Passive sensor systems record energy reflected from the surface of objects, such as trees, whereas radar energy can penetrate the canopy surface and interact with the vegetation elements such as leaves, branches, and trunks. These elements are large compared to the shorter radar bands (Appendix 1) such as the K-band and X-band but are small when compared to the longer L and P radar bands. The shorter wavelengths (i.e., K-band and X-band) are scattered more within a canopy whereas the longer wavelengths (i.e., L-band and P-band) are able to penetrate the canopy and in some cases even penetrate the soil before being scattered back to the radar's receiver.

The way in which a radar signal interacts with different objects, and therefore the intensity of the *backscatter* (returned signal), depends on the object's size, shape, surface roughness, angle of the incident microwave energy, and dielectric constant. An object's dielectric constant is a measure of the material's electrical properties with respect to the degree to which it absorbs, reflects, and transmits the incoming energy. Materials such as metal, water, and healthy vegetation have relatively high dielectric constants (meaning they reflect most the energy that strikes them) compared to soil, dead vegetation, or vegetation with very low water content (which generally absorb energy that strikes them). In other words, features such as a healthy forest will produce a brighter image than soil or a stressed forest.

The components that make up a vegetation canopy scatter and absorb radar energy hitting the canopy. The radar system measures the strength of the back-scatter (the portion of the emitted energy that is received by the radar antenna) and the time delay between when the energy was emitted and when it was received. These two types of information are used to measure vegetation structure.

Another useful property of radar systems is the polarity of the signal. When a radar emits a signal it leaves the transmitting antenna with either horizontal (H) or vertical (V) polarization (the direction of vibration of waves of electromagnetic radiation). After the signal interacts with features on the Earth's surface the antenna in either the horizontal or vertical direction receives it. The polarization of a particular data set can be HH, VV, HV, or VH where the first letter represents the polarization for the transmitted signal (horizontal or vertical) and the second letter is the polarization of the received signal. Using these different polarization configurations allows analysts to differentiate features based on how a feature modifies the polarization of the microwave signal. Creating a color composite using the different polarization combinations, it is possible to distinguish visually among different vegetation types (Fig. 4.11). Vegetation structure elements such as size, shape, and orientation have a definite albeit complex effect on polarization. The behavior of the polarization effects is also dependent on wavelength so polarization will behave differently depending on the wavelength of the radar signal.

Studies have shown that there is a relationship between the intensity of radar backscatter and forest biomass (Imhoff 1995). Longer wavelengths, such as the P-band, tend to be better predictors of biomass than the shorter wavelengths since the shorter wavelengths do not penetrate into the canopy as well as the longer wavelengths. Researchers are also seeking to better understand how biomass affects polarization. One drawback of using radar to estimate biomass is that biomass estimates tend to saturate at moderate biomass values so radar is not sensitive to variations within areas with high biomass (Imhoff 1995). Another problem is that surface wetness modifies the radar return adding more uncertainty to biomass estimates. Using radar to estimate biomass is also a labor-intensive effort since field surveys must be carried out to physically measure the biomass at several sites and then correlate this information with the data in the radar image. As research continues biomass estimation methods using radar might become an effective operational tool for measuring and monitoring biomass over large areas.

Forest characteristics such as height, density, and volume can also be measured using radar. As with estimating biomass, radar data using different wavelengths and polarization configurations are correlated with field data to see which configurations are best suited for measuring a particular characteristic.

Another technique for characterizing forest structure is *radar interferometry* (Section 5.1.3). The Shuttle Radar Topography Mission (SRTM) used this technique to create a near-global DEM using a radar system flown on the space shuttle. Interferometry use two radar images of the same area but which were acquired from slightly different locations. For the SRTM mission, one of the radar systems was mounted in the Space Shuttle cargo bay and the other was mounted on the end of a 60 m boom (Fig. 4.12). Two images can also be acquired using multiple passes by a satellite-based radar system as long as the exact distance between the two image acquisitions is known. If the distance between the two radar acquisitions is known, you can use sophisticated analysis techniques to calculate the height of objects on the ground. This method has been proven to produce high-quality DEMs (Gelautz *et al.* 2004) and research is

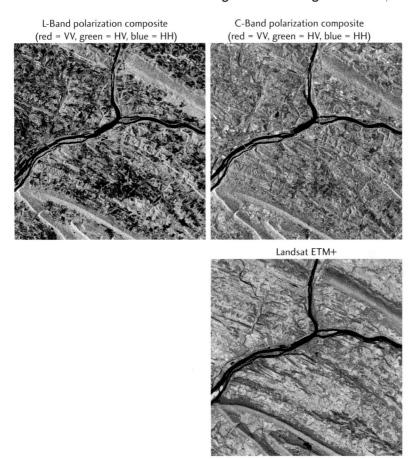

Fig. 4.11 Color composites can be created from radar data by combining images acquired with different polarization configurations. The top two images of an area around Sunbury, Pennsylvania, USA, show how radar data can be displayed as color images. The top two images are SIR-C/X-SAR data for L-band (5.8 cm wavelength) and C-band (23.5 cm wavelength). For each image the color composite was created by combining the following polarization combinations: VV, HV, and HH where the first letter is the transmitted polarization (either vertical or horizontal) and the second letter is the received polarization. Therefore, "HV" means that the signal was transmitted with a horizontal polarization and received with a vertical polarization. Combing different polarizations in a color composite helps you identify features on the ground (SIR-C/X-SAR data from October 6, 1994). The third image provides a view of the same area using an optical sensor (Landsat ETM+; bands 4, 5, 3 displayed; path 15; row 32; October 5, 2001). Credit: Ned Horning, American Museum of Natural History's Center for Biodiversity and Conservation.

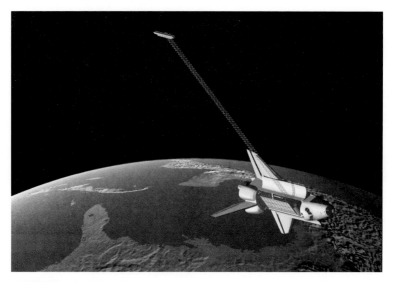

Fig. 4.12 The Shuttle Radar Topography Mission (SRTM) was launched on February 11, 2000 with the mission to record a near global elevation data set using an interferometric radar system. This system incorporated two radar antennas; one in the space shuttle cargo bay and the other on the end of a 60 m mast. Credit: NASA/JPL-Caltech.

ongoing to use radar interferometry to estimate tree heights and forest biomass (Kellndorfer *et al.* 2004). The main issue in calculating tree height is the necessity to measure the difference between the ground and the top of the canopy. Doing so requires the extraction of additional information. For more information on SRTM elevation data see Section 5.1.3.

With the increase in availability of satellite-based radar data, these data are increasingly being used to produce land cover maps and provide other information about habitat, especially as a complement to optical data or in areas with persistent cloud cover. While radar methods are still quite experimental with regard to the study of vegetation structure, research in this area is quite active (Kellndorfer *et al.* 2004, Treuhaft *et al.* 2004).

Radar data provide useful information. However, the techniques and software required to process radar data are still somewhat complex and, for the most part, beyond the capabilities of most conservation practitioners. In some cases, purchasing products derived from radar data such as land cover maps or collaborating with others who have experience working with radar data may be more feasible than buying the raw data and processing it yourself.

4.3.4.2 Lidar systems

Although lidar is probably best known for its use in creating digital elevation data, lidar systems show a lot of promise for the direct measurement of vegetation structural characteristics. Unlike radar and passive optical systems, lidar can directly measure vegetation structure and provide a vertical dimension largely missing in passive optical and radar data.

Lidar measures the distance between the sensor and a target by timing when the signal, a pulse of light, is transmitted and when received. Most of the laser systems used to measure vegetation structure use lasers that emit infrared light since vegetation is highly reflective in the infrared wavelengths, although certain bathymetric lidar systems utilize the water-penetration capabilities of green wavelengths.

Lidar systems use a pulsing laser and sensor that are flown in an airplane or onboard a satellite. In the simplest single pulse system, a laser pulses in rapid succession so the sensor collects data along a transect. The spacing of the pulses on the ground depends on the speed of the aircraft and the rate of the pulses being emitted. After a pulse hits a feature, the light is reflected back to the sensor. Only a portion of the light is reflected off of the top of the canopy and some of it continues down and interacts with other features within the canopy and other layers of vegetation (Fig. 4.13). The receiver in a lidar system measures the intensity of these returns. Discrete lidar systems only measure specific portions of this signal that correspond to peaks of returned energy. Some discrete systems only measure the first return, which is assumed to be the top of the canopy, while others measure multiple returns so that information about the vertical dimension of a forest can be inferred. More sophisticated lidar systems record the entire waveform so that rather than simply measuring the peaks in the returned signal the entire waveform is recorded (*waveform lidar*; Fig. 4.13).

Discrete lidar systems tend to have much higher spatial resolution because of their small footprint (size of the laser spot on the ground) and the rapid rate of emitting laser pulses (as high as 30,000 points per second). The primary advantage of waveform lidar is that it records more data from which to infer vegetation structure.

Lidar systems do not create images such as those created in typical optical remote sensing instruments. Although mapping lidar systems exist, the systems often used to measure forest structure provide points along a transect. A scanning lidar is a more recently developed system that provides enough points to enable an image to be constructed and is quite often used in marine, coastal, and wetland applications (Chapters 6 and 7).

The simplest measurement from a lidar system is the height of a canopy and the area covered by a canopy. With a well-designed sampling scheme and field plots to relate tree height with biomass, you can estimate biomass for very large areas, along with other forest stand characteristics. It is also possible to predict the percentage of light that is transmitted through different levels in the canopy. This is important when trying to understand how much light is available to organisms as you move from the top of a forest canopy to the forest floor.

By recording the intensity of the returned lidar signal you can derive a number of canopy structure indices. One of these indices is canopy volume, which is an

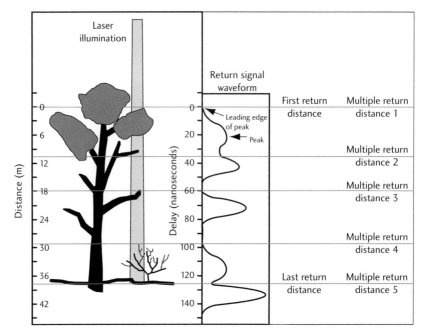

Fig. 4.13 When a laser pulse comes into contact with a forest, some of the energy is reflected from the top of the canopy but the rest enters the canopy and is reflected off of different elements of the tree, undergrowth, and eventually the ground. Depending on the type of laser being used, you can record varying amounts of data to understand the structure of the forest vegetation. The simplest lidar systems record only the first return distance. Other discrete-return systems record first and last and some record up to five discrete returns. The most sophisticated lidar systems can record full waveform data. Figure redrawn from Lefsky *et al.* (2002: 20), ©American Institute of Biological Sciences.

index that describes the surfaces of leaves and branches in three dimensions (Lefsky *et al.* 2002). Additional canopy indices will almost certainly be developed as lidar research continues. Canopy indices are potentially very important with respect to mapping habitats.

As of 2003, the only satellite-based lidar system used for vegetation studies is the Geoscience Laser Altimeter System (GLAS) onboard the Ice, Cloud, and land Elevation satellite (ICESAT). GLAS was developed primarily for measuring elevation and to determine ice sheet mass balance. There are a number of commercial and experimental airborne lidar systems acquiring data around the world. Scientists are only beginning to grasp the full potential of lidars for measuring vegetation structure and much research is going on in this arena (Behera and Roy 2002; Lefsky *et al.* 2002; Goodwin *et al.* 2006). Commercial airborne lidar systems exist. You can purchase aerial overflights of many locations with lidar and multispectral sensors. If you are interested in exploring the use of this technology, it may be well worth your time to contact some of these companies and ask them about the characteristics and capabilities of their systems. NASA is designing a satellite with a "vegetation-appropriate" lidar onboard called DESDYNI, planned for launch in 2014.

4.4 Summary

Satellite and airborne remote sensing provides a range of data and methods that can be used to study land cover, land use, and vegetation characteristics. You can successfully conduct simple analyses such as visual inspection of imagery. More complex techniques such as the creation of vegetation indices and land cover classification can be carried out with minimal training and experience. More complex analysis methods, especially those involving radar and lidar data, require more in-depth training. Fortunately, there are a number of high-level products derived from remotely sensed data that are available, with some available for free or at low cost. As these remote sensing systems improve, you can expect to see products that can be used to more precisely and accurately map features around the globe.

5

Terrain and soils

Building on the foundations of working with images and measuring land cover and vegetation in the previous two chapters, we now add the discussion of elevation and geology. Terrain attributes (such as elevation, slope, and aspect) and soil characteristics affect the distribution of most taxa and are therefore critical for effective biodiversity monitoring and conservation.

Remote sensing is the primary tool for collecting terrain information from local to global scales. This chapter will provide an overview of different types of terrain data that you can collect using remote sensing methods as well as how you can visualize and analyze these data. We will also highlight applications using terrain data to illustrate how they and their derived products can aid the conservation biologist or ecologist. In addition to landforms, this section will look at how remote sensing technology can provide information about geology and soils. Box 5.1 provides an example of how elevation data and satellite imagery helped in selecting field sites.

5.1 Elevation

The fundamental measurement used to create terrain data is elevation. In this section we discuss elevation measurements in detail. First, we define elevation and then describe common data formats. Next we present an overview of how

---

Box 5.1 Three-dimensional viewing for selecting field sites, a case study

In 1999, the American Museum of Natural History in New York and Institute for Ecological and Biological Resources in Vietnam were planning a major field expedition to Ngoc Linh in the forested mountains of central Vietnam. One of the tasks was to determine appropriate locations to establish base camps. This area is very mountainous and finding a level area large enough for over a dozen researchers proved to be a challenging task. To facilitate this process a Landsat Thematic Mapper (TM) satellite image was draped over a DEM and using three-dimensional visualization software expedition members were able to quickly locate relatively level areas that were conveniently located close to a water source and the sites that were to be visited during the expedition.

you can acquire elevation values and then we will present examples of how elevation data are useful in biodiversity conservation and how you can use these data to improve the geometric and radiometric qualities of remote sensing imagery. This section concludes with a discussion of some of the methods used to analyze and visualize terrain data.

5.1.1 What is elevation?

Before discussing the use of elevation data it is useful to define what is meant by "elevation" and other related terms. A general definition for elevation is that it is the vertical distance measured from a point to a reference surface. This may seem pretty straightforward, but accurately defining the location of a point or a reference surface in the vertical dimension can be quite difficult.

When measuring an elevation you need to define a reference surface. This reference surface is called a vertical datum. A common reference (or datum) for elevation measurements is sea level. Many maps, for instance, label elevation as meters or feet above sea level. So, how can one precisely measure sea level? If you were to go to the ocean and measure the height of the water would that be sea level? The answer is, probably not. The reference for "sea level" is meant to represent the mean level of the open sea, which is determined by regularly recording sea level using tidal gauges over a period of several years (DMA 1983).

Sea level is defined by a surface called the *geoid*. The geoid is defined by a surface of equal gravitational pull that can be thought of as the water surface if the ocean covered the entire earth. Due to differences in the Earth's gravitational forces caused by differences in the mass and density of the Earth's mantle and crust, the shape of the geoid is not smooth and it undulates above and below the *ellipsoid*, which is the mathematically defined shape of the Earth used for mapping (Fig. 5.1). The elevation measured between the geoid and a point on the Earth's topographic surface is called the *orthometric* height.

When you retrieve elevation values, it is important to know the reference from which they were derived. For instance, global positioning system (GPS) receivers calculate elevation relative to the ellipsoid (NIMA 1997). Most available digital elevation data are referenced to the geoid. The difference between the ellipsoid and geoid is called the geoid height. These values range from roughly +75 m (when the geoid is higher than the ellipsoid) to −100 m (when the ellipsoid is higher than the geoid) around the globe (Milbert and Smith 1996). To convert a GPS ellipsoid-based elevation reading into one relative to the geoid you can use a model of the geoid, such as those created by the United States National Oceanic and Atmospheric Administration's (NOAA) National Geodetic Survey (NGS), to calculate the offset for a particular area. Some GPS receivers have this conversion capability built in.

Once you have identified the reference, you can determine the elevation of a feature. Defining the point from which you are trying to measure an elevation depends on the methods you use to define that point. For example, if we are

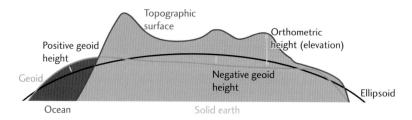

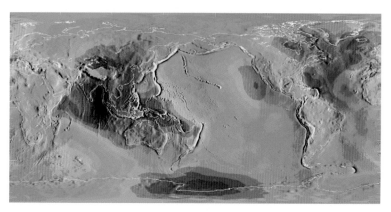

Fig. 5.1 Three representations of the Earth (*top*): geoid, ellipsoid, and the topographic surface. The ellipsoid is a solid form mathematically defined using two axes. The geoid is an irregular solid defined by a surface of equal gravity potential (sea level). Geoid height is the distance between the geoid and ellipsoid for a particular point on the globe. The lower map shows geoid heights for the globe. Red represents the maximum geoid height (85.4 m) and magenta represents the minimum geoid height (−107.0 m). Geoid heights were calculated using the WGS-84 reference ellipsoid and the EGM96 geoid model. Credits: Ned Horning, American Museum of Natural History's Center for Biodiversity and Conservation (*top*). US National Geodetic Survey, NOAA/NOS (*bottom*).

trying to determine the elevation of the Earth's surface in a forested region, we need to effectively see through the trees. Using traditional photogrammetric techniques (this is how most topographic maps have been made) a human would try to visually estimate the average height of the trees from aerial photographs and make the assumption that the terrain under the tree canopy was relatively similar to the changes in the surface defined by the top of the canopy. Using optical remote sensing imagery acquired from any digital imaging instrument holds the same challenge. While you can map the top of the canopy, you cannot see through the canopy to map the ground surface; so it is necessary to calculate an offset (usually the average tree height) to determine the ground surface elevation. Active remote sensing instruments can often penetrate the top of the canopy but they do not always accurately locate the ground surface. There is a radar technique called interferometry, discussed later and in Section 4.3.4, that can penetrate the top of the canopy but the signal typically does not reach the ground. In this case, the point being measured is somewhere between the ground and the top of the canopy and the exact location depends on a number of factors such as tree density and structure. Lidar, an active remote sensing instrument using lasers, is increasingly being used to provide accurate elevation data; using this technology it is possible to see patches of the ground through the canopy in all but the densest forests.

5.1.2 Representing three-dimensional surfaces

Now that you know what "elevation" means, how can it be stored as data? Perhaps the oldest technique used to illustrate terrain on a map is shading and sketching in mountains. Although these maps show relative changes in terrain there is no absolute elevation information. Contour lines have become the primary way to denote absolute elevation on topographic maps. Contours are lines that follow a single elevation. For example, a contour line on a map with a value of 100 m defines an imaginary line on the ground that is 100 m above mean sea level. With limited training and experience, you can get a pretty good idea of the topography of an area simply by looking at (reading) the contour lines. Some maps use shading to aid interpretation. If you digitize contour lines you can store them as vector lines or polygons in a geographic information system (GIS). With digital contour data, it is easy to create maps showing discrete ranges of elevations such as elevation values between 100 and 500 m (Fig. 5.2a).

Topographic data can also be represented digitally as gridded surfaces. In this form, the data are stored in an image, similar to a remotely sensed image, except the pixel values represent the elevation of the center point of each pixel (Fig. 5.2b). The most common term for gridded elevation data is Digital Elevation Model (DEM). In a DEM, elevation values (often referred to as "z" values since if latitude and longitude are "x" and "y" in a coordinate system, then elevation is "z") are stored in a grid with uniform cell spacing (i.e., 10 m, 90 m, 0.5 degrees) and the surface usually represents the bare Earth (Earth surface with no vegetation or artificial features). It is called a model because the "z" values are a representation or an abstraction of a surface. Another type of gridded model is a Digital Surface Model (DSM). This is similar to a DEM except the surface represents the top surface of features on the Earth such as a forest canopy or the tops of buildings.

The term Digital Terrain Model (DTM) is often used synonymously with DEM but a more accurate definition for a DTM is a DEM that also includes elevation data that better define topographic features. These extra data, called mass points and breaklines, define point and linear topographic features. Mass points are irregularly spaced points that define the elevation of prominent features that can be represented as a point such as the top of a peak or the

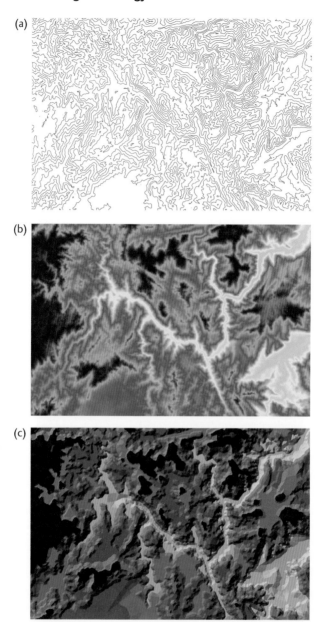

Fig. 5.2 Elevation data can be stored and displayed using different data models. Three common models are: (a) contours, (b) gridded, and (c) Triangulated Irregular Networks (TIN). These images were created using 90 m Shuttle Radar Topographic Mission (SRTM) data for an area in Quang Nam Province in central Vietnam. Credit: Ned Horning, American Museum of Natural History's Center for Biodiversity and Conservation.

bottom of a pit. Breaklines are linear features that define features such as ridge lines, drainage pathways, and shorelines. Using mass points and breaklines to create a DEM results in a product that more accurately includes topographic features defined by local maxima and minima, such as peaks, ridges, and rivers or the edges of abrupt changes in topography.

Another digital format for representing three-dimensional surfaces is Triangulated Irregular Networks (TIN). A TIN is a set of irregularly spaced mass points that are connected to form a set of contiguous, nonoverlapping triangles (Fig. 5.2c). Each triangle represents a facet, or plane, and each corner of the facet has a known elevation. It is a vector representation so it is a topological structure. A topological structure means that the lines and points in a TIN contain information about the neighboring points and triangles. When creating a TIN it is important to carefully select mass points. For example, mass points selected at points on the terrain with significant changes in slope or aspect such as peaks and valleys will ensure that the TIN accurately represents the terrain. A nice feature of a TIN is that it can "adapt" to changing terrain complexity by adjusting the number of mass points to capture important features. In other words, areas with a complex terrain would require more mass points than areas with minimal terrain variation.

Table 5.1 Advantages and disadvantages of using contour, grid, and triangulated irregular networks (TIN) digital representations of elevation data.

	Advantages	Disadvantages
Contours	• Easily digitized off of topographic maps • Compact file size	• Limited to discrete elevation data
Gridded Surface	• Easy to work with using GIS or image-processing software	• Often requires a lot of disk storage • Resolution is a constant—so not able to adapt to changing complexity of terrain
TIN	• Often required for spatial modeling • Smooth continuous representation of terrain • Efficiently stores data • Able to capture varying terrain complexity • Can be more efficiently displayed for three-dimensional visualization	• Requires significant human intervention to ensure mass points are well selected and accurate

With these different ways to represent three-dimensional surfaces, how do you know which is "best" for a particular situation? The choices are often limited to the tools and data you have available although in some cases a particular application or computer model will require a specific format. Fortunately, many GIS and image-processing computer software packages have processing methods to transform one elevation representation to another. Table 5.1 presents some of the advantages and disadvantages between contour, grid, and TIN digital representations of elevation data.

5.1.3 Acquiring elevation data

You can use a number of different methods to collect elevation data. Field measurements, such as those used to establish benchmarks (physical reference points with accurate elevation information) use various leveling and GPS techniques. The instruments used in these measurements are very precise levels using the same fundamental principles of a carpenter's level. Leveling produces very precise and accurate elevation information but it is time consuming and limited to recording point heights.

Remote sensing methods are used for more cost-effective elevation mapping over large areas. Traditionally, aerial photographs have been the primary source for recording topographic information. Using aerial stereo photographs (photographs of the same area acquired from different positions and therefore different look angles), it is possible to analyze and record three-dimensional information. The instruments (stereoplotters), originally created to make maps from aerial stereo photographs, were only capable of recording point heights and drawing contour lines on a map. Creating gridded elevation data was a tedious job requiring significant manual input. With the advent of computers, techniques were developed to automate the process of creating gridded surfaces. These methods make use of a technique, called autocorrelation, which matches portions of two stereo images and then measures the relative offset of individual pixels to calculate elevation values for each pixel. These elevation values correspond to the surface that is imaged resulting in the creation of a DSM. This image matching technique is also used for stereo satellite imagery. In fact, some satellite sensors, such as ASTER and PRISM from Japan, are designed to acquire an image of the same area twice in the same orbit by having a forward- and/or aft-looking sensor and a nadir (looking straight down) sensor. A near-global 30 m DEM prepared using ASTER imagery is described in Section 15.1.

Active remote sensing instruments are increasingly being used to create elevation data sets. There are two radar approaches for collecting elevation data. One, radar altimetry, collects point data and the other, radar interferometry, collects image data. A radar altimeter records spot heights, usually over water bodies, as the satellite orbits the Earth. The radar instrument measures the distance between the satellite and the water surface. Since the orbital parameters of the satellite are known with high precision, it is possible to calculate the distance between the satellite and a reference ellipsoid and with that information you can determine the elevation of the surface of water bodies.

Radar interferometry, or Interferometric Synthetic Aperture Radar (IFSAR), is discussed briefly in Section 4.3.4.1. This is the technique that was used to create the near-global (between 56° S and 60° N) Shuttle Radar Topographic Mission (SRTM) DEM. The spatial (horizontal) resolution of this data set is 30 m although it has been degraded to 90 m for most areas of the world outside of the United States. The vertical resolution of the SRTM data is 1 m with an absolute height error of roughly 8 m (Rodríguez *et al.* 2006).

In addition to the shuttle mission, satellite and airborne sensors are increasingly using radar interferometric methods to create detailed DEMs (Hensley *et al.* 2001). There are many different instrument designs for collecting radar interferometry data. For example, the frequency (wavelength) used affects how far a signal can penetrate tree canopies. The microwave frequency used for the SRTM data set records elevation heights that are well below the top of a forest canopy (Hofton *et al.* 2006). Higher frequencies (shorter wavelengths) can be used to record the elevation of the top of the canopy and lower frequencies (longer wavelengths) can be used to record the ground under the canopy. Because of physical limitations of radar, gaps or holes in the DEM can occur that result in missing data. There are a number of methods you can use to fill in these holes (Grohman *et al.* 2006). Using IFSAR methods, you can acquire topographic data for large areas quite rapidly and radars have the advantage of being able to work in rain and darkness.

Another remote sensing technique that uses an active sensor is topographic lidar. The basic principal of topographic lidar is similar to radar altimeters: determine and record the distance between the lidar instrument and a feature being measured for sequential points under the sensor as it travels over the Earth's surface. The location of the sensor as it sends and receives each pulse of light is determined through the use of a Global Positioning System (GPS) and an Inertial Measurement Unit (IMU). The GPS records the absolute position of the lidar instrument and the IMU measures the roll, tilt, and pitch of the platform carrying it, which is usually an airplane. Although lidar is not an imaging system in the same sense as the passive optical sensors, some lidar instruments, such as scanning lidar, are able to acquire a dense array of points sufficient to create an image using interpolation methods. The major disadvantage of lidar is that it can be difficult to acquire data through some clouds; and, since nadir lidar returns from water are not reliable, it is difficult to locate precisely the edge of water bodies (Fowler 2001).

DEM data sets derived from the above mentioned methods all have horizontal (x, y) and vertical (z) errors associated with them. Both horizontal and vertical errors are usually represented as a root-mean-square (RMS) error. RMS is calculated by summing the distances of the deviations of points from their true position and then taking the square root of the sum. This error information is usually contained in the data set's metadata and should be consulted so you have an indication of the severity of the errors inherent in the DEM. These errors will often become evident when you compare DEMs from two different sources. They each might have acceptable errors as defined by the mapping standards used to create them and they might look roughly the same but if you compare them pixel-by-pixel the differences become apparent.

In some cases the best topographic data are only available in a hardcopy (printed) format such as contours on a topographic map. There are a number of methods to assist the digitization of contour information. These methods range from manually digitizing to using sophisticated line-following software programs to partially automate the process. Once you have scanned the contour lines it is necessary to apply some form of interpolation or smoothing algorithm to fill in the empty space between contours in order to create a gridded DEM (Gousie and Franklin 2003).

5.1.4 DEM preprocessing

Often before you can use a DEM you need to apply some degree of preprocessing to enable its use as input for models or to derive other products. In this section we will address some of the common types of preprocessing you can perform.

The most common processing task is smoothing, which you can use to reduce the jagged effect of many DEMs that can cause problems when identifying topographic features such as ridges and valleys or calculating slope and aspect (Fig. 5.3). Smoothing can be accomplished with an image processing technique called filtering. To remove the high-frequency noise evidenced by the jagged appearance, you can use a low-pass filter. A low-pass filter replaces a pixel value with the average value of the surrounding values, which results in a smoothing of the image appearance. This is a common filtering method available in most image-processing software packages. It tends to minimize the noise in a DEM without significantly altering broader scale landforms (image smoothing is discussed further in Section 11.3.2).

Another issue that is a particular problem with the SRTM DEM is that there are holes representing areas of no data. There are generally two options to fill these holes: insert data from another DEM or use an algorithm such as *kriging*, or *polynomial interpolation*, to estimate elevation values. Elevation data from other sources can fill no-data holes in an SRTM DEM but you must do so with caution to ensure the patched area matches the elevation of the surrounding area. For example, if you want to patch a hole in an SRTM DEM with elevation values derived using optical satellite imagery, there is a good chance you will need to add (or subtract) an offset to (from) the patch so the elevation values of the two DEMs are relatively equal. Different methods are under development to normalize the fill data so that it fits properly within the SRTM DEM (Grohman *et al.* 2006).

Using an interpolation algorithm to fill holes in an SRTM DEM has the advantage of not requiring actual elevation data to replace the holes. However,

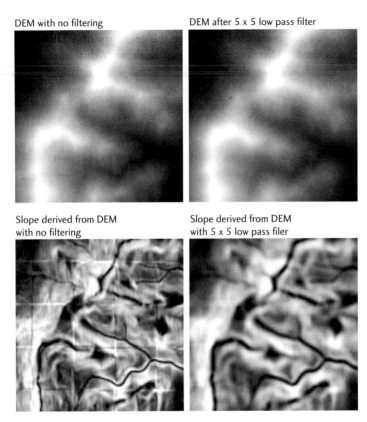

Fig. 5.3 Digital Elevation Models (DEMs) often have artifacts imbedded in the data that result from the way they were constructed. The negative effects of these artifacts can be reduced by smoothing the data through the application of a low-pass filter algorithm common in most image-processing packages. In the top DEM image you can see a blocky structure (caused by faint horizontal and vertical lines in the DEM) that is not part of the terrain in the original DEM. Creating a slope image from this DEM clearly shows that derived products will have spurious results. Applying a low pass filter reduces the severity of the artifacts. Expanding the low-pass filter beyond a size of 5×5 would smooth the data even more. Black represents the lowest elevation and slope values and white represents the highest values. The DEM covers the town of Ripton, Vermont, USA, and was subset from the USGS National Elevation Dataset 7.5' DEM. Credit: Ned Horning, American Museum of Natural History's Center for Biodiversity and Conservation.

the drawback is that the algorithm must make assumptions for the missing data based on existing data around the hole. This often is not a serious problem for small holes but it can produce erroneous results for larger holes.

In addition to these tasks for improving the usability of a DEM, some processing involves transforming the data by changing the geometry (such as changing the map projection) or the units of measurement used to record elevation values. Methods used to change the geometry of a DEM are similar to those described in Section 3.4.3, which dealt with this issue for remotely sensed imagery. Changing elevation units is usually a straightforward task that involves multiplying each cell by a factor to convert to the required unit.

5.1.5 Products derived from DEMs

Since DEMs provide a model of terrain they are often used to create secondary products that describe various physiographic features of a study area. We list below examples of the types of features applicable to ecology and biodiversity conservation. Topographic characteristics:

- Slope—steepness between two points.
- Slope aspect—orientation or direction of the slope.
- Contour lines—lines of equal elevation.
- Ruggedness index—relative measure of elevation difference between adjacent elevation cells.
- Viewshed delineation—area that is visible from a particular point.
- Topographically correct area—"true" surface area that takes into account slope as contrasted with planimetric area that can be measured directly from a map.

Topographic features:

- Ridges—ridge line.
- Peaks—conical convex landform.
- Channels—valley bottom.
- Pits—conical concave landform.
- Passes—low point connecting two peaks.
- Planes—flat areas.

Hydrologic analysis:

- Flow direction—direction of flow for each pixel.
- Flow accumulation—upstream area draining into each pixel.
- Stream order—a system of classifying stream segments based on the number of tributaries upstream that only changes at the confluence of two streams of the same order.
- Stream gradient—steepness of a stream channel.
- Watershed boundaries—delineation of a watershed.
- Watercourses—predicted stream channels.

Visual products:

- Shaded relief—an image of a DEM with three-dimensional effects created by illuminating the DEM by a virtual sun at a defined solar elevation (or zenith) and azimuth, often called hill shading.

- Enhanced relief—the appearance of relief in a shaded relief image is amplified by a multiplication factor to highlight subtle differences in relief.
- Virtual fly-through—a visual simulation where topographic data can be viewed from any dimension and perspective, and combined to display other data, such as land cover in a three-dimensional view.

To create these products, you need a DEM and appropriate, often specialized, software. For example, there are a number of software packages dedicated to hydrologic analysis and others that focus on extracting topographic features.

The quality of these derived products depends on the quality of the DEM and also the algorithm used to create it. As mentioned above, the extraction of terrain features can be improved by incorporating ancillary information such as mass points and breaklines into the process. This is especially useful in hydrologic analysis where it is important to have rivers and streams constrained to channels that have a continuous flow downhill. If you plan to use elevation data for hydrological analysis it is a good idea to work with a conditioned or hydrologically correct DEM (Hutchinson 1989; Kost *et al.* 2002). These conditioned DEMs are increasingly available (see Box 5.2) and if they are not available for a particular area the tools required to create one can be purchased, or in some cases, downloaded for free. Information about software that can be used to create products derived from DEMs can be found on the book's Web site.

5.1.6 Using DEMs to improve mapping accuracy

Elevation data are used to improve the geometric and radiometric accuracy of remotely sensed data. In this section we will further discuss these processes.

Box 5.2 HydroSHEDS

HydroSHEDS (**Hydro**logical data and maps based on **SH**uttle **E**levation **D**erivatives at multiple **S**cales) is a suite of mapping products that provide hydrographic information for regional- and global-scale applications in consistent georeferenced vector and raster formats (Lehner *et al.* 2006; USGS 2009). The data layers included in HydroSHEDS are: stream networks, watershed boundaries, drainage directions, and ancillary layers such as flow accumulations, distances, and river topology information. These data are available in a variety of resolutions ranging from 3 arcseconds (roughly 90 m at the equator) to 5 min (roughly 10 km at the equator) making it the most detailed near-global hydrographic dataset available in the public domain (USGS 2009).

5.1.6.1 Geometric corrections

The location of a feature in an image is affected by the height of that feature on the ground. As described in Chapter 3, elevation data are required in order to remove the geometric distortions caused by terrain using a process called orthorectification. To understand how the orthorectification process works you need to understand how terrain causes problems in the first place. This discussion will be limited to imaging optical sensors since terrain correction for radar is more complex and beyond the scope of this book. We will use an aerial camera to illustrate the principles as the basic concepts are applicable to other imaging sensors as well.

In a camera, an image is recorded after light rays, traveling in a straight path, enter the sensor's lens (or telescope) and then strike the image-recording surface or focal plane (Fig. 5.4). Since the image is recorded on a plane (the focal plane), distance measured along that plane will be proportional to a reference plane projected to the area being imaged. In Fig. 5.4 the reference plane is the base of the trees. Features with any height will appear to be displaced on the focal plane (Fig. 5.4). The amount of the displacement is directly proportional to the elevation above or below the reference plane of the feature being imaged.

If you know the elevation of the feature being imaged you can correct this displacement by moving the pixel to the correct location (i.e., moving a' to a in Fig. 5.4). This assumes that the image and the DEM are co-registered so that a pixel in the image can be matched with the correct elevation value.

5.1.6.2 Radiometric corrections

The position of the sun as well as topography can greatly influence the amount of light that is reflected off any given point on the Earth's surface. Although these topographic effects can improve our ability to visually interpret aerial or satellite imagery (Fig. 4.2), we usually try to reduce these effects for automated classification and feature extraction. Most automated classification and feature identification approaches work on the assumption that similar features will have similar reflectance properties. When a feature is partially or entirely covered by a shadow, however, the amount of light reflected back to the sensor can change dramatically. In the extreme case when a feature is entirely covered by a dark shadow, no light is reflected. This is particularly evident in the shadows associated with the clouds in the top image of Fig. 4.2 (white puffy features at the top and bottom of the right-side of the image). When a feature reflects no or very little light it is not possible to remove the shadow.

Another illumination effect, opposite from shadows, occurs when features are oriented in such a way that they become excessively illuminated. This can be seen in many mountainous areas when one side of the mountain is in a shadow and the other is brightly illuminated. This over illumination can cause reflectance values to be higher than what one would expect for a particular feature (Fig. 3.17).

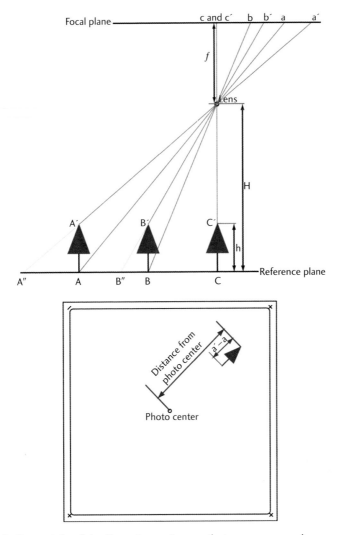

Fig. 5.4 Geometric distortions in an image that can occur when a scene is recorded by most passive sensors (cameras and scanners). The focal plane is the plane where the image is recorded (film or digital sensor). In this illustration, you can see that objects of any height will be radially displaced out from the center of the photo. The relative distances between the tree stems in the drawing on the top (points A, B, and C) are the same as the distances between their corresponding points on the focal plane (a, b, and c). The points on the focal plane that correspond with the tops of the trees (a′, b′, and c′) are also equally spaced but the distance between them is greater than the distances between the points a, b, and c. In the drawing below you can see that this causes objects with height to appear to "lay over" away from the center of the image. The farther the object is from the center and the higher it is, the more it will "lay over." The radial distortion (a′−a) can be corrected if the height of the objects and the flying height and focal length of the sensor are known. Using orthorectification software these principles are applied to offset pixels so they appear as if the scene being imaged was level with no relief. Credit: Ned Horning, American Museum of Natural History's Center for Biodiversity and Conservation.

Fortunately, there are algorithms that can reduce these effects. One common and relatively simple way to do this is to approximate the way the feature would be illuminated if it had a level orientation. The formula is:

$$L_H = L_T \left[\frac{\cos(\theta_S)}{\cos(i)} \right], \tag{5.1}$$

where L_H is the radiance for a horizontal surface, L_T is the radiance over sloped terrain, θ_S is the solar zenith angle and i is the sun's angle of incidence. The angle of incidence is the angle between the incoming light and an imaginary line perpendicular (normal) to the feature's slope (Fig. 5.5). It can be calculated by subtracting the slope of the feature from the solar zenith angle. This algorithm works on the assumption that the features on the surface are perfect diffuse reflectors (a Lambertian surface). Although some surfaces have near-Lambertian properties, none are perfect diffuse reflectors (Fig. 5.6).

There are more complex algorithms to compensate for the limitations of the simple cosine correction approach described above. One algorithm, called the Minnaert correction, raises the above formula to a power of a value between 0 (specular) and 1 (perfectly Lambertian) to differentiate types of land cover to account for the fact that features have varying degrees of diffuse reflection.

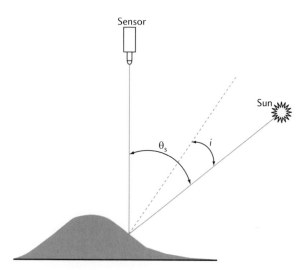

Fig. 5.5 In order to correct remotely sensed data for the uneven terrain illumination it is necessary to know the solar zenith angle (θ_S) and the sun's angle of incidence (i). The angle of incidence is the angle between the incoming light and an imaginary line perpendicular (normal) to the feature's slope. Credit: Ned Horning, American Museum of Natural History's Center for Biodiversity and Conservation.

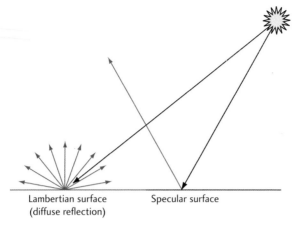

Lambertian surface   Specular surface
(diffuse reflection)

Fig. 5.6 Reflection of electromagnetic energy from features can range from specular to diffuse. Specular reflection causes the energy to be reflected at an angle that is equal to but opposite from the angle of incidence. Diffuse reflection causes the energy to be reflected equally in all directions. A surface that is a "perfect" diffuse reflector is called a Lambertian surface. Credit: Ned Horning, American Museum of Natural History's Center for Biodiversity and Conservation.

5.1.7 Three-dimensional analysis and visualization

You can also use digital elevation data to create stunning three-dimensional visual effects (Hirtz *et al.* 1999). By combining a DEM with a satellite image, land cover map, or other type of image data you can create static or dynamic visualizations. Static visualizations include shaded relief maps mentioned above and perspective views where you can simulate a wide range of viewing and environmental conditions by specifying the positioning of the viewer and the sun (Fig. 5.7). Some software programs include options to affect the atmospheric conditions by providing controls for haze and you can add features such as buildings and trees to the landscape to more accurately simulate the area being viewed.

Dynamic visualizations, or fly-throughs, simulate the experience you would have if you were in an aircraft flying over the terrain. You can fly over remotely sensed imagery or thematic maps.

Creating these visual products is not only fun, it is also an excellent way to convey the information in a thematic map or to illustrate how the landscape might change under a certain set of conditions. Being able to simulate the view of the landscape from an airplane, such as a fly-through, offers more realism than viewing the same landscape with static maps and these products are increasingly used as effective communications tools when interacting with the public (Box 5.3).

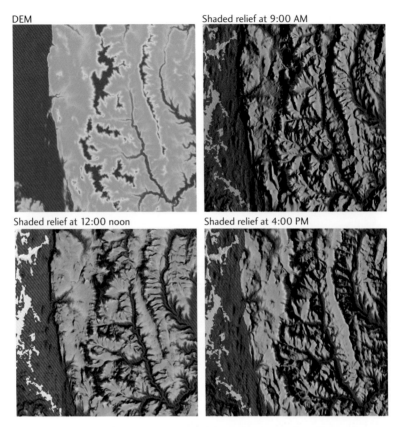

DEM

Shaded relief at 9:00 AM

Shaded relief at 12:00 noon

Shaded relief at 4:00 PM

Fig. 5.7 Shaded relief maps are a useful tool to visualize three-dimensional terrain features, as for the Green Mountains in central Vermont, USA, illustrated at different times of the day. The image in the upper right is a colored DEM with blue representing lower elevation values and red high values. The subsequent three shaded relief images represent the terrain illuminated on June 21 (the summer solstice) in the morning, noon, and afternoon. Note how the shadows appear on different sides of the mountains. We created using data from the 30 m USGS National Elevation Data set. Credit: Ned Horning, American Museum of Natural History's Center for Biodiversity and Conservation.

5.2 Geology and soils

Geology and soils play a significant role in shaping and controlling natural systems and therefore understanding the links to ecosystems is important for biodiversity conservation (Brilha 2002). Some researchers have also argued geology must be incorporated into conservation policies to ensure that some of the geologic wonders of the world are not destroyed (Brilha 2002). Geologic and soils mapping using remotely sensed imagery has been going on for decades and

Box 5.3 Fly-through animations for raising conservation awareness

The James River Basin Partnership in Missouri uses three-dimensional animated visualizations as a tool to familiarize the general public and decision makers with the area around the James River basin. These visualizations created by the Department of Geography, Geology, and Planning at Missouri State University use DEMs and remotely sensed imagery to illustrate urban sprawl and historic and current land cover, as well as predicted future land cover scenarios as the result of different management decisions. Providing a medium that appears more real than a static flat map allows people to understand easily the impact of different management decisions.

with the advent of new sensors the accuracy and precision of these maps are increasing.

5.2.1 Geology

Remote sensing methods are used extensively for mineral exploration and geologic mapping (Gupta 2003). For both of these endeavors, analysis of spectral information and landforms is important. Mapping landforms is relatively straightforward, through the interpretation of remotely sensed imagery and analysis of DEMs (Ustin *et al.* 1999). Geologic mapping, on the other hand, can be difficult because the substrate is often obscured by vegetation. When the substrate is visible, we can use the spectral information to identify the minerals that make up a rock. Libraries exist that contain digital spectral signatures of minerals obtained from laboratory measurements. We can use these reference spectral signatures to help us identify mineral content (Clark 1999; Hook *et al.* 1999). Geologists are arguably the most prolific users of hyperspectral imagery because it provides the detailed spectral information that can be compared with these spectral signatures in a library to distinguish mineral composition of exposed substrate.

When the substrate is covered by vegetation, the type of plants that cover the ground can be used as an indicator of the substrate (Ustin *et al.* 1999). The study of using vegetation as an aid in geological mapping is called geobotany. Since it is likely that much of the interpretation of geologic mapping units arose from inferences based on vegetation cover it is not surprising that geologic maps and vegetation maps of the same areas often are closely aligned. Because of the tight relationship between geology and vegetation, some people have used geological maps as a layer to aid in the automated classification process to create land cover maps (DuPuy and Moat 1996).

5.2.2 Soils

Information about soil type and soil moisture is important in biodiversity conservation for many reasons. Soil qualities affect the types of vegetation that can grow as well as faunal diversity. Soil data are also important for many types of modeling that require information about soil structure, such as erosion, runoff, and landslide susceptibility. Remote sensing methods are used to map various soil properties, but, as with geology, there are some limitations.

Soil mapping makes use of remote sensing instruments that measure reflected and emitted soil spectra in both optical and microwave wavelengths. You can directly measure soil characteristics when the soil is bare; however, if the soil is covered by vegetation its type must be inferred from the vegetation cover. As with geology, there are extensive libraries of digital soil spectra that can be used to identify the component materials that make up soils. Since soil composition includes a mix of organic and inorganic elements, it is typically much more difficult to identify these components than to identify rocks. Other properties, such as soil particle size and soil moisture (and vegetation cover) further complicate your ability to identify soil types.

In addition to soil type maps, soil moisture is a much sought-after data set. For the most part, soil moisture data derived from remote sensing refer to surface moisture. You can use models to derive the water content available at deeper layers in the soil (Scipal and Wagner 2004). Global soil moisture data are collected at frequent intervals using passive and active (radar) microwave instruments. These data typically have spatial resolutions ranging from 25 to 50 km (Scipal and Wagner 2004). One limitation of radar-derived soil moisture is that it is strongly affected by dense vegetation cover and for this reason this analysis does not perform well in the tropics. To measure soil moisture at finer scales, high-resolution aerial and satellite long-wavelength radar instruments (i.e., L-band and P-band) are more suitable (Moran *et al.* 2006). Two satellite-based radar instruments used to map global soil moisture are the European Remote Sensing Satellite (ERS) and the Advanced Microwave Scanning Radiometer (AMSR-E).

Although optical data are not ideal for directly measuring soil moisture, you can use them to monitor the water available to plants by creating drought indices. This can be done by monitoring changes in vegetation productivity through measuring changes in vegetation indices and land surface temperature (Nemani and Running 1989).

To map soil moisture more accurately and precisely, it is necessary to create models using *in situ* and remotely sensed data (Huete 2004). This approach is costly if large areas are to be covered and it requires a good deal of expertise (Scipal and Wagner 2004).

5.3 Summary

This chapter gives you an overview of how to derive terrain and soil information from remotely sensed data. Elevation data sets that cover the globe are increasingly available at finer spatial resolutions and in many cases these data can be freely downloaded from the Internet. You can also create your own elevation data sets or derive products that describe features in the terrain using specialized software and the proper data. Soil and geologic maps are available for many areas of the world but a consistent global-scale map is not available largely due to the complexities associated with reliably classifying different types of soils or substrate. Satellite based remote sensing sensors do record global soil moisture data but these data are often too coarse for use at local or landscape scale.

6

Marine and coastal environments

New remote sensing challenges arise from the addition of the water column to the remote sensing signal. At the same time, new opportunities for use of remotely sensed data are possible in the marine environment. Marine environments can have organisms in such great abundance that they are readily monitored using remote sensing. From measuring ocean productivity, to harmful algal blooms (HABs), to fisheries management, remote sensing is a key component of many efforts to manage and conserve marine ecosystems.

For example, the small giant clam, *Tridacna maxima*, is endangered in some areas of the Pacific, and because of commercial harvest pressure is listed in Appendix II of the Convention on the International Trade of Endangered Species (CITES, meaning they are not yet threatened by extinction but could become so if their trade is not tightly regulated). Andréfouët *et al.* (2005a) used field observations and remotely sensed data to study the productivity of the clam fishery in tiny (22.2 km^2, including a 9.9 km^2 lagoon) Fangatau Atoll (Eastern Tuamotu, French Polynesia). The fishery was under pressure due to the large (4 ton per year) export of clams to Tahiti. Remotely sensed data included a mosaic of aerial photographs (1.5 m resolution), a digital photograph taken from the International Space Station (red, green, blue, 5.6 m resolution), and Landsat TM imagery (30 m resolution). The authors classified each image of key lagoon habitats, using maximum likelihood supervised classification, with each image classified independently. They estimated the population size for the entire lagoon by multiplying the mean clam density in each habitat (from field data) by the total area of each habitat (in the maps made from the remotely sensed data). Amazingly, an estimated 23.65 $\pm$ 5.33 million clams (mean $\pm$95 percent confidence interval) inhabited the 4.05 km^2 area of suitable habitat in the lagoon. The high spatial resolution data (1.5 m aerial and 5.6 m astronaut photography data) both gave equivalent estimates of the biomass with good estimates of accuracy, but the Landsat 30 m data overestimated the population. The stock that is currently commercially available is about 40 percent of the total in the lagoon, indicating that if commercial harvest were to increase, there could be the need for additional management of the fishery. In this case, appropriate spatial resolution of 1–6 m in the photography was most important for getting accurate biomass estimates. However, the authors believed that even more accurate results could be obtained from data sources with both high spatial resolution, and more spectral resolution than was in the photograph, such as IKONOS or an airborne hyperspectral sensor.

In this chapter, we cover the basics of marine remote sensing, from deepwaters to shallow. We also give a brief look at the cutting edge of sensors and techniques for marine remote sensing. Sometimes the techniques will look very much like those applied in terrestrial remote sensing. Other times, the techniques will be unique to marine environments. The expansive scale of marine ecosystems has made remote sensing an important tool for understanding ecological processes and for conservation and management applications.

Remotely sensed data make important contributions to the major areas of concern for marine conservation: the response of the ocean to increased sea surface temperatures (SSTs) and atmospheric CO_2, sustainable management of shallow and deepwater fisheries, defining marine-protected areas, and managing declining coral reef ecosystems.

6.1 Separating the surface, water column, and bottom

There are similarities and differences in the technical challenges associated with remote sensing of terrestrial and aquatic habitats. In both terrestrial and aquatic environments we must contend with atmospheric scattering and absorption attenuating the light from the sun. Conceptually, you can equate this to the haze you see looking downward from an airplane, even on a relatively clear day. As you look further and further toward the horizon, the haze gets thicker and there is more scattering, and the source of the light you see may be reflected from many different locations on the Earth.

Remote sensing of aquatic environments adds new ways for noise to obscure the information you are seeking. A water surface reflects a large portion of the radiation that comes in from the sun. Depending on the relative position of the sun and the remote sensor, this reflection can be a blinding mirrorlike glint (see illustration of specular reflection in Fig. 5.6), or almost invisible to the eye. The light that passes through the water surface boundary is further attenuated by absorption and scattering in the water column. Some of this light is reflected upward from within the water column, and in areas of relatively clear water and a shallow depth, some of that light strikes the bottom surface and is reflected back toward the sensor. But before that signal is received and recorded, it must once again pass through the water column, the surface boundary and the atmosphere (Fig. 6.1). Studies from shipboard remotely sensed measurements of ocean color show that multiple variables can have large effects on the final calculated water-leaving radiance. For instance, sun angle, cloud cover, wind speed, and viewing geometry each had impacts on the order of 8–12 percent, with cumulative uncertainty as high as 60 percent; wind speed is the major source of uncertainty (Toole *et al.* 2000).

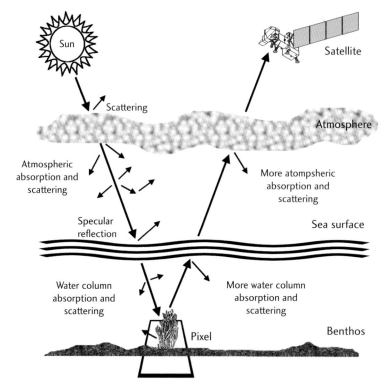

Fig. 6.1 A simplified schematic of the passage of light from the sun to the satellite sensor for remote sensing in marine and aquatic environments. The diagram shows both atmospheric absorption and scattering and the influence of the water column. Credit: Julie A. Robinson, NASA.

There are three major types of studies in shallow marine ecosystems, and for each one, separating the effects of the water column from the bottom signal is important. Some studies focus on the qualities of the water column itself, others are interested in modeling the attenuation of the water column in order to determine the depth of the bottom (bathymetry), and yet others are interested in measuring reflectance from the bottom surface that could be correlated to different habitats. For deeper marine ecosystems, different remote sensing techniques are used to focus on different types of properties of the water, from modeling ocean currents, to SST, to the biological content of the water column.

In studies of the properties of the water column itself, the bottom reflectance becomes the noise that needs to be eliminated before modeling absorption and scattering to infer the contents of the water. This contrasts with studies where benthic (bottom) composition is the focus, and the water column is the noise. Bathymetry studies using optical remote sensors rely on assumptions about the attenuation or reduction of light as it passes through the water column to estimate the depth. Some bathymetry measurements are also done with active sensors such as shipboard sonar and airborne lidar. In these cases water column effects can be more easily overcome; however, turbidity still has an impact on lidar and its effective maximum depth.

Whether studying the water column or the reflectance of habitats on the bottom, most marine remote sensing projects start with the atmospheric correction techniques discussed in Chapter 3, and then add corrections for surface glint or choppiness, and water column attenuation. We will describe how such corrections can be done, and what the considerations are for different types of aquatic conditions. Doing atmospheric and water column corrections adds additional steps to the analysis. The good news is that, depending on your information needs, you might be able to get by without doing all the corrections. Below we provide examples of all these possibilities.

6.1.1 Water types

Remote sensing of aquatic environments requires understanding the optical properties of the water, even when your measurement objective is habitat on the bottom. A lot of research over the years has gone into measuring the optical properties of the deep ocean waters in order to support the needs for global estimates of ocean productivity to support climate modeling. Unfortunately, deep, unproductive ocean waters are actually the simplest case for deriving water properties. The more complex the biology in the water column, the closer to land, or the shallower the water depth, the more difficult it is to predict the optical properties.

Two important processes lead to the attenuation in the amount of electromagnetic energy (light) as it passes through water. *Absorption* is the conversion of the light into heat or chemical energy (e.g., photosynthesis in phytoplankton). The main absorbers in the water column are phytoplankton, suspended particulate matter, dissolved organic compounds, and the water molecules themselves. Pure water strongly absorbs red and infrared light but has a much smaller effect on blue light (and this is why clear water is blue). *Scattering* happens primarily when the electromagnetic radiation "bounces" off of particles in the water and changes direction. The more sediment in the water, the greater the turbidity, and the more scattering occurs.

People often ask about how deep into the water a remote sensing instrument can "see." Most natural waters are not clear; they contain chlorophyll, sediments, and colored matter that affect three related parameters: photic zone depth (the ecologically relevant concept), Secchi depth (a field measurement), and spectral attenuation coefficient (a field or remote sensing measurement). Different wavelengths of light penetrate clear water to different depths. In aquatic remote sensing, *depth of penetration* is defined as being proportional to the inverse of the attenuation coefficient of the water, and there is a different depth of penetration for each wavelength. Depth of penetration corresponds to the

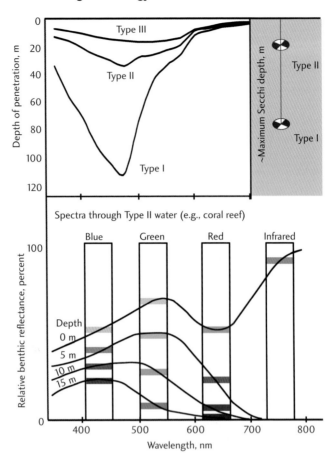

Fig. 6.2 Maximum Secchi depth and maximum depth of penetration by wavelength (proportional to Secchi depth) for different types of water (*top*), and the resulting attenuation of remote sensing reflectance from the bottom for Type II waters (*bottom*). The wavelength scale for the top and bottom graphs are the same. The black/white Secchi disk represents a field observation (all-white disks are often used in marine studies). In the benthic reflectance spectrum, the 0 m line shows no attenuation of the signal and each of the deeper lines show the differential attenuation of light at different wavelengths. The scaled cartoon in the upper right shows the deepest recorded Secchi depth of about 80 m in the Weddell Sea, Antarctica (Bledzki and Nagabhatla 2008). The top graph includes data of Jupp (1988), and the bottom graph includes the treatment of Green *et al.* (2000: 121) modified and combined to illustrate how depth of penetration and reflectance are related, used with permission.

point of disappearance of a Secchi disk that contrasts perfectly with the brightness of the water at that wavelength. Wavelengths shorter than 500 or even 580 nm (blues and greens) penetrate deep into water and can easily reflect off the bottom and back to the observer. Longer wavelengths (yellows and reds) do not penetrate very deeply; and infrared does not penetrate the water column at all (Fig. 6.2). As a rule of thumb for clear coastal waters such as over coral reefs (Type II), blue light penetrates to a maximum of about 25–30 m, green light penetrates to a maximum of about 15 m, red light to 5 m, near-infrared to 0.5 m, and infrared light is fully absorbed (Fig. 6.2; Jupp 1988).

As an example, Kratzer *et al.* (2003) used field data and SeaWiFS data to compare Secchi depth and spectral attenuation coefficient in the Baltic Sea. They focused specifically on photosynthetically active radiation (PAR), the wavelength range of photosynthetic response from 400–700 nm. In-water measurements showed that the spectral attenuation coefficient (usually represented as K_d) at 490 nm (blue-green, K_d [490]) was about 1.48 times higher than the spectral attenuation of PAR (K_d [PAR]). The depth of the euphotic zone was about 6.8 times the remote sensing optical depth ($K_d[490]^{-1}$). In this system, K_d [PAR] from SeaWiFS standard products could be used to estimate Secchi depth using the in-water empirical relationship K_d $[PAR] = 1.7$/Secchi depth.

Depending on what is in the water column, of course, each different wavelength will have additional absorption and scattering profiles. For example, Islam *et al.* (2004) investigated whether Landsat TM data (bands 1 and 2, blue-green and green, respectively) could be used to predict three different water quality parameters (total suspended sediment, Secchi depth, and chlorophyll concentration) in Moreton Bay, Australia. They collected water samples simultaneously with a Landsat overpass. Suspended sediments dominated some of the waters, and others were dominated by chlorophyll, with Secchi depths ranging from 1.2 to 6.2 m. Both suspended sediment and Secchi depth could be mapped from the TM imagery with an R^2 for the linear model of over 80 percent. However, the waters were so variable over time that the model worked reliably only for water samples taken concurrently to the imagery, illustrating some of the limitations of Landsat TM in this application. When there was a lot of sediment in the water, it was difficult to predict the chlorophyll concentration.

Marine scientists use two types of shorthand to discuss water properties, as an indication of how hard it might be to model their effects on the remote sensing signal. The formal classification of ocean waters often seen in the literature (Jerlov 1964) is Type I for extremely clear oceanic waters of low productivity, and Type II for clear coastal waters, such as those over many coral reefs, which typically have more attenuation. Type III waters are turbid, as with many estuarine waters. Some areas of upwelling may be so turbid they are not classified. To imagine these classifications in ecological terms, if the Secchi disk depth is less than 2 m, optical remote sensing will observe only the top meter or so of the water column, plus the surface (Arst *et al.* 2002).

Another shorthand description used for water types in marine geography encompasses some of the differences in water that are important for remote sensing as well as aquatic ecology (Fig. 6.3). *Blue water* is the deep open ocean, with optical properties nearly free of the influence of coastal processes and with low primary productivity. *Green water* is the zone of waters over continental shelves, around islands and archipelagos where coastal input influences ocean productivity, usually within 600 km of shore or less. Because of the nutrients available, green water is productive and contains phytoplankton, dissolved organic matter, and particulates. *Brown water* is even more heavily influenced by the shore, often within 60 km of shore or less. Brown water zones include shallow littoral zones and estuaries with higher turbidity and sediments. Most of the remote sensing algorithms for water column correction, ocean color, and ocean productivity were developed for blue water and extended to the clearer green waters. Studies of the ecologically interesting optical properties in nearshore brown waters are a major ongoing research focus and challenge in remote sensing.

Freshwater remote sensing offers similar challenges to marine environments. Like Type II and Type III waters, freshwater systems may have significant turbidity, and day-to-day changes in productivity, depending on precipitation, winds, and runoff characteristics. However, freshwater can be even more chal-

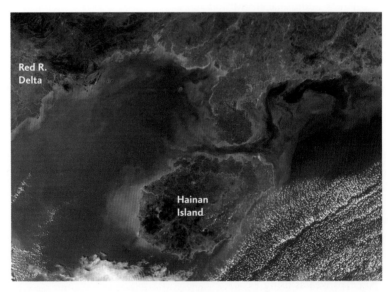

Fig. 6.3 The coastal waters of the Gulf of Tonkin show characteristic browns and greens from the presence of both sediment from the Red River delta of Vietnam and phytoplankton. "Blue waters" would be located to the southeast of Hainan Island, China, underneath the cloud cover (MODIS Aqua data, October 29, 2002; displayed in true color). Credit: Jacques Descloitres, MODIS Rapid Response Team, NASA/GSFC, and NASA Visible Earth.

lenging in some instances because there can be more variables simultaneously influencing the remote sensing observation (e.g., chemical composition, stratification, sediment, and algae). The only way to tease them apart is to use more advanced sensors, often with extensive ground observations, to separate the different factors and obtain the property you want to measure. For example, hyperspectral data will allow more precise determination of the presence of different types of chlorophyll which could then be related to algal populations.

In all types of aquatic environments, water chemistry—including colored dissolved organic matter (usually referred to as CDOM), and any unique chemistry of some freshwater bodies—can change rapidly and complicate interpreting even hyperspectral data. For both multispectral and hyperspectral data, excessive turbidity can completely obscure the remote sensing signal, limiting data to the top few centimeters of the water column. We discuss remote sensing of estuaries, freshwater wetlands, and lakes in Chapter 7.

6.1.2 Water column correction

If you are working in shallow aquatic ecosystems, you may need to model both benthic cover and water column, whether your primary interest is the water column, the benthic habitats, or both. When benthic cover is your interest, modeling the water column becomes important and water column correction is a recommended step for three types of applications:

1. Before a classification of benthic habitats. Studies have shown significant improvement in classification accuracy when a water column correction was added before classification, but the amount of improvement depends on the sensor used and the complexity of the habitats being distinguished. For example, simple distinction of coral, algae, sand, and seagrass will probably not benefit much from water column correction if the waters are shallow and uniform enough. The more variable the depth and the more heterogeneous the water properties, the more important water column corrections will be. For studies with multiple descriptive habitat classes using Landsat TM data, water column corrections have generally been shown to improve the classification accuracy significantly.

2. To establish a quantitative relationship between digital image data and marine features measured *in situ*. For example, after water column correction Mumby *et al.* (1997) could obtain good regressions for seagrass standing crop using the multispectral sensors SPOT XS and Landsat TM, as well as using airborne hyperspectral data.

3. To improve visual interpretation of images by removing variation in the perceived colors/contrast due to changing depth and water properties. A darker appearance of substrate due to increased depth can appear the same to the analyst as the darker appearance of benthic vegetation. Of course, the same confusion for visual interpretation can affect classification and modeling approaches listed above.

An ideal procedure for removing the influence of water depth on the remote sensing signal would require knowing the depth for each pixel in the image, and the attenuation characteristics of the water column (which depends on phytoplankton, suspended particulate matter, and dissolved organic compounds). If you knew that much about the water column, you probably would not need remote sensing to tell you what was on the bottom! The challenge of remote sensing is to derive environmental characteristics or properties directly from the imagery with limited or no input from other sources.

The Lyzenga (1978, 1981) method was one of the earliest approaches to compensate approximately for the effect of variable depth, but with an assumption of uniform water properties. Since the factors that influence the way that the bottom appears with depth in a specific image are similar regardless of what is on the bottom, using a ratio of two bands can cancel out the unknowns and produce a *depth-invariant bottom index* for the ratio between pairs of spectral bands. The index is the *y*-intercept of the plotted ratio of two bands, and the slope can be used as a derived *depth-invariant band* (Fig. 6.4) that can be used in subsequent analysis such as classifications. It is also possible to develop depth-invariant indices for certain bottom types based on ground truth data, and then use the position of the index to classify the bottom type for unknown pixels. The method works in Type I or Type II (clear) waters where light attenuation is primarily due to absorption by the water and not scattering of suspended particles. Lyzenga recommended that at least a crude atmospheric correction be applied before applying his water correction method. Because the index is pairwise for each band, it reduces the number of derived (depth invariant) bands by one degree of freedom, leading to one less new derived "band" for use in subsequent classifications. For example, the use of spectral information to do a depth correction using SPOT XS and Landsat MSS data was a disadvantage because after using some bands to do the water column correction only a single band (the *depth-invariant band*) remained for use in classifying different habitats (Green *et al.* 2000). Thus, these methods can only improve classification accuracy if you are starting with data that has at least three water-penetrating spectral bands. Landsat TM or ETM+ data just meets this minimum because the blue, green, and red bands all penetrate water to varying depths (Fig. 6.2). The general process of the Lyzenga method is illustrated graphically in Fig. 6.4.

From a remote sensing perspective, water column correction "cleans up" the data and, when appropriate, means the information used in the subsequent classification will produce more accurate results. Depth-invariant processing on each image can be very helpful if multiple scenes acquired at different times are used together, as it can help compensate for differences in tides or water clarity, both within a single image and among multiple images. From a practical perspective, the trade-off between additional labor and accuracy can differ depending on the objectives of the analysis. For example, depth correction was of little benefit to mapping geomorphological classes using band ratio techniques for the Millennium Coral Reef Maps project (Andréfouët *et al.* 2006). In

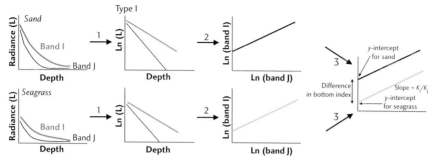

Fig. 6.4 Processes of water column correction, showing the steps involved in creating depth-invariant indices of bottom type for sand and seagrass. *Step 1*. Exponential attenuation of radiance with depth is made linear for bands I and J by taking the natural logarithm. (Band I has a shorter wavelength, and therefore attenuates less rapidly, than band J). *Step 2*. Plot of (transformed) band I against (transformed) band J for a unique substratum at various depths. Gradient of line represents the ratio of attenuation coefficients, K_I/K_J. The ratio is the same irrespective of bottom type. *Step 3*. Plotting multiple bottom types. Each bottom type has a unique y-intercept (regardless of its depth). The y-intercept therefore becomes a depth-invariant index of bottom type. Figure from Green *et al.* (2000: 123), used with permission.

addition, if water is too turbid or too colored then water corrections carried out independently of modeling other parameters will not work. Unfortunately, "too turbid" has not been well defined. Mumby *et al.* (1998) found at one site that if the horizontal Secchi distance at a depth of 0.5 m is on the order of 30–50 m, the Lyzenga method was beneficial before habitat classifications.

Although analysts still use the Lyzenga method, there have been many advances in water column correction over the intervening 30 years. Many of these are still conceptually linked to the ratio techniques of Lyzenga. Stumpf *et al.* (2003c) provide a modified method that is more applicable to data with limited spectral bands, such as SPOT and IKONOS. Modifications of the Lyzenga method have been developed for water of greater turbidity (Tassan 1996). Mishra *et al.* (2006) used principal components analysis (see general description in Section 4.3.2) to consolidate depth information across multiple bands, with homogeneous reference areas of seagrass used to calibrate a bathymetric map. Gagnon *et al.* (2008) compare uses of coarse bathymetry from sonar with other approaches using hyperspectral data alone for shallow benthic classifications of kelp and found better classification accuracies with the bathymetry estimated from the hyperspectral data than using the sonar-based bathymetry.

For hyperspectral data, there are many other possibilities for water column modeling. For example, Albert and Mobley (2003) provide an analytical model that works for deep and shallow Type II waters. The authors used a suite of parameters to describe the inherent optical properties of the water: absorption, backscatter, solar zenith angle, the viewing angle, and surface wind speed. For shallow waters, additional parameters added were bottom albedo, and bottom depth. Total accuracy of the analytical model in predicting remote sensing reflectance was >4 percent. Radiative transfer modeling approaches with hyperspectral data are available in customized modular software packages. For example, a package called Modular Inversion and Processing System developed by the German Aerospace Center, the Technical University of Munich and EOMAP GmbH & Co., has been used with airborne HyMap hyperspectral data (Heege *et al* 2003; Heege and Fischer 2004). With hyperspectral data as inputs, the model outputs estimates of aerosols; pixel-by-pixel sun glitter correction; atmosphere and water surface corrections; retrieval of water constituents in optically deepwaters; water column correction; and the classification of substrates such as coral reef, seagrass vegetation, and bottom sediments. This model is being used by the Australian Institute of Marine Science to map large areas of Australian coral reefs, such a Ningaloo Reef, Western Australia (Heege 2008). Related radiative transfer models and packages exist for other hyperspectral sensors and are used in other regions. When a satellite hyperspectral instrument is eventually developed for widespread use, there will likely be a consolidation and generalization in this area and validated modeling packages will become available as has happened for ocean color in deepwaters (described in more detail later in the chapter).

Although technically not a water column correction, another class of models needs mentioning here. *Coupled models* perform simultaneous atmospheric correction and ocean property retrieval. These were a major innovation in Type I waters (e.g., Maritorena *et al.* [2002]), becoming part of the ocean color and chlorophyll algorithms we will discuss later in this chapter. Both empirical models and quasi-analytical models (Lee *et al.* 2002) have been developed. Coupled models can also be important in Type II waters where chlorophyll in the water influences the reflectance of near-infrared radiation and can compromise the use of atmospheric correction algorithms (Siegel *et al.* 2000). However, in coastal waters, the algorithms have to be tuned to local conditions in order to get successful measurements of water properties, and this is an extremely active area of ongoing research in many of the major bays of the world.

6.1.3 Bathymetry

The approaches to depth correction discussed in the previous section assume the area of focus is on the bottom. For some conservation applications, knowing the water depth (bathymetry) or water properties can also be an important goal. This is particularly true in remote areas that may not have been well charted. Depending on the remoteness and logistical considerations, remote sensing can offer a cost-effective, though usually less accurate, alternative to traditional methods of field survey (Sandwell *et al.* 2002).

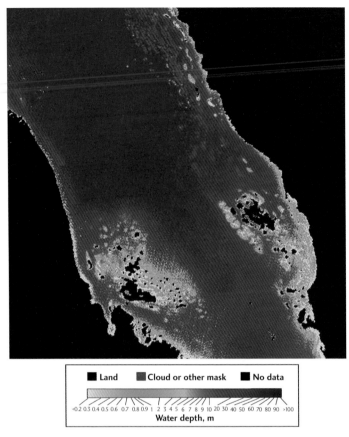

Land   **Cloud or other mask**   **No data**

<0.2 0.3 0.4 0.5 0.6 0.7 0.8 0.9 1 2 3 4 5 6 7 8 9 10 20 30 40 50 60 70 80 90 >100

Water depth, m

Fig. 6.5 Cloud-free shallow bathymetry map of the Southern Red Sea (Dahlak Archipelago, Eritrea, and Farasan Islands, Saudi Arabia), using all SeaWiFS data from launch through November 6, 2002 and the algorithm of Stumpf *et al.* (2003b,c). The algorithm was used to produce a global composite 1 km bathymetry map by computing median depths for each pixel for all SeaWiFS overflights to eliminate transient effects of clouds, sediment, and chlorophyll. Maps for any location in the world can be viewed online (Feldman and Kuring 2003). Credit: SeaWiFS Project, NASA/GSFC and GeoEye.

Although not designed for bathymetric mapping, the ready availability of multispectral data and the differential attenuation of different spectral bands by the water column discussed above make it possible to estimate bathymetry with multispectral data in clear waters. Green *et al.* (2000) provide worked examples of three representative approaches to estimating bathymetry using multispectral data as relevant to management applications. A newer modification of the Lyzenga method (Stumpf 2003c) also gives good results. Although not as accurate as measurements made in the field, such approaches can be applied to large geographical areas using multispectral data from SeaWiFS and MODIS to IKONOS (Stumpf *et al.* 2003c). For example, Stumpf *et al.* (2003b) created a 1 km-scale global shallow water bathymetry using the Stumpf (2003c) modification of the Lyzenga method and SeaWiFS data. Because SeaWiFS has high positional accuracy, each pixel over a specific location could be compared over time, and algorithms were used cumulatively on the full five-year set of SeaWiFS data to create the global bathymetry. Pixel values representing clouds could be excluded, until finally a cumulative cloud-free bathymetry map was constructed (Fig. 6.5).

Newer developments in analysis of hyperspectral imagery are also useful for mapping bathymetry. These are conceptually linked to the general approaches for water column modeling with hyperspectral data discussed above. For accurate bathymetry mapping, or work in turbid waters, the methods using passive optical remotely sensed data are limited. Although not discussed here in detail, if cost and logistics are no object, airborne lidar is the technique of choice for mapping coastal bathymetry (see more detailed discussions of lidar in Chapter 7). Multibeam bathymetry can also be developed from airborne systems; the classic sonar methods of bathymetry mapping from ships, remote sensing in their own right, can be combined with other optical data (Gagnon *et al.* 2008).

6.1.4 Top-down versus bottom-up approaches

The remote sensing techniques for making atmospheric and water column corrections are both types of what a remote sensing specialist calls radiative transfer modeling—mathematical models of the components affecting spectral radiance that reach the remote sensor. Such approaches in remote sensing are often classified as "bottom-up" and contrasted with the "top down" approaches of statistical classification methods such as maximum likelihood classification. If you have better understanding of the transmittance effects of specific elements in the water column, the radiative modeling can become very sophisticated.

Once a bottom-up model has been developed with detailed understanding, it does not always require detailed data to implement. For example, a new class of semi-analytical hyperspectral inversion models has been developed using simulations of the scattering of light. A nonlinear optimization routine can be used with the model to retrieve estimates of bathymetry and water properties from measured surface remote sensing reflectance data (Lee *et al.* 1998, 1999). You can also use the models to convert remote sensing reflectance back to known absorption spectra of phytoplankton pigments, allowing estimation of concentrations of chlorophyll-*a* (chl-*a*) and other accessory pigments (Lee and Carder 2004).

Top-down approaches do not try to understand all the individual components that make up the remote sensing signal. Instead, they look for general trends and patterns within the image that can be applied to make inferences about features or habitats of interest. They are generally easier to apply, and require less field

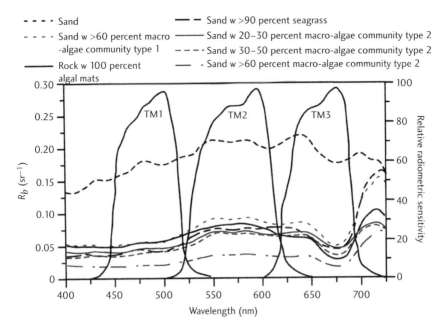

Fig. 6.6 Substrate reflectance spectra collected above the water for different reef-top assemblages in the Egyptian Red Sea. The radiometric sensitivity of Landsat TM for the first three bands (TM1, TM2, and TM3) is also shown. Figure from Purkis and Pasterkamp (2004), reproduced with kind permission from Springer Science+Business Media.

validation as well as less modeling in the remote sensing lab. However, the products are also usually less specific to the species or habitats of interest. The Lyzenga method of water column correction is a top-down method. More complex top-down methods include machine learning approaches and models that use fuzzy logic. A majority of classifications in this book (i.e., any that mention maximum likelihood classification methods) are top-down.

Bottom-up approaches build *spectral libraries* by making spectral measurements of all the components of the system in the field and then using them to build a model in an intensively studied environment. Other data may also be included in the models such as bathymetry and water properties. The model can then be applied in other similar areas to extract features or habitats of interest. These approaches are usually labor-intensive in the field and in the remote sensing lab, but the final model may be relatively easy to apply and the payoff can be very specific information about species or habitats.

Benthic habitat mapping can use either top-down or bottom-up approaches. As an example of a bottom-up approach, Purkis and Pasterkamp (2004) made measurements of reef-top reflectance spectra (Fig. 6.6) from above the water in the Egyptian Red Sea. They measured reflectance spectra and used them to train a supervised classification of Landsat TM imagery. To get the Landsat imagery to a state where it could be compared to the field-measured reflectance, Purkis and Pasterkamp (2004) first had to do atmospheric and radiometric correction, correction to compensate for refraction at the water–air boundary, water column correction, and depth correction. Using these techniques, they were able to distinguish several different communities of macroalgae, which are associated with the ecological status of reefs (community 1, 87 percent producer's and 90 percent user's accuracy; community 2, 67 percent producer's and 75 percent user's accuracy). We will discuss coral reef and seagrass remote sensing in more detail later in the chapter.

Because of the additional complication of the water column, species-specific questions in marine remote sensing are more likely to require a bottom-up approach—more so than would be required to answer similar questions in a terrestrial environment. As a rule of thumb for developing a remote sensing application, if you can generate a false color display of three bands that lets you visually distinguish the habitat or pattern of interest (with due caution to the possibly misleading effects of variable water properties and water depth), a top-down approach will probably serve, requiring less effort to implement. If not, you will need more complex modeling to map the area of interest, either through more advanced remote sensing techniques such as subpixel analysis, texture analysis, or combinations of techniques, or you may need to take a bottom-up approach.

6.2 Water properties

The measurement of water properties is most developed for remote sensing of the open ocean. We will also discuss related applications in estuaries and lakes in the next chapter (Chapter 7). Ocean remote sensing is a large discipline in its own right, and here we focus on some of the basic principles relevant to conservation biology. Deep ocean ("blue water") provides the most straightforward aquatic environment for remote sensing of water properties. Ocean color remote sensing began with NASA's Coastal Zone Color Scanner (CZCS) launched in 1978. This has been followed by the SeaWiFS and MODIS sensors which provide continuous standard ocean color products (Fig. 6.7). The main objective of much of the research has been to use observations of ocean color to estimate the primary productivity of the oceans for use in global climate models (ocean productivity is an important process impacting global carbon cycles) and in understanding how the oceans will respond to increased atmospheric CO_2 (Behrenfeld and Falkowski 1997; Carr *et al.* 2006; McClain *et al.* 2006). Ocean color data and techniques can also be applied to regional and local understanding of aquatic ecology. Smaller-scale studies can leverage the extensive work that has gone into developing standardized ocean color products.

All of the standard ocean color products depend on extracting remote sensing reflectance, R_{rs} from the signal reaching the satellite. Reflectance is discussed in

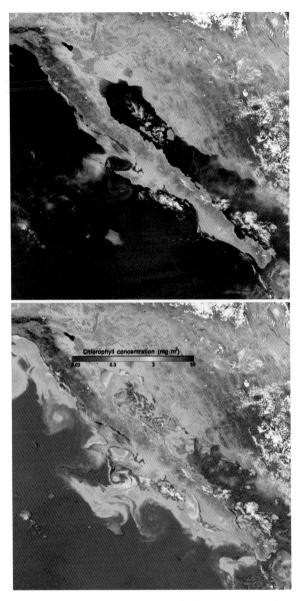

Fig. 6.7 SeaWiFS image of the waters around the Baja Peninsula on August 10, 2003. The top view shows the ocean in a true color display; the bottom image shows the standard chlorophyll product. Credit: SeaWiFS Project, NASA/GSFC, and GeoEye.

Chapter 3. *Remote sensing reflectance* is the radiance leaving the water L_u divided by the irradiance E_d that entered the water, or in more technical terms

$$R_{rs} = \frac{\text{water-leaving upwelling radiance}}{\text{incident downwelling irradiance}} = \frac{L_u}{E_d}. \tag{6.1}$$

Only about 10 percent of the total light detected by a satellite aimed at the ocean is water-leaving radiance, while the other 90 percent of the light comes from atmospheric effects such as scattering. To calculate normalized water-leaving radiance, you take the radiance signal received by the satellite and correct for atmospheric light-scattering and solar zenith angle. Normalized water-leaving radiance is the radiance that would be measured exiting the flat surface of the ocean with the Sun at zenith (directly overhead) and the atmosphere absent. Remote sensing reflectance calculated for each band is the fundamental measure for use in optical remote sensing of ocean color. In parallel to its calculation from satellite data, remote sensing reflectance can also be measured in the field by shipboard and in-water methods for use in calibration, model development, and validation (Toole *et al.* 2000).

A special software package for ocean color analysis (SeaDAS) is freely distributed for using data from MODIS and SeaWiFS, and standardized processed products are available for daily, eight-day, monthly, seasonal, and annual time periods. Access to all NASA ocean color data and systems is online (NASA Ocean Color 2009).

6.2.1 Chlorophyll

Phytoplankton is the major source of color in deep ocean water. Chlorophyll-*a* is the primary photosynthetic pigment in phytoplankton, and it absorbs relatively more blue and red light than green. Thus, the greener the color of ocean water (the greener the spectrum of backscattered sunlight) the higher the concentration of phytoplankton.

There are standard algorithms developed and validated for using multispectral data to estimate chl-*a* concentrations (and sometimes chl-*a* + phaeopigment concentration). Early algorithms were based on regressions of remote sensing of ocean radiance versus chlorophyll measured from ships.

More advanced algorithms, called semi-analytic (or semi-empirical or quasi-analytic) ocean color algorithms, combine analytical optical models of the effect of backscatter-to-absorption ratio on remote sensing reflectance with empirically derived terms for other components of the water, such as absorption coefficients for chlorophyll-*a* and detritus, and the backscattering (gelbstoff) coefficient. A large variety of these algorithms were evaluated with global empirical data under the SeaBAM project (O'Reilly *et al.* 1998). The standard chlorophyll-*a* product selected for the SeaWiFS sensor was the ocean chlorophyll 4 algorithm (OC4) which uses band ratios of the remote sensing reflectance (R_{rs}) of four bands (443, 490, 510, 555 nm). The coefficients of the equation are modified as the data set of ground observations expands, and the current version is OC4v4 (accuracy evaluated by O'Reilly *et al.* 1998):

$$C_a = 10^{(0.366 - 3.067\ R + 1.930\ R^2 + 0.649\ R^3 - 1.532\ R^4)},$$

where

$$R = \log_{10}\left\{\max\left[\frac{R_{rs}(433)}{R_{rs}(555)}, \frac{R_{rs}(490)}{R_{rs}(555)}, \frac{R_{rs}(510)}{R_{rs}(555)}\right]\right\}. \tag{6.2}$$

MODIS has slightly different bands than does SeaWiFS, so standard products are built from the ocean chlorophyll 3 algorithm (OC3) which uses band ratios of the remote sensing reflectance (R_{rs}) of three bands (443, 488, 551 nm).

$$C_a = 10^{(0.283 - 2.753\ R + 1.457\ R^2 + 0.659\ R^3 - 1.403\ R^4)},$$

where

$$R = \log_{10}\left\{\max\left[\frac{R_{rs}(443)}{R_{rs}(551)}, \frac{R_{rs}(488)}{R_{rs}(551)}\right]\right\}. \tag{6.3}$$

Cross-validation continues (e.g., Werdell *et al.* [2003]), and science teams released new merged chlorophyll products with data from both satellites in 2006.

6.2.2 Primary productivity

Chlorophyll-*a* products are combined with remotely sensed measures of SST and PAR to estimate ocean primary productivity. Algorithms have been developed to estimate global oceanic primary production from CZCS, SeaWiFS, and MODIS. The standard product selected for MODIS is based on the Vertically Generalized Production Model (VGPM) (Behrenfeld and Falkowski 1997), which calculates net primary production as a function of chlorophyll, available light, and the photosynthetic efficiency. Model inputs of chlorophyll and temperature data come from MODIS products, PAR from SeaWiFS, and estimates of euphotic zone depth from other global ocean models. An organized community of scientists evaluates and compares the many different versions of primary productivity models on a regular basis (e.g., Carr *et al.* [2006]).

Information on primary productivity is important for defining high-quality habitat for pelagic marine fisheries and satellite estimates of chlorophyll have been proposed as an input for defining and managing marine-protected areas (Hyrenbach *et al.* 2001). Short-term marine protected areas (either temporary or rotating, Wahle and Uravitch 2006) that track areas of productivity where key fish species congregate to feed could even be developed to better manage some fisheries.

Optical sensors such as SeaWiFS can also help to monitor oil spills. For instance, SeaWiFS documented the regional ocean productivity effects of an oil slick emanating from the tanker Jessica, which ran aground off the Galapagos

Islands in Ecuador in early 2001 while carrying 680,000 gallons of diesel fuel (Banks 2003). Scientists continued to monitor the movement of the spill and its effects on the Galápagos Marine Reserve, particularly the islands of Santa Fe, Santa Cruz, Isabela, and Floreana, through near daily data on the distribution chlorophyll-*a*, which affects ocean color, from SeaWiFS. The duration of an initial localized decrease in chlorophyll concentrations after the spill in comparison with concentrations from 1998 to 2000 was apparently short (about a month). The SeaWiFS data showed a subsequent increase in primary productivity (derived from the ocean color data through the relationship of these data to phytoplankton abundance and, hence, marine productivity), with variance consonant with the typically high variation for the region, particularly in response to El Niño/Southern Oscillation patterns. We discuss further applications of productivity in coastal and estuarine habitats in Chapter 7.

6.2.3 Harmful algal blooms

Given the success of marine remote sensing tools in measuring phytoplankton concentrations and ocean productivity, an obvious extension is to use remote sensing to target key species of phytoplankton, such as those that cause HABs. Figure 6.8 shows an example of annual observations of HABs in the Baltic Sea. HABs are sudden local or regional increases in the populations of species of plankton that produce neurotoxins. The toxins can be transferred through the food web and impact fish, shellfish, birds, marine mammals, and human use of marine resources. For example, red tides have had significant impacts on popu-

SeaWiFS, July 24, 2003   MODIS, July 10, 2005   MODIS, July 25, 2008

Fig. 6.8 A toxic bloom in the Baltic Sea of the cyanobacterium, *Nodularia spumigena*, discussed in Agence France-Presse and Reuters news reports, July 24, 2003. Such blooms have also been seen in subsequent years, and have been linked to increased nutrient runoff. They cause oxygen depletion that could impact fish survival. Satellite images, total chlorophyll data products, and reflectance at specific bands have been used in monitoring for harmful algal blooms (HABs). Credits: SeaWiFS Project, NASA/GSFC. and GeoEye; MODIS Ocean Color Project, NASA/GSFC.

lations of endangered manatees: a 1982 red tide killed about 10 percent (37) of the manatees in southwestern Florida (USA), and in 1996 killed about 35 percent (over 150) manatees in the same area. Such events are likely to have a significant impact on population viability (Marmontel *et al.* 1997). HABs in major coastal upwelling systems are a concern because of the global economic and conservation importance of these waters, and because of the impacts to fisheries and human health (Kudela *et al.* 2005).

In addition to identifying changes in ocean color correlated with HABs, remote sensing is also important in measuring the underlying physical and ecological factors that lead to blooms. These factors include wind regimes that influence upwelling–downwelling cycles, thermal stratification conditions, changes in nutrients and turbidity from onshore sources, and the normal seasonal succession of phytoplankton (Kudela *et al.* 2005). By combining oceanographic data and in-water sampling with remote sensing, advances have been made in understanding HAB occurrence and dynamics. For example, Tang *et al.* (2005) used remote sensing to evaluate a fall 1998 HAB of dinoflagellates (*Ceratium furca*) in the Bohai Sea, China. They used SeaWiFS chl-*a* data for the offshore waters (given the difficulties in interpreting the OC4 algorithm in coastal waters), SSTs from AVHRR, and wind speed and direction data from QuikSCAT, combined with hydrographic data collected by the State Oceanic Administration of China. The SeaWiFS data allowed mapping of the spatial distribution during the development and movement of the bloom. In addition, they were able to document that the bloom developed in the northern Bohai Sea along the frontal waters between the discharge of the Luanhe River and the coastal current, and not near the inputs of the Yellow River at its mouth on the southern Bohai Sea.

Perhaps the most sophisticated use of remote sensing of HABs has been developed for dinoflagellate (*Karenia brevis*) blooms in the Gulf of Mexico. Nearly annual occurrence of these red tides has been actively monitored by the state of Florida (USA) and the NOAA since 1999 (Stumpf *et al.* 2003a). Routine remote sensing supports models that monitor the movement of a previously identified HAB and detect new blooms and classify them as HAB or non-HAB. Interpretive and numerical modeling builds on the monitoring data to predict the movement of an identified HAB, and predict conditions favorable for formation of a new HAB. Region-specific algorithms have been developed that compensate for sediment scattering and track changes in a corrected estimate of chl-*a* to identify possible *K. brevis* in Florida gulf coast waters. Chlorophyll anomalies identified using the algorithm accurately identified *K. brevis* blooms over 83 percent of the time (Tomlinson *et al.* 2004). Under the monitoring and early warning system, blooms were identified in January 2000 and October 2001 in areas that had not been sampled by the state of Florida (Stumpf *et al.* 2003a). In order to refine approaches and increase accuracy, future improvements in the algorithms will combine the chlorophyll methods with backscattering, chl-*a* ratio, MODIS fluorescence data, winds, currents, and SST data (Hu *et al.* 2008).

6.2.4 Sea surface temperature (SST)

Some of the most valuable remote sensing observations of the Earth each day are the temperatures at the sea surface. Decades of satellite observations have helped to build our current understanding of El Niño/La Niña cycles, and the role of heat in the oceans as a primary driver of global climate. At their most basic level, these measurements have documented the rise in SSTs linked to global climate change.

The core scientific instruments for measuring SST have been AVHRRs which have flown on a variety of NOAA polar orbiting satellites since 1978. These instruments measure the thermal radiation (heat) given off by the surface of the ocean and then use it to calculate the temperature. Since 1999, MODIS radiometers have collected ocean temperature data with a larger number of narrower thermal infrared bands allowing more precise measurements. This has led to a large effort to develop improved atmospheric correction algorithms and standard SST products (Fig. 6.9).

SST products are a key component of global climate models, and are at correspondingly coarse spatial resolutions. AVHRR has a ground-sampled distance of ~1.1 km pixels, and MODIS sensors have 1 km pixels in the thermal

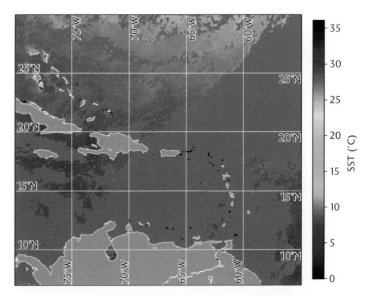

Fig. 6.9 Caribbean Sea Surface Temperature operational product provided 8 times per day from GOES Images (October 15, 2008). Products including True Color (MODIS), Chlorophyll-*a* (MODIS and SeaWiFS), Sea Surface Temperature (MODIS, POES, GOES, and TRMM), and Sea Surface Winds (QuikSCAT and DMSP) can be viewed and downloaded online (NOAA CoastWatch 2009). Credit: Ocean Watch, NOAA/NESDIS.

bands (with 250 and 500 m resolution in shorter wavelength bands). However, the spatial resolution for standard processed SST products from these instruments as distributed by NASA and NOAA are 9.88 km and 4 km for AVHRR (NOAA/NASA AVHRR Oceans Pathfinder Program V4 and V5, respectively), and 4.88 km for MODIS. The British/Australian Advanced Along Track Scanning Radiometer (AATSR) onboard the European Space Agency's ENVISAT has two operational SST products, a 1 km gridded SST product (GSST, Gridded Sea Surface Temperature Product) and a spatially averaged SST product at resolutions of 17 km, 50 km, 10′, and 30′ (ASST, averaged Sea Surface Temperature Product). Saunders *et al.* (2006) summarize the history of SST remote sensing.

A different technique is used by Advanced Microwave Scanning Radiometer for EOS (AMSR-E) on NASA's Aqua satellite. This instrument is a passive microwave radiometer. Since microwaves pass through cloud cover, they can measure ocean temperatures that would otherwise be obscured by clouds. However, the spatial resolution of microwave SST is about 50 km (1/4 degree).

SST can be important inputs into ecological models of species occurrence. For example, Azzellino *et al.* (2008) developed logistic regression models to predict the presence of three species of cetaceans (striped dolphin, *Stenella coeruleoalba*; fin whale, *Balaenoptera physalus*; and sperm whale, *Physeter macrocephalus*) based on SST measurements from 1996 to 2000 in the western Ligurian Sea. Santos (2000) reviewed the use of remotely sensed data for fisheries research as well as for fishing. Models with satellite data inputs for key species are used for predicting Chilean anchovy (*Engraulins ringens*) distribution, and are important for managing the fishery through El Niño oscillations (e.g., Nieto *et al.* [2001]; Yáñez [2004]). Of interest for endangered species conservation, AVHRR-derived SST data has been applied to understanding sea turtle migration routes with mixed results. Hays *et al.* (2001) attached satellite transmitters to five green turtles (*Chelonia mydas*), and found that their migration did not follow isotherms of SST. Coles and Musick (2000) and Harrison (2003) both used AVHRR SST data to correlate a data set of aerial surveys of sea turtles, with better success.

6.2.5 Predicting coral bleaching

One important application of SSTs in conservation is their use in predicting coral bleaching. Coral bleaching occurs when coral animals and their resident symbiotic algae (zooxanthellae) are stressed. The algae are expelled from the corals, often causing a loss of pigmentation. Stress may arise from a variety of factors such as water temperatures, UV exposure, water chemistry, siltation, and pathogens. A major correlate of many mass coral bleachings has been SST, which has led to concerns and debate about the impacts of global climate change on corals (Hoegh-Guldberg 1999; Hughes *et al.* 2003).

NOAA's Coral Reef Watch (Skirving *et al.* 2006) looks at daily SSTs and trends and has developed empirical approaches to predicting coral reef bleaching based on the temperature data. Data products and visualization tools are all distributed free online (Office of Satellite Data Processing and Distribution 2008).

Three different global nighttime SST products are produced operationally twice per week at 0.5×0.5 degree spatial resolution, and form the basis of an early warning system (Liu *et al.* 2003). *Sea Surface Temperature Anomaly* maps (Fig. 6.10) show the difference between estimated current temperatures and historic temperatures (called climatology). *Coral Bleaching Hotspot* maps show areas where the estimated SSTs exceed the maximum monthly climatology by $1°C$ or more. Coral bleaching events have been noted when the hot spot maps identify differences greater than $1°C$. *Degree Heating Weeks* (DHWs) indices (Fig. 6.10) describe the accumulation of thermal stress over a rolling 12-week period. One DHW equals one week at $1°C$ greater than the expected summer maximum. Two DHW equals either two weeks at $1°C$ greater than the expected summer maximum or one week at $2°C$ greater than the expected summer maximum, etc. There is a correlation with bleached corals when DHW >4, and a correlation with widespread bleaching and some mortality at DHW >8 (Wellington *et al.* 2001). These data are available globally, and are also compiled and monitored for 24 key reef sites linked to an automated coral bleaching alert system. The products have been used successfully to monitor catastrophic bleaching events such as the 2002 event at Australia's Great Barrier Reef (Liu *et al.* 2003).

Advance warnings of likely coral bleaching events allow managers to step up monitoring efforts at remote locations. In some cases, reef resource managers can even take actions to reduce other stresses on reefs during times of heat stress. For example, in the Florida Keys National Marine Sanctuary, activities of dive shops and tour boats are restricted during periods of heat stress to reduce the amount of sediment stirred up on the reef. Small differences in bottom topography and currents can mean that different corals experience different changes in temperature. A better understanding of the local patterns of heat stress can also help identify areas where corals are more adapted to swings in temperature or extended heat stress.

6.2.6 Salinity

Salinity is a key factor in the cycling of ocean systems. Weathering of minerals, evaporation, and sea ice formation increase the salinity of the ocean. Input of fresh water from rivers, precipitation, and sea ice melting decrease salinity. The ability to differentiate small changes in salinity has the potential to greatly improve our understanding of the global impacts of melting of polar ice, changing inputs from rivers, and changes in precipitation on the ocean system. To an Earth system scientist, this is important because of the connections between salinity, SST, and ocean circulation. Regional changes in precipitation can affect ocean circulation through salinity as well as heating to drive major ocean cycles such as El Niño events and are a fundamental part of the global climate.

In 2010, the Aquarius mission of NASA and the space agency of Argentina (Comisión Nacional de Actividades Espaciales, CONAE) plans to provide

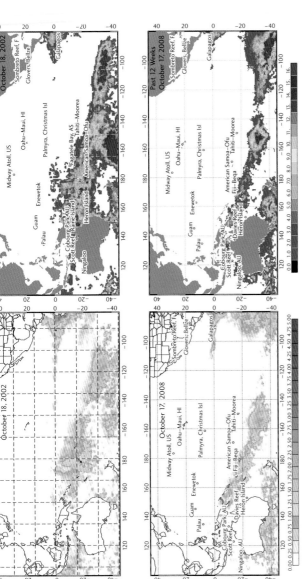

Fig. 6.10 NOAA Coral Reef Watch operational products around the time of a bleaching event in 2002 (Liu *et al.* 2003), and for the same time period in 2008. *Coral Reef Hotspots* compare the current SST with historical maximum monthly values ("climatology"), showing regions where SST is at least 1° greater than the maximum expected summertime temperature. The yellow to red colors indicate the potential for stress that could result in coral bleaching. *Degree Heating Weeks* (DHWs) indicate the accumulation of thermal stress that coral reefs have experienced over a previous period. One DHW is equivalent to one week of SST 1°C greater than the historical summertime maximum. Two DHWs is equivalent to either two weeks at 1° above the expected summertime maximum or one week of 2° above the expected summertime maximum. Orange and purple colors (DHWs > 10) indicate high and persistent SSTs that may lead to severe bleaching and possibly mortality, and are used to activate a global alert system. In the 2002 Great Barrier Reef Bleaching event, DHWs indicated more significant thermal stress than was shown by the hot spots alone. All products are available twice weekly online (NOAA Office of Satellite Data Processing and Distribution 2008). Credit: Office of Satellite Data Processing and Distribution, NOAA/NESDIS.

first-ever maps of seasonal and year-to-year variation in global sea surface salinity. Previously these estimations were only available from ship-based observations, or more local remote sensing analyses. The mission will include a radiometer to measure salinity (at 1.413 GHz, or L-band), and a scatterometer (microwave sensor to measure scattering from the sea surface) to measure and account for effects of sea surface roughness on the remote sensing signal reaching the radiometer. From the perspective of ecology and conservation biology, approaches developed for global salinity measurements may have applications at more regional scales to events such as freshwater incursions in marine habitats from inland floods or tropical storm rainfall.

6.2.7 Ocean circulation

Remote sensing is used to measure ocean circulation in two major ways: by following patterns in ocean color that indicate circulation movements or eddies, and using data from satellite radar altimeters that measure sea surface highs and lows. Although modeling of ocean circulation is probably best considered a specialty of physical oceanography, transport modeling methods with altimetry data can be an valuable method for modeling movements of planktonic larvae. Such models have important applications for the conservation of marine populations, and have been applied to a wide variety of species.

As an example, in seven years of monitoring after a decline in a spiny lobster (*Panulirus marginatus*) fishery in the Northwest Hawaiian islands, the population declined less and recovered more quickly at Necker Island (from standardized capture rates of 1 lobster per trap declining to 0.4 lobster per trap and then increasing to 0.7 lobster per trap). In contrast, the population at Maro Reef (670 km northwest) collapsed precipitously (from 1.8 lobsters per trap to 0.1 lobster per trap) and did not recover even after six years without fishing. The lobster larvae have an estimated 12-month pelagic stage, so understanding the influence of larval transport on recruitment was critical to understanding the fishery collapse. Polovina *et al.* (1999) used altimetry data from TOPEX/Poseidon to estimate current patterns. The current patterns drove a simulation model of the transport of the larvae from different banks and incorporated both spatial and seasonal dynamics. The model indicated that Necker would receive larval transport from other banks to the northwest and southeast as well as significant local recruitment. In contrast, the model showed that Maro had a much lower retention rate and actually exported larvae to Necker, while receiving little larval transport in return from Necker. Similar studies have since been done for a variety of pelagic larvae and locations (e.g., broader Hawaiian islands, Kobayashi and Polovina [2006]; New Zealand, Chiswell *et al.* [2003]; tropical Atlantic, Góes *et al.* [2007]). Using related techniques, Phinney *et al.* (2001) used archived satellite data of surface current patterns to assess whether spread of sea urchin *Diadema antillarum* mass mortality in the Caribbean was consistent with a waterborne pathogen.

6.3 Shallow benthic environments

In shallow waters observations of water properties and bottom properties are linked, but we now shift our focus to the bottom properties. Much of the exciting ecological work in this area relates to coral reefs and the use of remote sensing to map otherwise remote and inaccessible areas, and areas that are too large to be completely surveyed in the field (e.g., Florida Keys, Great Barrier Reef). Because of the significant declines in coral reefs worldwide over the last 3 decades and concern about responses of coral reefs to ongoing climate change and human impacts (i.e., Gardner *et al.* [2003]; Hoegh-Guldberg [1999]; Hoegh-Guldberg *et al.* [2007]), the bulk of active remote sensing research has been in the area of detecting and mapping habitats of interest in tropical zones where corals grow. The spatial scale of the distribution of coral reefs worldwide adds real challenges to conservation. Current networks of marine-protected areas are considered inadequate to protect coral reef diversity (Mora *et al.* 2006), and knowing where coral reefs occur is the first step in defining an effective set of marine-protected areas.

As discussed earlier in the chapter, after you remove atmospheric influences and sun glint the remaining remote sensing signal includes both reflectance from the water column and reflectance from the bottom if the water is shallow enough. The challenge is to differentiate the respective influences from each of these inputs. This can have important applications in mapping shallow benthic habitats, including seagrasses and coral reefs.

6.3.1 Coral reefs

The most basic needs for coral reef conservation are suitably scaled maps of habitats with enough information to identify ecological change. A component of the concept of the "health" of a coral reef is knowledge of the benthic cover—live coral, macroalgae, or sand—and the ability to readily detect changes in this cover.

Using a bottom-up approach based on thousands of spectral signatures taken from coral reefs, Hochberg and Atkinson (2003) evaluated the performance of a variety of existing and proposed sensors with different spectral bands in separating coral, algae, and sand endmembers (Fig. 6.11). "Endmembers" are the categories of cover type that may come from a bottom-up classification. Hyperspectral and narrow band multispectral sensors could distinguish the cover types, while broadband multispectral sensors (such as IKONOS, Landsat TM, and SPOT) overestimated coral cover by 24 percent. Spectral characteristics that distinguish coral from algae are in the range of 500–525 nm, and a satellite designed for remote mapping of coral reefs would have narrow (10–20 nm) spectral bands at a minimum of 480, 510, 540, and 570 nm wavelengths (Hochberg and Atkinson 2003, such bands also could be obtained from a hyperspectral sensor). A similar bottom-up approach could even begin at the

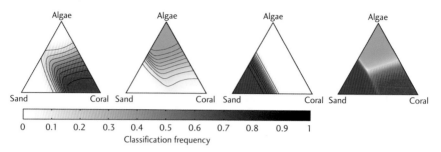

Fig. 6.11 Examples of a linear mixing analysis for distinguishing coral, algae, and sand end members in a classification. Each point in the triangle represents a pixel that includes some algae, some coral, and some sand. The top point of the triangle represents a pixel that is 100 percent algae, and the center point of the triangle represents a pixel that is 33.3 percent coral, 33.3 percent algae, and 33.3 percent sand. The intensity of the color represents the frequency with which that mixed pixel will be classified as the given cover type (the gray scale at the bottom shows that the darker or more intense the color shown in the triangles, the greater its classification frequency, i.e., the more often it is classified). The first three triangles show the classification frequency (number of spectra classified as a given bottom type divided by total number of spectra) for coral, algae, and sand, respectively. The fourth triangle is a red–green–blue composite for the combined classification frequencies, with coral represented by the intensity of the red, algae by green, and sand by blue. Yellow indicates the mixing boundary between coral and algae, magenta represents the boundary for coral and sand, and cyan for algae and sand. Credit: Eric Hochberg following the method of Hochberg and Atkinson (2003).

level of bio-optical modeling of photosynthetic pigments in corals (Hochberg *et al.* 2006).

6.3.1.1 Multispectral satellite data for mapping coral reefs

There are, as of 2009, no sensors in orbit designed to meet the spectral requirements for coral reef habitat mapping, which are quite different from land remote sensing and blue water remote sensing bands and spatial resolution. Prototype hyperspectral instruments (such as NASA's Hyperion and ESA's CHRIS) have helped to identify both the challenges and limitations of moving toward either global hyperspectral coverage, or an instrument more targeted to shallow coastal waters. In spite of this lack of optimal instruments, conservation need has driven innovation, and scientists have developed ways to use the sensors that are in orbit, including Landsat TM, SPOT, MODIS, IKONOS, and QuickBird, to help in coral reef management. One review of basic coral habitat mapping studies noted user accuracies for coral of 86 percent for Landsat TM and 76–93 percent for airborne multispectral imaging (Green *et al.* 2000). Unfortunately, Landsat TM classification accuracies for algal cover, important for trying to identify areas where living coral has died, are not as good (averaging 47 percent in Green *et al.* [2000]). Landsat is better than SPOT because its bands 1 and 2 cover the red reflectance maxima for brown and green algae (550 and 575 nm, Maritorena *et al.* 1994), and these cannot be distinguished by the broad (500–590 nm) range of SPOT XS band 1 (Green *et al.* 2000). For example, Phinney *et al.* (2001) could identify the overall increase in algal cover that followed mass mortality of sea urchins in the Caribbean (1983–4) using a retrospective analysis of Landsat TM data.

Given the dramatic and complex biological and geomorphological structure of coral reef systems, it is not surprising that spatial resolution can also limit applications of satellite sensors. Comparisons of airborne and satellite multi-spectral remote sensing suggest an optimal spatial resolution for most coral reef mapping of 1–10 m (Joyce and Phinn 2001; Andréfouët *et al.* 2003); these authors and others have examined the trade-offs between increased spatial resolution and decreased spectral resolution for benthic cover mapping using data such as IKONOS and QuickBird. One very practical way to decide what type of data to use is to find a study mapping similar types of habitats with similar depth ranges and water clarity, and model your own data selection and analysis techniques on what worked elsewhere.

Although habitat mapping is often the ultimate goal, maps of coral reef geomorphology (the major structures of the reef such as reef flat, reef crest, spur, and groove) are important contributors to global reef conservation. For example, Andréfouët *et al.* (2006) developed a technique for mapping reef geomorphology using a differencing technique with 30-m resolution Landsat data. Basically, a set of thresholds were used to mark where the major boundaries in reef zones occurred (Fig. 6.12). Using a hierarchical geomorphology classifi-cation scheme that could be applied worldwide to the many different types of tropical coral reefs, they created "Millennium Coral Reef" maps, the first uniformly collected data set on global coral reef extent. The extent of global hard reef classes in the Millennium map was 108,000 km^2. Compared to previous GIS compilations of nautical charts primarily focused on marine navigation, prior estimates of global reef extent (284,300 km^2; Spalding *et al.* 2001) are larger by a factor of 2.63. At the same time, nautical charts had underestimated the sedimentary areas associated with coral reefs by a factor of 1.85 (Andréfouët *et al.* 2006). Scientists may dispute which of the two maps represents a more ecologically relevant measure of global reef extent, but a standard product from uniform analysis of remotely sensed data at a single point in time provides a more useful baseline for monitoring change.

Even with all the innovations and successes above, many things that an ecologist or conservation biologist would want to learn from remotely sensed data are still very challenging—it is difficult to go beyond broad functional habitat categories (such as coral and algae), and species separation is very limited. It is hard to use satellite data to directly observe areas where there is coral bleaching (due to the temporal window for imagery collection), where there

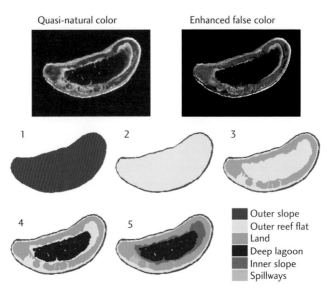

Fig. 6.12 Band thresholding and feature segmentation technique developed to extract reef geomorphology form Landsat TM data for the Millennium Coral Reefs Project (Andréfouët *et al.* 2006). Landsat TM image of Fangatau, Tuamotu Archipelago, French Polynesia (July 3, 1999) is shown in true color, and in a false color image enhanced to show shallow underwater structures. Image interpretation steps are as follows: *Step 1.* Identify the boundary between the outer slope and areas too deep to map using band 1 (blue) thresholding. *Step 2.* Identify the boundary between the outer slope and the rim using band 3 (red) thresholding. *Step 3.* Identify the area within the rim that is land using band 5 (infrared) thresholding. *Step 4.* Map the boundary between the rim and inner slope of the lagoon and the subsurface structures within the lagoon by growing a region of interest using band 3. *Step 5.* The final composite map is assembled by stacking these boundaries. Credit: Julie Robinson and Serge Andréfouët; Millennium Coral Reefs Landsat Archive, SeaWiFS Project, NASA/GSFC; Millennium Global Coral Reef Mapping Project, Institute for Marine Remote Sensing, University of South Florida; NASA/JSC.

has been a decline of corals and a shift to macroalgal cover (because of the challenges of change detection), or to estimate species richness or evenness (because of the difficulties in identifying species; Andréfouët *et al.* 2005b; Knudby *et al.* 2007). Until more ideal sensors for monitoring coral reef condition are placed in orbit, airborne hyperspectral campaigns with significant in-water collection of field data are the best way to do species-level or detailed habitat-level monitoring of corals. Even with these limitations on the ability of current satellite remote sensing to monitor reef health, the information gained from remotely sensed data for mapping reef structure and physical environment

(SST, winds, solar radiation, and water quality) are important for coral reef management (Mumby *et al.* 2004).

6.3.1.2 *Airborne hyperspectral imaging and coral reef mapping*

You can apply the same classification algorithms used in non-aquatic applications of hyperspectral image analysis in benthic habitat mapping. However, before using these approaches, you need to preprocess the data to estimate bottom reflectance (meaning atmospheric and water column corrections have to be done first) or employ an adaptive modeling scheme to account for spatial variations in water column properties and depth. General hyperspectral classification techniques are all applicable to benthic mapping, including spectral unmixing, spectral-angle mapping, matched filtering, mixture-tuned matched filtering, and spectral-feature fitting. Alternatively, some applications use forward modeling of measured field spectra to generate lookup tables, which are then used to classify the remotely sensed data. Further, beyond the basic classifications that assign pixels into one or more categories, the improved spectral resolution of hyperspectral data generally allows each pixel to be characterized in terms of the fraction of each cover type it contains (the endmembers)—this process is known as spectral unmixing.

Surveying reef spectra worldwide, Hochberg *et al.* (2003) grouped the majority of reef components into just 12 spectrally distinct categories: brown, green, and red fleshy algae; calcareous and turf algae; brown, blue, and bleached coral; gorgonian/soft coral; seagrass; terrigenous mud; and sand. The implication of this analysis, unfortunately for efforts to identify corals at the species level, is that many coral species are spectrally similar because of the similar origins of their pigments. Working with field data from Fiji and Indonesia, Holden and LeDrew (1999) found that differences in the morphology and condition of reef features impact the reflectance spectra and thus could be used to monitor reef health with hyperspectral data.

Lesser and Mobley (2007) used field spectral data and radiative transfer modeling to generate a lookup table for simultaneously estimating both bathymetry and percent cover of different types of coral classes using hyperspectral imagery in the Bahamas. The semi-analytical algorithms/modeling approaches discussed in Section 6.1.4 also have application to remote sensing of coral reef benthic cover using hyperspectral data. For example, Goodman and Ustin (2007) analyzed airborne hyperspectral data from NASA's Airborne Visible Infrared Imaging Spectrometer (AVIRIS) collected over Kaneohe Bay, Hawaii. The steps they used in this analysis were as follows: (1) The image was preprocessed including atmospheric correction and sun glint removal to provide water surface reflectance. (2) A semi-analytical model (also known as an inversion model, because it is being implemented in the inverse of the way it was developed, with absorption properties and generic bottom reflectance as the parameter inputs) was used to calculate water optical properties and bathymetry. (3) The same semi-analytical model was then used in the forward direction by inputting spectral endmembers (coral, algae, and sand), and the water properties and bathymetry from step 2 to produce an unmixed model output for the benthic classification. The maps of percent cover type for each endmember have real advantages for understanding the ecological structure of the reef cover and were comparable to available field data. Their approach required relatively little information on the water properties to use the model successfully.

It is also possible to use remote sensing to augment studies of ecosystem processes on coral reefs, beginning with the structure of the system, but also measuring environmental gradients across the reef such as variations in benthic light, temperature, and nutrients. For example, Brock *et al.* (2006) combined field deployment of a benthic chamber with habitat mapping from airborne hyperspectral imaging to estimate net calcification and excess production for coral reefs in Biscayne National Park, Florida.

6.3.1.3 Use of lidar and data fusion in coral reef mapping

Airborne lidar data is also widely applied for mapping coral reefs (lidar applications for depth mapping will be discussed in more detail in Chapter 7). For most applications, one frequency of laser is used for mapping reef structure and depth, and then a second multispectral or hyperspectral data source is used for information on the reef cover. For example, the USGS uses Scanning Hydrographic Operational Airborne Lidar Survey (SHOALS) combined with aerial photography and field data for mapping and monitoring of Pacific coral reefs (Cochran-Marquez 2005). Lidar measurement of rugosity (the roughness of the benthic surfaces as calculated from the lidar returns) is an important proxy for habitat structural complexity, and structural complexity is a useful predictor of reef biodiversity. Brock *et al.* (2004) used optical rugosity measured from NASA Experimental Advanced Airborne Research Lidar (EAARL) data over Biscayne National Park, Florida, USA to quantify the greater habitat complexity of the inshore patch reefs compared to outer bank reefs.

Airborne systems designed to collect hyperspectral and lidar data with a single processing system increasingly are being used. For example, a NOAA system called the Compact Hydrographic Airborne Rapid Total Survey (CHARTS) system combines SHOALS with a CASI hyperspectral sensor (Wozencraft *et al.* 2007). Another NOAA test system combined a different lidar system with a CASI-2 hyperspectral sensor (Sault *et al.* 2005). This is likely to be an area of ongoing technical development, and similar systems will eventually become available through the commercial market.

6.3.2 Seagrasses and kelp

Remote sensing is also used to map meadows of submerged seagrasses or forests of kelp. These distinctive marine habitats are representative of the possibilities and limitations for remote sensing of other submerged vegetation (see also wetland mapping in Chapter 7). The largest seagrass meadows can be visually observed in imagery from orbit (e.g., Robinson *et al.* [2001]; Fig. 6.13). Methods of seagrass mapping overlap significantly with methods for distinguishing benthic macroalgae from coral cover in tropical reef environments. Towed in-water photography, aerial photography, and satellite imagery have all been used as remotely sensed data for seagrass mapping. Visual mapping from aerial photography is probably the most accepted approach and the US National Wetlands Research Center and NOAA have a standard seagrass mapping protocol for color aerial photography (Finkbeiner *et al.* 2001). Applications have grown to include multispectral imagery and newer hyperspectral techniques.

Image selection can have a major influence on the ability to map seagrasses from satellite data. For example, Landsat TM images taken at low tide, and at the season with higher standing crop, will allow mapping of stands that are not seen in other images (Ferguson and Korfmacher 1997). Kelp maps from airborne multispectral data prepared for monitoring the commercial floating kelp harvest in Alaska were also highly dependent on collecting data at a standard tide level, although biomass estimates were less sensitive to tide level (Stekoll *et al.* 2006). As for remote sensing of coral reefs, if wind conditions are too high when the imagery is acquired, then it will be difficult to detect any signal reflected from submerged vegetation. Turbidity generally will limit the ability to detect seagrass. Interestingly, kelp can still be detected in turbid waters. In relatively clear waters, the kelp had strong reflectance in the red and infrared bands (5, 6, and 7) of Landsat MSS, but under turbid conditions the same kelp stand could be visualized by the contrast between the kelp and the turbid water as seen in the water-penetrating green band (MSS band 4; Jensen *et al.* 1980). Jensen *et al.* (1980) also showed successful mapping using both multispectral and X-band radar imagery, although these techniques do not seem to have been adopted in the ensuing years (e.g., Deysher [1993]; Stekoll *et al.* [2006]).

Mumby *et al.* (1997) did a comparative analysis of Landsat, SPOT, and CASI imagery with field measurements for remote sensing of seagrass standing crop. They handled water depth differences by calculating a depth-invariant bottom index for each pair of spectral bands (see discussion of Lyzenga method above). For the limited spectral bands in SPOT, this led to a single index value to be used in linear regressions; for Landsat and CASI data, the multiple indexes were used in a series of regressions to determine the degree to which each depth-invariant bottom index was related to seagrass standing crop. The SPOT index, Landsat band 1,2 (blue-green, green) depth-invariant index, and CASI green, red depth-invariant index all closely correlated with seagrass standing crop, and compared favorably to quadrat harvest methods.

Spectral libraries can be combined with satellite data to improve benthic habitat classifications (Purkis and Pasterkamp 2004). After using the *in situ* measurements as training data for the supervised classification (of sand, rubble, macroalgae, seagrass, and algal mats), Purkis and Pasterkamp 2004 found that

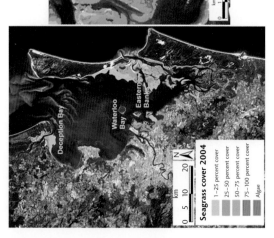

Fig. 6.13 Seagrass maps for the Eastern Banks in Moreton Bay, Australia (Phinn *et al.* 2006). Data from field transects collected in July 2004 (by Australian natural resource agencies and volunteers) were used to perform supervised classifications of Landsat TM and Quickbird satellite images (Landsat TM, August 8, 2004; Quickbird, September 17, 2004). High-spatial resolution data allowed classification to the species level. Maps ©2005 Commonwealth of Australia (Geoscience Australia), reproduced under public license.

adding depth information improved the classification accuracy from 53 to 76 percent. Pahlevan *et al.* (2006) compare techniques for using ancillary bathymetric data with the image-only Lyzenga depth corrections for classification of coral, seagrass, and algal cover types. Major types of ancillary data sets that are suitable for combining with remotely sensed data are reviewed by Robinson *et al.* (2006).

Airborne hyperspectral data can be a powerful tool for monitoring seagrass extent. For example, Peneva *et al.* (2008) used airborne HyMap hyperspectral imagery acquired at 2.9-m resolution to map seagrass cover classes and estimate seagrass areal coverage off the coast of Mississippi, USA. They collected field spectra at different water depths and tested performance of three types of supervised image classifications (maximum likelihood, minimum distance-to-means, and spectral angle mapper). The maximum likelihood method had the highest overall accuracy (83 percent). They also recommended the use of 3-m spatial resolution data for other seagrass mapping applications.

6.4 Summary

With the oceans covering about 70 percent of the Earth's surface, marine applications constitute a significant part of the field of remote sensing, primarily for the areas of global ocean modeling and global climate modeling. Satellites and techniques developed for global studies have applications to conservation and ecological management, including through understanding the physical ocean environment, ocean productivity, and shallow benthic habitat composition. From a bloom of microscopic plankton, to the movements of a cetacean, to the health of a coral reef, remote sensing is an important tool for spanning the spatial scale of the oceans and informing their conservation.

7

Wetlands—estuaries, inland wetlands, and freshwater lakes

Two major disasters, the Indian Ocean Tsunami of December 2004 and the flooding of New Orleans after Hurricane Katrina in August 2005, have heightened global awareness of the importance of wetlands for reducing wave energies and negative impacts of floods on coastal communities (Danielsen *et al.* 2005). Both situations have also led to research that uses remote sensing to help understand changes in coastal wetlands over regional scales. These types of studies would be difficult to complete with classic field methods because of the breadth of their spatio-temporal scopes. Remote sensing helps scientists to identify the most beneficial approaches to reduce wetland losses, and to target restoration programs.

Remote sensing can increase understanding of wetland change and provide an evidence base for policy makers. We will start with an example of a major analysis of the historical conversion of mangrove habitats prior to the Indian Ocean Tsunami, seeking insights into whether intact coastal wetlands provide protection. We will have a related example for the Louisiana coast and hurricane vulnerability later in the chapter. Giri *et al.* (2008) used more than 750 Landsat images to map tsunami-prone coastal areas of Indonesia, Malaysia, Thailand, Burma (Myanmar), Bangladesh, India, and Sri Lanka. Imagery was centered on four different time periods (as close as possible to the central calendar year, given cloud cover in many images): mid-1970s, 1990, around 2000, and 2005. Because of the size of the study area, they resampled data to the Albers equal area map projection, normalized for solar irradiance, and produced maps for each time period. The authors used supervised classification to map the water bodies and unsupervised classification (isodata cluster analysis) to classify the remaining images as mangrove, non-mangrove, or barren lands. Field data and high-resolution satellite images (QuickBird, IKONOS) were the source of map validation. They then produced post-classification change maps by subtracting the classifications of pairs of wetland maps, comparing 1975–90, 1975–2000, 1975–2005, 1990–2000, 1990–2005 and 2000–5. Changed areas were then compared by visual interpretation of the original imagery to identify the causes of the change (such as agriculture, aquaculture, and urban development). A set of local experts reviewed the maps and change maps at a workshop to validate the causes of change, using ground data, field data, and the high-resolution satellite images.

The study identified a net loss 12 percent of the mangrove forests in the region from 1975 to 2005, with present extent estimated at about 1,670,000 ha. Major geographical differences losses were linked to the approaches to mangrove management in different countries. The major causes of deforestation calculated across all the maps for the region were agriculture (81 percent), aquaculture (12 percent), and urban development (2 percent), but when each country was considered separately, there were broad differences in the major causes of deforestation. For example, in Thailand, mangrove loss was due to both agricultural conversion (50 percent) and aquaculture to support the global shrimp market (41 percent). Compared to field surveys and maps published by different regional and government authorities, this work provided a relatively objective source of information for decisions on the distribution of resources for the conservation and rehabilitation of mangrove forests. Such mapping can become a key input to economic analyses and land management actions aimed at reducing impacts of tsunamis in the future.

Mapping wetlands in ways that reflect both the physical components (such as elevation and tides) and vegetation components of the system is key for conservation efforts—from understanding wetland ecology, to identifying jurisdictional wetlands, to monitoring restoration projects, and to understanding environmental change. The principles and techniques discussed previously in this book for land and marine remote sensing come together in studies of the complex interfaces between water and land. In all types of wetland environments, techniques appropriate to land cover remote sensing can be used to classify wetland vegetation. Although limited by the presence of sediments, techniques developed for marine remote sensing also have important applications to the study of submerged wetlands and lakes. Because of the complex water–land interfaces, we also see a strong dependence on active remote sensing systems (lidar and radar). Active sensors provide the possibility to see through vegetation or standing water to map different layers of the environment from the hard bottom to the vegetation top.

In this chapter, we will begin by outlining the linkages between the remote sensing techniques covered in previous chapters on land vegetation and marine remote sensing, and their application to the different major wetland systems of estuarine, riverine, palustrine (marsh), and lacustrine (lake) wetlands (Schot 1999). Because there are similarities and differences between wetland remote sensing techniques and techniques used in studies of terrestrial vegetation, benthic marine, and deepwater marine environments, we have summarized the approaches and unique constraints for the different major ecological zones (upland/emergent vegetation, submergent vegetation, water column, and water depth) and for the different types of wetlands in Table 7.1. With these general principles, we move to examples of ecological or conservation-related uses of remote sensing for wetlands of different types. This ecological structure will first

Table 7.1 Summary of approaches to mapping different types of wetlands and ecological zones, with highlights of major constraints. As for all remote sensing, the match between spatial scale of remotely sensed data and the specific objective is an overarching constraint.

Ecological zone Wetland type	Approaches and unique constraints
Upland and emergent vegetation	
Estuarine	The most comprehensive applications use lidar terrain modeling to distinguish vegetation, substrate, sediments, and water to tell how "solid" the land is and to separate different marsh zones. Vegetation mapping techniques for multispectral data work well for uplands but are significantly more challenging for emergent vegetation. There is much research activity on the use of hyperspectral data for mapping marsh vegetation. For passive reflectance data, difficulties arise in distinguishing transitions between non-wetland, and infrequently inundated "high marsh." Difficulties also can arise in distinguishing boundaries between upland and emergent zones, because multispectral sensors cannot see through the vegetation to map standing water underneath. Some of these difficulties can be overcome by using appropriate timing of data collection relative to normal tides and storm tides. The need for data at specific known tide heights can limit usefulness of routinely acquired data from global sensor systems such as Landsat; the need for lidar or hyperspectral data drives many applications to airborne sensors. Mangroves have a strong IR signature. Seasonal changes become very important in mapping emergent annual grasses. Sedimentation can be so thick after a rainfall event, that multispectral analysis has trouble distinguishing sediment-laden water from other non-vegetated soils.
Riverine	Vegetation mapping techniques for multispectral data work well if the spatial resolution is sufficient to capture the width of the river-influenced vegetation corridor. In arid environments, seasonal imagery of bank-side vegetation can stand out because it stays green further into the dry season.
Palustrine	Vegetation mapping techniques for multispectral data work well, but active lidar from airborne sensors allows more sophisticated separation of water, vegetation, and sediments. Difficulties can arise in distinguishing upland and emergent vegetation, these can be solved with hyperspectral data (improving the ability to distinguish different key

vegetation types), and by informed use of seasonal changes. Annual and seasonal differences in inundation are often a goal of analysis, so use of multi-date imagery is often important. For seasonal wetlands, mapping soil types during non-inundated seasons and combining that map with a vegetation map during an inundated season can also be a useful technique.

Lacustrine   Vegetation mapping techniques for multispectral data work well if the spatial resolution is sufficient to capture the width of any beaches or lake-influenced vegetation. For shallow shorelines, the notes under palustrine wetlands apply. Lidar can be very useful for topographic mapping.

Submergent vegetation/substrate

Estuarine   The high sediment load in many estuarine environments is a key limitation to the information that can be obtained from multispectral imagery. Variable tidal submersion makes the time and date of image acquisition critical to any multispectral analysis. At the wrong date and time, an entire salt marsh may appear to be open water with submerged vegetation. Seagrass mapping has been successfully developed when sediment load does not obscure observation of the benthic zone.

Riverine   The high sediment load in many riverine environments limits multispectral imaging. Most clear rivers are relatively small, and not suited to the spatial resolution of global land imagers. Fusion of data layers, such as river boundaries mapped from digital orthophotos, can help in the interpretation of imagery acquired from satellite sensors.

Palustrine   Once again, sediment is the key limiting factor for the use of multispectral imagery to map submerged palustrine vegetation. Use of radar-based active imaging such a lidar, allows mapping of some bottom features through the sediment and water.

Lacustrine   In clear waters, remote sensing of the littoral zone can be similar to remote sensing of coral cover (Section 6.3). Compared to deepwater marine environments, freshwater lakes can have much more complex optical structure from the water column. An understanding of the bathymetry, water chemistry, and stratification of a particular lake will be important. Standard water column correction methods for marine "blue and green waters" are not going to work for freshwater lakes, and most lakes would need a custom model based on the specific makeup of inorganic and organic components determining the water color.

(continued)

Table 7.1 (Continued)

Ecological zone	Approaches and unique constraints
Water column	
Estuarine	The confluence of sediment with nutrient fluxes and heavy organic loads, make remote sensing of water columns with current multispectral satellite sensors very difficult (the "brown water" problem from Chapter 6). Experimental work is currently being done to develop and validate hyperspectral methods for understanding near-shore and estuarine waters.
Riverine	Aerial imaging is generally better suited to the scale of study of riverine water quality than is satellite remote sensing. Static mapping of water column content or quality along a river course is not usually feasible because of the broad changes of substrate type and sediment influx that occur along the length of a river. Using comparative imagery and ancillary maps of a watershed, remotely sensed imagery can be useful in identifying sources of influxes such as hot water, sediments, or sewage. Such analyses can be visual, as in identifying an unexpected change in the water appearance at a specific point along the river course.
Palustrine	The prevalence of sediment and variable nutrient loads make remote sensing of waters in palustrine wetlands very difficult. Use of hyperspectral or lidar can partly, but not completely overcome these problems.
Lacustrine	Remote sensing can be a tool in monitoring water quality of freshwater lakes. However, many lakes will require development of specific optical models for the lake based on field measurements of water components before remote sensing could be used to distinguish key features such as plankton and colored dissolved organic matter (CDOM). Evaporation of shallow lakes can be readily monitored by remote sensing, and hypersaline lakes can exhibit color changes related to faunal populations that are indicative of overall salinity changes.
Water depth/flood depth	For all but the clearest waters, multispectral imagery is not going to give a successful estimate of water depth in any of the wetland systems. Active systems such as lidar are the best methods for mapping bathymetry. Lidar can have the additional advantage of mapping depth of soft sediments or sands, in addition to the depth of the water. Large lakes may be suited to sonar or sounding profiles to measure bathymetry.

feature multispectral remote sensing of mangroves. Next, we discuss mapping of wetlands, emphasizing the ways to use multispectral, lidar, and radar data to better understand these complex systems. Shoreline mapping of lakes and rivers is the next topic. Finally we discuss the use of remote sensing to map water quality using hyperspectral, multispectral, and thermal data.

7.1 Mangroves

Mangroves, tropical forests that grow in sheltered saline tidal areas, are important for their role as nurseries in the life cycles of marine fishes, as wildlife habitat, and in stabilizing coastlines from erosion. However, they are under extensive pressure from agroforestry, shrimp fisheries and aquaculture, and coastal development, leading to declines in the extent of mangroves worldwide (Valiela *et al.* 2001). The dark green appearance of mangrove forests is very visible from orbit for larger stands (Robinson *et al.* 2001) and translates into a strong infrared signature that can stand out in stark contrast to other vegetation (Fig. 7.1).

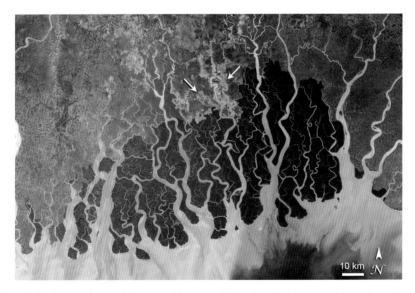

Fig. 7.1 True-color multispectral image of the Sundarbans, southwestern Bangladesh and southeastern India, the largest remaining tract of mangrove forest in the world. The dark green area is the mangrove forest. Aquaculture facilities can be seen at the northern border of the projected area (arrows). This image was created by merging several Landsat 7 images into a cloud-free composite (path, row 138, 45 and 137, 45; November 24, 1999, and November 17 and 26, 2000. Credit: Jesse Allen, NASA Earth Observatory, using data obtained from the University of Maryland's Global Land Cover Facility.

Green *et al.* (1998) reviewed a number of mangrove remote sensing studies (as they did for seagrasses—Section 6.3.2). They also provide an example at a single study site comparing different data sources, different analysis methods, and their limitations in mangrove mapping. They compared three data sources—Landsat TM, SPOT XS, and CASI (airborne multispectral flown with eight bands and 1 m spatial resolution)—for mapping mangroves in the Turks and Caicos Islands. They also used five different analysis methods: visual interpretation, calculation of NDVI followed by unsupervised classification, unsupervised classification of the raw image data, supervised classification, and unsupervised classification of principal components of band ratios. Principal components analysis used data from Landsat TM bands 3, 4, and 5, and the ratios of bands 3/5 and 5/4. Unsupervised classification was then performed on an image made up of the first three principal components. The 3/5 and 5/4 band ratios take advantage of the "red edge"—the rapid increase in chlorophyll reflectance that occurs between about 680 (red) and 730 nm (infrared) in plants including wetland species such as mangroves and reeds (*Phragmites,* see Fig. 7.2, Yang *et al.* 2008). The red edge comes from the functional responses of photosynthetic pigments to light—plants absorb light suitable for photosynthesis, but reflect the slightly longer wavelengths of near-infrared light, which would heat the leaves

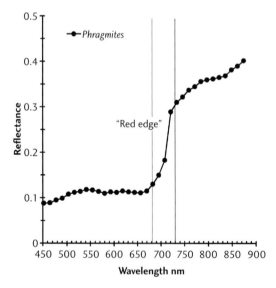

Fig. 7.2 Field-measured spectrum for a dense stand of *Phragmites*. Dense mono-specific stands of wetland vegetation can be readily mapped by remote sensing instruments based on the rapid change of the reflectance in the transition between red and infrared wavelengths (the "red edge"). Distinguishing species composition requires distinguishing much more subtle differences in the spectra. (Figure from Yang *et al.* 2008, used with permission.)

but are not suitable for photosynthesis. Thus, for Landsat TM, the ratio of bands 3/5 captures the ratio of the signal red/mid-infrared, and the ratio of bands 5/4 captures the ratio of mid-infrared/near-infrared. The red edge is nicely reviewed by Seager *et al.* (2005; they propose its use in finding extraterrestrial life by identifying vegetation on other planets).

Given the techniques of Green *et al.* (1998) outlined above, both Landsat and CASI data were suitable for discriminating mangrove from non-mangrove vegetation, but SPOT XS data were not able to distinguish mangrove vegetation. Since SPOT XS has been used successfully in other mangrove studies (e.g., Madagascar, Rasolofoharinoro *et al.* [1998]), they felt that the limited number of spectral bands was the root of the problem for identifying the vegetation types in these sites. Landsat TM and CASI data worked with unsupervised, supervised, and principal components classification methods, with the most accurate method (92 percent overall accuracy) from principal components. Surprisingly, Landsat TM and CASI classifications using principal components were of equivalent accuracy (92 and 96 percent, respectively). This result indicates that the increased spatial and spectral information from CASI (which also means more effort and expense in data acquisition and analysis) were not important for distinguishing mangrove and non-mangrove vegetation.

Green *et al.* (1998) also tried to distinguish specific stands of mangroves that were categorized based on canopy characteristics and dominant species. Landsat TM data could only be used to distinguish tall *Rhizophora* sp. canopies from other mangrove classes. The additional spectral and spatial information in the CASI airborne data made it possible to distinguish all nine mangrove habitat classes they had identified from field surveys. The most accurate analysis method was once again principal components analysis with band ratios followed by unsupervised classification (85 percent overall accuracy).

Forest canopy monitoring techniques, such as estimating leaf area index, also work well with mangroves (e.g., Kovacs *et al.* [2005], using IKONOS; Green *et al.* [1997], using Landsat TM and SPOT). Mangrove reforestation is expected to be a major tool for CO_2 sequestration (Okimoto *et al.* 2008), and leaf area index can be used in estimating carbon sequestration for stands of varying vigor. Remote sensing of mangroves has also been used to evaluate whether Ramsar designation of protected wetlands has been successful in slowing conversion to aquaculture (Seto and Fragkias 2007).

7.2 Salt and freshwater marshes

If you are interested in generating ecologically relevant maps of salt marshes or other complex coastal wetlands, you are likely to find that remotely sensed data from satellites is of limited usefulness. Although some researchers have created wetland extent and vegetation maps successfully using Landsat, SPOT, and even satellite-based synthetic aperture radar, most have found many limitations to using these data sources to make biologically meaningful maps of marshlands. Spatial resolution, spectral resolution, and lack of control of imagery acquisition relative to tides and winds limit the use of satellite data. Although tidal changes in water level are obviously a bane to researchers selecting from standard satellite data acquisition cycles in coastal salt marshes, the situation is not much easier in inland wetlands where annual cycles of inundation lead to difficulty in timing observations.

Airborne sensors are the primary source of remotely sensed data for mapping vegetation in marshes. Compared to satellite sensors, airborne sensors combine acquisition timing with high spatial resolution (about 1 m ground-sampled distance or better) and spectral characteristics (five bands multispectral in visible to near-infrared or better) that are ecologically relevant. Once you have commissioned an airborne mission, it is best to collect both lidar and targeted multispectral data together. Lidar will allow interpretation of the topography of the wetland, enabling mapping of different marsh zones regardless of overlying vegetation. The airborne multispectral data can be configured to meet the needs of the specific project for identifying vegetation zones. And the two data sets can be combined (often called "data fusion") to get more sophisticated maps that reflect vegetation cover, topography, and hydrology. While this is ideal, many researchers might not have the funding to do an elaborate, multisensor project, and it is possible to conduct good research addressing focused questions without the perfect set of airborne data.

7.2.1 Lidar mapping of wetland elevation

Wetland mapping (mapping of emergent vegetation in either salt marshes or freshwater marshes) relies extensively upon lidar because lidar allows for very high accuracy in mapping the elevation of the soil underneath most vegetation and any standing water. National topographic data sets such as USGS DEMs, GTOPO30, and NASA SRTM, do not have the elevational resolution to capture the ecologially relevant small differences in marsh elevation (Yang 2005). Because the laser pulses fire rapidly (around 25 kHz/s), the signal returned to the instrument partly reflects off trees and dense vegetation, and partly penetrates to the underlying soil. Canopy trees with broad crowns can also be problematic with double bounce occurring and adding noise. The raw data are a dense series of points with x, y, and z coordinates on the terrain referenced to an onboard GPS, as well as data on the intensity and delay of the return pulse. Software packages allow the removal of the vegetation "artifacts" to produce a DEM at the soil level (Fig. 7.3), and this post-processing is where there is a learning curve if you want to do the analyses yourself. In particular, one set of subtraction functions can be developed to subtract the ground from the canopy and get height under the tree crowns. You would use a slightly different subtraction function to get minute elevation changes on the ground below the canopy.

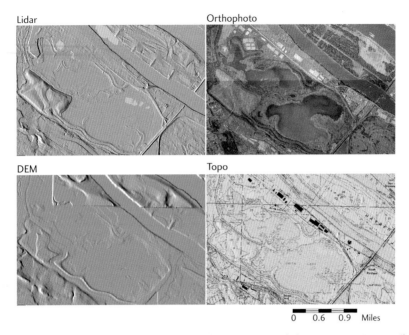

Fig. 7.3 Example of lidar data in wetland mapping. (a) lidar intensity image, (b) digital orthophoto, (c) digital elevation model (DEM), and (d) topographic map for the Smith and Bybee Lakes area of Columbia Slough, a remnant wetland of the lower Columbia River system in the Portland, Oregon, USA, metropolitan area. Data were extracted from the "Pilot LIDAR Project—Portland Metro Area," Oregon Department of Geology and Mineral Industries (Madin *et al.* 2009), which includes acquisition and public distribution of airborne lidar data through an online map server. Credit: Oregon Department of Geology and Mineral Industries.

The different commercial lidar systems vary in their recommended methods of post-processing, and the operator will usually provide the georeferencing of the data to GPS measurements from the flight lines. Often, you can pay the company contracted to fly the lidar survey to do other post-processing and deliver data that you can import directly into a GIS. In the GIS, built-in functions interpolate between the elevation points to create a triangulated irregular network (TIN) surface model. The TIN can be used as is in modeling, and can also be converted to a grid with a minimum mapping unit for combination with other data sources such as multispectral data. In interpolating the TIN, you may need to degrade the point density (e.g., from 10 to 100 cm elevation differences) because the data density of an elevation data layer can make the file size unmanageable.

As a rule of thumb, the vertical accuracy of x (easting), y (northing), and z (elevation) point data is determined by the accuracy of the lidar and the onboard

GPS, with accuracies of different systems ranging from ± 8 to 19 cm in marshes and grasslands (Hodgson and Bresnahan 2004; Montané and Torres 2006). Many studies of wetland habitats do not externally validate the accuracy of the DEM, and just use the relative heights. More information about elevation modeling can be found in Chapter 5.

Elevation models of wetlands can be important for predicting the outcomes of wetland restoration projects. To predict the development of an intertidal marsh following inundation of a formerly reclaimed area in the United Kingdom, Blott and Pye (2004) used lidar data to construct a digital terrain model of areas behind old seawalls. They combined the elevation model with observations of tidal flows (which at the study locations had a range of 8.5 m between lowest and highest astronomical tide) at analog locations to predict the flooding that would occur after the seawall was breached in multiple locations. Employing lidar data collected from government agency overflights, the authors were able to use their model and tide tables to predict tidal volumes and flow through the breaches. They also used the historical analogs to make predictions of the future extent of salt marsh, mudflat, and lagoon. Although the data have not yet been published, the general trend now that the breaches have occurred corresponds with the predictions (Simon Blott, personal communication).

7.2.2 Lidar mapping of wetland vegetation

When employing lidar to map wetland extent, analysts usually focus on elevation and discard the signal return from the vegetation as an artifact. For marsh vegetation, however, the first and last returns of each laser signal are quite useful. The first return is from the closer vegetation top, and the last return is expected to be from the soil elevation. However, if the vegetation canopy is too dense, the signal might not penetrate to the ground and you might only be able to map vegetation height regardless.

Rosso et al. (2006) used lidar and field surveys to study changes associated with the invasion of nonnative *Spartina alterniflora*, which is displacing and hybridizing with native *S. foliosa* and expanding across mudflats in San Francisco Bay. They originally sought to produce DEMs by hiring commercial overflights in two consecutive winters when vegetation was less dense than in spring or summer. However, the signal returned from *Spartina* patches compared to the surrounding mudflat was around 0.6 m higher, indicating that in this system, the lidar was not penetrating the vegetation (note that many other studies in salt marshes have not identified this problem, e.g., Montané and Torres [2006]; Yang [2005]; Morris et al. [2005]). In the vegetated patches, the last return was from the mid-range of the canopy in areas of new leaf growth. They constructed an elevation model by interpolating the elevation underneath the *Spartina* patches from the elevations of the surrounding mudflats. The signal returned from the vegetation could be used to map the *Spartina* distribution and compare it between the 2 years. They detected changes of 20 cm or more in elevation, identified effects of *Spartina* on the acretion and erosion patterns of the shoreline and mudflats, and could distinguish areas where *Spartina* was actively expanding.

Lidar was important for mapping habitat variables determining the distribution of a threatened beach plant, seaside amaranth (*Amaranthus pumilus*), a flowering annual of the Atlantic barrier islands (Sellars and Jolls 2007). Elevation was the most limiting topographic variable, with amaranth occurring within 1.23 m of local mean high water. Sellars and Jolls (2007) used airborne digital photography collected with the lidar overflights to map vegetation associations for the habitat model, and also included occurrence of seaside amaranth in previous years in the model. The models predicted 46 to 100 percent of the plant occurrences after field sampling of as little as 2 percent of the habitat to build and test the model.

7.2.3 Spectral characteristics used in mapping of marshes

Bottom-up approaches (Section 6.1.4) using spectral reflectance of marshes seek to identify species-specific signatures that can be used with hyperspectral imagery to create maps of wetland vegetation types. Bottom-up approaches also give a lot of insight into what is producing the reflectance signal classified using multispectral data.

Working in the Dutch Waddenzee, Schmidt and Skidmore (2003) used a handheld spectrometer at 1.5 m away from the vegetation to measure reflectance spectra of salt marsh plants at the stand/canopy level (as opposed to the plant level)— basically at the same level an ecologist would conduct quadrat sampling. Plant sampling was conducted in parallel to collecting spectral reflectance for 132 vegetation plots with 10–20 spectra taken for each plot. They grouped the vegetation sampling data using ordination analysis (a common statistical method in vegetation analysis) to identify 27 different salt marsh vegetation associations. The associations are familiar ones for ecologists working in coastal marshes—for example, *Salicornia* and *Salicornia–Sueda* for low marsh, *Juncus–Limonium* and *Juncus–Atriplex* for mid-marsh, and *Festuca* and *Elymus–Festuca* for high marsh (Fig. 7.4). They compared spectra for each pairwise set of vegetation associations to determine which wavelengths were important for distinguishing the associations. A set of normalization techniques standardized the spectra for differences in overall albedo without losing information in the areas of the spectra where most plants have maximum reflectance. All but 9 of the 27 vegetation types had a distinct signature, and most of these could be distinguished by using reflectance at just six wavelengths (Table 7.2).

A marsh that looks fairly homogeneous to the broad bands of Landsat can show more heterogeneity with the appropriate spectral bands and spatial resolution. Once the spectral signatures of vegetation in a specific area have been studied, a relatively small number of spectral bands may be needed to distinguish the target vegetation types. The challenge is to what degree such a spectral library gives insight for areas outside the area in which they were developed.

Of course, if satellite data are appropriate, it could be less expensive to buy IKONOS or QuickBird imagery than to fly an airborne mission. How do the

Table 7.2 Key wavelengths for distinguishing species of marsh vegetation, as identified by Schmidt and Skidmore (2003).

Frequency (nm)	Reflectance association
404	Blue chlorophyll absorption
628	Chlorophyll absorption
771	Near-infrared ridge
1398	Downward slope of near-infrared plateau
1803	Right flank of first shortwave infrared peak
2183	Second shortwave infrared peak

resulting maps compare with maps derived from airborne multispectral and hyperspectral data? Belluco *et al.* (2006) compared three airborne sensors with IKONOS and QuickBird data for mapping salt marsh vegetation in Venice Lagoon, Italy. The airborne sensors were Reflective Optics System Imaging Spectrometer (ROSIS, 115 bands in visible and near-infrared, 1 m spatial resolution), Compact Airborne Spectrographic Imager (CASI, 15 bands in visible and near-infrared, 1.3 m spatial resolution), and Multispectral IR and Visible Imaging Spectrometer (MIVIS, 20 bands visible and near-infrared, 72 bands in mid- and far infrared, 10 thermal bands, and 2.6 m spatial resolution). They combined the four IKONOS bands at 4 m resolution with the panchromatic band for 1 m spatial resolution. QuickBird also had four visible and near-infrared bands, but at 2.9 m spatial resolution. Field observations were the source of GPS-delineated boundaries for zones of five dominant genera—*Juncus, Spartina, Limonium, Sarcocornia,* and *Salicornia.* They atmospherically and geometrically corrected all data and compared unsupervised classifications (K-means) to supervised classifications (spectral angle mapping and maximum likelihood). Before classification, they reduced the many redundant bands in the hyperspectral ROSIS data to a set of four bands using the maximum noise fraction (MNF) transform (Green *et al.* 1988)—a technique related to principal components analysis.

The results of the comparisons of sensors and techniques (Belluco *et al.* 2006) were that both *Limonium*- and *Sacrocornia*-dominated zones could be accurately identified by all the sensors. *Juncus* patches were at a smaller scale of spatial heterogeneity and more often misclassified in all the analyses. *Spartina* in low marsh was classified less accurately because it included mixed signatures of solid vegetation and vegetation/bare soil. The data were able to document a significant shift in the dominant vegetation types from *Spartina* to *Salicornia* over a 1-year period. The hyperspectral (ROSIS) classifications were a little more accurate than the satellite data, especially for identifying *Juncus,* but IKONOS and QuickBird-derived classifications still had high overall accuracies ranging from 91 to 97 percent.

The greatest advantage in using hyperspectral data is the potential to classify vegetation and simultaneously infer the morphology and soil topography of the

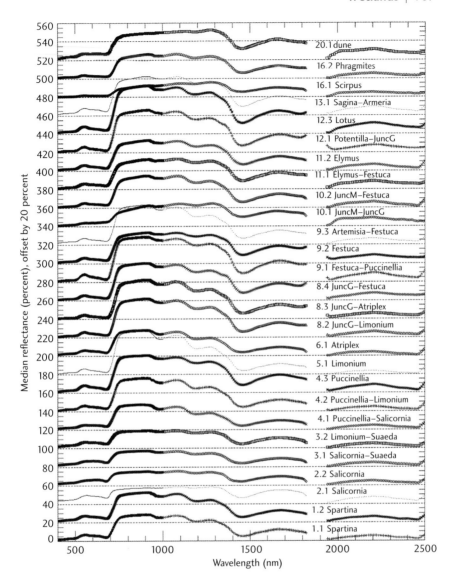

Fig. 7.4 Median normalized reflectance spectra for 27 salt marsh vegetation associations in the Waddenzee, the Netherlands. The scale for each spectrum is percentage reflectance with most spectra ranging from 0 to 50 percent at different wavelengths. Each spectrum is displayed stacked on the graph with the zero value offset by an additional 20 percent for each subsequent spectrum so that they can be distinguished (otherwise all 23 spectra would be plotted on top of each other). (Figure reprinted from Schmidt and Skidmore 2003: 96 with permission from Elsevier.)

marsh using spectral unmixing. In this approach, the first step is to identify pure pixels of homogeneous composition as representative of different endmembers (such as *Spartina, Limonium, Sarcoconia,* and soil), and then use a linear model to estimate the composition of mixed pixels (Silvestri *et al.* 2003). The next step is to combine empirical observations of the relationship between different species and mean soil elevation with the spectral unmixing analysis to create an inferred DEM of predicted soil elevations. Unique to wetland areas, vegetation is such a good indicator of soil elevation and inundation that the accuracies of DEMs produced in this way can be comparable to laser altimeters (e.g., a standard deviation of 5.3 cm in the data of Silvestri *et al.* [2003]).

Liu *et al.* (2005) developed spectral libraries for the monitoring of purple loosestrife (*Lythrum salicaria*), an invasive species that has spread through fresh-water marshes and pond edges in the United States. They conducted airborne flights of the Hudson River Valley using a Digital Airborne Imaging Spectrom-eter (DAIS) hyperspectral instrument at midday with 2 m spatial resolution. As the flights were taking place, field crews collected handheld spectra of various species, including purple loosestrife, along the flight lines. The airborne data were georectified and atmospherically corrected so they would be comparable to the field data. Using spectral match scores, they identified as "pure pixels" areas in the hyperspectral data that closely matched the reference spectrum of purple loosestrife and used these pure pixels as reference pixels for a supervised classi-fication of the hyperspectral data. Using this technique, the overall accuracy in identifying stands of purple loosestrife was >90 percent (compared to field verification). The approach allows targeting of areas likely to contain the invasive plant for additional field surveys and eradication campaigns.

7.2.4 Combining lidar and multispectral data

Sophisticated analyses are possible when combining airborne lidar and multi-spectral data with modeling to characterize wetland structure and vegetation. As an example, Morris *et al.* (2005) collected multispectral (red, green, blue, and near-infrared) and aerial lidar data over North Inlet, South Carolina. They obtained multispectral data from a set of October overflights timed close to solar noon and low tide. The commercial provider corrected radiometric non-uniformities along the edge of the flight lines, performed an atmospheric correction based on empirical observation of a calibration target, and georefer-enced the data so that each 0.7×0.7 m pixel was resampled to 0.5 m positional accuracy on a UTM projection. They collected lidar data through a different commercial data provider 2 years later, with overflights in January when the salt marsh vegetation was senescent. Vegetation removal algorithms were used to remove vegetation artifacts from the data and positional x, y, and z data in a UTM projection were delivered to the investigators. The raw data were con-verted to a TIN with 5×5 m mapping units. They completed ground surveys in the spring between the two overflights to accurately measure the elevation of stable benchmarks already in the marsh.

Artificial neural network modeling combined the two data sets, allowing the use of training data for iterative development of mathematical models that assign data to a specific category. They built a least squares logistic model for the four multispectral bands to categorize vegetation zones in the marsh (water, *S. alterniflora, Juncus*, forest, asphalt, and sand). The only classes with significant overlap were *Spartina* and *Juncus*, which had overall accuracies of 90 percent. Combining the marsh classification with the elevation data showed that *Juncus* grew in a much wider range of vertical habitats (80 percent between 0.30 and 0.98 m) compared to *Spartina* (80 percent between 0.22 and 0.48 m). A small positive increase in lidar elevation under *Spartina* was interpreted as being partly from interference of the vegetation with the lidar signal, and partly from the positive tendency of *Spartina* to trap sediments.

7.2.5 Radar mapping of wetlands

Synthetic aperture radar (SAR) has significant applications in wetland mapping. Working in the microwave part of the spectrum, radar systems use the measurement of backscatter to estimate surface roughness as well as soil and vegetation moisture content (Section 4.3.4.1). A real advantage of radar is that it can be used day or night and in almost all weather conditions. Henderson and Lewis (2008) provide a review of the use of imaging radar in understanding wetland ecosystems. Through 1990, applications focused on mapping flooded forest using mostly L-band SARs such as Seasat, and Shuttle Imaging Radar (SIR)-A and B. A major challenge in forested wetlands was the double bounce that occurs because the signal reflects off both the tree trunks and the smooth reflective surface of the water. The 1990s saw the use of C-band radar from SIR-C and the European Remote Sensing (ERS) SAR, and Radarsat (a Canadian satellite with US cooperation). Polarimetric analysis became more widely used—in which the change in the polarization of the signal provides additional information about the surface. A general rule of thumb from these studies was that L-band with HH polarization (L-HH) was better for flooded forests, and C-band with HH polarization (C-HH) was better for herbaceous wetlands (Kasischke *et al.* 1997).

Using polarized L-HH SAR data, flooded mangroves can be distinguished from non-flooded mangroves because the double bounce from the flooded mangroves produces a very different signal than the overall scattering observed for the non-flooded mangroves (Ramsey 1998). With multifrequency (L-band, C-band, and X-band) data, you can get information on hydrology, soil moisture, and vegetation type simultaneously.

The challenge in using SAR data is that the analysis of backscatter and polarization requires a different set of techniques from the analysis of multispectral data. Different software tools are needed. These are sometimes developed by the space agency operating the satellite, but still represent new tools to learn, even for someone experienced in other types of remote sensing. There are a number of different online tutorials to help a new user get started. Henderson and Lewis (2008) reviewed about 60 articles using SAR for mapping wetlands published since1998, a valuable resource for published studies. Not surprisingly, studies of the Amazon and major wetlands of the United States and Canada predominate the literature.

Henderson and Lewis (2008) also assess why some studies have been successful in using SAR to map wetlands, while others have not. A key factor for success is having a relatively simple environment to map, with fewer vegetation classes in fairly homogeneous patches. Unfortunately for ecological mapping, distinguishing flood areas from non-flooded areas is easier than distinguishing among wetland types. Another real challenge discussed by Henderson and Lewis is the lack of consistency or consensus for the recommended analysis techniques. If SAR data are suited to a mapping project, the best approach is to look for a study in a habitat as similar as possible to the one you are studying, and adopt those successful approaches as a model.

Ruan and Ren (2007) combined SAR and Landsat ETM + multispectral data to map palustrine wetlands and distinguish them from rice paddies along the shore of Hongze Lake, a large freshwater lake of significant importance to migratory birds in China. They used the digital numbers for six Landsat bands, the first four principal components from a PCA (Section 4.3.2), and a DEM in a classification and regression tree (CART) model developed with 1,500 field validation points. The CART-classified data were combined with a measure of the degree of SAR backscatter (classified as lowest, low, medium, and high), using a rules model, increasing the overall accuracy of the classification to 92.3 percent.

7.2.6 Using radar to map hurricane-related flooding

SAR is a key tool for mapping and monitoring floods (see also Chapter 9). In the context of flooded wetlands, Kiage et al. (2005) provide a review of the use of radar backscatter to map flooded areas. They describe their use of Radarsat-1 SAR to detect flooded areas in coastal Louisiana after the passage of Tropical Storm Isidore and Hurricane Lili in one week (September/October 2002). Images were C-band (5.6 cm wavelength) with HH polarization, with two images in the days prior to the hurricane, and one after. They filtered the images with a 3×3 pixel median filter to reduce noise, and then georeferenced to a Landsat TM image. Water level data from ground stations served as a source of ground reference data. Once the images were georeferenced, it was possible to use relatively simple "band math" (a mathematical operation with the digital numbers of two or more bands to create a new images) to detect changes in the imagery due to flooding. Flooded areas are associated with low radar backscatter because they have less surface roughness, so the simplest technique used by Kiage et al. (2005) was to identify dark areas in the radar image and assume they had all been inundated. They also used image differencing of the pixel digital numbers of images collected before and after the flooding. In the difference map, the brightest areas are those with a significant change in inundation. A third technique for comparing three dates of imagery was to assign the digital numbers from each date to a different color (red, green, and blue). In the resulting false color image, the hue of the color indicates the date of the change, while the intensity of the color represents the degree of the change. A fourth technique took the mean of the digital numbers in the two reference images and then subtracted this pixel value from the image after the hurricane. This final method was found to be the best for easily identifying the flooded areas. Because there was also radar backscatter caused by vegetation, the differencing methods above were better than use of a single radar image.

The imaging helped identify which wetlands had been most severely affected by the passage of the storms as possible remediation targets. Interestingly, Kiage *et al.* (2005) also did a preliminary analysis of Radarsat images of the flooding of New Orleans after Hurricane Katrina (August/September 2005), but the significant backscatter from reflection off of buildings made the radar data unsuitable for mapping the flooding. In this case, emergency response mapping was performed using multispectral data from SPOT.

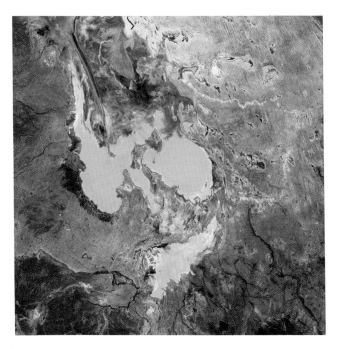

Fig. 7.5 Infrared bands can be used to highlight and distinguish water from land as shown in this Landsat ETM + image of Lake Eyre, Australia, showing the extremely rare (several times per century) inundation of this desert basin. The image is a 7, 4, 1 (shortwave infrared, near-infrared, and blue) false-color composite image (July 29, 1999). Credit: NASA Earth Observatory.

7.3 Shoreline mapping of lakes and rivers

If there is not too much interference with vegetation hiding the shoreline, multispectral imagery very easily identifies the interface between water and land (Fig. 7.5). For example, Landsat TM band 5 shows high contrast between land and water because mid-infrared light is strongly absorbed by water (even turbid water) and vegetation is strongly reflective in the same range (see also Fig. 6.12, step 3 for distinguishing reef from land). A histogram of TM band 5 has two sharp peaks due to these reflectance differences. If there are a large number of mixed pixels, the ratios of TM band 4/2 and 5/2 are good for delineating water boundaries (Frazier and Page 2000; Alesheikh *et al.* 2007).

Moore (2000) reviewed basic photogrammetric approaches to shoreline mapping with practical advice on how to match a technique to a project based on accuracy needed. For additional examples and approaches to using passive and active remote sensing to map flooding of lakes and rivers, see the section on floods (Section 9.3). Multiple teams of Russian scientists used photographic imaging from the *Mir* Space Station in studies of vegetation and shoreline change of the Caspian Sea (Lulla *et al.* 2000). Section 9.3 also summarizes the use of altimetry for monitoring lake height. Birkett and colleagues have a body of work using satellite laser altimetry as a tool for monitoring flooding of the Amazon (Birkett *et al.* 2002), and global lake heights such as the Aral Sea, Caspian Sea, Lake Issyk-Kul, and Lake Chad (e.g., Birkett [1994]; Birkett and Mason [1995]; Cretaux and Birkett [2006]).

7.4 Water quality mapping and monitoring

Approaches to water quality mapping include using multispectral, hyperspectral, and even radar imagery. Hyperspectral imaging overcomes the spectral limitations of multispectral sensors, and has great potential to aid understanding of water quality issues. Although the principles are basically the same as for ocean color (Section 6.2), the local complexities in understanding water quality of a specific system become increasingly challenging as you move along a continuum from open ocean to coastal ocean, to estuary, to freshwater lakes.

7.4.1 Hyperspectral remote sensing of water quality

Although there are no long-term operational hyperspectral sensors in orbit, a number of researchers have worked with experimental data from the Hyperion Imaging Spectrometer on the Earth Observing-1 platform. (Hyperion has been collecting requested data since 2001, with public acquisition requests accepted through the Earth Resources Observation and Science [EROS] data center. Requests from NASA-supported investigators are accepted directly by the NASA EO-1 Mission Science Office.) This instrument served as a pathfinder for future instrument development, and has 48 usable spectral bands in the visible and near-infrared. For water quality monitoring, periodic overflights of a satellite are more practical than regular airborne campaigns and it is likely that an operational hyperspectral sensor will eventually be placed in orbit. Brando and Dekker (2003) used Hyperion data to produce a full optical model of water quality in Moreton Bay, Australia, in a way analogous to the optical modeling that underlies standard ocean color products. They were able to map colored dissolved organic matter (CDOM), chlorophyll, and total suspended matter in these difficult "brown waters."

Scientists have adapted procedures used for mapping harmful algal blooms in oceans (Section 6.2.3) for understanding plankton and chlorophyll patterns in other waters. For example, Kallio *et al.* (2003) used an airborne image spectrometer (AISA), set to collect bands of 5–8 nm over the visible to near-infrared range of 450–750 nm, to estimate chlorophyll-*a* using a ratio of the near-infrared (700–710 nm) to red (660–665 nm) bands. This technique works well in oligotrophic to eutrophic lakes. In hypersaline lakes, such as the Dead Sea, Landsat TM data have been used successfully to identify green halophilic algae and red halophilic Archaea that bloom during periods of stratification (Oren and Ben-Yosef 1997). They used what is sometimes called the "algal index"—the ratio between Landsat TM bands 4 (near-infrared) and 3 (red). This index works because scattering reflectance in band 4 increases with algal concentration while absorption in band 3 also increases, and using the ratio reduces atmospheric effects.

7.4.2 Thermal mapping

Temperature is an important element of water quality in lakes and streams. Heat directly influences the biology of many aquatic organisms, and anthropogenic inputs of warm but clean water can have significant impacts on stream ecology. Thermal infrared imaging (TIR) is an option for monitoring thermal changes in rivers and streams. For example, Torgersen *et al.* (2001) studied thermal conditions in multiple watersheds in Oregon using an airborne forward-looking infrared system (capable of detecting thermal differences of $\pm 0.2°C$), accompanied by digital video imagery and field validation. They were able to map longitudinal patterns in stream temperature. Using ancillary data sets, the results gave insights into the factors that determined stream temperature including topography, riparian canopy, stream channel, water velocity, flow volume, and groundwater inputs.

It is also possible to use towed radar antennae to image the structure of the thermocline within lakes (Bradford *et al.* 2007, using a pulsed georadar system with linear dipole antennas operating at a frequency of 50 MHz with a corresponding wavelength of 0.65 m). The thermal boundary acted as a radar reflector and could be readily imaged from the towed system floating on the surface. This new methodology indicates the potential for future development in the area of radar monitoring of lake structure.

7.5 Summary

Just as the logistics of field sampling in wetlands can be challenging (picture yourself up to your hips in mud trying to collect a single ground validation point!), remote sensing in these areas also has unique challenges. The need to separate vegetation, sediment, soil, and water signatures has driven a lot of creativity and innovations in the use of remotely sensed data, and has stretched the bounds of the way many sensors are used, from radar and lidar to multi-spectral sensors. But it is also the challenges of doing field work in such important environments that makes remote sensing an asset—it provides the ability to make observations of ecological processes over broad spatial scales that might not otherwise be possible. Rather than settling for older map data, it is important to consider whether a newly developed map based on either satellite or airborne data might make important contributions to your application.

8

Atmosphere and climate

There is a compelling need for environmental managers to consider atmospheric and climatic impacts upon the systems they manage. Pounds *et al.* (2006) linked dramatic losses of frog species in the neotropical genus *Atelopus* to regional climate effects on the temperature and relative humidity of highland forests. They related frog disappearances to tropical air temperatures, finding that ~80 percent of the missing species were lost after relatively warm years. The strength of association between warm years and disappearing frogs was independent of elevation, latitude, or range size. Such an association of extinctions with warmer years leads to a paradox: the believed cause of death of the Atelopine frogs is chytridiomycosis due to outbreaks of the fungus *Batrachochytrium dendrobatidis*, but *Batrachochytrium* becomes more pathogenic at lower rather than higher temperatures. Pounds *et al.* posited a resolution to this paradox by coupling higher temperatures to increased evaporation rates resulting in more water vapor in the atmosphere. Higher atmospheric water vapor drives increased cloud cover over Monteverde and other sites where scientists observed disappearances. In this case, more clouds led to cooler days, because they reflected more solar radiation, but also to warmer nights as they decreased heat loss to the atmosphere. The net result was that the range of daily maximum and minimum temperatures was not only less but less in a way that favored chytrid fungi (which grow best at 17–25 °C). Preventing it from getting too hot by day or too cold at night, the increased clouds during warmer years kept the temperature "just right" for *Batrachochytrium* to infect frogs.

Conservation biologists recognize the significant impact that regional shifts in climate may have on populations of conservation concern (Hannah *et al.* 2005). However, much of the remote sensing work on the atmosphere and climate addresses global-scale phenomena, such as general circulation models (GCMs) of the atmosphere. Moving from these global scales to scales more appropriate to conservation work continues to be a significant challenge. Given that regional changes in climate and the resulting impacts on habitats and species of concern are difficult to predict, it is tempting simply to ignore the large set of observations available from atmospheric remote sensing and climate science as being too far removed from conservation.

While it may be challenging to bridge these disciplines, we believe it is necessary in order to provide unique opportunities to improve conservation management. There are three major reasons these bridges are important. The first goes back to fundamental principles of ecology. Climate, including temperature regime, precipitation, and cloud cover, determines many of the fundamental physical parameters that define the ecosystems we seek to understand and conserve. Second, for some species, atmospheric or climate data from remote sensing might provide critical insights that could dramatically change conservation planning. Finally, as understanding of the links between global and regional and local climate improves, we need to apply this understanding directly to ecosystem management. A central effort in the study of Earth system science has been the development of better sensors and observations to support ever more sophisticated climate models. As understanding moves from global to more regional and even local-scale processes, ecologists and conservation biologists will find immediate applications to the habitats and ecosystems in which they specialize.

We have designed this chapter and Appendix 6 to serve as an entrée to the very large field of atmospheric and climate remote sensing. Our objective is to provide enough information so that ecologists and conservation biologists will be aware of the types of data being collected and how they are used. We especially hope that by providing a primer, more ecologists and conservation biologists will have flashes of insight and find new applications for remotely sensed atmospheric data, climatic data, or associated climate models.

8.1 Climate and the physical environment

Those seeking to understand the geophysical drivers of populations, communities, or entire ecosystems of concern must confront the constraints and opportunities imposed by climate. Climate, defined as the average weather over time, largely determines the physical envelope in which all organisms exist. Climatic phenomena such as temperature, moisture, solar radiation, winds, and the resulting circulation of fresh and salt waters also provide the fundamental physical context for both biogeography and population ecology, two of the scientific pillars of conservation biology. Temperature is critical in setting the rates for the biochemical reactions that are the basis for life. The presence of liquid water is essential for life. And solar radiation in the form of visible light is necessary for photosynthesis—the primary energy source for life (Fig. 8.1). Robert Bailey, author of *Ecosystem Geography* and an early proponent of ecoregions as an organizing construct for conservation management, points to climate as the initial criterion in defining ecosystem boundaries and refers to it as the "prime controlling factor for ecosystems" (Bailey 1996).

Ecologists and conservation biologists cannot ignore climate. But how should we observe and try to understand climate and its impacts? Satellite imagery is an ideal tool, perhaps the preeminent tool, for gaining insights into weather and climate. Until the advent of satellite technology, the study of weather and climate

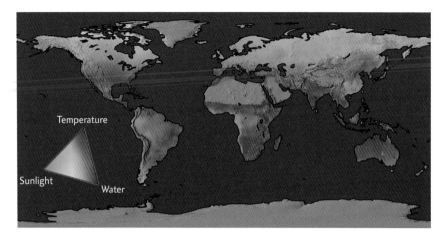

Fig. 8.1 The geographic distribution of potential climatic constraints to plant growth (and thus terrestrial net primary production) from various long-term climate statistics featuring temperature (in blue), water (in red), and sunlight (in green) as limiting factors; gray-colored areas are non-vegetated. (Adapted [modified] from Nemani *et al.* 2003 with permission from AAAS.)

depended upon ground observations and relatively brief measures taken from balloon- or rocket-borne instruments. Satellite imagery from space has revolutionized meteorology and climatology. Because it allows us to visualize radiation across the electromagnetic spectrum, satellite imagery can help us track the movement of heat (i.e., energy) and water (in visible clouds, invisible water vapor, and precipitation) in the atmosphere. The flows of energy and water fundamentally determine climate and, through climate, the conditions for life itself.

Of all the factors driving biodiversity loss, climate change is perhaps the least understood. Increasing our understanding requires us to become conversant in climatology. In 2007, the Intergovernmental Panel on Climate Change (IPCC) cited a global surface temperature increase of $0.74\,^{\circ}\text{C} \pm 0.18\,^{\circ}\text{C}$ from 1906 to 2005 with the rate of warming over the last 50 years almost double that for the entire 100-year period (Trenberth *et al.* 2007; Fig. 8.2). Furthermore, this report states that the equilibrium global mean surface air temperature warming resulting from a doubling of atmospheric carbon dioxide (CO_2) is likely (more than 66 percent probability) to lie within the range of 2.0–$4.5\,^{\circ}\text{C}$, with a most likely value of about $3\,^{\circ}\text{C}$ (Meehl *et al.* 2007). The timing of this warming depends upon the emission scenario (Fig. 8.3). The IPCC found it extremely likely (95 percent confidence or higher) that humans have exerted a substantial warming influence on climate since 1750 (Forster *et al.* 2007).

Analysis by Thomas *et al.* (2004) brought together the results of multiple modeling studies that assessed the impacts of different levels of climate change on

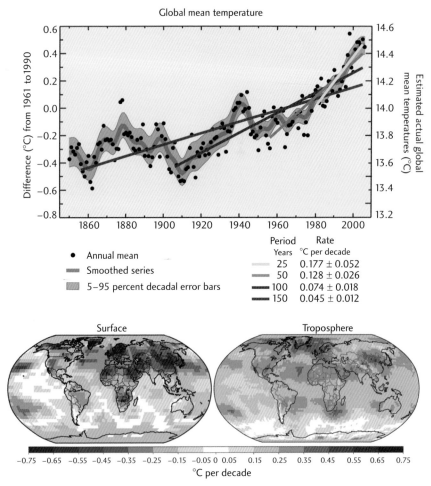

Fig. 8.2 Comparison of annual global mean observed temperatures (black dots, *top*) along with linear fits to the data. The left-hand axis shows anomalies relative to the 1961 to 1990 average temperature and the right-hand axis shows the estimated actual temperature (°C). Linear trend fits to the last 25 (yellow), 50 (orange), 100 (purple), and 150 years (red) are shown, and correspond to the periods 1981–2005, 1956–2005, 1906–2005, and 1856–2005, respectively. Note that for shorter recent periods, the slope is greater, indicating accelerated warming. The blue curve is a smoothed depiction to capture the decadal variations. To give an idea of whether the fluctuations are meaningful, decadal 5 to 95 percent error ranges about that line are given. The maps show global temperature trends from 1979 to 2005 estimated at the surface (*left*), and for the troposphere (*right*) from the surface to about 10 km altitude, from satellite sounder records. Gray areas indicate incomplete data. (Figure from Trenberth *et al.* 2007, with permission from Cambridge University Press.)

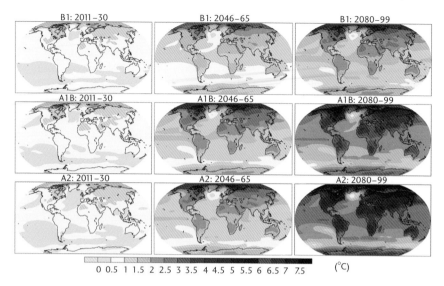

0 0.5 1 1.5 2 2.5 3 3.5 4 4.5 5 5.5 6 6.5 7 7.5 (°C)

Fig. 8.3 Multiple climate model mean result for annual mean surface warming (surface air temperature change, °C) for three different scenarios of greenhouse gas emission levels: B1 (*top*), A1B (*middle*), and A2 (*bottom*), and three time periods, 2011–30 (*left*), 2046–65 (*middle*), and 2080–99 (*right*). Each scenario assumes different emissions of greenhouse gases and the resulting radiative forcing: relatively low (B1), relatively moderate (A1B), and relatively high (A2). Temperature anomalies are relative to the average of the period 1980–99. (Figure from Meehl *et al.* 2007, with permission from Cambridge University Press.)

terrestrial species from a range of groups (plants, butterflies, frogs, reptiles, birds, mammals, etc.) in different geographical regions. They used minimal (0.8–1.7 °C), mid-range (1.8–2.0 °C), and high (>2.0 °C) scenarios of climate warming by the year 2050. In spite of concerns about the reliance on climate envelope modeling in the study, their results predicted that 18–35 percent (for minimal to high levels of warming) of terrestrial organisms in the regions affected would be committed to extinction, through irreversible population decline, as a result of climate change.

Predicting the effects of climate change on populations of organisms requires understanding the effects of temperature forcing on the water cycle. We use the term "forcing" to refer to a cause or an agent driving change(s) in a system. Water—whether in the form of clouds (liquid water and/or solid ice crystals), water vapor, surface waters, or surface snow and ice—has a dramatic effect on the amount of the Sun's radiation that reaches and is absorbed by the surface. Phase changes in water release or consume energy (which is known as latent heat) between Earth's surface and atmosphere (which is in turn known as the latent heat flux). This flux is the primary means by which the Earth system maintains, over time, a net radiative balance (Carleton 1991; Aguado and Burt 1999; Bonan 2002). Thus, Earth's interconnected energy and water cycles maintain a planetary homeostasis with regard to heat and water, enabling a global environment conducive to life, also known as the biosphere.

Because the heat capacity of water (i.e., the energy required to raise the temperature of a given amount of water by 1°C without a change in phase) is several times that of dry soils, the oceans serve as buffers of Earth's climate system (Mayes and Hughes 2004). Satellite images depicting day and night (or summer and winter) surface temperatures at the land/ocean interface demonstrate the higher heat capacity of the oceans and their resulting buffering potential in that ocean temperatures remain more constant than land temperatures. To a first order of approximation, atmospheric scientists seeking to understand and forecast Earth's weather and climate track water and electromagnetic radiation (in the form of heat), which moves this water.

Earth system science is the study of the Earth as an integrated system— including the flows of water and energy that determine the fundamental physical parameters that make the planet suitable for life. The discipline studying this integrated system should not be mistaken for the "lower case e" earth science that usually emphasizes geology. In the next few sections we will discuss the major indicators used to follow water and energy through the Earth system: clouds, aerosols, precipitation, winds, and temperature. For each indicator, we start with an example of the application of the data to conservation biology, provide a brief primer on its role in determining climate, and then provide an overview of how remote sensing is used in its measurement.

8.2 Clouds

Why should ecologists and conservation biologists concern themselves with clouds? Clouds are key drivers of temperature and the water cycle. For one example, we can return to the montane cloud forests of the neotropics, which contain high levels of species richness and endemism and are often areas of conservation concern. Work in Costa Rica (Lawton *et al.* 2001; Nair *et al.* 2003; Ray *et al.* 2006) has linked deforestation to changes in nearby tropical montane cloud forests through the medium of clouds. The researchers used 1 km spatial resolution visible imagery from the NOAA GOES system to map the frequency of cumulus cloud coverage on a per pixel basis over southern Nicaragua and Costa Rica. They also employed some higher spatial resolution Landsat imagery to check cumulus development. Their particular area of focus was the Cordillera de Tilaran range, which includes Costa Rica's Monteverde cloud forest. The team found cumulus cloud formation to be poor or completely absent over deforested areas in Costa Rica's Rio San Juan basin when compared to still-forested areas in neighboring Nicaragua. In addition, they employed the

Regional Atmospheric Modeling System of Colorado State University to run simulations of the atmospheric effects of different land covers: tropical evergreen forest and pasture. While both cover types resulted in cloud formation, the cloud base height (a critical measure for determining those areas that will be cloud covered on the ground) was a good deal lower over forest than over pasture during times of the day when the slopes would typically be shrouded in cloud. The authors suggested the mechanism for this change in cloud base height lay in reduced evapotranspiration after deforestation, which resulted in less moisture in the air flowing up the slopes of the mountains adjacent to the deforested lowlands. Higher cloud base heights can lead to cloud forests without clouds, and ultimately to the loss of species adapted to cloud forest conditions.

8.2.1 Clouds and climate

For those trying to observe the land surface by means of visual and infrared energy (the focus of much of this book), clouds are a problem to overcome because they obscure our view of Earth's surface. However, for atmospheric scientists seeking to view weather and climatic phenomena, clouds often become the object of observation. Clouds are so important because they are a visibly obvious driver and manifestation of the energy and water cycles that produce our climate.

Clouds, which consist of liquid water droplets and/or ice crystals, demonstrate the dual effects of water in the atmosphere. They reflect incoming solar radiation away from Earth's surface for a cooling albedo effect (albedo is the fraction of solar energy reflected by the Earth back into space). They also absorb some of the longer-wave radiation emitted by the Earth and in turn radiate some of this energy back to the Earth in a warming greenhouse effect.

Clouds cover roughly 68 percent of Earth's surface (Rossow and Schiffer 1999) (Fig. 8.4). Therefore, their impact on solar radiation's interaction with the Earth is great. Whether a cloud has a net cooling or net warming effect appears to depend on its altitude and optical thickness (i.e., a measure of how much light clouds intercept resulting from the thickness of the cloud and its vertical water or ice content; Carleton 1991). Different types of clouds correspond to different altitudes in the atmosphere and different weather phenomena. Appendix 6 covers operational and research systems designed to observe clouds from orbit. Tables A6.1 and A6.2 provide characterizations and images of the basic cloud types.

8.2.2 How cloud remote sensing works

The visible channels allow us to see most clouds and cloud edges, determining where clouds are present. The infrared channels, particularly those in the thermal infrared observing radiation emanating from the Earth system, measure the intensity (or brightness) of the thermal infrared emission from a cloud. This measure of the intensity of the radiation emitted by an object goes by the name

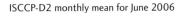

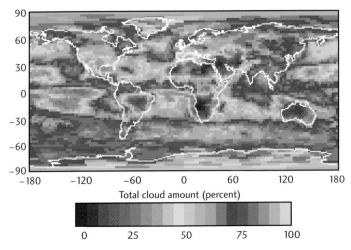

Fig. 8.4 Monthly mean total cloud amount for June 2006. A complete archive of cloud data sets is available online from the NASA Goddard Institute for Space Studies International Satellite Cloud Climatology Project (2007). Credit: International Satellite Cloud Climatology Project (ISCCP), NASA.

brightness temperature or radiative temperature and is different from the actual or kinetic temperature of the object (Mayes and Hughes 2004). Observations of cloud shape and texture in conjunction with cloud brightness temperature enable determination of cloud type. Cloud observers set threshold values for the radiances (i.e., the levels of brightness of the electromagnetic radiation received at the sensor) detected in the chosen visible and infrared channels and these enable a decision as to whether a particular pixel contains clouds or no clouds (Carleton 1991). Adjusting these threshold values can raise the sensitivity of a sensor to particular cloud types (Rossow and Schiffer 1999).

Combining visible and infrared imagery has long served as the basis for cloud detection and for separating detected clouds into various types. Bispectral methods classify clouds based upon the separation of dark and bright surfaces with visible band imagery in tandem with the separation of warm and cold surfaces with infrared imagery (Kidder and Vonder Haar 1995). These methods allow detection of low clouds (bright/warm), cloud-free areas (dark/warm), thin cirrus (dark/cold), and locations undergoing deep convection (bright/cold). Convection is the upward buoyant motion of gases and liquids heated from below, and it is also the main process of atmospheric heating during daytime hours (Mayes and Hughes 2004). Bispectral methods are a key tool in the development of cloud climatologies that contain information on cloud physical properties through time.

One of the longest running satellite-based cloud climatologies is the International Satellite Cloud Climatology Project (ISCCP), which the World Climate

Research Programme established in 1982. It began tracking cloud amounts and types globally in July 1983 using an international suite of satellite sensors. Figure 8.5 depicts the ISCCP cloud classification scheme, which uses cloud top pressure and cloud optical thickness measures derived from visible and infrared bands. The ISCCP makes 3-hourly monthly mean data sets available online for a large number of cloud parameters, including: total cloud amount, types of clouds, cloud top temperatures, cloud top pressures, cloud optical thickness, cloud water path (i.e., the column mass density of the cloud), as well as other atmospheric properties like tropopause and stratospheric temperatures and precipitable water at certain pressure levels (Kidder and Vonder Haar 1995; Rossow and Schiffer 1999).

As you go from cloud detection to cloud depiction, atmospheric imagery from operational satellites is typically presented in black and white. The convention among those producing cloud imagery products is to use a grayscale scheme to depict clouds in both visible and infrared channels in a similar manner so that

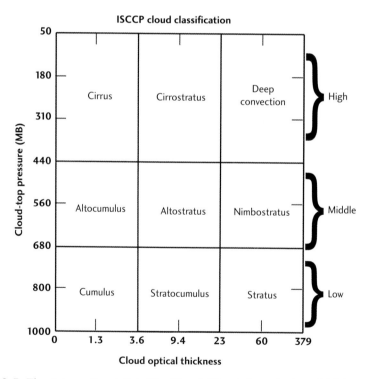

Fig. 8.5 The International Satellite Cloud Climatology Project (ISCCP) cloud classification scheme (NASA Goddard Institute for Space Studies International Satellite Cloud Climatology Project 2006). Credit: International Satellite Cloud Climatology Project (ISCCP), NASA.

higher and colder clouds appear as whiter while lower and warmer clouds show as grayer to blacker—whether you are looking at visible or infrared imagery. While this convention makes it easier to compare visible and infrared data, it does require displaying warmer clouds as darker even if they have higher brightness temperatures or thermal infrared radiances (Bader *et al.* 1995; Mayes and Hughes 2004). Some of the distinctive features of clouds when displayed by these conventions in satellite images are included in Table A6.1.

8.3 Aerosols

Aerosols or particulates are solid and/or liquid particles suspended in the atmosphere and range in size from ~2 nm to 1 mm (Mayes and Hughes 2004). They can arise from either natural or man-made sources. Natural sources include soil dust and sea salt (by far the largest sources of aerosol mass), volcanic emissions, sulfates from atmospheric chemical reactions, plant debris, soil organic matter, and microbial particles (pollen, bacteria, fungal spores, viruses, and algae). Industrial combustion and some biomass burning are significant human sources of aerosols (Bonan 2002). At smaller diameters (e.g., one μm and less), particles are just the right size to scatter and absorb incoming shortwave visible radiation from the sun. In fact, our blue sky is a manifestation of the Rayleigh scatter effect, whereby air molecules, but also atmospheric particles, scatter shorter wavelength light more readily than the light of longer wavelengths (Lillesand and Kiefer 1994). Thus, the shorter blue wavelengths of visible light scatter more than the other wavelengths, imparting their color to the sky around them.

The transatlantic transport of pathogens and contaminants within atmospheric dust may play a role in the decline of Caribbean coral reefs. This is the suggestion of Garrison *et al.* (2003) who posit that the deposition of particles from Africa may be the cause of significant damage to this marine ecosystem. They suggest that pathogenic microbes spread diseases and that chemical contaminants alter the resistance of coral reef organisms. Climatic drivers in the form of less intense convective disturbances and low rainfall in the Saharan region appear to be increasing the quantities of particles available for crossing the Atlantic Ocean. Imagery from the *Space Shuttle* and various satellites provides a unique visual record of these very large-scale events (Fig. 8.6).

Global movement of dust transports pesticides, fungal spores and rusts, and bacteria. The fungus *Aspergillus sydowii*, which cannot reproduce in seawater, has been implicated as a pathogen affecting sea fans or gorgonians (Griffin and Kellogg 2004). These authors also report that 10 percent of the microorganisms in Virgin Islands dust transport events were opportunistic human pathogens while 25 percent were plant pathogens. Fungal rust spores are especially strong candidates for long-distance aerial dispersal with their pathogens seeming to reestablish themselves in extinction–recolonization cycles in areas containing susceptible hosts, a survival strategy somewhat similar to that of migratory birds and insects (Brown and Hovmoller 2002). Of course, Caribbean dust

Fig. 8.6 Dust from a sandstorm blowing off northwest Africa. The dust plume covers hundreds of thousands of square miles as it is blowing west over the Atlantic Ocean (SeaWiFS, February 26, 2000). Credit: SeaWiFS Project, NASA/ GSFC and GeoEye.

events do not occur in isolation from other environmental phenomena. How the impacts of airborne pathogens combine with the stress of local anthropogenic effects and sea surface warming events to affect corals remains largely unknown.

Global transport of pollutant and natural (e.g., dust) aerosols is biologically important and also critical for understanding the radiative forcings in the Earth system. Estimates indicate that ~3 billion tons of soil move some distance within Earth's atmosphere each year and that a single gram of arid soil contains between 10,000 and 1,000,000,000 bacteria (Griffin 2005). The largest sources of atmospheric dust are the Sahara desert and Sahel region of North Africa and the Gobi, Taklamakan, and Badain Jaran deserts of Central Asia. The Sahara and Sahel contribute significant quantities of dust year-round (although in June through October the transport is to the mid-/northern Caribbean and North America while in November to May transport is to the mid-/southern Caribbean and South America). The Central Asian deserts launch most of their dust in the spring from February to May (Griffin and Kellogg 2004).

8.3.1 Aerosols and climate

Aerosols both directly and indirectly affect Earth's radiation budget (i.e., the balance of incoming and outgoing radiation). They do so directly by scattering solar radiation away from the Earth, thus cooling the planet's surface, or by trapping the longer wavelength radiation emitted by the Earth and preventing it from escaping into space, which results in a warming of Earth's surface. Indirectly, aerosols affect the planet's radiation balance and its water cycle by serving as the condensation nuclei for cloud formation; and clouds, of course, have their own significant impacts on radiation and water (Aguado and Burt 1999). In fact, we should consider aerosols the progenitors of clouds. However, clouds also affect aerosols in complicated ways by adding mass and, in some cases, directly forming new aerosols. Conversely, aerosol absorption of shortwave radiation leads to atmospheric heating that influences cloud formation and lifetime (Forster *et al.* 2007). Thus, clouds and aerosols are tightly coupled and it is difficult to understand the radiative forcing impacts of one without understanding the properties of the other.

As is the case with clouds, much uncertainty exists as to whether aerosols have a net cooling or net warming impact on surface temperatures once all their effects have been combined. Arriving at reliable estimates of the net radiative impacts of aerosols is no small matter given the lack of homogeneity in their temporal and spatial distributions in the atmosphere, which leads to pronounced regional and seasonal variability (Forster *et al.* 2007). In general, atmospheric aerosol lifetimes are only a week or less with smaller particles remaining in the atmosphere longer and larger particles falling out more rapidly (Ramanathan *et al.* 2001). Figure 8.7 depicts our understanding of the relative radiative forcing (both warming and cooling) effects of various environmental parameters and points to the relatively high levels of uncertainty surrounding the effects of aerosols. Research shows aerosols likely having a net cooling effect (Kaufman *et al.* 2002; Forster *et al.* 2007).

To make progress in understanding the impacts of human actions and natural changes on global temperature patterns, we need to reduce the uncertainty as to the effects of aerosols on climate. However, Anderson *et al.* (2003) point out that even assuming the highest possible values for aerosol negative forcing (i.e., a net cooling effect), their short lifetimes mean that relative to greenhouse gases, which have very long atmospheric lifetimes, aerosols do not accumulate in the atmosphere. Thus, the positive forcing (i.e., net warming effect) of greenhouse gases should exceed any potential aerosol cooling effect between the years 2030 and 2050. Interestingly, there also appears to be a "semi-direct effect" of aerosols on Earth's radiation budget due to the inhibition of afternoon cumulus cloud formation by smoke particles, which results in a net warming effect at that time of day (Koren *et al.* 2004).

The effect of aerosols on precipitation is even more poorly understood than their effects on temperature through radiative forcing. Precipitation does not occur or is delayed in polluted clouds and is suppressed by desert dust (Ramanathan *et al.* 2001; Kaufman *et al.* 2002). Ramanathan *et al.* (2001) contend that aerosols result in a "spinning down" of the hydrological cycle. This occurs for two reasons: (1) aerosol-induced reductions in surface solar radiation due to scattering and absorption lead to less surface heat and surface-driven convection

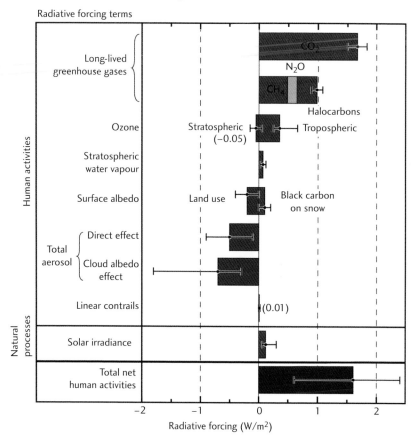

Fig. 8.7 Summary of principal components of the radiative forcing of climate change. All of these radiative forcings result from one or more factors that affect climate and are associated with human activities or natural processes. The values represent the forcings in 2005 relative to the start of the industrial era (about 1750). Human activities cause significant changes in long-lived gases, ozone, water vapor, surface albedo, aerosols, and contrails. The only increase in natural forcing of any significance between 1750 and 2005 occurred in solar irradiance. Positive forcings lead to warming of climate and negative forcings lead to cooling. The thin black line attached to each colored bar represents the range of uncertainty for the respective value. (Figure from Forster *et al.* 2007, with permission from Cambridge University Press.)

and (2) suppression of precipitation by aerosols due to their creation of many more small cloud droplets that coalesce less efficiently (NASA 2005a).

The climatic effects of aerosols depend upon whether they are in the stratosphere or the troposphere. Tropospheric aerosols are approximately 1000 times

MODIS AOT 8 year

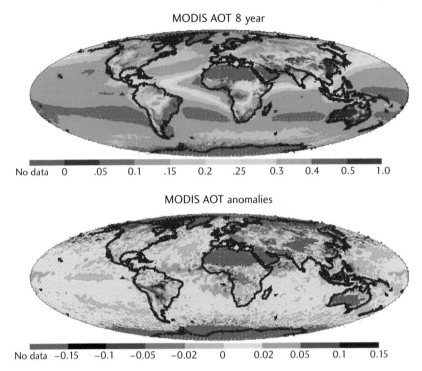

No data   0   .05   0.1   .15   0.2   .25   0.3   0.4   0.5   1.0

MODIS AOT anomalies

No data −0.15   −0.1   −0.05   −0.02   0   0.02   0.05   0.1   0.15

Fig. 8.8 Global mean aerosol optical depth from MODIS over 8 years (*top*, called AOT or aerosol optical thickness) and the deviation between the 8-year mean and the 2007 annual mean (*bottom*) as observed by the MODIS sensor aboard the Terra satellite. In the 8-year mean (*top*) high aerosol regions over northern and central Africa, southern and eastern Asia, parts of Central and South America, and oceanic regions down wind of these "hot spots" are shown in red. The anomalies plot (*bottom*), shows the impact of biomass burning in South America in 2007 with smoke spreading southward from the deforestation zone at 0–10° S latitude to coastal Uruguay and northern Argentina (in red). Biomass burning smoke in Indonesia and Central Africa was anomalously low in 2007 compared to the 8-year mean (blue). Eastern China shows a strong positive anomaly in 2007, with higher annual mean AOT than its already high 8-year mean. Credit: Richard Kleidman, Lorraine Remer, and Shana Mattoo, NASA Climate, NASA/GSFC.

more abundant than those in the stratosphere and are the primary drivers of radiative forcing (Kidder and Vonder Haar 1995). However, stratospheric aerosols can have a dramatic, if temporary, cooling effect on global climate following exceptionally large volcanic eruptions that inject large amounts of dust into the stratosphere where strong winds spread them quickly around the globe. The 1991 eruption of Mt Pinatubo in the Philippines is an example of such a dramatic occurrence in which stratospheric injection and winds aloft transformed the typically regional effects of aerosol emissions into an event of truly global impact (Bonan 2002).

8.3.2 Aerosols and biological productivity

In addition to their large role in determining Earth's radiative balance and their role as a potential source of pathogens, aerosols are important biologically because dust includes nutrients (iron, phosphates, and organic detritus) that may fertilize and raise the productivity of relatively nutrient-poor environments such as the central ocean regions (Barber and Chavez 1991). Behrenfeld *et al.* (1996) demonstrated that the Eastern Equatorial Pacific Ocean, an area characterized as high-nutrient (nitrate and phosphate) but low-chlorophyll (low phytoplankton biomass), is limited by a lack of iron. The IronEx II experiment documented that an increase in iron availability can stimulate phytoplankton productivity. A companion article (Turner *et al.* 1996) on this experiment showed that iron fertilization can have feedback effects on aerosol production and the sulfur cycle through the generation of sulfate particles. These particles then have their own climate impacts. Marine plankton are a major source of sulfate particles through their generation of the sulfate precursor dimethyl sulfide (DMS). Iron fertilization produced a marked increase in DMS concentrations through the stimulation of phytoplankton production.

In contrast to the Pacific, productivity in the North Atlantic Ocean appears to be more limited by nitrogen than iron. Pahlow and Riebesell (2000) showed that an anthropogenic increase in atmospheric nitrogen could account for an increase in the nitrogen–phosphorus ratio in that region. As the foundation of the trophic web, phytoplankton production is a fundamental factor determining the productivity of entire marine ecosystems.

Nutrients in dust may also affect terrestrial primary productivity in some nutrient-limited systems. Swap *et al.* (1992) concluded that part of the productivity of the Amazon rain forest depends upon trace elements contained in soil dust transported atmospherically from the Sahara desert and Sahelian regions of Africa. This raises the questions: could the incredible diversity of the tropical Amazon have roots in the transatlantic deposition of vital trace elements from the xeric regions of northern Africa and how has this deposition changed through time?

8.3.3 How aerosol remote sensing works

Combinations of visible and/or infrared imagery allow the detection of the aerosol optical depth of tropospheric aerosols. Aerosol optical depth (AOD) is a measure of atmospheric visibility or of how much light passes through a particular column of atmosphere (Fig. 8.8). The trick in determining aerosol optical depth is to isolate and define the fraction of radiance scattered by aerosols. You need to distinguish radiance from the surface from radiation scattered by aerosols. Thus, aerosol detection is easier over dark surfaces that do not reflect radiation (Kidder and Vonder Haar 1995; Mayes and Hughes 2004). Darker surfaces, like oceans and forests, allow better quantification of the scattering from particles and hence better measures of AOD (King *et al.* 1999). Early measures of AOD by the AVHRR sensor and sensors on the GOES and Meteosat satellites tended to rely on single wavelength observations of aerosols and focused on acquisitions over the oceans or dark land targets (Kaufman *et al.* 2002; Yu *et al.* 2006). Another heritage data set for aerosols comes from the NASA Total Ozone Mapping Spectrometer (TOMS) sensor and its use of ultraviolet channels that are particularly sensitive to light-absorbing aerosols. The French space agency Centre National d'Études Spatiales (CNES) developed the first satellite sensor devoted to taking aerosol observations over ocean and land, using measurements of light polarization. It is called POLDER (Polarization and Directionality of the Earth's Reflectances) and provides information on aerosol shape and composition.

Visual interpretation of satellite imagery can also add insight into aerosol transport. For example, SeaWiFS on the US commercial SeaStar satellite (also known as OrbView-2) was designed for monitoring ocean color. However, its images of dust plumes moving off the Sahara desert and out over the Atlantic Ocean have had a profound effect upon our appreciation of the transoceanic nature of these aerosol processes. For the ecologist or conservation biologist, useful aerosol data likely include imagery from a sensor like SeaWiFS that shows the location and direction of transport of dust and smoke plumes. Appendix 6 contains additional information on systems used to detect and measure characteristics of aerosols.

8.4 Precipitation

Water is an essential ingredient for life on Earth. Precipitation is that component of the water (or hydrologic) cycle in which water travels from the atmosphere to Earth's surface. Thus, precipitation ought to have some predictive power among the cluster of environmental variables often used to model the distribution of organisms.

Raxworthy *et al.* (2003) modeled the distribution of 11 chameleon species in Madagascar. Their tool was the Genetic Algorithm for Rule-set Prediction (GARP), a modeling approach that delineates ecological niches and allows prediction of geographic distributions of species. GARP brings together both environmental information, from either *in situ* or satellite sources, and species occurrence data from natural history collections and field surveys to generate rules outlining ecological niche spaces. In this case, Raxworthy *et al.* used precipitation data derived from the Meteosat geostationary satellite and ground-based rain gauges, along with land cover, topography, hydrology, and other climatological information, for the environmental layers. This information in conjunction with post-1988 species locality data resulted in an 85 percent success rate for predicting the presence and absence of the chameleon species. Some cases in which the models predicted the distributions of species in areas where they simply did not occur (i.e., areas of overprediction) led to the discovery of at least seven new species congeneric with those initially used in the models for the overpredicted areas. The conservation implications of this discovery are profound in that the Government of Madagascar was in the process of increasing its land area under protection, making information about areas of herpetological endemism extremely useful (Bates 2004).

8.4.1 The basics of precipitation

Precipitation occurs when cloud droplets, the constituents of clouds, grow large enough to overcome updrafts and fall to the surface before evaporation takes place. Natural and man-made aerosols provide cloud condensation nuclei upon which cloud droplets form. The type of precipitation experienced on the ground (rain, snow, etc.) depends upon the temperature of the atmosphere through which the precipitation falls on its way to Earth's surface. Aguado and Burt (1999) and Mayes and Hughes (2004) are good references for understanding the climatology of precipitation.

Whether rain or snow, precipitation typically comes from one of two types of clouds: (1) stratiform clouds, which are often located along frontal layers and horizontally continuous covering relatively broad areas of stable air, and (2) cumulonimbus clouds, which are vertically developed and produced by convective uplift, usually in unstable atmospheric conditions (Bader *et al.* 1995; Mayes and Hughes 2004). From above, convective precipitation tends to appear in relatively small, intense cells or cell clusters, which are several kilometers in diameter and may be either isolated clouds or bright spots within layered clouds. Stratiform precipitation, on the other hand, comes from long bands of clouds that are sometimes hundreds of kilometers long and $\sim$2–100 km in width (Bader *et al.* 1995). Local topography plays an important role in cloud formation. Precipitation is usually greatest on the upwind side of hills and mountains and decreases on the lee side, the side sheltered from the wind (Bader *et al.* 1995). This phenomenon gives rise to the rain shadow effect of clear skies and higher temperatures on the lee sides of upland areas (Mayes and Hughes 2004).

8.4.2 Ground-based radar

Ground-based radars occupy the vital intermediate position between rain gauges and satellite imagery for measuring precipitation. Radars detect rain and snow because the drops and ice crystals are large enough to scatter the electromagnetic energy pulses emitted by the radar as they travel back to the receiver. The droplets and ice crystals in clouds, on the other hand, are too small to backscatter energy at the long radar wavelengths, which are typically in the 5–10 cm range. Rain drops scatter radar pulses much better than the ice crystals of snowflakes (Kidder and Vonder Haar 1995). The radars most sensitive to snow send out pulses with wavelengths of 3 cm (Bader *et al.* 1995).

Ground-based weather radars transmit from a fixed point. Their beams increase in width and height as they extend outward from the transmitter. The vertical pattern of the backscattered echo from the precipitation helps meteorologists classify it as stratiform, convective, or a severe storm (Bader *et al.* 1995). Depending on the country, ground-based radar coverage ranges from nearly complete over populated areas to extremely sparse. In the United States, NOAA's National Weather Service relies upon a national network of Doppler radars, the NEXRAD network. Doppler radars take advantage of the fact that horizontal motions of the droplets or ice crystals shift the wavelength (and thus the frequency) of the backscattered echo returned to the radar, enabling not only the tracking of the storm movement but also measurement of wind speed and direction (Kidder and Vonder Haar 1995; Aguado and Burt 1999).

Ground-based radars face a number of challenges. They can miss low-altitude precipitation that may fall under the beam or miss low-level evaporation of precipitation due to a dry layer of air at the surface. Hills or other features block radar beams. Transient objects, such as aircraft, birds, or insects, may result in a backscatter signal. Temperature inversion layers (locations in the troposphere where temperature increases with altitude) can refract a radar beam downward causing it to pick up increased ground clutter. Secondary echoes from a previous pulse backscattered by a target outside a radar's range occasionally return to the radar receiver after the transmission of the next pulse, confounding the operator with a false-elongated echo (Burroughs 1991; Bader *et al.* 1995). Despite these challenges, ground-based radars are an extremely important tool for meteorology and climatology as satellite approaches to precipitation estimation and measurement depend heavily on them for calibration and interpretation.

Researchers have demonstrated the utility of Doppler weather surveillance radars (as well as other ground-based radars) for improving our understanding of bird migration (Fig. 8.9). Gauthreaux and Belser (2003, 2005) used radars to map migratory stopover areas and bird movements to and from these areas. They then compared these migration stopover maps with land cover maps derived from classified Landsat imagery. They found along the coastal plain of the northern Gulf of Mexico and Atlantic Ocean that stopover areas tend to be in riverine flood plains with upland areas used less and bottomlands used almost exclusively by the migrants. The widespread Doppler radar network, in conjunction with data from older weather radars, also allows mapping of the distribution and abundance patterns of bird migrants over time for the entire United States, providing season-to-season and year-to-year variations. Gauthreaux and Belser (2003) documented a significant decline in the number of migrant flights along the Texas and Louisiana coasts between three years in the mid-1960s and three years in the late 1980s.

8.4.3 How remote sensing of precipitation works

Detection of precipitation by satellite remote sensing of visible and infrared radiation is very challenging because only a small fraction of clouds generate precipitation at any one time. In addition, precipitation is patchy even within the confines of a given storm system. In the tropics year-round and in humid areas of

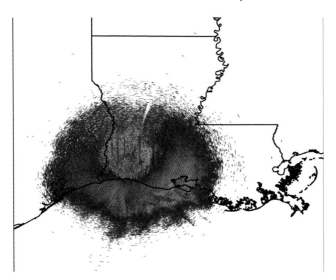

Fig. 8.9 Migratory land birds arriving in coastal Louisiana, USA, after a flight across the Gulf of Mexico near the peak of the spring migration lead to a strong signal (bright pink crescent) in NEXRAD Level II radar data collected at Lake Charles, Louisiana, USA on April 22, 1999 (18:26 UTC). Credit: National Wetlands Research Center, USGS.

the mid-latitudes during spring, summer, and fall, rain tends to arise from vertical convective processes. During frontal passage in the mid-latitudes and higher latitude areas, horizontal or advective processes tend to dominate precipitation formation. Therefore, remote sensing techniques that perform well in the tropics may not be suitable for higher latitudes (Carleton 1991; Kidder and Vonder Haar 1995). Also, since the visible and infrared radiation detected by many satellite sensors cannot penetrate thick clouds, the sensors cannot see precipitation falling from the bottom of clouds.

There are two choices for tracking precipitation with satellite remote sensing: indirect methods and direct methods. Indirect methods rely on the use of visible and infrared satellite imagery to view clouds from above and form relationships between cloud type and meteorological conditions in order to determine which clouds are likely to be raining or snowing and then estimate precipitation rates. Direct methods take advantage of two remote sensing technologies: (1) passive microwave radiometers that measure the brightness temperature of the precipitation and (2) active microwave radars that measure radiation backscattered from the precipitation itself, like ground-based radars. Both direct methods use microwave wavelengths capable of penetrating clouds (Burroughs 1991).

8.4.3.1 Indirect remote sensing of precipitation in the visible and infrared

Indirect methods of estimating precipitation use visible and infrared imagery, typically from geostationary satellites to take advantage of their frequent views of the clouds. These techniques work best for convective, as opposed to stratiform, precipitation. Three broad categories of techniques are used: cloud indexing, bispectral techniques, and life history methods. Kidder and Vonder Haar (1995) and Carleton (1991) contain good descriptions of these approaches.

Cloud indexing builds upon our ability to classify clouds according to type and assigns rain rates to these various cloud types. Visible imagery tends to work best for tropical, convection-oriented systems while infrared imagery tends to lead to better estimates in mid-latitudes, which are often characterized by advection or horizontal movement.

Bispectral techniques for precipitation are similar to the bispectral methods used in cloud detection and the development of cloud climatologies. They rely upon the combination of visible imagery for brightness and infrared imagery for cold versus warm designation. Bright (thick) clouds tend to precipitate more often than dark (thin) clouds. Although there are exceptions, cold clouds are more likely to precipitate than warm clouds. In general, clouds that are both cold and bright are most likely to yield precipitation. Bispectral techniques have been successful for separating weaker from more intense monsoons and tend to outperform the use of either visible or infrared data by themselves.

Life history techniques apply our knowledge of the developmental stages of clouds during their life cycles. For convective clouds, rain rates differ with the stages of the life cycle. Precipitation rates peak during the time when a cloud is rapidly growing and actually decline once it reaches maximum area. Life history approaches require geostationary imagery because high temporal resolution is necessary to get as many looks as possible at the developing clouds.

For convective clouds, high positive correlations also exist between cloud area, as detected by visible and infrared wavelengths, and the total volume of rainfall over a given amount of time. On the other hand, little correlation is evident between the visible brightness or the infrared temperature of a particular point in a convective cloud and the rain rate beneath that point (Kidder and Vonder Haar 1995). This latter issue underscores the limitations of indirect methods in that no relationship between visible and infrared measures and precipitation works at all times and in all places. Nevertheless, averaging estimates over a number of days can reduce the errors of precipitation estimates (Carleton 1991).

8.4.3.2 Precipitable water and snow cover

In addition to their use for the indirect estimation of precipitation, visible and infrared satellite imagery provide other data products relevant to understanding the water cycle. These include measures of total precipitable water and snow cover. Total precipitable water is the amount of liquid water, often measured in millimeters or centimeters, contained within a column of atmosphere if all the gaseous water vapor in that column were condensed to its liquid phase (NASA 2008d; University of Wisconsin 2008). Thus, it is an important measure of atmospheric water vapor, a vital precursor for precipitation.

Total precipitable water measurements, derived from water vapor bands and other infrared wavelengths, are available for the continental United States from the sounders on the NOAA GOES satellites. The European Meteosat's SEVIRI imager also produces a European and North African regional total precipitable water data product. Polar-orbiting sensors produce less frequent total precipitable water products. These include two research sensors: MODIS aboard the Terra and Aqua satellites (the MOD 05 product) and the NASA Atmospheric Infrared Sounder (AIRS) sensor, a revolutionary high-spectral resolution sounder with over 2000 channels aboard the Aqua satellite. Other total precipitable water products from polar-orbiting satellite sensors typically combine infrared imagery with passive microwave radiometer data. See Table A6.5 for more information on these products.

Snow and ice cover have very high albedos, reflecting much solar energy back into space. Snow also exhibits high infrared emissivity (i.e., a fraction or percentage expressing how efficient an object is at emitting radiation), which leads to rapid cooling and lower surface temperatures at night (Burroughs 1991; Aguado and Burt 1999). Thus, snow and ice have significant impacts on global, regional, and local energy balances. NOAA has generated snow and ice cover maps of the northern hemisphere since 1966, making these maps the longest satellite-derived environmental data set available (Ramsay 1998). NASA MODIS now provides maps of global snow cover (as well as ice cover on large inland water bodies). Table A6.5 also contains more information on snow and ice products.

8.4.3.3 Direct remote sensing of precipitation with microwaves

Direct methods of precipitation estimation rely on both the absorption and scattering of the microwave wavelengths by precipitation (microwaves are longer relative to visible and infrared wavelengths). Because microwaves are unaffected by the smaller droplets of non-precipitating clouds, such clouds are essentially transparent to microwave systems. Carleton (1991) and Kidder and Vonder Haar (1995) provide more detailed descriptions of the physics of passive and active microwave remote sensing.

Passive microwave systems detect precipitation by measuring its attenuation of the microwave radiation being emitted by Earth's surface, through the mechanism of changes in brightness temperature at the sensor. This is radiation of roughly 0.1 to 10 cm in wavelength corresponding to frequencies of 300 to 3 gigahertz (GHz, radar specifications are usually provided using frequency rather than wavelength). Ice scatters radiation while liquid precipitation both absorbs and scatters it—with absorption dominating. Both absorption and scattering increase with the frequency of the radiation sensed and with the rate at which it is raining. Ice scattering increases more rapidly as frequency increases than does scattering by rain. Based on these physical realities, passive microwave radiometry of precipitation focuses on three areas of the microwave portion of the electromagnetic spectrum. At frequencies below 22 GHz, absorption dominates while at those above ~60 GHz, scattering dominates. At frequencies between 22 and 60 GHz, both absorption and scattering play a role. Thus, below 22 GHz, atmospheric ice is largely transparent to the sensor and measurements are more sensitive to rain; above 60 GHz, measurements are more sensitive to ice.

Challenges for passive microwave remote sensing include cloud droplets, water vapor, and atmospheric oxygen, all of which can absorb microwave radiation and confuse precipitation estimates. Another major challenge is the large footprint or coarse ground spatial resolution of microwave radiometers. The measurement footprint is typically on the order of tens of kilometers. This large footprint is necessary because the longer the wavelength, the larger the antenna required to sense it (Kidder and Vonder Haar 1995). The trouble with large microwave footprints is the resulting large pixel sizes, which are almost certain to include several precipitation rates and potentially areas of no precipitation within any given pixel's brightness temperature measurement. So, most pixels showing precipitation are mixed pixels that contain areas of precipitation and areas without precipitation. Even those areas completely covered with precipitation often include precipitation occurring at various rates within the pixel.

Another challenge in using microwave remote sensing is distinguishing precipitation over land from soil moisture and standing water bodies such as lakes. To distinguish these, passive microwave radiometers take measurements in both horizontal and vertical polarizations. An ecological bonus of this approach is the ability to make coarse-resolution soil moisture measures with the microwave data (Fig. 8.10). This can be useful for understanding water and energy cycles as well as determining soil and vegetation properties. Soil moisture products from microwave radiometers rely on the high radiation emittance of dry soils and the low emittance from water surfaces to detect the lower and polarized emittances of wet soils (Kidder and Vonder Haar 1995). Microwave radiometers are also the source for long-term records of changing sea ice, perhaps the bellwether of climate change most readily appreciated by the public (Fig. 8.11). These sea ice records are an indispensable long-term climate data product derived from remote sensing. Appendix 6 describes systems for the direct remote sensing of precipitation.

8.4.4 A caveat regarding precipitation products

Unfortunately, the coarse spatial resolutions of most satellite precipitation products are difficult to relate to the scale of most field sites. Ground spatial resolutions for precipitation products are often on the order of several kilometers for the optical (visible and infrared) and active microwave systems and on the order of tens of kilometers for the passive microwave systems. If you require higher resolution data for your particular sites, a rain gauge is likely the best option. However, satellite data still provide the broader precipitation context in space and time, and may also provide historical information not otherwise available.

Aqua AMSR-E   August 20, 2008 ascending

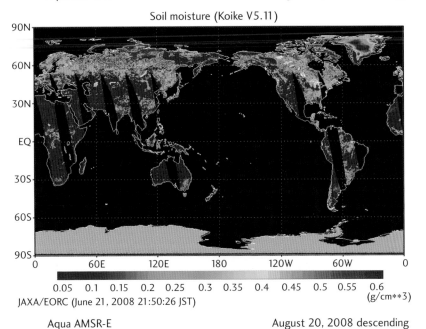

JAXA/EORC (June 21, 2008 21:50:26 JST)

Aqua AMSR-E   August 20, 2008 descending

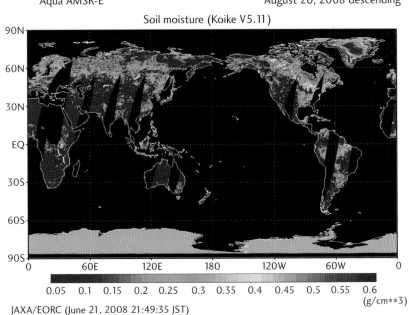

JAXA/EORC (June 21, 2008 21:49:35 JST)

Fig. 8.10 Soil moisture products are derived from data acquired by the Japanese AMSR-E sensor onboard the NASA Aqua satellite. The two images represent data collected during the ascending (top image) and descending (bottom image) orbits on June 20, 2008. Images © JAXA/Earth Observation Research Center (EORC), used with permission.

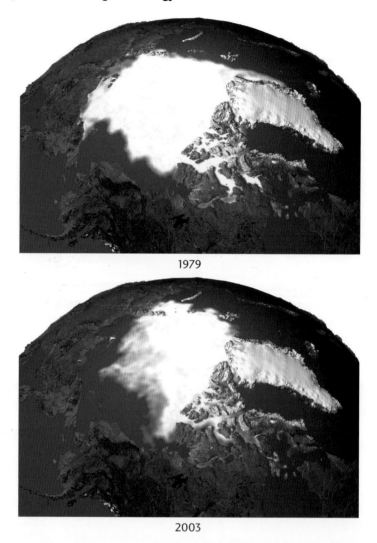

1979

2003

Fig. 8.11 Two images show significant differences in Arctic minimum sea ice in 1979 and 2003 (Comiso 2003). The images are derived from the SSM/I imager aboard the polar-orbiting DMSP satellites. Credit: Scientific Visualization Studio, NASA/GSFC and NASA Earth Observatory.

8.4.5 Global precipitation climatology product

In 1986, the World Climate Research Programme established the Global Precipitation Climatology Project (GPCP) with a goal of providing monthly mean global precipitation data on a $2.5° \times 2.5°$ latitude–longitude grid extending from 1979 to the present. The primary satellite observations for the GPCP are data from the polar-orbiting passive microwave radiometers, but also include

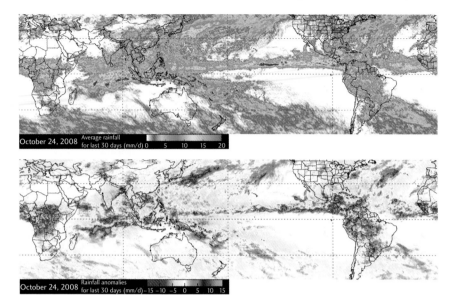

Fig. 8.12 Estimates of average rainfall (top) and rainfall anomalies (bottom) for the 30-day interval before October 24, 2008 are calculated using data from TRMM sensors. The anomalies are developed by comparison to the average value for the same period over the entire TRMM archive, which started in 1998 (NASA Goddard Space Flight Center 2009). Credit: Tropical Rainfall Measuring Mission, NASA/GSFC.

TRMM data (Fig. 8.12). However, infrared imagery from the geostationary satellites of the United States, Europe, and Japan is also part of the mix. Monthly mean data are available from 1979 to the present, as well as five-day pentads. Daily precipitation products extend back to 1997 (Robert Adler, personal Communication, 2006). Information on GPCP products is available on the Web.

8.4.6 Feedbacks between vegetation and precipitation

Rainfall and winter snowpack are major factors driving terrestrial primary production and the cycling of water is a fundamental property of ecosystems. However, biological systems are not merely passive recipients of moisture from the physical climate system; they also affect precipitation.

Satellite imagery has enabled us to monitor cloud formation and land cover and also to relate land cover and its changes to clouds. However, clouds alone do not necessarily result in precipitation. Convection is often necessary. Bonan (2002) describes the connections among precipitation, soil moisture, and evapo-transpiration. Vegetation cover, vegetation type, and soil moisture both influence, and are influenced by, precipitation. Evapotranspiration is the loss of water to the atmosphere from the land surface arising from a combination of direct evaporation from soils and transpiration from plant leaves. Impacts of vegetation on the atmosphere include higher leaf area index (Section 4.3) values' resulting in increased evapotranspiration in vegetated regions during the summer season, provided there is sufficient soil water available. Increased evapotranspiration cools Earth's surface and can lead to increased precipitation. Lower leaf area index values tend to produce the opposite effect, a warmer surface, and less precipitation. Deeper roots, which allow plants more reliable access to water, can also generate a cooler and wetter climate.

Albedo is an important component of the link between vegetation and precipitation. In general, vegetation has relatively low albedo values, with forest albedos less than those of grasslands and croplands which, in turn, are less than the albedos of highly reflective deserts. Thus, pastures created by the clearing of forests usually have higher albedo values than the forests that preceded them. These values can result in warmer and drier local climate due to decreased evapotranspiration, but the temperature story is complicated as you also need to factor in the cooling effects of the increased albedos in pastures (Bonan 2008). Another factor promoting warmer and drier climate is the decline in surface roughness once you go from forest to pasture. Decreased surface roughness means less surface turbulence resulting in generally lower transfers of both latent and sensible heat (sensible heat is heat transferred by the movement of air due to a temperature difference) to the atmosphere. To take matters a step farther, when dryland vegetation gives way to unvegetated areas, albedo increases and evapotranspiration goes down, further reducing precipitation in a feedback effect (Bonan 2002).

Different land covers with different albedos can induce increases in circulation at the boundaries of surface types, which can, in turn, generate precipitation. Models of mixed forest–farm landscapes produce convection not seen in models of areas with homogeneous vegetation (Bonan 2002). Anthes (1984) hypothesized that planting semiarid lands with alternating bands of dense vegetation on the order of 50–100 km in width would result in differential heating of the atmosphere resulting in mesoscale (20–200 km) circulations leading to significant increases in convective rainfall.

Pielke *et al.* (1999) modeled the effects of human-driven land cover change in south Florida on precipitation in that region. Their primary tool was the Regional Atmospheric Modeling System with which they ran simulations for the months of July and August. Model runs simulated two-month deep cumulus precipitation based upon the different land cover conditions in 1900, 1973, and 1993. Their model results showed a substantial impact on the hydrology of the region from landscape change. From 1900 to 1973, there was a 9 percent reduction in precipitation, with an 11 percent reduction from 1900 to 1993. Changes in land cover altered the spatial pattern of evapotranspiration resulting in a reduction in water flux to the atmosphere and less precipitation in the interior of the Florida peninsula. Unfortunately, limited ground-based measures of precipitation dating back to 1900 made validation of these modeling results difficult. Nonetheless, this work and that of many others demonstrate the importance of considering land cover when forecasting changes in climate.

Through observations and models, Webb *et al.* (2005) looked at the impact of declining forest cover on precipitation in Brazil's São Paulo state from 1962 to 1992. For measures of rainfall, they used monthly summaries of the number of rain days, total rainfall, and maximum daily rainfall from ground-based climate stations across the state. Their sources for forest cover data were the Continuous Fields Tree Cover Project from the University of Maryland (a global data set at 1 km ground spatial resolution for 1992 to 1993 derived from AVHRR imagery) and also historical maps of forest cover at 4.8 km resolution with particular focus on a 1962 map composed from aerial photographs. Forest cover in São Paulo state decreased by ~12 percent between 1962 and 1992. Webb *et al.* found no trend in total rainfall over the period of study. However, they did find a significant positive correlation between tree cover and mean annual rain days. In addition to a strong relationship to the number of rain days, areas with higher tree cover tended to have less interannual variability in rainfall. The authors noted the likely importance of other factors in determining the overall amount of rainfall in São Paulo state. In particular, they demonstrated the importance of distance to the coast in determining quantity of rainfall. They also point out that the majority of the state's forest had already disappeared by 1962 such that the most severe consequences of deforestation likely predate the data sets used in their study. In addressing the conservation implications of their work, these investigators made the case that larger areas of forest promote a more stable climate.

Zhang *et al.* (2003a,b) investigated the effects of vegetation cover in the previous winter and spring seasons on summer precipitation in China. As a measure of vegetation cover, they derived NDVI values from AVHRR satellite imagery for the periods July 1981 to September 1994 and July 1981 to December 2000. Precipitation data came from 160 ground stations of the China Meteorological Administration. Dividing the Chinese mainland into eight regions, the authors found different relationships between NDVI in the previous winter and spring and precipitation in the following summer. However, for most regions, there were positive correlations between previous season vegetation cover and summer rainfall in China, with precipitation in certain regions apparently sensitive to prior vegetation cover. Positive correlations were also found between initial soil saturation and subsequent summer rainfall over a period of 14 years in an Illinois study (Findell and Eltahir 1997).

8.5 Winds

Species management requires understanding of the dispersal of organisms. Biogeographic theory has often focused on the relationship of geographic proximity to organismal connectivity and dispersal (de Queiroz 2005; Kokko and Lopez-Sepulcre 2006; Nathan 2006). In organisms ranging from birds and insects to plants, winds are important for dispersal, and wind effects can over-come geographic proximity in influencing distribution patterns. For example, Muñoz *et al.* (2004) examined the distribution of mosses, liverworts, lichens, and pteridophytes (i.e., ferns, club mosses, and horsetails) in the extratropical islands of the southern hemisphere to determine whether the flora of these islands are better explained by wind connectivity, via "wind highways" over the Southern Ocean, or by simple geographic proximity. They used data from the SeaWinds scatterometer on the NASA QuikSCAT satellite to create matrices showing wind connectivity for the time period between June 1999 and March 2003 (Fig. 8.13). In 85 percent of the cases studied, wind connectivity resulted in higher correl-ation values than geographic proximity. In particular, mosses, liverworts, and lichens showed stronger floristic similarities associated with wind connectivity than geographic proximity, while for pteridophytes the effects of wind connect-ivity and geographic proximity were about equal. As a result, islands separated by great distances but linked by ocean winds (through wind connectivity) often had more similar floras than those closer together.

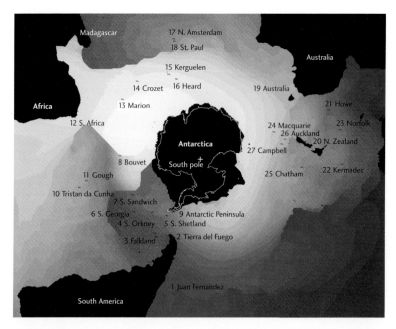

Fig. 8.13 Different gray tones represent different levels of wind connectivity for Bouvet Island (#8), South Atlantic Ocean, as measured by the SeaWinds scatte-rometer (February 1–10, 2002), with increasing connectivity depicted by going from dark to pale tones. The SeaWinds scatterometer only records wind properties over ocean water surfaces—land surfaces, ocean surfaces covered with ice, and areas with null connectivity values for this time period appear as black due to an absence of data. Figure from Muñoz *et al.* 2004, with permission from AAAS.

Winds also contribute indirectly to the long-distance dispersal of organisms through effects on sea surface circulation. Biologists have long noted that floating trees and even relatively large patches of earth, some containing rooted vegetation, may travel for hundreds of kilometers across the world's oceans (Wallace 1880). These rafts of debris appear to serve as platforms from which a wide range of terrestrial taxa can colonize new locations (de Queiroz 2005). Raxworthy *et al.* (2002) posit an "out of Madagascar" species radiation of chameleons around the Indian Ocean region as a result of oceanic dispersal events. Pole (1994) suggests that almost all the current vegetation on New Zealand arrived via long-distance dispersal after continental drifting events had isolated the island.

Ocean winds data and sea surface circulation patterns are contributing to a revolution in our understanding of long-distance dispersal and its role in historical biogeography (de Queiroz 2005). Passive dispersal by winds over relatively short distances is standard for a number of plants, arthropods, fungi, and microbes. However, wind-driven dispersal can also occur over much larger spatial scales, forming something akin to an aerial plankton in the jet streams (Brown and Lomolino 1998). Though less frequent than "typical" short-distance dispersal, a long-distance dispersal event can readily occur when strong vertical winds form under intense convection, which can be observed from atmospheric satellites as bright cumulonimbus clouds and the formation of low pressure systems.

As our ability to model the interaction of ground and wind improves, there are already indications that long-distance dispersal is more common than historically believed (Nathan *et al.* 2002, 2005). Important variables for modeling the dispersal of seeds include the horizontal wind velocity, the height at which the seed is released, the height of the surrounding vegetation, and the terminal velocity of the seed, that is, the unchanging maximum velocity reached by a falling seed (Soons *et al.* 2004). When conditions are right, the distances traveled can be long. In June 1998, hunters found concentrations of jack pine and white spruce pollen from central Quebec almost 3,000 km away in Repulse Bay, Northwest Territories within the Canadian Arctic (Campbell *et al.* 1999). The driver for this event was an unusually strong low pressure system.

While working in deforested areas of Scotland's Southern Uplands, Bacles *et al.* (2006) found that wind dispersal of seeds made a significant contribution to the genetic connectivity of the common ash, *Fraxinus excelsior,* in a severely fragmented landscape. They showed that seed dispersal by wind is up to six times more effective than pollen dispersal at maintaining genetic connectivity among landscape fragments for this tree, which is both wind-pollinated and wind-dispersed. Long-distance dispersal plays an important role here with at least 46 percent of seed-mediated gene flow coming from outside the sampled area of 900 ha. The authors cite modeling evidence supporting the idea that exposed deforested landscapes increase the likelihood that winged seeds will experience uplift and thus promote the long-distance dispersal of both seeds and pollen.

8.5.1 The basics of global winds

Fundamentally, winds result from changes in atmospheric pressure that lead to movements of air. Atmospheric pressure (effectively the mass of the air being pulled downward by gravity above a particular point on the Earth) responds to changes in atmospheric density and temperature. It also decreases with increasing altitude. Differences in atmospheric pressure result in pressure gradients. These pressure gradients drive winds with air moving from areas of higher pressure to areas of lower pressure in response to a pressure gradient force. One source of differing pressure gradients is the variable thickness of the atmosphere. The troposphere is thicker over the tropics (18 to 20 km) than at the poles (~8 km) resulting in different pressures at the same altitude as you go from low latitudes to high latitudes. Much of the description of atmospheric circulation in the paragraphs below comes from the treatments of Aguado and Burt (1999) and Mayes and Hughes (2004).

The Earth spins upon its axis and creates the Coriolis force that deflects the movement of air to the right of the pressure gradient force in the northern hemisphere and to the left of the pressure gradient force in the southern hemisphere. Thus, in the mid- to upper troposphere over much of the globe, winds tend to blow from west to east generating the upper westerlies. Friction with Earth's surface affects lower altitude winds in the so-called boundary layer, the first 1.5 km of the atmosphere. The friction is greater over the land surface than the oceans. This surface friction causes winds at very low altitude to blow more slowly and often in directions different from those at higher levels of the atmosphere.

Atmospheric circulation also responds to heating by the sun, Earth's heat pump. As this heating is greatest at the equator and lessens toward the poles, the planet's fluid media (i.e., the atmosphere and the oceans) move heat from the equator to the poles (Burroughs 1991). The movement of this heat defines atmospheric circulation and thus weather at the global scale. At the equator, solar heating causes the air to expand, rise, and travel toward the poles by convection, in the process generating an area of low pressure referred to as the equatorial low or the Inter-Tropical Convergence Zone (ITCZ). This rising air leads to clusters of convective clouds and precipitation that mark the ITCZ from space (Fig. 8.14). The wet tropics, the most biologically diverse areas of the planet, lie in the ITCZ, which offers the physical properties of heat, moisture, and light required for abundant life.

The rising air at the ITCZ tends to fall back toward Earth's surface and then flow back toward the equator. These thermally induced cells with downward flows around 30° N and S are known as Hadley cells. The downward flow forms subtropical high-pressure areas that produce the world's great deserts due to the loss of moisture in the descending and increasingly warmer air within these high-pressure systems. Hadley cells also generate surface winds known as the northeast trade winds north of the equator and southeast trade winds south of the equator.

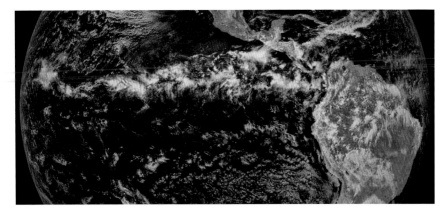

Fig. 8.14 The Inter-Tropical Convergence Zone (ITCZ) appears as a white horizontal band of clouds in this global scale image. The cloud data for this image were collected using NOAA's GOES-11 and were overlaid on color land cover classification data. Credit: GOES Project Science Office and NASA Visible Earth.

The ITCZ is not fixed at the equator but moves latitudinally north and south a few degrees with the changing seasons, especially influencing those areas around the edges of the tropics by giving them both pronounced wet and dry periods, for example, Africa's Sahel and sections of Central America.

At the poles, circulating Polar cells contribute to the generation of mid-latitude depressions or low-pressure systems while generating contrasting high-pressure regions at the highest latitudes. Dry air characterizes regions of high pressure. The Coriolis force acting upon the pressure gradient forces established by the high- and low-pressure regions of the Polar cells results in easterly winds at high latitudes and the poles. The Hadley cells and Polar cells, both thermally driven phenomena, in conjunction with the upper westerlies generate westerly winds in mid-latitudes (roughly 30–60° N and S latitudes) on both sides of the equator. These westerlies have a tremendous meteorological impact, being largely responsible for the west to east movement of most weather systems in the mid-latitudes. At places with a strong and rapidly developing pressure gradient force arising from the collision of different air masses at frontal boundaries, high-altitude jet streams may form. Jet streams travel in large waves of air, known as Rossby waves, around the globe. These waves, when especially pronounced, can deliver warm air from the subtropics to very high latitudes and conversely cold air from high latitudes to low latitudes. Thus, the mid-latitudes act as the transition zone between the warm, wet equatorial region and the cold, dry polar region. As a result, they have highly variable weather when compared to the weather at both low latitudes and high latitudes.

The preceding description of the Hadley and Polar cells implies they are constant and permanent features in the atmosphere. In reality, these cells are more indicative of long-term average conditions. Winds typically respond to semipermanent cells of high and low pressure that grow and diminish with changing seasons. Some of these semipermanent cells are dominant in winter and others in summer. The ITCZ also changes position over the course of a year. As lower altitude winds drive ocean currents, you see similarities in the locations of semipermanent pressure cells, their resulting winds, and the tracks of the world's major ocean currents.

8.5.2 How remote sensing of wind works

Several techniques are useful for the remote sensing of winds. Kidder and Vonder Haar (1995) offer a thorough treatment. Techniques are divided into two main groups: those tracking clouds and water vapor with visual and infrared bands, and those using active and passive microwave remote sensing to analyze the surface roughness of the oceans.

8.5.2.1 Tracking clouds and water vapor

The oldest and perhaps still most common method of determining wind vectors uses geostationary imagers to track cloud movements. Known as cloud-track or cloud-drift winds, these estimates take advantage of the high temporal resolution (every 15 to 30 min) offered by geostationary satellites. Wind speed and direction are estimated by measuring the vector difference in the location of a particular cloud divided by the time interval between the two images. This approach may be conducted manually by an analyst or automatically via computer. Problems with this method include its dependence on clouds (i.e., no clouds = no wind data) and obscuring by high-level cirrus of lower-level clouds. High-altitude clouds mask lower-altitude winds associated with certain storms. The best clouds to track for this method are those that move passively with the winds, especially low-level clouds or high cirrus. Tall cumulonimbus clouds do not move well with winds and are not good candidates for this method, nor are orographic clouds. Most, if not all, of the world's geostationary satellite systems produce operational wind products and, in several cases, maintain historical archives of them. Numerical weather models often require these products.

For cloud-free areas, the 6.5 to 7.0 μm water vapor bands allow tracking of winds through the movements of water vapor, which is invisible to the naked eye but detectable in these thermal infrared bands. These vapor-track wind measurements complement cloud-track wind measurements by detecting wind-driven movement in the middle troposphere, an area of the atmosphere not well represented by cloud tracking. Most errors in both cloud-track and vapor-track winds arise from incorrect estimates of cloud or water vapor height, which subsequently result in the assignment of incorrect altitudes to the derived wind vectors. Another technique for calculating winds in cloud-free areas from satellite

data takes advantage of temperature measures from sounder sensors and estimates of sea-level pressure to calculate the heights of pressure surfaces in the
atmosphere. This method is better for winds aloft, as satellite temperature
soundings are least accurate near the surface.

In addition to data from geostationary satellites, NOAA has developed an
experimental polar winds product using imagery from the polar-orbiting
AVHRR and MODIS sensors. Polar-orbiting satellites go nearly over the poles
on every orbit providing a relatively large number of daily observations for polar
regions. The NOAA products take advantage of the same cloud-track and water-
vapor track (for MODIS only) automated techniques developed for the geostationary sensors. Polar wind data are available on the Web.

8.5.2.2 Measurement of winds based on sea-surface roughness

Both active and passive microwave technologies allow detection of wind speed
and direction over the oceans. Scatterometers are active microwave sensors
(essentially specialized radars) that estimate sea surface wind vectors by means
of radar backscatter from ocean waves. Using antennae, scatterometers transmit
electromagnetic pulses to the surface of the ocean and receive a backscatter
return signal from that surface. Rougher surfaces with larger waves resulting
from higher-speed winds produce stronger backscatter signals than smoother
surfaces that generate less backscatter. Operating sensors include the SeaWinds
scatterometer aboard the NASA QuikSCAT satellite (Fig. 8.15) and the
Scatterometer on the ESA ERS-2 satellite. Both are in near-polar orbits. ESA
also launched an Advanced Scatterometer (ASCAT) in 2006 aboard its
METOP satellite (ESA 2008). SeaWinds senses an 1800 km swath of the
ocean's surface, allowing it to cover ~90 percent of Earth's oceans each day
(NASA 2008e).

Passive microwave sensors also provide ocean wind speed data products. These
sensors detect microwave radiation emitted from the sea surface and do not
transmit their own pulses of microwave radiation as radars do. Nevertheless, they
are able to detect changes in sea surface microwave emissions due to the effects of
winds on ocean surface roughness. Also helpful for remote detection of wind
speed is the formation of foam on the sea surface at wind speeds above 7 m/s.
The amount of foam increases with wind speed, and foam is readily detectable in
microwave bands due to its high emittance levels. Thus, tracking the amount of
foam allows an estimate of surface wind speed (Kidder and Vonder Haar 1995).
The US Department of Defense makes available, through NOAA, SSM/I
microwave wind speed products on the Web.

Measurement of the global tropospheric wind field (or winds as a function of
height globally) constitutes a major challenge for future wind remote sensing.
Such data would have a dramatic impact on weather prediction, climate modeling, and our understanding of other wind-driven phenomena. Going beyond
scatterometry, such data would provide us with satellite wind information over

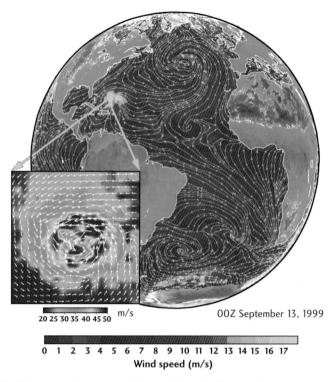

20 25 30 35 40 45 50 m/s   00Z September 13, 1999

0 1 2 3 4 5 6 7 8 9 10 11 12 13 14 15 16 17
Wind speed (m/s)

Fig. 8.15 Global wind patterns observed by the SeaWinds instrument onboard the QuikSCAT satellite, including extreme winds from Hurricane Floyd located west of the Bahamas (inset, September 13, 1999). White arrows show wind direction and the color coding represents wind speed. Credit: NASA/JPL.

the land surface. The sensor of choice for large-scale wind profiles is a Doppler lidar system, operating in the 10.6 μm band, which would use backscatter from naturally occurring particles at different angles in tandem with the velocity of the spacecraft to calculate a horizontal wind vector (Kidder and Vonder Haar 1995). Aircraft systems carrying prototype Doppler lidars are operating and providing wind vectors (R. Kakar, personal communication, 2006).

8.5.3 Winds and ocean productivity

Oceans have high heat capacities relative to the land and atmosphere, effectively making them the "heat buffers" of the Earth system. Existing ocean surface wind vectors allow us to track the drivers of ocean circulation—the means by which oceans move heat about the globe. In turn, these movements generate much of what we know as climate. Thus, wind data find a role in the growing field of climate forecasting in which forecasters seek to predict phenomena driven by longer-term interannual climate variability, such as ENSO events. On shorter timescales, meteorologists incorporate satellite wind vectors into numerical weather models, resulting in improved forecasts (NASA 2008e).

Winds blowing offshore along the west coasts of North and South America, southern Africa, and Australia circulate warm surface water away from the shore and foster the upwelling of deeper waters that bring nutrients to the surface and into the sunlight, resulting in high levels of productivity (Fig. 8.16). Coastal upwelling zones are so productive that while they account for only 0.1 percent of global ocean surface area, they produce 50 percent of the world's fisheries catch (Cox and Moore 2000). Ocean circulation patterns are also responsible for the dispersal of marine planktonic organisms, including the larvae of many species.

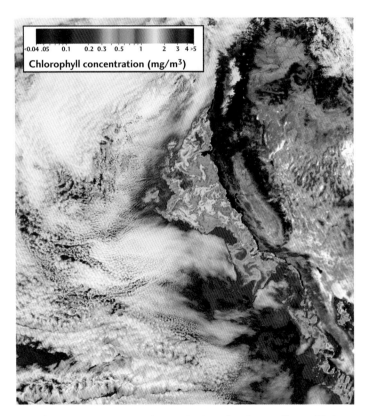

Fig. 8.16 This SeaWiFS image shows the result of upwelling off the coast of California, USA (October 6, 2002). With the surge of nutrients in upwelling zones, phytoplankton thrive and their concentrations rapidly increase. Ocean color sensors such as SeaWiFS and MODIS are used to map ocean productivity by monitoring phytoplankton pigment. Credit: Ocean Color Project, NASA/GSFC and GeoEye.

8.6 Temperature and the radiation budget

Temperature, through its effects on growing season, productivity, and connections to precipitation, is a primary determinant of species distributions and the quality of habitats under projected future conditions. Thus far, we have discussed the remote sensing of clouds, aerosols, precipitation, and winds, all key parameters in modeling and understanding climate on global, regional, and local scales. Measuring Earth's surface temperature is clearly one of the most fundamental observations in this regard. It is also one of the most complex.

8.6.1 Temperature and vegetation

At regional to global spatial scales, a number of studies have taken advantage of the historical AVHRR data record of more than 2 decades to compute NDVI values as proxies for biologically relevant parameters, such as plant growth. Myneni *et al.* (1997) documented increased photosynthetic activity in terrestrial vegetation from 1981 to 1991 using NDVI as a measure of photosynthetic activity. They also found an increase in the length of the growing season of 12 ± 4 days in the Northern Hemisphere north of $45\degree$ N. These changes occurred in association with pronounced warming temperatures over substantial areas of Alaska, northwestern Canada, and northern Eurasia. Slayback *et al.* (2003) extended this work for the period 1982–99 and added data sets and improvements in calibration as well as corrections for atmospheric effects. They also found increases in NDVI for latitudes from 35–75$\degree$ N with increases generally greater in the 1990s than the 1980s. Xiao and Moody (2005) sought to determine the climatological factors associated with changes in NDVI at different latitudes in the 1982 to 1998 time period. Temperature appeared to be a more important climatic correlate than precipitation for the enhanced greening trend seen in northern high latitudes and in western Europe. This team also highlighted areas of the globe that showed decreasing greenness as measured by NDVI. Most of these areas were in the Southern Hemisphere (southern Africa, southern South America, and central Australia). There were also large regions of the globe, including some in the high latitudes, which showed no trends in greenness over that time period and also other large areas that were undergoing increased greening but with no associations between these greening trends and trends in temperature or precipitation.

Nemani *et al.* (2003) derived LAI and fraction of photosynthetically active radiation (FPAR, the proportion of available radiation in photosynthetically active wavelengths [0.4–0.7 μm] absorbed by the vegetation canopy) values and then used these vegetation properties, in conjunction with modeled climate data, to estimate monthly and annual trends in net primary production. For 1982 to 1999, their data show a 6 percent increase in net primary production on a global basis, with the largest increase seen in tropical ecosystems. In fact, Amazonia accounted for 42 percent of the global rise in production. The authors also sought to determine the relative impacts of various climatic variables on plant growth via net primary production. To do so, they mapped the degree to which three major climatic variables effectively constrained net primary production and thus plant growth over time. These variables were: (1) temperature defined as growing season average temperature; (2) water through the vapor pressure deficit, the saturated vapor pressure at a given surface temperature minus the actual vapor pressure of the air; and (3) solar radiation from ISCCP cloud, Earth Radiation Budget Experiment, and other data. Nemani *et al.* estimated that water availability was the strongest limiting factor on vegetation growth for 40 percent of Earth's vegetated surface, while temperature most strongly limited growth over 33 percent and radiation was the dominate limiting factor over 27 percent of the planet's vegetated surface area (see Fig. 8.1; Nemani *et al.* 2003). Of course, these three climatic factors (heat, water, and light) tend to interact and become co-limiting but the effort to determine which climatic factors dominate in which areas of the globe provides a deeper level of understanding of the impacts of particular climate variables on life.

8.6.2 Temperature and species

At the species level, temperature information and other climate measures, especially precipitation, are vital to the growing field of ecological niche modeling. These models define ecological niche spaces for species statistically, using various environmental conditions within the species' known distribution to develop environmental envelopes for species. These envelopes, in turn, are mapped to a geographical niche space in order to provide a potential range map for modeled species. The climatic information for these models can come from climatologies, derived from both satellite and *in situ* sensors, as well as from scenarios derived from global or regional climate models (Pearson and Dawson 2003; Raxworthy *et al.* 2003; Thomas *et al.* 2004; Phillips *et al.* 2006). Ecological niche models and the data to run them are increasingly applied by those trying to understand the impacts on species of both climate variability (i.e., seasonal to interannual to multi-decadal changes in climate assumed to be of nonhuman origin) and anthropogenic climate change driven by our export of greenhouse gases into Earth's atmosphere. See Chapter 14 for more on ecological modeling.

There have been a large number of studies documenting the effects of changing climates on the planet's ecosystems and species, which have recorded changes in distributions and phenologies among other effects (e.g., Penuelas and Filella [2001]; Walther *et al.* [2002]; Parmesan and Yohe [2003]; Root *et al.* [2003]; Perry *et al.* [2005]; Parmesan [2005]). Habitat fragmentation and climate variability and change act synergistically to increase the potential impacts (Hannah *et al.* 2005). Land cover maps derived from satellite imagery allow you to fine-tune species distributions based upon climate change scenarios in ecological niche models by clipping those areas that no longer contain the required habitat for the species of concern. For example, a deforested area is unlikely to serve as habitat for a forest species and can therefore be excluded from that species' potential distribution (Phillips *et al.* 2006). Satellite remote sensing offers tools to ecologists and conservation biologists that allow for both the detection and monitoring of habitat fragmentation and climatic factors, as well as the potential to model the impacts of changes in these factors.

8.6.3 The basics of Earth's radiation budget and temperature

Measuring the solar radiation incident upon the Earth is an essential first step in understanding Earth's energy budget. The angle at which incident solar radiation strikes the Earth and what happens to it once it enters the Earth system (i.e., whether it is absorbed or reflected and where this occurs) largely determines the temperature for a particular location on Earth, but there are also regional and local factors that influence the temperature at a given location. Maintaining a habitable temperature at Earth's surface depends upon a global balance in net radiation, that is, a balance between incoming shortwave radiation (or irradiance) and outgoing longwave radiation. The entire Earth system, surface and atmosphere together, maintains this balance. Approximately $1368 \, \text{W}/\text{m}^2$ of solar radiation reaches the top of Earth's atmosphere. Although known as the solar constant, this figure is an annual average with a value varying $\pm$ 3.4 percent over the course of a year. In fact, the first successful satellite-based meteorological instrument, developed by Verner Suomi and flown aboard NASA's Explorer 7 in October 1959, detected incoming solar radiation and outgoing infrared radiation from the Earth in an early experiment to quantify these critical measures for Earth's radiation budget. Satellites allow the direct measurement of this parameter without the previously required correction for atmospheric effects. By measuring solar irradiance, satellite data also allow assessment of the potential effects of the 11-year solar sunspot cycle (Kidder and Vonder Haar 1995).

On average, the atmosphere (stratosphere and troposphere) absorbs about 25 percent of the incoming solar radiation. Clouds and atmospheric gases scatter back to space another 25 percent or so, leaving about 50 percent as Earth's insolation, or the downwelling solar radiation reaching Earth's surface. The Earth backscatters ~5 percent of this radiation back into space, giving a planetary albedo of almost 30 percent when combined with cloud and atmospheric scattering. Thus, Earth's surface absorbs about 45 percent of incoming solar radiation and the atmosphere absorbs about 25 percent. The atmosphere and surface of the Earth also emit longwave radiation, exchanging radiation between each other and emitting it to space. Energy transfers, essentially exchanges of sensible and latent heat between the surface and atmosphere, occur in such a way that surplus longwave radiation at the surface exactly matches the atmosphere's longwave radiation deficit (Aguado and Burt 1999; Mayes and Hughes 2004).

A number of factors influence the regional distribution of heat, and thus temperature, on our planet. Transfers of energy take time. So, there is a lag between the time and dates of maximum insolation and the time and dates during which we experience the greatest temperatures. For example, we typically experience the highest temperatures in the early afternoon between 2:00 and 4:00 PM and throughout the Northern Hemisphere during the months of July and August. Winds and ocean currents are the primary redistributors of heat on our planet, moving excess heat from lower latitudes toward the poles. Latitudinally, temperatures decrease as we travel toward the poles. Latitudinal temperature gradients are greatest during the winter season. Water has a higher heat capacity than dry soil so that temperatures over land tend to be warmer in summer and colder in winter than temperatures over nearby water bodies. Locally, south-facing slopes in the Northern Hemisphere receive more solar illumination than those facing other directions, which can result not only in higher temperatures but also in drier zones than on north-facing slopes.

On a local scale, land cover affects temperature. Tall vegetation reduces the amount of sunlight reaching Earth's surface by day and also tends to inhibit longwave radiation loss by night, reducing day–night temperature extremes. Large and dense urban areas generate their own temperature effects, referred to as urban heat islands due to the sometimes substantial increases in temperature experienced (Section 11.7; Aguado and Burt 1999).

8.6.4 Remote sensing of Earth's radiation budget and temperature

For over 25 years, the US Government has monitored levels of incoming radiation from the sun, that is, the total solar irradiance, through a series of sun-looking sensors. This line of irradiance monitors includes NASA's Solar Radiation and Climate Experiment (SORCE), which was launched in 2003 (LASP 2008). In concert with those instruments looking away from the Earth to determine levels of solar irradiance, another series of sensors have measured outgoing radiation by looking back at the Earth. Today, NASA Clouds and the Earth's Radiant Energy System (CERES) sensors provide this information. CERES sensors are broadband, scanning radiometers with three wide channels measuring total radiance: (1) in the range between 0.3 and more than 100 μm, (2) in the narrower electromagnetic range at 0.3–5 μm, and (3) in the 8–12 μm thermal atmospheric window (Parkinson *et al.* 2006). Ground spatial resolutions are 10 km or 20 km at nadir, depending upon the satellite carrying the CERES sensor. CERES provides radiation flux measurements, including both solar-reflected and Earth-emitted radiation, from Earth's surface to the top of its atmosphere. Because the CERES sensors are flying in tandem with higher resolution imagers that view clouds on the TRMM, Terra, and Aqua satellites, they are also enhancing our understanding of the impacts of cloud properties on radiative fluxes, perhaps the most important challenge to our knowledge of climate variability and change.

Moving from the radiation budget to temperature, we can divide the remote sensing of Earth's temperature into two broad categories: remote sensing of surface temperature and remote sensing of atmospheric temperature. Both depend upon atmospheric transmission of electromagnetic radiation. For surface temperature detection, the challenge is to get a clean transmission of radiation from Earth's surface, that is, to eliminate the noise of radiation coming from other sources, particularly the atmosphere.

8.6.4.1 Surface temperatures

Satellite imagers viewing electromagnetic radiation through the atmospheric windows located at 10.5 to 12.5 μm and 3.5 to 4.0 μm are the principal means for measuring land and sea surface temperatures (SSTs) from orbit. Atmospheric windows are ranges of wavelengths at which the atmosphere is largely transparent to radiation emitted by (or reflected from) the Earth and allow this radiation to transit the atmosphere with little absorption (Appendix 1). While these atmospheric windows do allow the transmission of surface radiation, atmospheric radiation still modifies this surface radiation preventing the receipt of a pure surface signal. Split-window and multiple-window techniques allow us to cancel out the atmospheric impacts (essentially the atmospheric temperature) on the brightness temperatures measured by the imager. The *split-window technique* takes advantage of the width of the 10.5–12.5 μm atmospheric window, which allows several multichannel sensors to have two channels within this one window. Taking the difference between the two observations made using two channels in the wide thermal window allows an observer to correct for atmospheric effects and improve estimates of surface temperature (see Kidder and Vonder Haar [1995] for a more detailed summary). The *multiple-window technique* adds observations from another atmospheric window, typically the one at $\sim$ 3.5–4.0 μm, to derive surface temperatures. After correcting for atmospheric effects, brightness temperature approximately equals emissivity multiplied by surface temperature. Land and water surfaces usually have emissivities close to 1.0 (in the 0.9–0.95 range) for infrared wavelengths, which means that the resulting brightness temperatures are very close to the surface temperature (Fig. 8.17).

At microwave wavelengths, open ocean emissivities are in the 0.45 to 0.65 range while those for land surfaces remain close to 1.0. Microwave measures of surface temperature are not impeded by clouds. The primary channels for microwave remote sensing of surface temperature are those at 6 GHz (for SST), 10 GHz, and 35 GHz—all of which are equivalent to 1–10 cm wavelengths (Burroughs 1991; Kidder and Vonder Harr 1995; R. Kakar, personal communication, 2006).

Many of the geostationary and polar-orbiting imagers with thermal channels produce surface temperature products. Some have done so for decades. The variability of land surface cover coupled with the greater diurnal changes seen in land versus ocean temperatures make satellite derivation of land surface temperatures and emissivities very challenging. Thus, the operational temperature products that do extend back in time tend to be SST products, which are discussed in more detail in Section 6.2.4. One long-term terrestrial data set comes from the work of Jin (2004) and his colleagues to develop an experimental global land surface temperature data set for snow-free land areas that spans 1981

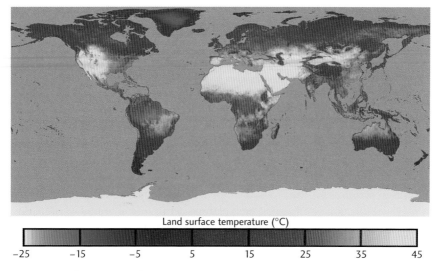

Land surface temperature (°C)

−25   −15   −5   5   15   25   35   45

Fig. 8.17 This MODIS-derived image product depicts land surface temperature for the entire month of July 2003 (Jin 2004). Credit: NASA/GSFC.

to 1998 and uses data from the NOAA AVHRR series of imagers. It gives 8 km monthly average maximum and minimum temperatures. To capture the diurnal variation in surface temperatures, it uses modeled products since the AVHRR imagers only view much of Earth's surface twice a day. The uncertainties of its temperature estimates are highest in the tropics.

In addition to surface temperature measures from the operational geostationary and polar-orbiting satellites, other satellite measurements seek to capture the more challenging parameter of land surface temperature. Table A6.6 includes examples from the NASA MODIS and Japanese ASTER sensor, which shares space with MODIS aboard the NASA Terra satellite.

8.6.4.2 Atmospheric temperatures

The remote sensing of atmospheric temperatures is the domain of sounder sensors that capture vertical profiles of the atmosphere and thus are often called vertical profilers. For sounders sensing the atmosphere, electromagnetic radiation from the surface is the noise to be eliminated. Transmittance of radiation through the atmosphere is a function of atmospheric temperature and the mixing ratio (the ratio of the density of a gas to the total density of the atmosphere) of any absorbing gases in it. Atmospheric temperature sounding in the infrared region of the spectrum takes advantage of the fact that carbon dioxide is well mixed within the atmosphere in well-known concentrations. So, at wavelengths where well-mixed carbon dioxide strongly absorbs infrared radiation ($\sim 4.3\,\mu$m and from 12 to $18\,\mu$m, centered on $15\,\mu$m), atmospheric transmittance is essentially a function of temperature. Thus, we can solve for temperature.

Carbon dioxide absorbs radiation differently at different wavelengths. At the center of these absorption bands (say, 15 μm), carbon dioxide absorbs almost all radiation from below the top of the atmosphere; and you are effectively only sensing radiation from the top of the atmosphere. However, as you move away from the center of these wavelength bands along different wavelengths, the absorption of radiation (i.e., the atmosphere's opacity) decreases and transmittance increases (Fig. 8.18).

Heights in the atmosphere are typically expressed as levels of atmospheric pressure. Quantitative atmospheric temperature profiles are produced using an algorithm that sums different brightness temperatures at different wavelengths while multiplying each by a coefficient known as a weighting function. This algorithm accounts for the physical temperature at any particular altitude's being a weighted function of brightness temperatures across several nearby wavelengths.

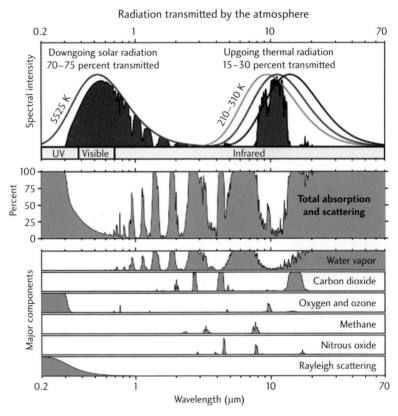

Fig. 8.18 Radiation being transmitted through the atmosphere is absorbed and scattered by different molecules (including carbon dioxide) and particulates. The absorption bands for specific wavelengths of electromagnetic energy are shown for each major molecule. Credit: Robert A. Rohde (2007), Global Warming Art, used with permission.

As with infrared imagers, clouds are also a problem for infrared sounder sensors. Microwave sounding allows us to avoid the cloud problem although, as explained for precipitation, this is at the cost of poorer ground spatial resolution. Microwave sounding of atmospheric temperature follows an approach similar to that described above for infrared sounding but uses one oxygen absorption band located at $\sim$50 GHz (roughly 0.5 to 0.6 cm in terms of wavelength) to take advantage of the fact that molecular oxygen is well-mixed in the atmosphere. Appendix 6 provides additional information about sounding techniques.

Working in the opposite direction, this sounding approach is also useful for deriving the concentrations of trace gases in the atmosphere. In those cases where a gas is not well mixed (e.g., ozone or water vapor) but where the temperature at a particular level of the atmosphere is known, we can use sounding techniques and the existing atmospheric transmittance to estimate the concentration of those trace gases in the atmosphere (Burroughs 1991; Kidder and Vonder Harr 1995; R. Kakar, personal communication, 2006).

8.6.5 Long-term temperature data sets

Those seeking to understand and model changes in land surface temperature over time rely on long-term records of land surface temperature that in turn depend on collections of ground station data stretching back hundreds of years in some cases. When using long-term measures of surface temperature, you must determine a starting point in time based upon an assessment of the quality and coverage of the ground-based station record for the area you intend to survey. For example, the NASA Goddard Institute for Space Studies (GISS) requires global measures of land surface temperatures through time for its modeling and assessment work. GISS begins many of its analyses of temperature change in the year 1880 because of its assessment that this date corresponds to the establishment of "a reasonably global distribution of meteorological stations" overcoming the generally poor spatial coverage of ground-based weather stations prior to that time (NASA Goddard Institute for Space Studies 2008). GISS Surface Temperature Analysis activities use ground station data from the Global Historical Climatology Network (GHCN), which is made available by NOAA on the Web and holds data from thousands of temperature, precipitation, and pressure stations around the world. The oldest data date back to 1697. This network represents an invaluable source of direct, long-term, digitized land surface temperature measurements for the study of climate change at both global and regional scales (Peterson and Vose 1997).

Building upon the GHCN and other sources of climate data, a relatively new global climatology known as WorldClim (also available on the Web) has compiled monthly averages of mean, minimum, and maximum temperature and also monthly precipitation for global land areas (excluding Antarctica) mainly covering the 1950 to 2000 time period (Hijmans *et al.* 2005). These global climate layers are available at the spatial resolution of 1 km^2, much higher than previous global efforts and developed with biogeographic applications in mind.

Records for satellite remote sensing of temperature extend back to 1979, following the launch in October 1978 of the NOAA TIROS N operational polar-orbiting satellite, which carried the AVHRR, HIRS/2 (the predecessor to today's HIRS/3 and HIRS/4 sensors), Microwave Sounding Unit or MSU (the predecessor to the Advanced Microwave Sounding Unit or AMSU), and Strato-spheric Sounding Unit sensors (Kidder and Vonder Haar 1995). In particular, this long-term record consists of atmospheric temperatures derived from the MSU. These observations show tropospheric temperature increases of 0.10 to 0.20 °C per decade (Wigley *et al.* 2006). Records from Earth's surface also show warming over that time period while measures from the stratosphere depict considerable cooling. These changes are in accord with the results of climate models.

8.7 Global climate modeling applications to ecology and conservation

General Circulation Models (GCMs), also called Global Climate Models, are numerical representations of the climate system, typically at global scales. The physical laws of the Earth system and the physical, chemical, and biological properties of its components form the basis for these models. GCMs initially focused on the physics of the atmosphere and the oceans, Earth's more fluid media, and described atmosphere and ocean dynamics. Typically, GCMs divide the Earth and its atmosphere into three-dimensional grids with horizontal resolutions on the order of tens to hundreds of kilometers and vertical resolutions of 200 m to 1 km. The resolutions of these grids have gotten finer over time due to increases in computer capability (Fig. 8.19). In order to represent physical processes that cannot be resolved at the spatial (or temporal) resolutions of these models (i.e., sub-grid scale processes), modelers use a technique known as parameterization to represent the processes collectively, essentially by area or time averaging the sub-grid phenomena to reach the appropriate larger scale of the GCM. For example, while individual clouds are usually too small to be resolved within the grid scale of a GCM, you can empirically derive the average percentage cloudiness and resulting heating profile for a model grid area and use this value to incorporate an important sub-grid phenomenon, that is, clouds, into the model.

As computational power and our understanding of other components of the Earth system have increased, GCMs have evolved to incorporate the land surface, ice (i.e., cryosphere), and living (i.e., biosphere) elements of our planet. Just getting the physics of the atmosphere and ocean dynamics right, given the chaotic aspects of Earth's climate system, continues to be a major challenge. While coupled atmosphere/ocean GCMs provide a fairly comprehensive view of

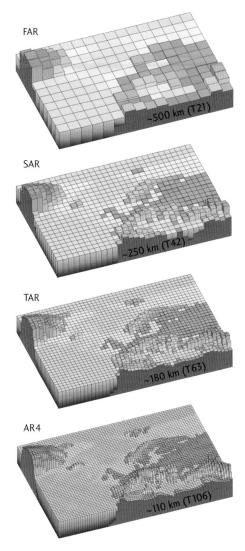

FAR

~500 km (T21)

SAR

~250 km (T42)

TAR

~180 km (T63)

AR4

~110 km (T106)

Fig. 8.19 Subsequent generations of climate models used in IPCC Assessment Reports have had improving spatial resolution: (First Assessment Report—FAR [IPCC 1990], Second Assessment Report—SAR [IPCC 1995], Third Assessment Report—TAR [IPCC 2001a], and Fourth Assessment Report—AR4 [2007]). As the horizontal grids become more refined in successive global models, northern Europe becomes more clearly resolved. While vertical resolution in both atmosphere and ocean models is not shown, it has increased comparably with the horizontal resolution, beginning typically with a single-layer slab ocean and 10 atmospheric layers in the FAR and progressing to about 30 levels in both atmosphere and ocean. Figure from Le Treut *et al.* 2007, with permission from Cambridge University Press.

the climate system, the ongoing challenge is to integrate chemical and biological processes into these physical models. An important goal is an integrated understanding of a coupled physical, chemical, and biological Earth system. Global-scale modelers seeking to relate biological changes to the physical climate changes tracked by GCMs have focused their efforts in two areas: the biogeochemical cycling of important elements, especially carbon, and the biogeography of functional types of vegetation. (Schneider 1992; Le Treut *et al.* 2007; T. Lee, personal communication, 2007)

The applications of GCM products are many. For example, given that changes in land cover due to deforestation can affect local and mesoscale precipitation, GCMs can explore whether large-scale tropical deforestation alters precipitation patterns at other latitudes and on other continents. Avissar and Werth (2005) used a NASA GISS GCM known as GISS GCM II, a global atmospheric model without a coupled ocean component, to test possible relationships between large-scale tropical deforestation and climate. They generated five sets of simulations called ensembles with each ensemble consisting of six separate 12-year model runs. In the simulations, Amazonia, Central Africa, and Southeast Asia were individually deforested and replaced by mixed shrub and grassland. They also ran other simulations in which all three wet tropical regions were deforested simultaneously. In the simulations, deforestation caused a significant reduction in precipitation locally, that is, within the deforested regions themselves. In addition, they found teleconnections (i.e., linkages between atmospheric circulation occurring across widely separated parts of the globe) whereby the impacts of the modeled deforestation spread throughout the equatorial regions and even to areas in the mid-latitudes and higher latitudes.

For example, the modeled deforestation of Amazonia had dramatic impacts on predicted rainfall in North America. Predicted rainfall decreased in the Gulf of Mexico region, particularly in Texas (which experienced a reduction of about 25 percent) and northern Mexico. Modeled Central African deforestation decreased precipitation in the Great Lakes region of the United States and also in Ukraine and Russia (north of the Black Sea). Modeled deforestation in Southeast Asia hit China, the Balkan Peninsula, and western Turkey especially hard. Precipitation decreases were counterbalanced by increases in other places. For example, the models of deforestation in each of the three major tropical regions predicted increased rainfall in the Arabian Peninsula and East Africa. The simulated simultaneous deforestation of all three wet tropical areas had different effects than a simple sum of the deforestation effects in each area. Avissar and Werth interpreted their results by noting that tropical deforestation considerably alters the release of both sensible and latent heat to the atmosphere, which then modifies zones of atmospheric convergence and divergence, shifting the pattern of the Polar Jet Stream and the precipitation it fosters. They went on to posit that the activation of Rossby waves is a likely vehicle driving these global teleconnections.

8.8 Summary and a potential way forward through ecological forecasting

From its early days providing images of clouds to weather forecasters, satellite remote sensing of the atmosphere has grown to include a very broad suite of sensors measuring and monitoring a number of climatic phenomena. In fact, the atmospheric sciences continue to control the lion's share of research budgets for civilian Earth remote sensing systems. So, there is a rich array of tools from which ecologists and conservation biologists can choose. However, this wealth of sensors remains largely unutilized by those applying satellite remote sensing to conservation biology and the management of natural resources. We are only beginning to explore the potential power of these atmospheric observations.

Perhaps one way forward lies in using these observations in conjunction with numerical models to provide us with ecological forecasts. Ecological forecasts are somewhat analogous to weather forecasts and the more recently available longer-term climate forecasts. They require a combination of satellite and *in situ* observations, physical and ecological models, and improved understanding of key processes for enhanced predictive capability. Ecological forecasts will depend upon the further integration of physical climate and other geophysical models with biological and ecological models, whether this occurs through direct model coupling (i.e., a two-way flow of information between model types) or simply by linking models through the incorporation of the outputs from one into another. Ecological forecasts will enable us to project how changes in atmospheric and climatic phenomena drive changes in ecosystems upon which we depend for a plethora of goods and services, as well as their associated biodiversity. Perhaps the use of satellite imagery and numerical models can catalyze a revolution in our ability to predict ecological changes akin to the revolution in meteorological forecasting they initiated more than a generation ago.

9

Disturbances: fires and floods

From space, much of Indonesia appeared to be on fire. One of the strongest El Niño/Southern Oscillation (ENSO) events of the twentieth century had generated drought conditions in the fall of 1997 and early 1998. These conditions, probably in concert with the impacts of logging, resulted in what has been called the largest fire disaster ever observed (Siegert *et al.* 2001). The powerful 1997–8 ENSO also led to extensive fires in Amazonia. The humid tropics, home to Earth's greatest concentrations of biodiversity, had long been thought to be fire resistant due to high-moisture levels in the leaf litter and the humidity of the understory. The massive fires of 1997–8 increased our understanding of the complex interactions between fire and humid tropical forests. Since the late 1990s, a new synthesis has emerged linking ENSO events, drought, logging, and fire in the wet tropics. This synthesis has sought to understand the impacts of these phenomena on tropical environments and also explain the role humans play in tropical fires and fire impacts. Remote sensing has been an important tool in forging this new synthesis of understanding. For example, NOAA's workhorse AVHRR sensor, the SeaWiFS sensor, and NASA's TOMS instrument were among the satellite tools available to provide imagery of the dramatic events of 1997–8 (Fig. 9.1).

In this chapter, we discuss the potential for remote sensing to detect, monitor, and increase our understanding of certain disturbance mechanisms affecting ecosystems. We focus on fires and floods, adding shorter sections at the end on two other drivers of disturbance, volcanoes and dams.

9.1 Fires and logging in the humid tropics

A key challenge lies in understanding the degree to which logging, even selective logging, is interacting with periodic droughts to drive fires in humid forests. Are humid tropical forests essentially immune to fire unless disturbed by human logging, or have they always been subject to climate-induced droughts and subsequent fires? The answer is crucial in determining our impact on these great storehouses of biodiversity and holds major implications for forest management. Part of the answer lies in looking backward in time. In Amazonia and

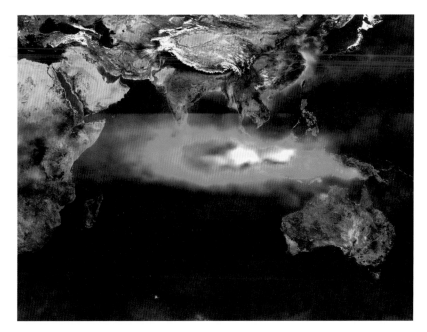

Fig. 9.1 NASA Total Ozone Mapping Spectrometer (TOMS) data depict pollution over Indonesia and the Indian Ocean on October 22, 1997, resulting from fires in Indonesia. White shows aerosols (smoke) remaining in the vicinity of the fires while green, yellow, and red represent increasing amounts of tropospheric ozone (smog) being moved to the west by high winds. The smoke and smog are moving at different rates and in some cases different directions. Source: Scientific Visualization Studio, NASA/GSFC.

the Guianas, charcoal found in soil samples points to major past fire events. Meggers (1994) found evidence of extreme ENSO events resulting in significant droughts, vegetational replacement, and cultural changes over the past 1600 years in the lowland forests of Amazonia. However, these events seem to happen rather infrequently with long fire return times of decades to centuries (Hammond and ter Steege 1998; Uhl 1998). Such findings place today's fire events in an historical context. Climatic variability, such as ENSO events, can drive significant fire events in humid tropical environments but these seem relatively rare. What happens when we add modern logging into the mix?

Siegert *et al.* (2001) used AVHRR optical imagery and SAR data from the European Remote-Sensing Satellite 2 (ERS-2) to locate and assess the extent of burned area from the 1998 fires in East Kalimantan. SAR images allowed viewing through the haze of the fires and also the clouds accompanying the rainfall that followed the drought. Focusing on East Kalimantan, these researchers estimated that fires damaged 5.2 ($\pm$ 0.3) million hectares (over 50,000 km^2). A vegetation cover map, derived from August 1997 SAR imagery taken prior to the fires, allowed detection of the type of forests burned. They also digitized the legal status of the land before the fire to try and determine the land use on burned lands, that is, whether fires occurred in natural forest concessions, pulpwood plantation forests, oil palm plantations, agricultural lands, or pro-tected areas. Relatively cloud-free Landsat TM data provided an independent reference for other sources of land use data. A primary goal of the project was to see whether logged forests were more affected by fire than undisturbed forests. The combination of radar, optical satellite data, and ground-based information on land use showed that only 5.7 percent of undisturbed forests were affected by fire, while 59 percent of the logged forest and 70.7 percent of the non-forest area were fire damaged. Fire impacts were also more extreme in logged forests, as 48 percent of logged forests experienced severe (50–80 percent of trees dead) or total (greater than 80 percent of vegetation killed) damage while only 4 percent of undisturbed forests experienced these levels of mortality. Furthermore, the time since logging had occurred strongly affected the fire impact. Nearly 49.5 percent of the burned area in forests logged within the past two years was severely impacted, while only 26.3 percent of the burned areas in forests logged farther back in time showed severe damage. Logging greatly increased fuel loads through logging slash, which opened the canopy to greater photon flux densities (photons per unit area per unit time at a surface) leading to drying and enhanced flammability. The percent of area burned was much higher near newly estab-lished logging roads (65 percent) than older logging roads (16 percent).

The results of Siegert *et al.* support the notion of positive feedbacks between logging and fire occurrence in which selective logging, associated logging roads and logging byproducts, and more open canopies make rainforests more suscep-tible to fire. Past fires tend to increase the probability of future fires, a result also found by Cochrane *et al.* (1999) in Amazonia where second fires were faster moving and much more intense, releasing roughly 10 times the heat of first fires. Thus, recurrent tropical forest fires not only have greater impacts than initial fires, they also promote future fires, reducing the fire return interval (Cochrane and Schulze 1998).

Nepstad *et al.* (1999) found that logging in Amazonian forests damaged 10–40 percent of the living biomass and reduced leaf canopy coverage by 14–50 percent. Uhl and Kauffman (1990) see a new era in which selective logging and associated human disturbances are transforming relatively nonflammable rain forests into flammable second growth communities, elevating fire into a dominant disturbance mechanism for humid tropical forests. While tropical forest systems do have a history of fire, the problem today lies in the increased frequency of fires due to human actions and the resulting forest fragmentation and degradation caused by these fires (Laurance and Williamson 2001; Cochrane 2003) (Fig. 9.2).

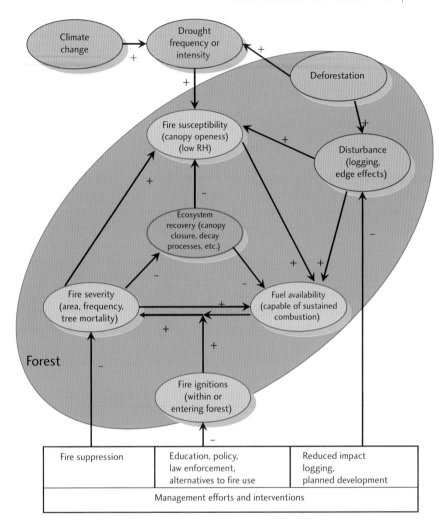

Fig. 9.2 A schematic by Cochrane (2003) demonstrates positive (+) and negative (−) feedbacks driving fire processes in tropical forests. Positions inside and outside light green shading indicate factors occurring inside and outside the forest respectively. Red ovals show factors controlling fire occurrence or behavior; brown ovals show those modifying the fire environment; and the darker green oval shows processes in opposition to fire (RH, relative humidity). The "Management efforts and interventions" box shows human actions that diminish tropical forest fires. Reprinted by permission from Macmillan Publishers Ltd: Nature (Cochrane 2003), ©2003.

9.1.1 Tropical fires and biodiversity

Studies attempting to document the effects of fires on tropical wildlife show mixed impacts. Ferry Slik *et al.* (2002) looked at the effects of fire and selective logging on tree species in East Kalimantan, Indonesia and found some decrease in the number of species up to 15 years after the fire, although the overall numbers of trees recovered to pre-disturbance values. In 1999, Fredericksen and Fredericksen trapped wildlife in a Bolivian humid tropical forest that had been disturbed by fire in 1995 and selectively logged in 1998 and compared their results to captures in an adjacent undisturbed forest (Fredericksen and Fredericksen 2002). They found that the abundance and species richness of small mammals and reptiles and amphibians tended to be higher while those of invertebrates tended to be lower in the disturbed areas. Kinnaird and O'Brien (1998) also found mixed responses with some taxonomic groups doing better and some worse in their study of the impacts on wildlife (mammals and birds) of the 1997 fires in the lowland rainforests of the Bukit Barisan Selatan National Park in Sumatra, Indonesia.

These studies are not yet conclusive and more work needs to be done on the combined effects of fire and logging and the degree to which they drive changes in the fundamental ecological structure of humid tropical forests. Early work suggests that tropical wildlife has adapted to certain types of tropical rainforest fire events. However, repeated burning or intensive logging after a fire are causes for serious concern if you want to retain the integrity of a tropical forest and avoid positive feedback loops resulting ultimately in a deforested landscape of scrub or grassland (Cochrane *et al.* 1999; van Nieuwstadt *et al.* 2001;).

9.1.2 Tropical fires and the atmosphere

The atmospheric effects of tropical fires (usually called biomass burning in this context) are considerable. Crutzen and Andreae (1990) summed across several sources and estimated that tropical fires release 1.8–4.7 Pg of carbon per year (1 Pg or petagram = 10^{15} grams), 30–80 percent of the amount of carbon released by the burning of fossil fuels, which totals 5.7 Pg carbon per year. While some of this carbon is taken up once again by regrowth of the vegetation burned, burning that accompanies deforestation leads to a net release of carbon to the atmosphere. Fires release a number of trace gases into the atmosphere, including those with greenhouse gas properties.

Fires also generate atmospheric aerosols. Section 8.3 discusses the direct and indirect effects of aerosols on Earth's climate. Biomass burning is a primary human source of atmospheric aerosols. These aerosols reflect incoming solar radiation and trap outgoing terrestrial radiation while also serving as condensation nuclei for cloud formation. Through such aerosol releases, fires have major impacts on Earth's radiation budget and its water cycle. For example, Rosenfeld (1999) used the unique satellite sensor combination aboard the United States–Japanese TRMM satellite to confirm that smoke from biomass burning shuts off warm rain-forming processes in tropical clouds. In addition to concerns about biomass burning and the climatic effects of greenhouse gases and aerosols, there are more direct human health issues. For instance, the Indonesian fires of 1997–8 increased mortality in Malaysia and lowered infant and fetal survival in Indonesia; one author implicated the fires in over 16,400 infant and fetal deaths across Indonesia (Jayachandran 2005; Lohman *et al.* 2007).

Whether you are concerned with the loss of tropical forests and biodiversity or climate change, the formidable feedback loop among fires, logging, and climate variability bears further investigation and monitoring. Remote sensing provides useful tools in this regard because it enables observations of fire patterns across large regions and allows us to connect these patterns to land cover change and atmospheric effects.

9.2 Remote sensing of fire and its aftermath

Remote sensing contributes to the study of fire in four phases: prefire assessment of vegetation conditions (fire danger rating), detection and monitoring of active fires, postfire assessment of the area burned and fire severity, and long-term postfire monitoring of vegetation recovery (C. Justice, personal communication 2007). Global remote sensing products specifically targeting fires tend to be of two types: (1) detections of active fires (i.e., thermal anomalies) via locations of "hot" pixels or (2) detections of the burned areas resulting from fires. Thus, remotely sensed fire products often focus on the middle two phases of fire study. The first and fourth phases (prefire assessment of vegetation conditions and long-term monitoring of vegetation recovery after fire) draw heavily upon the capabilities discussed in the chapter on the remote sensing of vegetation (Chapter 4).

9.2.1 Prefire assessment

Prefire assessment of vegetation conditions builds upon three types of information: fire fuels, the topography of the area, and past and current weather conditions. To some degree, remote sensing can provide all three. Efforts to develop fire potential indices use satellite-derived vegetation index values from an area of interest to derive fuel load estimates. Combining these estimates with weather data from stations and satellites along with land cover from classified satellite imagery provides the inputs for the fire potential index, which ranges from 0 (no fire risk) to 100 (very high fire risk) and can be continental in scope at spatial resolutions of 1 km (Burgan *et al.* 2000; Lopez *et al.* 2002). The correlation between the fire potential index and fire occurrence is strong, and index values increase as the day of the fire event approaches.

9.2.2 Fire detection and monitoring

Direct detection of fires from satellites uses the different brightness temperatures recorded in the shortwave thermal infrared (also known as mid-infrared) and the longwave thermal infrared channels to find fires. As defined in Section 8.2, brightness temperature or radiative temperature is a measure of the intensity of radiation emitted by an object as measured at a sensor. It is different from actual or kinetic temperature (although you can derive actual temperature from brightness temperature if you know the emissivity of an object and can account for atmospheric conditions). The approach most often used for fire detection is to detect differences in temperature between fire-affected target pixels (or portions of a pixel) and the neighboring background pixels (or portions of pixels) not affected by fire. Thus, this approach uses a contextual algorithm that compares values of a possible fire pixel(s) with values of neighboring pixels (i.e., the fire's context) and uses the difference between them to locate fires (Flasse and Ceccato 1996).

The heritage of satellite active fire detection dates back to the early days of the AVHRR sensor aboard NOAA meteorological satellites. Early AVHRR fire detection took great advantage of the fact that this sensor has infrared channels in the 3.55–3.93 μm range and in the 10.3–11.3 μm range of the electromagnetic spectrum (later augmented with another thermal channel in the 11.5–12.5 μm range). The basis for the fire detection algorithm lies in the different responses to high temperature targets by the 3.55–3.93 channel and the 10.3–11.3 channel. The 3.55–3.93 channel shows higher increases in brightness temperature relative to the longer wavelength 10.3– 11.3 channel, as fires contribute proportionately more radiance to the remotely sensed signal at the higher frequency wavelengths around 4 μm than at those around 11 μm (Dozier 1981; Giglio *et al.* 2003). This difference in brightness temperature responses is especially pronounced when one part of a pixel is considerably warmer than another part, as often happens with fire; it enables the location of sub-pixel-sized fires and, under controlled conditions, makes possible estimates of fire temperature.

Geostationary satellites with a shortwave (or mid-infrared) band at roughly 4 μm are also able to detect fires (Prins *et al.* 2001). The growing number of geostationary meteorological systems with shortwave bands offers the potential for global geostationary fire products of very high temporal resolution (Prins *et al.* 2006). The Spinning Enhanced Visible and Infrared Imager (SEVIRI) on the geostationary European Meteosat Second Generation spacecraft offers 3 km resolution imagery for characterizations of fire radiative power in Africa, the continent with the highest average annual biomass burning emissions (Roberts and Wooster 2007). Fire radiative power is a measure of a fire's emission of radiative energy (in watts) over the full wavelength range and is derived from the difference in brightness temperature between a fire pixel and pixels in the neighboring background area (Mottram *et al.* 2005). This measure of fire intensity is useful in estimating the amounts of fuel consumed by the fire.

Building on the AVHRR and early geostationary experiences, the NASA MODIS sensor was specifically designed with fire monitoring in mind. MODIS fire detection uses two channels at $\sim$ 4 μm, which saturate at different temperatures giving them different sensitivities to fires. There is also the necessary 11 μm channel for comparison with the shortwave channels. These channels collect information at 1 km spatial resolution. Other channels at 0.65 μm and 0.86 μm (250 m spatial resolution), 2.1 μm (500 m spatial resolution), and 12 μm (1 km spatial resolution) support the MODIS fire detection algorithm by masking clouds and allowing the rejection of false detections at coastal margins and those due to sun glint. There are two spacecraft (Terra and Aqua) carrying MODIS sensors in sun synchronous polar orbits. These two sensors, combined with their day and night fire detection capabilities (resulting from the fact that fire measurements rely largely upon radiation emitted by the Earth, as opposed to radiation reflected by the sun), allow MODIS to detect fires across most areas of Earth's surface four times a day (Parkinson and Greenstone 2000).

The MODIS fire detection algorithm proceeds in stages (Giglio *et al.* 2003). First, it classifies potential fire pixels. It then looks at pixels surrounding potential fire pixels to identify background (non-fire) pixels in order to try and determine what the signal from the potential fire pixel would be in the absence of a fire. The algorithm next subjects these neighboring pixels and the potential fire pixels to a series of tests to confirm their identity as fire pixels and eliminate false alarms due to sun glint, hot desert surfaces, and coasts and shorelines (which can exhibit significant differences in brightness temperature at the land–water margin). The probability of detecting fires depends upon the temperature and area of the fire as well as the biome in which it occurs. Using this algorithm in four biomes: tropical rainforest, temperate deciduous forest, boreal deciduous forest, and dry tropical savanna, Giglio *et al.* (2003) found that the smallest flaming fire, having at least a 50 percent chance of being detected under ideal daytime and nighttime observing conditions, was ~100 m^2 in size. Smoldering fires typically had to be 10 to 20 times larger to achieve the same probability of detection.

Assessments of the performance of the MODIS contextual fire detection algorithm used higher spatial resolution (30 m) Japanese Advanced Spaceborne Thermal Emission and Reflection Radiometer (ASTER) shortwave infrared data and also data from higher spatial resolution MODIS channels sensing at 250 m and 500 m. ASTER is well suited for this role as it has several thermal channels at higher spatial resolution than MODIS and also flies on the same Terra satellite carrying one of the MODIS sensors. Prescribed burns were the means for validating the ASTER data (J. Morisette, personal communication 2007). The MODIS team produces a variety of active fire products under the banner of MOD 14: MODIS Thermal Anomalies (Parkinson and Greenstone 2000). These include products showing active fires by day and night in individual MODIS scenes (also known as granules), eight-day daily composite fire products, and daily and monthly gridded summaries of fire products for climate modeling. A consistent MODIS time series of fire data dates back to November 2000. The Active Fire Product User's Guide for MODIS is available on line at http://modis-fire.umd.edu/documents/MODIS_Fire_Users_Guide_2.2.pdf. (Fig. 9.3)

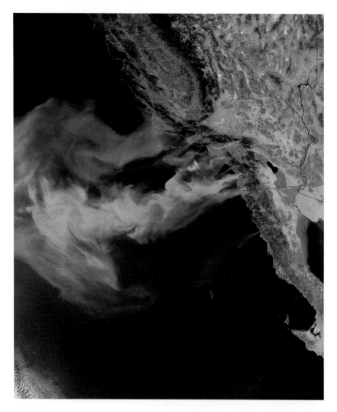

Fig. 9.3 A NASA Aqua satellite MODIS image depicts the locations of active fires (red dots) in southern California, United States of America, and northern Baja, Mexico (October 22, 2007; 21:00 UTC). Credit: MODIS Rapid Response System Image Gallery, NASA/GSFC.

The first and longest running record of global fire observations is the European Space Agency's (ESA) World Fire Atlas, which began in 1995 and has been producing monthly global fire maps since 1997 (Mota *et al.* 2006). ESA initially derived these monthly products from the Along Track Scanning Radiometer (ATSR) sensor aboard its ERS-2. The ERS-2 ATSR collects 1 km spatial resolution imagery from four visible and near-infrared channels and three channels in the thermal infrared, including one at 3.7 μm. The Atlas uses two fire algorithms to detect fires. One includes pixels with brightness temperatures at 3.7 μm greater than 312 K, while the other includes pixels in that wavelength with temperatures greater than 308 K. In 2002, ESA launched its Envisat mission carrying the Advanced Along Track Scanning Radiometer (AATSR), which provides continuity of measurements with ATSR. Envisat also carries the Advanced Synthetic Aperture Radar (ASAR), a C-band SAR with the ability to detect fires and burned areas through haze, smoke, and clouds, as well as the MERIS sensor with 15 visible to near-infrared channels. This combination of

ATSR–WFA 2008/06: 12051 hot spots (ALG02)

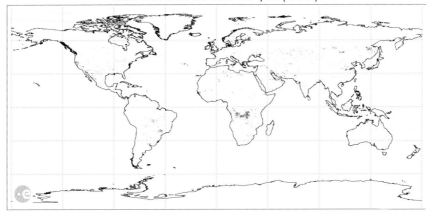

Fig. 9.4 World Fire Atlas map of hot spots for June 2008. Credit: AATSR World Fire Atlas, Data User Element of the European Space Agency.

sensors makes Envisat a very capable system for fire monitoring (Huang and Siegert 2004). Since 2003, the World Fire Atlas has used 1 km AATSR imagery. To reduce false detections due to sun glint and solar reflection from clouds and bare surfaces, the Atlas uses only nighttime data. Since fire activity tends to peak in the late afternoon and the satellite has a three-day revisit time at the equator, it tends to underestimate fire activity. However, it does so in order to limit the number of false alarms, essentially trading higher errors of omission for lower errors of commission (Arino *et al.* 2005). The World Fire Atlas offers a vital record of fire history that grows more valuable as the length of its time series increases. It is a standard data source for many satellite-based studies of fire impacts (Fig. 9.4).

Agencies trying to suppress fires frequently rely on aircraft sensors and increasingly on instruments aboard remotely piloted platforms, often referred to as unmanned aerial vehicles (UAVs) or unmanned aircraft systems (UASs), to detect and monitor active fires. These platforms are also useful for immediate postfire assessment. During Southern California fires in 2007, NASA made extensive use of a UAV called Ikhana, which carried the 12-channel Autonomous Modular Sensor (AMS) with visible and near-infrared channels as well as the key thermal channels, to support the US Forest Service (USFS) and other management agencies. UAVs have the advantage of being able to stay on station and observe particular fires for long periods of time. With the advent of Google Earth and similar systems, there are now convenient web-based locations to serve imagery from these observation platforms to a wide array of first responders and also the general public.

A tool of particular relevance to ecological researchers involves the use of MODIS imagery to generate e-mail or text message alerts containing locations of active fires for use by protected area and other land managers. This tool leverages the capabilities of the MODIS Rapid Response System to make fire products available to operational users every few hours.

The MODIS and ATSR/AATSR fire products allow us to look at the global distribution and seasonal variability of active fires over several years (Schultz 2002; Giglio *et al.* 2006). This information is fundamental for those trying to understand the effect of biomass burning emissions on climate. It is also vital to our understanding of how different regions and biomes respond to fire and how fire regimes might be changing. Finally, these products in conjunction with other information about land cover and anthropogenic land use should enable us to refine our understanding of the role fire plays in the conversion of ecosystems and associated changes in biodiversity.

9.2.3 Postfire assessment

MODIS also provides estimates of burned area through the automated detection of burn scars on the landscape. The burned area product uses daily land surface reflectance data at 500 m spatial resolution to detect changes in the land surface due to fires. Using the right sensor channels is crucial in this regard. MODIS channel 5 (1.23–1.25 μm) and channel 2 (0.84–0.88 μm) have shown the greatest ability to discriminate burned areas from unburned areas. A major challenge stems from the fact that wide field of view sensors like MODIS and AVHRR have large swaths and footprints and thus see the same point on Earth's surface from a number of different viewing points over time. So, the reflectance detected by the sensor from the same spot on Earth's surface may vary greatly as a function of sensor viewing geometry and solar angles. Differences in reflectance caused by differences in the sun-surface-sensor angle can be as large as or even larger than the differences in reflectance resulting from the fire-caused changes at the surface you seek to detect.

To deal with these effects, you could limit looks at a target area to only nadir views, that is, views looking straight down on the target from above. However, doing so would significantly decrease the number of observations of the target over time and thereby negate the primary advantage of wide field of view sensors, that is, many looks at the target over a given time period. In addition, off-nadir views can contain useful information. The MODIS algorithm for mapping burned areas embraces this challenge by using previous observations to compute predicted reflectances and associated uncertainties for given viewing angles on subsequent observations. A value known as the Bidirectional Reflectance Distribution Function (BRDF) gives the reflectance value of a target adjusted for viewing and illumination angle effects. It allows you to use the angular information contained in wide swath data sets to model the directional dependence of the reflectance received by the sensor. This approach helps distinguish actual surface reflectance differences from viewing angle and illumination differences. The MODIS channel 7 (2.1–2.2 μm) is a another useful component of the algorithm in that it allows the separation of reflectance changes arising from clouds, shadows, and differences in soil moisture. Iteration improves this algorithm's ability to detect true burned areas (Justice *et al.* 2006; Roy *et al.* 2006).

The USFS frequently establishes Burned Area Emergency Response (BAER) teams in the wake of major wildland fires. BAER teams seek to evaluate the condition of burned areas immediately after fires, often reporting out plans for erosion control and revegetation within seven days of fire containment (T. Bobbe, personal communication 2007). USFS has assessed the value of satellite imagery from a host of instruments including Landsat 5 TM and Landsat 7 ETM+, MODIS, and sensors on SPOT 4 and 5 for immediate postfire response through the BAER process (Clark *et al.* 2003). Shortwave infrared imagery appears to be particularly useful here as it is necessary to compute a normalized burn ratio (NBR), which is one method for mapping fire severity.

The calculation of the NBR is somewhat similar to the Normalized Difference Vegetation Index (NDVI) but arises from a different combination of satellite bands. With Landsat imagery, the formula for the NBR uses the per pixel reflectance values of band 4 (0.76–0.9 μm) and band 7 (2.08–2.35 μm) in the following manner to show the greatest distinction between unburned and burned areas.

$$NBR = (R4 - R7)/(R4 + R7)$$

In addition, to provide a quantitative measure of change, users typically take a difference or delta NBR by subtracting a postfire NBR measure from a prefire NBR measure.

$$delta\ NBR = NBR_{prefire} - NBR_{postfire}$$

To relate this band combination product to ecological characteristics on the ground after a fire, the USFS applies NBRs in conjunction with a ground-based measure of burn severity known as the Composite Burn Index (CBI). The CBI is plot-based and consists of evaluations and scorings for five vegetation strata at a site: substrates; herbs, low shrubs, and trees less than 1 m tall; tall shrubs and trees of 1–5 m; intermediate trees (sub-canopy); and large trees (upper canopy). Thus, the NBR and CBI unite satellite and field-based approaches for the measurement of burn severity. (Key and Benson 2005)

Burned area sensors also include radars, which have proven useful in observing forest burn scars due to strong decreases in radar backscatter across land cover classes (Siegert and Rucker 2000).

9.2.4 Some satellite fire products

Introductions for many satellite fire products are available on the Web. Sites containing compendiums of fire products include the Global Fire Monitoring Center (http://www.fire.uni-freiburg.de/) and the Fire Team pages of the Global Observation of Forest and Land Cover Dynamics (GOFC-GOLD; http://www.

fao.org/gtos/gofc-gold/index.html). The USGS maintains an online burn severity mapping page at http://burnseverity.cr.usgs.gov/. The growing number of fire
products available around the world offer many opportunities for collaboration.

9.3 Remote sensing of floods

Like fires, floods are agents of change, washing away the old and ushering in the
new. While we often view them as destructive, particularly for human infrastructure and nonaquatic organisms inhabiting floodplains (the intermittently submerged areas along rivers), floods are necessary for the maintenance of a number
of ecosystems (Fig. 9.5).

Rivers are both habitats and a primary source of ecological connectivity,
transporting water, nutrients, and organisms within and among ecosystems.
Much of the coupling between rivers and adjacent lands occurs on floodplains.
Here, flooding promotes ecological processes on seasonal timescales. In essence,
floods are part of a hydrologically based phenology driving the biogeochemistry
and biodiversity of floodplain systems. For example, the neotropical floodplains
of the Orinoco and Amazon rivers are critical nursery and growth environments
for a very high diversity of fish species living in these systems (estimates of fish
diversity in the Amazon Basin range from 2500 to 3000 species) (Goulding *et al.*
1996; Lewis *et al.* 2000). In addition to fishes, the floodplains are home to a rich
diversity of unique terrestrial fauna. Charismatic vertebrates include the world's
smallest monkey (the pygmy marmoset, *Callithrix pygmaea*), the world's largest

Fig. 9.5 ASTER image of flooding north of Gloucester, United Kingdom (August
1, 2007). Credit: Jesse Allen, NASA Earth Observatory using data provided by
NASA/GSFC/MITI/ERSDAC/JAROS and US/Japan ASTER Science Team.

rodent (the capybara, *Hydrochoerus hydrochaeris*) and largest mustelid (the giant otter, *Pteronura brasiliensis*), unusual birds such as the hoatzin (*Opisthocomus hoazin*) and the Amazonian umbrellabird (*Cephalopterus ornatus*), four caiman species, the world's heaviest snake (the anaconda, *Eunectes murinus*), and the large Amazon river turtle (*Podocnemis expansa*).

Flooding also has important ramifications for biogeochemistry and the cycling of important elements, such as carbon. Richey *et al.* (2002) used both active L-band radar data and passive microwave data to estimate the area and timing of flooding for rivers in the Amazon basin. They also took samples from the Amazon mainstem, tributary, and floodplain waters measuring the partial pressures of dissolved carbon dioxide at different water stages. Using these data and a gas transfer model, the team found that the waters of the Amazon export about 13 times more carbon directly to the atmosphere than they transport to the ocean at the mouth of this great river system. If these findings hold for other humid tropical forests, global estimates of carbon flux from the water to the atmosphere would be three times higher and help explain inverse model findings that show the tropics are not a net sink for carbon dioxide but actually are in balance or possibly are a net source—a major issue for our understanding of the global carbon cycle. Knowing where floods are and the extent of flooding is vital information for those tracking the condition of ecosystems and their inhabitants.

9.3.1 Passive and active remote sensing of floods

Satellite detection of inundation with most passive infrared remote sensors relies upon the strong absorption of electromagnetic radiation by water in the near-infrared wavelengths, roughly 0.8 to 1.3 μm, and an associated decline in reflectance values (Lillesand and Kiefer 1994; Brakenridge *et al.* 2005). The lower reflectance over water (Section 7.3) results in large differences in the land and water radiances (brightness recorded by the sensor) with lower radiances over water. An increase in the amount of surface water is an indicator of flooding. Researchers have taken advantage of this ability to measure flooded areas from satellites since the 1970s using Landsat imagery. Many satellite systems today have this capability, for example Landsat, ASTER, SPOT, AVHRR, MODIS, etc. (Smith 1997). In addition, thermal infrared imagery allows researchers to use the nighttime heat contrast between land and water to detect flooded lands after dark (Burroughs 1991). Thus, if you can get a clear look at the flooded area, traditional visible and infrared sensors can provide a good estimate of the area affected.

Unfortunately, clouds often block our view of flooded landscapes. In addition, emergent trees and other vegetation can obscure underlying open water, such as in floodplain forests. In such cases, you may need to turn to types of microwave imagery to observe the extent of a flood's impact. For assessments of inundation patterns across entire floodplains and over large wetlands in the neotropics, passive microwave remote sensing has provided monthly estimates of flooded area over multiyear periods (Hamilton *et al.* 1996, 2004; Sippel *et al.* 1998). Passive microwave sensors measure the electromagnetic radiation emitted by the Earth at relatively coarse spatial resolutions, typically tens of kilometers. However, they are able to receive radiation from the surface through clouds. Studies using this approach include those which have focused on the Pantanal wetland, 12 reaches of the Amazon River main stem and three major tributaries, the Llanos de Moxos floodplain in Bolivia, and the Llanos del Orinoco floodplain in Venezuela and Colombia. The technique used data at the 37 GHz frequency from the Scanning Multichannel Microwave Radiometer (SMMR), which flew aboard the NASA Nimbus-7 satellite and provided data with a ground spatial resolution of ~27 km. Specifically, this work used differences between the vertically and horizontally polarized brightness temperatures (expressed in kelvins) received at 37 GHz. Large brightness temperature difference values are characteristic of open water surfaces as opposed to rougher vegetated surfaces, which decrease the brightness temperature difference (Smith 1997). Maps and Landsat imagery provided the areas of rivers and lakes in order to discriminate them from flooded areas.

Other passive microwave imagers operate today. The Advanced Microwave Scanning Radiometer-E (AMSR-E) aboard the NASA Aqua satellite has a ground spatial resolution of ~14 km at 36.5 GHz. This resolution is too coarse for mapping the extent of any but the largest floods, yet easily capable of recording, as changes in brightness temperature, the surface area of floods as they pass fixed ground-based measurement sites located along many rivers (Brakenridge *et al.* 2007; R. Brakenridge, personal communication 2009). You can use these ground-based measures to calibrate satellite changes in brightness temperatures with certain levels of flooding.

For higher resolution detection and assessment of flooding in cloudy areas and areas with emergent vegetation, active microwave remote sensing through SARs is the tool of choice. Radars emit pulses of microwave radiation and read the backscattered return signal to form images of the surface below (Sections 4.3.4.1 and 7.2.5). Smooth flat waters of low surface roughness exhibit mirror-like or specular reflectance patterns in which the angle of incoming radiation and return angle of reflected radiation are the same (Lillesand and Kiefer 1994). Specular reflectance patterns yield low radar backscatter, or return signals because the energy is reflected away from the detector. Winds roughen water surfaces and increase radar backscatter to the satellite. Trees and other vegetation also result in higher backscatter signals (Smith 1997). Launches of radar satellites by Japan (PALSAR) in 2006 and Germany (TerraSAR-X) and Canada (RADARSAT-2) in 2007 have resulted in a relative wealth of SAR imagery with spatial resolutions of 100 m or less, and in some cases less than 10 m.

Townsend (2001) used data from the Canadian RADARSAT-1 SAR operating in C-band and horizontal (HH) polarization to map flooding beneath forest canopies in the Roanoke River floodplain under both leaf-on and leaf-off conditions. The overall accuracy for distinguishing flooded from non-flooded forests was 93.5 percent, with the classification of leaf-off scenes showing higher accuracies (98.1 percent) than leaf-on scenes (89.1 percent). Flooded forests showed more distinct and continuous returns with lower ranges in backscatter than non-flooded forests. USGS provided the validation data for this effort.

Experiments with airborne SARs have shown that multiple frequency, or multiple band, radars (e.g., those with both C and L bands) and radars with multiple polarizations (e.g., having both horizontal and vertical polarizations) are better able to detect flooding beneath forest canopies (Smith 1997).

Satellite altimetry is another technology with application to floods. Altimeters typically employ microwave radars or laser lidars. Lidars use pulses of shorter wavelength radiation often in the visible and near-infrared wavelengths, which lack the cloud penetration capabilities of microwave radars (Sections 4.3.4.2 and

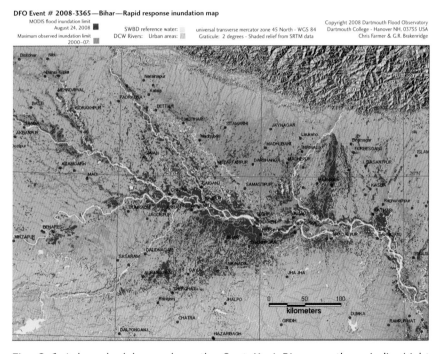

Fig. 9.6 A breached levee along the Sapt Kosi River, northern India (right portion of map) allowed the river to find a new path along this broad alluvial landscape, and forced the evacuation of several million people in August 2008. Scientists used optical (visible and infrared) satellite images from MODIS to map the maximum observed inundation limit for the 2000–7 time period (shown in blue) and the 2008 flooding (shown in red). The lightest blue color is permanent surface water inferred from the SRTM mission SAR data. Map by C. Farmer and G. R. Brakenridge, Dartmouth Flood Observatory, and provided by G. R. Brakenridge.

7.2.5). Radar altimeters (such as those on the European Space Agency's Envisat satellite and the French-US TOPEX/Poseidon and Jason satellite systems) and lidars allow researchers to estimate the surface heights of large lakes and rivers, in some cases providing the function of traditional water gauges (Birkett 1994; Smith 1997).

In the future, a combination of satellite-derived variables including water surface area from passive or active sensors, water surface height or elevation from altimeters, terrain topography from lidar- or interferometric radar-generated digital elevation models, and water velocity at the surface from radars or doppler lidars may all come together to allow the measurement of river discharge from space (Bjerklie *et al.* 2003). Rates of river discharge represent a key parameter for water managers everywhere, with applications for flood modeling.

The Dartmouth Flood Observatory (http://www.dartmouth.edu/~floods/index.html) is an excellent source for satellite-derived maps of active flooding across the globe (Fig. 9.6).

9.4 Other disturbance mechanisms

9.4.1 Volcanoes

Volcanoes are a major geological hazard due to the explosive nature of their eruptions, the severe risks from various types of volcanic flows, their release of deadly gases, and the threat to air traffic from ash clouds that can extend for hundreds of kilometers. The USGS Volcano Hazards Program (http://volcanoes.usgs.gov/) operates several volcano observatories that monitor active and potentially active volcanoes. Satellite imagery has played an important role in both volcano monitoring and research. The Alaska Volcano Observatory (AVO) has used the AVHRR instrument aboard the NOAA POES systems to monitor 150 potentially active volcanoes in the northern Pacific region, focusing on Alaska, the Aleutian Islands, and northeastern Russia. The 1.1 km spatial resolution AVHRR imagery in visible/near-infrared, shortwave infrared, and thermal infrared bands provides eruption alerts for volcanoes when temperatures rise above a background state (Ramsey and Dehn 2004). At the high latitudes monitored by the AVO, the number of AVHRR passes available on any given day range from 1 to 12. AVO uses the satellite data in conjunction with its own and Russian seismometer data.

Eruptions of the Bezymianny volcano on Russia's Kamchatka Peninsula in 2000 and 2005 offered opportunities for the combination of AVHRR imagery with higher resolution imagery from Japan's ASTER instrument aboard the NASA Terra satellite (Ramsey and Dehn 2004; Carter *et al.* 2007). ASTER has 15 m visible/near-infrared imagery, 30 m shortwave infrared imagery (in six channels, although these SWIR channels failed in 2008), and 90 m thermal infrared imagery (in five channels), allowing it to zoom in on volcanological phenomena. ASTER's data acquisition strategy calls for routine nighttime collection of shortwave and thermal infrared data, providing more imagery over the area of interest.

Two other applications of remote sensing for volcano observation are worth noting. One is the tracking of volcanic plumes post eruption. Another involves the use of interferometric radars and lidars to track the inflation of active volcanoes (i.e., deformation of the land surface), an indication of increasing pressure and a possible prelude to an eruption (J. LaBrecque personal communication, 2008).

May 15, 2006

July 17, 2000

Fig. 9.7 ASTER images from July 2000 and May 2006 depict the construction of the Three Gorges Dam on the Yangtze River, China. By May 2006, the almost complete dam spans the river and spray shoots through the gates at its center. Locks allowing passage around the dam lie to the north. Credit: Jesse Allen, NASA Earth Observatory using data provided courtesy of NASA/GSFC/MITI/ERSDAC/ JAROS and US/Japan ASTER Science Team.

9.4.2 Dams

Dams, especially large dams, are often a major form of anthropogenic disturbance to associated ecosystems. Satellite imagery is useful in tracking the development of large dams and their reservoirs. For example, ASTER imagery has allowed tracking of the land cover changes surrounding the construction of the Three Gorges Dam on central China's Yangtze River (Fig. 9.7). Remote sensing is also a useful tool for tracking changes on the landscape after dam removal.

Wu *et al.* (2006) were interested in documenting possible climatic effects resulting from the growing reservoir behind the Three Gorges Dam, the world's largest hydroelectric project. They employed a combination of monthly rainfall rate data from the NASA–Japanese TRMM satellite, land surface temperature data from the MODIS sensor on the NASA Terra satellite, available rain gauge data, and numerical simulations from the Pennsylvania State University—National Center for Atmospheric Research (PSU-NCAR) fifth generation Mesoscale Model (MM5) to address the dam's effect on rainfall and temperature. In particular, they found that the rise in the dam's water level from 66 to 135 m as it went into partial use in June 2003 corresponded with enhanced rainfall to the north of the Yangtze River in the valley between the Daba and Qingling mountains, but reduced precipitation in the immediate vicinity of the river. In parallel, daytime temperatures decreased by $0.67°C$ in the areas seeing the increased rainfall. It is important to note that inundation levels at the Three Gorges Dam were still rising after the time of this study. This research demonstrated that the climatic effects of the land use change associated with the Three Gorges Dam could be regional (~100 km) as well as local (~10 km) in scale.

9.5 Summary

From global to regional to landscape scales, satellite data increasingly provide tools for detecting and tracking disturbance processes. Disturbance events are often critical ecosystem phenomena whether they serve to reshape, restore, or maintain an ecosystem of concern. Our increasing ability to detect and track disturbance processes with remote sensing has led to the establishment of internet-based monitoring systems for fires and floods. These early efforts to provide open and timely data to all interested in these disturbance mechanisms offer a wealth of information of relevance to ecologists and conservation biologists. They also serve as a model for how to use remote sensing to monitor other disturbance processes (e.g., human land use change) of concern to our communities.

Part III

Putting remote sensing into practice: conservation and ecology applications

10
Landscape fragmentation

The country of Vietnam has long been recognized as an important region for biodiversity (Sterling *et al.* 2006). High-profile discoveries in the 1990s of many species new to science including large ones such as the Saola (*Pseudoryx nghetinhensis*), an 85 kg basal member of the cattle subfamily Bovinae and the first new genus of large land-dwelling mammal described since the okapi (*Okapia johnstoni*) in 1901, have focused the attention of national and international conservation organizations on Vietnam and surrounding countries in mainland Southeast Asia (Hurley *et al.* in prep.). Conservation action for these endemic, endangered species relies on a clear understanding of trends in habitat conversion. To track deforestation rates through time in Vietnam, Meyfroidt and Lambin (2008) combined remotely sensed data with landscape metrics such as number of patches, mean patch size, mean proximity index, and total core area index. They tested their analyses across a variety of land cover studies including those using Advanced Very High Resolution Radiometer (AVHRR), Landsat, SPOT, and MODIS data sources. They found that forest cover decreased nationally from the 1980s to the 1990s and then showed an increase between 1990 and 2000, due to plantation forests as well as natural forest regeneration. However, the effects of this forest transition on fragmentation metrics noted above differed across the country. For instance, in some places, such as central Vietnam where forest cover is relatively large and well connected, reforestation led to a decrease in forest fragmentation and secondary forests recovered rapidly. However in others, such as areas in the north where forest fragmentation dates back centuries and forests have therefore long been isolated, reforestation did not seem to have an impact on continued fragmentation and habitat loss.

In this chapter we detail the importance of fragmentation and landscape metrics to ecology and conservation, outlining when and where remotely sensed data can help in these analyses. We then discuss a subset of fragmentation metrics and point to some challenges in processing fragmentation data. We provide examples of composition and connectivity metrics illuminated with examples from the remote sensing literature. We talk about remote sensing and its utility in fractal dimension analysis and route network metrics and conclude by providing examples of where researchers have used remote sensing techniques for fragmentation analyses across scales from local to global.

10.1 Fragmentation basics

Conservation planners and ecologists frequently use remotely sensed data for characterizing landscapes, showing which land cover types are concentrated or dispersed, and which are contiguous or fragmented. Remotely sensed data can help us to differentiate the various features across a landscape. They can help us delineate "patches," homogenous areas that differ in appearance from their surrounding areas, as well as, in some cases, the "matrix," the most dominant element in a landscape (Forman and Godron 1986) and then to track the effects as well as the causes of fragmentation in a landscape (Strand *et al.* 2007).

We define fragmentation as the process of subdividing previously contiguous areas of a particular land cover (sometimes termed habitat) into patches surrounded by matrix or non-habitat elements. Landscape change, including fragmentation and habitat loss, due to anthropogenic pressures is one of the major challenges to conservation (Benton *et al.* 2003) and is considered a major threat to the viability and status of populations, species, and ecosystems around the world (Sih *et al.* 2000; Dirzo and Raven 2003; Fahrig 2003). Landscape fragmentation changes the relative proportions of different habitats on a landscape. Fragmentation may lead to a reduction in the total area of a particular land cover type and usually decreases the amount of the dominant habitat. It can also decrease individual patch size, result in a greater distance between patches (and therefore isolation of those patches), and increase the amount of "edge" (or perimeter-to-area ratio) of patches (Fahrig 2002, 2003; Bennett *et al.* 2006). Multi-temporal analyses of remotely sensed data can be employed to monitor this progression, predict its trajectory or rate, and contribute to anticipating its impacts (Hargis *et al.* 1998). Fragmentation can increase the rates of interactions like parasitism, predation, and herbivory between species and intensify edge effects and microclimate changes in patches. Fragmentation can lead to a loss of habitat for some species, but can also increase the quantity or quality of habitat for others.

Tools that can help predict the impact of fragmentation are crucial to land use planning, and understanding the patterns of extinction and recolonization in fragmented populations is key to their effective management (Fahrig and Merriam 1994; Kindlmann and Burel 2008). Increased understanding of landscape mosaics can help us to predict how suitable an area is for wide-ranging animals in need of large, continuous habitats as well as for smaller, specialized organisms that require specific habitats within traveling distance (such as amphibians moving between vernal pools or plants that only occur in vernal pools). Quantifying fragmentation can also help us to measure connectivity between patches so we can predict how organisms might move across increasingly modified landscapes including how diseases may spread between populations in different patches.

Fragmentation analyses tell us how "patchy" a landscape is. Land use planners and conservation professionals use fragmentation or landscape metrics to quantify and qualify the arrangement, size, and contiguity of patches, and the ratio of patch habitat to matrix. When assessing how fragmented a landscape is, you would look at the structure of the landscape, analyzing how many patches of each class you find. The size of the patches and the distance between patches of a species' habitat help predict dispersal capabilities. The shape of a patch affects the viability of a population in the patch. Edge metrics quantify physical or biological factors that occur at the boundary between different patches or between patches and matrix, that is, edge effects. The amount of "edge" or perimeter in relation to interior can significantly change the quality of a patch, sometimes for the better, sometimes for the worse depending on the species. When compared over time, these metrics help us to understand complex dynamic spatial and temporal processes and in particular to characterize, predict, and monitor habitat loss and fragmentation.

Landscape analysts use several terms that complement fragmentation, including dispersion, connectivity, "intactness," and isolation. Dispersion describes how clumped or randomly distributed patches are across a geographical area (McGarigal *et al.* 2002). Connectivity within a landscape denotes an organism's ability to disperse across the matrix among patches and its ability to survive in resource patches via, for instance, colonizing new patches, increasing population size in existing patches, or recolonizing patches in which a population was extirpated (Taylor *et al.* 1993). The degree to which patches are linked across space or to which they facilitate the movement of organisms can have significant impacts on the dynamics of species and ecosystem processes. Metapopulation dynamics, source–sink dynamics, and migratory behaviors, among other ecological phenomena, depend on the ability of individuals to move within and between habitat patches. Quantifying connectivity, identifying the linkages between patches in a landscape, and predicting their impacts on species is often a key component in developing species recovery plans, designing corridors and reserves, predicting the impacts of climate changes, and other activities that are central to conservation practice (Haddad *et al.* 2003).

Connectivity in a landscape is analyzed in relation to a particular species or process and it differs across scales. An "intact" area is generally defined as one of homogenous cover or continuous habitat (D'Eon *et al.* 2002) and isolated patches are ones surrounded by matrix with no connectivity to like patches. The concepts of "continuous" and "isolated" are, of course, different when applied to volant versus non-volant species. With the former, connected patches may not be physically contiguous, just within flying distance.

Effective fragmentation or landscape metrics are often based on both field and remotely sensed data. For instance, it may be time consuming to identify the size and boundaries of a forest patch using traditional ground-based survey techniques, whereas aerial or satellite images can sometimes immediately show the extent of the patch. However, viewing a patch that looks quite homogenous in terms of land cover from above can mask microclimatic features such as light, humidity, and wind that may vary from edge to interior of a patch. The remotely sensed view may not reveal ecological features such as which species of plants and animals are present within a patch. These characteristics can dictate quality of the patch microhabitat for different species, affecting germination of plants, predation and parasitism rates, prey availability, and presence of invasive species.

Remotely sensed data can help conservation biologists or ecologists differentiate fragmentation that stems from anthropogenic activities (natural resource harvesting such as logging; conversion of land for agricultural use or urban development; oil and gas exploration and extraction; and infrastructure development such as the creation of roads, utility corridors, oil and gas development, irrigation or transportation canals, etc.) from fragmentation resulting from natural disturbances (lightning-ignited fires, hurricane damage, etc.). Anthropogenic fragmentation can sometimes generate harder edges (more abrupt transitions between land cover types) and these patterns are generally feasible to detect from above.

Remotely sensed data can also help elucidate the history of an area, telling how long ago patches were created and for how long they have been isolated. However, some changes are easier to detect than others. For instance, Asner *et al.* (2002) investigated forest canopy damage in Amazonia, comparing different types of selective and conventional logging techniques. They matched on-the-ground data with Landsat 7 ETM+ products to determine what patterns could be detected in the Landsat images. They used images from the dry season for 1999 and 2000, 0.5–3.5 years after logging, calibrated the images to top-of-atmosphere radiance and then used an image texture analysis (3×3 convolution mask) to detect lateral variation (see Section 11.5 for more on texture analysis). In this case the image texture analysis was a way to look at finer scale effects of logging on forest structure, without actually mapping patches and calculating statistics as if each patch was homogeneous. They determined that there were differences in canopy damage and regrowth rates between the different logging methods (conventional versus reduced impact logging). Staging areas, or log decks, where felled trees were stored prior to transport, had the largest gap fractions immediately post cutting. Early successional plant species grew quickly in these gaps, reducing the gap fraction within 1.5 years post abandonment. These accounted for a small percentage (1–2 percent) of total harvested areas, even though they were the most conspicuous damaged areas observed from the ground as well as in satellite imagery. Tree-fall gaps, skid trails, and roads were significantly harder to identify using the Landsat reflectance data and the textural analysis, due to inadequate resolution. The authors concluded that Landsat textural analysis is helpful for identifying conventionally logged forests, but is not appropriate for tracking impacts of selective logging. Although not tested as part of this study, higher spatial resolution data could have been useful for detecting finer-scale logging patterns.

10.2 Fragmentation metrics

You can analyze land cover information processed from remotely sensed data to derive numerous variables that serve as measures of fragmentation and connectivity. These include total number of land cover types, patch size (smallest, largest, and average), patch density, perimeter-to-area ratio, core area index, fractal dimension, distance to nearest neighbor, contagion, juxtaposition index, road length, and road density (Haines-Young and Chopping 1996; Schumaker 1996). These measures are most useful when we can point to their specific effect on target organisms, processes, or habitats (e.g., road density affects habitat quality for elk: Lyon [1983]), but this kind of research is not yet well developed. For instance, few studies have empirical data looking at the correlation between connectivity and species richness (e.g., Goparaju *et al.* [2005]; Jha *et al.* [2005]).

You can calculate landscape metrics at three levels—patch, class, and landscape. Patches usually comprise one land cover type, although the definition of that cover type depends on the type of analysis that is being done and the focal species or question. Patches are described based on area, perimeter (edge), and shape (usually edge-to-area ratio) (Rex and Malanson 1990). Patches are grouped into "classes" based on similar defining characteristics such as vegetation, land use, dominant structural features (as with coral reefs), or soil. For example, you could run a class metric on all mangrove forest patches in the study area. The landscape level looks at all patches from all classes.

A suite of review papers nicely summarizes and categorizes the numerous existing fragmentation and connectivity metrics (e.g., Garcia-Gigorro and Saura [2005]; Calabrese and Fagan [2004]; Moilanen and Nieminen [2002]). These metrics differ in how easy they are to measure and calculate, their relevance to a broad variety of organisms, and their consistency across spatial scales (Johnson and Gaines 1985; Tischendorf 2001). Some metrics are highly correlated with one another, while others stand out as being uncorrelated (Riitters *et al.* 1995; O'Neill *et al.* 1999; Frohn and Hao 2006).

No single set of measurements can encapsulate patterns for all species or processes (Dale and Pearson 1997); the species and habitat characteristics of interest will frame the analysis. Generally scientists use four to five metrics in order to characterize patch composition, size, shape, and configuration and to adequately encompass the complexity of fragmentation processes. No consensus exists on how to group landscape metrics. Fundamentally, *composition* metrics quantify the variety, frequency, and area of landscape elements, *configuration* metrics encompass the shape and spatial relationship of these elements, and *connectivity* metrics focus on the spatial proximity of similar patches across the landscape. Other categories could group elements within composition, patch size/density, shape, configuration of landscapes, and route networks. Individual metrics often overlap several categories.

When selecting measures of fragmentation, analysts think about what is causing fragmentation of the landscape as well as the connectivity requirements

Table 10.1 Scale dependent behavior of class–landscape scale FRAGSTAT metrics.

| Class of metric | Response with increasing image pixel size | | Constant value | Complex pattern |
	Increase	Decrease		
Patch size, density, and variability	(1) Mean patch size (2) Patch size standard deviation	(1) Patch density	(1) Number of patches (2) Patch size coefficient of deviation	
Edge	(1) Total edge length	(1) Edge density		
Shape			(1) Landscape shape index (2) Mean shape index (3) Area-weighted mean shape index (4) Double log fractal dimension (5) Mean patch fractal dimension	
Core area	(1) Total core area (2) Mean core area per patch (3) Patch core area standard deviation (4) Mean core area per disjunct core (5) Disjunct core area standard deviation (6) Total core area index	(1) Core area density		(1) Number of core areas

Nearest-neighbor	(1) Mean nearest neighbor distance	(1) Nearest neighbor coefficient of variation
	(2) Nearest-neighbor standard deviation	
Diversity		(1) Shannon's diversity index
		(2) Simpson's diversity index
		(3) Modified Simpson's diversity index
		(4) Patch richness
		(5) Patch richness density
		(6) Relative patch richness
		(7) Simpson's unevenness index
		(8) Modified Simpson's unevenness index
Contagion and		(1) Interspersion and Juxtaposition index
dispersion		(2) Contagion index
Others	(1) Total landscape area	(1) largest patch index

Source: Table reprinted from Millington *et al.* (2003: 11), with permission from Elsevier.

of the organisms or process of interest (D'Eon *et al.* 2002). They might also think about the relative effects of fragmentation versus habitat loss (Fahrig 2003; Koper *et al.* 2007) and determine which is more relevant for the study. Other factors determining choice of metric include the complexity or processing time of the calculation and ease of interpretation of the results. To help guide selection of appropriate metrics and resolutions it is a good idea to review the literature for similar studies and, if data sources of multiple resolution are available, conduct a sensitivity analysis to determine what is most appropriate. Unfortunately, there is no rule of thumb to help with these choices, but Table 10.1 summarizes metrics appropriate for different scales. A final factor to consider is that it is problematic to analyze landscape metrics using land cover data derived from remotely sensed sources that are not properly validated. The land cover data that may form the basis for fragmentation metrics contain some level of error (often 80 percent or lower in accuracy). More significantly, the edge characteristics of habitat patches that are most important for measuring fragmentation often fall where a majority of the errors in land cover classification takes place (O'Neill *et al.* 1999). Any comparison of trends within or across landscapes also depends on comparable data sets that cover the appropriate time frame and similar "grain"—defined as the smallest level of spatial resolution of the data.

In summary, prior to undertaking landscape analyses, you should consider how each metric relates to the questions you are asking, focusing on issues of scale and applicability to the phenomenon or organism of interest (Schumaker 1996; Wiens 1997; Tischendorf and Fahrig 2000; Moilanen and Hanski 2001; Tischendorf 2001; McGarigal 2002).

10.3 Issues in processing fragmentation data

Metrics such as length, area, and frequency of patches across a landscape are easy to measure in most Geographical Information Systems (GIS). Generally, you incorporate satellite images into a GIS, undertake some level of preprocessing or classification-based mapping, and then use spatial software to compute the fragmentation statistics. You can find more sophisticated metrics in software like FRAGSTATS (McGarigal and Marks 1995; McGarigal *et al.* 2002), Patch Analyst Extension for ArcView, and r.le for GRASS (see Box 10.1). All of these software packages can process raster data, and FRAGSTATS and Patch Analyst are also capable of processing vector data (see below for discussion of raster and vector data).

Grain (resolution) and *extent* (the size of the study area or duration of the study) are both important parameters of scale that substantially affect your ability to undertake a landscape analysis. At a coarse resolution (large grain size), a landscape may appear homogenous and intact whereas a finer resolution (smaller grain size) analysis may differentiate patterns significant to the organism of interest. For instance, within the confines of a mature wet evergreen forest, there may be patches of disturbed land where harvesting or hurricanes had

Box 10.1 Fragmentation Software

FRAGSTATS is a popular software package available for free that encompasses a suite of fragmentation metrics (McGarigal et al. 2002).
r.le programs computes a variety of raster-based fragmentation metrics within GRASS GIS software. It is publicly available.

LEAP II uses an older version of FRAGSTATS that run under the Windows NT environment (Forest Landscape Ecology Program 1999–2000).

Patch Analyst is an extension to the ESRI ArcGIS and ArcView software for analyzing landscape patches and modeling patch attributes (Rempel 2008).

caused the forest composition to be predominately pioneer species. Larger grain analysis might be unable to distinguish the disturbed patches if the patches are generally smaller than the smallest unit of land cover data, while finer grained data might more readily identify the patches. Similarly, the extent of the analysis will influence the designation of habitat patches and the matrix. In our example above, the matrix is the mature forest as it is the most connected and dominant feature, while the patch is the area covered with pioneer species. Taking a broader look at the landscape we may find that agricultural lands surround the mature forest; in this case the forest is the patch and agricultural land is the matrix; the disturbed patches with pioneer species within the mature forest are too small to be distinguished in the analysis. You should find data sources with appropriate resolution to address the smallest patches of relevance to your objectives.

Vector data structures represent features as points, lines, or polygons whereas raster data are represented as an $n \times m$ matrix of grid cells. Raster and vector data sets differ in their representation of edges and therefore potentially in edge metrics. Vector data show a line in its digitized form, while raster data represent lines in stair-steps, likely representing a different overall line length. Because of the way these data are stored, vector files are smaller than corresponding raster data sets and relationships between neighboring features (topology) can be more efficiently stored with the vector data. Vector data can more accurately represent linear features (i.e., roads and rivers) and boundaries between features, since vector data can follow the irregular boundary or edge while raster data can only approximate the boundary in unit lengths equal to the grain size. As grain size decreases, the raster representation of a patch approaches the vector representation (Fig. 10.1). Raster data, on the other hand, are much easier to process so calculation of landscape metrics is faster and raster files can be used to represent continuous variables such as elevation, rainfall, and temperature.

Since the way the edge of a patch is represented differs with vector and raster data structures (Fig. 10.2), landscape metrics that make use of edge measurements will produce different results with vector versus raster data. The length of an edge will be greater with raster data because the boundary follows the edge of

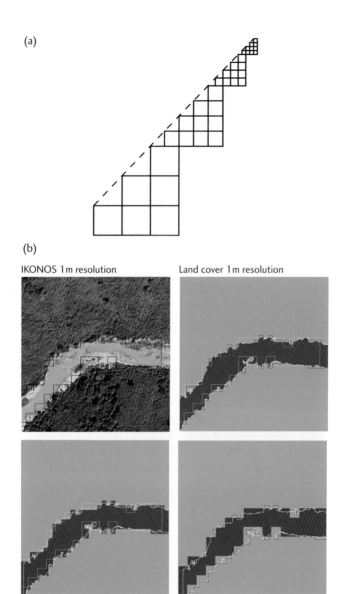

(a)

(b)

IKONOS 1m resolution   Land cover 1m resolution

Land cover 15 m resolution   Land cover 30 m resolution

Fig. 10.1 Vector data, shown as dotted line in (a), are effective and efficient in representing linear features such as roads and rivers. Raster data, shown as solid line, represent lines using stair-steps and are easier to process digitally than vector data. As grain size decreases, to the upper part of the drawing, the raster representation of a patch approaches the vector representation. In the IKONOS and land cover representations (b), the comparison of raster and vector representations can make a significant difference in the way a linear feature, such as a river, is mapped. Each image represents what would be classified as the river at the spatial resolutions of 1, 15, and 30 m. The white line represents the river/forest boundary mapped at 1 m resolution, the red line at 15 m, and the yellow line at 30 m. Credits: (a) Peter Ersts and (b) Ned Horning, American Museum of Natural History's Center for Biodiversity and Conservation.

Landsat TM image of a lake

Zoomed portion of water class with vector overaly

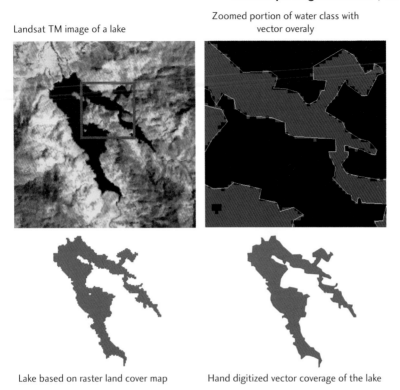

Lake based on raster land cover map

Hand digitized vector coverage of the lake

Fig. 10.2 The length of an edge will be larger in a raster representation of a feature than a vector representation. The image in the upper-left shows a Landsat TM image of a lake. The image was processed to create a land cover map and the Water class was extracted for this example. The image on the lower left shows how this feature appears when it is represented as a raster image and the image in the lower-right shows how the lake looks when it is digitized in a vector format. The image in the upper-right corner is a zoomed portion of the land cover map with the vector overlay (white line) superimposed on the raster version of the Water class (blue). The length of the perimeter of the raster representation is 30,894 m and the length of the vector perimeter is 23,665 m. Credit: Ned Horning, American Museum of Natural History's Center for Biodiversity and Conservation.

the raster cells instead of closely following the "natural" edge of a feature. Distance metrics (i.e., mean nearest-neighbor and nearest-neighbor standard deviation) increase with finer resolution (Millington *et al.* 2003). Landscape metrics dependent on the spatial configuration of patches are also very dependent on data structure (vector or raster) and resolution (McGarigal 2002). Some metrics are more sensitive to resolution than others (Table 10.1) and these factors need to be assessed when comparing landscape metrics created using data with a different resolution.

Since some software only uses raster data, it might be necessary to convert vector data to a raster format as a preprocessing step. Although this can be easily done in most GIS and remote sensing software packages, it does degrade the information in the data set (Wade *et al.* 2003). A more complete overview of the comparison between vector and raster data for landscape metrics can be found in Wade *et al.* (2003).

Below we have provided examples of some common landscape metrics and cases where remotely sensed data aided in these analyses.

10.4 Composition metrics

Remotely sensed data are particularly well suited for contributing to composition metrics, which generally depict types of patches (dry forest, agriculture, urban, habitat/nonhabitat, etc.). These metrics may include patch-type richness, evenness, and other diversity indices. There are a number of commonly used composition metrics (equations for composition metrics are provided in Box 10.2). The total *number of patches* in a landscape or the number of patches representing an individual class within the landscape can help indicate the level of fragmentation in a geographical area. Patch number is an important measure for studies of metapopulation dynamics and species interactions (Kareiva 1990). *Patch type richness* is another useful metric, representing the total number of land cover types (Cain *et al.* 1997; O'Neill *et al.* 1999). Patch type richness is partly driven by the number of classes that are recognized in a land cover classification and partly by the spatial resolution of the classification. Patch richness based on a classification that recognizes late, middle, and early secondary forest potentially will be higher than patch richness based on a classification that only focuses on secondary forest. So, the detail of the land cover classification can have a considerable impact on this as with other metrics. *Patch density* represents the number of patches per unit area and serves in comparisons of landscapes of different sizes. *Mean patch size* is an extremely important metric, again helping to identify the level of fragmentation. Landscapes with small mean patch sizes could be more fragmented (or harbor a diversity of microclimates, soil types, or topography) than those with larger mean patch sizes. Mean patch size does not represent number of patches in a landscape and is most useful when used in concert with total class area, patch density (or number of patches), and patch size variability.

Patch size standard deviation helps elucidate landscape heterogeneity. Greater variation in patch size connotes less uniformity across the landscape and can indicate different underlying processes influencing the landscape. *Patch size coefficient of variation* quantifies the relative variability in samples from populations with different means and is often used for comparing variability across different landscapes.

In one application of landscape metrics to a conservation question, Nagendra *et al.* (2008) compared the degree of fragmentation across forested areas under different management regimes in the Chitwan Valley in Nepal using a Landsat TM image from 1999 and an ETM image from 2000. They processed the images

---

Box 10.2 Composition metrics

Adapted from McGarigal (2002).

Patch Density

$$PD_i = \frac{n_i}{A}$$

The number of patches of the corresponding patch type (n_i) divided by total landscape area (A).

Mean Patch Size

$$MPS_i = \frac{CA_i}{n_i}$$

The sum of the areas of all patches of the corresponding patch type, divided by the number of patches of the same type (n_i).

Patch Size Standard Deviation

$$PSSD_i = \sqrt{\frac{\sum_{j=1}^{n_i}(a_{ij}-MPS_i)^2}{n_i}}$$

The square root of the sum of the squared deviations of each patch area from the mean patch size (MPS_i) of the corresponding patch type (i), divided by the number of patches of the same type (n_i). Note this is the population standard deviation, not the sample standard deviation.

Patch Size Coefficient of Variation

$$PSCV_i = \frac{PSSD_i}{MPS_i}(100)$$

The standard deviation in patch size $PSSD_i$ divided by the mean patch size (MPS_i) of the corresponding patch type (i), multiplied by 100 (to convert to percent); that is, the variability in patch size relative to the mean patch size.

---

for comparability using atmospheric correction, radiometric calibration, and radiometric rectification. They first geometrically registered the 1989 image to a 1:25,000 scale topographic map and then registered the 2000 image to this base layer. They combined the individual classifications from the two time periods to create an image to elucidate areas of modification (such as deforestation and reforestation) as well as those showing no change. They then used FRAGSTATS to derive mean patch size and patch density as well as mean shape index, Euclidean nearest neighbor, clumpiness, and interspersion and juxtaposition index to compare land cover across the different management regimes. Their results pointed to high rates of degradation and deforestation at the perimeters of protected land, in stark contrast to the buffer zone and community forest regions where local community groups actively participated in monitoring forest activities and managed for limited fragmentation while fostering regrowth. Community forest regions, where less wealthy individuals live and depend on management through forest protection, showed higher rates of regrowth in comparison with buffer zone regions where management focused on tree planting. The highest rates of large-scale clearing and fragmentation took place in the privately owned lands.

10.5 Configuration, edge, and connectivity metrics

Patch geometry strongly influences the number of individuals and species that can occupy a patch, the local conditions found in the patch, and the resources likely to be present. Species' home ranges, feeding requirements, or interactions with other species may require patches of a minimum area. Similarly, the shape of a patch determines its edge-to-interior that may limit or facilitate the persistence of any given species in the habitat or its ability to enter or leave the patch.

Configuration, or shape, metrics portray patch complexity. Circular patches are more compact than more complex shapes and the relationship between area and perimeter (or edge to interior) can be measured by its *compactness*. A higher compactness number—a full circle is the most compact shape—will denote a larger perimeter-to-area ratio. Patch shape can also be indicated by a *shape index*, which may be measured using a vector (circular) or raster (square) standard. *Core area index* measures perimeter to interior data—the percentage of a patch that is core area—from the perspective of a specific species (McGarigal 2002).

Edge effects are an important consideration when analyzing a fragmented environment. Edge factors such as wind, light, temperature, humidity, and predator presence may influence composition and structure of the vegetation in a patch and therefore viability of the patch for supporting different organisms. Each factor influences a different proportion of the patch and is in turn influenced by the patch's shape, orientation, and placement within the matrix. Organisms react in distinct ways to edges, with some unaffected, others avoiding edges and still others favoring them. Edge effects can penetrate several hundred meters into a patch.

The grain size of the data that you use can radically affect edge metrics. At a coarse resolution, edges may appear straight, whereas at finer resolution more detail in the form of dents and bulges along the edge will be observed. Thus, you should never compare edge metrics calculated at different scales.

You can measure several variables in order to characterize edges (equations for edge metrics are provided in Box 10.3). At the patch level, you may simply measure the perimeter of a patch. At class and landscape levels, *total edge* measures the perimeter of patches by summing the total edge length of patches in a given class or of all patches in the landscape. *Edge density* represents the amount of edge relative to the landscape area and can be useful in comparisons across landscapes of different sizes. When comparing landscapes of identical size, total edge and edge density would of course be redundant. The *edge contrast index* quantifies the contrast between a patch and its immediate neighborhood. The

Box 10.3 Compactness metrics

Adapted from McGarigal (2002).

<u>Compactness</u>

Compactness $= \frac{P^2}{A}$

The ratio is equal to 4π for a circle, and larger for all other figures. For digital pictures, P^2/A is computed by dividing the square of the length of the boundary by the number of pixels.

<u>Shape Index</u>

Vector

$$\text{SHAPE}_{ij} = \frac{p_{ij}}{2\sqrt{\pi^* a_{ij}}}$$

Raster

$$\text{SHAPE}_{ij} = \frac{0.25\ p_{ij}}{\sqrt{a_{ij}}}$$

Shape index is equal to the patch perimeter divided by the minimum perimeter for a maximally compact patch.

<u>Total Edge (TE)</u>

$$\text{TE}_i = \sum_{j=1}^{n_i} p_{ij}, \text{ and for the landscape level, } \text{TE} = \sum_{i=1}^{n} \text{TE}_i$$

Total edge is equal to the sum of the lengths of all edge segments of corresponding patch types.

<u>Edge Density (ED)</u>

At the class level:

$$\text{ED}_i = \frac{\text{TE}_i}{A}$$

Class edge density is equal to the sum of the lengths of all edge segments of corresponding patch types (total edge) divided by the total area.

At the landscape level:

$$\text{ED} = \frac{\text{TE}}{A}$$

Landscape edge density equals the sum of the lengths of all edge segments in the landscape divided by the total landscape area.

<u>Edge Contrast Index (EDGECON)</u>

$$\text{EDGECON}_{ij} = \frac{\sum\limits_{k=1}^{m} \left(e_{ijk} {}^* d_{ik}\right)}{p_{ij}} (100)$$

Where e_{ijk} is the total length of edge segments of the patch that border patches of class k, and d_{ik} is the degree of contrast between classes i and k.

<u>Contrast Weighted Edge Density (CWED)</u>

$$\text{CWED}_i = \frac{\sum\limits_{k=1}^{m} \left(e_{ik} {}^* d_{ik}\right)}{A}$$

where e_{ik} is the total length of edge between patches of class i and class k.

<u>Total Edge Contrast Index (TECI)</u>

$$\text{TECI}_i = \frac{\sum\limits_{k=1}^{m} \left(e_{ik} {}^* d_{ik}\right)}{\text{TE}_i} (100)$$

TECI is equal to the sum of the lengths of each segment in corresponding patch types multiplied by the corresponding contrast weight, divided by the sum of the lengths of all corresponding edge segments (total edge), multiplied by 100.

The Landscape Shape Index (LSI)

Vector

Raster

$$\text{LSI}_i = \frac{\text{TE}_i}{2\sqrt{\pi^* A}} \qquad \text{LSI}_i = \frac{\text{TE}_i}{4\sqrt{A}}$$

Sum of the lengths of all edge segments involving the corresponding patch type, divided by the square root of the total landscape area (A), adjusted by a constant for a circular standard (vector) or square standard (raster).

Core Area Index (CAI)

$$\text{CAI}_{ij} = \frac{a_{ij}^c}{a_{ij}}(100)$$

CAI_{ij} equals the patch core area divided by total patch area, multiplied by 100.

Contagion (CONTAG)

$$\text{CONTAG} = \left\{ 1 + \frac{\sum_{i=1}^{m}\sum_{k=1}^{m}\left[(P_i)\left(\frac{g_{ik}}{\sum_{k=1}^{m}g_{ik}}\right)\right]\cdot\left[\ln(P_i)\left(\frac{g_{ik}}{\sum_{k=1}^{m}g_{ik}}\right)\right]}{2\ln(m)} \right\}(100)$$

where P_i equals proportion of the landscape occupied by patch type (class) i, g_{ik} equals number of adjacencies (joins) between pixels of patch types (classes) i and k based on the double-count method, and m is the number of patch types (classes) present in the landscape, including the landscape border if present.

The Interspersion and Juxtaposition Index (IJI)

$$\text{IJI}_i = \frac{-\sum_{k=1}^{m}\left[\left(\frac{e_{ik}}{\text{TE}_i}\right)\cdot\ln\left(\frac{e_{ik}}{\text{TE}_i}\right)\right]}{\ln(m-1)}$$

IJI equals minus the sum of the length of each unique edge type involving the corresponding patch type divided by the total length of edge involving the same type, multiplied by the logarithm of the same quantity, summed over each unique edge type; divided by the logarithm of the number of patch types minus 1. The numerator is sometimes called the *entropy*, and it measures how evenly distributed the adjacency is to other classes. It is largest if the class is perfectly evenly interspersed, that is, e_{ik} is the same for each other class k. In this case the numerator is $\ln(m_i - 1)$. The denominator is a scaling factor that ensures that IJI lies between 0 and 1.

contrast weighted edge density allows for comparison between differently sized landscapes by calculating edge per unit area. The *total edge contrast index* measures the average edge contrast for a particular class by adding the lengths of each edge segment of a relevant patch type and multiplying the result by the corresponding contrast weight, dividing by the sum of the lengths of all edge segments of the same type and multiplying by 100 to convert to percentages. The *landscape shape index* quantifies the perimeter-to-area ratio for the entire land-scape based on the "average" patch characteristics at the class and landscape levels.

Wickham *et al.* (2007) noted that studies focusing on patch and edge statistics may not detect changes on the spatial scale at which we measure forests. They therefore analyzed forest loss in the Chesapeake Bay and the state of New Jersey using Landsat TM-derived land cover data to examine patch-based and area–density scaling measures of fragmentation. They found that patch size cumulative distributions were not sensitive to changes in forest loss. The area–density analysis used moving windows, with sizes ranging from 2.25 to 5314 ha. This analysis identified nonlinear patterns to the ratio of "dominant" forest (forest pixels surrounded by a neighborhood in which forest occupied the majority of pixels) to forest lost. The authors predicted from the area–density analysis that continued forest loss would result in a swift transition from predominantly forested to predominantly isolated forest patches across larger areas.

Bar Massada *et al.* (2008) used data from cameras mounted on helium balloons to develop vegetation maps and then calculate landscape metrics in northern Israel. They looked across four different spatial resolutions (25, 50, 75, and 100 cm) at metrics such as proportion of landscape, mean patch area, edge density, mean proximity index, patch density, and mean shape index and then used these metrics to do a fine-scale analysis of grazing and shrub clearing in this Mediterranean environment. They found that the finest resolution analyses were the most important in determining the effects of disturbance on the woody environments.

10.6 Fractal dimensions

Fractal dimensions are more complex metrics for interpreting fragmented land-scapes. Fractal geometry, first introduced by Benoit Mandelbrot (1967), analyzes complex geometrical shapes across different scales. One of the more important concepts brought to light by fractal geometry is that of self-similarity, wherein a shape, when magnified, retains its inherent shape. At any scale, a self-similar feature, like a coastline, will look similar. For example, zooming from a global view to a view with a magnifying glass the shape of the coastline will look similar. This is critical to edge metrics in particular, in that the length of the perimeter will depend on the scale at which you measure. Perimeter-to-area ratio is one of the most common metrics for estimating fractal dimension. O'Neill *et al.* (1999)

recommend that regional assessments should involve two shape measurements—average perimeter-to-area ratio for patch shape and fractal dimension for patch compaction. Geographical areas with higher mean perimeter-to-area ratios and fractal dimensions will exhibit more fragmentation.

10.7 Connectivity metrics

Connectivity metrics are often used in landscape analyses, capturing the overall level of isolation of patches, including the distance to similar patches and sometimes the degree of difference between neighboring patches (equations for connectivity metrics are provided in Box 10.2 and described below). The *nearest neighbor* metric measures the shortest edge-to-edge distance between two patches of the same class. The *mean nearest neighbor* distance can be interpreted at the class as well as landscape level. At the class level, it represents the average nearest neighbor distance for patches within individual classes. At the landscape level, it represents the mean of the nearest neighbor distances for the entire class. Nearest neighbor metrics are relatively easy to calculate but may poorly represent actual connectivity (Moilanen and Nieminen 2002). Researchers use point- or grid-based occurrence data within patches to modify nearest neighbor and model potential connectivity. Connectivity metrics have been used in the past for analyses of habitats for individual species, but they are increasingly used for multiple species (Calabrese and Fagan 2004). Observed emigration, immigration, or dispersal data between patches are obviously the best data for actual connectivity metrics (Calabrese and Fagan 2004) but remotely sensed data can help particularly in cases where some of the on-the-ground detail is unavailable.

Contagion is a raster-based metric that quantifies the degree of adjacency for pixels across a landscape. One of the most widely used connectivity metrics is the *interspersion and juxtaposition index* (IJI), which quantifies patch adjacency and patch configuration for classes or for the entire landscape. At the class level, it measures adjacency and configuration of one class in relation to the other classes. At the landscape level, it quantifies the interspersion of all the classes. IJI is one of the most commonly used metrics for fragmentation analyses.

Thus, remotely sensed data can help you visualize the relative dispersion, isolation, and connectivity between patches (Fig. 10.3). As one example, remotely sensed data can help you see potential corridors—physical linkages between patches that can serve to connect populations in different patches (Fig. 10.4) even when corridors do not comprise the same habitat as the patches they connect (Chetkiewicz *et al.* 2006). This, in combination with systematic studies of behavior, can help to determine which characteristics of corridors are useful in connecting patches for specific species when concerned about small population sizes or disconnecting populations when trying to manage infectious diseases. The size and shape of the corridor and its characteristics in relation to those of the matrix affect its utility for different species. We often assume that

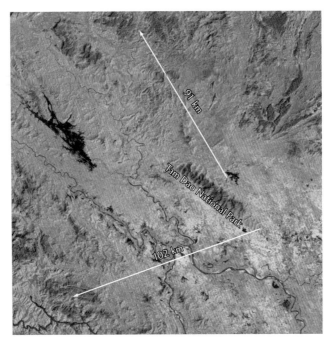

Fig. 10.3 Satellite image depicting Tam Dao National Park (dark brown area in the center of the image) in northern Vietnam, located northwest of Hanoi. The isolated granitic forested mountain ridge rises from the surrounding agricultural lowlands (in blue) so species unable to maintain populations in the agricultural areas need to travel long distances to find other forest habitat (arrows). Credit: Peter Ersts, American Museum of Natural History's Center for Biodiversity and Conservation.

movement is automatically facilitated by corridors and prevented by matrix in a binary fashion (Simberloff *et al.* 1992; Rosenberg *et al.* 1997; Baum *et al.* 2004) when in reality landscapes are complex and many factors affect movement (Puth and Wilson 2001). Corridors may serve as ultimate "sinks" (areas in which mortality exceeds reproduction and immigration) for organisms as well as highways between patches (Henein and Meriam 1990; Crooks and Sanjayan 2006). Organisms' behavior can determine whether a corridor is used to begin with, and corridor characteristics can be attractive to some species but not to others.

10.8 Route network metrics

Understanding the impact of roads on biodiversity is often a key element in mapping threats in a region. The roads can themselves serve as barriers that fragment landscapes and are often followed by accelerated land conversion in a

Fig. 10.4 A map of wildlife corridors along the Huong Son (Annamite) Range, central Vietnam, was based on data from a Landsat TM satellite image. Potential corridors unite larger forested regions (brown) in relation to surrounding matrix (red hatching) and are crucial in protected area planning for species with large home ranges. Credit: American Museum of Natural History's Center for Biodiversity and Conservation.

region. Roads can also serve as pathways for invasive species, including human access to otherwise remote areas. Route network metrics help depict fragmentation due to roads, utility corridors, or other linear features that divide contiguous patches. Common metrics include road length and road density, but the area or proportion of habitat within a specified distance of roads is another important metric. A special issue of *Photogrammetric Engineering and Remote Sensing* (Vol. 70, No. 12, December 2004) was dedicated to road-mapping tools.

Multiple studies have addressed the impact of roads on landscapes, including their contribution to fragmentation (Forman and Alexander 1998; Trombulak and Frissell 2000; Gucinski *et al.* 2001; Gaines *et al.* 2003). We can use high-resolution image data, including digital air photos, IKONOS, and QuickBird, as well as moderate-resolution TM, SPOT and IRS, to create data layers representing the layout of roads that in turn help to elucidate impacts on habitat patches across broad landscapes.

In many cases, remotely sensed data are particularly good at detecting linear features such as roads and paths. Features with sharp geometric contours or straight lines generally indicate human activity and remote sensing specialists can often detect them at sub-pixel levels. Lausch and Herzog (2002) suggest that remotely sensed data with sufficient detail, such as data from IKONOS or airborne sensors, could extract linear features such as small roads and rivers that may serve as barriers or corridors for certain species.

Weller *et al.* (2002) and Thomson *et al.* (2005) show how digital air photos (1 m pixels) can be used to calculate road metrics such as total length of road, road density, road effect zones, cumulative distance to roads, and core habitat areas in the western United States. The resulting metrics were compared with data from empirical studies demonstrating the potential negative impact of road density on species such as pronghorn (*Antelocarpa americana*), elk (*Cervus canadensis*), and Greater Sage-grouse (*Centrocercus urophasianus*).

10.9 Fragmentation analyses at different scales using remote sensing

Scientists have undertaken fragmentation studies employing remotely sensed data at a wide variety of spatial and temporal scales. Using Landsat TM and ETM+ imagery, Ferraz *et al.* (2005) measured several landscape metrics in central Rondonia, Brazil. While deforestation in this region is oft-studied, little was known about landscape-scale trends in these losses. The authors tracked forest fragments every other year from 1984 to 2002, measuring the proportion of each land-use class in the study area, patch density, largest patch index (the proportion of the landscape occupied by the largest patch of each land use), mean nearest neighbor distance, and the interspersion and juxtaposition index. From these data, they were able to detect changes in landscape dynamics and trends in logging: the majority of clear-cutting and selective logging took place in patches smaller than 5 ha. The patch density for mature forest initially increased over the first 12 years of the study and then reached a plateau. The mean distance between patches, in contrast, remained steady until 1996 and then doubled by 2002. Road metrics showed that 80 percent of deforestation took place within 3 km of a road.

The concepts of patches and corridors are also relevant in the marine realm. In addition to being able to detect different marine environments (Chapter 6), remote sensing instruments can identify potential "corridors" between them such as channels or inlets. Ocean color from SeaWiFS (Section 6.2) helps depict ocean productivity and potential feeding areas for various species and to detect changes in "patches" of these ecologically important areas through time. Károlyi and Grebogi (2007) for instance used SeaWiFS data to model the distribution of phytoplankton on the sea surface. TOPEX or other altimetry data can elucidate current speed and direction, providing insights into potential larval dispersal through corridors. For instance, researchers in New Zealand used TOPEX/ Poseidon altimetry data to model passive larval drifter trajectories, developing a statistical depiction of probability of retention time in eddies for weak-swimming organisms such as rock lobster larvae (Chiswell and Roemmich 1998; see Section 6.2.7 for more information and examples).

At the national scale, Harper *et al.* (2007) quantified forest fragmentation in Madagascar from the 1950s to 2000 using aerial photography and Landsat imagery. They found that core forest—more than 1 km from a non-forest edge—declined by almost 80 percent over the study period. Conversion to agricultural lands is one of the main drivers of fragmentation and remotely sensed data can help to quantify agricultural land use through time at local, regional, and national scales (Loveland *et al.* 1995; Senay and Elliot 2002; Kerr and Cihlar 2003; Liang *et al.* 2004).

Riitters *et al.* (2000) used AVHRR 1 km land cover data to determine perforated, edge, and transitional habitats for fragmentation analyses at the continental scale. Heilman *et al.* (2002) quantified forest fragmentation and strongly suggested that landscape indices should be carefully chosen at the continental scale. In particular, they recommended analyzing a comprehensive list of metrics (instead of selecting a subsection of metrics as others have suggested for finer-scale analyses, see O'Neill *et al.* [1999]) since we still know relatively little about interpreting spatial patterns at this scale and about the mechanisms and impact of forest fragmentation. Several authors have worked to improve methods for quantifying global forest fragmentation (Riitters *et al.* 2000; Wade *et al.* 2003), though to date other terrestrial biomes have not been sampled at this level.

10.10 Summary

As you can see, remotely sensed data is helpful across scales in landscape metric analyses. It is particularly helpful in differentiating features across a landscape; in identifying patches, patch sizes, and isolation; in discriminating between anthropogenic and natural fragmentation; and in elucidating the history of an area. You can use remotely sensed data to help map the patterns of fragmentation across a landscape or the causes of fragmentation. The most effective metric analyses for ecology and conservation are often a combination of field and remotely sensed data.

11

Human interfaces and urban change

For the first time in human history, more people live in urban areas than in rural areas, and the patterns of suburbanization and urban sprawl once characteristic of North America are now present globally (Obaid 2007). As conservation biologists seek to prioritize conservation efforts worldwide, urbanization and agricultural development emerge as two of the most extensive processes that threaten biodiversity. Suburban and rural sprawl are significant drivers of forest fragmentation and biodiversity loss (e.g., Murphy 1988; Radeloff *et al.* 2005). Data on human impacts is often averaged across political boundaries rather than biogeographic boundaries, making it challenging to use existing data sets on human demography in ecological studies and relate human population change to the changes in populations of other species.

Remotely sensed data can make major contributions to mapping human impacts in ecologically relevant ways. For example, Ricketts and Imhoff (2003) assigned conservation priorities (based on species richness and endemism) for the United States and Canada using several different types of remotely sensed data. For mapping urban cover, they used the map of "city lights at night" from the Defense Meteorological Satellite Program (Imhoff *et al.* 1997) to classify land as urbanized or not urbanized. For mapping agricultural cover, they used the USGS North America Seasonal Land Cover map (Loveland *et al.* 2000), derived from the Advanced Very High Resolution Radiometer (AVHRR), lumping five categories to create an agricultural land class. For ecological data, they used a compilation of ecoregion boundaries combined with range maps for over 20,000 species in eight taxa (birds, mammals, butterflies, amphibians, reptiles, land snails, tiger beetles, and vascular plants; Ricketts *et al.* 1999). Analyzing these data, Ricketts and Imhoff (2003) identified a strong correlation between species richness and urbanization. Of the 110 ecoregions studied, 18 ranked in the top third for both urbanization and biodiversity (species richness, endemism, or both); some of the ecoregions identified as priorities were not identified by a previous biodiversity assessment that did not include the remotely sensed mapping of urbanization (Ricketts *et al.* 1999).

A large body of remote sensing work focuses on urban management needs (Paulsson 1992; Liverman *et al.* 1998; Netzband *et al.* 2007). The rapid urbanization around the world has encouraged development of advanced methods for change detection to be applied in urban areas. In this chapter we will discuss the major data sources important for urban remote sensing, and highlight analysis techniques that are most appropriate for these data. Since change detection is a key theme of urban studies, we will focus on techniques and accuracy assessments for change detections studies. We will describe the uses of texture analysis to increase the information gleaned from remotely sensed data, and conclude with examples of complex urban analyses and studies of urban heat islands.

11.1 Importance of remotely sensed data for studying urban interfaces

Ecological studies of urban change benefit from the ability of remote sensing to document subtle types of urban change (such as the conversion of native forest patches to multiuse parks) as well as larger patterns of urban vegetation and heat island effects (Stefanov and Brazel 2007). The interaction between human systems and ecological systems are complex and require multidisciplinary approaches. The creation of protected areas can even trigger growth of human populations near reserves (probably driven by development and economic activities associated with creation and management of reserves; Liu *et al.* 2007; Wittemyer *et al.* 2008).

We can improve our understanding of the ecological impacts of land cover change by mapping not just the natural land cover being lost, but also the types of land cover that replace native vegetation. Exurban development (defined as low-density housing, 6–25 homes/km^2 within a landscape dominated by native vegetation) includes both urban fringe development (the expansion of exurban densities on the periphery of cities) and rural residential development (exurban densities away from urban areas, often on the periphery of national parks and public lands with high recreational value). Exurban development is relatively unstudied ecologically and is widespread with the potential to have significant effects on biodiversity (Hansen *et al.* 2005).

Techniques for the study of land cover and change detection (Chapter 4 and Coppin *et al.* 2004) are the foundation for studies of ecological change at urban, suburban, and exurban fringes. Most of the time, ecologists and conservation biologists studying biodiversity in urban interfaces use surrogate data sources such as population density from census data, or general purpose land cover maps. Some studies use economic data sets to partition urban areas into different zones (e.g., Kinzig *et al.* 2005). A number of studies simply note a general land cover class during field surveys and use those field notes to evaluate habitat fragmentation without any mapping efforts (e.g., Hope *et al.* 2003, Smith 2007). However, some studies classify remotely sensed imagery such as Landsat into a small number of categories (such as urban, exurban, and agriculture) to help in the selection of field sites and interpretation of survey data (e.g., Marzluff 2005; Shochat *et al.* 2004).

There are many more ways of using remote sensing to understand urban interfaces. Multidisciplinary studies of the effects of urbanization on ecosystems depend on understanding the patterns of urban change, which may require more than simply adding a few layers of social and economical information to existing land cover maps (Andersson 2006). A goal of this chapter is to provide enough information on how remote sensing can be important in studies of the effects of human settlements on the environment to allow you to identify situations where doing your own analysis of remotely sensed data could improve understanding.

Relatively simple land cover remote sensing analyses can add important insights into studies in urban areas. For example, Donnelly and Marzluff (2004) used digital orthophotos and Landsat TM data in a study of 29 reserves in developed areas. Rather than using standard land cover products imported directly into a GIS, they did their own classifications of land cover based on the proportions of pavement and vegetation: forest (>70 percent trees), urban forest (≥25 percent trees and 20–60 percent impervious surface), urban land (≥60 percent impervious surface), other (≥75 percent open water or bare soil). They classified reserves as exurban, suburban, and urban by the dominant land cover of the landscape in which they were embedded. The remote sensing analysis allowed objective classification of the reserves prior to field surveys for avian diversity, avian reproductive success, and vegetation. Through these analyses they were able to understand avian diversity in terms of the reserve size and degree of landscape urbanization, and to identify a negative impact of exotic shrubs on avian diversity in the most urban reserves.

Looking beyond classifications of land cover, additional techniques developed for urban remote sensing, such as techniques for studying urban heat islands and texture analysis, may have further applications within ecological contexts. In this chapter we will try to provide at least a small entrée into these areas as well as the ecological applications of urban land cover mapping.

11.2 Data sources for urban classification

As always, the spatial resolution of the data source needs to be appropriate to the question being addressed and the information desired. Møller-Jensen (1990) noted two types of objectives that might influence your approach to image classification. (1) Synthesizing: the purpose is to retrieve overall information about the major spatial trends in the image. For example, a study of general urban expansion on the surrounding landscape is a synthesizing purpose. (2) Analytical: the purpose is to learn detailed information about the smallest elements in the image. For example, resolving the type of housing being constructed in an area of urban expansion is an analytical purpose. The purpose in classification also influences the appropriateness of a given data source.

Since land cover and land use in cities is highly heterogeneous at small spatial scales, it may surprise you that for urban land use, increased resolution does not lead to increased classification accuracy using automated methods. Urban classification is often less accurate with SPOT (10 m panchromatic and 20 m multispectral) and Landsat TM (30 m multispectral) data than with Landsat MSS data at about 80 m spatial resolution (Toll 1985; Haack *et al.* 1987; Khorram *et al.* 1987; Martin and Howarth 1989). Compared to other land cover classes, built-up areas are spectrally heterogeneous at a very fine scale (Jensen 1983; Toll 1985; Møller-Jensen 1990). In Landsat MSS or MODIS data much of the subtle detail in the radiance from lawns, roofs, trees, and concrete has already been integrated into a single signal (Jensen 1983; Martin and Howarth 1989). Higher spatial resolution of the data reveals a pattern that is more complicated and more difficult to classify on a pixel-by-pixel basis. When using high-resolution data such as IKONOS, QuickBird, or airborne multispectral scanners, you must often use additional processing to improve the classification accuracy. Object-oriented image analysis techniques are usually employed with high-resolution data (e.g., Benz *et al.* 2004; Doxani *et al.* 2008) but this approach is site-specific and does not lend itself to automation. For synthesizing applications, use of lower resolution data might be a good alternative. Another rule of thumb is that detecting change requires lower spatial and spectral resolution than does a detailed classification (Jensen 1996).

For change detection studies, the date and time the imagery was acquired can influence the amount of information that can be obtained and the subsequent accuracy of the classification or change that is detected. Ideally you would acquire images at the same time of day, and use anniversary dates because they minimize the differences caused by seasonal vegetation changes, soil moisture changes, atmospheric effects, and varying sun angle (Jensen 1996). Choice of season might be important in areas where tree cover can interfere with distinguishing suburban areas from woodland. Because urban areas have expanded rapidly over the last 100 years (Obaid 2007), frequent imagery, or even combining data from different sensors, can add a temporal dimension that can be very important for understanding accompanying changes in ecosystem processes or species diversity.

Aerial photos with manual interpretation are a primary source of mapping information about urban areas because of their high spatial resolution and their long history of acquisition for government mapping of streets and other urban map features. However aerial photos have many drawbacks. The cost per unit area of acquiring photos and the manual interpretation of a large number of photos are expensive and time consuming (Møller-Jensen 1990). Automated classification methods that can handle building shadows, concrete and roof materials, and the other challenges at the spatial resolution of aerial photography are in use but are still under development. Although it is sometimes possible to get these photos from government sources for little or no cost, repeated series of photos are not always available.

Active sensors are also used extensively in urban remote sensing (see review by Gamba *et al.* 2005). Airborne lidar and radar, especially synthetic aperture radar from satellites such as European Remote Sensing Satellite 1/2 (ERS-1/2), provide urban land cover classification and allow the development of digital terrain models (Dell'Acqua *et al.* 2003; Engdahl and Hyyppa 2003). Lidar and radar have also found successful urban applications in monitoring subsidence, mapping flood risk, and mapping fault lines (e.g., Priestnall *et al.* 2000; Engelkemeir and Khan 2008). Driven by the need to better map flood risk in urban areas (National Research Council 2007), national and local governments in the United States are funding an increasing number of airborne lidar campaigns. These might become a valuable source of data for conservation applications in the future. In this chapter, we focus on passive optical data, but approaches for the use of lidar data in marine (Section 6.3.1) and wetland (Section 7.2.1) environments are also applicable to conservation in urban areas.

11.3 Data analysis techniques

The core techniques of urban land classification are related to the techniques for land use and land cover classification outlined in Chapter 3. For urban area mapping and change detection applications, there are some additional considerations we outline in this section.

11.3.1 Image rectification

Image rectification (realigning or "rubber-sheeting" a remotely sensed image to improve the spatial accuracy) can be very important in change detection for urban area studies (Section 3.4.3). For change detection in urban areas, there are special considerations in resampling algorithms. The nearest neighbor algorithm does not alter original pixel values, because it sets each new pixel to be the value of the nearest pixel in the original image. In contrast, cubic convolution resampling does alter original pixel values because it replaces the value of each pixel with the weighted average of the 16 closest pixels to the input coordinates (Fig. 11.1). If you need to preserve road features or urban boundaries as straight lines to improve visual interpretation, then cubic convolution will preserve straight lines and boundaries and might be preferable. On the other hand, if you want to do change detection, then you might want to preserve the radiometric values of the original pixels, and nearest neighbor resampling could be a better choice. If the data you are using have already been processed for positional accuracy, they have sometimes already been resampled using cubic convolution.

Image rectification for change detection can be an important source of error. In order to avoid identifying spurious areas of change using pixel-by-pixel change detection methods, image registration errors should be less than one pixel (Jensen 1996). Even when multiple images are rectified to the same coordinate system, they may need additional registration to each other (Howarth and Boasson 1983).

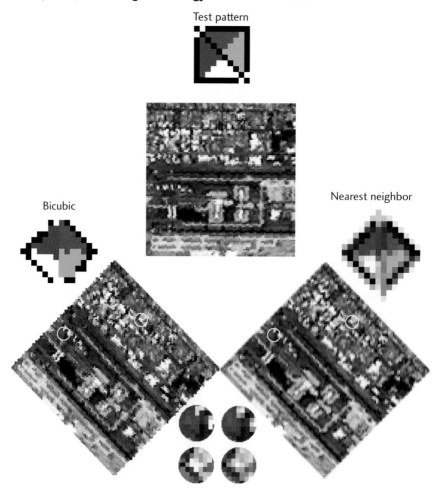

Fig. 11.1 Comparison of the effects of different resampling methods on a 45° clockwise rotation. Two different resampling methods are shown: nearest neighbor and bicubic (weighted average), with results for a 10×10 pixel test pattern as well as a 100×100 pixel portion of a Landsat image of the Phoenix, Arizona, USA, airport. Bicubic resampling preserves the reflectance of each pixel (the display of white for roofs, the gray for runways, and red for infrared vegetation, compare the areas that are circled and shown enlarged in the two rotated images), but makes linear features appear jagged (compare the appearance of the runways on the lower left side of the rotated images). Nearest neighbor resampling preserves the appearance of linear features (roads and runways) but the interpolation compromises the reflectance signal along the edges of features (note how the brightest reds and whites are lost in the nearest neighbor rotation of the Landsat scene, ETM+, bands 4, 3, 2, April 19, 2000). Credit: Julie A. Robinson, NASA/JSC with data from Landsat GeoCover Collection, NASA/GSFC.

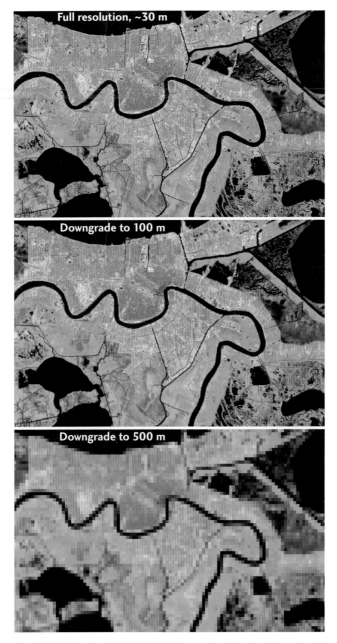

Fig. 11.2 Examples of downgraded resolution beginning with Landsat data shown in full resolution, downgraded by 30 percent to 100 m resolution using the average of all the pixels as the value for each new pixel, and downgraded to 500 m resolution in the same way. Note that as the image is downgraded the texture of the urban areas resulting from roads and building shadows is removed, while the more homogeneous wetland areas surrounding the city do not have such large changes in their appearance (Landsat ETM+ image of New Orleans, USA, bands 7, 4, 2, September 17, 2000. Credit: Julie A. Robinson, NASA/JSC with data from Landsat GeoCover Collection, NASA/GSFC.

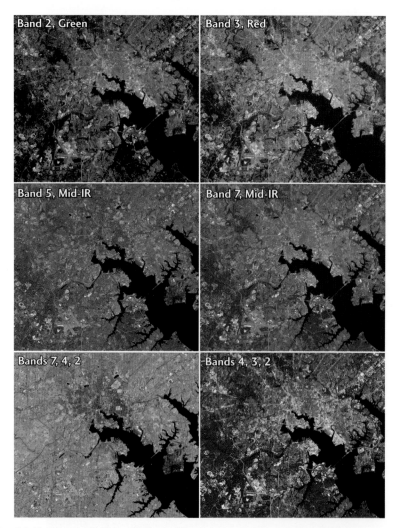

Fig. 11.3 The similarity of information in certain Landsat bands for city areas. Top row compares band 2 (green) and band 3 (red). The second row compares near infrared bands 4 and 7. The bottom row shows the two visual displays most commonly used for studies of urban areas using Landsat combination 7, 4, 2 and 4, 3, 2 (Landsat ETM+ image, Baltimore, Maryland, USA, October 5, 2001). Compare these urban representations to the common vegetation displays shown in Fig. 3.3. Credit: Julie A. Robinson, NASA/JSC with data from Landsat GeoCover Collection, NASA/GSFC.

11.3.2 Preprocessing

Data preprocessing (Sections 3.3 and 3.4) is useful in urban remote sensing analyses when it helps to improve final classification (such as by removing building shadows or unneeded resolution of buildings and streets that would otherwise confuse the classification). For example, image smoothing uses a spatial moving average or median to increase the homogeneity of the image. The software passes a filter over the image looking at a specified number of pixels around the target pixel, and replaces the central pixel with the mean or median of the pixels around it (Fig. 11.2). "Downgrading" high spatial resolution imagery in this way can be particularly useful for general classifications (i.e., urban, forest, and agriculture; Kam 1995).

Rather than averaging out the textural information, other techniques try to incorporate it into the analysis. Preprocessing to extract texture information (Section 11.5) can be used to add a supplementary band of data to the information for change detection. With data from some satellites, rather than downgrading the spatial information in the image, you can upgrade it by merging lower resolution multispectral data with higher resolution panchromatic data (Section 3.3.3). For example, you can preprocess SPOT HRV data to combine the information from the panchromatic sensor (P) with the multispectral (XS) sensor (e.g., Ehlers *et al.* 1990), and then use textural information as part of the classification (Section 3.5.2).

Principal components analysis (Section 4.3.2) can reduce the dimensionality of Landsat data (Townshend 1984); some analysts find this to be useful in urban applications, because the green and red reflectance of urban areas has fairly redundant information, as do infrared bands (Fig. 11.3).

11.3.3 Change detection algorithms

For many ecological studies in urban areas, both the current condition and the change from previous condition are of interest. Change detection (Section 4.2) can use image differencing, image ratios, and post-classification comparison. Ancillary data sets (such as land use maps or digital elevation models) can improve classification accuracy by structuring the probabilities of certain types of changes (e.g., Kam 1995). There are also sophisticated systems for incorporating texture, context, and additional information that allow further improvements in classification performance (e.g., Doxani *et al.* 2008; Møller-Jensen 1990; Stefanov *et al.* 2001).

As an example, Wang and Moskovitz (2001) used Landsat MSS images from 1972, and Landsat TM images from 1985 and 1997 to study the change in protected areas and the surrounding urban and suburban matrix of the greater Chicago metropolitan area. They used images from 1997 with ground validation data to develop a supervised maximum-likelihood classification linked to 24 ecological communities in the region, further divided into 55 subclasses. Historical photographs, topographic maps, and land management records were the ground reference data for supervised classification of the 1972 and 1985 imagery. Areas with the largest human impact could be assigned to multiple classes including unassociated woody (mixture of shrubs and trees that did not represent any native community), unassociated grassy (usually old fields), urban built-up, urban grass, and cropland. To have suitable regional classification accuracy, they condensed the ecological communities into eight community classes.

A number of the activities in this Chicago Wilderness study (Wang and Moskovitz 2001) highlight techniques that can be used to study land use change generally and especially at the urban interface (Fig. 11.4):

- To prepare the Landsat scenes for multitemporal comparisons, they used ground control points and transformed the images to UTM coordinates.
- To compare the lower spatial resolution MSS scene with the others, they resampled it using cubic convolution to match the spatial resolution of the Landsat TM imagery (essentially subdividing larger pixels into duplicate smaller pixels so the images would all have the same number of pixels).
- They completed supervised maximum likelihood classifications on the preprocessed images.
- They documented the changes that had occurred by post-classification comparison of the community classes.

Ecologists often seem more comfortable with land cover classifications that change detection between unclassified images, and often want to preserve the

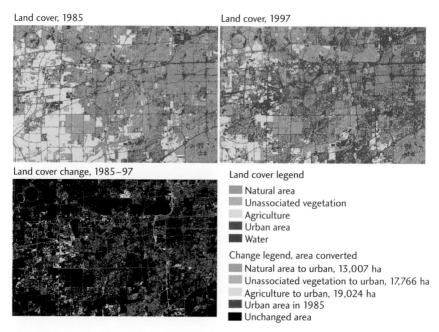

Land cover, 1985 Land cover, 1997

Land cover change, 1985–97

Land cover legend
▪ Natural area
▦ Unassociated vegetation
▫ Agriculture
▪ Urban area
▪ Water

Change legend, area converted
▪ Natural area to urban, 13,007 ha
▦ Unassociated vegetation to urban, 17,766 ha
▫ Agriculture to urban, 19,024 ha
▪ Urban area in 1985
▪ Unchanged area

Fig. 11.4 Land-cover change between 1985 and 1997 in Naperville, a western suburb of Chicago, Illinois, USA, mapped using post-classification comparison. Figure from Wang and Moskovitz (2001: 842), displayed in higher resolution than the original publication provided courtesy of the authors and with permission of Wiley-Blackwell.

maximum spatial and spectral resolution for this purpose. For the Chicago Wilderness study, the ecologically based land cover map was a major objective in its own right, and that drove the study to post-classification change detection. There are alternative methods that you could use to achieve different objectives. For example, you could rectify all the images to the most recent Landsat TM to reduce the amount of resampling. Alternately, you could down-sample all images to MSS resolution (this would more commonly be done if the goal were to distinguish the core built-up area of the city). Doing so would permit change detection by comparing digital numbers for a single band pixel-by-pixel or by looking at the ratio of the values of each pixel at two different times without doing any classification. Visual inspection of georeferenced images might be sufficient for mapping changes at the urban periphery (Robinson *et al.* 2000).

Visual interpretation of aerial photography was the primary method of incorporating remotely sensed data into one study of the effects of urbanization on avian diversity. Blair (2004) estimated cover of each land cover or land use type (buildings, pavement, lawn, grassland, and trees or shrubs) from aerial photography of urban fringe environments in California and Ohio. These land cover types were input into a principal components analysis, with the first principal component used as an index of urbanization. This index was then used in a statistical analysis of field measurements of nesting success, avian distributions, and diversity indices. The analysis identified patterns of species responses to urbanization—with some species disappearing and other species invading—and quantified a homogenization of the avifauna with increasing urbanization.

Post-classification change detection was used by Robinson *et al.* (2005) in their study of ecological effects of urban sprawl around Seattle. They hand-digitized polygons on digital orthophotos from 1974 and 1998, classified the polygons by visual interpretation, and did a statistical change analysis of areal trends. A policy of low-density zoning in rural areas resulted in unintended widespread exurban development. This development significantly reduced interior forest habitat, suggesting the potential for impacts on forest bird species.

A very different approach to urban change detection comes from the area of object-oriented analysis using fuzzy logic. (See Section 3.5.2.2, for additional descriptions of this approach.) Object-oriented analysis (Benz *et al.* 2004; Schöpfer and Moeller 2006) is well suited to urban studies because it uses both the reflectance values and other parameters such as object size, shape, texture, and neighborhood relations. Special software (such as eCognition®), when used iteratively, defines sets of criteria that will classify the data into hierarchical levels categorized by the size of their segments. Lower levels have a large number of small segments, which are nested inside higher levels with a small number of large segments (Fig. 11.5). This approach allows a vegetated area surrounded by urban features (a park) to be distinguished from a spectrally similar vegetated area that is surrounded by a natural matrix (perhaps indicating a spring, or a different soil type). Object-oriented analysis is a key technique for applications with high-resolution data but because it uses so much site-specific information, each model

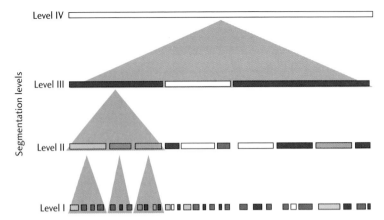

Fig. 11.5 This schematic diagram shows the structure of a classification scheme for object-oriented analysis. A set of nested segmentation levels are developed through iterative trials, so that a set of Level I classes are members of a single Level II class, etc. After defining the segmentation schemes, analysts then describe each class in terms of spectral ranges or band combinations, neighboring classes, and membership in higher segmentation levels. Figure from Stefanov *et al.* (2007: 152) reproduced with kind permission of Springer Science+Business Media.

is generally limited to the area for which the approach was developed (e.g. Doxani *et al.* 2008; Wentz *et al.* 2008).

11.4 Accuracy measurements for urban change

Early efforts to classify land use and land cover from single Landsat MSS scenes identified systematic sources of error. These include: (1) sensor resolution inadequate to the classification need, (2) ground scene or atmospheric variation from date to date, (3) selection of inappropriate categorical scheme, (4) inappropriate classification method or underlying assumptions, (5) faulty data set registration, and (6) quantitative errors due to manipulation or resampling of raster data. Other errors relate to particular aspects of the landscape in a particular scene. For example, many land cover researchers have had difficulty distinguishing bare soil of agricultural fields from urban and native vegetation.

You would think that the appropriate method for a given urban change question could be selected on the basis of its performance in previous studies. Although many authors have compared multiple classification and change detection methods, no clear pattern linking purpose and method has emerged (Powers 2005). In part, this is because accuracy assessment itself is not clear-cut. Accuracy assessment also depends on the type of data used, the analyst's training, and variability in what different studies consider as ground "truth." A comparison of Phoenix land use–land cover classifications by Wentz *et al.*

(2006) using satellite, aerial photograph, and ground observations determined that satellite imagery was best for regions with homogeneous land cover at the subpixel scale, but heterogeneous landscapes required higher resolution data or ground observations for accurate classification.

There are three types of metrics to describe the accuracy of a change detection analysis: (1) the accuracy of the classification (error matrix of reference data versus classified data), (2) accuracy of change detection (error matrix of all possible pairwise changes for reference data versus classified data), and (3) or change–no change accuracy (2×2 matrix of no change×change for reference data and classified data; Congalton and Green 1999). You should carefully select the accuracy metric to emphasize the types of errors that have the most impact on the interpretation of the changes. For example, errors in classifying recently cleared forest as pavement rather than bare soil could have serious impacts on the interpretation of changes in cropland in an exurban area. Such an error would be reflected more in the classification accuracy than in the change–no change accuracy. On the other hand, if most errors were from misalignment of multi-date images, or from different positions of shadows, there would be no clear pattern in the classification accuracy and the change–no change accuracy might be the most informative metric.

Methods that produce the highest classification accuracy do not necessarily detect change the most effectively or accurately. For example, in a classic study of urban change detection using SPOT XS data of the Toronto area, Martin and Howarth (1989) built a composite multi-date image showing change by selecting a band (such as Band 1) and displaying that band from the first image as green, and from the second image as red; with the colors in the composite image representing changes between the two dates. They found equivalent land cover classification accuracies (80 percent) using side-by-side visual inspection and supervised classification of the multi-date composite image. In contrast, their best *change detection* accuracy (60 percent) was with supervised classification of the multi-date image—visual inspection and post-classification change detection were less accurate.

The overall classification accuracy may not be representative of the classification accuracy for a given class. Martin and Howarth (1989) were among the first to illustrate this in urban change detection. As mentioned above, side-by-side visual analysis and supervised classification of a multi-date composite image had equivalent overall accuracy. However, the visual side-by-side comparison was 2.3–2.5 times better at identifying no-change pixels in urban areas and the supervised classification of the multi-date image was 4.3 times better at identifying no-change pixels in rural areas.

The level of classification detail used in the analysis is a major determinant of the accuracy of change detection. When Martin and Howarth (1989) collapsed their error matrix (Section 2.2.3) into change–no change categories, accuracies increased from 60 percent to greater than 90 percent. One way to avoid propagation of classification errors is to make sure that classification is focused on the particular research question and the level of detail needed. For example, if a regional view of change in an urban area is all that you require, a classification of two images as urban–not urban (or a multi-category analysis lumped into an urban–not urban scheme) followed by post-classification change detection could have greater accuracy than a typical multi-category land use classifications, followed by post-classification change detection and then a recoding of each change by whether it was a change to or from an urban class.

As for all change detection, beware that your software will do many things that might not be the best ways to measure change, so you have to be sure that the approach you use and the way you measure its accuracy are linked to the underlying change questions you are asking. For applications seeking to understand the effect of urban change on native species, the right change detection methods may depend on the life histories of the organisms. Different ways of measuring change in the same peri-urban area might be more appropriate for a study of decline of native plant species (where the vegetation types gained and lost would be important) than for a study of changes in densities of species of breeding birds (which might respond to broader types of change such as forest area lost to development).

11.5 Texture analysis

Remote sensing classification works best when the areas to be classified are relatively homogeneous at the spatial scale of the remotely sensed data. Some biomes, such as wooded grasslands, may show heterogeneous texture that is more difficult to classify using standard techniques. Many urban areas have heterogeneous patterns within a single land use class of interest, also leading to reduced classification accuracy. Importantly, as the resolution of the remotely sensed data increases, so does the influence of textural heterogeneity on the accuracy of the classification. This can be a disadvantage if the texture leads to errors in classification, or an advantage if you use an analytical technique that enhances the texture differences (Fig. 11.6). Although first developed for urban applications, texture analysis can also be useful in examining clear-cutting and forest fragmentation (Asner *et al.* 2002; see Section 10.1 for further development).

One solution to the problem of textural heterogeneity is to quantify the heterogeneity using texture analysis (often through employing a panchromatic band), and then add the texture analysis image map an additional parameter or data layer used in the classification. The ability to distinguish texture (i.e., the visual impression of coarseness or smoothness caused by the variability or uniformity of image tone or color) is a key element of our visual system (Avery and Berlin 1992). By doing a texture analysis, you can allow your classification algorithm to use some of that information as well.

In the most basic texture analysis, you pass a "filter" or "window" (where a very small number of adjacent pixels are considered in isolation) pixel by pixel

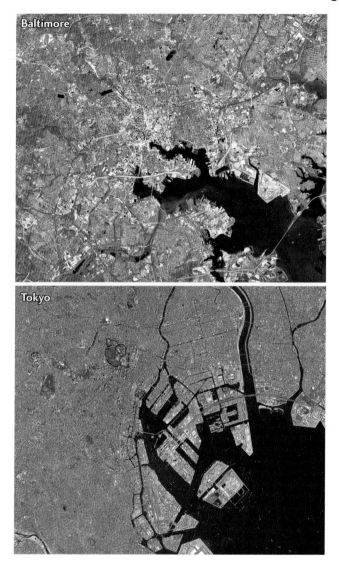

Fig. 11.6 ASTER images showing the differences in texture that accompany different urban densities. The pattern of a core urban center with decreasing density as you move away from the center is typical of US cities. The pattern of higher core density that is more uniform throughout the built-up area is typical of Asian cities. The result is that a city like Baltimore, Maryland, USA (April 4, 2000), has a coarser scale of Texture than does Tokyo, Japan (March 22, 2000). Credit: NASA/GSFC/METI/ERSDAC/JAROS and US/Japan ASTER Science Team.

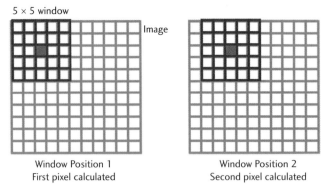

Fig. 11.7 Illustration of a 5×5 pixel filter being used for texture analysis. Once the filter has passed over the entire image, a new image is produced representing the texture as measured by the selected calculation. This representation is based on a tutorial by Hall-Beyer (2007), used with permission.

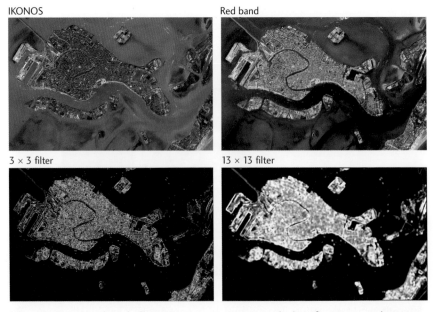

Fig. 11.8 It can be challenging to use automated classifications and texture filters with high resolution images such as this image of Venice, Italy, (a) taken from IKONOS (1 m spatial resolution, April 2, 2001). Texture analysis of higher resolution data becomes more challenging because more and more of the fine-scale texture is recorded in the image. The finer filters do not remove the contrast between buildings and streets, and this detail can be confusing to the automated classifiers. However, even with the coarser filter, the clumped pattern can be misinterpreted. (b) The red band of the image. (c) A 3×3 variance texture filter on the red band. (d) A 13×13 variance filter on the red band. Credit: Ned Horning, American Museum of Natural History's Center for Biodiversity and Conservation with data from NASA Earth Observatory and IKONOS image courtesy of GeoEye.

across the image (Fig. 11.7). A filter can vary from 3×3 to 15×15 or more pixels. Texture is quantified for the group of pixels within the moving window using a variety of statistical techniques, including coefficient of variance, auto-covariance, standard deviation, spatial autocorrelation, or even fractal dimension. Most researchers choose from among the different texture filters available in their remote sensing software, adjusting parameters such as the window size and statistical method. Generally, a trial and error approach is used, but a 3×3 window often works well for urban areas and Landsat TM images (Fig. 11.8). Texture analysis of higher resolution imagery becomes more challenging, because more and more of the fine-scale texture is recorded in the image (e.g., see comparison of filters applied to 15 m/pixel ASTER and 8 m/pixel astronaut photography in Fig. 11.9, Part B; Stefanov and Netzband 2005; Wentz *et al.* 2008).

Since 2000, remote sensing literature has contained a flurry of developments using Gabor or wavelet transforms as a less subjective method of setting texture analysis parameters (see review of mathematics of texture analysis in Zhang and Tan 2002). These are basically ways of downsampling the imagery at a series of spatial scales and then analyzing all the different images at different resulting spatial scales. Wavelet transforms are also important parts of "despeckling" tools you may use in photo analysis software. And just to connect a few more mathematical dots, speckle removal is also an important part of processing of SAR radar imagery. If you are interested in a deeper understanding of texture analysis, Ruiz *et al.* (2004) compared four different approaches for extracting texture from images of both forest and urban landscapes.

11.6 Complex urban land cover analyses

Stefanov *et al.* (2001) classified land cover in the Phoenix, Arizona metropolitan area using Landsat TM data to meet the needs of ecologists working in the Central Arizona-Phoenix Long Term Ecological Research site; their work is a great example of the application of basic land cover classification, texture analysis, and the inclusion of multiple data sets to improve classification accuracy. They georeferenced Landsat TM data from 1998 to Universal Transverse Mercator (UTM) coordinates using nearest neighbor resampling. Next, they applied an atmospheric correction using a packaged radiative transfer code (MODTRAN3) to derive surface reflectance. The visible and near-infrared bands were used to calculate a soil-adjusted vegetation index (a variant of NDVI) to represent vegetation greenness. A maximum-likelihood classification produced eight land cover classes (vegetation, undisturbed, water, disturbed–mesic residential, disturbed–xeric residential, disturbed–commercial, disturbed–asphalt, and disturbed–compact soil). In addition, they used the three visible bands to calculate spatial variance texture using a 3×3 pixel moving window.

ASTER, 15 m

Astronaut photography, 8 m

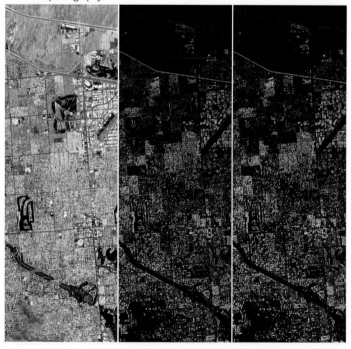

Fig. 11.9 Part A. *Top*: This side by side comparison shows an image of part of metropolitan Phoenix, Arizona, USA, taken from ASTER in 2000 on the left (bands 3, 2, 1) and a texture analysis of the images (using variance texture calculated using a 3×3 window on the ASTER visible and near-infrared bands), which shows the amount of built structures in this urban city. *Bottom*: The same area of Phoenix shown in a May 10, 2006 digital photograph taken from the International Space Station (red, green, blue bands shown on the far left). The yellow arrows mark the same location in the ASTER image and astronaut photograph, to help in comparing the different fields of view. To the right of the three-color display of the astronaut photograph, is a texture analysis of the three bands together, and of the green band alone (both texture images are variance calculated using a 3×3 window). Credit: William Stefanov, Image Analysis Laboratory, NASA/JSC with data from Scientific Visualization Studio, NASA/GSFC.

ASTER, 15 m

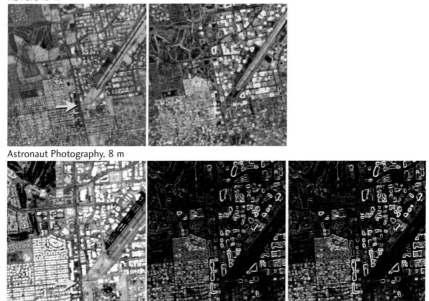

Astronaut Photography, 8 m

Fig. 11.9 Part B. Detail of the data shown in Fig. 11.9, Part A, enlarged by 100 percent to better display the pixel-level data and show the effects of spatial resolution (15 m for ASTER and 8 m for the astronaut photograph) on the variance filters.

The maximum likelihood classification alone was not sufficiently accurate in distinguishing the desired classes, so Stefanov *et al.* (2001) used post-classification recoding that combined the initial maximum-likelihood land cover classification, the spatial variance texture data, and several vector data sets (land use, water rights, and municipal boundaries). Using an expert (or hypothesis-testing) system, they could distinguish additional classes, including cultivated vegetation, cultivated grass, canals, and compacted soil. Once the expert system model was developed, they applied it to TM and ancillary data from 4 previous years to build a land cover data set from 1985 to 1998. They later modified the model to use higher resolution ASTER data in a study of landscape fragmentation and structure in the Phoenix metropolitan area (Stefanov and Netzband 2005). With further modifications the model could be applied more broadly to classify land cover change in areas such as Delhi, India (Wentz *et al.* 2008).

Moeller (2004, 2005) and Stefanov *et al.* (2007) also developed an object-oriented classification approach for change detection in the Phoenix metropolitan area to better quantify the effects of agricultural land use transitions on urban–suburban–exurban ecosystems. For the change detection analysis, spring season imagery from the Landsat MSS/TM/ETM+ and ASTER (part of the ASTER data is shown in Fig. 11.9) were key because that was the season when vegetation was most abundant in the natural desert landscape around Phoenix.

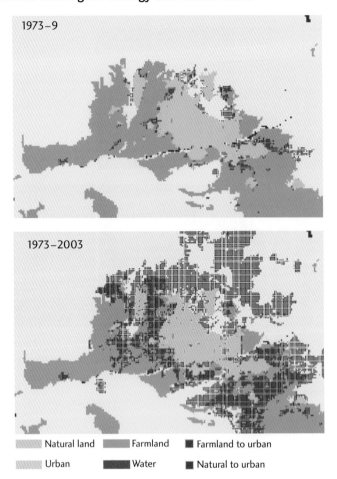

Natural land   Farmland   ■ Farmland to urban

Urban   ■ Water   ■ Natural to urban

Fig. 11.10 Change analysis for land cover in the Phoenix, Arizona, USA, metro-politan area based on a time series constructed from Landsat MSS, TM, ETM+, and ASTER data (8 scenes, 1973–2003). The top image shows the change from 1973 to 1979 and the bottom image shows the change from 1973 to 2003. The solid color areas represent the original land cover and the red hatch patterns show areas that were converted to urban cover, with the previous land cover visible through the hatching. Image courtesy of Matthias Moeller and William Stefanov, after Stefanov et al. (2001, 2007) reproduced with kind permission of Springer Science+Business Media.

They devised a two-level classification scheme. At Level I, the large segments were classified manually into urban, natural land, and farmland by looking at approximately 150 segments that the software identified in each image. Within each of the Level I classes, they subclassified small segments into a total of 14

Level II classes, separating urban classes by settlement density, and farmland by vegetation growth. Using the classification scheme, they were able to identify waves of development along the urban fringe, moving outward from the city center, and to quantify the transition of farmland to urban land and of natural land to urban land that had occurred from 1973 to 2003 (Fig. 11.10).

11.7 Urban heat islands

The expansion of urban areas includes the replacement of more natural habitats with human-constructed land cover, and also affects their emission of radiant heat energy. Urban features such as asphalt, cement, and roofing materials have much higher heat capacities than natural land cover such as forest. During the day, urban structures absorb thermal energy from sunlight, and the stored heat is reemitted during the night (Stone and Rodgers 2001). The general phenomenon of metropolitan areas being warmer than their surroundings is known as the *urban heat island effect.*

Remote sensing can be an important tool for understanding the link between urban change, land cover, and local climate. Stone and Rogers (2001) looked at high resolution thermal imagery (10×10 m airborne data collected by NASA's Global Hydrology and Climate Center) of Atlanta, Georgia. At this spatial resolution, they could identify individual parcels of single family homes. The thermal infrared data allowed them to calculate the total quantity of radiant heat per parcel per unit of time. There was a strong relationship between parcel size and net thermal emissions that was likely related to the quantity of exposed surface area. The lower-density housing patterns actually contributed more radiant heat energy than higher-density development.

Subsequent analyses of the accompanying high-resolution airborne multi-spectral imagery (Advanced Thermal and Land Applications Sensor with 10 m resolution and 15 multispectral bands, Stone and Norman 2006) were able to characterize the urban land use in more specific ways. They measured the area of impervious materials (driveways and building footprints), area of lawn and landscaping, proportion of overlying tree cover (from NDVI), and number of bedrooms (the area of the home and number of bedrooms were obviously not derived from remote sensing, but from tax records!). Such analyses have helped communities to better understand the contributions of lower-density suburban land use to urban heat island effects, and identified ways that planners can minimize these effects. For example, the Atlanta study estimated that a 25 percent reduction in the area of impervious and residential lawn space and an increase in average tree canopy cover from 45 to 60 percent would reduce the city's tendency to serve as a heat sink by 40 percent. Such information is being used to galvanize tree planting in temperate and subtropical cities, as communities seek to lower energy costs for cooling in summer.

Study of urban heat islands also informs understanding of human settlement patterns and decision-making processes. Although many ecologists have traditionally avoided study of areas with significant human alteration, it is obvious that human activities are an integral part of the function of urban ecosystems. Urban heat island effects are perhaps one of the most immediately observable results of human modification of the landscape (Brazel *et al.* 2000; Voogt and Oke 2003; Stefanov and Brazel 2007). An exciting area of interdisciplinary research involves studying the interactions between social factors, landscape, and atmosphere in urban centers. For example, landscaping and vegetation choices in neighborhoods in Phoenix correlates to microclimate, meaning there are economic inequities in exposure of people to extreme climatic conditions (Harlan *et al.* 2007; Jenerette *et al.* 2007).

11.8 Summary

As the world becomes increasingly urbanized, ecological studies on the urban fringe and within urban areas become important. Many field biologists working in urban and exurban environments simply add a notation of a land use class such as "park," "fallow field," or "suburb" to their field notes as they make observations seeking to understand the effects of urbanization on native species. We urge these scientists to consider whether use of mapping techniques could improve their studies. Similarly, other studies that use mapping have relied on census data delimited by political boundaries. We encourage researchers interested in urban interfaces to consider whether development of a custom map from remotely sensed data could give better information than simply loading whatever census data is available into a GIS. By using remote sensing to generate maps appropriate to the types of impacts being studied, you can gain much more information about patterns of transition in land cover, and about the spatial distribution of remnant habitats in the changing matrix of human-modified lands. Mapping human impacts is also important in global studies of the human footprint (Section 15.2.2; Sanderson *et al.* 2002). Another strength of remote sensing is the ability to look back in time using historical data from Landsat, SPOT, USGS digital orthophotos, and even astronaut photography. Classifications developed with field data in the present can be extrapolated to understand the history of urban expansion in the past, providing important insights into the impacts of urbanization on species distributions and other measures of biodiversity.

12

Protected area design and monitoring

Researchers interested in remote locations have developed monitoring schemes, sometimes called "Watchful Eye" monitoring, that use a time series of remotely sensed images to assess changes over time to a protected area or habitat. For instance, the European Space Agency (ESA) and UNESCO have set up repeat analyses of satellite imagery for World Heritage sites. The first area for which they developed this technique was the habitat of the critically endangered mountain gorilla (*Gorilla berengei berengei*) in the Virunga Mountains in Central Africa, including the Bwindi and Mgahinga National Parks in Uganda, the Virunga and Kahuzi-Biega National Parks in the Democratic Republic of Congo, and the trans-boundary Volcanoes Conservation Area (Fig. 12.1a). The project developed detailed maps of these inaccessible zones so that protected area managers can monitor the gorilla habitat. Previously, available maps were old and inaccurate (at times handmade), did not completely cover the range of the gorillas, and did not cross national boundaries. Because there was no systematic information from the ground regarding changes over time, researchers also used remotely sensed data to complete change detection analyses over the past two decades. Using both optical (Landsat series) and radar (ENVISAT ASAR) satellite data, researchers were able to quantify rates of deforestation between 1990 and 2003 and relate these rates to human migration rates into the area resulting from regional political instability. Researchers constructed the first digital base maps of the areas, digital elevation models (DEMs), and updated vegetation and land use maps (Fig. 12.1b). They faced significant problems in both field and laboratory activities, including lack of existing ground data, dense vegetation cover, and fairly continuous cloud cover. They therefore used a combination of ESA ENVISAT ASAR as well as Landsat and ESA Medium Resolution Imaging Spectrometer (MERIS) optical data. The radar images allowed them to quantify elevation and distances between trees and homes. Landsat and MERIS data helped identify forest cover types, with Landsat providing finer-scale images at less frequent intervals and MERIS serving lower-resolution images more frequently. National government and international conservation organizations are employing the resulting products to refine their antipoaching efforts, delineate the park boundaries, follow migrating gorilla groups across international boundaries, and plan for ecotourism (Fernández-Prieto *et al.* 2003, 2004, 2005).

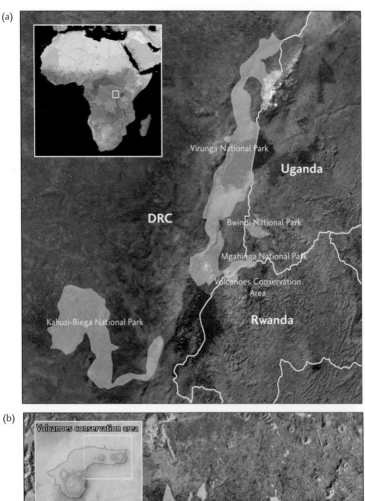

Fig. 12.1 (a) Central African region showing protected areas that harbor mountain gorillas and (b) Example partial land cover map of the Volcanoes Conservation Area developed from Landsat ETM+ data (path 173, row 61, January 31, 2003) and SRTM-based DEM. Credit: Jeff Silverman, American Museum of Natural History's Center for Biodiversity and Conservation.

Conservation biologists use remote sensing regularly in planning for and managing protected areas. In this chapter we will provide examples of how these data have been used for planning protected areas, from designing individual protected areas at the local scale to mapping out networks of protected areas at the regional or national scale. We then discuss how these kinds of data can be useful for managing and monitoring existing protected areas. Remotely sensed data are increasingly used to help integrate social and economic factors into protected area planning and monitoring and we provide several examples of this. We conclude the chapter with some resources available for global-scale monitoring of protected areas and with cautions regarding drawbacks to applying remotely sensed data to protected areas.

12.1 Planning for protected areas

Remotely sensed data have been used in designing individual and networks of protected areas. Governments and communities working to set aside areas for protection regularly employ multiple criteria such as irreplaceability, representation, and species richness in determining likely targets for conservation. Their mandate is often to concentrate on as small an area as possible to allow for competing demands for development and other human activities. Remote sensing and geographical information systems can help efforts to maximize the biodiversity represented within a minimum area, at both a network level and at an individual site level. The technologies can be very useful in protected area network design since multi-criteria decision-making requires consistent information on and definitions of biodiversity value, threats, and constraints. Maps derived from remote sensing, such as existing land use or status and trends in extent of biomes or species distributions, provide important input to such analyses.

12.1.1 Designing individual protected areas

Remote sensing is playing an increasingly important role in the planning and design of individual protected areas. Its primary purpose has been in planning boundaries for the potential protected area—using measures of biological and physical conditions such as land cover types and human disturbance (cf. Menon and Bawa 1997). As discussed in Chapter 10, remote sensing can provide measures of local and regional habitat fragmentation in comparison with the surrounding cover to help in planning boundaries.

As an example, when conservation biologists collaborated with governmental and nongovernmental organizations to develop a new national park in northeastern Madagascar, they identified 13 design criteria of which 4 relied on data from satellite imagery (Kremen *et al.* 1999). They wanted to identify the largest contiguous area of natural forest. This area needed to be primary or relatively undisturbed habitat; and it needed to encompass a suite of representative patches of the existing habitat types, including habitat mosaics and transitional zones, across the spectrum of environmental gradients. They wanted to identify any existing corridors that could encourage animal movement or support forest regeneration activities. They developed forest cover layers from a 1991 SPOT panchromatic satellite image using manual interpretation, refined by ground verification and aerial overflight data. From this panchromatic imagery, they were able to distinguish forested and deforested areas, as well as fragments of littoral forest–mangrove–marsh mosaics. They integrated these data layers with biological information on species distribution and population abundance, threats analyses, social and economic information on human settlements, land use and tenure, and commercial and subsistence market analyses to estimate the economic potential of forest management and conservation compared with that of deforestation activities. The integrated analysis yielded a proposal for balancing wildlife and human needs and ultimately led to the establishment of the largest national park in Madagascar (at that time).

Other researchers have used remotely sensed data to analyze the effects of drivers of biodiversity loss, such as climate change, on species representation in reserves (Araújo *et al.* 2004) or on analyses of the regions surrounding protected areas in order to identify possible corridors of habitat to connect existing protected areas (Plumptre 2002; Lees and Peres 2008).

12.1.2 Designing networks of protected areas

Planners have used remote sensing techniques to help design networks of protected areas in both terrestrial and marine environments. For instance, in the terrestrial realm, Das *et al.* (2006) used a systematic conservation planning approach to identify areas of high conservation value in the Western Ghats of India. They looked at surrogates of conservation value such as number of threatened and endemic plant and vertebrate species; area of unfragmented forest dry forests, and evergreen ecosystems; and location and extent of rare vegetation types to test whether the surrogates were correlated, identify irreplaceable sites based on all five surrogates, and then assess the representation of these factors in the existing protected area network. For the habitat analyses, they used two scenes from the Indian Remote Sensing satellite Wide Field Sensors at 188 m resolution for dates ranging from 2000 to 2003 selected to encompass the end of the wet season and middle of the dry season. They georeferenced the images with 1:250,000 topographic maps and used NDVI to classify the vegetation through a classification and regression tree approach (Section 3.5.2). They developed two possible reserve networks, one with minimal representation of each of the surrogates, the other with at least three occurrences of each species and 25 percent of each habitat type. They found that 70 percent of the irreplaceable areas in their analysis were outside the current protected area system and that amphibians, endemic tree species, and small mammals were particularly poorly represented in the current system even though the system met the minimal representation target for 88 percent of the species considered in the analysis.

In the marine realm, Louzao *et al.* (2006) noted that most marine protected area (MPA) systems are set up to protect benthic species and habitats so they tested the ability for MPAs in the western Mediterranean to protect highly mobile pelagic species, such as sea turtles, mammals, and sea birds. In particular, they focused on the distribution and oceanographic habitat use of the Balearic shearwater (*Puffinus mauretanicus*) during chick rearing periods (May to June) from 1999 to 2002. They used a hierarchical modeling approach to isolate the key environmental variables for shearwater habitat, identifying foraging sites using presence–absence data as well as abundance data. They combined at-sea surveys with measures of environmental variables such as sea surface temperature (SST) and chlorophyll *a* (chl *a*) using eight-day composites of 9 km pixel data. They used nighttime Pathfinder 4.1 SST imagery from AVHRR to measure

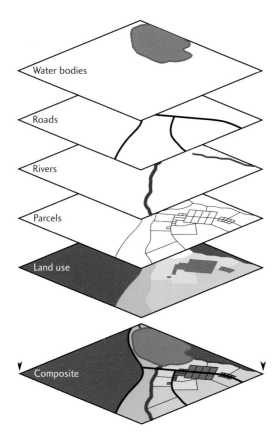

Fig. 12.2 Layers used in a typical gap analysis. Credit: Peter Ersts, American Museum of Natural History's Center for Biodiversity and Conservation.

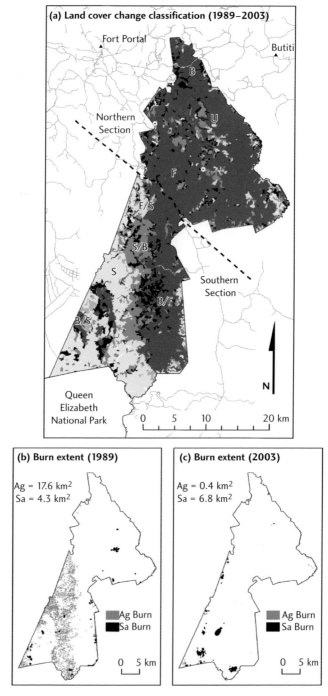

Fig. 12.3 (a) Land-cover change classification for a protected area in Kibale National Park, Uganda and (b & c) Total area burned in 1989 and 2003. Burns are divided by whether pre-burn land cover was agriculture (Ag) or savannah (Sa). Credit: Nadine Laporte, Woods Hole Research Center.

water temperature and derived chl *a* from SeaWiFS imagery (discarding values that fell beyond the range of SeaWiFS validation). They confirmed that greater understanding of wildlife habitat associations, incorporating life history and dynamism, would help to refine the feasibility, efficacy, and general design of networks of marine protected areas. They recommended for the western Mediterranean that regions harboring dense aggregations of shearwaters could serve as core regions with higher protection and management efforts, whereas areas where the species forages at lower abundance and density could be included in buffer regions around the core zones. This kind of zoning could extend protection beyond the breeding aggregation sites and protect pelagic species during both breeding and nonbreeding seasons.

Planners frequently use remotely sensed data in gap analyses for designing networks of protected areas, looking at what biological elements already exist within a protected area system, what elements they would like to have covered by that system, and identifying the gaps in the current system. Remote sensing can help in developing layers for gap analyses (Fig. 12.2) including mapping vegetation patterns and species ranges, visualizing locations managed primarily for biodiversity (e.g., national parks or wildlife refuges), identifying species not protected or underrepresented in these areas, and ultimately establishing conservation priorities based on these results (Scott *et al.* 1993). Gap analysis was first used in the United States on the island of Hawaii to examine the distribution of four endangered forest finches with respect to existing nature reserves. Only 10 percent of the birds' habitat overlapped with nature reserves and as a result new protected areas were created where the endangered birds were located.

Scott and colleagues at the Gap Analysis Project then undertook to develop spatially explicit models on species and assemblages of species across the United States (Scott *et al.* 1993; Scott and Jennings 1998) using Landsat imagery. They worked to develop a framework for assessing what we know about terrestrial vertebrate species distributions and vegetation types across the United States, stratifying existing data to focus future higher-resolution surveys efficiently. They first mapped vegetation alliance, then created GIS layers of existing conservation lands and of predicted distributions of native vertebrate species, and finally looked at the representation of vertebrate species and different land cover types in protected areas to identify gaps in land management and, by extension, in knowledge about species and natural communities. To undertake the land cover classification, the authors used an iterative system with the results from any particular step triggering a reconsideration of results from previous steps. They geographically registered the Landsat TM data and sorted it into 240 classes employing bands 1,2,3,4,5, and 7. Managers at the state level used the resulting Gap Analysis for a variety of purposes, including land use planning in southern California (Crowe 1996). The authors envisioned a suite of potential applications of the products, including being able to take a distribution map for a particular species and test the representativeness of existing locality information or develop hypotheses concerning species ranges, abundance, and reproductive success. Subsequent gap analyses have focused on broadening the representation of species covered to include groups that are commonly not considered, such as invertebrates (Jennings 2000).

12.2 Managing and monitoring protected areas

Many researchers have increasingly undertaken studies to track protected area status and trends using remote sensing technology (Bock *et al.* 2005; Courrau 1999; Curran *et al.* 2004; Dudley *et al.* 1999; Hockings 2003; Parrish *et al.* 2003; Rand 2002; Salami *et al.* 1999; Seto and Fragkias 2007; Vasconcelos *et al.* 2002). These methods are particularly useful in assessing the effectiveness of protected area management, with indicators derived from land cover change analyses (both inside and outside protected area boundaries) and various human disturbance layers.

In Uganda along the Albertine Rift, Plumptre *et al.* (2003; Plumptre 2002) assessed forest conversion to agriculture from the 1980s to the early 2000s and modeled future threats to the region's fragmented network of protected areas. The threats to the network of protected areas along the Rift varied across the regions and countries and include habitat loss, hunting, timber exploitation, and mining. The biologists melded traditional, fine-scale field surveys with remote sensing data to locate areas of active deforestation. The latter involved a time series of Landsat images, georeferencing Landsat-7 images to Landsat-5 images from NASA's Global Orthorectified Landsat data set products. They then developed a new regional mosaic to provide information that could be applied to ongoing development of management strategies for protected areas in this region and a baseline for future threats assessment and monitoring—critical for an area that has some of the highest human population densities in all of Africa.

Plumptre *et al.* (2003) used unsupervised classification and expert knowledge to create a map of forest loss for each of six protected areas separately (Bugoma, Budongo, Kagombe, Kasyoha-Kitomi, Kalinzu-Maramagamba, and Bwindi). They found the highest deforestation rates in the northern part of the protected area network, with substantial forest loss attributed to large-scale farming, and that much of the forest lost was located immediately adjacent to protected area boundaries. There is also evidence that deforestation is already taking place within park boundaries.

Remote sensing can provide unique information on the effectiveness of management strategies. For example, Laporte *et al.* (2008) employed Landsat satellite imagery acquired from 1989 and 2003 in order to assess correlations between land cover and management policies such as fire suppression and the eviction of farmers in Kibale National Park, Uganda. In this park, the Uganda Wildlife Authority used fire suppression and eviction of human communities to foster the conversion of agricultural lands to young forest and mixed bushland/woodland. These changes provided a greater quantity of habitat for monkey species in the short term and possibly for chimpanzees in the long term. However, the suppression of fires led to a decrease in grassland habitat, which may reduce population sizes of elephants and ungulates.

The 1989 and 2003 images were registered to an ortho-rectified Landsat image from 2001. The authors employed a nearest neighbor resampling method at a resolution of 28.5 m. They georeferenced the images using 35 ground control points located throughout the Landsat scene but clustered around Kibale National Park and surrounding areas. Change detection was undertaken using object-oriented analysis (with eCognition® 4.0) and Landsat bands 2, 3, and 4 of the 1989 and 2003 images. Researchers also identified and quantified burn scars across both images to determine changes in agricultural and savannah burning through time (Fig. 12.3). They found that suppression of fire correlates highly with the ratio of forest to savannah. They also suggested that ecosystem diversity and habitat for nonprimate mammals could be ameliorated through prescribed burning at selected locations, particularly in the north of the reserve.

In another example of protected area monitoring with remotely sensed data, Sánchez-Azofeifa *et al.* (2003) noted that the national park system in Costa Rica is extensive and the efforts to monitor park effectiveness are a significant priority for the government. Monitoring questions include: How well are individual park boundaries respected? Do the parks in general create a functioning network? Are the parks effective at conserving Costa Rica's biodiversity? The authors measured deforestation and forest regeneration within and around protected areas from 1960 to 1997, spanning baseline conditions as well as the period of high rates of deforestation that began in the 1970s. They studied land cover change via three data sets—1:250,000 topographic maps from 1960 aerial photography; 1970s land cover maps developed from Landsat MSS data (black and white prints); and Landsat TM data acquired from 1986 to 1997 (seven spectral bands and 28.5 m spatial resolution). No ground validation was available for the first two data sets, while they used validation data from 800 points for the TM images, with an overall classification accuracy of 92 percent. Cloud cover obscured parts of the TM data set, but mainly in regions without national parks or reserves.

The authors incorporated the land cover maps into a GIS database along with layers representing: (1) the location of national parks, (2) biological reserves and proposed biological corridors (1:50,000) as well as 0.5, 1 and 10 km buffer zones around these parks and reserves, (3) boundaries for conservation regions (1:200,000), and (4) Holdridge life zones (1:200,000). The study revealed that deforestation rates within Costa Rica's national parks and biological reserves were minimal, and that areas within the 1 km buffer around parks and reserves underwent a net forest gain from 1987 to 1997. The 10 km buffer zones, however, showed significant forest loss across the decades of the study. Thus, individual protected areas seem to be functioning effectively at conserving forest cover, but they may be increasingly isolated, precluding effective functioning of a national network of protected areas.

At a much broader scale, researchers have applied remote sensing and GIS techniques to develop a monitoring system for European networks of protected areas such as Natura 2000 (Groom *et al.* 2006). They have combined land cover maps derived from satellite data (Landsat TM, SPOT) with a digital terrain model and land use data (forest road networks, summer cottages, tourist locations) to analyze indicators such as "naturalness," "vulnerability," and "threat" for selected regions to help identify current state and track future changes in the landscape.

In the marine realm, Friedman *et al.* (2007a,b) combined field surveys for fish with satellite imagery to assess the efficacy of different kinds of protected areas in Hawaii for fish protection. For the past four decades, Hawaii has been developing a suite of Marine Life Conservation Districts, all of which vary in size, management goals, and habitat quality. They developed digital benthic maps using visually interpreted ortho-rectified aerial photography, IKONOS satellite imagery, and airborne hyperspectral imagery for near-shore waters (to 25 m depth). They based visual interpretation on habitat classifications of ecologically relevant location information (backreef, forereef, lagoon, etc.) as well as typological (patch reef, spur and groove, colonized pavement, etc.) strata. Their results showed that fish biomass was more than 2.5 times greater in marine protected areas than in areas open to fishing. Overall, the size of adult fish assemblages was larger and the larger size classes had greater numbers of individuals in MPAs when compared with areas under different management systems.

12.3 Integrating remotely sensed data and social and economic considerations into protected area planning and monitoring

Increasingly, remotely sensed data are being used to assess the location, extent, rate, and even anthropogenic drivers of changes in and around protected areas (Liu *et al.* 2001; Sánchez-Azofeifa *et al.* 2001; Sánchez-Azofeifa *et al.* 2003). Southworth *et al.* (2006) compiled a suite of studies in a 2006 volume of *Applied Geography* that queried the efficacy of parks as a conservation strategy, particularly in relation to human–environment trade-offs. They traced the history of land change research and its contribution to protected area design and assessment, noting that land change research has evolved over time from a focus on single-factor explanations of land use or land cover change to identifying multiple, interrelated factors occurring concurrently and at different scales within a landscape (Lambin *et al.* 2003). They call for the linking of remote sensing analyses and field studies to understand the social and institutional processes that impact land cover change and conservation. They point to the several papers within the volume and beyond that address these linkages (Messina *et al.* 2006; Nagendra *et al.* 2006; Southworth *et al.* 2002).

Researchers have begun to work on community mapping strategies with knowledgeable inhabitants living near potential and existing protected areas to better incorporate broad sets of values, experiences, and backgrounds in analyses of protected areas (Ban *et al.* 2008). Hernandez-Stefanoni *et al.* (2006) found a high level of congruence between habitat classifications in Quintana Roo, Mexico, done by rural Mayan communities and those done using cluster and detrended correspondence analysis of multispectral images. The authors show that indigenous knowledge can effectively complement remote sensing and field biology techniques.

Satellite imagery can also help managers to locate regions outside protected area boundaries where natural resource extraction could have a lesser impact on natural systems (Kairo *et al.* 2002). It is easy to fall into traps using satellite or other spatially explicit data where local human populations become secondary to externally defined "wilderness", for instance, or where human habitations are automatically considered a threat to local biodiversity. The limitations of remote sensing techniques that rely on optical reflectance in distinguishing primary from secondary forest, and in identifying human impacts under the canopy should be kept in mind (see Chapter 2 for an extensive discussion of other limitations of remotely sensed data).

12.4 Global-scale monitoring and resources for remotely sensed data and protected areas

At a global scale, remotely sensed data have been used to assess habitat status and degree of conversion within and around protected areas (Defries *et al.* 2005; Hoekstra *et al.* 2005). Researchers use remote sensing as a "coarse filter" to highlight target areas for more detailed examination regarding their importance to conservation (Townshend *et al.* 2002). You can scan through a number of resources to find data you need for global analyses relevant to protected areas (see Appendix 4).

For instance, *TerraLook*, previously called the Protected Area Archive, is a project led by the US Geological Survey that increases access to satellite images by making them available as simple georeferenced images (USGS 2008). *Terra-Look* was developed for users that have no knowledge of remote sensing or image processing, but who can benefit by access to images for management, communication, and other purposes. ASTER and Landsat satellite images are available free of cost. Users can download and visually interpret the images without the need for expensive software. The images include global historical Landsat data from around 1975, 1990, and 2000, plus global ASTER data from 2000 to the present. Although *TerraLook* includes visualization and analysis software, the standard image format allows users to utilize whatever GIS or Web mapping tools they wish. The images come bundled with image footprint overlays that delineate image boundaries, and metadata files that describe the acquisition and image data characteristics. Users can create their own collections of images from locations around the world. The *TerraLook* software allows users to overlay protected area boundaries and other relevant GIS shape files onto an image

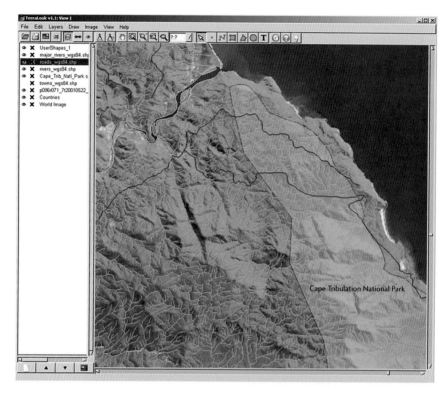

Fig. 12.4 TerraLook overlay showing a portion of the Cape Tribulation National Park in the Daintree River watershed, Far North Queensland, Australia. Layers show rivers in blue, protected area in orange, and roads in dark grey. Credit: Jeff Silverman, American Museum of Natural History's Center for Biodiversity and Conservation.

(Fig. 12.4), compare images from different time periods, measure area and distance, create and edit overlays, and perform many other activities with images and overlays. The data and software are all free online.

You should be cautious about using global data sets at an individual protected area level, as often they are not accurate at finer scales. The World Conservation Monitoring Center had compiled a global database of coral reef maps based on a wide variety of maps (Spalding *et al.* 2001). Using an automated algorithm for shallow bathymetry mapping and global SeaWiFS data (Stumpf *et al.* 2003a,b), and benefiting from the high positional accuracy of the SeaWiFS system, Green *et al.* (2006) generated a new global map of shallow coral reefs from SeaWiFS and used it to make positional corrections in the WCMC database. In some cases, reefs had significantly different locations compared to their original mapping in the WCMC database. This improved the accuracy of assessments combining databases of marine protected areas and the coral reef map layers.

Other resources are available that you can combine with remotely sensed data to plan and manage protected areas. As one example, the *World Database of Protected Areas* (WDPA) is the most comprehensive global data set on marine and terrestrial protected areas currently available. Compiled from a variety of sources, it is a joint venture of the United Nations Environment Programme and IUCN, managed by the World Conservation Monitoring Centre (UNEP-WCMC) in collaboration with the IUCN World Database on Protected Areas Consortium working with governments and collaborating NGOs. It consists of a Web-enabled spatial relational database platform with custom data editing, querying, downloading, and analysis facilities. Data on protected areas include name, designation or convention, total area, date of establishment, legal status, and IUCN Protected Areas Management Category. WDPA also stores the spatial boundary or location (where available) for each protected area in a GIS and includes an interactive map service along with a suite of relevant publications available for free download (WDPA 2009).

Protected Areas Learning Network (PALnet) is a Web-based interactive site that contains a substantial compilation of protected area management information. It is supported by IUCN and World Commission on Protected Areas scientists and practitioners as well as by partner individuals and institutions. The purpose of the site is to facilitate access to data for protected area managers, and to help with networking and sharing field-based experiences. Experts, organizations, documents, and project profiles can be searched or browsed by category, including region, biome, and threat on the Web site (PALnet 2009).

12.5 Summary and cautions about the use of remotely sensed data for protected area design and monitoring

While many of the major parks in the United States and Europe were declared prior to the availability of remotely sensed data, countries with newer protected area systems have been able to rely heavily on remote sensing in all stages of developing their networks. Costa Rica, for example, has led the field in using remotely sensed data in protected areas planning as well as monitoring (Powell *et al.* 2000; Sánchez-Azofeifa *et al.* 2001, 2003). Even in long-established protected area systems, managers are using remote sensing to track land cover changes through time both in and around protected areas, as well as to assess and monitor changes in remote areas. Remotely sensed data are extremely valuable for management of protected areas and remote sensing and GIS techniques provide a unifying framework within which to organize many kinds of data.

One thing to keep in mind when using remotely sensed data for planning and monitoring is that some vegetation structure changes may not be identifiable at the spatial and spectral scale available (Section 2.1). For forested regions, it is often not possible to detect differences between the protected forests and surrounding forests with higher intensities of land use (see challenges for forest remote sensing covered in Section 4.1). Also, remote sensors are not designed to detect individual organisms and therefore remotely sensed data are not able to discriminate "empty forests" (or most other habitats) from those rich in non-woody species. Remotely sensed data mainly informs us about structural entities—canopy cover for instance—and not what is living within or underneath that structure or how human communities interact with, and depend on, the forests. Thus remote sensing and satellite imagery cannot provide a direct measure of threats to biodiversity within parks at the species level. Assessing and monitoring the extent of certain types of habitats (e.g., wetlands, natural grasslands) using satellite imagery is more difficult than others (e.g., forests), making it more appropriate for habitats with easily distinguishable cover.

Other potential stumbling blocks relate to the temporal availability of remotely sensed data. For instance, managers often want to assess the rate of change in natural forest cover within protected areas yet this requires imagery from two or more dates. In humid tropical forests, it is often difficult to find images with comparable cloud cover from the same season in two different years. Also, the data available via remote sensing may not be available far enough back in time to understand the major drivers of land use change and threats to protected areas.

Despite these cautions, remote sensing has been and will continue to be an important tool for design and monitoring of protected areas. Its ability to provide uniform information about large areas where fieldwork can be challenging makes it instrumental for protected areas development and management.

13
Integrating field data

While the savannah elephant (*Loxodonta africana*) is listed by the International Union for Conservation of Nature (IUCN) as "vulnerable" because of declining abundance in some regions of Africa (Blanc 2008), populations in some protected areas of South Africa are growing rapidly (van Aarde and Jackson 2007). These populations can cause extensive modification of vegetation structure when their density increases (Owen-Smith 1996; Whyte *et al.* 2003; Guldemond and van Aarde 2007). Management methods such as culling, translocation, and birth control have not reduced density in some cases (van Aarde *et al.* 1999; Pimm and van Aarde 2001). Providing more space for elephants is one alternative management strategy, yet fundamental to this strategy is a clear understanding of habitat and landscape use by elephants.

Harris *et al.* (2008) combined remotely sensed data with Global Positioning System (GPS) and traditional ethological observations to assess elephant habitat use across three areas that span the ecological gradient of historical elephant distribution. They explored influences on habitat use across arid savannahs (Etosha National Park in Namibia) and woodlands (Tembe Elephant Park in South Africa and Maputo Elephant Reserve in Mozambique). The researchers focused on three main variables—distance to human settlements, distance to water, and vegetation type.

The authors used Landsat 7 ETM+ imagery to create vegetation maps for each location, employing supervised classification and maximum likelihood estimation. Across all sites, they recorded the coordinates of patches with different vegetation and of vegetation transitions to develop signatures for the maps. Elephants do not use all vegetation types, and it can be expedient to focus on presence rather than both presence and absence. Accordingly, the researchers used GPS to record the locations of elephants with the aim of identifying important land cover types for vegetation mapping. The authors mapped water locations in the wet and dry seasons using remotely sensed data and mapped human settlements using GPS, aerial surveys, and regional maps. They tracked elephants with radiotelemetry collars that communicated with the ARGOS satellite system, sending location data for most of the elephants over 24 h, and then remaining quiescent for the next 48 h to extend battery life.

From these analyses, the researchers determined that elephants travel only a few kilometers per day when the resources they need are present. Elephants, particularly females and during the dry season, most often were found in areas close to water, with high vegetation cover, and away from human settlements. This study provided insight into the relative importance of each variable, interactions among variables, and seasonal changes in habitat use. Water had the greatest influence on patterns of elephant presence, except when nearby forage was limited. These detailed inferences would not have been possible without integrating data from GPS technology, remote sensing, and behavioral observation.

Effective environmental management relies on accurate data describing the state of the environment and how it is changing. These data can be periodic snapshots that represent the environment at particular points in time recorded on an ad hoc basis or more consistently over time. You can collect snapshots with the intent of better understanding or quantifying the status of a particular area or use them to serve as a baseline for long-term monitoring.

Previous chapters that introduced fundamental remote sensing concepts and applications of remote sensing in various ecosystems also discussed many of the remote sensing methods used to support environmental management. This chapter addresses the use of field-based equipment that can complement aerial and satellite remote sensing.

13.1 Integrating field data and remotely sensed data

Remotely sensed data can support inventory and monitoring at local to global scales but must be validated or supplemented with data collected in the field in order to relate the remotely sensed data to the reality on the ground. Knowing when to use field-based measurements and which types of measurements are appropriate for a given objective can be confusing, especially given the growing overlap in capabilities of remote sensing instruments and field instruments.

13.1.1 Remote sensing versus field methods

Field data may be necessary when remotely sensed data are not available or when remote sensing techniques simply cannot measure the quantity of interest, but data collected in the field can also complement remote sensing methods in a number of ways. For example, as discussed in previous chapters, field data can validate remote sensing products. You might use data collected in the field to determine the accuracy of a land cover map (Wulder *et al.* 2006) or to train an algorithm to process a satellite image to create a land cover map (Homer *et al.* 2004). Detailed, site-specific data collected from the field also can also help establish the relationship between fine-scale abiotic and biotic data collected from the field and coarser scale data collected by remote sensing instruments mounted in aerial or satellite platforms. Several remote sensing-based data sets have arisen from this calibration approach, such as temperature (Sugita and Brutsaert 1993), reflectance (Liang *et al.* 2002), and biomass (Lu 2006). Field data can provide highly accurate measurements for a point or a small area. We can relate field data to remotely sensed data on meteorology (i.e., temperature, precipitation, and wind speed); soil conditions (i.e., moisture and temperature); water conditions (i.e., temperature, depth, sediment concentrations, water sediment load, and flow rate); or a host of other variables. Deciding when to use remote sensing methods of data collection in addition to field methods depends on the question you are trying to answer, the data you want to collect, the accuracy you need, and the resources you have.

Scientists use a variety of field-based instruments for environmental inventory and monitoring as a substitute for or in conjunction with remote sensing methods. Providing an exhaustive list of instruments for collecting field data is beyond the scope of this book so in the next sections we will focus on a few instruments that are commonly used to complement remote sensing, to support our example of combining data from these instruments with satellite or airborne remotely sensed data.

13.1.2 Handheld sensors: an intersection of remote sensing and field methods

Handheld sensors are a way of taking similar light-measuring sensors that can be flown in an aircraft or on a satellite, and using them in the field. Portable or handheld radiometers and spectrometers measure reflected and emitted energy from the ultraviolet, visible, infrared, and microwave portions of the electromagnetic spectrum. Just like their satellite instrument counterparts, radiometers and spectrometers record data from discrete portions, or bands, of the electromagnetic spectrum. Radiometers are sensors that record a few bands whereas spectrometers (Fig. 13.1) usually record many contiguous bands and create spectral curves like those from the hyperspectral sensors discussed in Chapter 2. Some of these sensors record images but most record energy from a single point or area. The size of the area (the footprint) depends on the distance between the sensor and the object being measured. Radiometers and spectrometers collect accurate spectral information about specific objects. Photographic cameras are a type of handheld sensor with up to three bands (usually recording red, green, and blue light intensity) and are discussed in Section 13.1.3.

You can use handheld sensors at the Earth's surface or high above the surface (from a balloon or in an aircraft, for example) to acquire data from a range of perspectives. The main characteristic of handheld sensors is that they are portable.

You can use field radiometers and spectrometers to determine spectral characteristics of different materials or objects that, in turn, may serve as reference data to calibrate airborne or satellite imagery. By selecting field, aerial, and satellite sensors that measure similar wavelengths of energy you can conduct multi-scale analyses by using the finer detailed data to calibrate or scale-up to the coarser data. For example, Cheng et al. (2006) conducted a study using a field

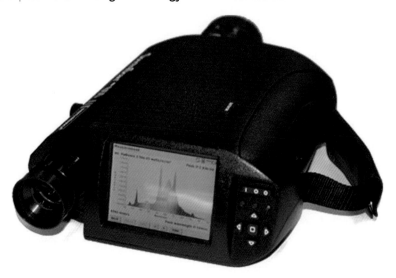

Fig. 13.1 An image of the Photo Research PR-655 SpectraScan spectroradiometer. A handheld scanner like this one is commonly used to collect spectral signatures in the field. Credit: Photo Research, Inc.

and an aerial spectrometer (AVIRIS) to test the quality of three MODIS products: normalized difference vegetation index (NDVI), enhanced vegetation index (EVI), and the fraction of photosynthetically active radiation absorbed by vegetation (fPAR). The analysis took place over a chaparral ecosystem in southern California. The results indicated that there was good agreement between the MODIS EVI product and EVI calculated using the field spectrometer and AVIRIS data. For NDVI, MODIS values were generally higher (indicating greater productivity) than the finer-scale data. The MODIS fPAR values were slightly higher than the fine-scale data but after a fire passed through the study area MODIS fPAR values were much higher (they should have been very close to 0). These types of multi-scale analyses are useful to provide confidence to broad-scale remote sensing products and to improve the quality of the algorithms used to create the products (Cheng *et al.* 2006).

You can also use these field sensors to monitor changes in spectral properties over time. Because of their portability, these sensors can acquire data at more frequent intervals and at finer resolutions than is possible with airborne or satellite instruments. This is helpful for monitoring the attributes or status of vegetation over time, and radiometers are frequently used to monitor agricultural crops (Zhang *et al.* 2002). You can also study plant phenology, for example, by measuring how the spectral reflectance of individual plants changes throughout the growth cycle (Karnieli 2003).

Radiometers that operate in the thermal infrared portion of the electromagnetic spectrum are useful for measuring water and soil surface temperature. Microwave radiometers can measure soil moisture and the moisture content of snow. As with the vegetation examples given earlier, data acquired from thermal and microwave radiometers can calibrate remotely sensed data acquired from satellite sensors and can be used to monitor changes in specific areas at short temporal intervals.

13.1.3 Ground-level field photography

Digital and film cameras are simple instruments often used in the field to record detailed images of a specific place. Although cameras record reflected electromagnetic energy, they are not designed to accurately quantify the magnitude of this energy in discrete bands. Usually photographs qualitatively document the appearance of a particular area when the photograph was acquired. If you can get information on the spectral response of the sensor in a high-end digital camera, it could be used as a quantitative three-band sensor; however, this information is not often available, as most cameras do not provide spectral information suitable for quantitative analysis.

Photographs often provide information to help classify and validate land cover mapping products derived from satellite imagery. Photographs can have greater information content than simple textual data, like a written site description. With sufficient detail, you can accurately identify the type of land cover from a photograph and use this information in the classification process.

Field photographs are taken from a different perspective than satellite or aerial images. Most field photographs have a severe oblique angle with much of the horizon showing, whereas satellite or aerial images typically have a nadir view (Fig. 13.2). This difference in viewing perspectives can make it difficult to identify the same feature on the two sets of images. With practice this may become easier.

You can also use photographs for monitoring the attributes of a given point in space. To monitor a point with photographs, it is critical to take repeat photographs of the exact same scene from the same location using the same camera direction, height, angle, and exposure settings (Hall 2001). It is preferable to permanently mark the location from which you will acquire the photographs (Fig. 13.3) and record the coordinates of that location with a GPS receiver. Repeat photographs also should be taken at the same time of year and time of day. These methods allow you to monitor changes in the scene over time, such as qualitative attributes of vegetation structure and composition (Van Willigen and Grodecki 2006), erosion, and changes in cover type. There is a paucity of software available for aiding in the comparison of repeat photography so comparisons are typically done using manual methods that involve visually comparing photographs of the same area and noting changes (Hall 2001).

Photographer location

Fig. 13.2 These two images cover approximately the same area in Quang Nam province in Vietnam. The bottom image is an oblique image taken from the ground (24 April 2002). The top image is a color composite from IKONOS (subset from image ID PO_91586, April 29, 2002). Notice how the different view perspectives make it difficult to identify the same features in the two images as marked by the letters: A and E—burn scars, B—forested mountain peak, C—paddy rice, D—houses in a village. Credit: Ned Horning, American Museum of Natural History's Center for Biodiversity and Conservation, IKONOS image courtesy of GeoEye.

Fig. 13.3 Permanent markers are helpful to ensure that repeated photographs are taken from the same location using the same orientation. This tool, known as the PicturePost, was developed as part of the Measuring Vegetation Health project (Measuring Vegetation Health Project 2007). Credit: Measuring Vegetation Health project.

As the availability of GPS-capable cameras increases, the process of recording this information will become automated. However, it is still useful to manually record the position and direction of the camera with a GPS receiver and compass. In addition to its value for repeat photography, information on location and direction facilitates matching the area captured in a photograph with the area represented in a satellite or aerial image. Some GIS software applications allow you to create a layer with points to denote the location where a photograph was acquired and to display the photographs acquired from that point. More feature-filled software also includes an arrow to indicate the direction from which the photograph was taken (Fig. 13.4). This type of software is quite useful for matching ground photographs with aerial or satellite imagery.

You can also use geocoded ground photographs to improve the accuracy of interpretation, classification, and analysis of remotely sensed data, such as satellite imagery, and the subsequent validation of their derived products. Photographs also illustrate the appearance of different land cover types in a map (Král and Pavliš 2006).

Fig. 13.4 This is a pair of screen captures from a desktop GIS that illustrates how locations from which photographs were taken (red squares) and the direction in which the camera was pointed (black arrow) can be displayed for visual analysis. Credit: Ned Horning, American Museum of Natural History's Center for Biodiversity and Conservation.

Although geocoded photographs are easy to acquire, they have traditionally been collected by remote sensing specialists who undertake site visits to multiple localities to record *in situ* measurements, estimates, or qualitative assessments, such as ground cover, biomass, canopy closure, or vegetation type. To complement photographs, it is helpful to create textual descriptions of the area being photographed or even to draw an annotated sketch of the area. This ancillary contextual information is useful for interpreting the photographs at a later time. Features visible by eye may not be evident in the photograph. For example, land use or vegetation composition might be difficult to determine from a photograph.

13.1.4 Telemetry

Telemetry is not often considered as part of the domain of remote sensing but it is an important tool for ecology and conservation employed since the early 1970s (Gillespie 2001). Telemetry is simply the transmission of remote data. These data can be from sensors in a satellite; on Earth's surface, where they record parameters such as temperature, wind speed, precipitation, and incoming solar radiance; or on an animal, enabling accurate tracking of the animal's location.

Telemetry systems can broadcast data using ground-based radios but these systems are limited by the distance between the transmitter and the receiver. For this reason satellite telemetry has become a popular approach for collecting remote data whether from mobile or stationary points. In satellite telemetry systems, the satellite receives data from a sensor on Earth's surface and then transmits the data to a receiver from which the data can be collected and subsequently analyzed. Some satellite systems, such as the Argos series of satellites and ground stations, are also able to record the location of the object transmitting data to the satellite. This location is determined using the Doppler shift of the transmitted signal created as the satellite passes over the object as the satellite orbits Earth (Fig. 13.5). The positional accuracy of satellite telemetry typically is on the order of hundreds of meters (Soutullo *et al.* 2007).

For higher positional accuracy (on the order of several meters), it is best to transmit position coordinates acquired with a GPS receiver (Hulbert and French 2001). Telemetry systems that transmit GPS coordinates often use ground-based

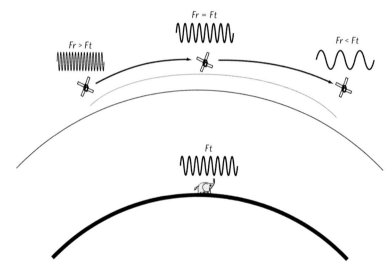

Fig. 13.5 Satellite telemetry systems receive data from a radio transmitter. Often these transmitters are mounted on a collar or other device attached to an animal. The location of the animal is determined by analyzing the Doppler shift as the satellite approaches then passes over the animal. As the satellite orbits over the radio transmitter there is a frequency shift in the radio signal. As the satellite approaches the animal, the received frequency (*Fr*) increases relative to the transmitted frequency (*Ft*) and as the satellite moves farther away the received frequency decreases. This is called the "Doppler shift." This method is capable of producing positional accuracy on the order of hundreds of meters. Credit: Ned Horning, American Museum of Natural History's Center for Biodiversity and Conservation.

radio networks and cell phone services. Satellite systems are also used when ground networks are not adequate.

Unfortunately, GPS receivers do not function underwater although for marine applications tags have been developed that receive a signal when the animal surfaces.

Very High Frequency (VHF) was the first telemetry technology used for animal tracking. A VHF system triangulates the location of the transmitter using two or more receivers. Each receiver provides information on its direction

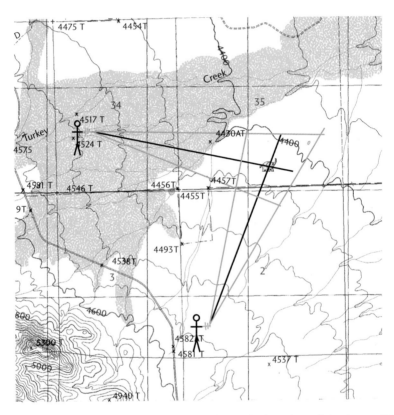

Fig. 13.6 A VHF telemetry system triangulates the location of the transmitter using two or more receivers. In this cartoon, the two people are holding directional antennas that can be used to determine the direction between the antenna and the radio transmitter mounted on a collar on the animal (black lines). By plotting the directions from two or more antennas on a map and noting where the lines cross, it is possible to determine the location of the transmitter. This technique is known as triangulation. The gray lines illustrate the approximate error associated with the measurement. In this case, the researchers would expect the true location of the animal to be within the polygon formed by the intersection of the four gray lines. Credit: Ned Horning, American Museum of Natural History's Center for Biodiversity and Conservation.

to the transmitter. By drawing lines on a map to indicate the direction from each receiver to the transmitter, and noting where the two lines cross, one can determine the location of the transmitter (Fig. 13.6). Accuracy of VHF telemetry ranges from a few hundred meters to a few kilometers. Advantages of VHF systems are that they can be less expensive and lighter than GPS telemetry units so they can be used to track smaller animals than can be monitored with the latter units.

Telemetry collars and tags that collect three or more signals from satellites can provide precise information on latitude and longitude. Information on elevation can be obtained with at least four satellites. Satellite tracking overcomes some of the drawbacks of traditional radio tracking, such as limited transmission radius and the need to follow an animal in the field (potentially across inaccessible terrain) to collect data. Telemetry collars or tags have been used in both marine and terrestrial systems to gather location data (Marcinek *et al.* 2001; Johnson *et al.* 2002).

Traditionally, marine systems have proven to be difficult environments within which to study movement patterns of organisms, yet this information is critical to effective fisheries management. As early as 1873, people were tagging Atlantic salmon in Maine's Penobscot River to elucidate their migratory patterns. The metal tags used had many drawbacks, including the necessity of recapture for data collection and potential for loss or damage. Recently, researchers have begun to use a suite of telemetry tags to transmit remotely sensed information on location and environmental variables for marine organisms.

Archival tags are small, long lasting (up to 10 years), and powerful. They can record water pressure (providing information on depth of dives), ambient light (used to estimate location), body temperature, and travel speed. They have to be retrieved, so are more often used for commercial fish or for animals like sea turtles that return to nesting areas. Pop-up archival tags are larger tags that detach from an animal 30, 60, or 90 days after being attached. Once detached, the tags float to the surface and then transmit data in batches to the *ARGOS* satellite for about two weeks, until the battery dies. The data are maintained when the battery is drained so if researchers recover the tag itself, they can retrieve all the data. Used for animals like white sharks (*Carcharodon carcharias*) that do not spend much time at the surface and are not commercially fished, pop-up archival tags can provide information on water pressure, ambient light, and body temperature.

Smart Position or Temperature Transmitting Tags, which can transmit data for up to two years, are used for animals that surface regularly for air (marine mammals, for instance) or that swim close to the surface (e.g., blue sharks, *Prionace glauca*, and makos, *Isurus* spp). When the antenna is at the surface, it sends data on geolocation, water pressure, speed, and water temperature to a satellite; when the antenna submerges, a saltwater switch turns off the tag. Researchers can estimate an animal's location by calculating shifts in the signals in successive transmissions.

Choice of tags, and even whether to use the tags, depends on trade-offs among reliability, cost, objectives of the project, and suitability of the tags given the size and behavior of an animal (Blake *et al.* 2001).

The Tagging of Pacific Predators project, led by several dozen researchers from the US NOAA Pacific Fisheries Ecosystems Laboratory, Stanford University's Hopkins Marine Laboratory, the University of California, Santa Cruz's Long Marine Laboratory, and across eight countries, has attached satellite tags to 22 different species of apex predators in the Pacific Ocean. Between 2000 and 2007, researchers tagged more than 2000 animals, including elephant seals (*Mirounga angustirostris*), white sharks (*Carcharodon carcharias*), leatherback turtles (*Dermochelys coriacea*), Humboldt squid (*Dosidicus gigas*), albatross (*Phoebastria* spp.), and sooty shearwaters (*Puffinus griseus*).

For instance, some of these investigators have been tracking movements of Atlantic bluefin tuna (*Thunnus thynnus*) from their spawning to feeding grounds. As with other top pelagic predators, the abundance of bluefin tuna is declining rapidly due to harvest. The abundance of western Atlantic bluefin tuna has decreased by more than 80 percent since 1970 (Block *et al.* 2005). Information on tuna movements and spawning ground visits by age class can inform management strategies and improve stock assessments. The researchers used archival and pop-up tags, combined with US pelagic longline observer and logbook catch data, to determine important spawning areas as well as age-related and seasonal variation in migratory patterns and habitat use (Stokesbury *et al.* 2004; Block *et al.* 2005). The implanted tags recorded data on pressure, light intensity, and ambient and internal temperature every 60, 120, or 128 s. Location of the tuna was estimated from light intensity data from the tags. Researchers identified two overlapping populations at the North Atlantic Ocean foraging grounds. One population spawns in the Gulf of Mexico, whereas the second spawns in the Mediterranean Sea. The scientists provided recommendations on when and where longline fisheries should operate within tuna spawning sites to reduce the incidental catch of tuna by pelagic longline fisheries.

13.2 Summary

Remote sensing is a powerful tool for inventorying and monitoring the environment. A number of tools that can be deployed in the field have been developed to allow you to more effectively relate conditions in the field with the data recorded by an airborne or satellite-based sensor. You can use tools such as digital cameras to record visual information about a landscape that can be compared with other remotely sensed data. Cameras can also be used as a stand-alone monitoring tool by acquiring and analyzing repeat photography of an area. Another monitoring tool is telemetry. Although not often thought of as a remote sensing tool, telemetry technology has been effectively integrated with remote sensing studies to determine habitat associations and migration routes.

14

Linking remote sensing with modeling

Conservation biologists and natural resource managers often require detailed, accurate information on natural resources or biodiversity elements such as species, landscapes, and ecosystems. Their patterns of occurrence and their responses to environmental disturbance or change are dynamic over space and time and may be mediated by complex ecological processes.

In most cases, our ability to directly measure or comprehensively map biodiversity elements is limited by human or financial resources, and logistical challenges such as difficulties in accessing terrain or short field seasons. In other situations, we might want to make quantitative inferences about, say, the kinds of environments that are most suitable for the persistence of an endangered species, or the influence of landscape modification on its highest-quality habitat. In these cases, developing models that explain and predict the patterns of biodiversity elements can help provide guidance at scales and resolutions that are not available through direct measurement.

For example, Goetz *et al.* (2007) employed lidar data to predict the bird species richness across a 5,315 ha temperate forest reserve, the Patuxent National Wildlife Refuge (PWNR) in the eastern United States. In this study, Goetz *et al.* derived and mapped several measures of forest canopy structure, including canopy height, and three descriptors of the vertical distribution of canopy elements. In addition to lidar, they also used optical remotely sensed data from two dates of Landsat ETM+ to derive NDVI during the growing season and the difference between the NDVI of leaf-on and leaf-off conditions (growing season versus winter).

Testing three different quantitative statistical models (stepwise multiple linear regression, generalized additive models, and regression trees) to predict bird species richness, the authors used field survey data on the birds of the PWNR that were collected at a series of fixed points across the reserve as the training data for the response variable (bird species richness). To calibrate the model, they combined the habitat descriptors with the survey data, usually reserving 25 percent of the survey data to validate each model's results. They found that the lidar-derived habitat measures were generally more effective than the Landsat ETM-derived measures in predicting bird species richness, explaining 30–45 percent of the observed variation in bird species richness. Using the best performing model, they generated a map of predicted species richness (Fig. 14.1)

Richness ■ 3.6 ▨ 6.1 ▨ 7.2 ☐ 9.5

Fig. 14.1 Map of forest bird species richness derived from a regression tree model using lidar data. Figure reprinted from Goetz *et al.* (2007) with permission from Elsevier.

that identified the key areas for birds in the reserve and can be used to guide future habitat management plans. (Note that this map was not field validated with new survey data to see how well its predictions were matched by field conditions.)

As we have discussed in many of the preceding chapters, remote sensing technologies can provide extensive data on Earth's physical and biological attributes. Satellite data in particular offer us the capacity to observe large areas of the Earth with synoptic, "wall-to-wall" perspectives on those attributes that are difficult if not impossible to obtain by making ground-based measurements. Even for accessible or well-studied areas, ground-collected data is almost never comprehensive or historically complete. By combining limited, field-generated data on socioeconomic and ecological phenomena with more extensive remotely sensed data, models can help us "scale-up" conservation-relevant assessments to address the societal needs for information on the status of biodiversity and ecosystems.

A wide variety of models, modeling approaches, and other quantitative methods that employ remotely sensed data are already in use in conservation biology. In this section, we will discuss what models are, the basic steps to constructing and testing models, the types of remotely sensed data that are commonly used in modeling efforts, and provide a series of examples of biodiversity-related models that integrate remotely sensed data at different eco-logical scales. For more information on specific statistical or methodological approaches to modeling, there are many good textbooks and journals that present both introductory and state-of-the-art discussions (see, e.g., Hilborn and Mangel [1997]; Burnham and Anderson [2002]; Mangel [2006]; Clark [2007]; McCarthy [2007]).

14.1 What are models?

Models are tools for expressing simplified descriptions of some aspect of the world and, usually, how it works (Fleishman and Seto 2009). Models can be qualitative or quantitative in nature and can be simple or complex. Models can help us make predictions about something that interests us, learn about the

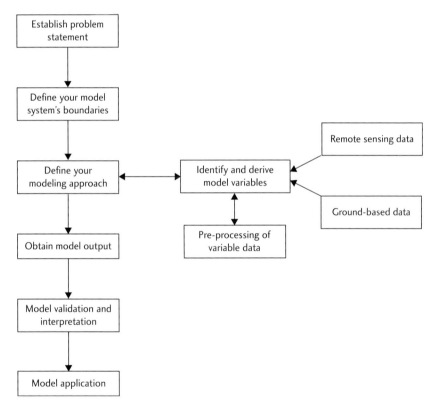

Fig. 14.2 Generalized diagram of the major steps in developing, constructing, and testing a model. Adapted from Fleishman and Seto (2009). Credit: American Museum of Natural History, Center for Biodiversity and Conservation.

interactions between parts of a system, and test hypotheses. Models are useful for exploring relationships between a response variable and factors that potentially play a role in directly or indirectly influencing its response.

Most used in ecology and conservation biology are mathematical predictions of a response variable of interest derived from some combination of other explanatory variables, for example the abundance of a species along a precipitation gradient, the influence of browsing intensity on patterns of vegetation communities, or the impact of urban sprawl on estuarine nutrient levels. For the purposes of this discussion, we will primarily focus on models that combine ground-based observation data with more extensive, remotely sensed data to explain the patterns of variability in the observed data and then make spatially explicit predictions about the value of a phenomenon of interest in unmeasured areas (Fig. 14.2).

Most remote sensing work translating data observed by a sensor to a map of interest is essentially already a model. Thus, it is natural to combine field data, remotely sensed data, and other information together in developing models to address questions of ecological interest.

14.2 How do I start? Steps to developing models

14.2.1 Establish problem statement

As with virtually any formal research endeavor, your first step is to explicitly formulate your reason for developing a model. Consider the intended use for the model, especially its desired outputs, and the context in which they will be used. This will in turn lead you to articulate whether the model will be more theoretical or applied in nature, useful for explaining general behavior of your model system or directed toward informing some sort of management decision. You will also have to assess the kinds of data that you already have at your disposal, plan the methods you intend to use, the degree of precision you require from the model, and the level of uncertainty that is acceptable to you or the perceived audience of the modeling results.

It can be useful at this point to begin writing a narrative that includes answers to some of the questions above, or to begin constructing a conceptual map of your model system. For example, Maina *et al.* (2008) set out to develop models of the relationship between ocean environments and coral reef bleaching or mortality due to thermal stress, and then identify areas across ~24.8 million square kilometers of the western Indian Ocean that have environmental conditions likely to have reduced incidences of coral reef stress (see Section 6.2.5 for more background on this issue). The authors first constructed a conceptual map that included the environmental variables and observational data they would use, and the modeling techniques, training data, and model evaluation steps they would follow (Fig. 14.3). (See Foundations of Success [2009] for a complete treatment of conceptual models.)

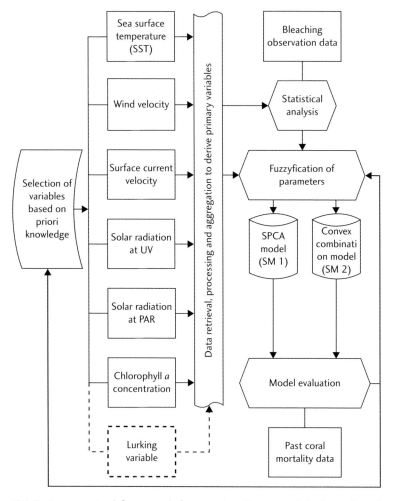

Fig. 14.3 A conceptual framework for constructing a model of coral reef susceptibility to environmental and thermal stress. Note the iterative process of variable selection and model evaluation implied by the two-way arrow that connects those steps. Figure reprinted from Maina *et al.* (2008) with permission from Elsevier.

14.2.2 Define your model system's boundaries

The next step in developing a model is to delineate the boundaries of the system you hope to investigate. You may choose to define the spatial boundaries of your model system according to biological or physical (geographical, hydrological, and topographical), political, or management jurisdiction considerations. Ideally, your model boundaries will encompass the full extent of the phenomenon you identified in your problem statement. Well-defined geographic areas, like ecoregions or life zones, can be useful since they are discrete areas with a relatively narrow range of climatic, geological, and biological characteristics and can have defined land use trends (Olson *et al.* 2001).

In practice, however, it is often difficult to delimit your system entirely along the lines of your biologically driven problem statement. For example, a migratory species' range may be too large to model in its entirety and so you may need to focus on its breeding grounds or even just a part of them. Defining model boundaries for large aquatic or long, linear freshwater systems can be challenging since these features often straddle political boundaries or have catchments that encompass large upstream and upslope areas. It is often the case that your data were collected within political boundaries that correspond to management priorities or jurisdictions. In these situations, it is especially important to make sure that your problem statement clearly spells out the geographical and temporal scope within which you want your model to be useful and to think about how your model boundaries may impact the conclusions of your study.

14.2.3 Define your modeling approach

Your next step will be to define your modeling approach. There are many different ways to differentiate or classify models. In turn, the mathematical or statistical techniques you decide to employ will dictate the modeling approach you select, your model system, and the types of data you may be able to compile. (See Hilborn and Mangel [1997] and Quinn and Keogh [2002] for more in-depth discussion of this and other topics concerning model selection. Also see Section 3.5.2.2 for brief descriptions of many mathematical approaches to modeling.) A few ways of characterizing models include:

- *Reductionist versus systems-based models.* A reductionist approach models components of a system separately, then may seek to aggregate those models into a larger model of the whole system. Systems-based models attempt to describe the interactions between the components of an entire system. These two opposing approaches are sometimes called "bottom-up" and "top-down" models, respectively (Section 6.1.4 discusses a related nomenclature for different approaches to using remotely sensed data in modeling the optical environment to understand the components of a remote sensing signal returned to the sensor).
- *Conceptual (qualitative) versus quantitative models.* Conceptual models try to express the nature (strength or direction) of the relationships between the components of a system, while quantitative models try to develop mathematical expressions (algorithms) that describe or predict a response variable.
- *Correlative versus mechanistic models.* Correlative, or phenomenological, models estimate the value of the response variable by "fitting" model parameters to the observed distribution of your data. For example, correlating known occurrence records of a species with a selection of environ-

mental variables to predict the distribution of high-quality habitat for the species. Mechanistic models, on the other hand, rely on detailed understandings of the limiting or driving factors that determine the behavior of your model's system. For example, you might predict the effects of urbanization on runoff and stream water levels based on known relationships between rainfall events, the area and distribution of impervious surfaces, and the configuration of watercourses within your study area.

- *Static versus dynamic models.* Static models are based on a single, discrete segment of time and reflect the system conditions during that time in their predictions. A vegetation map derived from a single Landsat TM image is an example of a static model. Dynamic models, on the other hand, include the passage of time as a model component and allow the interactions between variables to change as time progresses, such as a model of primary productivity across seasons.

It is worth mentioning at this point that in some situations it is difficult to define your modeling approach without a clear idea of what types of data or variables are to be included in your model. In this case, the order of step 3, defining your model, and step 4, identifying the model's variables, will be reversed.

14.2.4 Identify model variables

As we mentioned earlier, all models fundamentally seek to express a relationship, whether proven or hypothetical, between a variable of interest (the *dependent variable*) and one or more factors that are thought to cause a response in the dependent variable or be correlated with the patterns of response of the dependent variable. These factors are called *independent* or *predictor variables*. For example, a model might explore the response of a species' abundance to fluctuations in a variety of abiotic factors across a landscape. In this case, the variable of interest or dependent variable would be some measure of numbers of individuals of the species, and the predictor variables might be levels of certain nutrients, soil characteristics, or geomorphologic descriptors like slope or aspect.

For both practical and statistical reasons, models are unlikely to include all possible influences on the system or the dependent variable. Factors that have indirect influence on the dependent variable, called *exogenous variables*, are usually excluded from models in favor of a smaller number of factors that directly influence the model system's behavior, called *endogenous variables*. For example, a model of the relationship between the survival of a plant species and flooding events would likely include endogenous variables like floodwater levels and soil saturation as predictor variables, but exclude exogenous variables like rainfall or cloud cover even though these might influence floodwater levels.

Another critical element in selecting a model's variables is the influence of geographical and temporal scale on a model system. The extent and resolution (or grain) of the predictor variables will greatly influence the usefulness of your model and the precision and accuracy of its predictions. It is especially important to consider the scale at which the variable or process you hope to model is operating and the scale of your explanatory data. Attempting to model the daily movement of individual snails across a 100 m wide wetland using rainfall data whose resolution is 5 km will be an exercise in futility. Conversely, modeling the patterns of deforestation across the vast Amazon Basin with IKONOS data that has a resolution of 1 m would be inefficient if not practically impossible. Matching the temporal resolution of your data and your predictor variables is just as important—different remote sensing instruments have different periodicities of data capture that can facilitate or limit your ability to model phenomena that occur over short or long time frames.

Ideally, each explanatory variable chosen would be completely orthogonal, or perfectly unrelated, to all the other explanatory variables. Correlations or covariance between the explanatory factors can reduce the explanatory power of the model (Pearson 2007). In practice this is sometimes difficult to achieve, since environmental factors like temperature, elevation, and precipitation are often linked. Another hazard in selecting variables is overfitting, or the inclusion of too many explanatory variables in a model, which reduces the generality of the model (Tetko et al. 1995).

Sometimes the same explanatory variables can be used in multiple models that explain different, but complementary, aspects of the study system. For example, Brown et al. (2008) constructed models at two scales, population and landscape, to predict the invasion dynamics of a nonnative tree Syzygium jambos in the Luquillo Mountains of Puerto Rico. At the population scale, Brown et al. used field-based data on the life history structure of S. jambos to construct matrix projection models to estimate the finite rate of population increase (λ) for S. jambos at seven independent sites within the study area. They then modeled λ values as a function of several environmental variables derived from remote sensing—canopy cover derived from historical aerial photography (1930s era), leaf area index (LAI) derived from Landsat TM 5 data, evapotranspiration (ET) derived from Landsat TM and MODIS data, and climatic variables modeled from a digital elevation model (DEM). Using multiple, stepwise regression techniques, they obtained a map of predicted λ, or population growth rates, for the entire 11,300 ha of the Luquillo forest (Fig. 14.4a). At the landscape scale, the authors used an ecological niche modeling approach, Maxent (Phillips et al. 2006), to predict habitat for S. jambos in the study area as a function of the same environmental variables (Fig. 14.4b). Interestingly, different environmental variables were important in modeling the population dynamics and ecological niche of S. jambos. Past land use history and disturbances seemed most important for determining patterns of invasive success at fine spatial scales, while abiotic environmental variables modulated coarse-scale invasion dynamics.

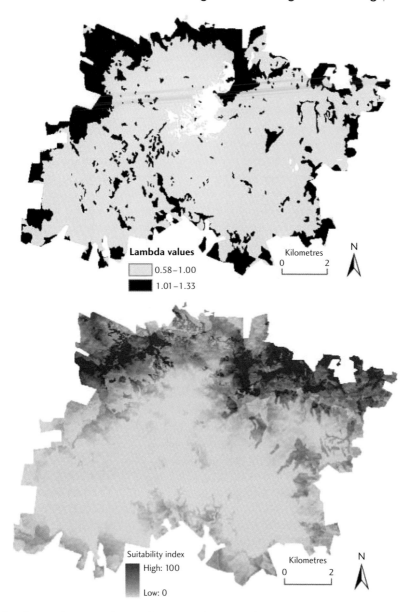

Fig. 14.4 Elements of an ecological niche model for the nonnative tree, *Syzygium jambos*, for the entire Luquillo forest, Puerto Rico. *Top*: Map of predicted , or population growth rates, from a stepwise multiple regression model derived from empirical population structure data and environmental variables. *Bottom*: Map of predicted suitable habitats for *S. jambos* from a Maxent ecological niche model derived from known occurrences of *S. jambos* and environmental variables. Figures reprinted from Brown *et al.* (2008) with permission from Wiley-Blackwell.

14.2.5 Test and validate your model

Assessing the accuracy of a model's predictions is commonly termed "validation" or "evaluation," and it is a vital step in model development (also see Section 2.2 for additional discussion of validation and accuracy assessment). Application of models, particularly to real world conservation issues, is not justifiable unless you have assessed the accuracy or limitations of their predictions. Validation and error quantification allow you to determine the suitability of a model for a specific use and perhaps to compare the performance of different modeling methods (Pearce and Ferrier 2000). Your ability to articulate the accuracy of your model will also be extremely important when you present and explain the model's results to decision makers or the general public.

There is no single validation approach that can be recommended for use in all modeling exercises; rather, your choice of validation strategy will be influenced by the aim of the modeling effort, the types of data available, and the modeling method used. However, all validation approaches seek to test the model's ability to explain the observed data and its variability (internal validation) *and* to assess the model's ability to make accurate predictions about other systems (external validation). Until a model has been externally validated, you should not consider it suitable for anticipating or predicting the response of the dependent variable in other systems.

The key to external validation is testing the model against new, independent data that were not used to build the model (see Pearson [2007] for a more detailed discussion of validation). We can refer to these as *test data* (sometimes called *evaluation data*) to distinguish them from the *calibration data* (sometimes called *training data*) that are used to build the model. This approach to more complex modeling is the same as the way calibration data are used to develop a supervised maximum likelihood classification model in land cover remote sensing, and test data used to validate it (Section 3.5.2.2)

Ideally one would collect test data independently from the training data used to calibrate the model (Araújo et al. 2005b). For example, Raxworthy et al. (2003) validated their models of reptile species distributions in Madagascar with data from a new round of field surveys. Other researchers have undertaken validation using independent data from different regions (e.g., Peterson and Shaw [2003]), data at different spatial resolution (e.g., Araújo et al. [2005a]; Pearson et al. [2002]), data from different time periods (e.g., Araújo et al. [2005b]), and data from surveys conducted by other researchers (Elith et al. 2006).

In practice, though, it may not be possible or feasible to obtain independent test data. In this situation it is common to partition the available data into calibration and test data sets (Pearson 2007). A variety of strategies are available for partitioning data, including:

1) A single split of the data into calibration and test data sets either randomly (e.g., Pearson et al. [2002]) or by dividing the data spatially (e.g., Peterson and Shaw; [2003]). Huberty (1994) provides guidelines for selecting the

relative proportions of data included in each category; using 70 percent for calibration and 30 percent for testing is common.

2) Bootstrapping, in which the data are split multiple times by sampling from the original set of data randomly with replacement (i.e., the same occurrence record could be included in the test data more than once) and a model is built for each successive split. Each models' performance is then assessed against the corresponding test data. Validation statistics are then calculated as the mean and range from the set of bootstrap samples (e.g., Buckland and Elston [1993]).

3) *K*-fold partitioning, of which jackknifing is an extreme form, splits the data into *k* parts of roughly equal size ($k > 2$) and each part is used as a test set with the other *k*-1 sets used for model calibration. Thus, if we select $k = 5$ then five models will be calibrated and each model will be tested against the excluded test data. Validation statistics are reported as the mean and range from the set of *k* tests. In jackknifing *k* is equal to the number of data points, with each data point excluded from model calibration during one partition (Fielding and Bell 1997).

How you characterize your model's accuracy will also depend on the kind of model you have constructed and the kinds of predictions or outputs your model provides. For many models with continuous output variables, statistics like R^2 are available to help determine the amount of variation in your data explained by a given model, as a function of the difference between the fitted (predicted) values and observed valued. For models that have categorical output, where predicted data may or may not be correctly assigned to given categories, other metrics are available that characterize the distribution of correctly versus incorrectly categorized values (Fielding and Bell 1997). Returning to the example of Brown *et al.* (2008) described earlier, the authors validated their two models differently; they assessed the population trajectory model, which provided continuous output, using an R^2 statistic that expresses how well the model fits the existing data, and they validated the niche model using a Receiver Operator Curve (ROC) plot to assess the percentage of the time the model can discriminate, or correctly predict, sites with or without the target species.

14.3 What remote sensing products are commonly used in modeling?

The wide variety of remotely sensed data on abiotic and biotic descriptors of the environment that are now available, and which are commonly in use in models applied to ecology and conservation biology models, have been the subject of many of the earlier chapters of this book. Rather than describe them again here, we will instead focus on the most commonly used types of products and some of the contexts in which they might be most useful. Fleishman and Seto (2009) provide a more in-depth discussion of the theoretical motivations for using particular types of data in ecological models. Most models will include a combination of types of data including some information on land cover, geomorphology or geology, and climatic conditions (Corsi *et al.* 2000).

In many cases, you may be interested in using multiple remote sensing products from different sensors as predictor variables in the same model. This is to be expected, since usually a combination of biotic and abiotic factors directly influence biological systems. Combining multiple types of spatial data will require some proficiency with geographic information system (GIS) software. You will need to spend time carefully co-registering the different data layers so that the data are accurately aligned in space and the values of each layer correspond to the correct position on the Earth.

It is likely that you will have to decide on the best way to deal with data layers with different resolutions or grain sizes. The two main approaches to dealing with this issue are either to subdivide the larger grain size data into pixels that correspond to the finest grain data (resampling) or to aggregate the finer grain data into larger pixels that correspond to the grain size of the coarser-resolution data, usually averaging the values of all the pixels that coalesce into each larger pixel. In many cases finer grain data will be desirable, but your choice depends on the extent of your model boundaries and the scale of the phenomenon you are trying to model. (See additional discussions of data preprocessing in Chapters 3, 4, and 11.)

Models that use data from multiple sources may also face data heterogeneity in that some of these data may be continuous variables while others are categorical. *Continuous* variables can have any value within the range of the variable, while *categorical* variables are constrained to a limited set of discrete states or values, such as a set of land use types or the integers 1–100. This is not usually difficult to deal with in terms of assembling your GIS data layers, but it may significantly influence the type of modeling approach, model algorithm, or statistical techniques you can use in your project.

14.3.1 Climate

As noted in Chapter 8, climatic conditions, together with weather, are the primary factors that drive and explain many ecological patterns and processes, especially at larger scales. Based on average precipitation and temperature alone, one could make fairly good estimates about the type of ecosystem you would expect to find, and, in turn, the kinds of plants and animals that would inhabit a region and perhaps even the kinds of land use likely to be present.

A tremendous amount of climate-related data is now available from ground-, air-, and space-based remote sensing instruments (Chapter 8). These data come in many forms, from raw data to highly processed products that summarize various components of climatic regimes and weather. Choosing the appropriate climatic data for your model should take into account the nature of the model system and your response variable in particular. The spatial and temporal resolution of the climate data needs to be carefully selected to make sense with respect to the phenomenon you want to model. Short-lived organisms, like many plant and invertebrate species, and rapidly shifting processes, such as water levels in aquatic systems, are influenced by short-term variability in weather such as daily temperatures, precipitation, and particular storm events, while longer-lived trees and sea circulation patterns may be more influenced by seasonal or annual fluctuations like mean monthly temperature, the difference between the coldest and the warmest months, or seasonal precipitation patterns. Migratory species' movement in response to seasonal changes may be affected by both long- and short-duration climatic conditions.

It can be useful to identify limiting conditions when modeling some organisms' population dynamics—metrics like the number of days below freezing or the intervals between precipitation events may influence the birth and death rates within a population, which in turn may determine the range limits of the species or the strength of that species' interactions with other species in your model system.

Variability in climate and weather over time is often an important factor in driving ecological processes, even if long-term averages remain the same. Some readily available climatological data that offer average values, but not the variance of the data, may not provide enough resolution for your model if your system is responsive to the temporal distribution of weather events, such as precipitation and major storms (recall the example of reductions in daily temperature variations leading to losses of the neotropical frog genus *Atelopus* discussed at the opening of Chapter 8.). Infrequent, extreme events often have a major influence in structuring ecosystems and landscapes or determining ecological dynamics.

14.3.2 Terrain and soils

It is likely that you will be interested in using additional predictor variables that describe the abiotic environment of your model system. Characteristics of the Earth's surface such as elevation, topography, soils, and water bodies, introduced in detail in Chapter 5, define the distribution of resources across landscapes and the ecosystem processes that transform them, influence climate and weather patterns, and define the many abiotic factors that help to delineate species' ecological niches and geographic ranges (Root 1988; Brilha 2002).

Your first step in incorporating terrain data into your model will be to obtain or construct a DEM or digital terrain model (DTM) (Section 5.1). Once you have a DEM or DTM, you will be able to derive a number of biologically or ecologically meaningful landscape characteristics following the suggestions in Chapters 5 and 7. A number of the most commonly used characteristics include:

Elevation—Elevation is associated with climatic conditions, soil types, and vegetation communities. Species' ranges are often limited by upper and lower elevation bounds, either due to the specificity of their habitat, their physiological tolerances, or by presence of another species or many species with which they interact.

Slope—The slope or steepness of terrain influences geological processes like erosion, runoff, and landslide potential, the vegetation communities and species that are able to establish within patches of the landscape, and patterns of land use.

Aspect—Along with slope, the orientation of terrain influences the amount of solar radiation that is incident on a site and thus helps to determine the local microclimate. Equator-facing slopes tend to be warmer and drier than poleward-facing slopes and often have very different suites of species and land uses associated with them.

Hydrology—Stream order and gradient help determine flow rates, streambed composition, the occurrence of pools and riffles and structure aquatic habitats (Wellborn *et al.* 2003). Watershed boundaries are helpful in defining the area of influence around aquatic systems and can be useful guides for delimiting management strategies and practices.

In addition to elevation and terrain characteristics, soil data are much sought after for use in many conservation models. Soil types and composition, mineral content, and moisture levels can all help to predict the distributions of species, land cover, and land uses. Soil characteristics are challenging to measure with remote sensing instruments, especially when vegetation is present. Nevertheless, digitized soil types maps are available for many areas and remotely sensed data on soils are available at a variety of resolutions from local to global.

14.2.3 Land cover

For many ecology and conservation biology models, land cover information (introduced in detail in Chapter 4) is often of critical importance. Data on vegetation characteristics, productivity, composition, and distribution can be fundamental to characterizing habitats, landscape connectivity, ecosystem function, and biodiversity value. Metrics of land cover widely used in conservation modeling include: vegetation indices such as vegetation structure, biomass, and primary productivity, and vegetation phenology.

14.3.4 Land use

The distribution, nature, and intensity of human activities are the drivers of a huge variety of changes in the world's ecosystems and all the biodiversity elements within them (Sanderson *et al.* 2002). Remotely sensed products can deliver information on many spatially defined categories of land use that can be used to investigate the influences of those uses on natural resources and processes. Land use data can also serve as a bridge between the biodiversity elements and social and economic factors to model the possible relationships between different development, management, or policy options and their impacts on elements of biodiversity (Kramer-Schadt *et al.* 2004; Lathrop *et al.* 2007)

Often the scale of human activity may require you to choose remotely sensed data of a particular resolution (Wickham and Riitters 1995). For example, to recognize urban areas it may be possible to use relatively coarse-grained data such as Landsat TM imagery, but to distinguish the nature of urban infrastructure or delineate the edges of urban features like small parks it may be necessary to work with finer resolution data from satellites such as IKONOS (1.4 m resolution) or QuickBird (multispectral or panchromatic data with 2.4 m and 0.6 m resolutions respectively). (See additional discussion of scale in urban remotely sensed data in Section 11.2.)

14.3.5 Landscape pattern descriptors

As we already discussed in Chapter 10, understanding the number, size, distribution and configuration of landscape elements, or patches, has enormous utility for anticipating the response of biodiversity to local and landscape-level changes. Relying on fundamental relationships from ecology, such as the island biogeography and the species–area relationship (MacArthur and Wilson 1967), and more recent studies that describe the area requirements of particular species or ecological functions, models that incorporate landscape pattern metrics are often capable of making accurate predictions of the distribution of species, species richness, communities, and ecological processes. Over time, landscape metrics can be useful to monitor or characterize the changes in landscape patterns (Lausch and Herzog 2002). Adequate definition of patch geometry, level of fragmentation and patch types are key in landscape modeling. For instance, the flow of energy and materials through ecosystems as well as species' vital rates and habitat associations can be tied to the different types of patches in a landscape and the resources and conditions they offer (see Scott *et al.* [2002]). Defining patches for your model will be dependent on both the scale of your response variable and the resolution of your data, since your ability to recognize differences in habitat types or areas of relatively homogeneous land cover will depend on the number and arrangement of your ground-based training data (Tuomisto *et al.* 1994).

Creating projections of land use and shifts in landscape patterns under different conditions can also help to elucidate the impacts of different land use policies. For example, Lathrop *et al.* (2007) assessed past land use changes and sought to predict the potential impacts of future change under alternative scenarios of development intensity on a large (600,000 ha) upland forest area within the New York City metropolitan region. First, to assess previous land use change in the model system, the authors obtained Landsat TM images of the area from three decadal periods (1984, 1995, and 2000) and created land cover maps with the aid of existing land use data and high-resolution digital ortho-photography and SPOT panchromatic imagery. To model the impact of future development, they created spatially explicit models that predicted the eventual results of development under two different scenarios of land use constraints: a "Low Constraint" scenario, under which all vacant, privately held land would be developed to the maximum extent allowable under current land use restrictions, and a "High Constraint" scenario, under which vacant, privately held land would be developed to the maximum extent allowable under tightened land use restrictions that provided increased protection of wetland or riparian buffers and steep slopes. To translate the impacts of development and buildout on the study area, the authors established indicators of forest and watershed condition based on the percentages of altered land cover, impervious surface, riparian zones in altered land covers, and remaining interior forest for each watershed within the study area.

The land cover analysis revealed general trends in the region between 1984 and 2000 of increasing altered land cover, impervious surfaces, and altered riparian zones, coupled with decreasing areas of interior forest, that led to a steady increase in the number of watersheds failing a priori thresholds for watershed integrity (Fig. 14.5). The models predicted substantial changes in land use within the study area leading to significant changes in watershed and forest condition, with the low constraint scenario leading to considerably more

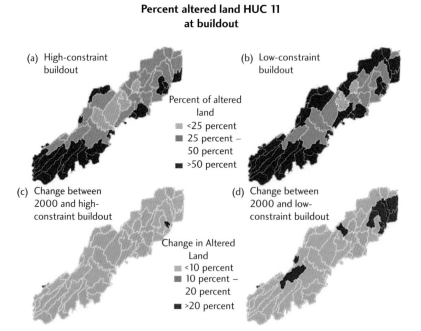

Fig. 14.5 (a) and (b) Maps of percent altered land, (c) and (d) estimated change of percent altered land (c and d) at buildout under two land use scenarios. Figure reprinted from Lathrop *et al.* (2007) with permission from Elsevier.

change than the high-constraint scenario. Population growth (26 percent versus 48 percent), the percentage of watersheds exceeding thresholds for altered land cover (47 percent versus 70 percent), the impervious surface (65 percent versus 80 percent), and altered riparian zones (20 percent versus 47 percent) were all substantially higher under the low constraint, status quo, scenario than under the higher constraint scenario. The percent of watersheds with >40 percent forest interior remaining was similarly expected to decline more steeply under the low-constraint scenario. Importantly, because the model was spatially explicit, the authors were able to make predictions about likely hot spots of development or watershed degradation that might attract greater attention in future management decisions.

14.4 Summary

Modeling helps us to explore the way that parts of natural systems interact and influence one another. This chapter provides an overview of the steps you might follow to developing a modeling project, some of the types of remotely sensed data you might use, and some of the contexts in which models can be useful. For many ecologists and conservation biologists, using remotely sensed data in models provides an opportunity to extrapolate field observations on species, habitats, or processes to much larger areas, potentially to the scale at which management decisions are made. As remotely sensed data become available on more biophysical characteristics of the planet, at higher spatial and temporal scales, modelers will be able to make more explicit and (hopefully) accurate inferences and predictions about ecological functions and they respond to human activities. To be successful, however, you must make the topic, scope, and methods of your model explicit as well as be careful to match the types of remotely sensed data you use with what you hope your model will explain.

15

Global conservation

On 24 December 1968, as they watched the half-illuminated earthrise over the surface of the moon, the crew of the *Apollo 8* lunar mission captured an image that changed humankind's view of our planet and our place on it. The earthrise image and other iconic global images like the "blue marble" photo taken by the crew of *Apollo 17* in 1972 gave us, for the first time, a global view of our fragile home within the vastness of space (Fig. 15.1). These early global images helped promote environmental awareness around the world and were instrumental in the development of the field of remote sensing (Lowman 1999). However, it would take some time for the research community to compile and use global-scale imagery from space in the ecological sciences.

Improvements in passive and active remote sensing systems placed in orbit by national governments and the growing commercial satellite sector have given us an "end-to-end" remote sensing capability that allows us to make measurements of important environmental phenomena from very local to global spatial scales (of course, airborne remote sensing systems have long enhanced our ability to capture information at local scales). Data depicting the social and economic drivers of biodiversity loss are also available globally from a variety of sources. These different data sets can now be brought together with powerful, affordable, spatially referenced computing technologies, e.g., GIS and GPS, which were unimaginable when the *Apollo* missions sent back their images. The entire *Apollo* spacecraft's computing power was less than that of today's mobile phone. Taken together, these advances have made it possible to grapple with the complexities and scale of addressing conservation challenges at the global level. This chapter elaborates the role of remote sensing as one among several catalysts driving the development of new approaches to ecology and conservation biology at the global level.

15.1 Remote sensing and the road to a global ecology

In the early 1980s, NASA initiated its Global Habitability program (NASA 1983; Waldrop 1986; Running *et al.* 2004). This program sought to answer the big question of how the biosphere partitions its energy and mass. This focus, in turn, resulted in an effort to track the biological productivity of the Earth's terrestrial biomes and how they responded to environmental changes. Synoptic

Fig. 15.1 Images that transformed our perceptions of the Earth and our role in its stewardship, the classic "Blue Marble" image taken by the *Apollo 17* crew on December 7, 1972 (*top*, AS17–148–22727) and "Earthrise," the rising Earth above the lunar horizon taken from the *Apollo 8* spacecraft on December 24, 1968 (*bottom*, AS08–14–2383). Credit: Image Science & Analysis Laboratory, NASA/JSC.

and repeated observations from space would be necessary to meet this challenge. Tucker *et al.* (1985) used NOAA weather satellite imagery from the AVHRR to classify land cover and map vegetation dynamics over a multi-month period

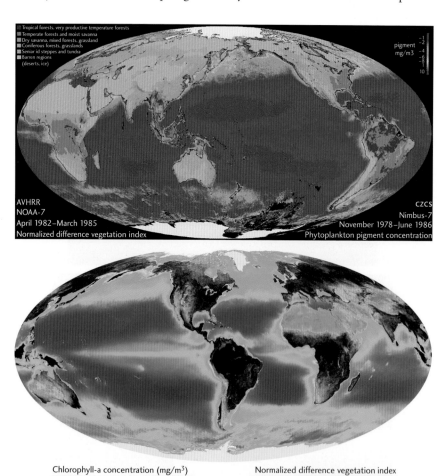

Fig. 15.2 A global biosphere composite image derived by compositing 3 years (1982 to 1985) of NOAA AVHRR land surface data and 7.5 years (1978 to 1986) of chlorophyll-*a* ocean color data from the Coastal Zone Color Scanner (CZCS) sensor aboard the *Nimbus-7* satellite (*top*). This 1989 image built upon the original published as a map supplement in *National Geographic* magazine (December 1988). A more recent view of the global biosphere composited from 10 years (September 1997 to September 2007) of data from SeaWiFS, using the normalized difference vegetation index for land and the concentration of chlorophyll-*a* for the oceans and large water bodies (*bottom*). Credit: Gene Feldman, Ocean Color Project, NASA/GSFC, SeaWiFS data courtesy of GeoEye.

across the entire continent of Africa. They introduced two continental data sets of major importance to ecologists, in effect demonstrating that satellites could observe global biological phenomena. One data set consisted of seasonal indices of the changing green-leaf biomass derived from 4 km AVHRR imagery used within a series of NDVI products. The onset of new green-leaf biomass tracked movements of the Intertropical Convergence Zone (see Section 8.5.1 for more on the ITCZ) and its related precipitation in a pulse of climate-generated new growth, showing the large-scale response of biology to climate. The other data set was a continent-wide classification of vegetation types obtained from the multi-temporal vegetation index products. As Tucker *et al.* (1985: p. 374) put it, "the results suggest the prospect for internally consistent mapping and repeated monitoring of the main cover types of continental areas based on the use of multitemporal coarse-resolution satellite data." Global ecology was born.

One sign of the rise of this new global ecology was the release in the December 1988 issue of *National Geographic* of the first remotely sensed image of the global biosphere under the title "Endangered Earth." This image combined two multi-year composites: a global composite of 4 km NASA CZCS data, depicting ocean color derived from sea surface phytoplankton (the green plants of the sea), and a global composite of vegetation greenness from 4 km AVHRR NDVI data. The resulting image offered the first global view of the living components of the Earth system (Fig. 15.2).

The early NDVI products from AVHRR were precursors of today's broader suite of global land ecological data products from sources such as NASA MODIS, the European SPOT Vegetation programme, and the ESA MERIS sensor. These data products include LAI/FPAR, evapotranspiration, land cover and land cover change, and net primary productivity (Running *et al.* 2004). We now have the capability to look at terrestrial net primary productivity (NPP) on an eight-day composited as well as monthly basis and detect trends and anomalies over time in various ecoregions. These NPP anomalies serve as early warning systems for a host of large-scale ecological conditions and are especially important in a time of changing climate (Nemani *et al.* 2003). Similarly, global ocean color products from MODIS and other sensors provide us a view of changing sea surface chlorophyll-*a* concentrations, which correlate with ocean primary production.

In addition to the question of how the primary productivity of the planet changes with time, another fundamental question for global ecologists is how various land covers are distributed across Earth's terrestrial surface. Knowing the distribution of terrestrial land covers and how they change over time is one important prerequisite for understanding not only the global condition of biodiversity but also how important elements, such as carbon and nitrogen, are cycling through ecosystems. In the early 1990s, Skole and Tucker (1993) employed higher resolution Landsat imagery, at tens of meters spatial resolution, to track levels of deforestation for the entire forested portion of Brazil's Amazon

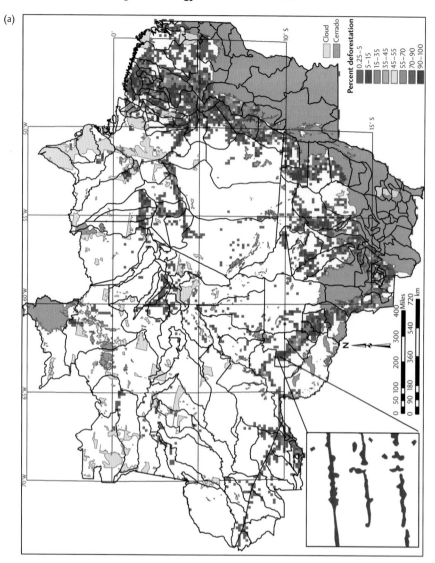

Fig. 15.3 (a) (continues).

Basin at two dates, 1978 and 1988 (Fig. 15.3). Using 1978 Landsat MSS and 1988 Landsat TM satellite data in a GIS, they digitized deforested areas in closed canopy forest through visual interpretation. Thus, the growing archive of moderate scale imagery from Landsat, which often includes multiple scenes of the same area of Earth's surface, enabled the assembly of large regional- to national-scale composites of land cover changes at a landscape scale. By landscape scale, we mean that this imagery was at the tens of meters scale rather than the kilometer scale. The scale matched that at which individual human decisions often directly affected landscapes and at which individuals could better view and understand

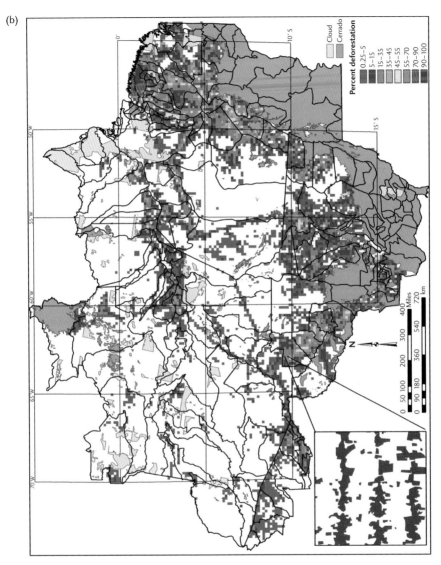

Fig. 15.3 Depictions of the percent deforestation within the Legal Amazon of Brazil from 1978 (a) and 1988 (b). The data were averaged into 16 × 16 km grid cells as shown in the lower left corner of each image. Adapted (modified) from Skole and Tucker (1993) with permission from AAAS.

the processes driving many types of changes. In addition to Landsat data availability, increasingly powerful computers (courtesy of Moore's Law and its implications for the increase in computational power over time) and the growth in GIS technology and remote sensing software tools allowed investigators to bring together hundreds of scenes of satellite imagery on common computer platforms to observe large-extent changes in land cover at relatively fine spatial resolutions. While not yet global, Skole and Tucker showed a way forward for the routine mapping of Earth's forested regions to look for deforestation and other processes placing biodiversity in jeopardy.

In Europe, the Joint Research Centre of the European Commission has been a leader in estimating global changes in forest cover. Achard *et al.* (2002) used Landsat TM imagery to assemble maps with 1 km^2 spatial resolution of the humid tropics in Latin America, Africa, and Southeast Asia. They also employed a sampling approach in which they focused their change detection on areas where a high proportion of deforestation was taking place as opposed to "wall-to-wall" measures of change throughout these entire regions. Their results showed 5.8 ± 1.4 million hectares of humid tropical forest were lost each year between 1990 and 1997, with a further 2.3±0.7 million hectares visibly degraded. As Earth's humid tropical forests are its greatest storehouses of terrestrial biodiversity, the importance of this information for conservation is clear. Information on forest loss is also a key data set for managing and trading carbon within the framework of efforts to reduce carbon emissions through the prevention of deforestation and forest degradation.

Despite demonstrations of how to assemble large data sets to understand forest loss over time, access to imagery was still an issue throughout the 1990s and into the first decade of the twenty-first century. A Landsat image costs several hundred US dollars, with comparable-scale imagery available at similar or even higher prices from other sources around the world. This situation changed rather dramatically around 2004 with the debut of a series of global Landsat data sets consisting of imagery from three different time periods available at very low cost to users. Perhaps even more importantly, there were no restrictions on a user's ability to redistribute the imagery (Tucker *et al.* 2004). These global data sets consist of Landsat MSS data from the mid-1970s, Landsat TM data circa 1990, and Landsat ETM+ data from circa 2000. The 30 m to 80 m data sets were orthorectified so that images from different dates could be easily compared to look for changes in land cover over a quarter century. Today, the cost for this global imagery has essentially gone to zero. NASA and the USGS are finalizing another global data set for the circa 2005 time period, the Global Land Survey 2005 (Gutman *et al.* 2008). In 2008, the USGS, in a major revision of its data pricing policy, announced that it would make all Landsat archive imagery available at no charge to the user. In terms of data access, this development ensures that the imagery will now be available for global assessments of habitat changes in Earth's land surface and coastal zones. Landsat data access has also made important contributions to mapping the global extent of coral reefs (see Section 6.3.1.1 for information on the Millennium Coral Reef Mapping Project). The imagery used in this effort is available on the Web (Robinson *et al.* 2006).

In addition, other global data sets now complement the land and ocean products available at both the several hundred meters to 1 km scales (building on decades of AVHRR data) and the global, landscape scale (30 m) products from Landsat and similar sensors. These include the SRTM digital terrain elevation data for the Earth's land surface between 56 °S and 60 °N latitudes, covering about 80 percent of Earth's landmass. This data set provides a near-global topography for the planet at approximately 30 m (available for the United States) and 90 m (available internationally) horizontal resolution (Slater *et al.* 2006). The Government of Japan in concert with NASA and USGS has developed a more complete global digital elevation product at approximately 100 m horizontal resolution from its ASTER sensor.

From the standpoint of a critical information layer to use in tandem with these and other remote sensing products, the United Nations Environment Programme (UNEP) World Conservation Monitoring Center (WCMC) has developed a World Database on Protected Areas (WDPA). This database has GIS layers of marine and terrestrial protected areas worldwide. WCMC is constantly working with national governments and nongovernmental organizations to improve this vitally important tool for global conservation (see Section 12.4 for more information on the WDPA).

Science, technology, and policy have now come together to enable us to achieve the global ecology envisioned in the 1980s. Remote sensing has played a key role but by no means the only role in bringing about global ecology. The creation of a host of global databases, with associated latitude and longitude coordinates from a large array of *in situ* information sources has certainly played a decisive role. It is up to the conservation community to translate these advances into appropriate products for global conservation. Our challenge is to develop the data systems and observation-fed models that allow us to integrate observations across multiple scales so that we can zoom in and then back out in space, placing local ecological processes into their broader geographic and environmental contexts and discovering linkages and feedbacks among physical, chemical, and biological phenomena occurring at transcontinental to sub-meter, and ultimately microscopic, scales.

15.2 Remote sensing and global conservation

The advent of Google Earth has popularized the notion of harnessing geospatial imagery to move from global to local spatial scales. However, we are only beginning to explore and appreciate the implications of this development for the ecological sciences generally as well as for specific applications to conservation practice. A research framework to take full advantage of our geospatial abilities is still largely lacking, which suggests that our ability to apply the results arising from this research lags even farther behind. There is important, and fascinating, progress being made on a number of fronts, however. Three topics in which global remote sensing applications are proving to be transformative both for the science and practice of conservation are described in the following sections.

15.2.1 Global priority setting for conservation

One of the areas in which the global conservation community has made tremendous investments has been in mapping specific priority areas for the conservation of biodiversity. The widely known slogan "think globally, act locally" has encouraged individuals to find ways in which they can contribute to conservation efforts close to home. At the same time, conservation biologists and international conservation NGOs have increasingly been asking, "How can we think globally so that we can decide where and how to act locally?"

These global-level efforts have varied according to the data and methods employed, but the majority of them result in maps with a number of regional-scale polygons defining the conservation unit and a ranking system making explicit the areas most in need of conservation effort. For example, Conservation International has identified biodiversity hotspots based upon global analyses of the concentration of endemic species and relative rates of habitat loss in the world's major biogeographic areas (Myers *et al.* 2000). The World Wildlife Fund, in contrast, has focused on delimiting "ecoregions," large units of land defined by a distinct assemblage of natural communities and species whose boundaries are meant to approximate the original extent of natural communities prior to major land use change (Olson and Dinerstein 1998; Olson *et al.* 2001). While neither of these highly influential approaches explicitly used remotely sensed data, they and others like them provide the all-important geospatial context for applying remote sensing to detect changes affecting biodiversity at global to regional scales. In essence, they are global maps of where we should be looking for change with remote sensing.

A global priority setting exercise that used remotely sensed data extensively, the Human Footprint/Last of the Wild project, was conducted by the Wildlife Conservation Society and the Center for International Earth Science Information Network to identify and highlight the world's areas most and least impacted by human activities (Sanderson *et al.* 2002). Using a global land cover product based on 1 km AVHRR data (Loveland *et al.* 2000), electrical power infrastructure data derived from nighttime imagery taken by meteorological satellites (Elvidge *et al.* 1997), and other data sets on population and infrastructure density, Sanderson's team described the Human Footprint as the signature of a novel Human Influence Index written across the world's landscapes. The Last of the Wild, in turn, were defined as the areas of relatively low Human Influence constituting the "wildest 10 percent" of each terrestrial biome, which represent critical priorities for conserving biodiversity in undisturbed patches (Fig. 15.4).

The large scales of these and other global priority-setting exercises have required thousands of hours of effort by ecologists with taxonomic and geospatial expertise to assemble the finished products. The positive result is that several conservation organizations have now identified key areas for conservation expenditures. However, ensuring that funds go to these priority areas continues to be a challenge in practice (Halpern *et al.* 2006). We are also developing a much

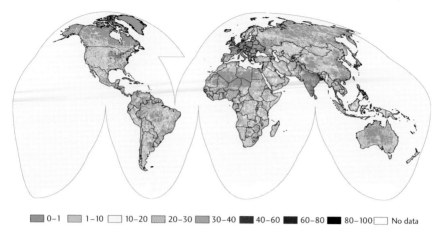

0–1 ▨ 1–10 ☐ 10–20 ▨ 20–30 ▨ 30–40 ▨ 40–60 ▨ 60–80 ■ 80–100 ☐ No data

Fig. 15.4 Part A. "The Human Footprint," a quantitative evaluation of human influence on the global land surface from data describing human population density, land transformation, access, and electrical power infrastructure normalized to reflect the continuum of human influence across each terrestrial biome defined within biogeographic realms. Satellite imagery from AVHRR (land cover) and DMSP (lights at night) contributed to this product and "The Last of the Wild" product. Figure from Sanderson *et al.* (2002), ©American Institute of Biological Sciences, used with permission.

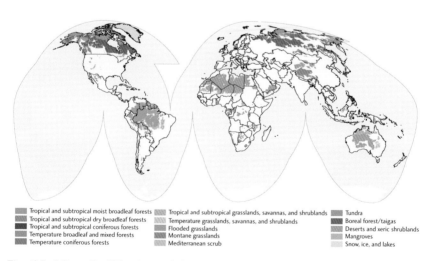

Tropical and subtropical moist broadleaf forests
Tropical and subtropical dry broadleaf forests
Tropical and subtropical coniferous forests
Temperate broadleaf and mixed forests
Temperate coniferous forests

Tropical and subtropical grasslands, savannas, and shrublands
Temperate grasslands, savannas, and shrublands
Flooded grasslands
Montane grasslands
Mediterranean scrub

Tundra
Boreal forest/taigas
Deserts and xeric shrublands
Mangroves
Snow, ice, and lakes

Fig. 15.4 Part B. "The Last of the Wild" maps the least human-influenced or 10 percent wildest areas in biomes within biogeographic realms. Figure from Sanderson *et al.* (2002), ©American Institute of Biological Sciences, used with permission.

better and more global understanding of what species live in which parts of particular landscapes, and increasingly seascapes. Knowing what lives where constitutes first-order information urgently needed by conservation biologists before any considerations of conservation action. Again, the scales of these global products lend themselves quite well to the application of remote sensing. In fact, priority-setting exercises have served as a catalyst for much of the growth in today's geospatial conservation community, which uses remote sensing as a standard tool in both its management and research toolkits.

15.2.2 Monitoring changes on earth's surface

Monitoring changes in land cover and land use, long a central application of remote sensing, is fast becoming another topic that can be tackled at the global scale. With the availability of daily, near global coverage of the Earth by MODIS and other relatively frequent imagery from active and passive sensors, we are now in a position to pinpoint areas of rapid deforestation, habitat conversion, or degradation. For example, Hansen *et al.* (2008) used MODIS and Landsat ETM+ imagery in tandem to measure the clearing of humid tropical forests during the interval 2000–2005. They estimated a 2.36 percent reduction in the area of humid tropical forests, a loss of over 27 million hectares in just five years, with Brazil and Indonesia accounting for over 60 percent of that total (Fig. 15.5). On a more regional basis, using data from the United Nation's Food and Agriculture Organization's global land cover products from 1990 to 2005,

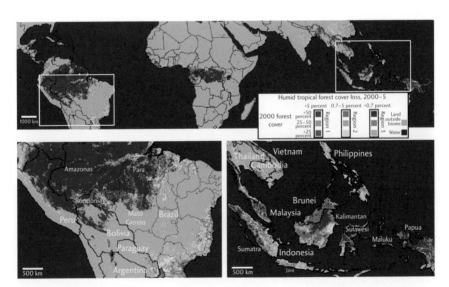

Fig. 15.5 Humid tropical forest cover in 2000 and forest cover loss between 2000 and 2005 derived using MODIS and Landsat imagery. Figure from Hansen *et al.* (2008) ©National Academy of Sciences, United States, used with permission.

Koh and Wilcove (2008) demonstrated that the majority of the extensive oil palm plantation expansions during that period came at the expense of tropical forests, despite oil palm producers' claims to the contrary. Examples such as these suggest we will increasingly be able to identify and respond quickly to the processes of habitat loss and conversion, with conservation efforts and policy initiatives targeted at the regions most under pressure.

15.2.3 Ecological forecasting

Complex global models of ecosystems that can provide predictions about the environmental consequences of different courses of action remain a goal for the conservation and ecological communities. Remote sensing appears poised to contribute to such models. However, the science of combining biological, economic, social, and political data streams in an integrated modeling system is still in its youth.

An important effort launched in 2001, the Millennium Ecosystem Assessment (MA), undertook the challenge of predicting the future quality of the environment under different policy scenarios to provide a scientific basis for making decisions about the conservation and development of the planet's biological resources. The MA focused on forecasting provisioning ecological services such as food, freshwater, and fuel, regulating services like air and water quality, and supporting services like primary production and nutrient cycling (Tallis and Kareiva 2006). In its interconnected models and submodels, the MA made extensive use of global data from remote sensing sources including global land cover products, climate products and models, primary productivity products, and atmospheric composition products. The MA was probably the most extensive ecological modeling effort ever developed and, importantly, explicitly included linkages between the social, economic, political, technological, and biological realms.

How can you directly relate remotely sensed maps of forest loss (or potentially other types of habitat loss) to changes in biodiversity elements, such as species? One common approach employs the species–area relationship, in which the number of species (S) directly relates to the amount of area (A) under consideration ($S = cA^z$), with (c) and (z) as fitted constants. Relating the species richness of an area to its size gives us a metric that couples our remotely sensed estimates of habitat loss to its an important biodiversity variable (Pimm and Raven 2000). This formula is the basis for many estimates of species loss due to human habitat alteration at large spatial scales, with remote sensing providing the necessary information for the area term.

15.3 A look ahead

Given that the tools are now largely in place to develop global conservation products, is there an international framework in which to bring them together?

In 2002, the Parties to the Convention on Biological Diversity (CBD) called for a significant reduction in the rate of biodiversity loss at the global, regional, and national level by the year 2010. The challenge lay in how to measure progress toward this 2010 Biodiversity Target. Millions had been spent, largely by conservation organizations and their donors, to develop global priorities for conservation (Brooks *et al.* 2006). These priority-setting exercises typically demarcated areas on maps that require protection and monitoring for adaptive management if we are to prevent further losses of biodiversity. Thus, we have a good sense of what large areas on Earth's land surface, and increasingly in its oceans (Roberts *et al.* 2002; Mora *et al.* 2006), are of the most importance for conservation. Our challenge lies in designing a framework to monitor and respond to changes in the status of these important areas over time, whether they are local sites or entire ecoregions. Pereira and Cooper (2006) propose one approach to this challenge, an integrated global and regional monitoring system for biodiversity that would utilize satellite imagery for tracking land cover changes in important regions and smaller areas, in conjunction with global and regional surveys and assessments of important taxa and selected habitats. In essence, this approach would marry the Earth observation efforts of the world's space agencies with the taxonomic and focused habitat assessments of the IUCN, Global Biodiversity Information Facility (GBIF), UNEP WCMC, BirdLife International, World Wildlife Fund, Conservation International, and many other organizations.

In 2003, an international partnership known as the Group on Earth Observations or GEO came together, rather quietly at first, to coordinate the satellite and *in situ* Earth observation programs of member nations. With over 70 national governments, the European Commission, and a host of participating organizations (including many United Nations bodies and other multinational entities) working together, GEO is in position to provide the global support structure to sustain a global conservation effort. Indeed, biodiversity is one of the nine principal focus areas selected by GEO. Through its focus on biodiversity, GEO members have called for the development of a global Biodiversity Observation Network (GEO BON), which is to be a system of systems coordinating satellite observations of ecosystems and other elements of biodiversity with *in situ* surveys and inventories of species and relevant genetic information (Scholes *et al.* 2008). The result will be global assessments of the status of and trends in the condition of biodiversity and a better understanding of where gaps exist in our knowledge. A primary constituent of GEO BON is the CBD. Since the membership of GEO includes the agencies within national governments charged with observing, and in many cases managing the condition of local environments, GEO appears set to become a significant force promoting the conservation of biodiversity in an integrated, global manner. Time will tell.

15.4 Summary

We are fortunate to live in a time in which existing remote sensing tools, computational technologies and associated software, GPS developments, and ecological modeling are providing the framework to practice truly global conservation. This is appropriate given the global nature of the threats to biodiversity and the global consequences of its decline. We know we are having a global impact on Earth's living systems. It is now time to begin to manage our impacts at a scale commensurate with that of our actions. The good news is that, increasingly, we have the tools to address this crisis. The choice of whether or not to do so is up to us. Our future, and that of life on this planet, is in our hands.

Part IV

Appendices

Appendix 1
The electromagnetic spectrum

The electromagnetic spectrum (EMS) is the term given to the entire range of electromagnetic (EM) radiation, from the short wavelength gamma rays to long wavelength radio waves. Electromagnetic radiation travels in the form of an oscillating wave at the speed of light. Because it travels as a wave, it is possible to categorize different types of EM radiation by wavelength or frequency. Wavelength is determined by measuring the distance between two consecutive wave peaks and this is measured in distance units such as micrometers (μm) and meters (Fig. A1.1). Frequency is the number of wave cycles passing a point in a second and is measured in hertz (Hz), which is equivalent to cycles per second (Fig. A1.1). Since all wavelengths of EM radiation travel at the same speed it is possible to derive a frequency if you know the wavelength and vice versa. The formula to convert between frequency and wavelength is $v = c/\lambda$ or $\lambda = c/v$ where $c =$ the speed of light (3×10^8 m/s), $\lambda =$ wavelength, and $v =$ frequency.

For most remote sensing applications, we divide the EMS into three broad categories: visible, infrared, and microwave (Fig. A1.2). Visible light includes those wavelengths visible to the human eye, ranging from 0.4 to 0.7 μm. Just beyond (longer wavelengths) visible light is the infrared portion of the spectrum. We divide this into the near-infrared (0.7–1.3 μm), mid-infrared (1.3–3 μm), and thermal-infrared (3–14 μm) regions. Microwaves are the longest wavelengths commonly used in remote sensing, ranging from wavelengths of 1 millimeter (mm) to 1 meter (m).

In remote sensing, it is common for those working with optical remote sensing, which includes the visible and infrared portions of the EMS, to use "wavelength" when describing the bands or channels of a particular sensor. For microwave remote sensing (e.g., radar), it is far more common to use "frequency" when describing the particular portion of the EMS being detected.

EM radiation coming off of the Earth's surface is a combination of reflected solar energy and energy emitted from the Earth. The source of reflected EM radiation is the sun. However, much of this energy is scattered or absorbed in the atmosphere before it reaches the Earth's surface (Fig. A1.3). Visible, near-infrared, and mid-infrared energy coming off the Earth's surface are almost

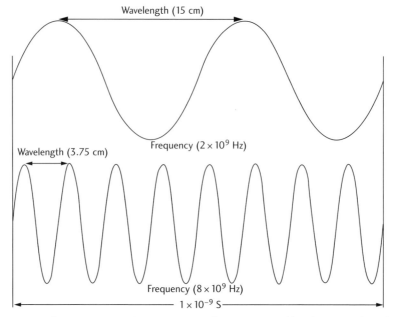

Fig. A1.1 Electromagnetic (EM) waves can be categorized by their wavelength or frequency. Wavelength is the distance between two consecutive wave peaks and frequency is the number of waves that pass a point over a period of time. Since EM waves travel at the same speed, the speed of light, it is possible to calculate the frequency if the wavelength is known and vice versa. The top wave has a longer wavelength and a lower frequency than the wave at the bottom. Credit: Ned Horning, American Museum of Natural History's Center for Biodiversity and Conservation.

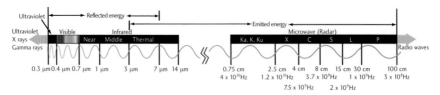

Fig. A1.2 Remote sensing uses a broad range of wavelengths of electromagnetic (EM) radiation. The segments of the microwave portion of the electromagnetic spectrum (EMS) used by radar instruments are commonly denoted by letters. Figure redrawn with modifications from Turner *et al.* (2003: 307), with permission from Elsevier.

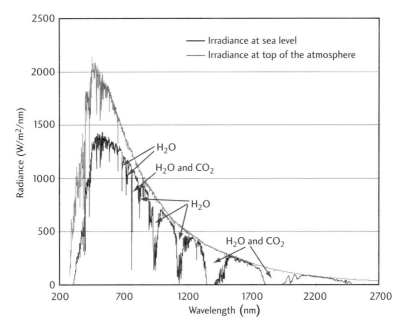

Fig. A1.3 Only a portion of the electromagnetic energy emitted by the sun actually reaches the Earth's surface. This graph compares the intensity (irradiance) of different wavelengths of electromagnetic (EM) energy at the top of the atmosphere with the intensity at sea level. This difference occurs because particulates and certain molecules in the atmosphere such as water and carbon dioxide reflect and absorb specific wavelengths of EM energy thereby reducing the solar energy that reaches the Earth's surface. The data on top of the atmosphere irradiance are from the 2000 ASTM Standard Extraterrestrial Spectrum Reference E-490–00 and the data for sea-level irradiance are from ASTM G173–03e1 Standard Tables for Reference Solar Spectral Irradiances: Direct Normal and Hemispherical on 37° Tilted Surface. Credit: Ned Horning, American Museum of Natural History's Center for Biodiversity and Conservation.

entirely comprised of reflected energy. However, as you enter the thermal infrared portion of the spectrum the amount of emitted energy increases and reflected energy decreases. This emitted energy reaches a peak at roughly 10 μm in the thermal infrared portion of the spectrum.

Please see remote sensing text books for more details about the EM spectrum.

Appendix 2
Image-processing software

In Chapter 3, we describe four different types of image-processing software. In this appendix, we list a number of specific software packages in each of the categories described. In each category, we start with a list of proprietary software, followed by open source software. With two exceptions, proprietary software listed below is sold commercially. In the case of open source software, the application and the source code are freely distributed. Most open source alternatives listed below provide support for several languages other than English. More information about open source software is available in Appendix 3.

We base the relative cost information on the price for a new (not an upgrade) single node-locked software license for a commercial company. Please use this information only as a guide. If you want to purchase any of these software applications, it is important that you contact the software company or a vendor to request a price quote. Many of the software companies listed below offer special discounts for education and nonprofit institutions or for multiple licenses. The legend for cost is:

- NC = no cost
- $ ≤ $1000
- $$ = $1001–2500
- $$$ = $2501–4500
- $$$$ = $4501–10,000
- $$$$$ ≥ $10,000

This list is not exhaustive but it can be used to help you become more familiar with some of the more common image-processing software alternatives. Only software packages that can read multiband imagery are considered. More information about software is available on the book's Web site.

A2.1 Graphics Software

A2.1.1 Proprietary

Adobe Photoshop: http://www.adobe.com

This is a powerful image-processing package created for the graphic arts and digital photography communities. Photoshop works with Windows and Macintosh operating systems. Cost = $.

Avenza Geographic Imager: http://www.avenza.com/

A plug-in that extends Photoshop's capabilities by providing tools to work with geospatial imagery such as remotely sensed images. Geographic Imager works with Windows and Macintosh operating systems. Cost = $.

A2.1.2 Open Source

GIMP: http://www.gimp.org/

The GNU Image Manipulation Program is an image-processing package created for the graphic arts and digital photography communities. As of this writing, no geospatial tools are available but they will likely be developed. GIMP works with Windows, Macintosh, Linux, and Unix operating systems. Cost = NC.

A2.2 Geographic information system (GIS) software

A2.2.1 Proprietary

ESRI ArcGIS: http://www.esri.com

An integrated collection of GIS software. Plug-ins are available from ESRI and other vendors to add advanced image-processing functionality to ArcGIS. ArcGIS works with the Windows operating system. Cost = $$.

Mapinfo Professional: http://www.mapinfo.com

A mapping GIS application with image visualization and some image manipulation capabilities. Mapinfo works with the Windows operating system. Cost = $$$$.

Manifold: http://www.manifold.net

An inexpensive desktop GIS with image visualization and image manipulation capabilities. Manifold works with the Windows operating system. Cost = $.

A2.2.2 Open Source

Quantum GIS (QGIS): http://www.qgis.org/

A desktop GIS with an interface to GRASS that provides advanced image-processing capabilities. QGIS works with Windows, Macintosh, Linux, and Unix operating systems. Cost = NC.

uDig: http://udig.refractions.net

A desktop GIS written in Java with image visualization capabilities. uDig works with Windows, Macintosh, Linux, and Unix operating systems. Cost = NC.

MapWindow: http://www.mapwindow.org/

A desktop GIS initially developed at Idaho State University. MapWindow works with the Windows operating system. Cost = NC.

A2.3 Specialized remote sensing software

A2.3.1 Proprietary

Leica Geosystems ERDAS IMAGINE Professional: http://gis.leica-geosystems.com

A suite of software products for working with remotely sensed imagery. ERDAS IMAGINE works with Windows operating systems. Cost = $$$$.

ITT Visual Information Solutions ENVI: http://www.ittvis.com

An image-processing package developed on the IDL programming language. ENVI works with Windows, Macintosh, Linux, and Unix operating systems. Cost = $$$$.

PCI Geomatica Core: http://www.pcigeomatics.com/

An image-processing package with a number of add-on modules available for advanced processing. Geomatica works with Windows, Linux, and Unix operating systems. Cost = $$$.

Clark Labs IDRISI Andes: http://www.clarklabs.org/

Focused on raster GIS but includes many image-processing capabilities and is designed to run on low-end Windows computers. IDRISI works with Windows operating systems. Cost = $$.

Definiens Developer: http://www.definiens.com

Designed to quickly extract accurate and reliable geo-information from any kind of remotely sensed imagery. Definiens Developer works with Windows and Linux operating systems. Cost = $$$$$.

Leica Geosystems ER Mapper Professional: http://gis.leica-geosystems.com

A desktop image-processing package. ER Mapper Professional works with the Windows operating system. Cost = $$$$.

MicroImages TNTmips: http://www.microimages.com/

A desktop image-processing and GIS package. TNTmips works with Windows, Linux, and Unix operating systems. Cost = $$$$.

MultiSpec: http://cobweb.ecn.purdue.edu/~biehl/MultiSpec

A freely available image data analysis system with good image classification capabilities. This is developed and maintained by faculty at Purdue University. MultiSpec works with the Windows and Macintosh operating systems. Cost = NC.

SPRING: http://www.dpi.inpe.br/spring/

A GIS and remote sensing image-processing package developed by Brazil's National Institute for Space Research (INPE). SPRING works with Windows and Linux operating systems. Cost = NC.

A2.3.2 Open source

OpenEV: http://fwtools.maptools.org/

Primarily used for image visualization and basic processing. The most up-to-date version is being maintained as part of the FWTools package. OpenEV works with Windows and Linux operating systems. Cost = NC.

Open Source Software Image Map (OSSIM): http://www.ossim.org
A high-performance image-processing library. A user interface called ImageLinker provides easy access to many of the available functions. OSSIM works with Windows, Macintosh, Linux, and Unix operating systems. Cost = NC.

Geographic Information System GIS (GRASS): http://grass.itc.it/

A raster and vector GIS and image-processing package that has been under development since 1982. It includes capabilities that rival many proprietary packages. Much has been done to make the program more user-friendly. The user group is very active. GRASS works with Windows, Macintosh, Linux, and Unix operating systems. Cost = NC.

52°North ILWIS Open: http://52north.org

This was formally a proprietary GIS and remote sensing image-processing package that has been released as open source. ILWIS Open works with the Windows operating system. Cost = NC.

A2.4 Numerical analysis software

A2.4.1 Proprietary

The MathWorks MATLAB: http://www.mathworks.com/

A high-level programming language and interactive environment. An image-processing toolbox is available to facilitate working with imagery. MATLAB works with Windows, Macintosh, Linux, and Unix operating systems. Cost = $$.

ITT Visual Information Solutions IDL: http://www.ittvis.com

A high-level programming language for data visualization and analysis with strong support for fundamental image-processing tasks. IDL works with Windows, Macintosh, Linux, and Unix operating systems. Cost = $$$.

Wolfram Research Mathematica: http://www.wolfram.com/

A high-level programming environment for data visualization and analysis. Mathematica works with Windows, Macintosh, Linux, and Unix operating systems. Cost = $$.

A2.4.2 Open source

FreeMat: http://freemat.sourceforge.net

Provides a large subset of the functionality available in MATLAB. FreeMat works with Windows, Macintosh, Linux, and Unix operating systems. Cost = NC.

Octave: http://www.gnu.org/software/octave/

A high-level programming language for numerical computations. Octave works with Windows, Macintosh, Linux, and Unix operating systems. Cost = NC.

Scilab: http://www.scilab.org/

A software package for numerical computations in a powerful computing environment. An image-processing toolbox called SIP is also available. Scilab works with Windows, Macintosh, Linux, and Unix operating systems. Cost = NC.

Appendix 3
Open source software

These are exciting times in the open source geographic information system (GIS) and remote sensing software arena. Previously, most of the open source GIS development projects focused on building software libraries with powerful functionality. Unfortunately, these packages were, for the most part, inaccessible to the typical user who wanted an application that was easy to install and use. This situation is rapidly changing.

A3.1 What is open source software?

Open source software is defined as software that has the source code freely available and is licensed so that it can be freely distributed and modified as long as appropriate credit is provided to the developers. There are several licensing options for open source software but all of them follow these basic rules. More information about open source software and the variety of licenses is available at the Open Source Initiative Web page (http://www.opensource.org/).

Open source software development efforts are often dedicated to creating applications or creating software libraries. Libraries are software modules designed for specific tasks such as importing and exporting images or providing image projection capabilities. These libraries are shared among different projects, thereby significantly reducing the amount of time to develop or improve an application. For example, the GDAL library is designed to read and write dozens of different common image and vector formats. Integrating this library in an application quickly provides advanced image import capabilities. Since many open source applications use GDAL, when improvements are made to that library these enhancements become available to all the applications.

In the geospatial arena, there is growing activity related to the use and development of open source software. This was evidenced by the formation of the Open Source Geospatial Foundation (OSGeo, http://osgeo.org) in early 2006. Open source software is a viable and evolving resource for research and conservation organizations around the world. Through the utilization of open source applications, researchers and practitioners have the opportunity to influence the development of these tools by providing feedback on current and future functionality.

A3.2 Where does open source software fit in?

Open source software can be a replacement for or a complement to proprietary software. A lot depends on your situation. If you work for an organization with proprietary software, you might consider open source software to fill in for functionality not provided by your proprietary software or you may just find that the open source version does some tasks better than the software you have already. If you are new to the world of remote sensing or GIS, open source software is a great place to start since it is free. If it meets your needs then you are all set and if you need functionality not available from open source packages you can consider purchasing proprietary software or working with the open source community to develop the functionally you need.

A3.3 So, how can you help?

If you are a computer programmer, your potential contribution is fairly straight-forward but what if you are an end user with no programming experience? Simply using the software and providing input to the development team about the interface, additional functionality, and bugs is appreciated. Writing new or commenting on existing documentation is another area where users can help. Most of these software projects have discussion lists and some of these are focused specifically on users. The best advice is to download the software, play around with it, and share your thoughts. If you like it, pass on the good news to your friends and colleagues.

A3.4 What is out there and where can I get it?

There are open source applications to meet most of your geospatial needs including desktop and server GIS, map and feature servers, image processing, and spatial databases. A number of open source applications are listed in Appendix 2. More information about open source geospatial software and the communities that support it is available at the OSGeo Web site: http://osgeo.org.

Appendix 4
Satellites and sensors

Below is a list of some of the satellite sensors used in ecology and biodiversity conservation. The list is ordered from fine to coarse resolution starting with optical sensors and ending with radar sensors. This list was adapted from Strand *et al.* (2007) and is far from exhaustive.

We base the relative cost information on the price for a commercial company. Please use it only as a guide. If you want to purchase imagery, it is important that you contact the vendor to request a price quote. The price can vary depending on your location. Sometimes special prices are available or can be negotiated for education or nonprofit institutions. A list of some Internet archives that distribute free remotely sensed data are listed at the end of this appendix.

The legend for cost is:

- NC = no cost
- $ ≤ $1000
- $$ = $1001–2500
- $$$ = $2501–4500
- $$$$ ≥ $4500

A4.1 Optical

GeoEye-1
URL: http://www.geoeye.com
Spatial resolution: Panchromatic: 41 cm, Multispectral; 1.65 m
Image coverage: 15.2 km swath width
Spectral bands: 1 Panchromatic: 450–900 nm; 4 Multispectral: 450–520, 520–600, 625–695, and 760–900 nm
Repeat frequency: 2–8 days
Launch year: 2008
Cost: $$$$

QuickBird
URL: http://www.digitalglobe.com
Spatial resolution: Panchromatic: 61 cm, Multispectral: 2.44 m
Image coverage: 16.5 km swath width

Spectral bands: 1 Panchromatic: 450–900 nm; 4 Multispectral: 450–520, 520–600, 630–690, and 760–900 nm
Repeat frequency: 1–3 days
Launch year: 2001
Cost: $$$$

IKONOS-2
URL: http://www.geoeye.com
Spatial resolution: Panchromatic: 1 m, Multispectral; 4 m
Image coverage: 11.3 km swath width
Spectral bands: 1 Panchromatic: 525.8–928.5 nm; 4 Multispectral: 450–520, 520–600, 630–690, and 760–900 nm
Repeat frequency: 1–3 days
Launch year: 1999
Cost: $$$$

SPOT 5/HRG
URL: http://www.spotimage.fr
Spatial resolution: Panchromatic: 2.5 m, Multispectral: 10 m, SWIR: 20 m
Image coverage: 60 km × 60 km
Spectral bands: 1 Panchromatic: 480–710 nm; 4 Multispectral: 500–590, 610–680, 780–890, and 1580–1750 nm
Repeat frequency: 2–3 days
Launch year: 2002
Cost: $$

CORONA (panoramic photographic imagery)
URL: http://edc.usgs.gov/products/satellite/declass1.html
Spatial resolution: 2–8 m
Image coverage: 230 km × 15 km
Spectral bands: Visible spectrum (black-and-white photographs)
Repeat frequency: Variable
Launch year: 1959
Cost: $

RESOURCESAT 1 IRS/P6 (three instruments LISS-3, LISS-4, and AWiFS)
URL: http://www.nrsc.gov.in
Spatial resolution: LISS-3: 23.5 m, LISS-4: 5.8 m, AWiFS 56 m
Image coverage: LISS-3: 142 km swath; LISS-4: 24 km (MX mode), 70 m (Pan mode); AWiFS 740 km
Spectral bands: LISS-3 and AWiFS: 520–590, 620–680, 770–860, and 1550–1700 nm
LISS-4: 520–590, 620–680, and 770–860 nm
Repeat frequency: LISS-4: 5 days, LISS-3 and AWiFS: 24 days
Launch year: 1996, 2003
Cost: LISS-3: $, LISS-4: $$

ALOS AVNIR-2

URL: http://www.jaxa.jp/projects/sat/alos/index_e.html
Spatial resolution: 10 m
Image coverage: 70 km swath width
Spectral bands: 420–500, 520–600, 610–690, and 760–890 nm
Repeat frequency: 2 days
Launch year: 2006
Cost: $

SPOT 4/HRVIR

URL: http://www.spotimage.fr
Spatial resolution: Panchromatic 10 m, Multispectral 20 m, SWIR 20 m
Image coverage: 60 km × 60 km
Spectral bands: 1 Panchromatic: 610–680 nm, 4 Multispectral: 500–590, 610–680,780–890, and 1580–1750 nm
Repeat frequency: 2–3 days
Launch year: 1998
Cost: $$

Terra/ASTER

URL: http://asterweb.jpl.nasa.gov/
Spatial resolution: Visible and near-infrared (VNIR): 15 m, Shortwave infrared (SWIR): 30 m, and Thermal infrared (TIR): 90 m.
Image coverage: 60 km × 60 km
Spectral bands: 4 VNIR: 520–600, 630–690, 780–860, and 780–860 nm (last band is pointed aft and thus allows automated generation of digital elevation models [DEMs]); 6 SWIR: 1600–1700, 2145–2185, 2185–2225, 2235–2285, 2295–2365, and 2360–2430 nm; 5 TIR: 8125–8475, 8475–8825, 8925–9275, 10250–10950, and 10850–11650 nm
Repeat frequency: 16 days; acquisitions are scheduled
Launch year: 2000
Cost: $

Landsat/TM and ETM+

URL: http://edc.usgs.gov/guides/landsat_tm.html
Spatial resolution: Panchromatic: 15 m, Multispectral: 30 m, Thermal: 60 m
Image coverage: 185 km × 170 km
Spectral bands: 1 Panchromatic (only on ETM+): 520–730 nm; 7 Multispectral: 450–520, 520–600, 630–690, 760–900, 1550–1750, 10400–12500, and 2080–2350 nm
Repeat frequency: 16 days
Launch years: Landsat TM 4 and 5 1982 and 1984, Landsat ETM+ 1999
Cost: NC

Landsat/MSS (historical data only)
URL: http://edc.usgs.gov/guides/landsat_mss.html
Spatial resolution: Landsat 1–3: 56 m × 79 m, Landsat 4–5: 68 m × 82 m
Image coverage: 185 km × 185 km
Spectral bands: 4–5 Multispectral: 500–600, 600–700, 700–800, 800–1100, and 10400–12600 nm (this last band is available only on Landsat 1–3)
Repeat frequency: Landsat 1–3: 18 days, Landsat 4–5: 16 days
Launch years: 1972, 1975, 1978, 1982, and 1984
Cost: NC

ENVISAT-1/MERIS
URL: http://earth.esa.int/dataproducts/
Spatial resolution: Ocean: 1040 m × 1200 m, Land and coast: 260 m × 300 m
Image coverage: 1150 km swath width
Spectral bands: VIS-NIR: 15 bands selectable across range: 400–1050 nm (bandwidth programmable between 2.5 and 30 nm)
Repeat frequency: 3 days
Launch year: 2002
Cost: $

Terra/MODIS
URL: http://modis.gsfc.nasa.gov/
Spatial resolution: Bands 1 and 2: 250 m, Bands 3–7: 500 m, and Bands 8–36: 1 km
Image coverage: 2330 km swath width
Spectral bands: Bands 1 and 2: 620–670, 841–876; Bands 3–7: 459–479, 545–565, 1230–1250, 1628–1652, and 2105–2155 nm; Bands 8–36: 12 bands ranging from 405 to 965 nm and 17 bands ranging from 1360 to 14385 nm
Repeat frequency: Near daily
Launch year: 2000
Cost: NC

NOAA KLM/AVHRR
URL: http://www2.ncdc.noaa.gov/docs/klm/index.htm
Spatial resolution: 1.1 km
Image coverage: 3000 km swath width
Spectral bands: Multispectral: 580–680, 725–1000, 1580–1640, 3550–3930, 10300–11300, and 11500–12500 nm
Repeat frequency: 1 day
Launch year: 1978
Cost: $

SPOT VEGETATION
URL: http://www.spot-vegetation.com
Spatial resolution: 1.15 km at nadir

Image coverage: 2200 km wide, variable length
Spectral bands: VIS: 610–680 nm, NIR: 780–890 nm, SWIR: 1580–1750 nm
Repeat frequency: 1 day
Launch year: 1986
Cost: NC

SeaWIFS/OrbView-2
URL: http://www.geoeye.com/products/imagery/orbview2
Spatial resolution: 1.1 km
Image coverage: 1500 km × 2800 km
Spectral bands: 8 bands at 402–422, 433–453, 480–500, 500–520, 545–565, 660–680, 745–785, and 845–885 nm
Repeat frequency: 1 day
Launch year: 1997
Cost: $

A4.2 Radar

TerraSAR-X
URL: http://www.infoterra.de/
Spatial resolution: Spotlight: 1 m, StripMap: 3 m, ScanSar: 16 m
Image coverage: Spotlight: 10 km × 10 km, StripMap: 30 km swath width, ScanSar: 100 km swath width
Spectral bands: Microwave: X-Band 9.6 GHz
Polarization: Single: HH and VV, Dual: HH/VV
Repeat frequency: 11 days
Launch year: 2007
Cost: $$$$

ALOS (Advanced Land Observing Satellite)/Phased Array type L-band Synthetic Aperture Radar (PALSAR)
URL: http://www.jaxa.jp/projects/sat/alos/index_e.html
Spatial resolution: Hi-res: 7–44 m or 14–88 m (depends on polarization and look angles), ScanSAR mode: <100 m, Polarimetry mode 24–88 m
Image coverage: High resolution mode: 70 km, Scan SAR mode: 250–360 km, Polarimetry mode: 30 km
Spectral bands: Microwave: L-Band 1270 MHz
Polarization: Single: HH and VV, Dual: HH/VV and VV/HH
Repeat frequency: 3 days
Launch year: 2006
Cost: $

ENVISAT/ASAR
URL: http://envisat.esa.int/instruments/asar/
Spatial resolution: Image, wave, and alternation polarization modes: 30 m, Wide swath mode: 150 m, Global monitoring: 1 km
Image coverage: Image and alternating polarization modes: Swath width up to 100 km, Wave mode: 5 km swath width, Wide swath and global monitoring modes: 400 km swath width or greater
Spectral bands: Microwave: C-band
Polarization: Single: HH and VV, Dual: VV/HH, HV/HH, and VH/VV
Repeat frequency: 35 days; acquisitions are scheduled
Launch year: 2002
Cost: $

Radarsat-1
URL: http://www.asc-csa.gc.ca/eng/satellites/default.asp
Spatial resolution: Fine mode: 8 m, Standard mode: 25 m, ScanSAR: 50–100 m, Extended: 25–30 m
Image coverage: Fine mode 50 km × 50 km, Standard mode 100 km × 100 km, ScanSAR 300 km × 300 km to 500 km × 500 km, Extended 75 km × 75 km to 170 km × 170 km
Spectral bands: Microwave: C-band: 5.3 GHz
Polarization: Single: HH
Repeat frequency: 24 days
Launch year: 1995
Cost: $$

A4.3 Free remotely sensed data archives

NOAA CoastWatch Retrospective Data Products: Provides access to AVHRR-derived sea surface temperatures, with links to other archives of POES and GOES data. Available at: http://www.nodc.noaa.gov/dsdt/cw/.

Warehouse Inventory Search Tool (WIST). Operated by NASA to provide access to Earth science data products from NASA and affiliated centers. Available at: http://wist.echo.nasa.gov/~wist/api/imswelcome.

Gateway to Astronaut Photography of Earth: Operated by NASA to provide access to photographs acquired by astronauts since the early 1960s. Available at: http://eol.jsc.nasa.gov/default.htm.

Global Land Cover Facility (GLCF): Operated by the University of Maryland and it freely distributes selected Landsat MSS, TM, and ETM+ imagery for the globe. Available at: http://landcover.org.

Global Visualization Viewer (GLOVIS): Operated by USGS and it freely distributes the entire Landsat MSS, TM, and ETM+ image archive. Available at: http://glovis.usgs.gov/.

Landsat Coral Reef Data Archive: Developed by NASA to host Landsat ETM+ images of coral reef areas and also eventually to serve as the archive for NASA-sponsored Millennium Coral Reef Maps using the data. Available at: http://oceancolor.gsfc.nasa.gov/cgi/landsat.pl.

TerraLook: Operated by USGS and it freely distributes easy-to-use jpeg satellite images from the Advanced Spaceborne Thermal Emission and Reflection Radiometer (ASTER) sensor and Landsat sensors with user-friendly software already incorporated allowing visual interpretation and comparison, a good place to start for the beginning satellite user. Available at: http://terralook.cr.usgs.gov/.

SPOT VEGETATION distribution site: Hosted by the Flemish institute for technological research (VITO) to distribute free SPOT VEGETATION imagery. Available at: http://free.vgt.vito.be/.

Links to other Internet databases and lists containing detailed information about satellites and sensors are on the book's Web site.

Appendix 5
Visual interpretation

Visual interpretation in the context of remote sensing is the task of visually identifying and describing features you see in an aerial or satellite image. This often overlooked ability is perhaps the most important skill one can learn when working with remotely sensed imagery. Even when using computer algorithms to identify features and create classified maps, you can improve your ability to train the algorithm or assess the accuracy of the output with strong visual interpretation skills. This age-old skill remains an important tool in an image analyst's toolbox.

More information about the advantages of visual interpretation is in Section 3.5.1

A5.1 What do you need to interpret images?

So, what do you need to interpret an image? The most basic requirement is that you have an image that is of sufficient quality to be able to discern features. If you are taking the image to the field, it is a good idea to protect the image either by laminating it or covering it in a plastic bag to keep it clean and dry. If you plan to write on the image make sure you have a pen, pencil, or marker that will write on the image and not be ruined by water. Fine-tipped indelible markers are often a good choice, but whatever you use it is a good idea to bring extras and to test writing on the image before you go to the field. If the image was printed using a wax printer, it can be difficult to write on it using a pen or pencil.

If you do not want to write directly on the image, you can tape a transparency overlay to the image and then write on the overlay. Using this method, it is important to write on the overlay some sort of reference information so you can pair the overlay with the correct image in case they become separated. You should also mark the corners of the image or some obvious features in the image on the overlay so that you can correctly position the overlay onto the image in case the overlay slips or is removed from the image.

When preparing an image for printing, it can be helpful to print a fine grid or tic marks to mark lines of latitude and longitude or meter divisions, if a map projection such as UTM is being used (Fig. A5.1). These markings can help you

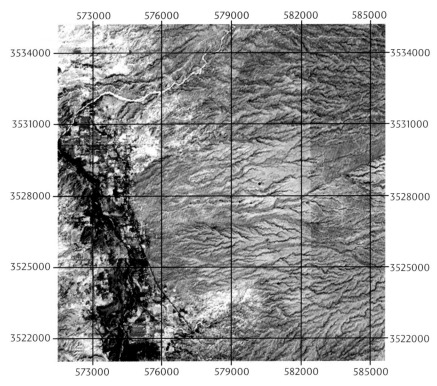

Fig. A5.1 Overlaying a grid on an image can help locate features in the field if you are using a GPS receiver. In this Landsat ETM+ image (path 35, row 38, September 12, 2000) of southeastern Arizona, USA, the grid lines represent UTM northing and easting coordinates. Credit: Ned Horning, American Museum of Natural History's Center for Biodiversity and Conservation.

locate yourself on the image when you are in the field if you are using a GPS receiver.

Being familiar with the area you are interpreting can also be invaluable. Your familiarity will help you to more readily identify features thereby furthering the learning process of relating the abstract features in an image to the actual features on the ground. When you see a similar feature in an image from an unfamiliar area, you will be able to make some educated guess as to what it is.

A5.2 Different levels of interpretation

Throughout your life, your brain is constantly learning to interpret features you see. As a baby, you are aware that you see something but you have no idea what it is. As you get older, you begin to identify features that you see and after more time you begin to put these features into some sort of context. Over time, the context within which the feature is placed can become quite complex. For example, a baby might see a feature from a window of a car and as the baby gets older she might recognize it as a building. With a little more time, she discovers that it is a school and then she realizes that this is a school that she will attend with her friends in her neighborhood but not with her friends from another town.

Interpreting imagery follows a similar progression. At the simplest level we can see that there is a distinct feature and with a little more experience or information we can identify that feature. With even more experience or information, we can put the feature into context. For example, you might see a linear feature in a dense forest (Fig. A5.2). After some thought you could come up with a list of possible features such as a road, stream, trail, or electrical lines. After spending more time looking at the image, you might see small clearings that occur along the line. You might expect these clearings could be log landings or may be camps for building a road. After further analysis, you discover that the line extends well

Fig. A5.2 In this Landsat ETM+ image of central Vietnam, you can see a blue linear feature passing from the upper left to lower right portion of the image (path 125, row 49, April 21, 2003; bands 4, 3, 2 RGB display as per Fig. 3.3). At first glance, you might think the feature is a river. After interpreting the image, you might (correctly) conclude that this is a road. Credit: Ned Horning, American Museum of Natural History's Center for Biodiversity and Conservation.

over 100 km and it runs between two large towns. With all of this information, you deduce that the feature is a new road being constructed to link the two towns. This is a reasonable assumption but it would still be useful to validate it, especially if your interpretation is going to have a significant impact on an important decision.

In addition to your own experience, the spatial resolution of the image will greatly influence what you can interpret in an image. The more detail you can see, the more information you have to work with to identify a feature. Increasing the spatial extent can provide additional information to put the feature into the proper spatial context.

A5.3 The elements of image interpretation

When we interpret a feature in an image, we use a number of cues to determine what it is and to put it into the appropriate context. Deliberately thinking about these different cues can help you deduce the identification of features.

A5.3.1 Color and tone

Color and tone are the fundamental qualities that affect the other visual cues described below. As you begin to look at remotely sensed imagery, you will associate specific colors and tones to certain features. For example, in Fig. A5.2 you would associate the brownish color with some sort of vegetation. In Fig. A5.1 you can see two shades of green separated by a line running from the top to bottom of the image. This dramatic change in tone is significant, but why is it there? Knowing that the image is from Arizona would help and with some interpretation experience you might realize that the green represents grassland with the darker green being healthier grassland than the light green on the left. It is likely that this difference is caused by a fence and the area on the left is grazed more heavily than the area on the right.

When working with color and tone you must be careful since the same image can look quite different depending on the band combination used and the enhancements that are applied. Figure A5.3 illustrates the same image as Fig. A5.2 with different band combinations and enhancements. Adjusting for these differences becomes easier with experience. As you become more experienced with image interpretation, you will likely want to stick to one or two different band combinations and enhancement methods to avoid confusion.

Fig. A5.3 These two images are representations of the same data set used to create the image in Fig. A5.2, but they were processed and displayed differently. The top image uses the same band combination as Fig. A5.2, but the enhancement is different. The lower image was created using a different set of bands (bands 7, 4, 2 RGB display as per Fig. 3.3). Credit: Ned Horning, American Museum of Natural History's Center for Biodiversity and Conservation.

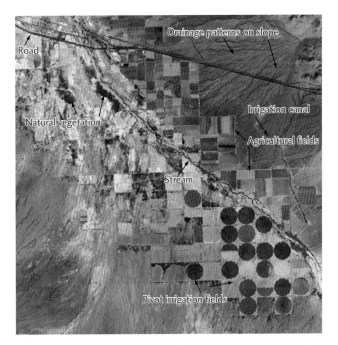

Fig. A5.4 In this Landsat ETM+ image of southeastern Arizona, USA, a number of features are labeled (path 35, row 38, September 12, 2000). Note that man-made features tend to be rectilinear and natural features are irregular in shape. Credit: Ned Horning, American Museum of Natural History's Center for Biodiversity and Conservation.

A5.3.2 Size and shape

Size and shape are the primary cues used to identify many features, especially man-made ones. Rectilinear and circular features often indicate human influence such as agriculture, urban developments, or infrastructure. Figure A5.4 has a number of features labeled.

The spatial resolution of the image greatly influences the size and shape of features within it (Fig. A5.5). Knowing the scale at which an image is printed can be helpful to more accurately identify features since you will be able to estimate the dimensions of the feature on the ground.

A5.3.3 Texture and pattern

Texture and pattern, are often described using words like "rough," "smooth," "fuzzy," "irregular," and "even." Texture and pattern are also greatly affected by spatial resolution (Fig. A5.6). In many cases texture in an image is caused by shadows cast by the feature(s) on the ground. One example of this is the difference in appearance between natural and plantation forests (Fig. A5.7).

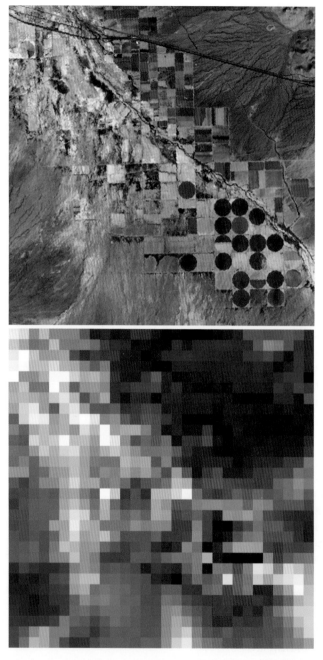

Fig. A5.5 The spatial resolution of the Landsat image from Fig. A5.4 compared with a MODIS image from the same day (September 12, 2000). The difference between these two images is that the Landsat ETM+ image (path 35, row 38) has a resolution of 30 m and the MODIS image has a resolution of 500 m. Note how the shape and size of features are different. Credit: Ned Horning, American Museum of Natural History's Center for Biodiversity and Conservation.

Fig. A5.6 A variety of textures are visible in this IKONOS image covering a part of the Chiricahua Mountains in southeastern Arizona, USA. Many of the blue areas representing soil are quite smooth. The texture of the vegetated areas (red areas) varies from quite smooth to rough. In this image, the rougher texture vegetated areas represent tall trees and the smoother areas are dense shrub and grass (subset from image ID PO_138307, June 12, 2003). Credit: Ned Horning, American Museum of Natural History's Center for Biodiversity and Conservation, IKONOS image courtesy of GeoEye.

The surface of the canopy of a natural forest is very uneven due to the uneven age distribution of trees and consists of a variety of different species. This causes significant shadowing at the top of a forest canopy causing the natural forest to appear rougher. Plantations, on the other hand, are usually planted in even-age stands and these canopies are typically quite uniform in height and therefore cast fewer shadows and have a smoother texture.

A5.3.4 Shadows

Shadows are often considered a contaminant in remote sensing, but for visual interpretation shadows can provide important clues to help us identify an object. Shadows can help accentuate relief (Fig. 4.2). The characteristics of a shadow depend on the location of the sun (elevation and azimuth) and the height of the object. The appearance of an object can change significantly due to changes in the sun's position, which is affected by the time of day and the time of year the image was acquired. The length of a shadow can provide information about how tall a feature is. Taller features cast longer shadows.

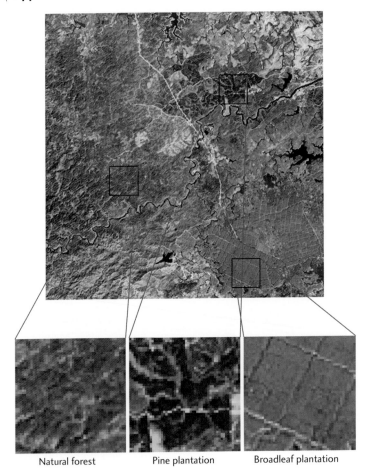

Natural forest   Pine plantation   Broadleaf plantation

Fig. A5.7 Even-aged plantation forests can be easy to distinguish from natural forest because they appear smoother in texture with a more uniform tone, as shown in this Landsat ETM+ image of central Vietnam (path 125, row 48, November 6, 2000). This is because the upper surface of a tree canopy of an even-aged plantation is not as rough and therefore casts fewer shadows than a natural forest. It also consists of a single species. Credit: Ned Horning, American Museum of Natural History's Center for Biodiversity and Conservation.

A5.3.5 Relative and absolute location

The location of a feature can provide information to help identify it by putting it into a geographic context. For example, a vegetated area in the middle of an urban environment might indicate a park. In Fig. A5.8, you can see a number of labeled features. The golf courses stick out because they are just about the only part of the image with green (red in the image) grass. If this feature were in the

Fig. A5.8 Sometimes more information than that available in the image must be used to validate your interpretation. In this Landsat ETM+ image (path 35, row 38, September 12, 2000) of the area around Sierra Vista, Arizona, USA, a military base, city, airport, and golf courses are labeled. Notice the similarity between the military base and the town. Credit: Ned Horning, American Museum of Natural History's Center for Biodiversity and Conservation.

middle of a rangeland, you might interpret it as a spring or in a desert it might be an oasis. The airport has a characteristic shape and since it is so close to this town you might make the assumption that it is a public airport. Then again, if you knew that this was a military airport you might be able to make the assumption that the buildings are actually part of a military base rather than a town. More information would be necessary to make the determination.

A5.3.6 Time

When interpreting an image, it can be import to know when the image was acquired. This is especially true in areas that experience significant seasonal changes. For example, if you look at an image of a deciduous forest during the leaf-off period you might mistake it for an area of non-forest if you were not aware that the image was acquired during a time when trees had shed their leaves. In this case it might be helpful to have imagery from two dates, one leaf-on and the other leaf-off to highlight clearly the deciduous forest (Fig. A5.9).

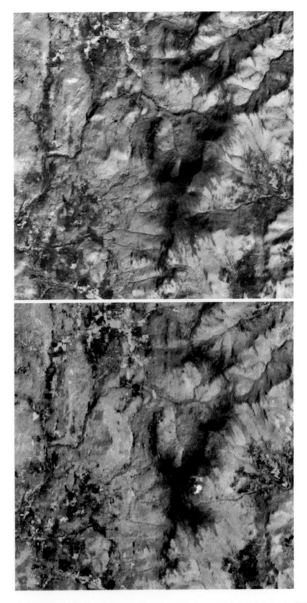

Fig. A5.9 Using images from different times of the year can be helpful to identify features that appear different during different seasons. This set of Landsat ETM+ images of the southwestern part of Vermont, USA (path 13, row 30), shows dramatic seasonal differences. The top image was acquired on October 20, 2000 after most of the leaves had fallen from the deciduous trees. Looking at this image, it appears as if most of the area is non-forest except for the ridgeline. The lower image was acquired on July 30, 1999 and you can see the forests quite well. By comparing these two images you can easily locate blocks of evergreen coniferous trees that have retained their needles and therefore appear red in the October image. Credit: Ned Horning, American Museum of Natural History's Center for Biodiversity and Conservation.

If you are familiar with the land use for a particular area, knowing when an image was acquired can also help you identify certain features and increase the precision of your interpretation. For example, knowing the planting schedule for particular crops and the image date might allow you to identify the type of crop growing in an agricultural area.

A5.4 Practice, practice, practice

Visually interpreting imagery is not all that difficult and with some experience you can become proficient. We are constantly interpreting features around us but in the case of remotely sensed images the perspective of looking at features from above is quite different from the one we are accustomed to. The more you work with remotely sensed imagery the better you will become at identifying features.

To get started, view some remotely sensed imagery of an area with which you are familiar. Once you are able to orient yourself, you will begin to identify features in the image familiar to you on the ground. It is also a good idea to take imagery with you when you take trips to the field. Orient yourself using a GPS receiver and compass or use ground features that are easily identified in the image. Compare what a view looks like in the field and then see what it looks like in an image. Look to see how well you can identify subtle differences in the image. If you see certain patterns or colors that you cannot identify, try and visit those areas to see what is causing the difference.

Sometimes you will see differences in tone in the image that cannot be identified in the field. This can be due to a number of reasons but two common ones are that (1) the situation in the field has changed due to seasons or possibly a change in land cover or (2) the image bands used to create the image might be sensitive to wavelengths of light that are not visible to you. For example, if a near-infrared band was used to create the image you might notice subtle differences within a forest canopy due to water stress or other factors and in the field you will not see these differences since we cannot see into the infrared portion of the spectrum.

With basic knowledge of remote sensing you will be able to determine why certain features look the way they do. In cases where you are unable to identify a feature or explain its appearance, you might need to consult someone with more experience or improve your knowledge of remote sensing.

Appendix 6
Systems for observing climate and atmospheric phenomena

A6.1 Clouds

The primary sensors for cloud remote sensing are on the operational weather satellites managed by NOAA in the United States and equivalent agencies of other governments worldwide (such as EUMETSAT, as well as the weather satellite programs of Japan, India, Russia, and China). The sensors on these satellites include visible and infrared wavelength bands (wavelength bands are often called channels by meteorologists) to separate clouds into categories based on cloud types. See Table A6.3 for information about sensor spatial resolutions.

With circular orbits taking them nearly over the Earth's poles approximately every 100 min, NOAA POES systems acquire global coverage on a daily basis (Kidwell 1998). At any given time, NOAA typically operates at least two POES spacecraft, one capturing data over the United States in the morning and one in the evening. Their sensors include the AVHRR, an imager with a mixture of channels ranging from the visible to the thermal infrared portions of the electromagnetic spectrum. Sun synchronous satellite orbits pass very near the poles of the Earth, thus they are often referred to as polar orbiters or polar-orbiting satellites. These high-inclination orbits ensure that they have constant equator crossing times, causing them to view any given point on the Earth at approximately the same time every day. Polar-orbiting or sun synchronous satellites generally image any given area of the Earth no more than once or twice per day (Kidder and Vonder Haar 1995).

Tracking rapidly developing storm systems requires more frequent observations. Geostationary satellites address this need by maintaining an equatorial orbit that is synchronized with the Earth's rotation on its axis, keeping them in a constant position above the equator (Bader *et al.* 1995). They are essentially an unblinking eye staring at and scanning over and over again the full disk of the Earth. Scanning large swaths of surface area, imagers on geostationary satellites generate a new full Earth disk image approximately every 15 to 30 min, depending on the imager (Schmetz *et al.* 2006; NOAA Satellite and Information Service 2008). Given the much higher satellite altitude required to remain in geostationary orbit (~36,000 km over the Earth as opposed to ~800–900 km for sun synchronous satellites), sensors aboard these satellites often have lower or coarser

Fig. A6.1 NOAA GOES-E full disk infrared image from September 16, 2008. Credit: Geostationary Satellite Server, NOAA/NEDSIS.

ground spatial resolutions than those aboard polar orbiters (Kidder and Vonder Haar 1995). Also, due to the curvature of the Earth, the equatorially based geostationary systems do not obtain useful imagery of high latitude regions (Fig. A6.1).

Five geostationary satellites strategically placed around the equator image all longitudes of the globe. There are two NOAA GOES satellites, GOES-*E* and GOES-*W*, at 75 and 135° W longitude, respectively. The European geostationary satellites or Meteosats maintain a position above the prime meridian (0° longitude). The Japanese meteorological satellites are part of the MTSAT series (which replaced Japan's Geosynchronous Meteorological Satellite series) and orbit at 140° E longitude. Completing the global system of geostationary satellites is India's INSAT series (with the latest meteorological satellites now being called MetSat) consisting of several satellites operated for both meteorology and communications. The primary orbit is 74° E longitude (Kidder and Vonder Haar 1995). Although different geostationary weather satellites offer different channel combinations, all feature channels sensing in the visible and thermal

GOES channel 1 visible   GOES channel 2 shortwave IR

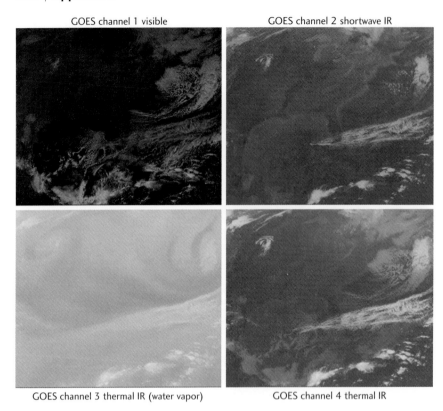

GOES channel 3 thermal IR (water vapor)   GOES channel 4 thermal IR

Fig. A6.2 The eastern United States and part of Mexico as observed from the first four channels of the GOES Imager (October 30, 2008 at 16:45 UTC). Credit: GOES Project, NOAA and NASA.

infrared portions of the electromagnetic spectrum (Fig. A6.2). More information on these geostationary imagers is available in Table A6.3.

NOAA operational meteorological satellites also capture vertical temperature profiles from sounders. Sounders are sensors that take measures or "soundings" of a vertical column of the atmosphere at different altitudes, providing a third dimensional counterpart (depth) to the two-dimensional views afforded by the AVHRR imagers onboard. Section 8.6.4.2 contains a description of the operation of sounders.

In addition to passive visible and infrared remote sensing of clouds by imagers and sounders, active sensors employing visible and infrared bands (i.e., lidars) along with passive microwave sensors and active microwave sensors (i.e., active microwave sensors are radars) have proven useful for detecting clouds and understanding their internal properties, such as vertical structure. Active sensors allow us to see inside clouds, augmenting the temperature profiles from sounder

Table 8.A6.1 Cloud heights and types.

Cloud heights	Altitude	Cloud types and characteristics	View from a satellite
Low	Below 2 km	Stratus, Stratocumulus, Nimbostratus—layered clouds often presenting complete blankets of cloud to observers from above and below; nimbostratus yield light precipitation	Stratus clouds of all types appear smooth, closed, relatively featureless, and cover large areas of up to hundreds of kilometers; stratocumulus often look like streets of cloud
Middle	2–6 km	Altostratus, Altocumulus—cumulus clouds generally puffier, patchier, more open, and with greater vertical development than stratus; also cumulus are generally indicative of more unstable air than stratus that usually form under stable conditions	Cumulus clouds mostly appear lumpy and consist of individual cells or clusters of cells; they have gaps between cells; clouds cover 1 km or so in diameter—smaller than stratus clouds
High	Above 6 km	Cirrus, Cirrostratus, Cirrocumulus—almost exclusively composed of ice crystals; lack of water makes them vertically thin and wispy; transmit higher amounts of incoming radiation due to fewer particles per unit volume than water clouds; include aircraft contrails	Cirrus clouds are often so thin as to be hard to detect with visible imagery; they can be striated in texture and cover large areas; cirrus cloud identification remains a major challenge for meteorologists and climatologists
Cumulonimbus (Low to High)	extending to 12–18 km	very tall storm clouds with columns reaching from troposphere often into lower stratosphere; tops often have anvil shapes; indicative of highly unstable fast rising air, turbulence, and downdrafts; aircraft avoid them	Clouds associated with uplift and the dramatic changes accompanying storm systems are very bright

Sources: Aguado and Burt (1999); Carleton (1991); Kidder and Vonder Haar (1995); Mayes and Hughes (2004).

Table 8.A6.2 Ground-based views of cloud types (images from NASA CERES S'COOL Project at http://asd-www.larc.nasa.gov/SCOOL/cldchart.html).

Height	Type	Type	Type
Height	Type	Type	Type
Low	**Stratus** (by Pequot Lakes Elementary School)	**Cumulus** (by Lin Chambers)	**Stratocumulus** (by Kevin Larman)
Low	**Nimbostratus** (by Robert Sepulveda)		
Middle	**Altostratus** (by Lin Chambers)	**Altocumulus** (by Mandana Khaiyer)	
High	**Cirrus** (by Kevin Larman)	**Cirrostratus** (by Doug Stoddard)	**Cirrocumulus** (by Jeff Caplan)
Low to High		**Cumulonimbus**	

radiance measures and offering more direct observations of other parameters derived using imager data in conjunction with certain algorithms (e.g., cloud optical depth). NASA launched two satellites in 2006 that emit pulses of electromagnetic radiation and measure the returning signals in order to lessen our uncertainty about cloud effects on radiative forcing of climate change. They

Table 8.A6.3 Some satellite systems for cloud detection and characterization.

System and status (orbit and operational/research)	Channels (μm)	Spatial resolution (except for radar and lidar, this is ground spatial resolution)
NOAA GOES Imager (NOAA Satellite and Information Service 2008 at http://noaasis.noaa.gov/NOAASIS/ml/imager.html)	5 #1 Visible (0.55–0.75) #2 Shortwave IR (3.8–4.0)	Visible = 1 km Shortwave = 4 km #3 Thermal = 8 km
Geostationary Operational	#3 Thermal IR (6.5–7.0) for water vapor #4 Thermal IR (10.2–11.2) #5 Thermal IR (11.5–12.5)	#4 Thermal = 4 km #5 Thermal = 4 km
European Meteosat SEVIRI	12	3.0 km with broadband channel #12 at 1.0 km
(Schmetz et al. 2006 at http://oiswww.eumetsat.org/WEBOPS/msg_interpretation/PowerPoints/Channels/schmetz7july.doc)	#1 Visible (0.56–0.71) #2 Visible (0.74–0.88) #3 Near IR (1.50–1.78)	
Geostationary Operational	#4 Shortwave IR (3.48–4.36) #5 Thermal IR (5.35–7.15) for water vapor #6 Thermal IR (6.85–7.85) for water vapor #7 Thermal IR (8.3–9.1) #8 Thermal IR (9.38–9.94) #9 Thermal IR (9.8–11.8) #10 Thermal IR (11.0–13.0) #11 Thermal IR (12.4–14.4) #12 Visible-Near IR Broadband (~0.4–1.1)	
Japanese MTSAT Imager (Japan Meteorological Agency 2008 at http://www.jma.go.jp/jma/jma-eng/satellite/about_mt/8.Major_Characteristics_of_the_meteorological_payload.html)	5 Visible (0.55–0.90) IR 1 (10.3–11.3) Thermal	Visible = 1.0 km IR 1–IR 4 = 4.0 km

(continued)

Table 8.A6.3 (Continued)

System and status (orbit and operational/research)	Channels (μm)	Spatial resolution (except for radar and lidar, this is ground spatial resolution)
Geostationary Operational	IR 2 (11.5–12.5) Thermal IR 3 (6.5–7.0) Thermal for water vapor IR 4 (3.5–4.0) Shortwave	
Indian MetSat-1 (renamed Kalpana-1) Very High Resolution Radiometer 2 (VHRR/2)	3 Visible (0.55–0.75) Thermal IR (10.5–12.5) Thermal/H2O vapor (5.7–7.1)	Visible = 2 km Thermal Channels = 8 km
(Slides by P.C. Joshi at GOES-R User Conference January 2008 available through http://www.goes-r.gov/downloads/) Geostationary Operational		
NOAA POES AVHRR (http://noaasis.noaa.gov/NOAASIS/ml/avhrr.html) Sun Synchronous Operational	6 #1 Visible (0.58–0.68) #2 Near IR (0.725–1.0) #3A Shortwave IR (1.58–1.64) #3B Shortwave IR (3.55–3.93) #4 Thermal IR (10.3–11.3) #5 Thermal IR (11.5–12.5)	1.09 km
DMSP OLS (http://www.ngdc.noaa.gov/dmsp/sensors/ols.html) Sun Synchronous Operational	3 Visible/Near IR Telescope (0.4–1.1)	2 Telescopes = 550 m in fine mode or 2.7 km in smooth mode

	Thermal IR Telescope (10.0–13.4) Visible photo multiplier tube for night viewing (0.47–0.95)	
NASA Terra and Aqua MODIS (Parkinson and Greenstone 2000; MODIS Atmosphere web site http://modis-atmos. gsfc.nasa.gov/index.html)	36 (ranging from 0.405 to 14.385)	Channels 1–2 = 250 m Channels 3–7 = 500 m
Sun Synchronous Research	Some Relevant Products: MOD 06 Cloud Product— daily global products at 1 km or 5 km for cloud optical thickness, effective cloud-particle radius, cloud-particle phase (ice vs. water, clouds vs. snow), cloud-top temperature, cloud height, effective emissivity, cloud fraction, and cirrus reflectance at 1.375 μm (useful for hard to detect cirrus clouds) MOD 35 Cloud Mask— daily global product at spatial resolutions of 1 km and 250 m, shows where the clouds are	Channels 8–36 = 1 km
CloudSat Cloud Profiling Radar (http://cloudsat.atmos. colostate.edu/instrument) Sun Synchronous Research	1 at 94 GHz (~3,000 μm or 3 mm) for this active radar instrument	500 m Vertical and 2 km Along-Track Sampling and 1.4 km Cross-Track
CALIPSO Cloud-Aerosol Lidar with Orthogonal Polarization (CALIOP) (http://www-calipso.larc. nasa.gov/about/payload. php#CALIOP) Sun Synchronous Research	2 Active lidar instrument with 2 wavelengths = 0.532 and 1.064 μm	30–60 m Vertical 333 m Horizontal 100 m Footprint

are the Canadian–American CloudSat and the French–American CALIPSO (Langenberg 2005). Both these satellites provide vertical profiles of internal cloud properties.

MODIS on both the NASA Terra and Aqua spacecraft, which have morning and afternoon equator crossing times respectively, is a research imager developed to test how additional wavelength channels improve our ability to detect and observe atmospheric, oceanic, and terrestrial phenomena. It has 36 channels compared to AVHRR's six but builds strongly upon the AVHRR heritage. The MODIS Cloud Product (MOD 06) includes daily global products at 1 km or 5 km horizontal resolution for cloud optical thickness, effective cloud particle radius, cloud-particle phase (ice vs. water, clouds vs. snow), cloud-top temperature, cloud height, effective emissivity, cloud fraction, and cirrus reflectance (useful for hard to detect cirrus clouds). MODIS also produces a Cloud-Mask Product (MOD 35), a daily global product at spatial resolutions of 1 km and 250 m that shows where the clouds are. (Parkinson and Greenstone 2000; NASA 2008a)

A6.2 Aerosols

Several research satellites include image products such as aerosol optical depth (AOD) that target aerosols. Sensors useful for detecting aerosols, AOD, and other aerosol characteristics are the NASA MODIS sensor on the Terra and Aqua satellites, its partner Multi-angle Imaging SpectroRadiometer (MISR) sensor on the Terra spacecraft, and the European Space Agency ENVISAT satellite's Advanced Along Track Scanning Radiometer (AATSR) and Medium Resolution Imaging Spectrometer (MERIS) sensors. Two next-generation ozone sensors are quite useful for aerosol monitoring: the Dutch–Finnish Ozone Monitoring Instrument (OMI) on the NASA Aura spacecraft and the SCIAMACHY sensor on ENVISAT. Finally, CALIPSO applies active remote sensing via laser pulses to the detection of the vertical profile of aerosols. Table A6.4 contains additional information about many of these systems.

If we are ever to reduce the major uncertainties associated with the radiative effects on climate by aerosols and the clouds they produce, no single sensor will be adequate. Integration of information from many sensors will yield the greatest advances (Yu et al. 2006). With this in mind, the 2006 launch of the CloudSat and CALIPSO satellites added their sensors to a growing "A-Train" series of satellites carrying sensors of direct relevance to both aerosols and clouds. In early 2008, the A-Train consisted of the Aqua, Aura, PARASOL, CloudSat, and CALIPSO satellites, all flying in an afternoon orbit (~1:30 P.M. equator crossing time) formation within 8 min of each other. The suite of sensors carried by these satellites provides global measures of a wide range of cloud optical properties and aerosol properties as well as cloud layering information (Langenberg 2005).

Table 8.A6.4 Some satellite systems for the remote sensing of aerosols.

System	Characteristics
NASA Total Ozone Mapping Spectrometer (TOMS) (http://toms.gsfc.nasa.gov/aerosols/aerosols_v8.html)	Designed for stratospheric ozone monitoring; observed dust aerosols and biomass burning over land with two ultraviolet (UV) bands; limitation— large (50 km) footprint (King et al. 1999; Yu et al. 2006)
CNES Polarization and Directionality of the Earth's Reflectances (POLDER) (http://parasol-polder.cnes.fr/en/index.htm)	Uses series of wavelength bands from UV to near IR along with camera able to observe same Earth target from different angles; multi-angle sensing allows it to use differences in polarization between light reflected from the Earth's surface and light reflected from atmospheric aerosols to measure AOD and other aerosol properties (Kaufman et al. 2002); flew on two Japanese Advanced Earth Observation Satellite (ADEOS) missions; now on CNES PARASOL satellite; ground spatial resolution of 6 km (Yu et al. 2006)
GeoEye's SeaStar Sea-viewing Wide Field-of-view Sensor (SeaWiFS) (http://oceancolor.gsfc.nasa.gov/SeaWiFS/)	Has ability to tilt (to avoid sun glint) and bands in the blue portion of visible spectrum making it useful for capturing AOD over the world's oceans (King et al. 1999)
NASA Terra and Aqua MODIS (http://modis-atmos.gsfc.nasa.gov/MOD04_L2/index.html)	MODIS Aerosol Product (MOD 04) uses eight MODIS bands to capture AOD over oceans and vegetated land surface as well as aerosol size distribution over oceans and aerosol type over land; ground pixel size for these MODIS products = 1 km; MODIS aerosol products also benefit from multiple MODIS cloud products; global coverage almost daily (King et al. 1999; Yu et al. 2006)
NASA Terra Multi-angle Imaging SpectroRadiometer (MISR) (http://www-misr.jpl.nasa.gov/index.html; http://eosweb.larc.nasa.gov/PRODOCS/misr/level3/overview.html#data)	Measures solar radiance in four wavelength bands (0.446, 0.558, 0.672, and 0.866 μm) and in nine view angles allowing detection of AOD and aerosol type over oceans and land, including bright desert surfaces; ground pixel size is 1.1 km; collects global imagery approximately every week (King et al. 1999; Yu et al. 2006)
European ENVISAT Advanced Along Track Scanning Radiometer (AATSR) and Medium Resolution Imaging Spectrometer (MERIS)	AATSR is a multi-angle sensor designed for capturing sea-surface temperatures; MERIS is an ocean, land, atmosphere imager providing critical cloud-top information; both sensors useful for aerosol collection (King et al. 1999)

(continued)

Table 8.A6.4 Continued

System	Characteristics
(http://envisat.esa.int/instruments/)	
Dutch-Finnish Ozone Monitoring Instrument (OMI) on NASA Aura spacecraft (http://aura.gsfc.nasa.gov/instruments/omi/index.html)	An imaging spectrometer (hyperspectral sensor) measuring between 0.27 and 0.5 μm with 0.5 nm spectral resolution and 13 $\times$ 24 km binned spatial resolution; capable of distinguishing aerosol types (e.g., smoke, dust, andsulfates)
European ENVISAT SCIAMACHY (http://envisat.esa.int/instruments/)	An imaging spectrometer measuring between 0.24 and 1.7 μm and in selected regions between 2.0 and 2.4 μm with three viewing angles
CALIPSO (http://www-calipso.larc.nasa.gov/about/)	Distinguishes aerosol size and shape, useful when determining whether aerosols arose from human or nonhuman sources
Stratospheric Aerosol and Gas Experiment (SAGE) (http://www-sage3.larc.nasa.gov/)	No longer operating but data available from this series of missions that used a limb-scanning technique to view columns of stratospheric aerosols (this technique scans a column of atmosphere at the edge of the Earth, i.e., at the Earth's limb, as the sun appears and disappears from view at sunrise and sunset); viewed the atmosphere "off to the side" of the spacecraft; SAGE observed aerosols (as well as atmospheric gases) in bands ranging from the UV portion of the electromagnetic spectrum to just beyond 1.0 μm in the near IR; produced an Aerosol Extinction product

A number of ground-based networks provide vital measures of AOD and other aerosol properties. The most extensive in terms of both spatial and temporal coverage is the Aerosol Robotic Network, known as AERONET, which is actually a federation of networks with calibrated sun photometers and radiometers at ~200 sites around the world (NASA 2008b; Yu *et al.* 2006). Sun photometers are sensors that measure only direct sunlight, not scattered light, and do so in specific wavelengths. The more particles in the atmosphere, the less sunlight reaches the photometer. In addition to providing well-calibrated aerosol climatologies, the ground-based networks also validate the space-based measures

Table 8.A6.5 Some satellite systems for measuring precipitation and related phenomena.

System	Type	Product characteristics
NOAA GOES Sounders (http://cimss.ssec.wisc.edu/goes/realtime/realtime.html)	Geostationary operational sounders using various thermal IR channels, including water vapor channels	Total Precipitable Water Vapor at effective spatial resolution of 14 km, generated every hour for continental United States
European Meteosat SEVIRI (http://nwcsaf.inm.es/HTMLContributions_v1.0/TPW/Prod_TPW_v1.0.htm)	Geostationary operational imager using various thermal IR channels, including water vapor channels	Total Precipitable Water every 15 min at ~5 km spatial resolution for Europe, North Africa, and adjacent areas
NASA Terra and Aqua MODIS (http://modis.gsfc.nasa.gov/data/dataprod/dataproducts.php?MOD_NUMBER = 05)	Sun Synchronous research imager using near IR and thermal IR channels, including water vapor channels	MOD 05 Total Precipitable Water offers global coverage at 1 km (daylight only) and 5 km (day and night) (http://modis.gsfc.nasa.gov/data/dataprod/pdf/MOD_05.pdf) MOD 10 Snow Cover provides maps of global snow cover (as well as ice cover on large inland water bodies) both daily and as 8-day composites at 500 m spatial resolution; allowing tracking of snow and ice cover persistence, an important parameter for documenting changing winter conditions over time (http://modis.gsfc.nasa.gov/data/dataprod/pdf/MOD_10.pdf)
NASA Aqua Atmospheric Infrared Sounder (AIRS) (http://www-airs.jpl.nasa.gov/)	Sun synchronous research hyperspectral sounder with 2,378 channels operating in IR from 3.7 to 15.4 μm plus four channels in visible to near IR wavelengths of 0.4 to 1.0 μm for cloud and surface properties	Global Atmospheric Water Vapor Profiles; also vertical structure of water vapor through depiction of isohyet surfaces (i.e., surfaces of constant water vapor amount); spatial resolution of 13.5 km for

(continued)

Table 8.A6.5 Continued

System	Type	Product characteristics
		IR channels and 2.3 km for visible/near IR channels; global coverage every 1 to 2 days (Parkinson et al. 2006)
DMSP SSM/I (Kidder and Vonder Haar 1995)	Sun synchronous operational microwave imager measuring brightness temperatures at four microwave frequencies (with along track × cross track ground spatial resolutions in parentheses following each): 19.4 GHz (69 × 43 km), 37.0 GHz (37 × 29 km), and 85.5 GHz (15 × 13 km) in both horizontal and vertical polarizations and 22.2 GHz (50 × 40 km) in vertical polarization only (Cavalieri 1992)	Daily, 3-day, weekly, and monthly maps of columnar water vapor, cloud liquid water, and rain rate (http://www.ssmi.com/ssmi/ssmi_description.html#dates; http://nsidc.org/data/nsidc-0032.html)
NASA and Japan Aerospace Exploration Agency (JAXA) Tropical Rainfall Measuring Mission (TRMM) Microwave Imager (TMI) (http://trmm.gsfc.nasa.gov/homepage.html)	Low inclination orbit of 35° providing coverage of tropics and areas just north and south between 35° north and 35° south latitude; Research passive microwave imager measuring microwave radiation in 9 channels at 5 frequencies (10.7, 19.4, 21.3, 37, and 85.5 GHz) at spatial resolutions ranging from 37 to 4.6 km as one goes from 10.7 to 85.5 GHz (Parkinson et al. 2006; R. Kakar, personal Communication, 2006)	Surface rainfall and products related to three-dimensional structure of atmospheric precipitation; monthly rainfall maps over oceans only at 5° resolution; also combination products with TRMM Precipitation Radar and other satellite products—the latter available approximately every 3 h (http://trmm.gsfc.nasa.gov/trmm_rain/Events/TRMMSeniorProp_1.pdf; http://precip.gsfc.nasa.gov/index.html)
NASA and JAXA TRMM Precipitation	Research active microwave radar in 35° low inclination	Ground resolution of ~5 km, a vertical resolution

Radar (http://trmm.gsfc.nasa.gov/overview_dir/pr.html)

orbit that emits radiation at a frequency of 13.8 GHz and measures radiation backscattered by precipitation

of 250 m (i.e., it can observe vertical slices of rainfall as small as 250 m), and can detect rain falling at rates as light as 0.7 mm/h; provides vertical profiles of rain and snow from ground surface to 20 km in surface rainfall product, rainfall type product, and products related to three-dimensional structure of atmospheric precipitation; monthly rainfall maps (ocean and land) at 5° resolution (http://trmm.gsfc.nasa.gov/overview_dir/pr.html; http://trmm.gsfc.nasa.gov/trmm_rain/Events/TRMMSeniorProp_1.pdf)

NASA and JAXA TRMM Visible and Infrared Scanner (VIRS) (http://trmm.gsfc.nasa.gov/overview_dir/virs.html)

Research imaging radiometer in 35° low inclination orbit with five visible and IR channels at 0.63, 1.61, 3.75, 10.8, and 12 μm and a ground spatial resolution of 2.5 km

Offers indirect approach to precipitation through provision of cloud context (i.e., cloud brightness and temperature) data; also serves as important bridge for transitioning TRMM microwave results to those from operational visible and IR polar- and geostationary-orbiting systems (http://trmm.gsfc.nasa.gov/trmm_rain/Events/TRMMSeniorProp_1.pdf; http://trmm.gsfc.nasa.gov/overview_dir/virs.html)

NASA and JAXA TRMM Lightning Imaging Sensor (LIS) (http://trmm.gsfc.nasa.gov/overview_dir/lis.html)

Research staring imager in 35° low inclination orbit that stares at a given point below for 80 s to allow estimation of lightning flashing rate; accounts for both cloud-to-cloud and cloud-to-ground lightning

Allows estimation of lightning flashing rate, a measure of storm intensity; lightning is a strong indicator of convective activity and useful for the nowcasting of severe storms; potential precursor for a geostationary

(continued)

Table 8.A6.5 Continued

System	Type	Product characteristics
	in day and night storms ~4 to 7 km in size	operational instrument (http://trmm.gsfc.nasa.gov/overview_dir/lis.html; http://thunder.msfc.nasa.gov/lis/)
NASA Aqua's Advanced Microwave Scanning Radiometer-EOS (AMSR-E) from Japan (http://www.ghcc.msfc.nasa.gov/AMSR/data_products.html)	Research passive microwave radiometer measuring both horizontally and vertically polarized microwave radiation at six frequencies and spatial resolutions: 89.0 GHz at 6×4 km, 36.5 GHz at 14×8 km, 23.8 GHz at 32×18 km, 18.7 GHz at 27×16 km, 10.65 GHz at 51×29 km, and 6.925 GHz at 74×43 km, which results in 12 channels (Parkinson et al. 2006)	Produces brightness temperature, water vapor, cloud liquid water, sea surface temperature over oceans, land surface soil moisture on 25-km grids, global rain rates over land and oceans at 5.4 km ground spatial resolution, snow water equivalent over land, sea-ice concentration at 12.5 km and 25 km ground resolutions, and ocean surface wind speed products (http://www.ghcc.msfc.nasa.gov/AMSR/data_products.html; http://eospso.gsfc.nasa.gov/ftp_docs/amsr-e.pdf)
NOAA Interactive Multisensor Snow and Ice Mapping System (IMS) (http://www.ssd.noaa.gov/PS/SNOW/)	Operational products from NOAA polar-orbiting AVHRR imagery, DMSP SSM/I passive microwave radiometry, and geostationary imagery from NOAA GOES, European Meteosat, and Japanese geostationary satellite series	Daily snow and ice cover products at 4-km resolution for Northern Hemisphere are produced on a daily basis; coarser spatial resolution products date back to 1966 (http://www.ssd.noaa.gov/PS/SNOW/; http://nsidc.org/data/g02156.html; Ramsay 1998)

Table 8.A6.6 Some Satellite Systems for Measuring Temperature.

System	Type	Product characteristics
NASA Terra and Aqua MODIS (http://modis.gsfc.nasa.gov/data/dataprod/pdf/MOD_11.pdf)	Sun Synchronous research imager using thermal IR channels for this measurement	MODIS Land Surface Temperature and Emissivity Product (MOD 11), a global research product over cloud-free land surfaces obtained at 1 and 5 km ground spatial resolutions using the split-window technique; includes daily and 8-day gridded products; the accuracy specification at 1 km resolution under clear skies is 1 K (http://modis.gsfc.nasa.gov/data/atbd/atbd_mod11.pdf; http://www.icess.ucsb.edu/modis/LstUsrGuide/usrguide.html)
Japanese Advanced Spaceborne Thermal Emission and Reflection Radiometer (ASTER) sensor aboard NASA Terra satellite (http://asterweb.jpl.nasa.gov/)	Sun Synchronous research imager using thermal IR channels for this measurement	ASTER Surface Kinetic Temperature Product (AST08) has higher ground spatial resolution of 90 m; provides land surface temperature estimate for each of ASTER's five thermal IR channels and information from another ASTER product, the Surface Leaving Radiance Thermal Infrared Product (AST09T) that is accurate to within 1.5 K for homogeneous scenes; ASTER also generates a Surface Emissivity Product (AST05) (http://asterweb.jpl.nasa.gov/data_products.asp; http://asterweb.jpl.nasa.gov/content/03_data/01_Data_Products/release_surface_kinetic_temperatur.htm; http://asterweb.jpl.nasa.gov/content/03_data/01_Data_Products/release_surface_emissivity_product.htm)

(continued)

Table 8.A6.6 Continued

System	Type	Product characteristics
NOAA POES AVHRR; NOAA GOES sensor(s); NASA Terra and Aqua MODIS; NOAA POES High Resolution Infrared Radiation Sounder (HIRS); NASA-Japan TRMM Microwave Imager (TMI); NASA Aqua's Advanced Microwave Scanning Radiometer-EOS (AMSR-E) from Japan (http://podaac.jpl.nasa.gov/; http://coastwatch.noaa.gov/)	Variety of both operational and research sensors in geostationary, sun synchronous, and low inclination orbits measuring sea surface temperature	Sea Surface Temperatures (SST) products served through Jet Propulsion Laboratory's Physical Oceanography Distributed Active Archive Center (PODAAC) (http://ghrsst.jpl.nasa.gov/), NOAA Comprehensive Large Array-data Stewardship System (CLASS) (http://www.class.noaa.gov/nsaa/products/welcome), and NOAA CoastWatch Project (http://coastwatch.noaa.gov/cw_index.html); depending on data set, AVHRR satellite record of SST begins in 1981 or 1985; includes global daily gridded 100 km data sets produced from 8 km imagery generated from AVHRR imager and HIRS sounder; recent SST (ocean color and sea surface winds) products available through CoastWatch project for US coastal areas extending several hundred miles offshore and including Great Lakes; TMI and AMSR-E passive microwave sensors measure SST through non-raining clouds with CoastWatch making recent TMI data available and Japan's Earth Observation Research Center providing AMSR-E global browse products (http://coastwatch.noaa.gov/interface/interface.html; http://sharaku.eorc.jaxa.jp/cgi-bin/adeos2/amsr/l3brws/l3brws_top.cgi?lang = e; Parkinson and Greenstone 2000)

(continued)

Table 8.A6.6 Continued

System	Type	Product characteristics
NOAA POES High Resolution Infrared Radiation Sounder (HIRS), Advanced Microwave Sounding Unit-A (AMSU-A), AMSU-B and its follow-on sensor the Microwave Humidity Sounder (MHS); NOAA GOES Sounder (http://www2.ncdc. noaa.gov/docs/klm/ index.htm; http:// noaasis.noaa.gov/ NOAASIS/ml/sounder. html)	Operational sun synchronous and geostationary sensors measuring atmospheric temperature	Atmospheric Temperature products; HIRS is a 20-channel IR sounder providing atmospheric temperature profiles from surface to ~40 km altitude and encompassing a ground area of 19 to 20 km when looking directly down at the Earth in a nadir view, the newest edition of HIRS (known as HIRS/4) encompasses a ground area of 10 km; HIRS flies aboard NOAA POES satellites with AMSU-A, a 15-channel microwave sounder taking temperature soundings from the Earth's surface to an altitude of about 45 km even when clouds present; AMSU-A collects information in roughly 50 km-diameter cells when looking directly beneath the satellite; AMSU-B and its follow-on instrument the MHS, first launched on NOAA-18, are microwave sounder sensors on POES satellites also measuring profiles of atmospheric humidity; GOES Sounder is operational IR system with 19 channels, one of which is visible channel used for cloud detection (http://www.ncdc.noaa.gov/oa/ podguide/ncdc/docs/intro.htm; Kidder and Vonder Haar 1995)
NASA Aqua Atmospheric Infrared Sounder (AIRS)	Sun synchronous research hyperspectral sounder	Atmospheric and Surface Temperature Products; next generation HIRS sensor with 2,378 channels for bands in the ranges of 3.74 to 4.61 μm, 6.2 to 8.22 μm, and 8.8 to 15.4 μm; nadir ground footprint for data is 15 $\times$ 15 km and temperature profile

(continued)

Table 8.A6.6 Continued

System	Type	Product characteristics
		accuracies are 1 K for every 1 km layer of the troposphere and 1 K for every 4 km layer in the stratosphere up to an altitude of 40 km; makes temperature measures at many more atmospheric levels than other sounders and achieves temperature profile accuracies in the troposphere comparable to those obtained by balloon-borne radiosondes but with advantage of global coverage; AIRS flies with AMSU-A microwave sounder (http://disc.gsfc.nasa. gov/AIRS/documentation/ v4_docs/ V4_Data_Release_UG.pdf; Parkinson and Greenstone 2000; http://www-airs.jpl.nasa. gov/)

and related modeling efforts. Ground-based lidars are also in use to retrieve aerosol profiles and assess cloud vertical structure. For example, the Micro-pulse Lidar Network (MPLNET) is co-located with certain AERONET sites (Yu *et al.* 2006; NASA 2008c).

A6.3 Precipitation

Since 1987, the workhorse passive microwave satellite radiometers have been the Special Sensor Microwave Imager (SSM/I) imagers aboard the polar-orbiting Defense Meteorological Satellite Program (DMSP) satellites of the US Department of Defense. SSM/I brightness temperatures are converted into higher level precipitation products, such as maps of rain rate. NOAA makes data products available from SSM/I sensors on multiple satellites through its Comprehensive Large Array-data Stewardship System (CLASS) at http://www.class.noaa.gov/nsaa/ products/welcome. Table A6.5 includes more information on the SSM/I sensors and their products as well as the other precipitation sensors mentioned in the paragraphs below.

Two experimental microwave radiometers build upon the heritage of SSM/I and its predecessors: the Japanese Advanced Microwave Scanning Radiometer-EOS (AMSR-E) on the NASA Aqua satellite and the TRMM Microwave Imager (TMI) on the Tropical Rainfall Measuring Mission (TRMM). AMSR-E, a Japanese sensor flying aboard a US satellite, is another example of the high degree of international collaboration that characterizes satellite remote sensing of the Earth System. The AMSR-E data products augment the very important long-term sea-ice data set for monitoring climate change.

Those seeking to improve measures of precipitation have long dreamed of placing a rain radar in space. The joint US-Japanese TRMM brought these dreams to fruition with the first satellite-borne rain radar. Launched in 1997, TRMM carries a complete suite of precipitation instruments: a passive microwave TMI, the active microwave Precipitation Radar, and a five-channel Visible and Infrared Scanner (VIRS), which provides indirect measures of precipitation as a complement to the more direct measures from the microwave sensors. Having all types of rain sensors on one platform enables the cross-calibration of results from the different approaches to rainfall estimation (Kidder and Vonder Haar 1995). In addition, there is a Lightning Imaging Sensor (LIS) aboard TRMM. Access to TRMM data products is available at http://disc.sci.gsfc.nasa.gov/data/datapool/TRMM/.

A6.4 Temperature

Operational infrared sounder sensors (e.g., the High Resolution Infrared Radiation Sounder or HIRS on NOAA polar-orbiting satellites) have used 20 channels to divide the atmosphere into a number of different layers and to sense the temperature of these layers. Newer research sounders (e.g., the Atmospheric Infrared Sounder or AIRS sensor on the NASA Aqua satellite) use many more channels to divide the atmosphere into even thinner layers for temperature detection.

Sounding of the Earth's limb is a technique often used for detection of temperatures in the stratosphere. Limb sounding does not sense radiation from the Earth's surface, only that from the atmosphere. It does this by scanning a column of atmosphere at the edge of the Earth (i.e., at the Earth's limb) as the sun appears and disappears from view at sunrise and sunset, typically viewing the atmosphere "off to the side" of the spacecraft (Burroughs 1991; Kidder and Vonder Harr 1995; Lillesand and Kiefer 1994; Mayes and Hughes 2004; R. Kakar, personal communication, 2006; DLR 2008).

References

Achard, F., Eva, H. D., Stibig, H. J., et al. (2002) Determination of deforestation rates of the world's humid tropical forests. *Science,* **297**: 999–1002.

Aguado, E. and Burt, J. E. (1999) *Understanding Weather and Climate.* Prentice Hall, Upper Saddle River, NJ.

Albert, A. and Mobley, C. D. (2003) An analytical model for subsurface irradiance and remote sensing reflectance in deep and shallow case-2 waters. *Optics Express,* **11**: 2873–890.

Alesheikh, A. A., Ghorbanali, A., and Nouri, N. (2007) Coastline change detection using remote sensing. *International Journal of Environmental Science and Technology,* **4**(1): 61–66.

Anderson, T. L., Charlson, R. J., Schwartz, S. E., et al. (2003) Climate forcing by aerosols—a hazy picture. *Science,* **300**: 1103–04.

Andersson, E. (2006) Urban landscapes and sustainable cities. *Ecology and Society,* **11**(1): 34, 1–7.

Andréfouët, S., Kramer, P., Torres-Pulliza, D., et al. (2003) Multi-site evaluation of IKONOS data for classification of tropical coral reef environments. *Remote Sensing of Environment,* **88**: 128–43.

——. Gilbert, A., Yan, L., et al. (2005a) The remarkable population size of the endangered clam Tridacna maxima assessed in Fangatau Atoll (Eastern Tuamotu, French Polynesia) using in situ and remote sensing data. *ICES Journal of Marine Science,* **62**(6): 1037–48.

——. Hochberg, E. J., Chevillon, C., et al. (2005b) Multi-scale remote sensing of coral reefs. In R. L. Miller, C. E. D. Castillo, and B. A. McKee, eds. *Remote Sensing of Coastal Aquatic Environments, Technologies, Techniques and Applications,* pp. 299–317. Springer, The Netherlands.

——. Muller-Karger, F. E., Robinson, J. A., et al. (2006) Global assessment of modern coral reef extent and diversity for regional science and management applications, a view from space, Keynote Paper. In Y. Suzuki, ed. *Proceedings of the 10th International Coral Reef Symposium,* pp. 1732–45. Japanese Coral Reef Society, Tokyo, Japan, Okinawa.

Anthes, R. A. (1984) Enhancement of convective precipitation by mesoscale variations in vegetative covering in semiarid regions. *Journal of Climate and Applied Meteorology,* **23**: 541–54.

Araújo, M. B., Cabeza, M., Thuiller, W., et al. (2004) Would climate change drive species out of reserves. An assessment of existing reserve-selection methods. *Global Change Biology,* **10**: 1618–26.

——. Thuiller, W., Williams, P. H., et al. (2005a) Downscaling European species atlas distributions to a finer resolution: implications for conservation planning. *Global Ecology and Biogeography,* **14**(1): 17–30.

——. Pearson, R. G., Thuiller, W., et al. (2005b) Validation of species-climate envelope models under climate change. *Global Change Biology,* **11**: 1504–13.

Arino, O., Plummer, S., and Defrenne, D. (2005) Fire disturbance: the ten years time series of the ATSR World Fire Atlas. *Proceedings of the MERIS-AATSR workshop 2005,* Frascati, Italy, September 2005. Accessed on the Web on August 31, 2007 at: http://envisat.esa.int/workshops/meris_aatsr2005/participants/342/paper_Arino.pdf.

Arst, H., Haltrin, V. I., and Arnone, R. A. (2002) Informative water layer, determined by attenuation depth, in water bodies of different turbidity. *Proceedings of the Marine Technology Society Oceans 2002 MTS/IEEE Conference,* 1968–72.

Arvidson, T., Gasch, J., Goward, S. N., et al. (2001) Landsat 7's long term acquisition plan—an innovative approach to building a global imagery archive. *Remote Sensing of Environment,* **78**: 13–26.

Asner, G. P., and Martin, R. E. (2008) Airborne spectranomics: mapping canopy chemical and taxonomic diversity in tropical forests. *Frontiers in Ecology and the Environment,* **7**: doi:10.1890/070152.

——. Keller, M., Pereira, R., et al. (2002) Remote sensing of selective logging in Amazonia: assessing limitations based on detailed field measurements. *Landsat ETM + and textural analysis. Remote Sensing of Environment,* **80**(3): 483–96.

——. Knapp, D. E., Broadbent, E. N., et al. (2005) Selective Logging in the Brazilian Amazon. *Science,* **310**: 480–82.

Avery, T. E., and Berlin, G. L. (1992) *Fundamentals of Remote Sensing and Airphoto Interpretation.* Macmillan, New York.

Avissar, R., and Werth, D. (2005) Global hydroclimatological teleconnections resulting from tropical deforestation. *Journal of Hydrometeorology,* **6**: 134–45.

Azzellino, A., Gaspari, S. A., Airoldi, S., et al. (2008) Biological consequences of global warming, does sea surface temperature affect cetacean distribution in the western Ligurian Sea? *Journal of the Marine Biological Association of the UK,* **88**(Special Issue 06, Sep 2008): 1145–52.

Bacles, C. F. E., Lowe, A. J., and Ennos, R. A. (2006) Effective seed dispersal across a fragmented landscape. *Science,* **311**: 628.

Bader, M. J., Forbes, G. S., Grant, J. R., et al. (1995) *Images in Weather Forecasting: A Practical Guide for Interpreting Satellite and Radar Imagery.* Cambridge University Press, Cambridge.

Bailey, R. G. (1996) *Ecosystem Geography.* Springer-Verlag, New York.

Ban, N. C., Picard, C., and Vincen, A. C. J. (2008) Moving toward spatial solutions in marine conservation with indigenous communities. *Ecology and Society,* **13**: 32.

Banks, S. (2003) SeaWiFS satellite monitoring of oil spill impact on primary production in the Galápagos Marine Reserve. *Marine Pollution Bulletin,* **47**: 325–30.

Bar Massada, A., Gabay, O., Perevolotsky, A., et al. (2008) Quantifying the effect of grazing and shrub-clearing on small scale spatial pattern of vegetation. *Landscape Ecology,* **23**: 327–39.

Barber, R. T. and Chavez, F. P. (1991) Regulation of primary productivity rate in the equatorial Pacific. *Limnology and Oceanography,* **36**: 1803–15.

Bates, J. (2004) Satellite, historic data lead to discovery of new species. *Space News,* January 5, 2004.

Baum, K. A., Haynes, K. J., Dillemuth, F. P., et al. (2004) The matrix enhances the effectiveness of corridors and stepping stones. *Ecology,* **85**: 2671–76.

Behera, M. D. and Roy, P. S. (2002) Lidar remote sensing for forestry applications: the Indian context. *Current Science,* **83**(11): 1320–27.

Behrenfeld, M. J. and Falkowski, P. G. (1997) Photosynthetic rates derived from satellite-based chlorophyll concentration. *Limnology and Oceanography,* **42**: 1–20.

——. Bale, A. J., Kolber, Z. S., et al. (1996) Confirmation of iron limitation of phytoplankton photosynthesis in the equatorial Pacific Ocean. *Nature,* **383**: 508–11.

Belluco, E., Camuffo, M., Ferrari, S., et al. (2006) Mapping salt-marsh vegetation by multi-spectral and hyperspectral remote sensing. *Remote Sensing of Environment,* **105**: 54–67.

Bennett, A. F., Radford, J. Q., Haslem, A., et al. (2006) Properties of land mosaics: implications for nature conservation in agricultural environments. *Biological Conservation,* **133**: 250–64.

Benton, T. G., Vickery, J. A., and Wilson, J. D. (2003) Farmland biodiversity, is habitat heterogeneity the key? *Trends in Ecology and Evolution,* **18**: 182–88.

Benz, U. C., Hoffman, P., Willhauk, G., et al. (2004) Multi-resolution, object-oriented fuzzy analysis of remote sensing data for GIS-ready information. *Journal of Photogrammetry and Remote Sensing*, **58**: 239–58.

Birkett, C. M. (1994) Radar altimetry: a new concept in monitoring lake level changes. *EOS, Transactions of the American Geophysical Union*, **75**(24): 273–75.

Birkett, C. M. and Mason, I. M. (1995) A new global lakes database for a remote sensing program studying climatically sensitive large lakes. *Journal of Great Lakes Research*, **21**(3): 307–18.

Birkett, C. M., Mertes, L. A. K., Dunne, T., et al. (2002) Surface water dynamics in the Amazon Basin: zpplication of satellite radar altimetry. *Journal of Geophysical Research*, Special Issue, **107**(D20): 8059, 26.1–26.21.

Bjerklie, D. M., Dingman, S. L., Vorosmarty, C. J., et al. (2003) Evaluating the potential for measuring river discharge from space. *Journal of Hydrology*, **278**: 17–38.

Blair, R. (2004) The effects of urban sprawl on birds at multiple levels of biological organization. *Ecology and Society*, **9**(5): 2 [online], 21.

Blake, S., Douglas-Hamilton, I., Karesh, W., et al. (2001) GPS telemetry of forest elephants in Central Africa: results of a preliminary study. *African Journal of Ecology*, **39**: 178–86.

Blanc, J. (2008) Loxodonta africana. In: 2008 IUCN Red List of Threatened Species. Accessed at www.iucnredlist.org. [Retrieved on April 26, 2009.]

Bledzki, L. A. (Lead Author) and Nagabhatla, N. (Topic Editor) (2008) Secchi disk. In C. J. Cleveland, ed. *Encyclopedia of Earth*, Environmental Information Coalition, National Council for Science and the Environment, Washington, DC. [Retrieved September 8, 2008]. http://www.eoearth.org/article/Secchi_disk.

Blott, S. J. and Pye, K. (2004) Application of LIDAR digital terrain modelling to predict intertidal habitat development at a managed retreat site: Abbotts Hall, Essex, UK. *Earth Surface Processes and Landforms*, **29**: 893–905.

Blumberg, D. G. and Zhu, G. (2007) Using a hierarchical multi-resolution mechanism for the classification and semantic extraction of landuse maps for Beer-Sheva. *Israel. International Journal of Remote Sensing*, **28**(15): 3273–89.

Bock, M., Xofis, P., Mitchley, J., et al. (2005) Object-oriented methods for habitat mapping at multiple scales—Case studies from Northern Germany and Wye Downs. *UK. Journal for Nature Conservation*, **13**: 75–89.

Bonan, G. B. (2002) *Ecological Climatology: Concepts and Applications*. Cambridge University Press, Cambridge.

Bonan, G. B. (2008) Forests and climate change: forcings, feedbacks, and the climate benefits of forests. *Science*, **320**: 1444–49.

Bradford, J. H., Johnson, C. R., Brosten, T., et al. (2007) Imaging thermal stratigraphy in freshwater lakes using georadar. *Geophysical Research Letters*, **34**: L24405, 5.

Brakenridge, G. R., Nghiem, S. V., Anderson, E., et al. (2005) Space-based measurement of river runoff. *Eos, Transactions of the American Geophysical Union*, **86**: 185–88.

Brakenridge, G. R., Nghiem, S. V., Anderson, E., et al. (2007) Orbital microwave measurement of river discharge and ice status. *Water Resources Research*, **43**: W0405, doi:10.1029/2006WR005238.

Brando, V. E. and Dekker, A. G. (2003) Satellite hyperspectral remote sensing for estimating estuarine and coastal water quality. *IEEE Transactions on Geoscience and Remote Sensing*, **41**: 1378–87.

Brazel, A. J., Selover, N., Vose, R., et al. (2000) The tale of two climates: Baltimore and Phoenix LTER sites. *Climate Research*, **15**: 123–35.

Brilha, J. B. (2002) Geoconservation and protected areas. *Environmental Conservation*, 29: 273–76.

Brock, J. C., Wright, C. W., Clayton, T. D., et al. (2004) LIDAR optical rugosity of coral reefs in Biscayne National Park, Florida. *Coral Reefs*, 23: 48–59.

Brock, J. C., Yates, K., Halley, R., et al. (2006) Integration of coral reef ecosystem process studies and remote sensing. In L. L. Richardson and E. F. LeDrew, eds. *Remote Sensing of Aquatic Coastal Ecosystem Processes*, pp. 111–31. Springer, Dordrecht, The Netherlands.

Brooks, T. M., Mittermeier, R. A., da Fonseca, G. A. B., et al. (2006) Global biodiversity conservation priorities. *Science*, 313: 58–61.

Brown, J. H. and Lomolino, M. V. (1998) *Biogeography*. Sinauer, Sunderland, MA.

Brown, J. K. M. and Hovmoller, M. S. (2002) Aerial dispersal of pathogens on the global and continental scales and its impact on plant disease. *Science*, 297: 537–41.

Brown, K. A., Spector, S., and Wu, W. (2008) Multi-scale analysis of species introductions: combining landscape and demographic models to improve management decisions about non-native species. *Journal of Applied Ecology*, 45: 1639–48.

Buckland, S. T., and Elston, D. A. (1993) Empirical models for the spatial distribution of wildlife. *Journal of Applied Ecology*, 30: 478–95.

Burgan, R. E., Klaver, R. W., and Klaver, J. M. (2000) Fuel models and fire potential from satellite and surface observations. Available on the Web at USFS-Wildland Fire Assessment System site at: http://www.fs.fed.us/land/wfas/firepot/fpipap.htm [Accessed on December 4, 2007.]

Burnham, K. P., and Anderson, D. R. (2002) *Model Selection and Multi-Model Inference: A Practical Information-Theoretic Approach*, 2nd edn. Springer, New York.

Burroughs, W. J. (1991) *Watching the World's Weather*. Cambridge University Press, Cambridge.

Cain, D. H., Riitters, K., and Orvis, K. (1997) A multi-scale analysis of landscape metrics. *Landscape Ecology*, 12: 199–212.

Calabrese, J. M., and Fagan, W. F. (2004) A comparison-shopper's guide to connectivity metrics. *Frontiers in Ecology and the Environment*, 2: 529–36.

Campbell, I. D., McDonald, K., Flannigan, M. D., et al. (1999) Long-distance transport of pollen into the Arctic. *Nature*, 399: 29–30.

Carleer, A. P., Debeir, O., and Wolf, E. (2005) Assessment of Very High Spatial Resolution Satellite Image Segmentations. *Photogrammetric Engineering and Remote Sensing*, 71: 1285–94.

Carleton, A. M. (1991) *Satellite Remote Sensing in Climatology*. Belhaven Press, London.

Carr, M. E., Friedrichs, M. A. M., Schmeltz, M., et al. (2006) A comparison of global estimates of marine primary production from ocean color. *Deep-Sea Research II*, 53: 741–70.

Carter, A. J., Ramsey, M. S., and Belousov, A. B. (2007) Detection of a new summit crater on Bezymianny Volcano lava dome: satellite and field-based thermal data. *Bulletin of Volcanology*, DOI: 10.1007/s00445–007–0113-x.

Cavalieri, D. J. (1992) Introduction. In D. J. Cavalieri, ed. NASA *Sea Ice Validation Program for the Defense Meteorological Satellite Program Special Sensor Microwave Imager: Final Report*, NASA Technical Memorandum 104559, Washington, DC.

Chen, P., Srinivasan, R., Fedosejevs, G., et al. (2003) Evaluating different NDVI composite techniques using NOAA-14 AVHRR data. *International Journal of Remote Sensing*, 24(17): 3403.

Cheng, Y., Gamon, J. A., Fuentes, D. A., et al. (2006) A multi-scale analysis of dynamic optical signals in a Southern California chaparral ecosystem: a comparison of field. *AVIRIS and MODIS data*. *Remote Sensing of Environment*, 103(3): 369–78.

Chetkiewicz, C. L. B., Clair, C. C. S., and Boyce, M. S. (2006) Corridors for conservation: integrating pattern and process. *Annual Review of Ecological Systems*, **37**: 317–42.

Chiswell, S. M. and Roemmich, D. (1998) The East Cape Current and two eddies: a mechanism for larval retention? *New Zealand Journal of Marine and Freshwater Research*, **32**: 385–97.

Chiswell, S. M., Wilkin, J., Booth, J. D., et al. (2003) Trans-Tasman Sea larval transport: is Australia a source for New Zealand rock lobsters? *Marine Ecology Progress Series*, **247**: 173–82.

Clark, J., Parsons, A., Zajkowski, T., et al. (2003) Remote sensing imagery support for burned area emergency response teams on 2003 Southern California wildfires. USDA Forest Service Remote Sensing Applications Center report, RSAC-2003-RPT1. Available on the Web at: http://www.fs.fed.us/eng/rsac/baer/2003-RPT1.pdf [Accessed on January 2, 2008.]

Clark, J. S. (2007) *Models for Ecological Data: An Introduction*. Princeton University Press, Princeton, NJ.

Clark, R. N. (1999) Spectroscopy of rocks and minerals, and principles of spectroscopy. In A. N. Rencz, ed. *Remote Sensing for the Earth Sciences*, 3rd edn. American Society for Photogrammetry and Remote Sensing, Bethesda, MD.

Cochrane, M. A. (2003) Fire science for rainforests. *Nature*, **421**: 913–19.

Cochrane, M. A. and Schulze, M. D. (1998) Forest fires in the Brazilian Amazon. *Conservation Biology*, **12**: 948–50.

Cochrane, M. A., Alencar, A., Schulze, M. D., et al. (1999) Positive feedbacks in the fire dynamic of closed canopy tropical forests. *Science*, **284**: 1832–35.

Cochran-Marquez, S. A. (2005) Moloka'i benthic habitat mapping. US Geological Survey Open-File Report 2005–1070.

Coles, W. C. and Musick, J. A. (2000) Satellite sea surface temperature analysis and correlation with sea turtle distribution off North Carolina. *Copeia*, **2000**(2): 551–54.

Comiso, J. C. (2003) Warming trends in the Arctic from clear sky satellite observations. *Journal of Climate*, **16**(21): 3498.

Congalton, R. (1988) Using spatial autocorrelation analysis to explore the errors in maps generated from remotely sensed data. *Photogrammetric Engineering and Remote Sensing*, **54**: 587–92.

Congalton, R. and Green, K. (1999) *Assessing the Accuracy of Remotely Sensed Data: Principles and Practices*. Lewis Publishers, New York.

Coppin, P., Jonckheere, I., Nackaerts, K., et al. (2004) Digital change detection methods in ecosystem monitoring: a review. *International Journal of Remote Sensing*, **25**(9): 1565–96.

Corsi, F., de Leeuw, J., and Skidmore, A. K. (2000) Modeling species distribution with GIS. In L. Boitani and T. Fuller, eds. *Research Techniques in Animal Ecology*. Columbia University Press, New York.

Courrau, J. (1999) Monitoring protected area management in Central America: a regional approach. *Parks*, **9**: 56–60.

Cox, C. B. and Moore, P. D. (2000) *Biogeography: An Ecological and Evolutionary Approach*. Blackwell Science, Oxford.

Cretaux, J. F. and Birkett, C. (2006) Lake studies from satellite radar altimetry. *Comptes rendus Géoscience*, **338**(14–15): 1098–112.

Crooks, K. R., and Sanjayan, M. A. eds. (2006) *Connectivity Conservation*. Cambridge University Press. Cambridge, MA.

Crowe, R. E. (1996) Use of gap analysis in regional planning in southern California. In J. M. Scott, T. Tear, and F. Davis, eds. *Gap Analysis: A Landscape Approach to Biodiversity*

Planning, pp. 221–38. American Society for Photogrammetry and Remote Sensing (ASPRS), Bethesda, MD.

Crutzen, P. J. and Andreae, M. O. (1990) Biomass burning in the tropics: impact on atmospheric chemistry and biogeochemical cycles. *Science*, **250**: 1669–78.

Curran, L., Trigg, S., McDonald, A., et al. (2004) Lowland forest loss in protected areas of Indonesian Borneo. *Science*, **303**: 1000–03.

Dale, V. H., and Pearson, S. M. (1997) Quantifying habitat fragmentation due to land-use change in Amazonia. In W. F. Laurance and R. O. Bierregaard, eds. *Tropical Forest Remnants, Ecology, Management and Conservation of Fragmented Communities*, pp. 400–10. The University of Chicago Press, Chicago, IL.

Danielsen, F., Sorensen, M. K., Olwig, M. F., et al. (2005) The Asian tsunami: a protective role for coastal vegetation. *Science*, **310**: 643.

Das, A., Krishnaswamyc, J., Bawab, K. S., et al. (2006) Prioritisation of conservation areas in the Western Ghats. *India: Biological Conservation*, **133**: 16–31.

de Queiroz, A. (2005) The resurrection of oceanic dispersal in historical biogeography. *Trends in Ecology and Evolution*, **20**: 68–73.

DeFries, R. S. and Townshend, J. R. G. (1994) NDVI-derived land cover classifications at a global scale. *International Journal of Remote Sensing*, **15**: 3567–86.

DeFries, R. S., Hansen, A., Newton, A. C., et al. (2005) Increasing isolation of protected areas in tropical forests over the past twenty years. *Ecological Applications*, **15**: 19–26.

Dell'Acqua, F., Gamba, P., Lisini, G., et al. (2003) Improvements to urban area characterization using multitemporal and multiangle SAR images. *IEEE Transactions on Geoscience and Remote Sensing*, **41**(9): 1996–2004.

D'Eon, R., Glenn, S. M., Parfitt, I., et al. (2002) Landscape connectivity as a function of scale and organism vagility in a real forested landscape. *Conservation Ecology*, **6**: 10.

Dennis, R. A., Mayer, J., Applegate, G., et al. (2005) Fire, people and pixels: linking social science and remote sensing to understand underlying causes and impacts of fires in Indonesia. *Human Ecology*, **33**(4): 465–504.

Deysher, L. E. (1993) Evaluation of remote sensing techniques for monitoring giant kelp populations. *Hydrobiologia*, **260**/261: 307–12.

Dirzo, R., and Raven, P. H. (2003) Global state of biodiversity and loss. *Annual Review of Environmental Resources*, **28**: 137–67.

DLR. (2008) Definition and conversion of volume mixing ratio. The World Data Center for Remote Sensing of the Atmosphere. Accessed on the Web at http://wdc.dlr.de/data_products/SERVICES/PROMOTE_O3/vmr.html.

DMA (1983) *Geodesy for the layman, DMA*. Technical Report 80–003. United States Defense Mapping Agency.

Donnelly, R. and Marzluff, J. M. (2004) Importance of reserve size and landscape context to urban bird conservation. *Conservation Biology*, **18**(3): 733–45.

Doxani, G., Siachalou, S., Tsakiri-Strati, M., et al. (2008) An object-oriented approach to urban land cover change detection. *The International Archives of the Photogrammetry, Remote Sensing and Spatial Information Sciences*, **37**(B7): 1655–60.

Dozier, J. (1981) A method for satellite identification of surface temperature fields of subpixel resolution. *Remote Sensing of Environment*, **11**: 221–29.

Droj, G. (2007) The applicability of fuzzy theory in remote sensing image classification. *Studia Universitatis "Babes-Bolyai"—Informatica*, **52**(1): 89–96.

Dudley, N., Hockings, M., and Stolton, S. eds. (1999) *Measuring the Effectiveness of Protected Area Management. Partnerships for Protection*. Earthscan, London.

Dupuy, D. J. and Moat, J. (1996) A refined classification of the primary vegetation of Madagascar based on the underlying geology: using GIS to map its distribution and to assess its conservation status. In W. R. Lourenço, ed. *International Symposium on the 'Biogeography de Madagascar'*. Paris, France.

Ehlers, M., Jadkowski, M. A., Howard, R. R., et al. (1990) Application of SPOT data for regional growth analysis and local planning. *Photogrametric Engineering and Remote Sensing*, **56**: 175–80.

Elith, J., Graham, C. H., Anderson, R. P., et al. (2006) Novel methods improve prediction of species' distributions from occurrence data. *Ecography*, **29**(2): 129–51.

Elvidge, C. D., Baugh, K. E., Kihn, E. A., et al. (1997) Relation between satellite-observed visible-near infrared emissions, population, economic activity and electric power consumption. *International Journal of Remote Sensing*, **18**: 1373–79.

Engdahl, M. E. and Hyyppä, J. M. (2003) Land-cover classification using multitemporal ERS-1/2 InSAR data. *IEEE Transcations on Geoscience and Remote Sensing*, **41**(7): 1620–28.

Engelkemeir, R. M. and Khan, S. D. (2008) Lidar mapping of faults in Houston. *Texas, USA. Geosphere*, **4**(1): 170–82.

ESA. (2008) *MetOp: Meteorological Missions*. Accessed at http://www.esa.int/esaLP/LPmetop.html.

ESA Earth Observation Science and Applications Department, Ionia. (2009) *ATSR World Fire Atlas*. Accessed at http://dup.esrin.esa.int/ionia/wfa/index.asp. [Modified January 14, 2009.]

Fahrig, L. (2002) Effect of habitat fragmentation on the extinction threshold: a synthesis. *Ecological Applications Appl.*, **12**: 346–53.

Fahrig, L. (2003) Effects of habitat fragmentation on biodiversity. *Annual Review of Ecology, Evolution, and Systematics*, **34**: 487–515.

Fahrig, L. and Merriam, G. (1994) Conservation of fragmented populations. *Conservation Biology*, **8**: 50–59.

Faundeen, J. L., Williams, D. L., and Greenhagen, C. A. (2004) Landsat yesterday and today: an American vision and an old challenge. *Journal of Map and Geography Libraries*, **1**: 59–74.

Feldman, G., and Kuring, N. (2003) *Remote Sensing of Coral Reefs: SeaWiFS Bathymetry and Data Archive Proof-of-Concept*. SeaWiFS Project, NASA Goddard Space Flight Center, Greenbelt, MD. Accessed at: http://oceancolor.gsfc.nasa.gov/cgi/reefs.pl [Last updated December 4, 2003.]

Ferguson, R. L. and Korfmacher, K. (1997) Remote sensing and GIS analysis of seagrass meadows in North Carolina, USA. *Aquatic Botany*, **58**: 241–58.

Fernández-Prieto, D., Hernández, M., Arino, O., et al. (2003) Building Environment for Gorilla: a new action in the joint UNESCO-ESA initiative to support the World Heritage Convention. *Proceedings of the 2003 Int. Geoscience and Remote Sensing Symposium (IGARSS 2003)*, Toulouse, France, July 21–25, 2003.

Fernández-Prieto, D., Hernández, M., Arino, O., et al. (2004) Managing world heritage sites from space: the BEGo project. *Proceedings of the 2004 Earsel Symposium*, Dubrovnik, Croatia, May 2004.

Fernández-Prieto, D., Hernández, M., and Seifert, F. M. (2005) Protecting world heritage from space: the activities of ESA. Proceedings of International Symposium in Remote Sensing of the Environment (ISRSE), Saint Petersburg, June 2005.

Ferraz, S. F. D., Vettorazzi, C. A., Theobald, D. M., et al. (2005) Landscape dynamics of Amazonian deforestation between 1984 and 2002 in central Rondonia. Brazil, assessment and future scenarios. *Forest Ecology and Management*, **204**: 69–85.

Ferry Slik, J. W., Verburg, R. W., and Kebler, P. J. (2002) Effects of fire and selective logging on the tree species composition of lowland dipterocarp forest in East Kalimantan, Indonesia. Biodiversity and Conservation, 11: 85–98.

Fielding, A. H., and Bell, J. F. (1997) A review of methods for the assessment of prediction errors in conservation presence/absence models. *Environmental Conservation*, 24: 38–49.

Findell, K. L. and Eltahir, E. A. B. (1997) An analysis of the soil moisture-rainfall feedback, based on direct observations from Illinois. *Water Resources Research*, 33: 725–35.

Finkbeiner, M., Stevenson, B., and Seaman, R. (2001) *Guidance for Benthic Habitat Mapping, an Aerial Photographic Approach*. NOAA Coastal Services Center, Charleston, SC.

Flasse, S. P. and Ceccato, P. (1996) A contextual algorithm for AVHRR fire detection. *International Journal of Remote Sensing*, 17: 419–24.

Fleishman, E., and Seto, K. C. (2009). Applications of remote sensing to ecological modeling. Network of Conservation Educators and Practitioners. Retrieved from http://ncep.amnh. org.

Forman, R. T., and Alexander, L. E. (1998) Roads and their major ecological effects. *Annual Review of Ecological Systems*, 29: 207–31.

Forman, R. T., and Godron, M. (1986) *Landscape Ecology*. Wiley, New York.

Forest Landscape Ecology Program. (1999–2000) *LEAP II*. Sault Ste, Marie, ON. Accessed at http://www.ai-geostats.org/index.php?id=102&no_cache=1&sword_list[]=leap. [Viewed January 3, 2009.]

Forster, P., Ramaswamy, V., Artaxo, P., et al. (2007) Changes in Atmospheric Constituents and in Radiative Forcing. In S. Solomon, D. Qin, M. Manning, et al. eds. *Climate Change 2007: The Physical Science Basis. Contribution of Working Group I to the Fourth Assessment Report of the Intergovernmental Panel on Climate Change*, Cambridge University Press, Cambridge and New York.

Foundations of Success (2009) *Using Conceptual Models to Document a Situation Analysis: An FOS How-To Guide*. Foundations of Success, Bethesda, MD. Accessed at http://fosonline. org/Site_Documents/Grouped/FOS_Conceputal_Model_Guide_April2009.pdf. [Viewed 19 May, 2009.]

Fowler, R. (2001) Topographic lidar. In D. F. Maune, ed. *Digital Elevation Model Technologies and Applications: The DEM Users Manual*, American Society for Photogrammetry and Remote Sensing, Bethesda, MD.

Frazier, P. S. and Page, K. J. (2000) Water body detection and delineation with Landsat TM data. *Photogrammetric Engineering and Remote Sensing*, 66: 1461–68.

Fredericksen, N. J. and Fredericksen, T. S. (2002) Terrestrial wildlife responses to logging and fire in a Bolivian tropical humid forest. *Biodiversity and Conservation*, 11: 27–38.

Friedman, A., Brown, E., and Monaco, M. E. (2007a) Coupling ecology and GIS to evaluate efficacy of marine protected areas in Hawaii. *Ecological Applications*, 17: 715–30.

Friedman, A., Brown, E., and Monaco, M. E. (2007b) Defining reef fish habitat utilization patterns in Hawaii: comparisons between marine protected areas and areas open to fishing. *Marine Ecology Progress Series*, 351: 221–33.

Frohn, R., and Hao, Y. (2006) Landscape metric performance in analyzing two decades of deforestation in the Amazon Basin of Rondonia, Brazil. *Remote Sensing of Environment*, 100: 237–51.

Gagnon, P., Scheibling, R. E., Jones, W., et al. (2008) The role of digital bathymetry in mapping shallow marine vegetation from hyperspectral image data. *International Journal of Remote Sensing*, 29(3): 879–904.

Gaines, W., Singleton, P., and Ross, R. (2003) *Assessing the Cumulative Effects of Linear Recreation Routes on Wildlife Habitats on the Okanogan and Wenatchee National Forests*. U.S. Department of Agriculture, U.S. Forest Service, and the Pacific Northwest Research Station, Portland, OR.

Gamba, P., Dell'Acqua, F., and Dasarathy, B. V. (2005) Urban remote sensing using multiple data sets: past, present, and future. *Information Fusion*, 6(4), 319–26.

Garcia-Gigorro, S., and Saura, S. (2005) Forest fragmentation estimated from remotely sensed data, is comparison across scales possible? *Forest Science*, 51: 51–63.

Gardner, T. A., Côté, I. M., Gill, J. A., et al. (2003) Long-term region-wide declines in Caribbean corals. *Science*, 301(5635): 958.

Garrison, V. H., Shinn, E. A., Foreman, W. T., et al. (2003) African and Asian dust: from desert soils to coral reefs. *BioScience*, 53: 469–80.

Gauthreaux, S. A. and Belser, C. G. (2003) Radar ornithology and biological conservation. *The Auk*, 120: 266–77.

Gauthreaux, S. A. and Belser, C. G. (2005) Radar ornithology and the conservation of migratory birds. USDA Forest Service General Technical Report, PSW-GTR-191, 871–75.

Gelautz, M., Paillou, P., Chen, C. W., et al. (2004) A comparative study of radar stereo and interferometry for DEM generation. In *Proceedings of the FRINGE 2003 Workshop (ESA SP-550)*. December 1–5, 2003, ESA/ESRIN, Frascati, Italy. H. Lacoste. Published on CDROM, p. 15.1.

Giglio, L., Descloitres, J., Justice, C. O., et al. (2003) An enhanced contextual fire detection algorithm for MODIS. *Remote Sensing of Environment*, 87: 273–82.

Giglio, L., Csiszar, I., and Justice, C. O. (2006) Global distribution and seasonality of active fires as observed with the Terra and Aqua Moderate Resolution Imaging Spectroradiometer (MODIS) sensors. *Journal of Geophysical Research*, 111: G02016.

Gillespie, T. (2001) Remote sensing of animals. *Progress in Physical Geography*, 25(3): 355–62.

Giri, C., Zhu, Z., Tieszen, L. L., et al. (2008) Mangrove forest distributions and dynamics (1975–2005) of the tsunami-affected region of Asia. *Journal of Biogeography*, 35: 519–28.

Gislason, P. O., Benediktsson, J. A., and Sveinsson, J. R. (2006) Random Forests for land cover classification. *Pattern Recognition Letters*, 27(4): 294–300.

Glenn, E. P., Huete, A. R., Nagler, P. L., et al. (2008) Relationship between remotely-sensed vegetation indices, canopy attributes and plant physiological processes: what vegetation indices can and cannot tell us about the landscape. *Sensors*, 8: 2136–160.

Góes, C. A., Lorenzzetti, J. A., Gherardi, D. F. M. , et al. (2007) Modeling spiny lobster larval dispersion in the tropical Atlantic using satellite data. Anais XIII Simpósio Brasileiro de Sensoriamento Remoto, April 21–26, 2007, INPE, Florianópolis, Brazil, pp. 4595–602.

Goetz, S., Steinberg, D., Dubayah, R., et al. (2007) Laser remote sensing of canopy habitat heterogeneity as a predictor of bird species richness in an eastern temperate forest, USA. *Remote Sensing of Environment*, 108(3): 254–63.

Goodman, J. A. and Ustin, S. L. (2007) Classification of benthic composition in a coral reef environment using spectral unmixing. *Journal of Applied Remote Sensing*, 1(011501): 1–17.

Goodwin, N. R., Coops, N. C., and Culvenor, D. S. (2006) Assessment of forest structure with airborne LiDAR and the effects of platform altitude. *Remote Sensing of Environment*, 103(2): 140–52.

Gopal, G. and Woodcock, C. (1994) Theory and methods for accuracy assessment of thematic maps using fuzzy sets. *Photogrammetric Engineering and Remote Sensing*, 60: 181–88.

Goparaju, L., Tripathi, A., and Jha, C. S. (2005) Forest fragmentation impacts on phytodiversity: an analysis using remote sensing and GIS. *Current Science*, 88: 1264–74.

Goulding, M., Smith, N. J. H., and Mahar, D. J. (1996) *Floods of Fortune: Ecology and Economy Along the Amazon*. Columbia University Press, New York.

Gousie, M. B. and Franklin, W. R. (2003) Constructing a DEM from grid-based data by computing intermediate contours. Eleventh ACM International Symposium on Advances in Geographic Information Systems, New Orleans, LA.

Green, A. A., Berman, M., Switzer, P., et al. (1988) A transformation for ordering multi-spectral data in terms of image quality with implications for noise removal. *IEEE Transactions on Geoscience and Remote Sensing*, **26**: 65–74.

Green, E. P., Clark, C. D., Mumby, P. J., et al. (1998) Remote sensing techniques for mangrove mapping. *International Journal of Remote Sensing*, **19**: 935–36.

Green, E. P., Mumby, P. J., Edwards, A. J., et al. (1997) Estimating leaf area index of mangroves from satellite data. *Aquatic Botany*, **58**(1): 11–19.

Green, E. P., Mumby, P. J., Edwards, A. J., et al. (2000) *Remote Sensing Handbook for Tropical Coastal Management: Coastal Management Sourcebooks 3*. UNESCO, Paris.

Green, E. P., Wood, R., Stumpf, R. P., et al. (2006) All our eggs in one basket: the present state of tropical marine biodiversity conservation. In Y. Suzuki, et al., eds. *Proceedings of the 10th International Coral Reef Symposium, Okinawa, 28 June-2 July, 2004*, pp. 1504–10. Japanese Coral Reef Society, Tokyo, Japan.

Gregorio, A. D. and Jansen, L. J. M. (2000) *Land Cover Classification System (LCCS): Classification Concepts and User Manual*. FAO, Rome, Italy.

Griffin, D. W. (2005) Clouds of desert dust and microbiology: a mechanism of global dispersion. *Microbiology Today*, November 05, pp. 180–82. Accessed on the Web at http://www.socgenmicrobiol.org.uk/pubs/micro_today/pdf/110506.pdf.

Griffin, D. W. and Kellogg, C. A. (2004) Dust storms and their impact on ocean and human health: dust in Earth's atmosphere. *EcoHealth*, **1**: 284–95.

Grohman, G., Kroenung, G., and Strebeck, J. (2006) Filling SRTM voids: the delta surface fill method. *Photogrammetric Engineering and Remote Sensing*, **72**: 213–16.

Groom, G., Mücher, C. A., Ihse, M. et al. (2006) Remote sensing in landscape ecology: experiences and perspectives in a European context. *Landscape Ecology*, **21**: 391–408.

Gucinski, H., Furniss, J. J., Ziemer, R. R., et al. (2001) *Forest Roads: A Synthesis of Scientific Information*. Department of Agriculture, U.S. Forest Service, Pacific Northwest Research Station, Portland, OR.

Guldemond, R., and van Aarde, R. (2007) The impact of elephants on plants and their community variables in South Africa's Maputaland. *African Journal of Ecology*, **45**: 327–35.

Gupta, R. P. (2003) *Remote Sensing Geology*. Springer Verlag, New York.

Gutman, G., Brynes, R., Masek, J., et al. (2008) Towards monitoring land-cover and land-use changes at a global scale: the global land survey 2005. *Photogrammetric Engineering and Remote Sensing*, **74**: 6–10.

Haack, B., Bryant, N., and Adams, S. (1987) An assessment of Landsat MSS and TM data for urban and near-urban land-cover digital classification. *Remote Sensing of Environment*, **21**: 201–13.

Haddad, N. M., Bowne, D. R., Cunningham, A., et al. (2003) Corridor use by diverse taxa. *Ecology*, **84**(3): 609–15. doi: 10.1890/0012–9658(2003)084[0609:CUBDT]2.0.CO;2.

Haines-Young, R., and Chopping, M. (1996) Quantifying landscape structure: a review of landscape indices and their application to forested landscapes. *Progress in Physical Geography*, **20**: 418–45.

Hall, F. C. (2001) *Photo Point Monitoring Handbook: Part A-Field Procedures*. Gen. Tech. Rep. PNW-GTR-526. Portland, OR: US Department of Agriculture, Forest Service, Pacific Northwest Research Station, **48**: 2.

Hall-Beyer, M. (2007) The GLCM Tutorial Home Page, Version: 2.10, Department of Geography. University of Calgary, Canada. Accessed at http://www.fp.ucalgary.ca/mhall-bey/tutorial.htm [Last updated February 21, 2007.]

Halpern, B. S., Pyke, C. R., Fox, H. E., et al. (2006) Gaps and Mismatches between Global Conservation Priorities and Spending. *Conservation Biology*, **20**: 56–64.

Hamilton, S. K., Sippel, S. J., and Melack, J. M. (1996) Inundation patterns in the Pantanal wetland of South America determined from passive microwave remote sensing. *Archiv für Hydrobiologie*, **137**: 1–23.

Hamilton, S. K., Sippel, S. J., and Melack, J. M. (2004) Seasonal inundation patterns in two large savanna floodplains of South America: the Llanos de Moxos (Bolivia) and the Llanos del Orinoco (Venezuela and Colombia). *Hydrological Processes*, **18**: 2103–16.

Hammond, D. S. and ter Steege, H. (1998) Propensity for fire in Guianan rainforests. *Conservation Biology*, **12**: 944–47.

Hannah, L., Lovejoy, T. E., and Schneider, S. H. (2005) Biodiversity and climate change in context. In T. E. Lovejoy and L. Hannah, eds. *Climate Change and Biodiversity*, Yale University Press, New Haven, CT and London.

Hansen, A. J., Knight, R. L., Marzluff, J. M., et al. (2005) Effects of exurban development on biodiversity: patterns, mechanisms, and research needs. *Ecological Applications*, **15**(6): 1893–905.

Hansen, M. C., Defries, R. S., Townshend, J. R. G., et al. (2003) Global percent tree cover at a spatial resolution of 500 meters: first results of the MODIS vegetation continuous fields algorithm. *Earth Interactions*, **7**: 1–15.

Hansen, M. C., Stehman, S. V., Potapov, P. V., et al. (2008) Humid tropical forest clearing from 2000 to 2005 quantified by using multitemporal and multiresolution remotely sensed data. *Proceedings of the National Academy of Sciences*, **105**: 9439–44.

Hargis, C. D., Bissonette, J. A., and David, J. L. (1998) The behavior of landscape metrics commonly used in the study of habitat fragmentation. *Landscape Ecology*, **13**(3): 167–86. doi: 10.1023/A:1007965018633.

Harlan, S. L., Brazel, A. J., Jenerette, G. D., et al. (2007) In the shade of affluence: the inequitable distribution of the urban heat island. *Research in Social Problems and Public Policy*, **15**: 173–202.

Harper, G. J., Steininger, M. K., Tucker, C. J., et al. (2007) Fifty years of deforestation and forest fragmentation in Madagascar. *Environmental Conservation*, **34**: 325–33.

Harris, G. M., Russell, G. J., van Aarde, R. I., et al. (2008) Rules of habitat use by elephants Loxodonta africana in southern Africa: insights for regional management. *Oryx*, **42**(1): 66–75.

Harrison, K. L. (2003) Correlation of AVHRR SST with the presence of loggerhead turtles. *Proceedings of the International Geoscience and Remote Sensing Symposium, 2003, IEEE International*, **4**(21–25): 2374–76.

Hashim, M., Watson, A., and Thomas, M. (2004) An approach for correcting inhomogeneous atmospheric effects in remote sensing images. *International Journal of Remote Sensing*, **25**(22): 5131–41.

Hays, G. C., Dray, M., Quaife, T., et al. (2001) Movements of migrating green turtles in relation to AVHRR derived sea surface temperature. *International Journal of Remote Sensing*, **22**: 1403–11.

Heege, T. (2008) Hyperspectral seafloor mapping and direct bathymetry calculation in littoral zones. Encora Coastal Portal. Accessed at http://www.encora.eu/coastalwiki/Hyperspectral_seafloor_mapping_and_direct_bathymetry_calculation_in_littoral_zones. [Modified September 25, 2008.]

Heege, T., and Fischer, J. (2004) Mapping of water constituents in Lake Constance using multi-spectral airborne scanner data and a physically based processing scheme. *Canadian Journal of Remote Sensing*, 30(1): 77–86.

Heege, T., Häse, C., Bogner, A., et al. (2003) Airborne multi-spectral sensing in shallow and deep waters. *Backscatter*, 1: 17–19.

Heilman, G. E., Stritholt, J. R., Slosser, N. C., et al. (2002) Forest fragmentation of the conterminous United States: assessing forest intactness through road density and spatial characteristics. *BioScience*, 52: 411–22.

Henderson, F. M. and Lewis, A. J. (2008) Radar detection of wetland ecosystems: a review. *International Journal of Remote Sensing*, 29: 5809–35.

Henein, K., and Merriam, G. (1990) The elements of connectivity where corridor quality is variable. *Landscape Ecology*, 4: 157–70.

Hensley, S. R., Munjy, R., and Rosen, P. (2001) Interferometric synthetic aperture radar (IFSAR). In D. F. Maune, ed. *Digital Elevation Model Technologies and Applications: The DEM Users Manual*. American Society for Photogrammetry and Remote Sensing, Bethesda, MD.

Hernandez-Stefanoni, J. L., Pineda, J. B., and Valdes-Valadez, G. (2006) Comparing the use of indigenous knowledge with classification and ordination techniques for assessing the species composition and structure of vegetation in a tropical forest. *Environmental Management*, 37: 686–702.

Hijmans, R. J., Cameron, S. E., Parra, J. L., et al. (2005) Very high resolution interpolated climate surfaces for global land areas. *International Journal of Climatology*, 25: 1965–78.

Hilborn, R., and Mangel, M. (1997) *The Ecological Detective*. Princeton University Press, Princeton, NJ.

Hirtz, P. H., Hoffman, H., and Nüesch, D. (1999) Interactive 3D landscape visualization: improved realism through use of remote sensing data and geoinformation. *Computer Graphics International. Proceedings*, 243: 101–08.

Hochberg, E. J. and Atkinson, M. J. (2003) Capabilities of remote sensors to classify coral, algae, and sand as pure and mixed spectra. *Remote Sensing of Environment*, 85: 174–89.

Hochberg, E. J., Atkinson, M. J., and Andréfouët, S. (2003) Spectral reflectance of coral reef bottom-types worldwide and implications for coral reef remote sensing. *Remote Sensing of Environment*, 85: 159–73.

Hochberg, E. J., Apprill, A. M., Atkinson, M. J., et al. (2006) Bio-optical modeling of photosynthetic pigments in corals. *Coral Reefs*, 25: 99–109.

Hockings, M. (2003) Systems for Assessing the Effectiveness of Management in Protected Areas. *BioScience*, 53: 828–32.

Hodgson, M. E. and Bresnahan, P. (2004) Accuracy of airborne lidar-derived elevation: empirical assessment and error budget. *Photogrammetric Engineering and Remote Sensing*, 70: 331–39.

Hoegh-Guldberg, O. (1999) Climate change, coral bleaching and the future of the world's coral reefs. *Marine and Freshwater Research*, 50(8): 839–66.

Hoegh-Guldberg, O., Mumby, P. J., Hooten, A. J., et al. (2007) Coral reefs under rapid climate change and ocean acidification. *Science*, 318(5857): 1737.

Hoekstra, J. M., Boucher, T. M., Ricketts, T. H., et al. (2005) Confronting a biome crisis: global disparities in habitat loss and protection. *Ecology Letters IUCN*, 8: 23–29.

Hofton, M., Dubayah, R., Blair, B., et al. (2006) Validation of SRTM elevations over vegetated and non-vegetated terrain using medium footprint lidar. *Photogrammetric Engineering and Remote Sensing*, 72: 279–85.

Holden, H. and LeDrew, E. (1999) Hyperspectral identification of coral reef features. *International Journal of Remote Sensing*, **20**: 2545–63.

Homer, C., Huang, C., Yang, L., et al. (2004) Development of a 2001 National Landcover Database for the United States. *Photogrammetric Engineering and Remote Sensing*, **70**(7): 829–40.

Hook, S. J., Abbott, E. A., Grove, C., et al. (1999) Use of multispectral thermal infrared data in geological studies. In A. N. Rencz, ed. *Remote Sensing for the Earth Sciences*, 3rd edn. American Society for Photogrammetry and Remote Sensing, Bethesda, MD.

Hope, D., Gries, C., Zhu, W., et al. (2003) Socioeconomics drive urban plant diversity. *Proceedings of the National Academy of Science*, **1000**(15): 8788–92.

Horning, N. and McPhearson, T. (2005) *Viewing Landsat TM Images with Adobe Photoshop*. American Museum of Natural History, Center for Biodiversity and Conservation. Available from http://biodiversityinformatics.amnh.org. [Accessed on December 31, 2008.]

Howarth, P. and Boasson, E. (1983) Landsat digital enhancement for change detection in urban environments. *Remote Sensing of Environment*, **13**: 149–60.

Hu, C., Luerssen, R., Muller-Karger, F. E., et al. (2008) On the remote monitoring of Karenia brevis blooms of the west Florida shelf. *Continental Shelf Research*, **28**: 159–76.

Huang, S. and Siegert, F. (2004) ENVISAT multisensor data for fire monitoring and impact assessment. *International Journal of Remote Sensing*, **25**: 4411–16.

Huberty, C. J. (1994) *Applied Discriminant Analysis*. Wiley Interscience, New York.

Hulbert, I., and French, J. (2001) The accuracy of GPS for wildlife telemetry and habitat mapping. *Ecology*, **38**: 869–78.

Huete, A. (2004) Remote sensing of soils and soil processes. In S. L. Ustin, ed. *Remote Sensing for Natural Resource Management and Environmental Monitoring*, 3rd edn. American Society for Photogrammetry and Remote Sensing, Bethesda, MD.

Huete, A., Liu, H. Q., Batchily, K., et al. (1997) A comparison of vegetation indices over a global set of TM images for EOS-MODIS. *Remote Sensing of Environment*, **59**(3): 440–51.

Huete, A., Didan, K., Miura, T., et al. (2002) Overview of the radiometric and biophysical performance of the MODIS vegetation indices. *Remote Sensing of Environment*, **83**: 195–213.

Hughes, T. P., Baird, A. H., Bellwood, D. R., et al. (2003) Climate change, human impacts, and the resilience of coral reefs. *Science*, **301**(5635): 929.

Hurley, M. M., Sterling, E. J., Lunde, D., et al. (In Prep.) High levels of novel vertebrate species diversity in Vietnam: implications for conservation.

Hutchinson, M. F. (1989) A new method for gridding elevation and streamline data with automatic removal of pits. *Journal of Hydrology*, **106**: 211–32.

Hyrenbach, K. D., Forney, K. A., and Dayton, P. K. (2001) Marine protected areas and ocean basin management. *Aquatic Conservation, Marine Freshwater Ecosystems*, **10**: 437–58.

Imhoff, M. L. (1995) Radar backscatter and biomass saturation: ramifications for global biomass inventory. *IEEE Transaction on Geoscience and Remote Sensing*, **33**: 511–18.

Imhoff, M. L., Lawrence, W. T., Stutzer, D. C., et al. (1997) A technique for using composite DMSP-OLS "city lights" satellite data to map urban area. *Remote Sensing of Environment*, **61**: 361–70.

Islam, A., Gao, J., Ahmad, W., et al. (2004) A composite DOP approach to excluding bottom reflectance in mapping water parameters of shallow coastal zones from TM imagery. *Remote Sensing of Environment*, **92**: 40–51.

JAXA Earth Observation Research Center (2009) *Soil Moisture (Koike V5.11)*. Accessed at http://sharaku.eorc.jaxa.jp/cgi-bin/adeos2/amsr/l3brws/l3brws.cgi?lang=e&sat=P1&ad=

A&prd=SM0_Koi&ver=new&map=E0&y=2008&m=10&d=30&ny=2008&nm=10
&nd=30. [Modified January 26, 2009.]

Jayachandran, S. (2005) *Air Quality and Infant Mortality During Indonesia's Massive Wildfires in 1997.* UCLA Economics Online Papers, 358. Accessed on the web November 27, 2007 at: http://ideas.repec.org/p/cla/uclaol/358.html#provider.

Jenerette, G. D., Harlan, S. L., Brazel, A., et al. (2007) Regional relationships between surface temperature, vegetation, and human settlement in a rapidly urbanizing ecosystem. *Landscape Ecology*, **22**: 353–65.

Jennings, M. D. (2000) Gap analysis: concepts, methods, and recent results. *Landscape Ecology*, **15**: 5–20.

Jensen, J. R. (1983) Urban/suburban land use analysis. In R. N. Colwell, ed. *Manual of Remote Sensing*, 2nd edn., pp. 1571–666. American Society of Photogrammetry, Falls Church, VA.

Jensen, J. R. (1996) *Introductory Image Processing: A Remote Sensing Perspective.* 2nd edn. Prentice-Hall, Upper Saddle River, NJ.

Jensen, J. R. (2005) Introductory digital image processing: a remote sensing perspective. Pearson Prentice Hall, Upper Saddle River, NJ.7458, 544.

Jensen, J. R., Estes, J. E., and Tinney, L. (1980) Remote sensing techniques for kelp surveys. *Photogrammetric Engineering and Remote Sensing*, **46**: 743–56.

Jeong Chang, S. (2003) Modelling the accuracy of image data reprojection. *International Journal of Remote Sensing*, **24**: 2309–21.

Jerlov, N. G. (1964) Optical classification of ocean water. In J. E. Tyler, ed. *Physical Aspects of Light in the Sea*, pp. 45–49. University of Hawaii Press, Honolulu, Hawaii.

Jha, C. S., Goparaju, L., Tripathi, A., et al. (2005) Forest fragmentation and its impact on species diversity: an analysis using remote sensing and GIS. *Biodiversity and Conservation*, **14**: 1681–98.

Jin, M. (2004) Analysis of land skin temperature using AVHRR observations. *Bulletin of the American Meteorological Society*, **85**: 587–600.

Johnson, C., Heard, D., and Parker, K. (2002) Expectations and realities of GPS animal location collars: results of three years in the field. *Wildlife Biology*, **8**: 153–59.

Johnson, M. L., and Gaines, M. S. (1985) Selective basis for emigration of the prairie vole, Microtuso chrogaster: open field experiment. *Journal of Animal Ecology*, **54**: 399–410.

Joyce, K. E. and Phinn, S. R. (2001) Optimal spatial resolution for coral reef mapping. *Proceedings of the International Geoscience and Remote Sensing Symposium*, 2001, *IEEE International*, 619–21.

Jupp, D. L. B. (1988) Background and extensions to depth of penetration (DOP) mapping in shallow coastal waters. *Proceedings of the Symposium on Remote Sensing of the Coastal Zone*, Gold Coast, Queensland, **IV.2**, 1–19.

Justice, C., Giglio, L., Boschetti, L., et al. (2006) *Algorithm Technical Background Document, MODIS Fire Products Version 2.3.* Accessed on the Web on August 3, 2007 at: http://modis.gsfc.nasa.gov/data/atbd/atbd_mod14.pdf.

Kairo, J. G., Kivyatu, B., and Koedam, N. (2002) Application of remote sensing and GIS in the management of mangrove forests within and adjacent to Kiunga Marine Protected Area. *Lamu, Kenya. Environment, Development and Sustainability*, **4**: 153–66.

Kallio, K., Koponen, S., and Pulliainen, J. (2003) Feasibility of airborne imaging spectrometry for lake monitoring— a case study of spatial chlorophyll a distribution in two mesoeutrophic lakes. *International Journal of Remote Sensing*, **24**: 3771–790.

Kam, T. S. (1995) Integrating GIS and remote sensing techniques for urban land-cover and land-use analysis. *Geocarto International*, **10**(1): 39–48.

Kareiva, P. (1990) Population dynamics in spatially complex environments: theory and data. *Philosophical Transactions of The Royal Society B*, **330**: 175–90.

Karnieli, A. (2003) Natural vegetation phenology assessment by ground spectral measurements in two semi-arid environments. *International Journal of Biometeorology*, 47(4): 179–87.

Károlyi, G., and Grebogi, C. (2007) Chaotic advection and fractality: applications in oceanography. Oceans 2007—Europe, 18–21 June, 1–5.

Kasischke, E., Melack, J., and Dobson, M. (1997) The use of radar for ecological applications: a review. *Remote Sensing of Environment*, **59**: 141–56.

Kaufman, Y. J., Tanre, D., and Boucher, O. (2002) A satellite view of aerosols in the climate system. *Nature*, **419**: 215–23.

Kellndorfer, J., Walker, W., Pierce, L., et al. (2004) Vegetation height estimation from Shuttle Radar Topography Mission and National Elevation Datasets. *Remote Sensing of Environment*, **93**(3): 339–58.

Kerr, J. T., and Cihlar, J. (2003) Land use and cover with intensity of agriculture for Canada from satellite and census data. Global Ecology and Biogeography, **12**: 161.

Key, C. H. and Benson, N. C. (2005) Landscape assessment: ground measure of severity, the Composite Burn Index; and remote sensing of severity, the Normalized Burn Ratio. In D. C. Lutes, R. E. Keane, J. F. Caratti, et al., eds. 2005. *FIREMON: Fire Effects Monitoring and Inventory System*, USDA Forest Service, Rocky Mountain Research Station, Ogden, UT. Gen. Tech. Rep. RMRS-GTR-164-CD: LA1–51. Accessed on the Web on January 4, 2008 at: http://frames.nbii.gov/projects/firemon/FIREMON_LandscapeAssessment.pdf.

Khorram, S., Brockhaus, J. A., Cheshire, H. M., et al. (1987) Comparson of Landsat MSS and TM data for urban land-use classification. *IEEE Transactions on Geoscience and Remote Sensing, GE-25(2)*, 238–43.

Kiage, L. M., Walker, N. D., Balasubramanian, S., et al. (2005) Applications of Radarsat-1 synthetic aperture radar imagery to assess hurricane-related flooding of coastal Louisiana. *International Journal of Remote Sensing*, **26**: 5359–80.

Kidder, S. Q. and Vonder Haar, T. H. (1995) *Satellite Meteorology: An Introduction*. Academic Press, San Diego, CA.

Kidwell, K. B. (1998) NOAA *Polar Orbiter Data User's Guide*. U.S. Department of Commerce, National Oceanic and Atmospheric Administration, National Environmental Satellite, Data, and Information Service, National Climatic Data Center. Accessed on the Web at http://www2.ncdc.noaa.gov/docs/podug/index.htm.

Kindlmann, P., and Burel, F. (2008) Connectivity measures: a review. *Landscape Ecology*, **23**: 879–90.

King, M. D., Kaufman, Y. J., Tanre, D., et al. (1999) Remote sensing of tropospheric aerosols from space: past, present, and future. *Bulletin of the American Meteorological Society*, **80**: 2229–59.

Kinnaird, M. F. and O'Brien, T. G. (1998) Ecological effects of wildfire on lowland rainforest in Sumatra. *Conservation Biology*, **12**: 954–56.

Kinzig, A. P., Warren, P. S., Martin, C., et al. (2005) The effects of socioeconomic and cultural characteristics on urban patterns of biodiversity. *Ecology and Society*, **10**: 23.

Knudby, A., LeDrew, E., Newman, C., et al. (2007) Progress in the use of remote sensing for coral reef biodiversity studies. *Progress in Physical Geography*, **31**: 421–34.

Kobayashi, D. R. and Polovina, J. J. (2006) Simulated seasonal and interannual variability in larval transport and oceanography in the Northwestern Hawaiian Islands using satellite remotely sensed data and computer modeling. *Atoll Research Bulletin*, **543**: 365–90.

Kogan, F. N. (2001) Operational Space Technology for Global Vegetation Assessment. *Bulletin of the American Meteorological Society*, **82**: 1949–64.

Koh, L. P., and Wilcove, D. S. (2008) Is oil palm agriculture really destroying tropical biodiversity? *Conservation Letters*, **1**: 60–64.

Kokko, H. and Lopez-Sepulcre, A. (2006) From individual dispersal to species ranges: perspectives for a changing world. *Science*, **313**: 789–91.

Koper, N., Schmiegelow, F. K. A., and Merrill, E. H. (2007) Residuals cannot distinguish between ecological effects of habitat amount and fragmentation: implications for the debate. *Landscape Ecology*, **22**: 811–20.

Koren, I., Kaufman, Y. J., Remer, L. A., et al. (2004) Measurement of the effect of Amazon smoke on inhibition of cloud formation. *Science*, **303**: 1342–45.

Kost, J., Verdin, K., Worstell, B., et al. (2002) *Methods and Tools for the Development of Hydrologically Conditioned Elevation Data and Derivatives for National Applications.* 2nd Annual Conference on Watershed Modeling. Las Vegas, NV.

Kovacs, J. M., Wang, J., and Flores-Verdugo, F. (2005) Mapping mangrove leaf area index at the species level using IKONOS and LAI-2000 sensors for the Agua Brava Lagoon, Mexican Pacific. *Estuarine, Coastal and Shelf Science*, **62**(1–2): 377–84.

Král, K., and Pavliš, J. (2006) The first detailed land cover map of Socotra Island by Landsat/ETM + data. *International Journal of Remote Sensing*, **27**(15): 3239–50.

Kramer-Schadt, S., Revilla, E. l. o. y., Wiegand, T., et al. (2004) Fragmented landscapes, road mortality and patch connectivity: modelling influences on the dispersal of Eurasian lynx. *Journal of Applied Ecology*, **41**(4): 711–23. doi: doi:10.1111/j.0021–8901.2004.00933.x.

Kratzer, S., Håkansson, B., and Sahlin, C. (2003) Assessing secchi and photic zone depth in the Baltic Sea from satellite data. *Ambio*, **32**: 577–85.

Kremen, C., Razafimahatratra, V., Guillery, R. P., et al. (1999) Designing the Masoala National Park in Madagascar Based on Biological and Socioeconomic Data. *Conservation Biology*, **13**: 1055–68.

Kudela, R., Pitcher, G., Probyn, T., et al. (2005) Harmful algal blooms in coastal upwelling systems. *Oceanography*, **18**: 184–97.

Lambin, E. F., Geist, H. J., and Lepers, E. (2003) Dynamics of land use and land cover change in tropical regions. *Annual Review Environmental Resources*, **28**: 205–41.

Langenberg, H. (2005) Inside information. *Nature*, **437**: 468–69.

Laporte, N. T., Walker, W., Stabach, J. A., et al. (2008) Monitoring forest-Savanna dynamics in Kibale National Park with satellite imagery (1989–2003): implications for the management of wildlife habitat. In R. Wrangham and E. Ross, eds. *Science and Conservation in African Forests: The Benefits of Long-Term Research*, pp. 38–50. Cambridge University Press, Cambridge.

LASP (2008) *SORCE: Solar Radiation and Climate Experiment.* University of Colorado Laboratory for Atmospheric and Space Physics (LASP). Accessed on the Web at http://lasp.colorado.edu/sorce/index.htm.

Lathrop, R., Tulloch, D., and Hatfield, C. (2007) Consequences of land use change in the New York–New Jersey highlands, USA: landscape indicators of forest and watershed integrity. *Landscape and Urban Planning*, **79**(2): 150–59.

Laurance, W. F. and Williamson, G. B. (2001) Positive feedbacks among forest fragmentation, drought, and climate change in the Amazon. *Conservation Biology*, **15**: 1529–35.

Lausch, A., and Herzog, F. (2002) Applicability of landscape metrics for the monitoring of landscape change, issues of scale, resolution and interpretability. *Ecological Indicators*, **2**: 3–15.

Lawton, R. O., Nair, U. S., Pielke, R. A., et al. (2001) Climatic impact of tropical lowland deforestation on nearby montane cloud forests. *Science*, **294**: 584–87.

Le Treut, H., Somerville, R., Cubasch, U., et al. (2007) Historical Overview of Climate Change. In S. Solomon, D. Qin, M. Manning, et al. eds. *Climate Change 2007: The Physical Science Basis. Contribution of Working Group I to the Fourth Assessment Report of the Intergovernmental Panel on Climate Change*, Cambridge University Press, Cambridge and New York.

Lee, Z. and Carder, K. L. (2004) Absorption spectrum of phytoplankton pigments derived from hyperspectral remote-sensing reflectance. *Remote Sensing of Environment*, **89**: 361–68.

Lee, Z., Carder, K. L., Mobley, C. D., et al. (1998) Hyperspectral remote sensing for shallow waters: 1. A semianalytical model. *Applied Optics*, **37**: 6329–38.

Lee, Z., Carder, K. L., Mobley, C. D., et al. (1999) Hyperspectral remote sensing for shallow waters: 2. Deriving bottom depths and water properties by optimization. *Applied Optics*, **38**: 3831–43.

Lee, Z., Carder, K. L., and Arnone, R. A. (2002) Deriving inherent optical properties from water color, a multiband quasi-analytical algorithm for optically deep waters. *Applied Optics*, **41**: 5755–72.

Lees, A. C., and Peres, C. A. (2008) Conservation value of Remnant Riparian Forest Corridors of varying Quality for Amazon Birds and Mammals. *Conservation Biology*, **22**: 439–49.

Lefsky, M. A., Cohen, W. B., Parker, G. G., et al. (2002) Lidar remote sensing for ecosystem studies. *BioScience*, **52**(1): 19–30.

Lehner, B., Verdin, K., and Jarvis, A. (2006) *HydroSHEDS Technical Documentation: Version 1.0.* World Wildlife Fund US, Washington, DC.

Lesser, M. P. and Mobley, C. D. (2007) Bathymetry, water optical properties, and benthic classification of coral reefs using hyperspectral remote sensing imagery. *Coral Reefs*, **26**: 819–29.

Lewis, W. M., Hamilton, S. K., Lasi, M. A., et al. (2000) Ecological Determinism on the Orinoco Floodplain. *BioScience*, **50**: 681–92.

Liang, S., Fang, H., Chen, M., et al. (2002) Validating MODIS land surface reflectance and albedo products- methods and preliminary results. *Remote Sensing of Environment*, **83**(1): 149–62.

Liang, S., Fang, H., Hoogenboom, G., et al. (2004) Estimation of crop yield at the regional scale from Modis observations. *International Geoscience and Remote Sensing Symposium Proceedings*, **3**: 1625–62.

Lieng, E., Schuler, D. V., Kastdalen, L., et al. (2005) *Classification of Land Cover Using Decision Trees and Multiple Reference Data Sources.* 31st International Symposium on Remote Sensing of Environment in Saint Petersburg, Russia, June 20–24, 2005. Accessed on the web at: http://www.isprs.org/publications/related/ISRSE/html/papers/629.pdf.

Lillesand, T. M. and Kiefer, R. W. (1994) Remote Sensing and Image Interpretation. Wiley, New York.

Liu, G., Skirving, W., and Strong, A. E. (2003) Remote sensing of sea surface temperature during 2002 Barrier Reef coral bleaching. *Eos, Transactions of the American Geophysical Union*, **84**(15): 137–44.

Liu, G., Allen, J., Lu, K., et al. (2005) *Using a Self-Built Hyperspectral Library for Identifying and Mapping the Invasive Species Purple Loosestrife.* Proceedings of PECORA 16 "Global Priorities in Land Remote Sensing" October 23–27, 2005, Sioux Falls, SD, 10.

Liu, J., Linderman, M., Ouyang, Z., et al. (2001) Ecological degradation in protected areas: the case of Wolong Nature Reserve for giant pandas. *Science*, **292**: 98–101.

Liu, J., Dietz, T., Carpenter, S. R., et al. (2007) Complexity of coupled human and natural systems. *Science*, **317**(5844): 1513–16.

Liu, W. and Wu, E. Y. (2005) Comparison of non-linear mixture models: sub-pixel classification. *Remote Sensing of Environment*, **94**: 145–54.

Liverman, D., Moran, E. F., Rindfuss, R. R., et al., eds. (1998) *People and Pixels: Linking Remote Sensing and Social Science*. National Academy Press, Washington, DC.

Lohman, D. J., Bickford, D., and Sodhi, N. S. (2007) The burning issue. *Science*, **316**: 376.

Lopez, A. S., San-Miguel-Ayanz, J., and Burgan, R. E. (2002) Integration of satellite sensor data, fuel type maps and meteorological observations for evaluation of forest fire risk at the pan-European scale. *International Journal of Remote Sensing*, **23**: 2713–19.

Louzao, M., Hyrenbach, K. D., Arcos, J. M., et al. (2006) Oceanographic habitat of an endangered Mediterranean Procellariiform: implications for marine protected areas. *Ecological Applications*, **16**: 1683–95.

Loveland, T. R., Merchant, J. W., Brown, J. F., et al. (1995) Seasonal land-cover regions of the United States. *Association Of American Geographers*, **85**: 339.

Loveland, T. R., Reed, B. C., Brown, J. F., et al. (2000) Development of a global land cover characteristics database and IGBP DISCover from 1-km AVHRR data. *International Journal of Remote Sensing*, **21**: 1303–30.

Lowman, P. D., Jr. (1999) Landsat and Apollo: the forgotten legacy. *Photogrammetric Engineering and Remote Sensing*, **65**: 1143–47.

Lu, D. (2006) The potential and challenge of remote sensing-based biomass estimation. *International Journal of Remote Sensing*, **27**(7): 1297–328.

Lu, D. and Weng, Q. (2007) A survey of image classification methods and techniques for improving classification performance. *International Journal of Remote Sensing*, **28**(5): 823–70.

Lu, D., Mausel, P., Brondízio, E., et al. (2004) Change detection techniques. *International Journal of Remote Sensing*, **25**(12): 2365–401.

Lulla, K. P., Dessinov, L., Evans, C. A., et al. eds. (2000) *Dynamic Earth Environments: Remote Sensing Observations from Shuttle–Mir Sissions*. Wiley, New York.

Lyon, L. J. (1983) Road Density Models Describing Habitat Effectiveness for Elk. *Journal of Forestry*, **81**: 592–613.

Lyzenga, D. R. (1978) Passive remote sensing techniques for mapping water depth and bottom features. *Applied Optics*, **17**: 379–83.

Lyzenga, D. R. (1981) Remote sensing of bottom reflectance and water attenuation parameters in shallow water using aircraft and Landsat data. *International Journal of Remote Sensing*, **2**: 71–82.

MacArthur, R. H., and Wilson, E. O. (1967) *The Theory of Island Biogeography*. Monographs in Population Ecology. Princeton University Press, Princeton, NJ.

Madin, I., Watzig, R., Percy, D., et al. (2009) *Pilot LIDAR Project - Portland Metro Area*. Oregon Department of Geology and Mineral Industries, Portland, OR. Accessed at http://lidar.geos.pdx.edu. [Viewed January 22, 2009.]

Maina, J., Venus, V., McClanahan, T. R., et al. (2008) Modelling susceptibility of coral reefs to environmental stress using remote sensing data and GIS models. *Ecological Modelling*, **212**(3): 180–99.

Mandelbrot, B. (1967) The Fractal Geometry of Nature. *Science*, **156**: 636–42.

Mangel, M. (2006) *The Theoretical Biologist's Toolbox: Quantitative Methods for Ecology and Evolutionary Biology*. Cambridge University Press, Cambridge.

Marcinek, D., Blackwell, S., Dewar, H., et al. (2001) Depth and muscle temperature of Pacific bluefin tuna examined with acoustic and pop-up satellite archival tags. *Marine Biology*, **138**: 869–85.

Maritorena, S., Morel, A., and Gentili, B. (1994) Diffuse reflectance of oceanic shallow waters, influence of water depth and bottom albedo. *Limnology and Oceanography*, **39**(7): 1689–703.

Maritorena, S., Siegel, D. A., and Peterson, A. R. (2002) Optimization of a semianalytical ocean color model for global-scale applications. *Applied Optics-LP*, **41**: 2705–14.

Markham, B., Storey, J. C., Williams, D. L., et al. (2004) Landsat sensor performance: history and current status. *Geoscience and Remote Sensing, IEEE Transactions on*, **42**(12): 2691–94.

Marmontel, M., Humphrey, S. R., and O'Shea, T. J. (1997) Population viability analysis of the Florida Manatee (*Trichechus manatus latirostris*), 1976–1991. *Conservation Biology*, **11**(2): 467–81.

Martin, L. R. G. and Howarth, P. J. (1989) Change detection accuracy assessment using SPOT multispectral imagery of the rural-urban fringe. *Remote Sensing of Environment*, **30**: 55–66.

Marzluff, J. M. (2005) Island biogeography for an urbanizing world: how extinction and colonization may determine biological diversity in human-dominated landscapes. *Urban Ecosystems*, **8**: 157–77.

Mas, J. (1999) Monitoring land-cover changes: a comparison of change detection techniques. *International Journal of Remote Sensing*, **20**(1): 139–52.

Mas, J. (2003) An artificial neural networks approach to map land use/cover using Landsat imagery and ancillary data. In *Geoscience and Remote Sensing Symposium, 2003. IGARSS '03. Proceedings. 2003 IEEE International*, pp. 3498–3500 vol.6.

Mas, J. F. and Flores, J. J. (2008) The application of artificial neural networks to the analysis of remotely sensed data. *International Journal of Remote Sensing*, **29**(3): 617.

Mayes, J. and Hughes, K. (2004) *Understanding Weather: A Visual Approach*. Arnold, London.

McCarthy, M. A. (2007) *Bayesian Methods for Ecology*. Cambridge University Press, Cambridge.

McClain, C., Hooker, S., Feldman, G., et al. (2006) Satellite data for ocean biology, biogeochemistry, and climate research. *Eos, Transactions of the American Geophysical Union*, **87**(34): 337.

McGarigal, K. (2002) Landscape pattern metrics. In A. H. El-Shaarawi and W. W. Piegorsch, eds. *Encyclopedia of Environmetrics*, Vol. 2, pp. 1135–42. Wiley, Sussex, UK.

McGarigal, K. and Marks, B. J. (1995) *FRAGSTATS: Spatial Pattern Analysis Program for Quantifying Landscape Structure*. USDA Forest Service.

McGarigal, K., Cushman, S. A., Neel, M. C., et al. (2002) *FRAGSTATS: Spatial Pattern Analysis Program for Categorical Maps*. University of Massachusetts, Amherst, MA. Available at the following web site, www.umass.edu/landeco/research/fragstats/fragstats.html. viewed 03 January 2009.

McPhearson, P. T., and Wallace, O. C. (2008) *Remote Sensing Applications to Biodiversity Conservation*. Available at: http://ncep.amnh.org.

Meehl, G. A., Stocker, T. F., Collins, W. D., et al. (2007) Global Climate Projections. In S. Solomon, D. Qin, M. Manning, et al. eds. *Climate Change 2007: The Physical Science Basis. Contribution of Working Group I to the Fourth Assessment Report of the Intergovernmental Panel on Climate Change*, Cambridge University Press, Cambridge and New York.

Meggers, B. J. (1994) Archeological evidence for the impact of mega-Nino events on Amazonia during the past two millennia. *Climatic Change*, **28**: 321–38.

Meinel, G. and Neubert, M. (2004) *A Comparison of Segmentation Programs for High Resolution Remote Sensing Data.* XXth Congress of the International Society for Photogrammetry and Remote Sensing, Istanbul, Turkey.

Menon, S. and Bawa, K. S. (1997) Applications of geographic information systems, remote-sensing, and a landscape ecology approach to biodiversity conservation in the Western Ghats. *Current Science,* 73(2): 134–45.

Messina, J. P., Walsh, S. J., Menab, C. F., et al. (2006) Land tenure and deforestation patterns in the Ecuadorian Amazon: conflicts in land conservation in frontier settings. *Applied Geography,* 26: 113–28.

Meyfroidt, P., and Lambin, F. (2008) Forest transition in Vietnam and its environmental impacts. *Global Change Biology,* 14: 1–18.

Milbert, D. and Smith, D. A. (1996) Converting GPS height into NAVD88 elevation with the GEOID96 GEOID height model. GIS/LIS '96. American Society for Photogrammetry and Remote Sensing, Denver, CO.

Millington, A. C., Velez-Liendo, X. M., and Bradley, A. V. (2003) Scale dependence in multitemporal mapping of forest fragmentation in Bolivia: implications for explaining temporal trends in landscape ecology and applications to biodiversity conservation. *ISPRS Journal of Photogrammetry and Remote Sensing,* 57: 289–99.

Mishra, D., Narumalani, S., Rundquist, D., et al. (2006) Benthic habitat mapping in tropical marine environments using QuickBird multispectral data. *Photograpmmetric Engineering and Remote Sensing,* 72: 1037–48.

Moeller, M. S. (2004) Monitoring long term transition processes of a metropolitan area with remote sensing. *Proceedings of the International Geoscience and Remote Sensing Symposium, IEEE International,* 5: 3398–401.

Moeller, M. S. (2005) Remote sensing for the monitoring of urban growth patterns. *Proceedings of the 3rd International Symposium Remote Sensing and Data Fusion Over Urban Areas and 5th International Symposium Remote Sensing of Urban Areas, ISPRS, International Archives of Photogrammetry, Remote Sensing and Spatial Information Sciences,* 36: Part 8/ W27, 6.

Moilanen, A., and Hanski, I. (2001) On the use of connectivity measures in spatial ecology. *Oikos,* 95: 147–51.

Moilanen, A. and Nieminen, M. (2002) Simple connectivity measures in spatial ecology. *Ecology,* 83: 1131–45.

Møller-Jensen, L. (1990) Knowledge-based classification of an urban area using texture and context information in Landsat-TM imagery. *Photogrammetric Engineering and Remote Sensing,* 56: 889–904.

Measuring Vegetation Health Project (2007) Available at http://mvh.sr.unh.edu/ [Accessed December 5, 2007.]

Montané, J. M. and Torres, R. (2006) Accuracy assessment of lidar saltmarsh topographic data using RTK GPS. *Photogrammetric Engineering and Remote Sensing,* 72: 961–67.

Moore, L. J. (2000) Shoreline mapping techniques. *Journal of Coastal Research,* 16(1): 111–24.

Mora, C., Andrèfouët, S., Costello, M. J., et al. (2006) Coral reefs and the global network of marine protected areas. *Science,* 312(5781): 1750–51.

Moran, M. S., Mcelroy, S., Watts, J. M., et al. (2006) Radar remote sensing for estimation of surface soil moisture at the watershed scale. In C. W. Richardson, A. S. Baez-Gonzalez, and M. Tiscareno, eds. *Modeling and Remote Sensing Applied in Agriculture (US and Mexico).* INIFAP, Aquascalientes, Mexico.

Morris, J., Porter, D., Neet, M., et al. (2005) Integrating LIDAR elevation data, multi-spectral imagery and neural network modeling for marsh characterization. *International Journal of Remote Sensing*, **26**: 5221–34.

Morrison, M. L., and Hall, L. S. (2002) Standard terminology: toward a common language to advance ecological understanding and application. In J. M. Scott, P. J. Heglund, M. L. Morrison, et al., eds. *Predicting Species Occurrences: Issues of Accuracy and Scale*, pp. 43–52. Island Press, Washington, DC.

Morton, D. C., Defries, R. S., Shimabukuro, Y. E., et al. (2005) Rapid assessment of annual deforestation in the Brazilian Amazon using MODIS data. *Earth Interactions*, **9**: 1–22.

Mota, B. W., Pereira, J. M. C., Oom, D., et al. (2006) Screening the ESA ATSR-2 World Fire Atlas (1997–2002). *Atmospheric Chemistry and Physics*, **6**: 1409–24.

Mottram, G. N., Wooster, M., Balzter, H., et al. (2005) *The Use of MODIS-Derived Fire Radiative Power to Characterise Siberian Boreal Forest Fires*. 31st International Symposium on Remote Sensing of Environment in Saint Petersburg, Russia, June 20–24, 2005. Accessed on the web at: http://www.isprs.org/publications/related/ISRSE/html/papers/681.pdf.

Mumby, P. J., Green, E. P., Edwards, A. J., et al. (1997) Measurement of seagrass standing crop using satellite and digital airborne remote sensing. *Marine Ecology Progress Series*, **159**: 51–60.

Mumby, P. J., Green, E. P., Clark, C. D., et al. (1998) Benefits of water column correction and contextual editing for mapping coral reefs. *International Journal of Remote Sensing*, **19**: 203 210.

Mumby, P. J., Skirving, W., Strong, A. E., et al. (2004) Remote sensing of coral reefs and their physical environment. *Marine Pollution Bulletin*, **48**: 219–28.

Muñoz, J., Felicisimo, A. M., Cabezas, F., et al. (2004) Wind as a long-distance dispersal vehicle in the southern hemisphere. *Science*, **304**: 1144–47.

Murphy, D. D. (1988) Challenges to biological diversity in urban areas. In E. O. Wilson, ed. *Biodiversity*, pp. 71–76. National Academy Press, Washington, DC.

Myers, N., Mittermeier, R. A., Mittermeier, C. G., et al. (2000) Biodiversity hotspots for conservation priorities. *Nature*, **403**: 853–58.

Myneni, R. B., Keeling, C. D., Tucker, C. J., et al. (1997) Increased plant growth in the northern high latitudes from 1981 to 1991. *Nature*, **386**: 698–702.

Nagendra, H., Pareeth, S., and Ghate, R. (2006) People within parks—forest villages, land-cover change and landscape fragmentation in the Tadoba Andhari Tiger Reserve, India. *Applied Geography*, **26**: 96–112.

Nagendra, H., Pareeth, S., Sharma, B., et al. (2008) Forest fragmentation and regrowth in an institutional mosaic of community, government and private ownership in Nepal. *Landscape Ecology*, **23**: 41–54.

Nair, U. S., Lawton, R. O., Welch, R. M., et al. (2003) Impact of land use on Costa Rican tropical montane cloud forests: sensitivity of cumulus cloud field characteristics to lowland deforestation. *Journal of Geophysical Research*, **108**(D7): 4206.

NASA (1983) *Land-Related Global Habitability Science Issues*. NASA Technical Memorandum 85841. NASA Office of Space Science and Applications, Washington, DC.

NASA (2005a) *Aerosols: More Than Meets the Eye*. NASA Facts. FS-2005–9–072-GSFC. Accessible on the Web at http://eospso.gsfc.nasa.gov/ftp_docs/NASA-Facts-Aerosols.pdf.

NASA (2005b) NASA—*Satellite Data to Track Wildlife: Elephants in Space*. Accessed on the web on May 1, 2008 at: http://www.nasa.gov/vision/earth/lookingatearth/elephants_space.html.

NASA (2008a) *MODIS Atmosphere page*. Accessed on the Web at http://modis-atmos.gsfc.nasa.gov/index.html.

NASA (2008b) *AERONET: Aerosol Robotic Network page.* Accessed at http://aeronet.gsfc.nasa. gov/new_web/index.html.

NASA (2008c) *The Micro Pulse Lidar Network: MPLNET page.* Accessed at http://mplnet. gsfc.nasa.gov/.

NASA (2008d) *MODIS Data Product Non-Technical Description - MOD 05 page.* Accessed at http://modis.gsfc.nasa.gov/data/dataprod/nontech/MOD05.php.

NASA (2008e) *Winds: Measuring Ocean Winds from Space.* Accessed at http://winds.jpl.nasa. gov/missions/quikscat/index.cfm and at http://winds.jpl.nasa.gov/aboutScat/index.cfm.

NASA (2008f) *Ocean Color Image Gallery.* Accessed at http://oceancolor.gsfc.nasa.gov/cgi/ image_archive.cgi?c=ALL. [Modified November 10, 2008.]

NASA Goddard Institute for Space Studies International Satellite Cloud Climatology Project (2006) *Cloud Analysis - Part 7: Cloud Types and Layer Structure.* Accessed at http://isccp. giss.nasa.gov/climanal7.html. [Modified June 2, 2006.]

NASA Goddard Institute for Space Studies International Satellite Cloud Climatology Project (2007) *ISCCP D2 Monthly Means and Climatology.* Accessed at http://isccp.giss.nasa.gov/ products/browsed2.html. [Modified August 22, 2007.]

NASA Goddard Institute for Space Studies (2008) *GISS Surface Temperature Analysis.* Accessed at http://data.giss.nasa.gov/gistemp/.

NASA Goddard Space Flight Center (2009) *TRMM Tropical Rainfall Measuring Mission.* Accessed at http://trmm.gsfc.nasa.gov/trmm_rain/Events/thirty_day.html. [Modified January 27, 2009.]

NASA Goddard Space Flight Center Climate and Radiation Branch (2009) *MODIS View of the Global Aerosol System and 2007 Anomalies.* Accessed at http://climate.gsfc.nasa.gov/ viewImage.php?id=230. [Modified January 27, 2009.]

NASA Goddard Space Flight Center GOES Project (2009) *GOES Project Science.* Accessed at http://goes.gsfc.nasa.gov/goeseast-lzw/east_coast/. [Modified January 28, 2009.]

NASA Jet Propulsion Laboratory (1999) *Photojournal—PIA02455: SeaWinds Global Coverage with Detail of Hurricane Floyd.* Accessed at http://photojournal.jpl.nasa.gov/catalog/ PIA02455. [Modified September 13, 1999.]

NASA Ocean Color (2009) *Ocean Color Web, NASA Goddard Space Flight Center.* Accessed at http://oceancolor.gsfc.nasa.gov. [Last Updated January 15, 2009.]

Nathan, R. (2006) Long-distance dispersal of plants. *Science*, **313**: 786–88.

Nathan, R., Katul, G. G., Horn, H. S., et al. (2002) Mechanisms of long-distance dispersal of seeds by wind. *Nature*, **418**: 409–13.

Nathan, R., Sapir, N., Trakhtenbrot, A., et al. (2005) Long-distance biological transport processes through the air: can nature's complexity be unfolded in silico? *Diversity and Distributions*, **11**: 131–37.

National Research Council (Committee on Floodplain Mapping Technologies, Board on Earth Sciences and Resources, Division on Earth and Life Studies) (2007) *Elevation Data for Floodplain Mapping.* The National Academies Press, Washington, DC.

Nemani, R. R. and Running, S. W. (1989) Estimation of regional surface resistance to evapotranspiration from NDVI and thermal-IR AVHRR data. *Journal of Applied Meteorology*, **28**: 276–84.

Nemani, R. R., Keeling, C. D., Hashimoto, H., et al. (2003) Climate-driven increases in global terrestrial net primary production from 1982 to 1999. *Science*, **300**: 1560–63.

Nepstad, D. C., Verissimo, A., Alencar, A., et al. (1999) Large-scale impoverishment of Amazonian forests by logging and fire. *Nature*, **398**: 505–08.

Netzband, M., Stefanov, W. L., and Redman, C. eds. (2007) *Applied Remote Sensing for Urban Planning, Governance and Sustainability.* Springer-Verlag, Heidelberg.

Nieto, K., Yanez, E., Silva, C., et al. (2001) *Proceedings of the International Geoscience and Remote Sensing Symposium, 2001. IEEE International*, 7: 2985–87.

NIMA (1997) *Department of Defense World Geodetic System 1984: Its Definition and Relationships with Local Geodetic Systems.* NIMA Technical Report TR8350.2 3rd ed. National Imagery and Mapping Agency, Bethesda, MD.

NOAA CoastWatch (2009) NOAA *CoastWatch Central Operations Homepage*, NOAA *Satellite and Information Service, National Environmental Satellite, Data, and Information Service.* Camp Springs, MD. Accessed at http://coastwatch.noaa.gov/. [Viewed January 22, 2009.]

NOAA National Environmental Satellite, Data, and Information Service (2009) *Geostationary Operational Environmental Satellites—East (GOES - E) Full disk infrared image.* Accessed at http://www.goes.noaa.gov/goesfull.html. [Modified January 26, 2009.]

NOAA Geostationary Operational Environmental Satellite (GOES) Project Science Office (2008) *The Intertropical Convergence Zone.* Accessed via NASA Visible Earth 2008 at http://visibleearth.nasa.gov/view_rec.php?id=643. [Modified February 26, 2008.]

NOAA Satellite and Information Service (2008) GOES *Imager Instrument.* NOAA *National Environmental Satellite, Data, and Information Service (NESDIS), Satellite Services Division.* Accessed at http://noaasis.noaa.gov/NOAASIS/ml/imager.html.

Office of Satellite Data Processing and Distribution (2008) *Coral Bleaching Products*, NOAA *Satellite and Information Service, National Environmental Satellite, Data, and Information Service.* Camp Springs, MD. Accessed at http://www.osdpd.noaa.gov/ml/ocean/coral_bleaching.html. [Last updated December 2008.]

O'Neill, R. V., Ritters, K. H., Wickham, J. D., et al. (1999) Landscape pattern metrics and regional assessment. *Ecosystem Health*, 5: 225–33.

O'Reilly, J. E., Maritorena, S., Mitchell, B. G., et al. (1998) Ocean color chlorophyll algorithms for SeaWiFS. *Journal of Geophysical Research*, 103(Cll): 24937–53.

Obaid, T. A. (2007) *State of World Population 2007.* United Nations Population Fund, New York.

Okimoto, Y., Nose, A., Ikeda, K., et al. (2008) An estimation of CO2 fixation capacity in mangrove forest using two methods of CO2 gas exchange and growth curve analysis. *Wetlands Ecology and Management*, 16: 155–71.

Olson, D. M. and Dinerstein, E. (1998) The Global 200: a representation approach to conserving the Earth's most biologically valuable ecoregions. *Conservation Biology*, 12: 502–15.

Olson, D. M., Dinerstein, E. Wikramanayake, E. D., et al. (2001) Terrestrial ecoregions of the world: a new map of life on earth. *Bioscience*, 51(110): 933–38.

Oren, A. and Ben-Yosef, N. (1997) Development and spatial distribution of an algal bloom in the Dead Sea: a remote sensing study. *Aquatic Microbial Ecology*, 13(22): 219–23.

Ostrom, E. and Nagendra, H. (2006) Insights on linking forests, trees, and people from the air, on the ground, and in the laboratory. *Proceedings of the National Academy of Sciences*, 103(51): 19224.

Owen-Smith, N. (1996) Ecological guidelines for water points in extensive protected areas. *South African Journal of Wildlife Resources*, 26: 107–12.

Pahlevan, N., Valadanzouj, M. J., and Alimohamadi, A. (2006) A quantitative comparison to water column correction techniques for benthic mapping using high spatial resolution data. ISPRS Commission VII Mid-term Symposium "Remote Sensing, From Pixels to Processes," Enschede, the Netherlands, May 8–11, 2006, pp. 286–91.

Pahlow, M. and Riebesell, U. (2000) Temporal trends in deep ocean Redfield ratios. *Science*, 287: 831–33.

PALnet (2009) *Protected Areas Learning Network. IUCN.* Accessed at http://www.parksnet. org. [Viewed January 3, 2009.]

Parkinson, C. L. and Greenstone, R. eds. (2000) *EOS Data Products Handbook.* Volume 2. NASA Goddard Space Flight Center, Greenbelt, MD. Available on the Web at http:// eospso.gsfc.nasa.gov/ftp_docs/data_products_vol2.pdf.

Parkinson, C. L. Ward, A., and King, M. D. eds. (2006) *Earth Science Reference Handbook: A Guide to NASA's Earth Science Program and Earth Observing Satellite Missions.* NASA, Washington, DC.

Parmesan, C. (2005) Biotic response: range and abundance changes. In T. E. Lovejoy and L. Hannah, eds. *Climate Change and Biodiversity,* Yale University Press, New Haven, CT and London.

Parmesan, C. and Yohe, G. (2003) A globally coherent fingerprint of climate change impacts across natural systems. *Nature,* 421: 37–42.

Parrish, J. D., Braun, D. P., and Unnasch, R. S. (2003) Are we conserving what we say we are? Measuring ecological integrity within protected areas. *BioScience,* 53: 851–60.

Paulsson, B. (1992) *Urban Applications of Satellite Remote Sensing and GIS Analysis.* The World Bank, Washington, DC.

Pearce, J., and Ferrier, S. (2000) Evaluating the predictive performance of habitat models developed using logistic regression. *Ecological Modelling,* 133: 225–45.

Pearson, R. G. (2007) *Species' Distribution Modeling for Conservation Educators and Practitioners. Synthesis. Network of Conservation Educators and Practitioners.* American Museum of Natural History. Retrieved from http://ncep.amnh.org.

Pearson, R. G. and Dawson, T. P. (2003) Predicting the impacts of climate change on the distribution of species: are bioclimate envelope models useful? *Global Ecology and Biogeography,* 12: 361–71.

Pearson, R. G., Dawson, T. P., Berry, P. M., et al. (2002) Species: a spatial evaluation of climate impact on the envelope of species. *Ecological Modelling,* 154: 289–300.

Peneva, E., Griffith, J. A., and Carter, G. A. (2008) Seagrass mapping in the northern Gulf of Mexico using airborne hyperspectral imagery: a comparison of classification methods. *Journal of Coastal Research,* 24: 850–56.

Penuelas, J. and Filella, I. (2001) Responses to a warming world. *Science,* 294: 793–95.

Pereira, H. M. and Cooper, H. D. (2006) Towards the global monitoring of biodiversity change. *Trends in Ecology and Evolution,* 21: 123–29.

Perry, A. L., Low, P. J., Ellis, J. R., et al. (2005) Climate change and distribution shifts in marine fishes. *Science,* 308: 1912–15.

Peterson, A. T., and Shaw, J. J. (2003) Lutzomyia vectors for cutaneous leishmaniasis in southern brazil: ecological niche models, predicted geographic distributions, and climate change effects. *International Journal of Parasitology,* 33: 919–31.

Peterson, D. L. and Parker, V. T. (1998) *Ecological Scale: Theory and Applications.* Columbia University Press, New York.

Peterson, T. C. and Vose, R. S. (1997) An overview of the global historical climatology network temperature database. *Bulletin of the American Meteorological Society,* 78: 2837–49.

Phillips, S. J., Anderson, R. P., and Schapire, R. E. (2006) Maximum entropy modeling of species geographic distributions. *Ecological Modelling,* 190: 231–59.

Phinn, S., Roelfsema, C., Dekker, A., et al. (2006) *Remote Sensing for Coastal Ecosystem Indicators Assessment and Monitoring.* SR 30.1 Final Report, Maps, techniques and error assessment for seagrass benthic habitat in Moreton Bay. Coastal CRC Technical Report No 76. CRC for Coastal Zone, Estuary and Waterway Management, Brisbane, Australia.

Phinney, J. T., Muller-Karger, F., Dustan, P., et al. (2001) Using remote sensing to reassess the mass mortality of Diadema antillarum 1983–1984. *Conservation Biology*, 15: 885–91.

Pielke, R. A., Walko, R. L., Steyaert, L. T., et al. (1999) The influence of anthropogenic landscape changes on weather in south Florida. *Monthly Weather Review*, 127: 1663–73.

Pimm, S. L. and Raven, P. (2000) Extinction by numbers. *Nature*, 403: 843–45.

Pimm, S. L. and van Aarde, R. J. (2001) Population control: African elephants and contraception. *Nature*, 411: 766.

Plumptre, A. J. (2002) *Extent and Status of the Forests in the Ugandan Albertine Rift.* Unpublished report to UNDP/GEF and WWF.

Plumptre, A. J., Laporte, N., and Devers, D. (2003) Section 9: threats to sites. In A. J. Plumptre, M. Behangana, E. Ndomba, et al., eds. *The Biodiversity of the Albertine Rift. Albertine Rift Technical Reports*, 3: 112.

Pole, M. (1994) The New Zealand flora—entirely long-distance dispersal? *Journal of Biogeography*, 21: 625–35.

Polovina, J., Kleiber, P., and Kobayashi, D. R. (1999) Application of TOPEX/POSEIDON satellite altimetry to simulate transport dynamics of larvae of spiny lobster, Panulirus marginatus, in the Northwestern Hawaiian Islands, 1993–1996. *Fishery Bulletin*, 97: 132–43.

Pounds, J. A., Bustamante, M. R., Coloma, L. A., et al. (2006) Widespread amphibian extinctions from epidemic disease driven by global warming. *Nature*, 439: 161–67.

Powell, G., Barborak, J., and Rodriguez, M. (2000) Assessing representativeness of protected natural areas in Costa Rica for conservation biodiversity: a preliminary gap analysis. *Biological Conservation*, 93: 41–53.

Powers, A. C. (2005) *Simulating Patterns of Uncertainty in Postclassification Change Detection. Proceedings of the 8th International Conference on GeoComputation. University of Michigan*, July 31–August 3, 2005, 13.

Priestnall, G., Jaafar, J., and Duncan, A. (2000) Extracting urban features from LiDAR digital surface models. *Computers, Environment and Urban Systems*, 24(2): 65–78.

Prins, E. M., Feltz, J. M., and Schmidt, C. C. (2001) *An Overview of Active Fire Detection and Monitoring Using Meteorological Satellites.*. Proceedings of the AMS 11th Conference on Satellite Meteorology and Oceanography, Madison, WI, October 15–18, 2001, pp. 1–8.

Prins, E. M., Govaerts, Y., and Csiszar, I. GOFC/GOLD Fire Monitoring and Mapping Implementation Team 2nd Workshop on Geostationary Fire Monitoring and Applications, EUMETSAT, Darmstadt, Germany, December 4–6, 2006. Accessed on the web on July 27, 2007 at: http://gofc-fire.umd.edu/products/pdfs/Events/2nd_GOFC_Geo_Workshop_Report percent 20final.pdf.

Purkis, S. J. and Pasterkamp, R. (2004) Integrating in situ reeftop reflectance spectra with Landsat TM imagery to aid shallow-tropical benthic habitat mapping. *Coral Reefs*, 23: 5–20.

Puth, L. M., and Wilson, K. A. (2001) Boundaries and corridors as a continuum of ecological flow control, lessons from rivers and streams. *Conservation Biology*, 15: 21–30.

Quinn, G. P., and Keogh, M. J. (2002) *Experimental Design and Data Analysis for Biologists.* Cambridge University Press, Cambridge, UK.

Radeloff, V. C., Hammer, R. B., and Stewart, S. I. (2005) Rural and suburban sprawl in the U.S. Midwest from 1940 to 2000 and its relation to forest fragmentation. *Conservation Biology*, 19(3): 793–805.

Ramanathan, V., Crutzen, P. J., Kiehl, J. T., et al. (2001) Aerosols, climate, and the hydrological cycle. *Science*, 294: 2119–24.

Ramsay, B. H. (1998) The interactive multisensor snow and ice mapping system. *Hydrological Processes*, **12**: 1537–46.

Ramsey, E., III. (1998) Radar remote sensing of wetlands. In R. Lunetta and C. Elvidge, eds. *Remote Sensing Change Detection: Environmental Monitoring Methods and Applications*, pp. 211–43. Ann Arbor Press, Chelsea, MI.

Ramsey, R. and Dehn, J. (2004) Spaceborne observations of the 2000 Bezymianny, Kamchatka eruption: the integration of high-resolution ASTER data into near real-time monitoring using AVHRR. *Journal of Volcanology and Geothermal Research*, **135**: 127–46.

Rand, D. (2002) *Forest Fragmentation Near Tai National Park, Ivory Coast*. PAMS department, University of Canterbury, Christchurch, New Zealand. http://www.cybermagic.co.nz/resources/content/20010822.htm. [Accessed in December 2005.]

Rasolofoharinoro, M., Blasco, F., Bellan, M. F., et al. (1998) A remote sensing based methodology for mangrove studies in Madagascar. *International Journal of Remote Sensing*, **19**: 1873–86.

Raxworthy, C. J., Forstner, M. R. J., and Nussbaum, R. A. (2002) Chameleon radiation by oceanic dispersal. *Nature*, **415**: 784–87.

Raxworthy, C. J., Martinez-Meyer, E., Horning, N., et al. (2003) Predicting distributions of known and unknown reptile species in Madagascar. *Nature*, **426**: 837–41.

Ray, D. K., Nair, U. S., Lawton, R. O., et al. (2006) Impact of land use on Costa Rican tropical montane cloud forests: sensitivity of orographic cloud formation to deforestation in the plains. *Journal of Geophysical Research*, **111**: D02108, doi:10.1029/2005JD006096.

Rempel, R. (2008) *Patch Analyst*. Centre for Northern Forest Ecosystem Research (Ontario Ministry of Natural Resources), Lakehead University Campus, Thunder Bay, Ontario. Accessed at http://flash.lakeheadu.ca/~rrempel/patch/index.html [Modified January 17, 2008.]

Rex, K. D., and Malanson, G. P. (1990) The fractal shape of riparian forest patches. *Landscape Ecology*, **4**: 249–58.

Riaño, D., Brondízio, E., Salas, J., et al. (2003) Assessment of different topographic corrections in Landsat-TM data for mapping vegetation types. *IEEE Transactions on Geoscience and Remote Sensing*, **41**(5): 1056–61.

Richards, J. A. and Jia, X. (1986) *Remote Sensing Digital Image Analysis*. Springer, New York.

Richey, J. E., Melack, J. M., Aufdenkampe, A. K., et al. (2002) Outgassing from Amazonian rivers and wetlands as a large tropical source of atmospheric CO_2. *Nature*, **416**: 617–20.

Ricketts, T. and Imhoff, M. (2003) Biodiversity, urban areas, and agriculture: locating priority ecoregions for conservation. *Conservation Ecology*, **8**(2): 1. [online], 15.

——. Dinerstein, E., Olson, D., et al. (1999) *Terrestrial Ecoregions of North America: A Conservation Assessment*. Island Press, Washington, DC.

Riitters, K. H., O'Neill, R. V., Hunsaker, C. T., et al. (1995) A factor analysis of landscape pattern and structure metrics. *Landscape Ecology*, **10**: 23–29.

——. Wickham, J. D., O'Neill, R., et al. (2000) Global-scale patterns of forest fragmentation. *Conservation Ecology*, **4**: 3.

Roberts, C. M., McClean, C. J., Veron, J. E. N., et al. (2002) Marine biodiversity hotspots and conservation priorities for tropical reefs. *Science*, **295**: 1280–84.

Roberts, G. and Wooster, M. J. (2007) New perspectives on African biomass burning dynamics. *Eos, Transactions of the American Geophysical Union*, **88**: 369–70.

Robinson, J. A., McRay, B., and Lulla, K. P. (2000) Twenty-eight years of urban growth in North America quantified by analysis of photographs from Apollo, Skylab and Shuttle-Mir. In K. P. Lulla, L. Dessinov, C. A. Evans, P. W. Dickerson, and J. A. Robinson, eds.

Dynamic Earth Environments: Remote Sensing Observations from Shuttle-Mir missions, pp. 25–42, 269, 270. Wiley, New York.

——. Lulla, K. P., Kashiwagi, M., et al. (2001) Conservation applications of astronaut photographs of Earth: tidal flat loss (Japan), elephant impacts on vegetation (Botswana), and seagrass and mangrove monitoring (Australia). *Conservation Biology*, 15: 876–84.

——. Andréfouët, S., and Burke, L. (2006) Data synthesis for coastal and coral reef ecosystem management at regional and global scales. In L. L. Richardson and E. F. Ledrew, eds. *Remote Sensing of Aquatic Coastal Ecosystem Processes*, pp. 279–305. Springer, Dordrecht, The Netherlands.

Robinson, L., Newell, J. P., and Marzluff, J. M. (2005) Twenty-five years of sprawl in the Seattle region: growth management responses and implications for conservation. *Landscape and Urban Planning*, 71: 51–72.

Rodríguez, E., Morin, C. S., and Belz, J. E. (2006) A global assessment of the SRTM performance. *Photogrammetric Engineering and Remote Sensing*, 72: 249–60.

Rohde, R. A. (2007) *Global Warming Art: Radiation Transmitted by the Atmosphere*. Accessed at http://www.globalwarmingart.com/wiki/Image:Atmospheric_Transmission_png. [Modified June 13, 2007.]

Root, T. (1988) Environmental factors associated with avian distributional boundaries. *Journal of Biogeography*, 15(3): 489–505.

——. Price, J. T., Hall K. R., et al. (2003) Fingerprints of global warming on wild animals and plants. *Nature*, 421: 57–60.

Rosenberg, D. K., Noon, B. R., and Meslow, E. C. (1997) Biological corridors: form, function, and efficacy. *BioScience*, 47: 677–87.

Rosenfeld, D. (1999) TRMM observed first direct evidence of smoke from forest fires inhibiting rainfall. *Geophysical Research Letters*, 26: 3105–08.

Rosso, P. H., Ustin, S. L., and Hastings, A. (2006) Use of lidar to study changes associated with Spartina invasion in San Francisco Bay marshes. *Remote Sensing of Environment*, 100(33): 295–306.

Rossow, W. B. and Schiffer, R. A. (1999) Advances in understanding clouds from ISCCP. *Bulletin of the American Meteorological Society*, 80: 2261–87.

Rouse, J. W., Haas, R. H., Schell, J. A., et al. (1973) *Monitoring Vegetation Systems in the Great Plains with ERTS*. Third ERTS Symposium, NASA SP-351 I.

Roy, D., Boschetti, L., and O'Neal, K. (2006) *MODIS Collection 5 Burned Area Product MCD45 User's Guide Version 1.0*. Accessed on the Web on August 24, 2007 at: http://modis-fire.umd.edu/documents/MODIS_Burned_Area_Users_Guide_1.0.pdf.

Ruan, R. and Ren, L. (2007) Identification of inland fresh water wetland using SAR and ETM + data. Proceedings of the IEEE International Geoscience and Remote Sensing Symposium, 2007, pp. 4592–95.

Ruiz, L. A., Fdez-sarría, A., and Recio, J. A. (2004) Texture feature extraction for classification of remote sensing data using wavelet decomposition: a comparative study. Proceedings of the XXth ISPRS Congress, July 12–23, 2004, Istanbul, Turkey, pp. 1109–14.

Running, S. W., Nemani, R. R., Heinsch, F. A., et al. (2004) A continuous satellite-derived measure of global terrestrial primary production. *BioScience*, 54: 547–60.

Salami, A. T., Ekanade, O., and Oyinloye, R. O. (1999) Detection of forest reserve incursion in south-western Nigeria from a combination of multi-date aerial photographs and high resolution satellite imagery. *International Journal of Remote Sensing*, 20: 1487–97.

Sánchez-Azofeifa, G. A., Harriss, R. C., and Skole, D. L. (2001) Deforestation in Costa Rica: a quantitative analysis using remote sensing imagery. *Biotropica*, 33: 378–84.

Sánchez-Azofeifa, G. A., Daily, G. C., Pfaff, A., et al. (2003) Integrity and isolation of Costa Rica's national parks and biological reserves: examining the dynamics of land-cover change. *Biological Conservation*, **109**: 123–35.

Sanderson, E. W., Jaiteh, M., Levy, M. A., et al. (2002) The Human Footprint and the Last of the Wild. *BioScience*, **52**: 891–904.

Sandwell, D. T., Gille, S. T., and Smith, W. H. F. eds. (2002) *Bathymetry from Space: Oceanography, Geophysics, and Climate*. Geoscience Professional Services, Bethesda, MD.

Santos, A. M. P. (2000) Fisheries oceanography using satellite and airborne remote sensing methods, a review. *Fisheries Research*, **49**: 1–20.

Sault, M., Parrish, C., White, S., et al. (2005) A sensor fusion approach to coastal mapping. *Proceedings of the 14th Biennial Coastal Zone Conference*. New Orleans, Louisiana, 17–21 July 2005.

Saunders, R. W., Watts, J. G., O'Carroll, A. G., et al. (2006) The measurement of the sea surface temperature by satellites from 1991 to 2005. *Journal of Atmospheric and Oceanic Technology*, **23**: 1573–82.

Schmetz, J., Govaerts, Y., Konig, M., et al. (2006) A short introduction to METEOSAT Second Generation (MSG). In V. Zwatz-Meise and J. Kerkmann, eds. *MSG Channels Interpretation Guide: Weather, Surface Conditions and Atmospheric Constituents* [EUMET-SAT], Accessed on the Web at http://oiswww.eumetsat.org/WEBOPS/msg_interpretation/PowerPoints/Channels/schmetz7july.doc.

Schmidt, K. S. and Skidmore, A. K. (2003) Spectral discrimination of vegetation types in a coastal wetland. *Remote Sensing of Environment*, **85**: 92–108.

Schneider, S. H. (1992) Introduction to climate modeling. In K. E. Trenberth, ed. *Climate System Modeling*, Cambridge University Press, Cambridge.

Scholes, R. J., Mace, G. M., Turner, W., et al. (2008) Towards a global biodiversity observing system. *Science*, **321**: 1044–45.

Schöpfer, E., and Moeller, M. S. (2006) Comparing metropolitan areas—a transferable object-based image analysis approach. *Photogrammetrie, Fernerkundung, Geoinformation*, **4**: 277–86.

Schot, P. P. (1999) Wetlands. In B. Nath, L. Hens, P. Compton and D. Devuysteds, eds. *Environmental Management in Practice*, Vol. 3, pp. 62–85. Routledge, London.

Schultz, M. G. (2002) On the use of ATSR fire count data to estimate the seasonal and interannual variability of vegetation fire emissions. *Atmospheric Chemistry and Physics*, **2**: 387–95.

Schumaker, N. H. (1996) Using landscape indices to predict habitat connectivity. *Ecology*, **77**: 1210–25.

Scipal, K. and Wagner, W. (2004) *Global Soil Moisture Data and Its Potential for Climatological and Meteorological Applications*. The 2004 Eumetsat Meteorological Satellite Conference. Prague, Czech Republic.

Scott, J. M., and Jennings, M. (1998) Large-area mapping of biodiversity. *Annals of the Missouri Botanical Garden*, **85**: 34–47.

Scott, J. M., Davis, F., Csuti, B., et al. (1993) Gap analysis: a geographic approach to protection of biological diversity. *Wildlife Monographs*, **123**: 3–41.

Scott, J. M., Heglund, P. J., Morrison, M., et al. (Eds.). (2002) *Predicting Species Occurrences: Issues of Scale and Accuracy*. Island Press, Washington, DC.

Seager, S., Turner, E. L., Schafer, J., et al. (2005) Vegetation's red edge: a possible spectroscopic biosignature of extraterrestrial plants. *Astrobiology*, **5**: 372–90.

Sellars, J. D. and Jolls, C. L. (2007) Habitat modeling for *Amaranthus pumilus*: an application of light detection and ranging (LIDAR) data. *Journal of Coastal Research*, **23**: 1193–202.

Senay, G. B., and Elliot, R. L. (2002) Capability of AVHRR data in discriminating rangeland cover mixtures. *International Journal of Remote Sensing*, **23**: 299–312.

Seto, K. C. and Fragkias, M. (2007) Mangrove conversion and aquaculture development in Vietnam: a remote sensing-based approach for evaluating the Ramsar Convention on Wetlands. *Global Environmental Change*, **17**: 486–500.

Shochat, E., Stefanov, W. L., Whitehorse, M. E., et al. (2004) Urbanization and spider diversity: influences of human modification of habitat structure and productivity. *Ecological Applications*, **14**: 268–80.

Siegel, D. A., Wang, M., Maritorena, S., et al. (2000) Atmospheric correction of satellite ocean color imagery, the black pixel assumption. *Applied Optics*, **39**: 3582–91.

Siegert, F. and Ruecker, G. (2000) Use of multitemporal ERS-2 SAR images for identification of burned scars in south-east Asian tropical forest. *International Journal of Remote Sensing*, **21**: 831–37.

Siegert, F., Ruecker, G., Hinrichs, A., et al. (2001) Increased damage from fires in logged forests during droughts caused by El Nino. *Nature*, **414**: 437–40.

Sih, A., Jonsson, B. G., and Luikart, G. (2000) Habitat loss: ecological, evolutionary and genetic consequences. *Trends in Ecology and Evolution*, **15**: 132–34.

Silvestri, S., Marani, M., and Marani, A. (2003) Hyperspectral remote sensing of salt marsh vegetation, morphology and soil topography. *Physics and Chemistry of the Earth, Parts A/B/C*, **28**: 15–25.

Simberloff, D., Farr, J. A., Cox, J., et al. (1992) Movement corridors: conservation bargains or poor investments? *Conservation Biology*, **6**: 493–504.

Sippel, S. J., Hamilton, S. K., Melack, J. M., et al. (1998) Passive microwave observations of inundation area and the area/stage relation in the Amazon River floodplain. *International Journal of Remote Sensing*, **19**: 3055–74.

Skirving, W., Strong, A. E., Liu, G., et al. (2006) Extreme events and perturbations of coastal ecosystems, sea surface temperature change and coral bleaching. In L. L. Richardson and E. F. LeDrew, eds. *Remote Sensing of Aquatic Coastal Ecosystem Processes*, pp. 11–25. Springer, Dordrecht, The Netherlands.

Skole, D. and Tucker, C. (1993) Tropical deforestation and habitat fragmentation in the Amazon: satellite data from 1978 to 1988. *Science*, **260**: 1905–10.

Slater, J. A., Garvey, G., Johnston, C., et al. (2006) The SRTM data "finishing" process and products. *Photogrammetric Engineering and Remote Sensing*, **72**: 237–47.

Slayback, D. A., Pinzon, J. E., Los, S. O., et al. (2003) Northern hemisphere photosynthetic trends 1982–99. *Global Change Biology*, **9**: 1–15.

Smith, L. C. (1997) Satellite remote sensing of river inundation area, stage, and discharge: a review. *Hydrological Processes*, **11**: 1427–39.

Smith, P. G. R. (2007) Characteristics of urban natural areas influencing winter bird use in Southern Ontario, Canada. *Environmental Management*, **39**(3): 338–52.

Song, C., Woodcock, C. E., Seto, K. C., et al. (2001) Classification and change detection using Landsat TM data: when and how to correct atmospheric effects? *Remote Sensing of Environment*, **75**: 230–44.

Soons, M. B., Heil, G. W., Nathan, R., et al. (2004) Determinants of long-distance seed dispersal by wind in grasslands. *Ecology*, **85**: 3056–79.

Southworth, J., Nagendra, H., and Tucker, C. M. (2002) Fragmentation of a landscape: incorporating landscape metrics into satellite analyses of land cover change. *Landscape Research*, **27**: 253–69.

Southworth, J., Munroe, D. K., and Nagendra, H. (2006) Editorial introduction to the special issue: are parks working? Exploring human–environment tradeoffs in protected area conservation. *Applied Geography*, **26**: 87–95.

Soutullo, A., Cadahia, L., Urios, V., et al. (2007) Accuracy of Lightweight Satellite Telemetry: a case study in the Iberian peninsula. *Journal of Wildlife Management*, 71(3): 1010–15.

Souza, C., Firestone, L., Silva, L. M., et al. (2003) Mapping forest degradation in the Eastern Amazon from SPOT 4 through spectral mixture models. *Remote Sensing of Environment*, 87(4): 494–506.

Spalding, M. D., Ravilious, C., Green, E. P., et al. (2001) *World Atlas of Coral Reefs*. University of California Press, Berkeley, CA.

Stefanov, W. L. and Brazel, A. J. (2007) Challenges in characterizing and mitigating urban heat islands—a role for integrated approaches including remote sensing. In M. Netzband, W. L. Stefanov, and C. Redman, eds. *Applied Remote Sensing for Urban Planning, Governance and Sustainability*, pp. 117–35. Springer-Verlag, Heidelberg, Germany.

Stefanov, W. L. and Netzband, M. (2005) Assessment of ASTER land cover and MODIS NDVI data at multiple scales for ecological characterization of an arid urban center. *Remote Sensing of Environment*, 99(1–2): 31–43.

Stefanov, W. L., Ramsey, M. S., and Christensen, P. R. (2001) Monitoring urban land cover change: an expert system approach to land cover classification of semiarid to arid urban centers. *Remote Sensing of Environment*, 77(2): 173–85.

Stefanov, W. L., Netzband, M., Möller, M. S., et al. (2007) Phoenix, Arizona, USA: applications of remote sensing in a rapidly urbanizing desert region. In M. Netzband, W. L. Stefanov and C. Redman, eds. *Applied Remote Sensing for Urban Planning, Governance and Sustainability*, pp. 137–64. Springer-Verlag, Heidelberg, Germany.

Steininger, M. K. (1996) Tropical secondary forest regrowth in the Amazon: age, area and change estimation with Thematic Mapper data. *International Journal of Remote Sensing*, 17: 9–27.

Stekoll, M., Deysher, L., and Hess, M. (2006) A remote sensing approach to estimating harvestable kelp biomass. *Journal of Applied Phycology*, 18: 323–34.

Sterling, E. J., Hurley, M. M., and Minh, L. D. (2006) *Vietnam: A Natural History*. Yale University Press, New Haven, CT.

Stokesbury, M., Teo, S., Seitz, A., et al. (2004) Movement of Atlantic bluefin tuna (Thunnus thynnus) as determined by satellite tagging experiments initiated off New England. *Canadian Journal of Fisheries and Aquatic Sciences*, 61: 1976–87.

Stone, B., and Norman, J. M. (2006) Land use planning and surface heat island formation: a parcel-based radiation flux approach. *Atmospheric Environment*, 40: 3561–73.

Stone, B., and Rodgers, M. O. (2001) Urban form and thermal efficiency: how the design of cities influences the urban heat island effect. *Journal of the American Planning Association*, 67(2): 186–98.

Story, M. and Congalton, R. (1986) Accuracy assessment: a user's perspective. *Photogrammetric Engineering and Remote Sensing*, 52: 397–99.

Strand, H., Höft, R., Strittholt, J., et al. eds. (2007) *Sourcebook on Remote Sensing and Biodiversity Indicators*. Secretariat of the Convention on Biological Diversity, Montreal, Technical Series no. 32, 201.

Stumpf, R. P., Culver, M. E., Tester, P. A., et al. (2003a) Monitoring Karenia brevis blooms in the Gulf of Mexico using satellite ocean color imagery and other data. *Harmful Algae*, 2: 147–60.

——. Holderied, K., Robinson, J. A., et al. (2003b) *Mapping Water Depths in Clear Water from Space. Proceedings of the 13th Biennial Coastal Zone Conference*, Baltimore, MD, July, 23–27, 2003, 5pp. Accessed at http://eol.jsc.nasa.gov/newsletter/CoastalZone/default.htm.

—— ——. and Sinclair, M. (2003c) Determination of water depth with high-resolution satellite imagery over variable bottom types. *Limnology and Oceanography*, **48**(1, part 2): 547–56.

Sugita, M. and Brutsaert, W. (1993) Comparison of land surface temperatures derived from satellite observations with ground truth during FIFE. *International Journal of Remote Sensing*, **14**: 1659–76.

Swap, R., Garstang, M., Greco, S., et al. (1992). Saharan dust in the Amazon basin. *Tellus*, **44B**: 133–49.

Tallis, H. M. and Kareiva, P. (2006) Shaping global environmental decisions using socio-ecological models. *TREE*, **21**: 562–67.

Tang, D., Kawamura, H., Oh, I. S., et al. (2005) Satellite evidence of harmful algal blooms and related oceanographic features in the Bohai Sea during autumn 1998. *Advances in Space Research*, **37**: 681–89.

Tassan, S. (1996) Modified Lyzenga's method for macroalgae detection in water with non-uniform composition. *International Journal of Remote Sensing*, **17**: 1601–07.

Taylor, P. D., Fahrig, L., Henein, K., et al. (1993) Connectivity is a vital element of landscape structure. *Oikos*, **68**: 571–73.

Tetko, I. V., Livingstone, D. J., and Luik, A. I. (1995) Neural network studies. 1. Comparison of Overfitting and Overtraining. *Journal of Chemical Information and Computer Science*, **35**: 826–33.

Thiha, Webb, E. L., and Honda, K. (2007) Biophysical and policy drivers of landscape change in a central Vietnamese district. *Environmental Conservation*, **32**: 164–72.

Thomas, C. D., Cameron, A., Green, R. E., et al. (2004) Extinction risk from climate change. *Nature*, **427**: 145–48.

Thomson, J. L., Schaub, T., Culver, N. W., et al. (2005) *Wildlife at a Crossroads*. Energy Development in Western Wyoming. The Wilderness Society, Washington, DC.

Tischendorf, L. (2001) Can landscape indices predict ecological processes consistently? *Landscape Ecology*, **16**: 235–54.

Tischendorf, L. and Fahrig, L. (2000) On the usage and measurement of landscape connectivity. *Oikos*, **90**: 7–19.

Toll, D. L. (1985) Landsat-4 Thematic Mapper scene characteristics of a suburban and rural area. *Photogrammetric Engineering and Remote Sensing*, **51**: 1471–82.

Tomlinson, M. C., Stumpf, R. P., Ransibrahmanakul, V., et al. (2004) Evaluation of the use of SeaWiFS imagery for detecting Karenia brevis harmful algal blooms in the eastern Gulf of Mexico. *Remote Sensing of Environmnt*, **91**: 293–303.

Toole, D. A., Siegel, D. A., Menzies, D. W., et al. (2000) Remote-sensing reflectance determinations in the coastal ocean environment, impact of instrumental characteristics and environmental variability. *Applied Optics LP*, **39**(3): 456–69.

Torgersen, C. E., Faux, R. N., McIntosh, B. A., et al. (2001) Airborne thermal remote sensing for water temperature assessment in rivers and streams. *Remote Sensing of Environment*, **76**: 386–98.

Townsend, P. A. (2001) Mapping seasonal flooding in forested wetlands using multi-temporal Radarsat SAR. *Photogrammetric Engineering and Remote Sensing*, **67**: 857–64.

Townshend, J. R. G. (1984) Agricultural land-cover discrimination using Thematic Mapper spectral bands. *International Journal of Remote Sensing*, **5**: 681–98.

Townshend, J. R. G., Huang, C., Kalluri, S. N. V., et al. (2000) Beware of per-pixel characterization of land cover. *International Journal of Remote Sensing*, **21**: 839–43.

Townshend, J. R. G., DeFries, R. S., Zhan, X., et al. (2002) MODIS 250 m and 500 m time series data for change detection and continuous representation of vegetation characteristics.

Analysis of multi-temporal remote sensing images. In L. Bruzzone and P. Smits, eds. *Proceedings of the First International Workshop on the Analysis of Multi-temporal Remote Sensing 2001, Trento, Italy*, pp. 233–40. World Scientific, London.

Tran, L. T., Wickham, J., Jarnagin, S. T., et al. (2005) Mapping spatial thematic accuracy with fuzzy sets. *Photogrammetric Engineering and Remote Sensing*, 71: 29–36.

Trenberth, K. E., Jones, P. D., Ambenje, P., et al. (2007) Observations: surface and atmospheric climate change. In S. Solomon, D. Qin, M. Manning, et al., eds. *Climate Change 2007: The Physical Science Basis. Contribution of Working Group I to the Fourth Assessment Report of the Intergovernmental Panel on Climate Change*, Cambridge University Press, Cambridge and New York.

Treuhaft, R. N., Law, B. E., and Asner, G. P. (2004) Forest attributes from radar interferometric structure and its fusion with optical remote sensing. *Bioscience*, 54(6): 561–71.

Trombulak, S. C., and Frissell, C. A. (2000) Review of ecological effects of roads on terrestrial and aquatic communities. *Conservation Biology*, 14: 18–30.

Tucker, C. J. and Sellers, P. J. (1986) Satellite remote sensing of primary production. *International Journal of Remote Sensing*, 7: 1395–416.

Tucker, C. J., Grant, D. M., and Dykstra, J. D. (2004) NASA's global orthorectified Landsat data set. *Photogrammetric Engineering and Remote Sensing*, 70: 313–22.

Tucker, C. J., Townshend, J. R. G., and Goff, T. E. (1985) African land-cover classification using satellite data. *Science*, 227: 369–75.

Tuomisto, H., Linna, A., and Kalliola, R. (1994) Use of digitally processed satellite images in studies of tropical rain forest vegetation. *International Journal of Remote Sensing*, 15(8): 1595. doi: 10.1080/01431169408954194.

Turner, M. D. (2003) Methodological reflections on the use of remote sensing and geographic information science in human ecological research. *Human Ecology*, 31(2): 255–79.

Turner, S. M., Nightingale, P. D., Spokes, L. J., et al. (1996) Increased dimethyl sulphide concentrations in sea water from in situ iron enrichment. *Nature*, 383: 513–17.

Turner, W., Spector, S., Gardiner, N., et al. (2003) Remote sensing for biodiversity science and conservation. *Trends in Ecology & Evolution*, 18(6): 306–14.

Uhl, C. (1998) Perspectives on wildfire in the humid tropics. *Conservation Biology*, 12: 942–43.

Uhl, C. and Kauffman, J. B. (1990) Deforestation, fire susceptibility, and potential tree responses to fire in the eastern Amazon. *Ecology*, 71: 437–49.

University of Wisconsin (2008) *The CIMSS (Cooperative Institute for Meteorological Satellite Studies) Realtime GOES Page*. Accessed on the Web at http://cimss.ssec.wisc.edu/goes/realtime/realtime.html.

US Geological Survey (2008) *TerraLook: Satellite Imagery to View a Changing World*. Sioux Falls, SD. Accessed at http://terralook.cr.usgs.gov. [Modified September 4, 2008.]

US Geological Survey (2009) *HydroSHEDS*. Sioux Falls, South Dakota, USA. Accessed at http://terralook.cr.usgs.gov. [Accessed May 12, 2009.]

Ustin, S. L., Smith, M. O., Jacquemond, S., et al. (1999) Geobotany: vegetation mapping for Earth sciences. In A. N. Rencz, ed. *Remote Sensing for the Earth Sciences*, 3rd edn. American Society for Photogrammetry and Remote Sensing, Bethesda, MD.

Valiela, I., Bowen, J. L., and York, J. K. (2001) Mangrove forests: one of the world's threatened major tropical environments. *BioScience*, 51: 807–15.

van Aarde, R., and Jackson, T. (2007) Megaparks for metapopulations: addressing the causes of locally high elephant numbers in southern Africa. *Biological Conservation*, 134: 289–97.

——. Whyte, I., and Pimm, S. L. (1999) Culling and the dynamics of the Kruger National Park African elephant population. *Animal Conservation*, 2: 287–94.

Van Nieuwstadt, M. G. L., Sheil, D., and Kartawinata, K. (2001) The ecological consequences of logging in the burned forests of East Kalimantan, Indonesia. *Conservation Biology*, 15: 1183–86.

Van Willigen, G., and Grodecki, A. (2006) *Land Manager's Monitoring Guide_Photopoint Monitoring* (p. 15). Queensland Government Department of Natural Resources. Accessed on the web on December 4, 2007 at: http://www.nrw.qld.gov.au/monitoring_guide/indicators/photopoints/index.html.

Vasconcelos, M., Mussa, J., Araujo, A., et al. (2002) Land cover change in two protected areas of Guinea-Bissau (1956–1998). *Applied Geography*, 22: 139–56.

Vieira, C. A. O., Mather, P. M., and Aplin, P. (2004) *Assessing the Positional and Thematic Accuracy of Remotely Sensed Data.* XXth Congress of the International Society for Photogrammetry and Remote Sensing. Istanbul, Turkey.

Voogt, J. A. and Oke, T. R. (2003) Thermal remote sensing of urban climates. *Remote Sensing of Environment*, 86: 370–84.

Wade, T. G., Riitters, K. H., Wickham, J. D., et al. (2003) Distribution and Causes of Global Forest Fragmentation. *Conservation Ecology*, 7: 7.

Wahle, C. M. and Uravitch, J. A. (2006) *A Functional Classification System for Marine Protected Areas in the United States.* National Marine Protected Areas Center, Silver Spring, MD.

Waldrop, M. M. (1986) Washington embraces global earth sciences. *Science*, 233: 1040–42.

Wallace, A. R. (1880) *Island Life.* Macmillan and Co., London.

Walker, P. A. and Peters, P. E. (2007) Making sense in time: remote sensing and the challenges of temporal heterogeneity in social analysis of environmental change-cases from Malawi. *Human Ecology*, 35(1): 69–80.

Walther, G. R., Post, E., Convey, P., et al. (2002) Ecological responses to recent climate change. *Nature*, 416: 389–395.

Wang, H. and Ellis, E. C. (2005) Image misregistration error in change measurements. *Photogrammetric Engineering and Remote Sensing*, 71: 1037–1044.

Wang, Y. and Moskovitz, D. (2001) Tracking fragmentation of natural communities and changes in land cover: applications of Landsat data for conservation in an urban landscape (Chicago Wilderness). *Conservation Biology*, 15: 835–842.

Webb, T. J., Woodward, F. I., Hannah, L., et al. (2005) Forest cover-rainfall relationships in a biodiversity hotspot: the Atlantic forest of Brazil. *Ecological Applications*, 15: 1968–1983.

Wellborn, G. A., Skelly, D. K., and Werner, E. E. (2003) Mechanisms creating community structure across a freshwater habitat gradient. *Annual Review of Ecology and Systematics*, 27: 337–363.

Weller, C., Thomson, J., Morton, P., et al. (2002) *Fragmenting Our Lands: The Ecological Footprint from Oil and Gas Development.* The Wilderness Society, Washington, DC.

Wellington, G. M., Glynn, P. W., Strong, A. E., et al. (2001) Crisis on coral reefs linked to climate change, *Eos. Transactions of the American Geophysical Union*, 82: 1–5.

Wentz, E. A., Stefanov, W. L., Gries, C., et al. (2006) Land use and land cover mapping from diverse data sources for an arid urban environments [sic]. *Computers, Environment, and Urban Systems*, 30(3): 320–346.

Wentz, E. A., Nelson, D., Rahman, A., et al. (2008) Expert system classification of urban land use/cover for Delhi, India. *International Journal of Remote Sensing*, 29(15): 4405–4427.

Werdell, P. J., Bailey, S., Fargion, G., et al. (2003) Unique data repository facilitates ocean color satellite validation, *Eos. Transactions of the American Geophysical Union*, 84(38): 377, 387.

Wertz, J. R. and Larson, W. J. eds. (1999) *Space Mission Analysis and Design.* 3rd ed. Kluwer Academic Publishers, Dordrecht.

Whyte, I., van Aarde, R., Jackson, T., et al. (2003) Kruger's elephant population: its size and consequences for ecosystem heterogeneity. In J. T. du Toit, K. H. Rogers and H. C. Biggs, eds. *The Kruger Experience: Ecology and Management of Savanna Heterogeneity*, pp. 232–248. Island Press, Washington, DC.

Wickham, J. D., and Riitters, K. H. (1995) Sensitivity of landscape metrics to pixel size. *International Journal of Remote Sensing*, 16(18): 3585. doi: 10.1080/01431169508954647.

Wickham, J. D., Riitters, K. H., Wade, T. G., et al. (2007) Temporal change in forest fragmentation at multiple scales. *Landscape Ecology*, 22: 481–489.

Wiens, J. A. (1997) The emerging role of patchiness in conservation biology. In S. T. A. Pickett, R. S. Ostfeld, M. Shachak, G. E. Likens, eds. *The Ecological Basis of Conservation, Heterogeneity, Ecosystems, and Biodiversity*. Chapman & Hall, New York.

Wigley, T. M. L., Ramaswamy, V., Christy, J. R., et al. (2006) Executive Summary in. In T. R. Karl, S. J. Hassol, C. D. Miller, and W. L. Murray, eds. *Temperature Trends in the Lower Atmosphere*. Steps for Understanding and Reconciling Differences. A Report by the Climate Change Science Program and the Subcommittee on Global Change Research, Washington, DC.

Wittemyer, G., Elsen, P., Bean, W. T., et al. (2008). Accelerated human population growth at protected area edges. *Science*, 321(5885): 123–126.

World Database on Protected Areas (WDPA), (2009) *World Database on Protected Areas (WDPA)*. World Conservation Union (IUCN) and UNEP World Conservation Monitoring Centre (UNEP-WCMC). Accessed at http://www.wdpa.org/.

Wozencraft, J. M., Macon, C. L., and Jeff, L. W. (2007) CHARTS-Enabled Data Fusion for Coastal Zone Characterization. Proceedings of the Coastal Sediments '07 Conference, American Society of Civil Engineers, 1827–36.

Wu, L., Zhang, Q., and Jiang, Z. (2006) Three Gorges Dam affects regional precipitation. *Geophysical Research Letters*, 33: L13806, doi:10.1029/2006GL026780.

Wulder, M. A., Franklin, S. E., White, J. C., et al. (2006) An accuracy assessment framework for large-area land cover classification products derived from medium-resolution satellite data. *International Journal of Remote Sensing*, 27(4): 663–83.

Xiao, J. and Moody, A. (2005) Geographical distribution of global greening trends and their climatic correlates: 1982–1998. *International Journal of Remote Sensing*, 26: 2371–90.

Yáñez, E., Silva, C., Nieto, K., et al. (2004) Using satellite technology to improve the Chilean purseine fishing fleet. *Gayana*, 68(2): 578–85.

Yang, J., Artigas, F. J., Wang, Y., et al. (2008) Mapping salt marsh vegetation using hyperspectral imagery. In W. Ji, ed. *Wetland and Water Resource Modeling and Assessment: A Watershed Perspective*, pp. 21–28. CRC Press, Boca Raton, FL.

Yang, X. (2005) Use of LIDAR elevation data to construct a high-resolution digital terrain model for an estuarine marsh area. *International Journal of Remote Sensing*, 26: 5163–66.

Yu, H., Kaufman, Y. J., Chin, M., et al. (2006) A review of measurement-based assessments of the aerosol direct radiative effect and forcing. *Atmospheric Chemistry and Physics*, 6: 613–66.

Zadeh, L. A. (1965) Fuzzy sets. *Information and Control*, 8: 338–53.

Zhang, J. and Foody, G. M. (2001) Fully-fuzzy supervised classification of sub-urban land cover from remotely sensed imagery: statistical and artificial neural network approaches. *International Journal of Remote Sensing*, 22(4): 615–28.

Zhang, J. and Tan, T. (2002) Brief review of invariant texture analysis methods. *Pattern Recognition*, 35: 735–47.

Zhang, J., Dong, W., Ye, D., et al. (2003a) New evidence for effects of land cover in China on summer climate. *Chinese Science Bulletin*, 48: 401–05.

Zhang, J., Dong, W., Fu, C., et al. (2003b) The influence of vegetation cover on summer precipitation in China: a statistical analysis of NDVI and climate data. *Advances in Atmospheric Sciences*, **20**: 1002–06.

Zhang, N., Wang, M., and Wang, N. (2002) Precision agriculture—a worldwide overview. *Computers and Electronics in Agriculture*, **36**(2–3): 113–32.

Zhang, X. Y., Friedl, M. A., Schaaf, C. B., et al. (2003) Monitoring vegetation phenology using MODIS. *Remote Sensing of Environment*, **84**: 471–75.

Zhang, Y. (2004) Understanding image fusion. *Photogrammetric Engineering & Remote Sensing*, **70**: 657–61.

Index